P9-BZO-551

READER'S DIGEST
WHY *in the* WORLD?

Clarence Robinson
94 Clarence St
Shoalhaven

WHY IN THE WORLD? was edited and designed by
Reader's Digest (Australia) Pty Limited

First edition Copyright © 1994
Reader's Digest (Australia) Pty Limited, 26-32 Waterloo Street, Surry Hills, NSW 2010
Copyright © 1994 The Reader's Digest Association Limited
Copyright © 1994 The Reader's Digest Association, Inc.
Copyright © 1994 The Reader's Digest Association (Canada) Ltd
Copyright © 1994 Reader's Digest Association Far East Ltd
Philippines copyright 1994 Reader's Digest Association Far East Ltd
Copyright © 1994 Reader's Digest South Africa (Pty) Limited
Copyright © 1994 Reader's Digest (New Zealand) Ltd

National Library of Australia cataloguing-in-publication data:

Why in the world?

Includes index.
ISBN O 86438 473 4.

1. Questions and answers.

032.02

Imagesetting by Wysiwyg Design Pty Ltd, Sydney
Colour separation by Colourscan Overseas Co. Pte Ltd, Singapore
Printing and binding by Toppan Printing Co., (S) Pte., Ltd, Singapore

COVER PHOTOS, READING LEFT TO RIGHT FROM TOP: Australasian Nature Transparencies/Dave Watts; Weldon Trannies; Horizon International;
Mary Evans Picture Library; The Image Bank/Luis Castaneda; Reuters Australia; Bruce Coleman; The Australian Picture Library; Mary Evans
Picture Library; The Image Bank/R Kristofik; Mary Evans Picture Library; Bruce Coleman/J&D Bartlett; Horizon International/Soames
Summerhays; Auscape/Reg Morrison; Mirror Australian Telegraph Publications; Australian Museum National Photographic Index/P Green;
The Image Bank/Butch Martin; The Australian Picture Library/Universal Pictorial Press, London; Hutchison Library/Jeremy Horner;
The Australian Picture Library/Zefa; The Australian Picture Library/W Hodges; The Image Bank/Stephen Marks; Horizon International.

READER'S DIGEST

WHY *in the* WORLD?

*Revealing answers to searching questions
about almost everything*

LONDON ■ NEW YORK ■ SYDNEY ■ AUCKLAND ■ CAPE TOWN ■ MONTREAL ■ HONG KONG

CONTENTS

CONTRIBUTORS

Principal writer Denis Wallis

Other writers and specialist contributors

Lesley Dow   Jim Heath, MSc   Michael Henderson, MA, MB, BChir   Patricia Holdway, PhD
Nelson Kenny   Peta Landman   Terence Lindsey   Alison Pressley
Jesse P. Shore *Senior Curator of Sciences, Powerhouse Museum, Sydney*   David Underhill

Advisers and consultants

G. Ted Ankrum *NASA Senior Scientific Representative in Australia*
Niels H. Aschengreen   Carol Ashworth
Herbert Beauchamp, BSc *Toxic Chemical Committee of the Total Environment Centre*
John Burland, DSc, FEng, FICE *Professor of Soil Mechanics,*
Imperial College of Science, Technology and Medicine
Les Billingsley (CTex) ATI, DipEd *Applied Science, Sydney Institute of Technology*
Michael Box, PhD *School of Physics, University of New South Wales*
Dr R. Brasch, AM, OBE
Andrew Brown *Western Australian Threatened Species and Communities Unit,*
Department of Conservation and Land Management
Debbie Callister *Director, TRAFFIC Oceania*
Mehmet Çelebi, PhD *United States Geological Survey, Menlo Park*
Russell B. Chapman *Manager, Motion Picture and Television Imaging, Kodak Australia*
Brian Coleman, ASTC, BSc, DipEd *Teacher of Textile Chemistry*
Dr A. F. Collings *CSIRO Division of Applied Physics*
Minas T. Coroneo, MSc, MS, FRACS, FRACO *Associate Professor of Opthalmology, University of New South Wales*
John Deeth *Civil Aviation Authority, Australia*
Angus Gidley-Baird, PhD *Department of Veterinary Physiology, University of Sydney*
Phoebe Joy Ho *Haematology Registrar, Royal Prince Alfred Hospital, Sydney*
Paul Holper, BSc (Hons), DipEd *CSIRO Division of Atmospheric Research*
David Jupp *Chief Engineer, Australis Media Pty Ltd*
Tony Larkum *Associate Professor, School of Biological Sciences, University of Sydney*
F. E. M. (Ted) Lilley, BSc, MSc, PhD *Senior Fellow in Earth Sciences, Australian National University, Canberra*
Nick Lomb, BSc, PhD *Curator of Astronomy, Sydney Observatory*
Colin C. Mickleburgh   Malcolm Moore, BE   Richard Moran
Max Mosher *Senior Information Officer, Energy Information Centre, Sydney*
Frank Newnes *Century Yuasa Batteries Pty Ltd*
Frank W. Nicholas *Associate Professor of Animal Genetics,*
Department of Animal Science, University of Sydney
James Pennington
Cathy Sage, BA, DipEd, GradDipAg *Communications Officer, CSIRO Division of Soils*
Geoff Senz *Manager, NRMA Technical Advisory Group, National Roads and Motorists' Association*
Linsey Siede *Managing Director, AC Rochester Australia, Ltd*
Helen Sim *CSIRO Australia Telescope National Facility*
Brian Travis   Sam Watts
Michael R. Willison *Research Engineer, Centre for Photovoltaics, University of New South Wales*

Picture researcher	**Researchers**	**Indexer**	**Photographer**
Annette Crueger	Ursula Dubosarsky Andrew Hobbs	Juliet Richters	Nick Rains

Artists

David Carroll   Jon Gittoes   Oliver Rennert

THIS AWESOME UNIVERSE

By telescope and cosmic probe we are slowly exposing its secrets and solving its mysteries. A revealing journey among the red giants, white dwarfs and black holes explores the remote and remarkable frontiers of space

Why do stars twinkle? PAGE 30

Why do some planets have rings? PAGE 29

Why do we talk about the Man in the Moon? PAGE 19

The moment when time began

Why is it said that the Universe began with a big bang?

In the beginning, say most scientists, there was nothing. It may seem absurd to believe that something – indeed, everything in the Universe, including the Earth, Sun, Moon and all the planets and stars – could come from nothing, but astronomers and physicists assert this with increasing confidence.

To make the point, they start with the Universe as we understand it today. Albert Einstein believed that the Universe is static and doesn't change. Since then, others have shown that the Universe is constantly expanding. The key to that deduction was found by the American astronomer Edwin Hubble. In 1923, he discovered that the awesome vastness of outer space contains thousands of millions of star systems similar to our Milky Way, a galaxy of 100 000 million stars. Light from these other galaxies is what astronomers call 'red-shifted'. Light emitted by an approaching star turns bluer as its wavelength gets shorter; that from a receding star has a longer wavelength and becomes redder. Hubble knew from this principle, the Doppler effect, that most galaxies are moving away. If they are doing that, it follows that they must in the past have been much closer and the Universe much smaller.

At some moment in the far-distant past the Universe began to expand. Physicists calculate this as 15 000 million years ago. Working backwards towards that precise point, they can describe what was happening just a fraction of a second after the Universe was born. At one-hundredth of a second, it was something about the size of a pea, compressed in a way that is difficult for most of us to comprehend. Its temperature was so high that it defies our imagination. From that – and the nothingness before it – came everything we know as our Universe. With it also came the great void of space, so vast that light takes thousands of millions of years to cross it.

So far, physicists cannot say what gave birth to that initial pea-sized ball of matter. Nor can they go back much farther than a moment when the Universe was only one-hundredth of a second old. In their thinking, the gap between that moment and that of the actual creation, the big bang, is gigantic. More happened in that time than in the next million years.

For two decades, from the 1940s to the 1960s, many physicists believed that the Universe is in a steady state. For them, there was no big bang: the Universe has always existed and will exist for ever. They

*A **medieval view** of the Universe, depicted by a woodcut in Martin Luther's Bible of 1534, shows God as its Orderer, with Earth at its centre, a belief that had lasted for centuries*

agreed that it is expanding, but held that it is not really changing because, as old galaxies die, new ones take their place.

This steady-state theory was not seriously challenged until the early 1960s. Then, Martin Ryle and a team of astronomers at Cambridge University were studying powerful radio waves sent out by galaxies in distant space. The sources, known as radio galaxies, are so far away that the waves have taken thousands of millions of years to reach us. The team at Cambridge discovered that the remotest zones of outer space hold many more radio galaxies than those much closer to us. From this finding the team argued that the Universe was undoubtedly different all those years ago. If it had changed, how could anyone suggest that it is in a steady state?

In 1965, the steady-state theory took another sharp blow. Two American astronomers, Arno Penzias and Robert Wilson (who later shared the Nobel prize for their work) discovered cosmic microwaves coming from outer space. Working on satellite communications at the Bell Telephone Laboratories in New Jersey, they picked up a strange signal, a form of radiation. The signal seemed to come from no single source, such as the Sun. Wherever they directed their instruments, they detected it, as if it came from a radioactive blanket stretching across the sky. What they had found, they believed – and a majority of scientists now agree with them – were the remains of radiation from the first big bang, the cataclysmic moment when our Universe was born.

Why doesn't the Sun burn out?

If you fail to stoke a fire, its flames at some time will die. Yet the great fire of the Sun has burned nonstop for about 5000 million years with no apparent sign of going out. We, on Earth, soak up a tiny fraction – perhaps one-hundred-millionth – of the Sun's vast energy. The rest of its awesome output of heat and light vanishes beyond the planets and into space.

People in many cultures regarded the Sun as a miraculous gift from the gods, quite different from earthly fires and therefore not likely to fail them unless the gods were made angry. We now know that the Sun will eventually burn away. Tests show that its temperature fluctuates. Since 1979, it seems to have cooled by one-tenth of 1 per cent, but that is not a sign that the great fire is going out. Space

scientists believe that, because of the Sun's volatile nature, this minor change may soon be reversed.

The Sun is composed of almost 75 per cent hydrogen and 25 per cent helium, plus much smaller amounts of oxygen, carbon, neon, nitrogen, magnesium, iron and silicon. It is known as a main sequence star, one that shines by burning hydrogen. At the Sun's heart, the hydrogen was once compressed with such force that it started a nuclear reaction. In this giant furnace, the hydrogen is converted by nuclear fusion into another combustible gas, helium, in a reaction similar to that in an H-bomb. Thus, the Sun is both burning fuel and creating it. As the hydrogen store diminishes, its stock of helium grows. The light and heat coming now from the Sun were actually produced in its core many millions of years ago.

When we burn fuel on a fire, we are converting matter – wood or coal – partly

GAMBLER'S LUCK GAVE SCIENCE A BOOST

The big-bang theory and some landmark discoveries in astronomy came from one of the most remarkable and unlikely teams in the history of science. In 1923, at Mount Wilson Observatory, near Los Angeles, a one-time mule skinner, gambler and roustabout of little education linked up by chance with a polished, cultured and potentially brilliant young astronomer.

When Mount Wilson was under construction, Milton Humason drove mule teams loaded with equipment up the mountainside. His keen interest in his cargo and how it fitted into what was then the world's biggest telescope led to work as the observatory's cleaner and odd-job man. When the night telescope assistant suddenly fell ill, young Milton stepped in, and showed such natural skill that he became permanent telescope operator and observing aide.

With Humason, astronomer Edwin Hubble struck up a partnership that, over thirty years, was to win world renown. In operating the telescope and photographing faint galaxies, Humason showed ability equal, if not superior, to that of any professional astronomer in the world. With his colleague's help, Hubble made his famous discovery of separate galaxies – groups, mainly of stars, bound together by gravity and marking specific regions in space.

Together, the pair produced a classification of the galaxies. Then, they measured the spectra of distant galaxies, the sum and frequency of light emitted by their millions of stars. They found to their surprise that the light is red-shifted – each spectral line has a longer than normal wavelength – showing that the galaxies are moving away. They found, too, that the more distant galaxies are receding at greater speed. The ratio of the speed of recession to distance is known as Hubble's Constant. From Hubble's discovery of receding galaxies came the big-bang theory explaining

the origins of the Universe. The time that has elapsed since the big bang is sometimes referred to as Hubble Time.

Before his death in 1953, Hubble helped complete the Hale Reflector on Mount Palomar. His partner, Humason, who died in 1972, will for ever be remembered as the odd-job man who seized his chance when the moment came, and won a lasting place in the history of astronomy.

The rare team of astronomer Edwin Hubble and one-time gambler and roustabout Milton Humason (above) made discoveries that led to the big-bang theory. An artist's impression shows the Hubble space telescope, one of the most remarkable satellites yet launched, which was named in honour of the astronomer

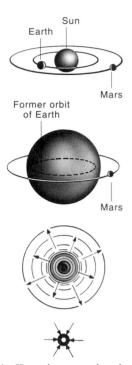

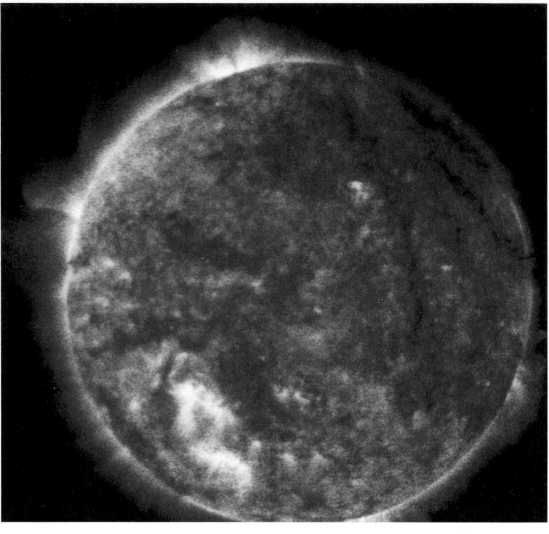

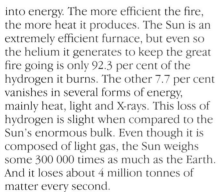

An X-ray image, *relayed from a space rocket, produced this close-up of the Sun and its corona, the outer part of the solar atmosphere. In time, the Sun will begin a series of death throes (above), engulfing the Earth and other planets to become a red giant. Its outer layers will vanish to leave a white dwarf*

into energy. The more efficient the fire, the more heat it produces. The Sun is an extremely efficient furnace, but even so the helium it generates to keep the great fire going is only 92.3 per cent of the hydrogen it burns. The other 7.7 per cent vanishes in several forms of energy, mainly heat, light and X-rays. This loss of hydrogen is slight when compared to the Sun's enormous bulk. Even though it is composed of light gas, the Sun weighs some 300 000 times as much as the Earth. And it loses about 4 million tonnes of matter every second.

Scientists predict that the Sun has enough hydrogen to keep the fire going for another 5000 million years, about as long again as it has already burned. If humans still inhabit the Earth at that time, they and all other life will perish in a terri-fying holocaust.

Before its great fire dies, the Sun will turn into a red giant, bloated to about 100 times its current size. First, it will engulf Mercury and then Venus, the nearest planets. The Earth's atmosphere, which normally shields it from the intense heat of the Sun, will drift away. Then the Earth's oceans will boil and vanish in

steam. Without the cooling effects of its atmosphere and oceans, Earth itself will turn into a massive ball of fire. Mars will disintegrate next.

The Sun will become what astronomers call a 'white dwarf', a star with a tiny, white-hot core. Now very unstable, it will produce no energy. Gradually, like the heart of a dying fire, it will change colour, turning in this case from white to yellow and red until, finally, as a black dwarf, it disappears from sight.

If that sounds depressing, take heart! If the Sun switched off its power tomorrow, it would be ten million years before its surface cooled sufficiently for anybody on Earth to feel the chill. In 5000 million years' time, humans may well have found an answer to impending doom.

Why doesn't the Sun grow bigger?

The Sun is a giant ball of hydrogen and helium gas. And it is on fire. If we heat a balloon of gas, it expands. That is why a hot-air balloon rises. Because the air in the balloon has expanded under heat, it is

lighter than normal air, and capable of lifting a basketful of people into the sky.

If the same principle applies, it seems logical to expect that the Sun's heat would make its own volume expand. We know that it doesn't do so. In fact, to most people, the Sun seems to behave with complete reliability – a constant and unchanging source of light and heat.

A solution to the problem of why the Sun doesn't grow in size was found in the 1920s by a British astronomer, Arthur Eddington. He argued that, if the Sun consists solely of gas, its force of gravity should draw that gas into a small and fairly tight ball. Because the Sun doesn't collapse in this way, another force keeps it in a balanced state. That force, he and others deduced, is heat. As gravity pulls inwards, heat pushes outwards. One force cancels out the other. Those twin forces, pulling equally, ensure that the Sun can't get any bigger. Nor for a long time can it become any smaller.

From these deductions came others. Already, the Sun's force of gravity was known. Eddington then calculated how much heat was needed to produce an equivalent and balancing force, and found that it was millions of degrees. At its heart, the Sun's temperature is 15 million°C (27 million°F). American physicist George Gamow worked out that a pin-head brought to the same temperature, if that were possible, would set fire to everything within a radius of 100 km (60 miles). So vast is the Sun's ball of gas that by the time heat reaches the surface it has cooled to a modest 5800°C (10 400°F).

The Sun's surface is in a state of constant turbulence as hot streams of gas break through. Cooler gas, more condensed and therefore heavier, sinks downwards into the furnace. These great flows are visible from Earth, giving the Sun a mottled appearance of light (hot) areas and dark.

Why does the Sun have spots?

The Sun is not only a turbulent mass of hydrogen and helium gas. Enormous electric currents generate vast magnetic fields, which come and go as dark spots on the Sun's surface. These spots form in groups, grow in intensity and number, reaching a peak every eleven years.

Sunspots were first seen in ancient times. But it was not until the nineteenth century that their cyclical nature was first discovered. A German amateur astronomer, Heinrich Schwabe, hoping to see a new planet pass in front of the Sun's shining disc, became interested instead in some dark spots on its surface. For about seventeen years, he sketched the position and density of these spots and, by 1843, had established their pattern. He noted that their peak coincided with a brilliant display by the aurora borealis and aurora australis (northern and southern lights).

Early this century, American astronomer

George Hale added to Schwabe's work. He discovered that sunspots produce intense magnetic activity and that those with strongest force are about 8000 times as powerful as the Earth's magnetic field at its surface.

Subsequent work has shown that sunspots, many of which are several times the size of the Earth, are part of vast solar storms. From time to time, magnetic fields reach the Sun's surface from far below. They block the flow of heat and light from the core so effectively that, where they appear – marked by a dark patch – the surface is at least 1000°C (1800°F) cooler than adjacent areas.

If these flare-ups occur near the centre of the Sun's disc and facing the Earth, they can produce a magnetic storm in our polar regions. Radio reception is crackly, compasses go awry, and our weather may suddenly change.

Solar flares may also upset migratory birds, which sometimes navigate by the Earth's magnetic field. In 1988, a solar storm sent clouds of electrically charged protons and other subatomic particles into space. At the time, some 3000 homing pigeons were racing from France to England. Bad weather obscured the Sun and the stars, by which the birds usually steer. They switched to their in-built emergency direction-finders only to find them jammed by solar fallout. Few birds reached their home lofts. Race organisers and pigeon owners were puzzled about the disappearance until scientists explained how the pigeons were deceived.

High-energy particles from solar flares pose a serious risk also for astronauts, threatening them with radiation sickness and cancer. Manned space missions are usually postponed if intense solar storms are anticipated.

Celestial fireworks light up the northern skies whenever the aurora borealis puts on its display. Auroras occur also in the southern hemisphere – the aurora australis. All are linked with the Sun's magnetic storms. Charged particles in the solar wind interact with gases in our atmosphere, producing an ever changing array of white and multicoloured lights

Why does the Sun rise in the east?

As the Earth moves in its orbit round the Sun, it also spins – at about 1600 km/h (1000 mph) at the equator. It took many centuries for astronomers to make that point. In about 350 BC, the Greek philosopher Heracleides first advanced the theory that the Earth turned, not the sky. Nobody believed him.

In the 1620s, Galileo Galilei noticed that spots on the Sun changed their position. He deduced that the Sun was actually revolving, and argued that in his view the Earth did the same. In 1633, the Catholic Church demanded a public renunciation. Galileo was forced to declare that the Earth was fixed. How, after all, could we walk on Earth if it were constantly spinning like a top? In 1992, after a long inquiry, the Church finally acknowledged its error.

In time, other astronomers showed indisputably that the Earth and other planets revolve but at different speeds. In 1851, the matter was proved without doubt. In a dramatic demonstration, French physicist Jean Foucault suspended

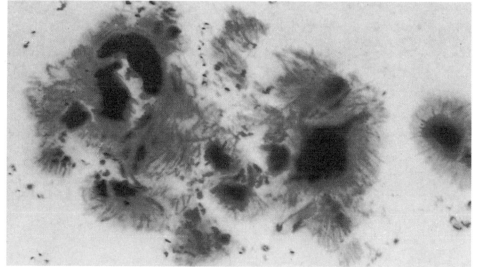

Vast solar storms bring the Sun out in spots. The dark patches are extensive magnetic fields on its surface, which reduce light and heat. Most are many times the size of Earth

a long pendulum from the ceiling of the Panthéon in Paris and set it swinging. As it swung, its tip left a mark in a patch of sand underneath. A heavy weight tends to swing in the same direction, but hour by hour the position of the mark changed. Beneath the pendulum the Earth was turning – as all visitors could see.

All planets except Venus rotate from west to east, so it is always the east that gets the first glimpse of the Sun. That never changes, no matter where the Sun is in the zodiac or where the Earth is in relation to the Sun.

You can test that for yourself with a table lamp and a globe of the Earth, if you have one. If not, use a ball. Switch on the lamp and pretend that it is the Sun, and that the globe or ball is the Earth (even though the Sun is big enough to swallow up 1.3 million Earths). On the ball, draw America, Europe/Asia or Australia, whichever is most familiar to you. Turn your globe or ball slowly from west to east. If you are looking from above, that is anti-clockwise. As you will see, the Sun's light always falls first on a continent's eastern side, and travels during the day gradually to the west. One complete turn of the ball represents a day in the life of our planet.

Proof positive *that the Earth rotates came from physicist Jean Foucault in Paris in 1851. He set a giant pendulum swinging so that it cut a path in a layer of sand. During the day, the path gradually changed, showing that the Earth itself must be turning*

PLOTTING YOUR STAR SIGN

*A **fanciful map** of the southern sky by James Barlow in 1790 shows signs of the zodiac on its perimeter and emblems representing constellations. The Babylonians first observed the Sun's orbit, and divided it into twelve segments. These they named after the group of stars that seemed to be closest to the Sun. The names are our zodiac signs: Aries, Taurus, Gemini, Cancer, Leo, Virgo, Libra, Scorpio, Sagittarius, Capricorn, Aquarius and Pisces*

Observers in centuries past soon discovered that the Sun moves through the sky in two basic ways. Every day it rises along our eastern horizon, reaches its highest point at noon, and sets in the west. Day by day, throughout the year, it moves gradually eastward relative to the stars, a fact you can easily check.

Go outside just after sunset, and pick out a bright group of stars in the western sky. Move your position so that the stars line up with a fixed object, such as a telegraph pole or lamp standard. If you look at the same stars from the same spot about a week later, you will find that they have moved closer to the horizon and nearer to the Sun. In a few more weeks, the stars will not be visible, because they will have set before the Sun goes down.

If you could plot the Sun's position relative to the stars for a year, you would find that it completes a circle, which astronomers call the ecliptic. The Babylonians gave names to the Sun's position month by month. Astronomers use these, translated and modified through the centuries, to indicate the Sun's position. And astrologers refer to them in predicting your future.

If you have ever wondered about why the dates of your star sign seem so peculiar, there is a simple explanation. The Sun is directly above the equator twice a year, on March 21 and September 23. These are known as the equinoxes. When the constellations were named all those years ago, the northern hemisphere spring equinox on March 21 coincided with the beginning of the constellation Aries. Because of this, Aries was assigned approximately the first twelfth of the year, starting with March 21. The other signs were given the succeeding twelfths.

To say that the Sun is 'in Aries' means that from our viewpoint the two are roughly in the same direction. In fact, the stars are far removed, millions of times farther out in space than the Sun is from the Earth.

Uncovering the Moon's secrets

Why do we always see the same side of the Moon?

In 1609, soon after the telescope's invention, the great Italian astronomer, Galileo Galilei, adapted it as a means of studying the night sky, its first use in astronomy. Galileo's telescopes were crude by our standards (his first magnified objects about three times), but they showed him the heavens as nobody had seen them before. For all that, his overall view of the Moon, though clearer, was not much different from that seen by the first humans about three million years ago or by Babylonian astronomers in 2000 BC.

Whether we look at the Moon with our naked eyes or with the most powerful telescopes, we see only one face of it. To understand why this is (and perhaps to explain it to a child) try this simple illustration, in which you will act as the Earth and the child as the Moon. Stand on a spot and get the child to move in a circle round you by stepping to the side, face turned towards you all the time. As the child moves, you turn slowly so that you are constantly facing one another. When both you and the child have turned a full circle, you will be back where you started without either of you having seen the back of the other. But that can happen only while you keep your rotations perfectly synchronised. If the child made only 99.999 per cent of a turn in every complete orbit, you would eventually see his or her back.

The Moon rotates once on its axis in the twenty-seven and a third days that it takes to complete a circuit around the Earth. If it rotated slightly faster or slower, the other face would gradually come completely into view. But that doesn't happen. The rotation of the Earth and of the Moon are so perfectly synchronised to keep the Moon's other face hidden that they might almost be meshed by gears.

Can that precision be accidental? You might believe so, except that many other moons – the satellites of Mars and Jupiter, for example – show only one face to their parent planets. For so many moons in the solar system to act in this way is no coincidence. They are governed by what astronomers call 'tidal locking'.

When our Moon was molten rock, a bulge developed on its side facing towards Earth. This bulge, a tide in the molten rock, was caused by the Earth's gravitational pull, which acts more strongly on the Moon's closer face than on its far side. As the Moon spun, the tidal bulge of fluid rocks rose and fell, rubbing against material deeper in the Moon's core and gradually slowing down the Moon's spin. While there was a difference between the time it took the Moon to rotate on its axis and for it to revolve round the Earth, tidal friction continued to slow down its spin. Only when the Earth and its moon were perfectly synchronised did the braking action of tidal friction cease. But when it did, the Moon's other face was hidden from direct view for ever.

Fortunately, we no longer rely on a direct view from Earth to give us information about the Moon and other heavenly bodies. In 1959, the Soviet Union's space probe Lunik III sent us the first pictures of the far side of the Moon, since when dozens of other missions by the Soviets and by the United States have added enormously to our knowledge.

Why are there eclipses?

During your lifetime you can expect to see about thirty-six total eclipses of the Moon and perhaps forty-eight partial eclipses. Eclipses of the Sun are much rarer. Like any solid objects bathed in light, the Earth and the Moon, both lit by the Sun, cast shadows into space. The Sun's light comes from a wide disc and not a single point. This gives the Earth a shadow with a soft and lighter edge known as the penumbra. When the Sun, Earth and Moon are in a direct line, the Moon moves into the darkest part of the Earth's shadow. It loses much of the Sun's light, and becomes totally eclipsed, turning a coppery red. The red light is weak sunlight, bent by the Earth's atmosphere, a kind of sunset glow all round the edges of the Earth, some of which reaches the Moon. If you were on the Moon during an eclipse, that is indeed what you would see – the Earth outlined by a trim of fiery red.

If the Moon passes into only the penumbra, the lighter part of the Earth's shadow, it will grow dimmer, as you can see with the naked eye. This is a partial eclipse. If at that time you were standing on the Moon, you would see part of the Sun blacked out. If you had a thermometer, you would soon notice that outside

The Moon's other face, which we never see, was photographed in 1969 by astronauts in lunar orbit on the Apollo 11 spacecraft. The large crater is about 80 km (50 miles) in diameter

your spacesuit the temperature had dropped sharply, because the Moon's surface quickly loses its heat.

Eclipses of the Moon occur only when the Moon is full – that is, when the Sun and the Moon are on opposite sides of the Earth. Because the Earth is so much larger than the Moon, it casts a large shadow, which varies according to the Moon's distance from the Earth. For this reason, the Moon may take as long as 105 minutes to move through the Earth's shadow, making eclipses of the Moon much longer than those of the Sun. Also, they can be seen by everybody facing the Moon at the time.

Eclipses of the Sun are caused by the Moon passing between the Earth and the Sun. All goes dark, because the Earth is in the Moon's shadow. For about seven minutes, the Sun may be seen only as a vague circle, glowing dimly at its perimeter. The eclipse is visible only in a region some 275 km (170 miles) wide. Close by, people may see only a partial eclipse.

You may wonder why an eclipse of the Moon doesn't occur every twenty-nine and a half days, whenever the Moon is full. The reason is that, for an eclipse to take place, the Moon's path in the sky must be close to what astronomers call the ecliptic – the Sun's path in the sky relative to the stars. But the Moon's orbit is tilted a little above or a little below. Only at two points, or nodes, do the Moon's path and the ecliptic coincide, putting the Moon into Earth's shadow.

Because eclipses are comparatively rare, people in centuries past have had good reason to study them. Eclipses were recorded as early as 750 BC. In ancient

times, they were seen as messages from the gods, so Babylonian and Greek astronomers paid them particular attention. Predicting an eclipse was like delivering an advance message from a supreme being, and ancient astronomers discovered how to do so with considerable accuracy. Some people believe that the great stones of Stonehenge were arranged so that ancients could predict when lunar eclipses would occur.

Why does the Moon change shape?

An easy way to understand why the Moon changes its shape is to hold a tennis ball in sunlight and view it from different angles. As you move, the sunlit part of the ball will take on the different shapes that are so familiar when you look at the Moon. When the Sun is behind the ball, you will get a thin crescent. Move slightly until the crescent covers half the ball, and you will see the shape of a quarter Moon. With the Sun behind you – but not directly behind – you will see what is called a gibbous Moon; the reflected light, convex in shape, covers more than half but less than a complete circle.

If the Moon is visible at the same time as the Sun, hold the ball in sunlight and at arm's length, so that you can no longer see the Moon. Sunshine on the ball will give you an exact replica of the Moon. It is easy to see why. Because it is so far away from the Moon and the ball, the Sun is shining on both at almost the same angle.

As it moves, Spaceship Earth allows us to see the Moon from different positions

on different days. Thus, the sunlit part that we see is constantly changing shape. Conventional names describe these different shapes: a new Moon is the crescent at its thinnest and just as it starts to grow once more. During the next twenty-nine and a half days, the span between one new Moon and the next, the Moon will appear in all its forms until finally it wanes to its slimmest – the old Moon – before disappearing.

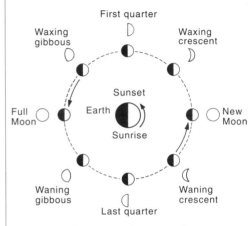

Waxing and waning, *the Moon orbits our planet every 27⅓ days. Its phases, as seen from Earth, are shown in the outer circle*

Why doesn't the Moon have air and water?

Long before the first astronauts landed there in 1969, astronomers had calculated that the Moon had no air. They suspected that it had no water either.

They were right on both counts. The Moon has no atmosphere, and lunar rocks brought back from that first landing contain no water. (Most Earth rocks hold 1 or 2 per cent.) To preserve the lunar rocks in their original condition, the National Aeronautics and Space Administration (NASA) stores them in its Planetary Materials Laboratory in Houston, Texas, in an atmosphere of dry nitrogen – which is absolutely waterless.

The Moon has no air or water because its gravity is too weak to hold on to an atmosphere or to any water vapour. It may seem strange that there isn't at least some thin air or some wispy clouds of vapour clinging to the Moon. The reason is linked to what is called escape velocity.

When astronauts take off into space, their vehicles need sufficient speed – escape velocity – to enable them to shake off the pull of Earth's gravity. The Earth's escape velocity is 11.2 km (7 miles) a second. That of the Moon is only 2.4 km (1.5 miles) a second. Anything moving faster than that and away from the Moon will head off into space. A speed of more

The Sun vanishes *during a total eclipse, but its fiery corona – its atmosphere – is still visible and provides a magnificent spectacle. Such a blackout of the Sun occurs when the Earth passes directly into the shadow cast by the Moon. A solar eclipse is never seen for more than seven minutes and forty seconds, and occurs only in a region some 275 km (170 miles) wide. The Moon's shadow is divided into a dark central umbra and a lighter region known as the penumbra. Where the umbra falls, the eclipse is total; within the penumbra region, it is partial*

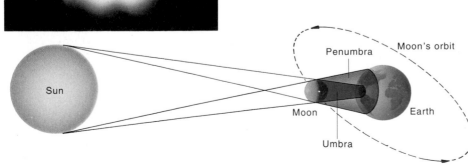

WANTED – A REASON FOR THE MOON

Venus and Mercury have no moons. The Earth has a moon that is larger in relation to its own size than the moons of giant planets. Mars has two small moons, and the gas giants – Jupiter, Saturn, Uranus and Neptune – each have several. Far-distant Pluto, a midget among planets, has a moon about half its own size.

Astronomers still cannot answer the basic question of why some planets have several moons and others have none. Nor can they say for certain how moons – satellites of bigger celestial bodies – came into being.

English astronomer George Darwin considered the problem last century, and concluded that the Earth and Moon were originally one. The fast-spinning Earth flung part of itself into space, leaving a great hole that became the Pacific Ocean. Scientists discount this theory, mainly because they say that the Earth's spin, which is the same now as it was originally, is too slow to throw a Moon-sized body into orbit. In addition, analysis of rocks brought back from the Moon shows too many differences between them and rocks on Earth.

A second theory is that the Earth and Moon were formed separately, along with all the planets. If that were so, nobody can explain satisfactorily why they are now composed of different material – the Earth with a metallic core and the Moon of solid rock. Another theory held by some astronomers is that the Earth and Moon were formed of different material at different times. The Moon followed an orbit that took it close to Earth, and the pull of Earth's gravity trapped it as a satellite.

A more recent idea is that a large asteroid hit the Earth soon after its creation 4600 million years ago. The immense shower of debris from the collision was thrown into space where it eventually formed the Moon.

Whatever happened – and one day astronomers will provide a full explanation – an accident we cannot explain gave us inspiration for poetry and romance.

The stuff of poetry and drama, too, the Moon provides the dominant imagery in Shakespeare's A Midsummer Night's Dream

than 8640 km/h (5368 mph), the Moon's escape velocity, sounds very fast. But molecules of gas regularly go as fast as that and sometimes much faster. At times, when the Sun is overhead, the temperature of rocks on the Moon rises to 110°C (230°F). High temperatures mean higher molecular speeds. Given time, any gas or water molecule on the Moon would reach a speed higher than that of the escape velocity – high enough for it to leave the Moon and never return. Any atmosphere and water on the Moon in ancient times would eventually have zoomed away into space.

Why does the full Moon look as big as the Sun?

The diameter of the Moon is only 3476 km (2160 miles), about the distance from London to Beirut. The Sun, diameter 1.39 million km (864 000 miles), is roughly 400 times as big. Yet when we look at a full Moon in the sky it seems to be about the same size as the Sun. The apparent sizes match so closely that occasionally the Moon's disc shuts out the Sun's light completely, causing a full eclipse.

What we see as a similarity in size is just an accident of time. The Moon, though much smaller, looks as big as the Sun because it is much closer. On average, the Sun is about 150 million km (93 million miles) distant, 389 times farther away from us than the Moon.

In the past, the Moon was much closer. At one time, 1200 million years ago, it was as close as 18 000 km (11 200 miles) and would have appeared about twenty times as big as it does today. Gradually, it is moving away, an effect of the Earth's tides. Gravitational pull from the Moon causes our oceans – 70 per cent of the Earth's total area – to bulge. If the Moon is over the Atlantic, the pull causes a bulge in that ocean and another in the

Indian Ocean on the far side of the globe. These bulges are seen by us as tides, and their frictional effect, acting like brakes, slows down the Earth's rotation, lengthening our day by about one second in 62 500 years.

This gradual slowing of the Earth allows the Moon to spin more quickly, inducing it to move away. The Earth's rotation also has an effect on the tides, drawing the bulges eastwards. This great shift of water affects the Earth's gravitational force, exerting a sideways tug on the Moon that also causes a gradual speed-up in its orbit. In this process, the lunar orbit itself is growing bigger so that, even though the Moon is travelling faster, it will take longer to make its sweep around the Earth. Calculations show that this process will go on for several million years, until eventually the Moon takes fifty-five days to complete its orbit, twice its current time of twenty-seven and a third days. That doesn't mean that we will eventually see

The fiery globe of the Moon sinks over the sea. Large as it seems, it was once closer and looked about twenty times its size today

the far side of the Moon, because as the Moon takes longer to complete its orbit, the Earth's spin will slow down, keeping the two bodies in step, like a well-trained couple of ballroom dancers.

Why is the force of gravity lower on the Moon?

An Olympic Games held on the Moon, if that were possible, would produce some remarkable results. High jumpers would soar six times as high, broad jumpers would leap much farther, shot putters and hammer throwers would hurl their missiles astonishing distances. All this would result from the fact that gravity on the Moon is only one-sixth of that on Earth. Thus, a 6-kg (13-lb) bag of potatoes bought in an earthly market would weigh only 1 kg (about 2 lb) on the Moon.

In 1665, the 23-year-old Isaac Newton first explained the force of gravity, and drew up a mathematical formula, known as Newton's laws, by which we can calculate gravitational pull on the Moon's surface or elsewhere. Newton explained that all objects exert the force of gravity. The attraction between two bodies, such as the Moon and the Earth, depends on their mass – the greater their mass, the stronger the attraction – and also on their distance apart, measured from the centre of each body.

Newton's laws still work extremely well, and are used in guiding spacecraft. As Apollo 8 headed towards the Moon and came under the influence of its gravitational pull, astronaut Bill Anders commented, 'I think Isaac Newton is doing most of the driving now.'

A spacecraft falling towards the Moon would take longer and not hit so hard as

one dropping to Earth. The Moon's mass is much less than that of the Earth's. For one thing, the Moon is much smaller – only about one-quarter of the Earth's diameter of 12 800 km (8000 miles). Also, the Moon is made of lighter material. On average, a cubic centimetre (0.06 cu in) of rock from the Moon weighs only 3.3 grams (0.1 oz) compared with 5.5 grams (0.2 oz) for a cubic centimetre of Earth.

For these reasons, gravity on the Moon is much less than that on Earth, both of which Newton's laws enable us to calculate precisely.

Why did astronauts go first to the Moon?

When President Kennedy announced plans for the Apollo program on May 25, 1961, the aim was to get men to the Moon and back, safely, before the decade was out. The target was the Moon – not Mars, Venus or Jupiter – and nobody seriously considered any other.

Distance was the key. The Moon is much closer to us than anything else in the solar system. On average, it is 384 400 km (238 900 miles) away. The closest that Venus comes is about 110 times that distance, and Mars is twice as far as Venus. Except for the Moon, those are our nearest neighbours.

Apollo took four days to reach the Moon. If the destination had been Mars, Neil Armstrong and his team would have taken at least 270 days. Another factor is that the Moon's gravity is much weaker than that of Mars or Venus. Apollo would have needed to carry much more fuel – not just for the longer journey but to generate the lift-off force to free itself from gravitational pull before heading back. The escape velocity from the Moon is 2.4 km (about 1.5 miles) a second; from Mars 5.1 km (3.2 miles); and from Venus l0.3 km (6.4 miles) a second – more than four times as fast.

Made to measure for astronauts in Apollo's crew, each pressure suit had seventeen layers and was worn over a water-cooled undergarment. The suits were heavy – 72.5 kg (160 lb) – but on the Moon weighed only a sixth of that. Edwin 'Buzz' Aldrin (right) takes a walk, with Neil Armstrong and Apollo 11 reflected in his visor

Why did astronauts need spacesuits for a Moon landing?

The Moon has no atmosphere – no air of any kind. Astronauts could have breathed by carrying tanks of oxygen, as sea divers do, but they faced other hazards that called for special suits.

Because the Moon has no air, the spacesuits were pressurised to keep each astronaut's body at the normal atmospheric pressure on Earth of 1 kg per sq cm (14.7 lb per sq in). Had they stepped from their suits, the spacemen would have experienced something worse than the bends sometimes suffered by divers. Their bodies might have exploded.

The astronauts also had to be shielded from fierce heat. Even on Earth, dark-coloured rocks, which absorb heat, can become too hot to handle. The Moon has no atmosphere to reduce the Sun's energy, and in full sunlight the temperature rises to 110°C (230°F), higher than the boiling point of water.

Earth has a built-in thermostat to control the Sun's heat. Our atmosphere, mostly oxygen and nitrogen, warms up and carries heat away from hot land surfaces. Oceans cover 70 per cent of the

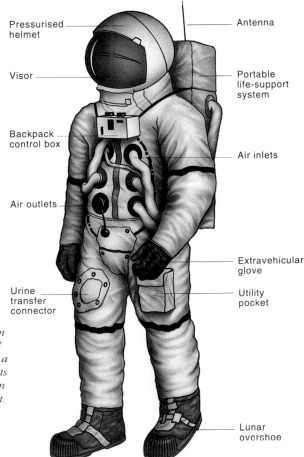

Pressurised helmet
Visor
Backpack control box
Air outlets
Urine transfer connector
Antenna
Portable life-support system
Air inlets
Extravehicular glove
Utility pocket
Lunar overshoe

Earth's surface. Because water absorbs a great deal of heat before warming up, these vast seas effectively control sudden swings in temperature.

The Moon has none of these advantages. With no atmosphere to penetrate, the Sun's intense ultraviolet light arrives unscreened. Spacesuits had special visors to filter out the UV rays. The garments' thick fabric gave protection too against micrometeorites – minute dust particles that hit the Moon at high speeds, sufficient to make a naked spaceman feel as though he'd entered a sandblaster.

Why does the Moon have so many craters?

The Moon is a museum, a showcase of ancient craters, some of them more than 150 km (nearly 100 miles) wide. For centuries, scientists debated their origin. In Galileo's time, and until the 1890s, it was accepted that the craters were the vents of huge but extinct volcanoes. This was a reasonable assumption, because they looked much like Earth's volcanoes: roughly circular and always ringed by a steep-sided, mountainous ridge.

American geologist Grove Karl Gilbert was the first to question that theory, asking why the Moon's craters were at ground level, not on mountain peaks. A few years later, in 1929, another American, astronomer Forest Moulton, argued successfully that meteorites hitting the

Moon with explosive impact at 108 000 km/h (67 000 mph) would create circular craters, and throw up a mountainous ridge around them.

Most of the Moon's craters date back about 4000 million years. Before that time, the Moon was constantly growing, because its gravity attracted debris floating around in space – large and small rocks, dust and asteroids. Some of these space missiles were hundreds of kilometres in diameter, and they left craters so vast that we can see some from Earth with the naked eye.

When the bombardment lessened, radioactive elements in the Moon's collection of debris caused massive flows of lava. Surface rocks melted to a depth of 200 km (125 miles). For 500 million years, lava flooded over the Moon's battered face, wiping out some craters and forming those wide dark shadows, known as *maria* (seas), so obvious today.

About 3000 million years ago, the lava flows stopped. More recent meteor strikes have made fresh and sometimes quite massive craters but, had astronauts landed on the Moon in ancient times, they would have seen a landscape much as it is today.

The Moon isn't alone in showing the scars of such a battering. Space probes to other planets reveal similar evidence. It's a sure sign of worlds lacking air and water, which over millions of years can slowly chisel and mould a new face, as they have done on planet Earth.

Why does the Moon sometimes shine by day?

A full Moon shines by day behind peaks in Oregon, USA. Bright as it is, the Moon reflects only a fraction of its received light

The Moon has no light of its own. What we see as moonlight is reflected light from the Sun. Even though moonlight at times turns night almost into day, the Moon's reflective power is very poor. Compared with a field of snow, which reflects almost 100 per cent of the light falling upon it, the Moon reflects only 7 per cent – about the same amount as dark volcanic rock.

But 7 per cent of sunlight is still impressively bright. Sometimes, when the Moon rises during the day, it is bright enough to outshine a dull patch of surrounding sky. Whenever this happens, the Moon will be visible. Even a thin, crescent Moon will stand out plainly.

Why doesn't the Moon fall down?

One commonplace statement that used to be indisputable is that what goes up must surely come down. The launching of spaceships and satellites has shown the argument to have flaws. The heavens are now littered with junk that went up but may never come down.

Why does the Moon, which hangs in the sky like a giant balloon and is pulled by Earth's gravity, not come crashing down on us? The concern, a fear in times gone by, is based on an illusion. The Moon may appear to be motionless, but it is moving in a steady orbit round the Earth. We find that hard to detect, because the Moon is on average 384 400 km

Bombarded by meteors, *the Moon is pockmarked by craters dating back thousands of millions of years. Eratosthenes, a young crater, was photographed by Apollo 17 astronauts in 1972*

(238 900 miles) away. Objects close to us appear to be moving more swiftly than when they are farther away. For example, an aircraft taking off seems to be going very fast to observers on the runway; high in a cloudless sky its movement may be difficult to detect.

The Moon's movement round the Earth is much like that of a ball swung steadily in a circle on the end of a string. The ball tries to fly off in a straight line (as it would do if the string broke) but the string keeps it swinging in a circle. Imagine that the Earth's gravity is the piece of string. The Moon's velocity, about 3700 km/h (2300 mph), is enough to keep it trying constantly to fly off into space. Earth's gravity, which lessens with distance, is still strong enough to keep the Moon within its orbit.

As a young man in the 1660s, Sir Isaac Newton pondered the problems of why the Moon doesn't come crashing down and why it doesn't fly into space. Newton wasn't the first to observe that objects tossed in the air fell to Earth, and the story that he discovered gravity when an apple fell on his head is possibly a piece of popular legend. Perhaps a falling apple, seen as he looked out on an orchard from his study window, inspired him. He reasoned quite rightly that, if objects on Earth were pulled by its gravity, so possibly was the Moon.

While other physicists had argued that this force didn't apply to heavenly bodies Newton believed that it did. Among other principles, he established that the Earth and Moon each have a gravitational pull, one on the other, which keeps them interacting in perfect balance.

The same principle applies to communications and other satellites orbiting the Earth. They are given sufficient velocity to hold a steady orbit. That doesn't mean that they are not falling: indeed, they are. But, as they fall, the Earth's surface is curving constantly away from them, so that they never get any closer.

Why do we say 'once in a blue Moon'?

A sixteenth-century rhyme by an anonymous author counsels us that, 'If they say the Moon is blue, We must believe that it is true.'

The statements of poets and song writers about the Moon are rightly open to question. But in Edinburgh on September 26, 1950, Scottish astronomer Charles Wilson focused his telescope on the Moon and measured its spectrum – its breakdown of colours. He proved that the Moon on that night was blue. Later, Wilson deduced that the Moon's blueness

was caused by oily particles floating high in the atmosphere. The debris came from a forest fire across the Atlantic in Canada, of such intensity that smoke and dust were swept thousands of metres upwards on convection currents.

What we see as light is a combination of colours, from red at one end of the spectrum to blue, indigo and violet at the other. Atmospheric dust tends to give light from the Sun or the Moon a reddish hue. This is because fine dust breaks up the light's combination of colours, scattering the blue and leaving the red to come through more strongly.

That is why we often get a red sky at night or in the morning. The Sun is low, and its light passes through more dust particles than when it is high in the sky. At the other extreme, large particles of water vapour scatter sunlight's basic colours almost equally, making the clouds look white (or grey and foggy).

Medium-sized particles, such as those from the forest fire, scatter red light more effectively than blue light. The red light is filtered out, vanishing against the blackness of the night, and we see that phenomenon – a blue Moon.

Why are blue Moons so rare that we have a saying about them? It's unusual for medium-sized particles of dust or other matter to be swept into the atmosphere. Fine dust is easily blown high into the sky. Water vapour, too, rises readily, and cold air condenses it into large particles which, when heavy enough, will fall as rain or hail. But, once in a blue Moon, a huge fire or a volcanic eruption will send up particles of just the right size to give our poets and astronomers something to sing about.

Why do we talk about the Man in the Moon?

Open a children's story book, and you're likely to find a drawing of the Man in the Moon. For many people, the Moon, with its combination of light and dark areas, looks like a man's face.

The Man in the Moon is always young, freshly discovered by each pair of eyes that sees him for the first time. And he is also ancient, dwelling in the Moon right down the ages, immortal as the rocks and dust of the Moon's geological face. And for those who travel for the first time to the opposite hemisphere, the Man in the Moon may have an unfamiliar face. Britons who visit South America or Australia assert – quite correctly – that their friendly figure from the north has suddenly turned upside down.

*A **friendly face** beaming down from the Moon is a familiar character in story books. This cartoon was drawn in the 1920s*

A galaxy of space explorers

Space exploration began when humans first looked at the sky. Ancient skywatchers noted the position of the Moon and the patterns of stars. Inquiring minds wondered about the drama above – why the Sun rose, why the Moon changed shape, why some stars were brighter, and what portents such matters held.

Throughout history, philosophers, scientists, engineers and imaginative writers have speculated about the nature of our unfolding Universe. Jointly, they took astronomy from the realms of theologians to make its basics a matter of everyday understanding.

The first astronomical records, kept with surprising accuracy 4000 years ago in Mesopotamia, were used more for astrology than science. Wars were planned according to the position of Saturn or Mars, and the ability to offer such advice gave astrologers great power.

The Greeks questioned this reliance on the supernatural. The most illustrious of their astronomers, Claudius Ptolemy, who worked in Alexandria in the second century AD, put forward theories that lasted some 1400 years. He assumed that the Earth was spherical, that it was the centre of the cosmos, and that a natural motion – rotation – drove all planets. He was the first to design a system, named after him, that accurately predicted planetary motions.

For more than 1000 years astronomy and much other learning remained dormant. Then, when Ptolemy's ideas were revived, they acquired the force of religious dogma. Powerful forces in the Church, keen to insist that the Earth was the centre of the Universe, silenced any who argued. Radical thinkers put their own lives at risk.

When the Polish cleric Nicolaus Copernicus proposed that the Sun controlled the planetary system, he was accused of heresy. A luckless follower, Giordano Bruno, was burned at the stake. Not surprisingly, Copernicus withheld publication of his great treatise, *De Revolutionibus Orbium Coelestium* (Concerning the Revolutions of the Heavenly Bodies) until just before he died in 1543. The book remained on the Papal Index of forbidden books until 1835.

The courageous and inspiring work of Copernicus was followed by that of Tycho Brahe, a Danish nobleman. His studies, plus observations collected from others in many parts of Europe, contradicted the general theory, dating

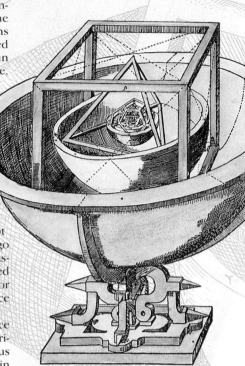

An ingenious model of the solar system was built by Johannes Kepler in 1596. He said that the six known planets were spaced according to the five solids of classical geometry. His laws of planetary motion, developed later, made astronomy into a modern science

Greek astronomer Claudius Ptolemy put the motionless Earth at the centre of the Universe. His ideas lasted about 1400 years

The scientific genius of Isaac Newton ended for ever the long-standing separation that astronomers had given to the Earth and celestial realms. Newton's laws of motion and concepts of gravity led him to develop theories that govern space travel today

back to the Greeks, that the heavens are constant and unchanging.

King Frederick II of Denmark gave Brahe immense funds, said to be more than a ton of gold, to set up the world's first observatory, Uraniborg (Castle of the Heavens) on the island of Hven. There, dependent basically on the naked eye, Brahe and his assistants recorded precise planetary positions for more than twenty years. His work led him to doubt the Copernican model of the cosmos, and he drew up a new one in which the Sun moves round the Earth but all other planets orbit the Sun.

Brahe trained a remarkable young assistant, Johannes Kepler, who produced his famous and quite radical laws of planetary motion. In 1609, Kepler published his *Astronomia Nova* (New Astronomy) which overturned the belief that the solar system moves uniformly and in perfect circles. Astronomy became a science based on physics.

Italian mathematician Galileo Galilei, the first to use the telescope in astronomy, built an instrument that made distant objects look thirty times closer. He saw the Moon, planets and stars as no one had seen them before. His ideas, too, were condemned. In 1633 he was made to 'abjure, curse and detest' before the Inquisition the opinion that the Earth moves round the Sun. Galileo advanced theories of terrestrial motion – acceleration, velocity, speed and inertia – and opened the door for Newton and other renowned explorers of space.

Born on Christmas Day 1642, Isaac Newton was destined to become one of the great mathematicians and thinkers of all time. He ended for ever the idea that the Earth and other planetary bodies are separate and independent. He is best known for discovering the law of gravity, but also he solved the problems of planetary motion. A close friend, Edmond Halley, used Newton's laws to work out the orbit of the comet that bears his name.

For nearly 400 years, space exploration depended almost entirely on what could be seen by telescope. Much of that work was done by amateur astronomers, among whom none won any greater renown than Sir William Herschel, a Hanoverian musican who settled in England in 1757 to escape military service.

Along with exploration by telescope came three and a half centuries of scientific space fiction, much of it about life on the planets. Kepler himself in his *Somnium seu Astronomia Lunari* (Dream, or Astronomy of the Moon) wrote about spirits travelling from Earth to an inhabited Moon across a bridge of shadow created during an eclipse.

In the 1600s, Cyrano de Bergerac depicted journeys on a vast scale, some by rocket. About 250 years later, Jules Verne, who understood the problems of escaping from Earth's gravity, wrote in *From the Earth to the Moon* of a giant gun launching a vehicle into space from a site just 240 km (150 miles) from Cape Kennedy, a fluky prediction. Just before the turn of this century, H. G. Wells wrote his classic fantasy of space literature, *The War of the Worlds* (which Orson Welles later adapted for radio with such remarkable effects) and followed it soon after with *The First Men in the Moon*.

For centuries men had made firework rockets, but by the 1930s liquid-fuel rockets seemed to be the only way to power space flight. German pioneers, notably Captain Walter Dornberger and Wernher von Braun, worked in utter secrecy to perfect a liquid-fuel rocket, a war weapon that was the prototype of future spaceships. In 1944, the giant V-2 missile carrying a ton of explosive and travelling at 5800 km/h (3600 mph) was launched against Britain. It was a superb and terrifying technological success, but came too late to change the course of the war.

Von Braun was not alone in seeing the possibilities of liquid-fuel rockets. Soviet scientists, too, were at work and in 1957 launched Sputnik I, the first satellite. Two years later, they had a triple triumph: Lunik I went past the Moon and Lunik II reached it, crash-landing on its surface. Lunik III sent the first photographs of the Moon's far side.

The race was on in earnest. In 1961, Soviet cosmonaut Yuri Gagarin became the first man in space, but finally, in 1969, the United States struck back with a spectacular achievement watched worldwide on televison. Astronaut Neil Armstrong and his team were the first

Science fiction gave impetus to space research. In Round the Moon, *Jules Verne wrote of a spacecraft fired from a gun*

men on the Moon. Since then, hardly a year has passed without significant probes into space. Exploration by land-based telescopes and manned spaceships has been backed by the astonishing feats of unmanned vehicles and robots. With every mission, they add to the knowledge of the cosmos that began with skywatchers many thousand years ago.

Rockets in World War II *developed by Wernher von Braun paved the way for today's flights into space. Von Braun perfected a liquid-fuel rocket, the V-2, which in 1944 hit Britain. Later he worked on the US space program, helping to produce rockets for the first Moon landings. During that era came the idea for a space shuttle, a reusable vehicle. Space shuttle Discovery (above) blasts off in 1990*

Journeys that stun the mind

Why do we doubt that life exists in space?

In the 1950s, British astronomer Fred Hoyle pointed out that, when Earth was created, its elements were mixed in the right proportions for life to emerge. Living organisms have almost equal numbers of carbon and oxygen atoms. Too little oxygen would have deprived the Earth of rock and soil; too much would have denied existence to the basic molecules in living organisms.

One by one, probes far into space have revealed conditions so different from anything on Earth that it seems that life as we know it is unlikely anywhere else in our solar system. Our galaxy has 100 000 million stars and other bodies. So far we have tested comparatively few planets and their satellites, but many scientists say that the possibility of life exists on only three of them.

In 1976, Viking 1 and Viking 2 examined the soil on Mars for signs of microscopic life. None was found, but nobody is yet bold enough to close the casebook. Mars has many different environments. One of them could have something resembling our bacteria.

Europa, a moon of Jupiter, and Titan, the largest satellite of Saturn, are other possibilities. Space probes show that beneath Europa's outer shell is an enormous well of liquid, which may be water. Europa has no oxygen, and none of the Sun's warmth pierces its shell. However, some dark and oxygen-less places on Earth's seabed hold primitive forms of life. Similar life could perhaps exist in Europa's darkest caverns.

Titan's atmosphere consists of nitrogen and methane. Its surface resembles Earth's – landmasses surrounded by oceans. The oceans aren't water, but they may be a kind of petroleum, formed by weak sunlight and volcanic heat acting on methane. Scientists are reluctant to say that those oceans cannot support life.

Despite all these doubts, a $100-million, ten-year program began in October 1992 to search for signals from other civilisations. The quest, by the United States' National Aeronautics and Space Administration (NASA), is called SETI, the search for extra-terrestrial intelligence. On an intensive scale, it is in two parts: one targets 1000 specific stars; the other scans vast regions of the sky. The world's largest radio telescope at Arecibo in Puerto Rico and others at Greenbank, West Virginia, and Goldstone in California's Mojave Desert explore the northern skies. Australia's Parkes radio telescope

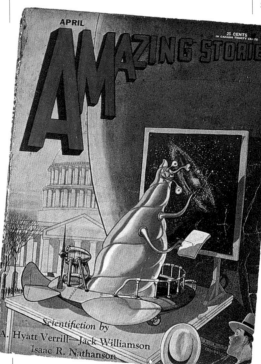

Life in space is a never-ending source of inspiration for sci-fi writers, and has been for many years. This cover, with an artist's impression of a creature from another planet, is from a magazine of the 1930s

surveys the south. Results go to a computer so powerful that it can make 1000 million tests every second to sift messages sent possibly by an alien civilisation from signals occurring naturally in space.

What do researchers expect to find? With luck, a simple (but alien) message indicating, 'We are here … we are here.' If the quest yields nothing, it will confirm what some already believe – that through a remarkable combination of events Earth alone received all the necessities of life. That will provide another good reason to protect it. If we ruin our planet, we'll have nowhere else to go.

Why does it take so long to reach the planets?

Without the magical propellants of sci-fi space travel, we have to rely on chemical rockets to power our spacecraft. Whether their fuel is solid or liquid, the principle is the same: the space vehicle goes off like a firework rocket. Hot exhaust gases thrusting downwards blast the spacecraft beyond the pull of Earth's gravity and towards its target.

Chemical rockets have limits – practical and economic. Take speed: Voyager 2, the fastest space probe yet launched, is travelling at 18.5 km (11½ miles) a second. By the hour – 66 600 km (41 400 miles) – that sounds impressively fast, equal almost to doing a return journey from London to Australia twice in sixty minutes. But for space travel it's a snail's pace. Mars, which at times is the planet closest to us, is on average about 78 million km (48 million miles) distant. Even if a spaceship could travel to Mars at 18 km (11 miles) a second in a straight line, the journey would take seventy-nine days. American and Russian provisional plans for manned missions to Mars estimate that crews will spend two years on a return journey. Spacecraft have to follow a curved path made up of various orbits usually governed by the Sun's gravity. And they need to aim at where their target will be, not where it is when they set off, a task requiring precise navigation to ensure that the vehicle doesn't zoom past its goal and fly for ever into space.

It's reasonable to expect that propulsion systems will improve. But even if we take everything at its best – boundless energy, a spaceship with ultimate powers of acceleration and the ability to fly in a straight line – nobody knows the limits of human endurance in space. To travel faster requires a faster breakout from the

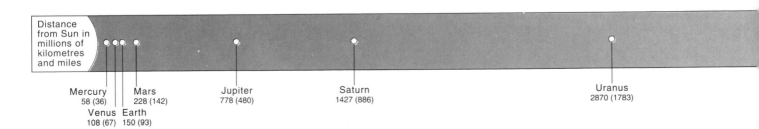

Distance from Sun in millions of kilometres and miles

Mercury
58 (36)

Venus
108 (67)

Earth
150 (93)

Mars
228 (142)

Jupiter
778 (480)

Saturn
1427 (886)

Uranus
2870 (1783)

Pluto

Sun

Mercury

Mars

Venus

Earth

Neptune

Uranus

Saturn

Jupiter

ond, 19.6 m per second after two seconds, and so on.) Physicists express that acceleration as 1 g – one times the force of gravity. Space scientists say that a journey in which the craft accelerates at 1 g is possibly the limit of human endurance. To guarantee a landing on Mars, the brakes would have to be applied, and the spaceship would need to decelerate at 1 g for the second half of the trip. At that rate, the journey would take only forty-nine and a half hours.

But what about trips to more distant planets? If you are planning to go aboard, you'd better take something to read. The closest that Neptune comes to Earth is 4300 million km (2672 million miles) – fifty-five times as far as Mars. At 1 g and in a straight line, the journey would take fifteen and a half days. When your skipper or ground control applied the brakes at the halfway mark, you'd be travelling at a sizzling 6529 km (4057 miles) a second.

Journeys to the stars would be more formidable, because a new speed limit would come into force – the speed of light. As Einstein demonstrated, nothing can travel faster than 300 000 km (186 000 miles) a second. Even if our spaceship could accelerate at 1 g until it reached 99 per cent of the speed of light, then decelerated at 1 g in the final stretch, a trip to Proxima Centauri, our nearest star, would take five years and four months.

Five years-plus is how we on Earth would time the journey. But, strangely, the astronauts would find the trip much faster. As Einstein predicted in his theory of relativity, the spaceship's clocks would slow down compared with those on Earth. A voyage across our whole galaxy – one that takes light 100 000 years to make – might happen while the astronauts had

An epic journey into space was the theme of Stanley Kubrick's movie, 2001, released in 1968, a year before the first Moon landing

constraints of Earth's gravity. All motorists know that fast acceleration from a standing start thrusts them back in their seats. Similarly, a spacecraft's rapid lift-off creates within the vehicle an artificial gravity that presses its occupants fiercely downwards. High speed over a long journey would make limbs feel useless, and possibly damage the heart.

Without air resistance, an object falling from a height accelerates at a rate of 9.8 m (32 ft) per second every second. (A falling apple, for example, will reach a speed of 9.8 m per second after one sec-

Meet our neighbours in the solar system. The illustration on the right shows the relative size of the nine planets, including the Earth; the chart below gives the average distance of each from the Sun. An easy way to remember them and their order is through the following mnemonic, in which the initial letters are those of the nine planets: Men Very Easily Make Jugs Serve Useful Nocturnal Purposes. The Sun's gravity keeps the planets moving round it. Pluto's eccentric orbit at present takes it closer than Neptune to the Sun

Neptune
4500 (2800)

Pluto
5970 (3700)

their morning coffee. Even journeys across the immense distances between galaxies, reckoned in thousands of millions of years at the speed of light, might be possible. Those left on Earth would age at the normal rate. When the astronauts returned from the stars after a five-year trip, by their reckoning, they would land in a world that had aged by several million years.

It's reasonable to assume that one day spacecraft will travel at 30 000 km (18 600 miles) a second, one-tenth the speed of light. At that speed, a trip to the nearest star would occupy about half a lifetime. Space scientists have considered what to do if nobody applies for that kind of holiday. They have seriously discussed sending teams of robots into space on a kind of planet-hopping mission.

The first team would arrive in, say, forty years. On landing, it would set up a factory to build two replica spaceships, mining the materials from an asteroid. Each new craft would head off to another target, and repeat the operation, while the parent robots transmitted data to Earth about their landing site and its surrounding system.

If all went well, the number of space probes would double every forty years. In 1000 years' time, some thirty million space laboratories and their robots would be doing field work among the stars.

Why is Venus called the Morning Star?

Venus, known sometimes as the Brilliant Light of Love, can outshine everything in our view except the Sun and the Moon. But we see it only in the early morning or evening, which is why it is known as both the Morning Star and the Evening Star. The nicknames, commonly applied many years ago by people who had little idea of the true nature of Venus, are misnomers. Venus is not a star but a planet. Like Earth, it orbits the Sun, travelling closer

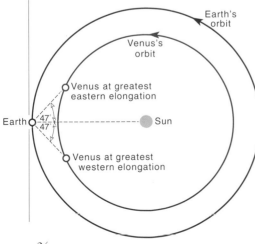

Radar mapping by the Magellan probe produced this image of Venus's northern hemisphere. Radar pulses pierce the dense clouds hiding the planet, and bounce back to reveal the pitted nature of its terrain. Venus is named after the Roman goddess of love. Inset: a detail from The Birth of Venus by Botticelli

to it than we do – on average about three-fifths of our distance.

Astronomers can plot Venus's position by measuring the angle between a line joining the Earth to Venus, and a line from the Earth to the Sun. Because Venus is closer to the Sun than we are, the angle between the Sun and Venus, as seen from Earth, never gets much larger than 45 degrees, an eighth of a circle. If you can see Venus in the eastern sky, daylight for most people will be no more than three hours away. Thus, Venus appears in the early morning and vanishes when the Sun is up. See Venus in the west, the so-called Evening Star, and night is about to fall. Like the Moon, Venus has phases, which you can see quite clearly if you watch

Light of Love and Earth's twin are two names given to Venus, which is known also as the Morning Star and the Evening Star. Like Earth, it is a planet, but its orbit is much closer to the Sun. At its greatest eastern elongation, we see Venus shining as an evening star; at its greatest western elongation, it appears as a morning star, to herald the dawn and vanish soon after

regularly with a good pair of binoculars. It is at its brightest – visible often at noon – when the angle between the planet and the Sun is 39 degrees. Its crescent then corresponds to that of the Moon five days after a new Moon.

When we see the bright light of Venus, we are in fact not seeing the planet itself but its atmosphere. Venus is completely enshrouded in swirling, unbroken clouds, which reflect 76 per cent of its received sunlight. These clouds, made up almost entirely of carbon dioxide, mask the planet in secrecy, blocking all attempts to view its surface by telescope. But recent advances in radar and space exploration have enabled us to peek through the curtain, and assess the planet's forbidding environment and cratered terrain.

Because of its similarity in size, slightly smaller than the Earth in diameter, Venus is often referred to as Earth's twin sister. We now know that size and mass are among the few things they have in common. Because Venus is closer to the Sun, it is logical to expect that it would be warmer there than on Earth. Data sent back by spacecraft show that it is astonishingly warmer. Its average surface temperature is about 460°C (860°F), over four times that of boiling water. Venus has a runaway greenhouse effect, caused by its enormous volume of carbon dioxide – more than 7500 times as much as the Earth's. Atmospheric pressure is almost 100 times as high.

From Earth, Venus can be a beautiful sight, a worthy choice by the Romans when they named it after their goddess of love and beauty. But they didn't know what we know about the planet's torrid temperament, a hellhole where life is impossible and where even the most intrepid of human explorers may never be able to land.

Why does Venus spin backwards?

All planets in the solar system, including the Earth, spin from west to east. But not Venus. This planet, about the same size as the Earth but much closer to the Sun, revolves from east to west, and does so very slowly.

Strangely, its day is longer than its year. Whereas the Earth turns full circle once in twenty-four hours, Venus spins once in a little more than 243 of our days. In less

than that time. – 225 days – it makes a complete trip round the Sun. That orbit is so short because Venus is on average only 108 million km (67 million miles) from the Sun and its orbit is almost circular. Those of other planets are elliptical and therefore longer.

Even though Venus is comparatively close to us, much about it remained a mystery until quite recently. Because it is shrouded in dense cloud, astronomers cannot see and measure its rotation rate by watching it through a telescope. Radar beams, bounced off the planet's surface, and many space probes have given us data about its rate and direction of spin.

So far, nobody has explained its retrograde rotation. One theory proposed that about 4600 million years ago, when the solar system formed, an accident stopped the infant planet Venus dead in its tracks. A likely event was a collision with another young planet, from which Venus emerged spinning in reverse. But in 1980, mathematicians analysed Venus's movement, and knocked on the head the notion that its backward spin came from an early collision. Meanwhile, astronomers pore over data from spacecraft and an array of other modern technology in their attempts to find an answer. It remains one of the most puzzling aspects of this most mysterious and inhospitable of planets.

Why is Mars known as the Red Planet?

Even with the naked eye, most of the surface of Mars looks rusty red in colour. And areas that look green are in fact red, an optical illusion caused by contrasting light and dark areas.

Astronomers have given many explanations for these various colours. Some argued that the green areas were vegetation and red regions were oceans. Then, in 1934, American astronomer Rupert Wildt gave a new theory: the browns, yellows and reds on Mars came from iron oxide – rust. Examine a rusting corrugated-iron roof, and you will see iron oxide in many of its colours.

When the Viking 1 and Viking 2 spacecraft landed on Mars in 1976, their instruments scooped up and analysed surface material. They proved that Wildt's theory was indeed right. Mars is covered with rusty, red sand, which is often whipped 30 km (nearly 20 miles) high by winds blowing at more than 100 km/h (62 mph).

These intense storms occur particularly when Mars is closest to the Sun, and the planet may be hidden by dust for months. When the dust settles, it is thoroughly mixed, giving Mars a surface of almost uniform rusty redness.

Sunset on Mars *was recorded in 1976 by the Viking 1 lander, part of which can be seen at bottom right in this colour-enhanced image. Contours around the Sun result from the imaging system. The spacecraft analysed surface samples, and found them to be iron-rich clays, a form of rust*

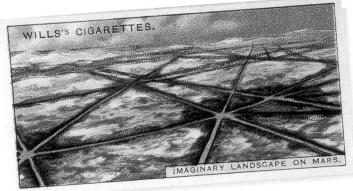

WILLS'S CIGARETTES.

IMAGINARY LANDSCAPE ON MARS.

A cigarette card of the 1930s gives an imaginary view of Mars and its canals. Reports of 'irrigation channels' led to beliefs and fears that intelligent beings inhabited the planet

Why was Mars said to have canals?

On Hallowe'en Night, 1938, radio listeners in New York were startled to hear a man's voice saying, 'Ladies and gentlemen, I have a grave announcement to make. Incredible as it may seem, strange beings who landed in New Jersey tonight are the vanguard of an invading army from Mars.' Orson Welles, doing a radio dramatisation of the H. G. Wells novel, *The War of the Worlds*, sent his audience into a panic. For more than sixty years, the notion that there might be life on Mars had been spreading. In 1877, Italian astronomer Giovanni Schiaparelli said that he had identified *canali* on the Red Planet. In Italian, *canali* means 'grooves' or 'channels'. But the word was translated into English as *canals* – and the myth was up and running. Canals signified intelligent life; beings lived on Mars who were capable of carrying out vast engineering projects and even of building spaceships with which to invade and attack the Earth. Popular-science articles surmised that these canals were designed perhaps to save a dying planet by transporting water from the poles to the arid heartland. The argument had some logic. Because gravity on Mars is low, only about two-fifths that on Earth, water vapour in the atmosphere soon leaks into space. The planet, said the pop-scientists, had a perpetual problem to stop its farmlands from drying out, and its engineers were solving it.

Once one astronomer had seen *canali*, others saw them too. Percival Lowell, a wealthy American astronomer, set up his own observatory in Flagstaff, Arizona, took hundreds of photographs and, in 1896, published maps of Mars showing a network of some 500 canals or aqueducts. These, he reasoned, were used to supply water for irrigation.

Helping to cloak the planet in mystery was the difficulty of seeing it clearly. Earth's turbulent atmosphere and Mars's frequent dust storms make moments of high clarity rare. Thus, astronomers who glimpsed what they thought were Martian-made waterways often had no chance to confirm their beliefs. The human imagination often leads the eye. A series of unconnected dots can quickly take on a coherent pattern, especially if that pattern is suddenly obliterated by dust or clouds.

Edward Maunder, a British astronomer who was one of many observers to insist that Mars had no canals, decided to test the theory that the so-called canals were optical illusions. Inside a group of circles he made a number of irregular, spotlike marks. He lined up some schoolchildren so that they could barely distinguish the

INTO THE VALLEY OF DEATH WENT THE MARS ROVER

California's Death Valley is so similar to the Martian landscape that scientists have carried out tests there for a planned mission to Mars in 1996.

The mission, initiated by Russia, also involves scientists and engineers from France and other European countries, including Austria, Germany and Finland. The California-based Planetary Society, which is helping the Russians, invited them to Death Valley to test out a radio-controlled dune buggy over the kind of terrain it might meet on Mars. NASA scientists named one area in the Californian desert Mars Hill, after analysing data sent back from Mars by Viking space probes.

The buggy, being developed in St Petersburg, must be able to operate partly on its own, reacting to its video cameras and other sensors in recognising and avoiding pitfalls and traps. Space scientists say that a mobile robot of this kind, which can do tests over a wide area, has a considerable advantage over stationary probes, which see no farther than the horizon.

Controlled by radio, a mobile robot is tested in Death Valley, which has features matching the harsh landscape on Mars

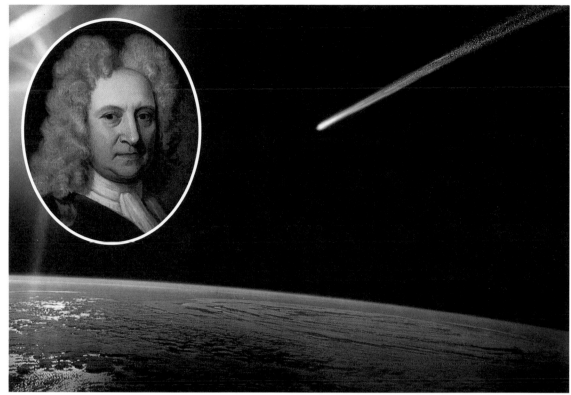

Halley's Comet puts on a spectacular show as it streaks across the night sky during its latest appearance in 1986. The comet is named in honour of Edmond Halley who suggested in 1705 that it reappears every seventy-six years. Inset is a portrait by R. Phillips of the famous astronomer, aged about sixty

spots, and asked them to draw what they saw. All of them connected the spots into straight lines, similar to those that Lowell had put on his maps.

Since the days of Lowell and Orson Welles, the Viking and Mariner space probes have mapped Mars in exquisite detail. We now know for sure that the canals were indeed optical illusions, but Mars does have water – frozen as ice. When Viking 1 and Viking 2 landed on the planet, their cameras revealed a bleak and forbidding landscape. No Martians roamed the dry and dusty wastes, but we still can't prove that the Red Planet has always been lifeless.

Why do comets get smaller?

Down the ages, comets have been objects of fear. Unlike the planets and the stars, which kept an orderly and reliable place in the night skies, comets were streaks of light that came suddenly and in a few weeks disappeared.

Their ghostly appearance – a fuzzy ball with a luminous tail – resembled, some said, the head of a demented woman, shrieking a warning from above. The word comet comes in fact from the Greek *kome*, meaning 'hair'. Without doubt, comets warned of bad news, some catastrophe in waiting. Inevitably, disaster came. Down the ages, prophets and soothsayers have always found something to support their predictions.

For many centuries, astronomers have tried to unravel the mystery of the vanish-

ing comet. Some argued that once a comet had gone from sight it had gone for good. In 1705, Edmond Halley suggested that a comet he had seen in the sky in 1682 had appeared before. Studying the records, he found that comets were seen in 1456, 1531 and 1607. He argued that this was the same comet coming back about every seventy-six years. He predicted that the comet, which was subsequently named in his honour, would be seen again in 1758. On Christmas night, 1758, a German amateur astronomer spotted the comet, sixteen years after Halley's death.

Astronomers explain that comets take an elliptical orbit round the Sun. The paths of some are comparatively short. Biela's Comet, now extinct, was seen every six and three-quarter years; others do not return for many centuries.

Comets are massive rocky balls bound together by frozen gases and ice. Each time they approach the Sun some of the gases are warmed and freed, and ice boils away. Sometimes, great chunks of rock fly off. In 1846, Biela's Comet broke in two. The twin halves did a lap of honour in 1852, before bursting into fragments. For a time, the fragments put on their own fireworks show, peppering the Earth with meteors every November until finally, by the 1980s, the last remnants of Biela were no longer to be seen.

Halley's Comet came back again in 1986, but the millions who saw it were generally disappointed, a sign perhaps that it, too, is growing smaller and may one day vanish from sight.

Why do comets have tails?

It is one of the wonders of astronomical research that we can tell what distant planets are made of without the need for space probes to visit them. As long ago as 1862, Swedish physicist Anders Ångström noted that dark lines in the solar spectrum – a breakdown of the Sun's light – were in exactly the same position as they would have been in light that was passing through hydrogen. He deduced correctly that hydrogen is a major constituent of the blazing Sun.

By a similar process we can tell what comets are made of, and we know that their chemical structure is different from that of other members of the solar system. In 1950, after studying their structure, American astronomer Fred Whipple described comets as 'dirty snowballs'. He discovered that they are composed largely of water and gases, all of which when frozen at very low temperatures turn into various kinds of ice. Bound up in these ices are dust particles.

When a comet nears the Sun, some of the ice vaporises, surrounding the comet with a cloud of dust and gas. When sunlight passes through this cloud, it lights it up, enveloping the comet in a fuzzy glow. As well as heat, the Sun creates a breeze, the solar wind, caused by electrically charged particles heading in all directions. This breeze blows the fuzzy cloud in a kind of slipstream behind the comet. That is why all comets have a luminous tail, which never faces towards the Sun.

Why are the outer planets so enormous?

If you could have taken a trip on Voyager 1 to look at Jupiter, the Lord of the Heavens, you would have seen something quite different from Earth and our nearer neighbours, Mercury, Venus and Mars.

The inner planets are rocky and tiny when compared with such mammoths as Jupiter, Saturn, Uranus and Neptune, which look today much as they did when they were first formed some 4600 million years ago. These remote planets are sometimes called 'the gas giants', because they are composed largely of hydrogen and helium, which make up about 98 per cent of the Universe. Hydrogen and helium are made of very light atoms. The lighter an atom, the more quickly it will move. If it is heated, it moves faster still. Only a planet of vast size and with a strong gravitational force can keep such unruly atoms in check; it holds on to them more easily if it is cold.

Astronomers have for long debated why the gas giants exist at all, and why such a change in character takes place in the distance between Mars, the last of the rocky planets, and Jupiter, the first of the gas giants. Many believe that the solar system formed from a vast cloud of swirling dust and gas. Most of the dust and gas collapsed to the centre of this mass, and formed the Sun. Part of the rest was pulled together by gravitational attraction, and made up the planets.

The Sun contracted, became hotter, and erupted in an atomic fire, blowing away most of the nearby dust and gas. As they warmed up, the planets closer to the Sun lost their hydrogen and helium, leaving only their rocky cores. The outer planets, too far from the Sun's heat, kept their lighter gases. This explains their immense size. Jupiter, the largest planet in the solar system, has a diameter of about 143 000 km (89 000 miles), eleven times that of the Earth. To fill its great volume would require more than a thousand Earths.

Vast as they are, the outer planets are extremely light in density – only 1.4 grams per cu cm, about a quarter the density of typical material from the Earth.

Among these remote giants is an odd-ball that doesn't quite fit the pattern. Pluto, the Guardian of the Dark, is smaller than our Moon and extremely cold. It is believed to be completely covered by frozen methane, a gas that turns to ice at -182.5°C (-296.5°F). Astronomers puzzle over how this midget got out there among the giants. One theory is that it was once a moon of Neptune, and during an extraordinary close encounter between that planet and Triton (Neptune's largest moon) escaped to take up its own lonely orbit far out in space.

Why is Neptune blue?

In California, it was 9 pm on August 24, 1989. Some 2.7 million people sat ready to watch 'Neptune All Night', a TV spectacular that promised the first pictures of the planet, almost as soon as they were received by 130 scientists at the Jet Propulsion Laboratory (JPL) in Pasadena.

Voyager 2 made its closest approach to the planet when it passed over the north pole of Neptune at 9 pm Californian time, its cameras focused. Because of the vast distances involved (Neptune was then 4400 million km/2750 million miles from Earth), it was about 1 am before the images were seen at JPL. When the pictures were screened on TV soon after, people reacted with cries of delight. Nobody had expected Neptune, in full colour, to be such a beautiful sight, a glorious and spectacular shade of blue.

Until Voyager 2's epic journey, Neptune's cold world was almost a total mystery. The giant planet, with a diameter nearly four times that of the Earth, was first noticed by Galileo in 1612, but he failed to recognise it as a newcomer. Observing the moons of Jupiter, he saw what he believed to be a star nearby, and after further study even commented that he thought the 'star' had changed position (as only a planet would). Perhaps because he feared trouble with the Church, he failed to follow up his discovery. It was

Four moons hover *near Jupiter, largest of all planets, in this photograph taken by a Voyager spacecraft. Farthest from the camera is Io, then Europa, Ganymede and Callisto (bottom right)*

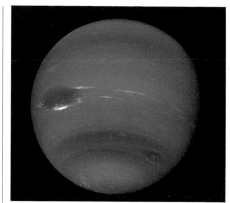

Cries of delight greeted images of Neptune sent from Voyager 2. The photograph shows the planet's true colour and some clouds

not until 1846 that Neptune was identified as a new planet.

We now know that Neptune, inexplicably, is racked constantly by savage storms and winds three times as strong as the worst Earth tornado. Like Uranus, with which it is linked, it has an atmosphere made up chiefly of hydrogen and helium. One difference is that the gases surrounding Neptune contain ethane, a constituent of the natural gas methane. The methane absorbs red light, giving the planet its distinctive shade of blue.

Why do some planets have rings?

For centuries, the strange rings around Saturn have presented astronomers with a major puzzle. Galileo's telescope was too weak to give him a clear view. He surmised first that Saturn had a bulge on each side, and then that he was looking at three planets in one. A few years later, in 1614, German astronomer Christoph Scheiner thought that the bulges were in fact two crescents: Saturn was a planet with handles! Forty years on, Christiaan Huygens, the Dutch mathematician and physicist who invented the pendulum clock, studied the planet with a more powerful telescope, and said that Saturn was surrounded by a flat ring, which encircled the planet at its equator. In 1665, French-Italian astronomer Gian Domenico Cassini observed that there were two rings, one inside another.

Saturn's rings shine more brightly than the planet itself, and they are gigantic, stretching some 272 000 km (169 000 miles), more than twenty times the diameter of the Earth. Since Cassini's discovery – known still as the Cassini division – other astronomers have puzzled over what makes up Saturn's rings and those

surrounding other giant and distant planets, Jupiter, Uranus and Neptune.

All these planets, because of their size, have tremendous gravitational force. In the 1850s, French astronomer Édouard Roche considered what would happen if the Moon were closer to Earth and therefore under a much stronger gravitational pull. He reasoned that what is known as the 'tidal effect' of the Earth on the Moon – which tends almost to lift its surface, as the Moon's gravity moves our oceans – would impose such a strain that the Moon would break into pieces. Applying that reasoning to the rings around Saturn and other planets, Roche deduced that they could not be solid sheets of matter.

Since then, Voyager probes have sent back a mass of data about the rings surrounding the distant gas giants, but nobody has yet explained convincingly why the rings were formed. One favoured theory takes up Roche's point that rings form when a moon, or perhaps an icy

comet, comes too close to a large planet and gets torn apart by gravity. As pieces break away, they go into independent orbits around the planet, and through constant collisions eventually become clouds of fine dust and gas.

To support this moon-crunching theory, astronomers assert that only the largest planets, with the strongest gravity, have rings. The rings differ in puzzling ways – some are extremely thin and dark, and reflect no light – but do not exist around the smaller inner planets, Mercury, Venus, Earth and Mars.

A counter-argument is that the rings formed in the earliest days of the solar system from the same material that made up the planets. For a time, the large planets may have resembled a flattened disk of gas and dust. Gravity pulled the more solid material into a smaller space, condensing it eventually into a planet. The remaining dust and gas tightened into the ring systems that we see today.

Rings around Saturn have long puzzled astronomers and, despite evidence sent back by spacecraft, they still search for an answer. In these Voyager 2 photographs the rings' faint colours have been enhanced by computer. Impurities in the ice of dust particles making up the rings is one reason given for their varying colours. The image below was taken 43 million km (27 million miles) from the planet, that on the left within 5000 km (3000 miles)

Fiery jewels in the night sky

Why are some stars known as pulsars?

The heaviest stars die explosively, signalling their end with a brilliant flash of light called a supernova. Astronomers know that a supernova's radiance is not quite the finish, but it is without doubt the beginning of the end.

When a supernova dies, it leaves behind a small ball of highly concentrated matter, composed entirely of subatomic particles known as neutrons. This discovery was made by two British radio astronomers, Anthony Hewish and Jocelyn Bell. In 1967, they picked up strange but regular signals from outer space. Dismissing the idea that the signals came from

inhabitants of some other civilisation, they realised they had found a source of pulsating energy in space.

Since that discovery at Cambridge, England, astronomers have found hundreds of other radio beacons in the skies, and say that a million more exist, waiting to be identified. These stars flash signals in much the same way that the rotating lantern of a lighthouse sends out a distinctive message. They are the remnants of supernovas, are only some 25 km (15½ miles) in diameter, and vary in their rate of spin. The fastest rotates at about 642 revolutions per second; others turn only once in that time.

Like lighthouses, spinning beacons are readily identified, because their radiation sweeps across the skies, giving out a

steady pulselike beat. For this reason, these stars are known as pulsars.

Pulsars, or neutron stars, consist of matter compressed so tightly that it is difficult for us to comprehend. If we could recover a pinhead-sized piece of a neutron star, it would weigh about a million tonnes – roughly equal to twelve vessels the size of the USS *Nimitz*, the world's largest warship.

The gravity on a neutron star is so intense that, if by some misfortune you were to land on one, you would suffer instant death. The force would flatten your body, spreading it thinner and thinner over a wide area until it could be flattened no more. Finally, you would become a wafer of crushed flesh and bone just one atom thick.

Why do stars twinkle?

It's a wonderful experience to go into the countryside on a pitch black night, far from the glare of city lights, and stare upwards at the awesome array of stars in the heavens. Alas, places where you can do that are becoming fewer. No wonder, then, that more people who have discovered the joy of star-gazing are travelling sometimes great distances to enjoy this magical pleasure.

The night sky is filled with stars of many different ages, but all have life spans of many millions of years. Astronomers can identify stars at various stages of development – at their birth, in the prime of their lives and amid the throes of death.

Stars are born when a cloud of gas, mainly hydrogen, is compressed under the force of its own gravity. That's how our Sun, which is also a star, came into being. If you have ever blown up a bicycle tyre with a hand pump, you will know that the pump gets hotter as the gas is compressed. So it is when a gas cloud draws itself into a tighter and tighter blob. If the temperature at the centre of the condensed cloud rises to 10 million°C (18 million°F), its hydrogen explodes like an H-bomb. This reaction turns the hydrogen into helium, which adds fuel to the fire, and a star is born.

By studying our Sun, we get a guide to the nature of other stars. We know that the heaviest stars burn more furiously, and use up their fuel more quickly. Lightweight stars don't burn so brightly, but their life might be 100 times that of a star with the weight of our Sun.

The British astronomer Edmond Halley first discovered early in the eighteenth

Fine filaments of luminous gas flow from a roughly circular shell. They are remnants of supernova Vela, 1500 light years distant

century that the stars moved, and then deduced that even the closest were many millions of miles away. For a speck of light to be visible on Earth from that distance meant, he argued, that it must come from a source as large as our Sun.

If Sirius, the brightest star, had a fire as big as the Sun's, Halley said it must be 19 million million km (about 12 million million miles) distant. His calculation, like Sirius itself, was way out, but Halley had no way of telling the relative brightness of the two stars. Sirius is in fact more than four times as far away – 82 million million km (52 million million miles).

The light from the Sun doesn't twinkle, because our star is so close to us. Nor does the light from the planets, which is steady because they reflect light from the Sun. Stars make their own light, and it twinkles because it travels so far. Also, because it is weakened by distance, starlight doesn't pass so easily through the Earth's atmosphere, which adds to the twinkling effect.

The light from individual stars varies in intensity. But whether they shine brightly or dimly, their remoteness and resultant lack of power at that range still give them that nursery-rhyme twinkle.

Celestial signposts, the stars have guided ships for centuries. A 1575 woodcut shows crew in the stern navigating by means of an astrolabe, an instrument for measuring the height of the Sun or the stars above the horizon. The table lists what appear from Earth to be the brightest stars. A star may shine brightly because it is comparatively near or because it is particularly luminous

THE TEN BRIGHTEST STARS	
NAME	*CONSTELLATION*
SIRIUS	Canis Major
CANOPUS	Carina
RIGIL KENTAURUS	Centaurus
ARCTURUS	Boötes
VEGA	Lyra
CAPELLA	Auriga
RIGEL	Orion
PROCYON	Canis Minor
ACHERNAR	Eridanus
HADAR	Centaurus

ASTRONOMY CAN MAKE YOU A STAR

Peering at the stars through a home made telescope on Christmas night 1980, Roy Panther identified a new comet, the first to be discovered by a British astronomer for fifteen years. Three weeks later, David Branchett, viewing the night sky from his bedroom window and using only a pair of ordinary binoculars, saw a bright glare in the sky. Still unidentified, it is called Branchett's Object.

Remarkably in an age when nations spend enormous sums on technology for exploring space, the world's amateur astronomers – 15 000 of them in Britain, 250 000 in the United States – continue to make outstanding contributions to our knowledge of the stars.

Star-gazing is a rewarding pastime that offers a sense of adventure and excitement. A major discovery, such as that of a comet, can bring immortality. Four comets are named after George Alcock, long acclaimed as one of the world's most famous amateur astronomers, who discovered them all through binoculars.

You don't need elaborate or expensive equipment to become a star-watcher. Most likely you already have the essentials – a reclining chair and a pair of binoculars. Star maps, to be found in many books, will help you to sort order from chaos. Find somewhere away from the glare of street and house lights. Using a weak torch to avoid dazzle, try to relate your star map to the patterns of the night sky. Several thousand stars are visible to the naked eye, but binoculars will add clarity to your viewing.

If you have a camera – almost any kind will do – photographing star patterns will help your understanding, and give valuable references for future work. Clamp your camera to something firm, and use a cable release to avoid camera-shake. Experiment with time-exposures of different lengths, anything from thirty seconds to ten minutes, with your lens set on infinity. Work at first with black-and-white film. If you learn to develop your own film and enlarge your prints, which is not difficult, you will get even more pleasure from your star-watching.

To speed your progress, join an astronomical society, where you will find experienced amateurs keen to give advice, particularly about equipment. Some groups operate their own observatories for members who don't own a telescope.

One glance at the sky on a clear and moonless night will demonstrate that it offers an infinite source of fascinating and useful study, with the incentive that professional astronomers can never keep watch on it all.

Great discoveries have come from amateurs using simple equipment

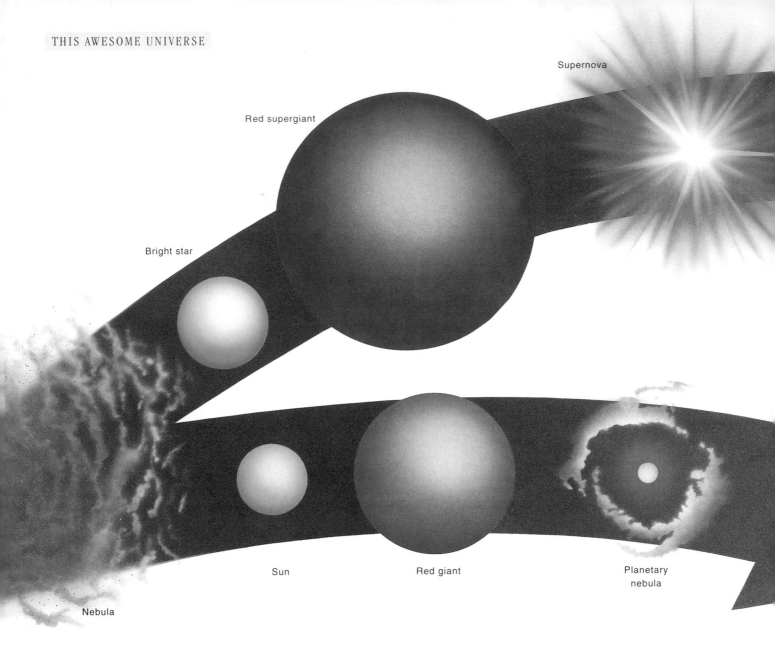

Supernova

Red supergiant

Bright star

Sun

Red giant

Planetary nebula

Nebula

Why do stars die?

A star's life is fixed at birth. It depends on its weight – how much matter it holds. A star is born when a cloud of hydrogen gas becomes so compressed that it explodes in a nuclear reaction. The greater the star's mass, the more fiercely will it burn, and the shorter will be its life.

The nuclear furnace that gives the stars their light is exactly the same as that in our star, the Sun. Like the Sun, the stars are both burning fuel and creating it. The nuclear reaction that brought the stars to life turns hydrogen into helium. Gradually, the hydrogen store is depleted by the light and heat given off by the star. In time, all stars will burn out, as will our Sun in about 5000 million years.

The heavyweight stars – those of vast bulk – last only about one-thousandth as long as the Sun. Lightweight stars may burn for 500 000 million years, 100 times

as long, but their light is much weaker. As a star begins to fail, it doesn't flicker out. Suddenly, it expands to about 100 times its size to become what astronomers call a red giant. The heart of the fire dies, but nuclear reactions continue farther from the core, swelling the star's perimeter. The outer layers of gas vanish into space, leaving eventually just the dead heart, still glowing with white heat, the corpse of a once shining star. These visible remnants are known as white dwarfs. In time, as they cool, they change colour to yellow, orange and red, until their light finally fades from view for ever.

Why do some stars become black holes?

Imagine taking a powerful torch and trying to shine it from a dark cave into the blackness outside. Strangely, no light emerges: a mysterious force swallows the

beam, refusing to allow any trace of it to leave the cave. It would be a terrifying predicament. If the force inside the cave stopped light from emerging, nothing else could possibly escape – including you. If a rescue mission came, all its members would be sucked into the cave, never to leave it.

In practice, of course, no human could live for even a fraction of a second in an environment where the force of gravity traps light. But that is what astronomers say happens in black holes, the most bizarre star corpses of all. We cannot see them, because they give out no light.

The term 'black holes' was first used in 1967 by Professor John Wheeler at a New York meeting of the Institute for Space Studies. He was describing stars that have collapsed completely because of the tremendous force of their own gravity.

Other astronomers have since theorised that, if the core of a supernova, an exploding star, is heavier than the mass

Pulsar/neutron star

Black hole

White dwarf

Black dwarf

A star is born *in a nebula, a cloud of glowing gas or dust in space. The gas is mainly hydrogen which, because of its own gravity, draws itself into a tighter mass. When a gas is compressed, as in a bicycle pump, it grows much hotter. In a nebula, temperatures rise to 10 million°C (18 million°F) and start nuclear reactions. The hydrogen turns into helium, a process that creates enormous energy – and the star begins to shine. How it progresses depends on its mass. A heavyweight star with a mass twenty times that of the Sun has a shorter life and a spectacular death before ending as a black hole*

A sun dies *when its nuclear fuel runs out. Our Sun, which is an average star, has a mass of some 2000 million million million million tonnes and a core temperature of about 10 million°C (18 million°F). Heavyweight stars burn rapidly, generating at their heart temperatures of 4000 million°C (7000 million°F). All suns, as they exhaust their fuel, swell to become bloated red giants. Then, slowly, they shrink, puffing out rings of gas before turning into dense white dwarfs. These shine feebly for an immense time before losing the last of their heat. All that remains of each sun in the end is a cold black dwarf*

of three Suns, it cannot end up as a pulsar, a spinning neutron star. Under the force of its gravity, the core shrinks virtually to nothing. However, the gravitational pull remains across a region several kilometres wide, from which nothing can escape, not even light.

If black holes emit no light, how do we know they are there? In recent years, astronomers have found some evidence. The gravitational pull from a black hole can draw gas from a companion star. Gas spiralling into the hole gives off X-rays. Thus, by searching for X-rays, astronomers can locate black holes. Also, they have noticed that a visible star in the region of a suspected black hole deviates slightly in its course. By assessing the star's size, they can calculate the force needed to shift it. One star in the constellation Cygnus (the swan) was seen to swing round an invisible companion. It was responding to a force equal to that made by ten Suns.

Since then, in July 1992, two American astronomers have located a black hole with the mass of 1000 million Suns, 100 times more powerful than any previously discovered. Its volume would fill the entire solar system. This black hole, in a galaxy known only by its star catalogue number, NGC 3115, is some 30 million light years from Earth.

We know that neutron stars have astonishing mass, but nothing as awesome as that of a black hole, which exerts a gigantic gravitational pull. An individual's weight depends on the force of gravity. For example, on the Moon, where gravity is weaker, we would all weigh less. Within 6 m (20 ft) of some black holes, a 1-kg (about 2-lb) packet of sugar would tip the scales at 1 million million tonnes.

Why do some stars explode?

All stars end their lives spectacularly, but some explode with such force and shine so brightly that their deaths can be seen from Earth with the naked eye.

In February 1987, astronomers in the southern hemisphere saw an obscure star suddenly send out a brilliant light, charged with more energy than in all the rest of the visible Universe combined. The star, seen previously only by telescope, had died to become Supernova 1987A.

Astronomers traced its history back to a massive star, known only by a catalogue number, Sanduleak -69° 202, which was about twenty times the size of our Sun. Massive stars burn more furiously and with a shorter life. This one lasted only eleven million years, so it died in infancy, compared with the 10 000 million years that is the Sun's life expectancy. When a

Into the black hole *goes a spaceship, never to be seen again, in this still from a Disney movie. Black holes exert such enormous gravitational force that not even light can escape from them*

massive star's supply of hydrogen runs low, it expands to become a red supergiant. But at its centre remains a compact core of helium which, as the pressure and temperature of the star continue to rise, fuses in a nuclear reaction into carbon, a heavier element. The nuclear furnace turns the carbon into still heavier elements, including neon, silicon and iron.

The dying star assembles concentric rings of five or six different elements until the process breaks down. Now the furnace stops producing more energy, and starts to consume it. The heavyweight's centre suddenly becomes very unstable, and in a few seconds all is blown apart.

In August 1885, the Hungarian Baroness de Podmaniczky spotted a remarkable supernova during a party. She set up a telescope on her lawn, and invited guests to view the stars. Turning the telescope towards the Andromeda Nebula, she saw the brightest supernova ever to be seen in an outer galaxy. The supernova, some 2 million light years from the Earth, shone briefly with a light at least fifteen million times that of the Sun.

Why do some stars wobble?

Astronomers keeping constant watch on far-distant stars claim that some of them occasionally show a mysterious wobble, deviating strangely from their predicted path. At first, such claims brought scepticism, and suggestions that the telescope itself had wobbled.

Now it is believed that some stars do wobble in response to the gravitational pull of massive but unseen companions. The wobble is so slight that it is scarcely detectable, but astronomers now believe that it is caused by the gravitational pull of a planet circling the star.

So far, even with the most modern telescopes, nobody has yet seen a planet beyond our solar system. One difficulty is that a star's glare outshines anything in its vicinity, but a way of detecting these hidden planets is to analyse the star's light. A wobbling star sends out light of a changing wavelength – reduced while the star moves towards the Earth and lengthened while it is moving away. Watch on the star Gamma Cephei shows that the wavelength of its light changes, indicating that the star is influenced by a body that is 1.6 times as massive as Jupiter, a giant with 318 times the mass of Earth.

IN THE END, THERE MAY BE A NEW BEGINNING

Astronomers' theories about the big bang and an expanding Universe are so hard for most of us to comprehend that scientists have tried to explain them in everyday terms.

Here is one analogy that may help to clarify the idea of an expanding Universe. Take a balloon and inflate it sufficiently to allow you to paint its surface with dots to represent many of the bodies in space. As you blow up the balloon, the dots move farther away from the centre and from one another. The Universe is, of course, three dimensional. So try, if you can, to visualise that suspended inside the balloon is a cloud of dust, with each separate particle – a heavenly body – keeping its own relative place as the space inside grows bigger.

The picture is roughly right but for two faults. One is that, as the balloon grows bigger, so do the painted dots. In an expanding Universe, the galaxies move constantly outwards but, unlike the dots, they do not expand. Another flaw is that the dust particles inside the balloon move outwards individually. As the Universe expands, the space between the galaxies continues to grow. The force of gravity within each galaxy keeps its members in order and stops them drifting away.

The Universe expands because of the cataclysmic force that came with its birth, but it would be wrong to think of the big bang as a kind of bomb, whose explosion sends splinters into space. Until that moment, 15 000 million years ago, there was no space. The big bang created it and everything within it.

Astrophysicists debate whether the Universe will expand for ever. It depends, they believe, on gravity, the force that one body exerts on another. Surprisingly to most people, the force that binds the Moon to the Earth, for example, also acts between one galaxy and another. If there were no gravitational force, the Universe would expand much more quickly. Gravity slows it down.

Eventually, the pull of gravity could put such a brake on the Universe's expansion that it comes to a halt – and switches suddenly into reverse. The pieces will start on a long return journey, a collision course that could end where it all started in another big bang. Another side to the argument is that the total mass of the Universe – its constituent parts – is not great enough to allow gravity to take over in that way. In which case, the expanding Universe may be for ever.

Gravity will decide whether the Universe continues to expand, as it has done since the big bang. The smallest sphere above represents the Universe almost at birth. Others (going clockwise) show galaxies moving apart from one another. The pull of gravity could in time end the expansion, or (lower spheres) the Universe could expand for ever

FOCUS ON PLANET EARTH

Daylight comes, night falls, the seasons change. We take it all for granted until suddenly the restless Earth rebels. The ground shakes, storms rage, the mutinous seas pour in. Refreshing insights into the myriad wonders of our world

Why do oceans have waves? PAGE 60

Why can light be turned into electricity? PAGE 70

Why do we sometimes get fogs? PAGE 57

New light on a puzzling world

Why does the Earth spin?

The astronomers of the ancient world believed that the Earth controlled the Universe. Today, we know that our planet and the eight others in the solar system are ruled by the Sun, and have been since they were formed 4600 million years ago. We know also that it is impossible to consider the Earth in isolation. The ancients regarded the Earth as something quite different from the rest of the cosmos and arrived at many false conclusions.

The Earth spins and so do all the other planets. They were sent into a spin when the solar system was created. Many theories explain how that happened, but as yet the world's scientists disagree on the specific details.

The first of the modern theories arose when telescopes gave astronomers a new view of the sky. In 1612, soon after the telescope's invention, German astronomer Simon Marius detected what looked like a luminous cloud, a nebula, in the Andromeda constellation. Similar discoveries of nebulas followed. Nearly two centuries later, in 1798, a French astronomer, Pierre-Simon de Laplace, reasoned that the pull of gravity could shrink these gas clouds into solid matter. As the spinning cloud was pulled into a tighter and tighter mass, it threw off rings of gas, each of which shrank further to form the planets. Laplace's theory is called the nebular hypothesis.

Laplace's ideas were accepted for about a century, since when other theories have for a time supplanted it. In 1944, German astronomer Carl von Weizsäcker took the nebular hypothesis and improved it. He suggested that the whirling cloud of gas first formed what he called planetesimals, small bodies that combined with each other and later turned into planets.

Whichever theory finally gains acceptance, a central fact remains: our planet and the others originated from a spinning cloud of gas. When a piece of a spinning object breaks away, it continues to spin in the same direction as its parent. Thus, the Earth and all other planets, except Venus, spin from west to east but at quite different speeds. (Scientists still can't explain the retrograde motion of Venus. Until 1961, when radar beams pierced its dense cloud cover, the nature of even its terrain was a mystery.)

And just as an artificial satellite can be made to follow a set path round the Earth controlled by our planet's gravity, so the Earth and its companions make a regular orbit round the Sun. The Sun's gravitational pull keeps them and the Earth in check across nearly 12 000 million km (7300 million miles) of space.

A Moon's eye-view shows Earth and a background of stars. Just as the Moon orbits our planet, so do the Earth and its eight companions travel round the Sun

Why is the Earth round?

It's customary in the northern hemisphere to think of Australia and the antipodes as being Down Under. To the collective mind's eye of those Up Top comes a bizarre picture, particularly bewildering to children, of people on the other side of the globe standing upside down. And the question is sometimes asked why they don't fall off.

What keeps us all standing upright, without falling into space or slipping down the sides of the globe, is the same force that makes our planet a sphere. We are kept in place by gravity. Wherever we are, our legs point in the general direction of the sphere's centre, 6370 km (3960 miles) below. Without that force, our atmosphere would have vanished

long ago, and our seas would have spilled into space.

Earth's gravity pulls everything towards the planet's centre. That is why Earth cannot be anything but a globe. Study other shapes – a cube, pyramid, ovoid – and you can see that only a sphere has every part of the parcel packed as closely to the centre as possible.

Why isn't the Earth a perfect sphere?

It is nearly 2500 years since learned Greeks first showed that the Earth is round. Not until the early 1600s did scientists believe that it might not be a perfect sphere. Other celestial bodies, such as the Sun and the Moon, were perfectly round and, as could be seen with a naked eye, they kept that shape as they moved in the sky. There was no reason to think that the Earth was different.

When astronomers first pointed telescopes at the sky, they found evidence to disturb their ideas. Looking at Jupiter and Saturn, they saw that these planets are elliptical, and their shape never changes. What's more, seventeenth-century scientists observed that the planets bulge round the middles: they are flatter on top and bottom.

It took Sir Isaac Newton to explain the fact. If an object spins, its components try to move in a straight line, instead of flying smoothly round the bend. Countless examples occur in our everyday lives to demonstrate that. If you ride in a car, you are swung outwards as it takes a corner. Laundry in a spin dryer flies onto the drum instead of staying in its centre. The faster something revolves, the greater the force. That is why children sitting on the outside of a roundabout are at greater danger of being thrown off than those nearer the centre.

Newton's laws of motion explained this centrifugal force – the tendency of a spinning object to 'fly from the centre'.

A point on the Earth's equator moves from east to west at a speed of 1670 km/h (1040 mph). Nearer the poles, the spin is much slower. The spin is faster at the equator because any point there is taking a bigger circle: it needs to travel farther to complete each revolution.

The effect on the Earth of these different speeds is to create a bulge where it moves faster. Centrifugal force at the equator throws it outwards. If the Earth's mass were greater, the pull of its own gravity would counteract that outward thrust. The Sun, for example, spins very rapidly, reaching 7260 km/h (4500 mph) at its equator, but its own gravity keeps it more or less in shape. Jupiter spins at

The Earth's spin creates *a centrifugal force similar to that on a fairground ride. Its outward thrust gives the planet a bulge round its middle*

perfectly round. It involved comparing distances and angles measured at different places. In 1736, two French expeditions set off, one going to Lapland to measure the Earth's curvature near the North Pole and the other to Peru to take readings near the equator. They discovered that the Earth bulges slightly: its diameter across the equator is 43 km (27 miles) greater than its diameter measured from pole to pole.

Satellite surveys show that the Earth's girth is at its biggest slightly south of the equator, where the diameter swells by 7.6 m (25 ft). The announcement, in 1959, brought headlines about a pear-shaped world. The description is grossly exaggerated. To an astronaut, unaided by instruments, our planet looks like a perfect sphere.

a much greater speed of 45 770 km/h (28 400 mph), but its gravitational pull is far less than the Sun's and it, like Saturn, cannot resist being spun out of shape.

Until the age of satellites, it was more difficult to prove that the Earth is not

Why, when we jump upwards, do we always land in the same place?

At the equator, where it spins more quickly than elsewhere, the Earth travels at 1670 km/h (1040 mph). If it is spinning as fast as that, it seems reasonable to expect that somebody jumping straight into the air would land on a different spot. The Earth, after all, would surely have moved beneath the jumper's feet.

The argument was raised frequently in days when astronomers first claimed the Earth to be a spinning globe. We know now that in a moving object everything moves. That is why we use seat belts in aircraft and automobiles. A child who is not strapped into a safety seat flies forwards if the car stops suddenly, because the infant, like everything else in the vehicle, travels at the vehicle's speed. If that were not so, it would be impossible on a train to toss a magazine across the aisle to a friend. And a rifle bullet fired at the same speed as the train could never leave the barrel.

When Galileo Galilei argued the matter, he put a convincing case. Imagine, he

SIZING IT UP BY SUN AND CAMEL

For thousands of years most people believed the Earth to be flat. That isn't surprising. When they stood on a hilltop and looked at the valley below, the land appeared to go endlessly into the distance, as far as the eye could see. From a coastal headland or boat, the sea on a calm day looked as flat as could be. If the Earth were round, as some suggested, why didn't we fall off the edge?

Nearly 2500 years ago, Greek thinkers concluded that the Earth is a sphere. Aristotle, in 340 BC, gave as evidence the curved edge of Earth's shadow appearing on the Moon during a lunar eclipse. A sphere is the only shape that casts a circular shadow from any angle. Therefore, Aristotle argued, the Earth must be a sphere. After determining the shape of the Earth, the Greeks calculated its size. In about 240 BC, the Greek astronomer Eratosthenes, who lived in Alexandria, set out to measure the Earth's circumference.

On a trip south to Syene (modern-day Aswan) at the summer solstice, when the Sun was directly overhead, he noticed that its rays at noon fell straight down a well. A year later, on the same date and at the same time, the shadow of the gnomon on a sundial in Alexandria showed that the Sun was about 7 degrees south, not directly overhead. Assuming the Earth to be round, then the distance from Syene to Alexandria was 7/360ths (about one-fiftieth) of the total circumference.

Eratosthenes knew, from the time it took a camel caravan to travel from Syene to Alexandria, that the distance between the two cities was 5000 *stadia*. (One *stadium* is roughly ⅙ km or about 180 yd.) He calculated the Earth's circumference to be 250 000 (50 x 5000) *stadia* – that is, about 42 000 km (26 000 miles). His was a more accurate assessment than Christopher Columbus had when he sailed westwards in 1492. Columbus believed that Earth's circumference was about 29 000 km (18 000 miles). Today's accepted circumference at the equator is quite close to Eratosthenes's figure: 40 075 km (24 901 miles).

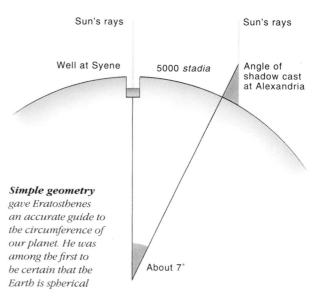

Simple geometry gave Eratosthenes *an accurate guide to the circumference of our planet. He was among the first to be certain that the Earth is spherical*

said, that you climb the highest mast of a ship sailing in reasonably calm seas so that the deck lies immediately below you. If you drop something from that height, it falls to the deck, not into the sea, even though in that time the ship has sailed on.

Everything resting on our planet moves at the speed of the Earth's spin, including the planet's atmosphere. If we jump on the spot, we come down on the spot, because we retain that speed. If we throw a ball in the park or hurl a javelin in a stadium, both will arrive where our arms sent them – ignoring the wind, of course.

Why is the Earth a magnet?

The ancient Chinese and Greeks discovered that magnetite, a form of iron ore, has properties that we call magnetism. They knew that this natural magnet responds to something in the Earth, taking up a certain position if allowed to move freely. It took centuries to discover that the Earth itself is a giant magnet.

William Gilbert, physicist and physician to Queen Elizabeth I of England, was the first to suggest it. In 1600, he said that the Earth behaves like a giant bar magnet, a theory not seriously disputed until early this century. We know now that at intervals ranging from thousands to millions of years, the Earth's magnetic field springs a surprise: it changes direction. Over a period of a couple of thousand years, the north magnetic pole becomes the south, and south becomes north. That fact discredits any idea that a magnetic rod, perhaps massive deposits of iron, runs from north to south. The polarity of a bar magnet does not change. Another factor is that a magnet loses its force when heated. The enormous heat of the Earth's core would soon destroy a bar magnet.

Why the Earth has a magnetic field puzzled scientists until the 1960s. The answer lies possibly in electromagnetism. If you wrap some wire round a strip of steel, then pass an electric current through the wire, the steel becomes a magnet. Turn off the current and you switch off the magnetism.

Now we believe that the Earth's magnetism comes from electric currents generated deep within the planet. We know that a molten mass makes up the Earth's outer core. This layer, about 2200 km (1380 miles) thick, separates the Earth's mantle and the solid but white-hot inner core. Geologists think that it is probably a vast sea of molten nickel and iron.

The lower edge of the mantle and the inner core are vastly different in density and temperature. These differences cause convection currents in the molten outer core, so that it circulates slowly. As the

Electric currents formed within the planet probably give Earth its vast magnetic field. The force resembles that used in some scrapyard electromagnets (left). But in them the power can be cut to turn off the magnet

Earth spins, this fluid layer enables the crust and mantle to rotate faster relatively than the inner core. A movement of electrons in the mantle and within the inner core sets up a natural dynamo, generating electricity. The fluid, nickel-iron alloy of the outer core is too hot to become a natural bar magnet, but it is an excellent conductor of electricity. As the Earth's dynamo generates power, it turns the outer core into a vast magnet, stretching from north to south through the planet.

Scientists believe that the Earth was given a magnetic field as a birthday present from the Sun. Our planet was born from a fierce storm of dust, which held metallic particles. As these passed through the Sun's magnetic field, they created their own electric current, and captured magnetism for the Earth. The constant movement of the planet's outer core keeps the electromagnet working.

It's a good job it does. The Earth's magnetic field protects us from much of the Sun's dangerous radiation. On the solar wind, electrified atomic particles fly away at supersonic speeds. The force of our planet's magnetic field reaches about 60 000 km (37 300 miles) into space on the side facing the Sun. This acts on the Sun's radiation, deflecting the solar wind away from the Earth. For all that, the Earth's magnetic field is not particularly strong. Jupiter's is some ten times as powerful, giving off bursts of radio waves with energy about a million times that in one of Earth's great bolts of lightning.

Why does the Earth's magnetism change direction?

Towards the end of the seventeenth century, British astronomer Edmond Halley, of comet fame, was the first to investigate a theory that the Earth's magnetic field is moving. Modern tests show that it is drifting about one degree westwards every five years. The field is not only moving, but it is losing strength. It is about 6 per cent weaker now than it was 150 years ago. The drifting and weakening are probably related, signs that the field is slowly swinging right round.

At its strongest, the field is quite weak. Scientists measure it with a magnetometer, an instrument so sensitive that users remove their wristwatches and belts, because the metal in them affects the reading. Magnetometers are scaled in fractions of a tesla. This unit, recognised internationally, is based on the force required to make a compass needle point east to west – that is, at right angles to its normal direction. On that scale, the Earth's magnetic field measures only 0.00005 tesla. The force from an ordinary toy horseshoe magnet is several hundred times stronger.

Some 700 000 years ago, the Earth's magnetic field pointed in the opposite direction. What is now north was south. We know this because the sensitivity of the magnetometer allows geologists to test rocks for the merest traces of magnetism. As molten rocks cooled and solidified, they trapped tiny particles of iron. The iron became magnetised in the direction of the Earth's magnetic field at that time, giving us a fossilised picture of the field in ages past. Using palaeomagnetism, the study of the magnetic field preserved in ancient rocks, scientists know that the field has reversed its polarity. They know also that in the past its strength weakened as the field drifted.

These changes occur irregularly and slowly, each one taking about 1000 to 2000 years. During the last four million years, there have been ten periods of reversed polarity. And the Earth is not alone. The Sun's magnetic field, from which Earth's magnetism probably came, changes direction. Sunspots, which flare up every eleven years, are signs of this.

Movements within the Earth's various layers generate electrical energy, which turns the fluid outer core – possibly an alloy of nickel and iron – into a giant electromagnet. Our best estimates show that this core fluid moves about 25 m (80 ft) westwards every day, shifting the Earth's magnetism as it does so.

Does such a shift hold serious dangers? Scientists aren't sure. The danger comes from electrified particles in the solar wind. Without our magnetic field to deflect them, they would constantly bombard the Earth.

Why does a compass needle point to the north?

In 800 BC, the Greeks mined a natural magnet, lodestone, in their province of Magnesia (now in Turkey), which gave us our word magnet. The ancient Chinese used magnets some 2000 years ago. The

OLD-TIME AID STILL POINTS THE WAY

Magnetic compasses still find a place among the equipment aboard modern aircraft

For all our skill at finding new and faster ways to travel, the basic method of navigating from one point to another remains the same for us as it was for medieval sailors. Nobody has yet devised a simpler and more reliable aid than the magnetic compass. When the stars are blacked out by cloud, and fog obscures all landmarks, the compass – controlled by the Earth's magnetic field – points the way home for travellers on land, in the air and at sea. Even the most advanced navigation systems rely to some extent on the compass. All gyrocompasses, which are used in aircraft, ships and spacecraft, are used with a magnetic compass to help stabilise them. Because sunspots often distort radio signals, high-tech navigational aids that depend on radio beams from one or more transmitters can be unreliable. For this reason, seagoing vessels of more than 150 tonnes must carry a magnetic compass, and air pilots are trained in compass navigation to an accuracy of 0.5 degree. They need to be: at a speed of 1930 km/h (1200 mph) a 1-degree error results in an aircraft being 500 m (550 yd) off course in one minute.

Trustworthy as it is, because it always points to the Earth's north magnetic pole, a compass bearing can be misleading. That isn't the compass's fault. The Earth's magnetic field constantly changes. Readings taken in London over the past 400 years show that the difference between it and the geographic North Pole – known as the declination – has varied by as much as 35 degrees. As well, electromagnetic forces in the upper atmosphere cause hour-by-hour and even minute-by-minute changes.

Everybody who uses a compass, even walkers on a mountain track, needs to understand declination, or magnetic variation, a reading that varies from region to region. To find true north, the correct amount of variation must be added to or subtracted from magnetic north. Observatories round the world monitor that variation every few days. Sudden changes can outdate even new maps and charts, and those requiring the latest information rely on computer models, which calculate the changes mathematically. The results are used by aircraft making long international flights and also by America's space shuttle.

Greeks and the Chinese knew that lodestone, a form of iron ore known as magnetite, carries a remarkable force. Two pieces in close proximity will suddenly cling together, with one sometimes changing its alignment to join the other. Lodestone means 'leading

Simple and reliable, the compass has changed little since this one of 1750

stone'. The Chinese found that a small shard of it, if allowed to swing freely through 360 degrees, will always point in a particular direction. It is possible that they made the first compass in the first century AD by balancing a lodestone on a smooth board. This device was used not for navigation but for fortune-telling. The earliest evidence we have of mariners' compasses came centuries later. In 1180, the English scholar Alexander Neckam mentioned their use. In 1269, a French military engineer named Petrus

Peregrinus described how a piece of iron wire could be magnetised by rubbing it with lodestone. If placed on a lightweight piece of floating wood, it came to rest pointing north–south.

At about the same time, the Chinese magnetised thin sheets of iron, cut them into the shape of fish, and floated them on water. Sailors steered by primitive compasses, setting a piece of magnetised iron on a floating cork.

The magnetic compass undoubtedly helped the great explorers of the fifteenth century, but floating compasses were unreliable, particularly in heavy seas. In the next 200 years came first the dry compass, with a disc mounted on a needle point, and then compasses set on gimbals to keep them horizontal.

A compass needle, whether made of lodestone or steel, is a magnet reacting to the laws of magnetic attraction and repulsion. The north pole of one bar magnet attracts the south pole of another: like poles repel, opposite poles attract. When a compass needle points to the north, it is reacting to the Earth's magnetism, which is caused by fluid motions in the planet's liquid outer core.

The Earth's two magnetic poles were wrongly named. According to the laws of magnetism, the north pole of a compass points to the south magnetic pole not to its north, but most people today agree that to rename them would be too confusing. That is why many scientists call the opposite ends of a compass needle the north- and south-seeking poles. Because the Earth's geographic and magnetic poles are in different places, a compass doesn't point to the true north, a fact that Chinese philosophers recognised in about 1050. The north magnetic pole, in Canada's northeast, is some 1600 km (1000 miles) from the geographic pole. In some places the error, known as the magnetic variation, doesn't matter much. From the equator, for example, the two poles would seem to be close together. In the Arctic or Antarctic it is of the greatest importance, and travellers there would quickly get lost if they failed to observe the difference.

Why doesn't the Earth have craters like the Moon's?

Four thousand million years ago, the Moon was bombarded with massive rocks from space, causing the craters in its surface that we can see from Earth. The Moon is a close neighbour, so how did our planet escape this missile attack?

You might guess that space debris of a size that scarred the Moon would have disintegrated on its way to Earth. Our atmosphere would have burned up rocks or torn them apart. You would be wrong. We know now that stony objects more than about 150 m (165 yd) across will hit the Earth intact – and pack a giant wallop.

Iron meteorites are stronger. At some time between 25 000 and 50 000 years ago, an iron-nickel meteorite, about 50 m (55 yd) in diameter, hit the United States near present-day Winslow, Arizona, at an estimated 11 km (7 miles) a second. The impact caused the Barringer Crater, about 200 m (220 yd) deep and 1.2 km (¾ mile) wide. That meteorite was a midget compared with those hitting the Earth 4000 million years ago. Some were several hundred kilometres across. If such a meteorite struck Britain today, it could wipe out London, Birmingham and Glasgow in one hit. When a giant meteorite struck Earth, the atmosphere had no effect on it: in fact, the meteorite's rear didn't feel the impact until the front was buried 20 km (12 miles) deep.

The Earth isn't crater-scarred now, because since that time it has put on a new face. The old craters were worn away, or ploughed into the deeper rocks beneath the planet's crust. The Earth is geologically active. The tectonic plates that make up the Earth's crust shift and fold, bringing tremors and earthquakes. Sometimes, these tectonic plates plunge deep, carrying down and burying surface matter. Craters above a moving plate were swallowed up.

Most of the Earth's surface features are comparatively new. The Atlantic Ocean, for example, is no older than 175 million years. Unlike the Moon, which has no air or water to erode its scars, the Earth has a constantly changing face, one that will continue to weather for as long as anyone can foresee.

A *space missile* blasted the Barringer Crater in the Arizona desert. The meteorite was a midget compared with those that once hit the Earth

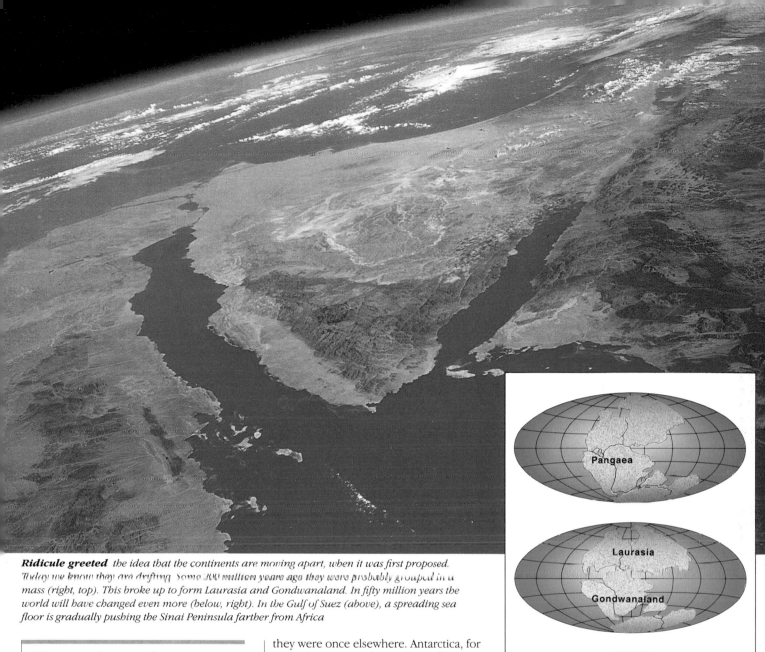

Ridicule greeted *the idea that the continents are moving apart, when it was first proposed. Today we know they are drifting. Some 200 million years ago they were probably grouped in a mass (right, top). This broke up to form Laurasia and Gondwanaland. In fifty million years the world will have changed even more (below, right). In the Gulf of Suez (above), a spreading sea floor is gradually pushing the Sinai Peninsula farther from Africa*

Why are the continents drifting apart?

If you took some scissors and cut out the continents from a world map, you would have an interesting jigsaw puzzle. You might be surprised to see that some of the pieces fit snugly together: South America's east coast matches Africa's west; southern Australia locks onto Antarctica; India slots neatly against the horn of Africa.

When geologists examine the rocks in these now far-apart continents, they find that those in Brazil and southwest Africa, for example, are of a similar type and age. Both have what are known as shield areas, with rocks more than 2000 million years old. When these regions are closely examined, the rocks' structure – what might be called their grain – matches up. They show similar effects from the land-shaping forces of glaciation, erosion and volcanic activity. Also, similar fossils of plants and animals exist in matching regions. Some continents have features suggesting that

they were once elsewhere. Antarctica, for example, has coal, the product of ancient, lush forests; and central Africa shows signs of erosion by huge ice sheets.

In 1620, Francis Bacon, the English philosopher, was first to point out the match-up between South America and Africa. Nearly three centuries later, German meteorologist Alfred Lothar Wegener suggested that all the continents were once a single landmass, which he called Pangaea, the Greek for 'all land'. He theorised that they had probably floated apart on the oceans. He called the movement 'continental drift'.

The idea that great landmasses could move was ridiculed. Wegener was wrong about how they had moved, but quite right in his theory of drift. In the 1950s, geophysicists began to study magnetic fields in rocks on the ocean floor, and found that some are magnetised in one direction and some in another. Since being magnetised by the Earth's magnetic field, the rocks have moved.

American geologist William Ewing showed in 1956 that a mountain range

curved down the middle of the Atlantic Ocean, went around Africa and into the Indian Ocean. From there, it continued to Antarctica and into the Pacific, making up a sub-ocean system that girdled the world. Occasionally, its highest peaks showed up as islands. This system became known as the mid-ocean ridge. Further study showed that the Earth's outer shell, or lithosphere, is broken into sections known as tectonic plates. These plates, seven major and twenty or so minor, average 100 km (60 miles) in thickness. Tectonic plates range in size up to 100 million sq km (40 million sq miles) in area, roughly five times the size of the United States and Canada combined.

When geologists had the techniques and equipment to drill into the ocean bed, they discovered that the rocks became younger towards the mid-ocean ridge, showing that material rising from deep inside the Earth spreads slowly across the seabed, gradually pushing the plates apart.

The continents have drifted for at least 2500 million years, and continue to move at an annual rate of 20 to 75 mm (⅘ to 3 in). But not all the movement is under the oceans. Part of a continent can split from the rest, in a process called rifting. Such a shift created the Atlantic Ocean, 175 million years ago. The Red Sea was formed in this way, as part of a rift that still goes on. Siberia, too, has an active rift system, which created Lake Baikal.

The movement of the Earth's plates and landmasses resting on them doesn't mean that the planet is getting bigger. When plates move away in one place, they converge in others. And when they collide, the effects can be catastrophic, crumpling mountain ranges, causing great earthquakes, opening up volcanoes and ocean trenches. The world's highest mountains, the Himalayas, were formed when the Indian plate collided with the Asian, some fifty million years ago.

Why doesn't our air supply vanish into space?

Early astronomers believed the Universe to be filled with air. If only they could find a suitable vehicle, perhaps a chariot drawn by birds, travel to the Moon would be much like a journey to some distant country. These days we know that adventurers into space need special suits and oxygen.

Not until 1648 was it shown that the Earth's atmosphere thins out with altitude. French physicist Blaise Pascal conducted an experiment to prove it. He sent his brother-in-law up a mountainside to test the air pressure with tubes of mercury. Pascal predicted that, higher up the mountain, lower air pressure would support a lower level of mercury in each tube. If the Earth's atmosphere didn't vary, the mercury level would not change.

Pascal was right, of course. If the Universe were filled with air, then planets and other bodies would gradually slow down in their orbits. Eventually, the Moon would crash to Earth, and Earth itself would inevitably succumb to the gravitational pull of the Sun, ending its life in the solar furnace.

Earth's atmosphere probably evolved in stages after the planet was born, 4600 million years ago. It came from a chemical interplay between solid and fluid matter. Scientists believe that at first it was mainly hydrogen and helium. These gases, light in composition and subjected to enormous heat from the Sun, had the velocity to escape the pull of Earth's gravity, and most of them vanished into space.

As the Earth's crust cooled, enormous volumes of carbon dioxide, water, methane and ammonia poured out from the fiery mass below, much as gases spew from active volcanoes today. Then, about 4500 million years ago, when the Earth's temperature had fallen below 100°C

Few believed *Blaise Pascal (left) when he asserted that the air thins out with altitude. He proved his theory by taking a tube of mercury and showing that in the city and on a mountain he got quite different readings. High in the Himalayas, a mountaineer with an oxygen mask proves the point again*

(212°F), water vapour condensed and fell as rain. The ocean basins began to fill.

Some 3000 million years ago, the atmosphere held little free oxygen. A complicated series of interactions between ultraviolet light from the Sun, methane, ammonia and water created an ozone layer. This blocked much of the ultraviolet light, which is harmful to life. Nitrogen, produced from ammonia, became the Earth's dominant gas.

Geological evidence shows that about 2000 million years ago primitive plant life began slowly to convert carbon dioxide into oxygen. This process continues steadily, so that today our atmosphere is roughly 78 per cent nitrogen, 21 per cent oxygen, plus traces of other gases.

If you turn on the gas tap of a kitchen stove, the gas soon spreads into the room. That is because the gas burner has no gravitational pull of its own. The Earth's gravity keeps its gases locked around it. To escape, they need to achieve the speed of astronauts in a space rocket – at least 11.2 km (7 miles) a second – and this, luckily for us, they cannot do.

TAKING A WEIGHT OFF YOUR MIND

Most people know that barometers, which used to be commonplace items in the home, measure air pressure – the weight of the atmosphere, which varies according to altitude and its water vapour content. At sea level, standard air pressure as measured on a barometer is 1013 millibars, or 760 mm (29.9 in) of a column of mercury.

Surprisingly, because we rarely notice it, the atmosphere presses on all of us with crushing force. Its total weight is nearly 5000 million million tonnes. Above each of us is a column of air weighing about a tonne. At sea level, the pressure is almost a kilogram on every square centimetre of the body (15 lb per sq in). At an altitude of 5500 m (18 000 ft), it is only half as much.

Most of us live close to the bottom of an ocean of air, whose weight has been compared with the pressure of deep water on a fish. The fish survives because it has an in-built mechanism to equalise the weight of water that otherwise would crush it. We don't notice the atmosphere's weight, because our inner body pressure, pushing out, matches the force pushing in.

In the main, atmospheric pressure concerns us only when we move out of our usual environment – for example, by taking a holiday in a high-altitude resort. There, because pressure is lower and the air contains less oxygen, we may find ourselves short of breath, particularly when walking or doing strenuous exercise. Problems arise, too, when flying in the unpressurised cabin of an aircraft. The pressure inside our eardrums, no longer equal to that outside, may give us a strange sensation and even some pain. By swallowing, we soon even things up.

Early barometers were impractical until Daniel Quare made one in 1695 that could be moved without spilling the mercury. Right: his improved version of 1705

Why doesn't the Earth bump into other planets?

It's a favourite theme for science-fiction movies. The Earth is on a collision course with another planet. Unless we move fast, we face certain destruction …

Rest assured, it couldn't happen. Earth remains vulnerable to a strike from an asteroid, one of the myriad and relatively small bodies that, along with our planet, orbit the Sun. Astronomers estimate that there may be at least a million asteroids with a diameter of more than 100 m (110 yd). The orbital path of some of these crosses that of the Earth. Any of these could hit us, but our danger of crashing into any other planet in the solar system is negligible for several thousand years and perhaps for ever.

Eight other planets – Mercury, Venus, Mars, Jupiter, Saturn, Uranus, Neptune and Pluto – share that system. At present, none has an orbit that crosses that of the

Earth. Venus passes closest, but still misses us by 42 million km (26 million miles) – 110 times more distant than the Moon and a wide safety margin indeed.

Alas, for our total peace of mind, we don't know that the planets won't change their orbits. Scientists now recognise that the solar system is chaotic, meaning that it is impossible to determine precisely what will happen within it for immensely long times ahead. Some computer studies show that, in the next 100 million years, the outer planets – Jupiter, Saturn, Uranus, Neptune and Pluto – will show signs of 'orbital wobble', deviating slightly from their current courses.

We need more powerful computers to tell us what, over millions of years, will be the cumulative effects of the gravitational pulls of all the planets, one on another. But it is quite likely that, when we have those computers, they will assure us that the solar system is stable for the next 500 million years, long enough to calm even the most chronic worriers among us.

Mighty forces show their power

Why is the Earth's core hot?

If you were to ride down the world's deepest mine, 3777 m (2.34 miles) below the surface at Carletonville, South Africa, you would indeed feel as though you were going into the heart of the Earth. The gold mine's temperature, 55°C (131°F), might make you believe that you

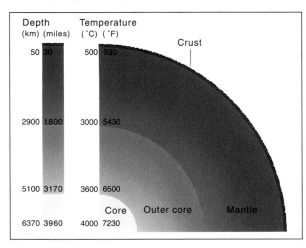

Depth (km) (miles)	Temperature (°C) (°F)	
50 30	500 930	Crust
2900 1800	3000 5430	
5100 3170	3600 6500	
6370 3960	4000 7230	Core Outer core Mantle

had penetrated deep into the Earth's mantle, towards the fiery furnace below. You would be grossly mistaken.

The world's deepest hole was begun by the Soviet Union in 1970, and descends for some 13 km (8 miles) beneath Zapolarny, on the Kola Peninsula, a short distance from the Finnish border. By 1995, this geological probe will reach 15 km (nearly 9½ miles), but even then it will be a mere pinprick, about halfway into the Earth's crust and no more than 0.23 per cent of the 6370-km (3960-mile) journey to the Earth's centre.

Our planet's structure is much like that of an onion, built layer upon layer. Unlike the layers in an onion, which are basically the same in form and density, the four major layers that make up the Earth – the

A slice through the Earth's centre would show that it is built of four main layers, and at its heart has an atomic furnace generating enormous heat

crust, the mantle and the outer and inner core – vary considerably. The Earth's crust, about 1 per cent of the total volume, is comparably much thinner than an onion's outer skin. A clingwrap covering on a basketball would perhaps give a more accurate comparison.

Beneath the Earth's thin crust is the mantle, which accounts for 82 per cent of the Earth's total volume and descends nearly 3000 km (over 1800 miles) to the molten outer core. Some 2000 km (1200 miles) deeper still is the central core, our planet's dense and fiery heart.

The core is not merely hot. It has the white heat of an atomic furnace – for that is what it is – a ball of energy produced by radioactive elements in decay. Geophysicists estimate that the temperature at the core is perhaps 4000°C (7230°F), which diminishes gradually to about 3000°C (5430°F) at the boundary between the outer core and the mantle. But not all the heat comes from radioactive decay. Much of it, say some scientists, was generated when the Earth was born from a whirling cloud of gas. In all probability, the gas cloud formed planetesimals, small bodies

CUTTING EARTHQUAKES DOWN TO SIZE

The magnitude of an earthquake is defined as the absolute measure of its strength, related to the energy released by the shock. It is usually measured on the Richter scale, devised by American seismologist Dr Charles F. Richter in 1935. Measurements are taken by a standard seismograph 100 km (62 miles) from the quake's epicentre; for accuracy, readings usually come from several seismographs.

The scale is open-ended – that is, it has no upper or lower limits. Also, it is logarithmic; each increase of one unit represents a tenfold increase in an earthquake's magnitude and roughly a thirty-times increase in the energy released as seismic waves. A Magnitude 1 tremor could be detected only by a seismograph. One of Magnitude 2, ten times the wave amplitude or size, is about the smallest that humans can detect.

A Magnitude 8 earthquake has 10 000 times the amplitude of one of Magnitude 4 and according to where it struck, would have devastating results. The 1976 Tangshan earthquake, which killed some 650 000 people, measured 7.9 on the Richter scale. Perhaps the largest known earthquake struck north of Quito, Ecuador, and is estimated to have been 8.9 on the Richter scale. It generated as much force as 125 million tonnes of TNT; the Hiroshima atomic bomb had one ten-thousandth the explosive power.

Scientists doubt that a more powerful earthquake is possible. This is because they believe that no volume of rock within the Earth's crust could withstand a higher stress. It would shatter before such a force was reached, releasing vast amounts of energy but sparing us from an even more awesome explosion.

The Richter scale is just one way of assessing the nature of an earthquake. Others look at an earthquake's intensity,

which is determined by assessing the degree to which the shaking is noticeable in a particular area, the amount of visible deformation of the Earth's surface, and damage to buildings. Whereas the Richter scale provides one measurement, intensity scales may give several. Points equidistant from an earthquake's epicentre may experience different levels of intensity, according to the geology of the regions: for example, buildings on soft soil will suffer more than those on hard rock.

Intensity scales are criticised for a lack of sophistication, but their results are regarded as useful in determining the vulnerability of areas to earthquake damage.

Shock waves from an earthquake are detected on sensitive instruments known as seismographs and measured on a scale devised by Charles Richter (right)

*A **gaping canyon*** *opened up beneath a main street of Anchorage, Alaska, when an earthquake struck on Good Friday, 1964. The street and its buildings dropped into the chasm. Massive ocean waves swept across the Pacific to Japan and Antarctica*

that smashed together, creating enormous kinetic energy – and subsequently heat – as Earth and other planets in the solar system were formed.

Today we have a detailed picture of the planet's structure, built up this century by piecing together information from several sources. Earthquakes pose awesome problems for our cities, but for scientists they offer the key to understanding the mechanisms that control the planet's interior. An earthquake's primary or pressure (P) waves will pass through rocks, gases and liquids. Its secondary force, the shear (S) waves, move with side-to-side vibrations, and penetrate only solids. Thus, when receiving one and not the other, geologists can plot regions of gases and liquids. Seismographic recordings of P waves tell geologists the nature and density of the Earth's core. That's how we know that the inner core is solid. The heavier materials have sunk beneath a molten sea of iron and nickel.

Why can't we predict earthquakes?

Less than twenty years ago, it seemed that science had at last found the key to forecasting serious earth tremors. To worldwide astonishment, Chinese officials in 1975 evacuated the Manchurian city of

Haicheng after warnings of an earthquake, and possibly saved 100 000 lives.

The Chinese had noted two clues: a series of small tremors and a rising and falling water table. Their seismologists gave not only a warning: they predicted the earthquake's precise strength – 7.3 on the Richter scale. A year later, as many as 650 000 people died in a massive earthquake at nearby Tangshan, and the Chinese detected no real warning signs.

Every year, more than a million earthquakes are recorded – 1000 a day in Japan alone. Most are so low in energy that only sensitive instruments can trace them. Others, striking with sufficient force to devastate a town, occur about every two weeks, but fortunately under the sea or far from habitation.

Only in the past thirty years have we fully discovered, through the study of plate tectonics, just what causes an earthquake. Tectonic plates, some larger than continents, make up the Earth's outer layer, and are in constant motion as they float on oceans of molten rock. Their movement builds up a complex variety of stresses deep underground. Sometimes, one plate slips over another, slowly producing enormous strain. Or the two may collide, perhaps with cataclysmic effect.

It is precisely this variety of possibilities that makes accurate prediction of a major earthquake so difficult. Into that web of

complexity can be woven another: just as no two earthquakes are exactly alike, nor are regions that are prone to major shocks. California, for example, sits above two plates; Japan is perched above three. In America, most earthquakes start on land; in Japan, they usually come from below the ocean bed.

Picking a major earthquake from a minor tremor is in essence the problem, a one-in-a-million quest on which Japan and the United States, in particular, spend vast sums. The minor shocks cannot be ignored, because scientists believe they may be precursors of a catastrophic strike. Nor must their effects be overestimated: imagine, if you will, the evacuation of a metropolis for an earthquake that didn't happen. To log the gentle murmurings of the Earth's crust, Japanese seismologists have buried sensitive instruments in wells more than 3 km (2 miles) deep to screen them from traffic vibrations above.

Quake watchers are not depending on science alone. For centuries, observers have noted the strange behaviour of animals and birds sometimes hours before a disaster. We know that dogs can hear sounds denied to humans. Perhaps animals pick up the distant rumblings of an impending shock wave, and begin to panic. The trouble, alas, is that not all earthquakes give us a warning, or strike where we might expect.

Why do some regions have earthquakes?

Every day, seismologists record about 3000 earthquakes. About 90 per cent of these occur in a region that almost encloses the Pacific Ocean, and most of the others in a band stretching from Spain and the northern Mediterranean, through the Himalayas and Indonesia. The two zones meet near New Guinea.

The Earth is made up of layers. Its shell or lithosphere is broken into seven huge slabs, each roughly 100 km (60 miles) thick. Squeezed between the large, rigid plates are some twenty smaller ones. Driven possibly by strong thermal currents, the plates move independently over the asthenosphere, a partially molten mass in the upper mantle. Plates often converge and collide. Frequently, one plate may slide beneath another. A map of the world's earthquakes would define the boundaries of the Earth's tectonic plates.

Earthquakes occur occasionally outside these recognised zones. Seismologists give two main reasons: first, there may be excessive stress within the plate itself, due maybe to a violent upthrust from below. Or the cause may even be human: underground nuclear testing, the seepage of liquid wastes deep into the Earth's crust, or pressure from the weight of water stored in a dam.

Why do giant waves appear in the oceans?

The gentle waves we see rolling across a beach are induced by soft breezes which, if they turn stormy, usually give us adequate warning. But sometimes a coastline

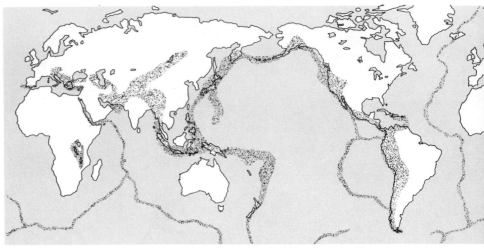

Most earthquakes occur in clearly defined zones (shaded) that girdle the Earth. A map of these regions outlines the major tectonic plates of the Earth's crust, which move and often collide

may be hit by a giant wave that seems to come from nowhere.

Such waves, commonly but incorrectly called tidal waves, are properly known as tsunami, the most feared of all. They result from earthquakes or, less usually, volcanic eruptions beneath the ocean bed. The initial energy may be so vast as to drive a series of waves at high speed across the Pacific from Japan to California and back again. The deeper the ocean where the shock occurs, the greater the speed of the waves, which may follow one another at intervals of anything between five minutes and an hour. Their speed in the open ocean has been recorded at more than 800 km/h (500 mph).

Usually, they pass unnoticed by the crews of small vessels out at sea. This is because in deep water the waves may rise only 20 cm (8 in) or so above others. When a tsunami reaches a coastal shelf, its force builds up in the shallows. Resistance slows down the front of the wave, causing its faster-moving back to pile up. Eventu-

ally, the wave breaks with devastating force, sweeping aside anything movable in its path. In 1737, a tsunami broke on Cape Lopatka, Siberia, and marked the cliff face 64 m (210 ft) above sea level.

Why do volcanoes suddenly erupt?

Shake a bottle of champagne, free the cork from its bindings and … POP. The cork flies out to hit the ceiling, followed often by bubbling champagne. In principle, that is why and how many volcanoes suddenly erupt.

The Earth's crust and the upper part of its mantle is a jigsaw of seven major tectonic plates and perhaps twenty minor ones. These pieces drift slowly on an enormous sea of molten matter. In regions of volcanic activity – generally where the plates grind together – one plate may slide beneath another. As it does so, it is forced downwards. The farther it goes, the hotter it becomes. Eventually, it melts in the fierce heat of the mantle, the massive zone that lies beneath the Earth's crust.

Often, the plate discharges water, which turns instantly into steam. A mixture of water and silica can be explosive. The amount of silica decides the viscosity of the molten rock – whether it is a thin, runny discharge or stiffer, with the consistency of cement.

If the silica content is low and that of the water high, steam bubbles, acting like those in champagne, will expand in lava of low viscosity and shoot fiery debris from the volcano's cone. If the mixture is low in water but high in silica, lava will set round the volcano's dome, building it higher and higher. If the proportions of both silica and water are high, the thickness of the discharge will trap steam bubbles until they suddenly explode, possibly with all the fury of a major eruption.

A killer wave heads for land in a print by nineteenth-century Japanese artist Katsushika Hokusai

Why can't we predict volcanic eruptions?

Our chances of saying with certainty that a volcano is about to erupt seem better than those of forecasting an earthquake. In the first place, the trouble spots are more easily identified. We know that a volcano has erupted in the past, that it is still active and may erupt again. The problem is: when?

Volcanologists say there is no single clue, but records of related events such as earthquakes give considerable guidance – not in predicting a pattern of volcanic behaviour but about where the world's scientists should concentrate their resources.

Early this century, Japanese scientists noticed that before an eruption the Usu and Sakurajima volcanoes tended to swell gradually near their summits. After the eruption, the swelling subsided. During World War II, the Japanese finally succeeded in making an instrument, a tiltmeter, that was sensitive enough to detect a slight bulging of the ground on which it stood. Since then, advanced technology has produced tiltmeters using laser beams to give volcanologists highly accurate evidence of ground movement.

By using the twin techniques – monitoring the rumblings of earthquakes and any swelling in a volcano's summit – scientists have advanced considerably their efforts to predict eruptions. To these measures they have added a few others, such as tracing the movement of molten rock in a volcanic zone and analysing the

Vesuvius erupts and its fury is depicted on an early lantern slide. Mainland Europe's only active volcano has buried three cities and killed thousands of people. It last erupted in 1944

gases that seep from fissures. Notable early successes were to predict eruptions of the Hawaiian volcano, Kilauea, in December 1959 and at the nearby village of Kapoho a few weeks later. Soon, Hawaii had become a renowned centre for volcanic research, attracting scientists from the world's high-risk regions.

Though precise prediction remains difficult, many lives already have been saved. Also, early warning of a likely eruption enables emergency teams to test promising countermeasures. For example, in the mid-1970s the United States Air Force bombed Hawaii's Mauna Loa in a bid to relieve the mounting pressure of lava near its summit. In 1973, on an island off the coast of Iceland, scientists successfully slowed down a lava flow by dowsing it with cold water.

More recently, volcanologists have tried many ways to stem and divert the flow from Sicily's Mt Etna, Europe's most active volcano. In 1992, when Etna erupted again, they erected earthworks and barriers, and helicopters dumped concrete blocks into lava-oozing holes high on the mountain. The outcome of such measures is often doubtful, because nobody can predict with certainty which new direction the flow will take. Thousands

of people live or have holiday homes on the mountain: saving one community often endangers another. Despite the criticism, scientists believe that every battle brings them closer to winning the war – against the might of Etna and other volcanoes throughout the world.

Why do volcanoes pop up in surprising places?

The evidence of volcanoes, past and present, is almost everywhere on the face of the Earth. Many countries have the ancient craters and cones of long-extinct volcanoes; others have rich remains of fiery eruptions, showing as strangely shaped needles spiking the landscape, as vast plains of basalt, or in spectacular outcrops of igneous rock.

Today, more than 600 active volcanoes breathe their sulphurous smoke and fire into our atmosphere. Most are strung along boundaries between the giant tectonic plates that make up the Earth's shell. Indonesia and its adjacent regions, lying along one such boundary, has more than 100 active volcanoes.

Another site of volcanoes is where two plates move apart, allowing a flow of

Molten lava flows on Hawaii from Mt Kilauea, said by islanders to be the home of Pele, goddess of fire

magma – molten matter from within the Earth's mantle – to well up between the plates. Usually, this happens underwater. The seas cool the magma, creating a new layer of ocean bed. The Mid-Atlantic Ridge, a range of underwater mountains running from Iceland to the Antarctic, was built up gradually in this way.

Volcanoes and earthquakes are closely linked. But, just as earthquakes sometimes occur far from the margins of tectonic plates, so occasionally do volcanoes suddenly appear in unexpected places. Hawaii, with its string of volcanic islands, is one such region, lying far from the edges of its Pacific plate. Geologists explain that the Hawaiian volcanoes arise from 'hot spots' – weak areas in the plate's structure. These yield under pressure, and allow magmas to penetrate to the surface, forming over millions of years a chain of progressively older volcanoes.

Volcanoes sometimes explode with cataclysmic power, spreading silicate dust and sulphuric acid into the upper atmosphere. When Mt Pinatubo, in the Philippines, erupted in June 1991, it increased the amount of dust and acid aerosols in the stratosphere at least sixty times, and within three months had temporarily warmed the upper atmosphere by 3°C (6°F). For all that, volcanoes are believed to be essential to the maintenance of life on Earth. Some scientists believe that the Earth's atmosphere and its oceans came originally, aeons ago, from the planet's seething mass. Elements that make up our air and water are often found in the same proportions in the fiery steam and smoke seen billowing skywards from active volcanoes.

Why do some countries have hot springs?

Play golf on a course in the thermal zone of New Zealand's North Island and you could, if you are fanatically foolish, find yourself trying to retrieve a wayward ball from a bubbling mud pool. Book into a hotel there and you would almost certainly take a morning shower in water heated by the region's geysers. Catch a trout in Lake Rotorua and you could cook it in a nearby hot spring.

Such hydrothermal phenomena are by no means unique to New Zealand. They exist worldwide. In many places, such as Iceland, they are part of inhabitants' everyday lives, providing hot water for the laundry and guarding crops against frost. At Lardarello, Italy, a power station using geothermal energy has provided the town with electricity since 1904.

Hot springs are created in a volcanic region when rainwater trickles through the ground until it meets porous rock, which traps it like a sponge. What follows is much like the action in a pressure cooker, in which water boils at a temperature higher than its normal 100°C (212°F).

The water in the rocky sponge is under pressure from water above. Consequently, as water absorbs heat from molten rocks below, it may reach 250°C (482°F) without boiling. Cold water, heavier than hot, fills up the sponge, driving heated water to the surface. In its upward journey, it loses pressure. How much decides whether it emerges from a fissure in the ground as a bubbling spring of hot water or as a geyser, a spectacular blast of steam.

Jets of steam and boiling water roar up from a weakness in the Earth's crust to give Iceland a source of geothermal power. The lagoon offers a hot bath all year round

Why do islands emerge from the sea?

Ceaselessly, beneath the oceans, volcanoes silently spew out lava every day, cloaked by the seas above them. At some points, where tectonic plates gradually pull apart, magma flows out from deep within the Earth's mantle to change the seabed, often creating a chain of submarine volcanoes stretching for thousands of kilometres. In time, as their cones build up, some of these undersea volcanoes may reveal themselves as islands.

A spectacular example is Surtsey, a volcanic island that was suddenly born off Iceland in 1963, amid a cloud of ash and steam. Just as volcanic islands are suddenly born, so with comparable swiftness they may die. In August 1883, the island of Krakatoa, between Java and Sumatra, exploded with terrifying effects in the greatest volcanic blast on record. Waves swamped coastal towns in Java and Sumatra, killing 36 000 people. A plume of black vapour rose 80 km (50 miles) into the atmosphere and volcanic dust drifted round the world for months.

Krakatoa's child is what Malays call the volcano that emerged in 1928 close to where Krakatoa raged. The newcomer (right) is expected to grow for some 600 years

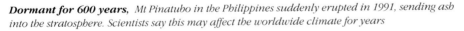

Dormant for 600 years, Mt Pinatubo in the Philippines suddenly erupted in 1991, sending ash into the stratosphere. Scientists say this may affect the worldwide climate for years

Lifting the fog on climate

The world's largest continuous sand area, Saudi Arabia's Empty Quarter (top), has summer heat of 50°C (122°F). Antarctica's cold in 1983 dropped to a record -89.2°C (-182.6°F)

Why does our climate stay much the same?

You may feel that our summers are sometimes too hot and the winters bitterly cold, but year in and year out the climate is ideal for us. Few places on Earth are unfit for human existence. Even in Antarctica, most of which never sees temperatures above freezing point, and amid the baking heat of the Sahara, where the ground heats up sometimes to 84°C (183°F), people know how to survive for long periods, if they need to.

Not so in space where hopes of finding life, or conditions suitable for it, are fast running out. Our near neighbours, Mars and Venus, were once strong candidates. Since then, space probes have told us that Mars is bitterly cold, with temperatures averaging -60°C (-82°F). Venus, mean temperature 460°C (860°F), is a fiery hellhole where any living creature would soon roast to death. An analysis of the atmosphere on these planets explains why they can't support life, but our planet can and does.

In 1965, Mariner 4 tested the Martian atmosphere with radio waves, and confirmed what astronomers had detected about twenty years earlier. Mars has a thin layer of carbon dioxide but no oxygen or nitrogen. Space probes to Venus show

that its atmosphere is some ninety times denser than Earth's, and contains 7600 times more carbon dioxide. One neighbour has too little carbon dioxide, the other far too much.

Carbon dioxide is vital for our survival. It traps the Sun's heat, keeping our climate reasonably balmy. Its presence explains why our planet has always had water. The carbon dioxide, which is produced in two basic ways, acts as an essential component of the Earth's built-in thermostat. Volcanic eruptions release enormous volumes of carbon dioxide. Some dissolves in rain, and is absorbed by rocks as they weather. Independently, animals – people among them – take in oxygen and exhale carbon dioxide. Trees and plants use the carbon dioxide and produce oxygen.

Together, these processes keep the Earth's supply of carbon dioxide intact. They work in a wonderful balance. If our planet's temperature were suddenly to fall in a new Ice Age, less water would evaporate. That, in turn, would

mean lower rainfall. With less rain, erosion and weathering of rocks would slow down, releasing less carbon dioxide. Scientists believe that volcanic action would go on, boosting the carbon dioxide in our atmosphere. That would trap more of the Sun's heat. The temperature would rise again, increasing evaporation and rainfall. A similar balancing act would counter any warming of our planet – unless we continue to put too much carbon dioxide into the atmosphere and the greenhouse effect speeds out of control.

Why does El Niño upset the weather?

As swimmers know, the sea's temperature often varies considerably within a short distance. According to currents flowing at the time, the water in one spot may be quite warm, in another distinctly cold.

Ocean currents, warm and cold, have enormous influence on the world's weather. In recent years, meteorologists have kept closer watch on a strange and little understood Pacific Ocean current known as El Niño. Some scientists believe that it causes drastic changes in weather patterns, and may be closely linked with global warming.

Nobody is sure what causes El Niño. It could be volcanic activity on or just below the ocean bed, or an unexplained interaction between the sea and the atmosphere. One controversial claim is that the 1991 eruption of Mt Pinatubo, in the Philippines, triggered El Niño that year. The

Floods and drought followed the phenomenon, El Niño, after it appeared in 1983. Warm currents swept across the Pacific, changing wind patterns, and upsetting the weather in North and South America, Australia and much of Asia

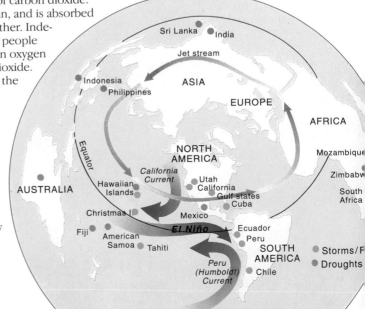

Four angels *ruled the winds, in the minds of ancient scholars, who puzzled about why Earth had steady breezes. A detail from a map of 1664 shows one angelic ruler*

mysterious current was first discovered in the seventeenth century by fishermen based at Spanish ports along the Pacific coast of South America. They named it El Niño – the Christ child – because it flows at Christmastime, but not every year. It lasts usually between fourteen and eighteen months, and may vanish for anything from three to eight years.

El Niño flows from New Guinea and the Micronesian islands some 14 000 km (9000 miles) across the Pacific to coastal regions of Peru. It seems to coincide with a warming of the sea north of New Guinea, when water temperatures may reach 30°C (86°F).

Records show that unusually warm seas in the Pacific, Indian and South Atlantic oceans in spring are followed by summer drought in western Africa. El Niño, a particularly powerful current, moves enormous volumes of exceptionally warm water. As it does so, it heats the air above, shifting it to the north and south. Warm water piles up off South America, leaving colder currents in the western Pacific, along eastern Australia.

The Earth's atmosphere is a complex system. What happens in one region can influence the whole. The Pacific Ocean, equal in area to all the landmasses combined, is a major factor in the world's weather. Although nobody can prove what brings a drought to one region and freak winds and rains to another, it's likely that fickle El Niño plays a major part. In February 1992, satellite images showed a clear link between El Niño and floods in southern California, an event that normally occurs about once in fifty years.

Partnering El Niño is La Niña – the girl child – a cold Pacific current flowing back to the west along the equator that may have upset weather worldwide in 1990. Fierce storms hit northern Europe, Australia experienced a deluge and parts of South America a drought. For all our high-tech devices, we are a long way yet from understanding precisely how the world's weather machine works.

Why does the Earth have steady winds?

Winds can be a blessing or a curse. We delight in gentle summer breezes, and sometimes cringe with fear in the face of gales and hurricanes. Winds generate power of enormous magnitude. If we could harness the world's winds blowing steadily at, say, 30 km/h (about 20 mph),

their combined energy at any moment would exceed the output of a great power station working nonstop for 5000 years.

Winds blow because temperature varies from place to place. Higher temperatures cause air to rise, lowering air pressure. As air rises in one region, cold air moves in from another. The cold air sinks and increases air pressure. The Earth's atmosphere seeks constantly to balance its areas of high and low pressure.

In this process, air currents cause what are sometimes called local winds – the kind experienced in many coastal regions. By day, the land warms up, lowering the air pressure above it. The sea, slower to warm, keeps its atmosphere cooler and at greater pressure. That is why breezes often blow onshore late in the day and into the night. In mountainous regions, cool air rolls downwards at night to replace warmer air rising from the valleys.

When Christopher Columbus sailed to the New World in 1492, he found that steady, east–west winds drove him on. When he returned across the Atlantic, he first sailed northwards and picked up westerlies to take him home. That was a

A WEATHER VANE TO CROW ABOUT

High above buildings in many parts of the world, a weather vane tells which way the wind blows. Usually, above the arrow itself, the vane has a symbolic figure of some kind – and more often than not it is a cockerel. But whether the vane has a cockerel or other figure surveying all, the device is frequently referred to as a weather cock.

According to St Mark's gospel, when Jesus sat with his disciples at the Last Supper, He said to Peter: 'Verily I say unto thee, That this day, even in this night, before the cock crow twice, thou shalt deny me thrice.' In the ninth century, to commemorate this prediction, Pope Nicholas I ordered that a cockerel should surmount the highest steeple or pinnacle of every cathedral, abbey and church in Christendom. Weather vanes were already in use so, to give the cockerel a place higher than anything else, the figure was mounted above the vane.

From the earliest times, it was known that a wind from a certain direction usually brought a particular kind of weather. Wind indicators were installed more as a means of predicting the weather than to indicate merely shifts in the wind.

Weather vanes *got a new look when cockerels were added in the ninth century*

Looking like a river, heat shimmers across a plain where emus head for distant scrub. Ground radiation provides most of our summer warmth

discovery of the greatest importance, and brought a steady growth in trade – hence, the term trade winds. From then on, sailors knew they could count on steady winds to deliver them and their cargo.

It took nearly 200 years before scientists could explain trade winds. In 1686, Edmond Halley argued that, if the air was evenly heated, we would have no winds. Because tropical air is warmer, he said, cool air moves in to take its place. But he couldn't explain why prevailing winds don't blow constantly from the poles towards the equator.

In 1735, the problem interested a British lawyer named George Hadley. He reasoned that the Earth's spin, from west to east, moves faster at the equator than winds travelling towards it. The spin deflects the winds, so that north of the equator trade winds blow steadily from the northeast, and south of the equator from the southeast. Where they meet, in the doldrums, there is little or no wind.

Air moving from the equator to replace that from the poles suffers an opposite shift. Because the Earth spins more slowly at the poles, air moving towards them travels faster than the ground. This turns the winds into westerlies. In 1835, French physicist Gaspard de Coriolis calculated mathematically how the difference in the Earth's speed of rotation from one region to another influences prevailing winds. Scientists know the phenomenon as the Coriolis effect.

Why is summer hotter than winter?

If we have thought about it at all, most of us would say that summer is warmer because the Sun is closer and therefore hotter. The nearer you are to a fire, the warmer it feels. It's a reasonable explanation, but it isn't so. Pursue the matter

further, and it's likely you will get nearer to the truth. Before long, somebody will argue that without doubt the Sun is closer, because in summer it is almost directly overhead.

That, indeed, is the key to the matter. It is not the Sun's distance from the Earth that makes the difference between summer and winter, but the angle at which it shines down on us. On June 21, the northern hemisphere's longest day, the Sun is overhead at the Tropic of Cancer, and beams its heat straight down on that region. When it moves south to the Tropic of Capricorn, giving the southern hemisphere its longest day on December 21, the Sun slants its rays northwards at a considerable angle, so that its heat is distributed over a much larger area. While the southern hemisphere enjoys summer, because the Sun is closer to being directly overhead, the northern hemisphere is wrapped in winter.

Two other factors make summer warmer. One is that, because of the Sun's position, days are longer. The Sun delivers its heat for more hours of the day. Most of us probably believe that pleasant summer warmth comes from the Sun heating the air around us. Again, that isn't so. Most of the heat we enjoy comes as radiation from the ground. You may have noticed that on a hot, sunny day the ground shimmers. Those smoky

waves rising from its surface are signs of radiating heat. Little air is heated directly by the Sun.

The Sun's heat comes as high-frequency radiations, some of which – infrared energy – is exactly the same as that coming from an electric fire. These radiations pass through the atmosphere, and strike the Earth, warming it very quickly in summer. Soon, the ground sends heat back, but in long-wave radiations that do warm the air. The warm air rises; cooler air replaces it and warms up. In time, this constant interchange of air increases the overall temperature. Low cloud may trap heat, and the air gets steadily warmer. That is why some days in summer when the sky is covered in cloud are often oppressively hot.

Why do we give names to cyclones?

If you want impending storms to carry a true note of menace, give them a name. Researchers say that a warning about Hurricane Claud or Cyclone Amanda will have citizens scuttling for shelter or leaving low-lying coastal regions, when

threats of an anonymous storm, no matter how severe, usually go unheeded.

Hurricane, cyclone and typhoon are synonyms for the same weather phenomenon. They describe raging spirals of wind and rain that are born near the equator over seas with a surface temperature of at least 27°C (81°F). The spirals twist anti-clockwise in the northern hemisphere and clockwise in the southern. At their centre or eye, a calm area of low pressure some 32 km (20 miles) across draws winds towards it at speeds that reach about 320 km/h (200 mph).

Clement L. Wragge, a nineteenth-century Australian weatherman, is credited with being the first person to name cyclonic storms. He chose biblical names, such as Rakem, Sacar, Talman and Uphaz. The modern vogue for giving cyclones more common names is said to have started during World War II, when an American radio operator was overheard whistling the popular song, 'Every little breeze seems to whisper Louise', as a storm warning was broadcast to US aircraft. The storm was named Louise.

From 1963 until 1979, the US Weather Bureau gave only female names to hurricanes, but in 1975 the Australian weather service began to allocate male and female names equally. The World Meteorological Service followed suit in 1978. Names are applied alphabetically from A to W, and those given to particularly destructive cyclones or hurricanes are not used again. Thus there is now a shortage of popular female names from early in the alphabet, and weathermen have in recent times called upon less common names such as Alicia and Chantal.

Dew sparkles on woodland grass in the early-morning sunlight. Dewdrops (shown also in close-up) are formed from vapour in the atmosphere, not from moisture given off by plants

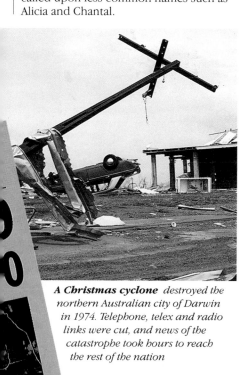

A Christmas cyclone destroyed the northern Australian city of Darwin in 1974. Telephone, telex and radio links were cut, and news of the catastrophe took hours to reach the rest of the nation

Why does dew form?

Aristotle, the Greek philosopher who had an explanation for most of the commonplace events that puzzled his fellows, was wise about dew. It is produced, he said, in serene weather and in calm places. Even though it may seem that the early-morning grass is always covered with shoe-soaking dew, that isn't so. Dew is fussy stuff. It comes only in certain conditions, and these usually promise fine weather.

For dew to form, the day must be fine and warm, and followed by a still, cooler evening and night, in which the sky must be clear or almost cloudless. If you were to walk on a lawn or into a grassy meadow at twilight, and hold something cold – a hand mirror or tumbler of ice – just above the surface, you would soon find it coated with water droplets: condensed vapour.

On a clear night, the ground radiates the day's warmth into the skies. The ground becomes much cooler, causing vapour to condense. On an overcast night, clouds send that heat back to the ground, so that it never gets cold enough to form dew.

You may wonder why dew forms on a lawn and not, say, on the soil of flower beds. It is not that grass attracts dew, but that the plants in flower beds keep the ground warmer. You can check this for yourself by shielding a patch of grass from the night sky. You will need a piece of cotton cloth – a tablecloth will do – and some sticks or canes. On an evening when conditions seem right, stretch the cloth over the canes about 30 cm (1 ft) above the lawn. Next morning, before the Sun has dried things out, you will find that everywhere, except beneath the cloth, the lawn is covered with dew.

Why, sometimes, is the ground covered with frost? During the night, the air has got progressively colder. Cold air, heavier than warm air, has formed a layer at ground level, turning the water vapour that would otherwise be dew into frost.

Cauldron of the world's weather

Nothing affects our lives more than the weather. By it, we eat or starve, prosper or face ruin. Its capricious shifts decide our moods, our leisure, our wellbeing. It determines where we live, whether homes stand or fall. For many of the world's inhabitants it is an ever-present matter of life and death. The inescapable fact is that the weather is always there: and what it is today, right now, it may not be tomorrow or even in an hour's time.

Some people ask why, if the Earth's atmosphere spins with the planet and at the same speed, we should not have the same weather all the time, an endless succession of windless days. Luckily for us, the world's weather is constantly changing. If it brings fierce storms, it gives us also gentle rains, the enveloping silence of snow, dappled clouds and golden sunshine – the stuff of both poetry and everyday conversation.

Four interacting factors determine our weather. The first is the Sun, about 1.3 million times the size of the Earth. The Sun's enormous nuclear furnace reaches at its heart a temperature of some 15 million°C (27 million°F). Even though the Sun is about 150 million km (93 million miles) away, it radiates to Earth a steady supply of energy, some 281 million million kilojoules every hour (nearly 78 million million kilowatt hours), about the same as we use in a year. All that solar power is estimated to be only one two-thousand-millionth of the Sun's awesome total output.

A second element is the Earth itself. As it orbits the Sun, it spins from west to east at 1670 km/h (1040 mph) at the equator. This rotation creates what is known as the Coriolis effect. In 1835, French mathematician Gaspard de Coriolis observed that an object moving across a turning surface veers to the left or right, according to the direction of the spin. If the Earth were stationary, the trade winds would blow from north to south in the northern hemisphere and vice versa.

As the Earth moves in orbit round the Sun, it maintains a fixed tilt – an angle of 23½ degrees to the plane of its path. Thus, part of the planet is closer to the Sun and part farther away. This tilt gives us our seasons, with different parts of the Earth receiving more or less of the Sun's energy.

A third factor, essential to life itself, is the Earth's atmosphere, a blanket of air that keeps the planet comfortably warm. It is almost impossible to say how high that blanket goes. Some 75 per cent of its mass lies below 8800 m (29 000 ft), the height of Everest. Higher than that, its density gradually decreases, but faint traces are still found at altitudes above 8000 km (5000 miles).

Apart from providing air for all living plants and creatures, the atmosphere acts as an insulator. It shields us from the Sun's rays that would otherwise scorch some places with 80°C (176°F) heat by day. By night, the temperature there would fall to -140°C (-220°F).

Gravity keeps this mixture of gases – roughly four-fifths nitrogen, one-fifth oxygen – in place. Another minute but vital ingredient of the Earth's atmosphere is carbon dioxide, which helps to stabilise temperatures near the planet's surface and in the upper atmosphere.

The atmosphere's most important influence on our weather comes from its enormous store of water. This exists as vapour, drops of water and ice crystals, and rises to heights exceeding 13 500 m (44 000 ft). If all this moisture fell at once as rain, the entire Earth would be covered with 25 mm (1 in) of water. The atmospheric blanket has several layers. The lowest, known as the troposphere, varies in thickness, rising about 8 km (5 miles) high at the North and South poles to twice that height at the equator. This layer, a mere film when compared

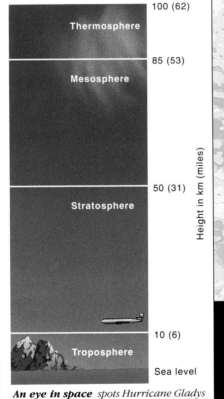

100 (62)

Thermosphere

85 (53)

Mesosphere

50 (31)

Stratosphere

Height in km (miles)

10 (6)

Troposphere

Sea level

An eye in space spots Hurricane Gladys swirling over Florida. Apollo 7 took the photograph at an altitude of 180 km (112 miles). The diagram shows part of Earth's atmosphere. Most of the weather occurs in the lowest layer, the troposphere

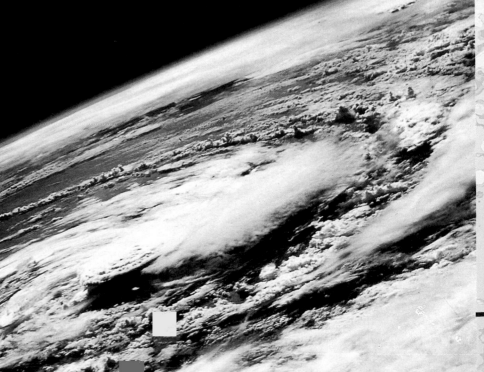

The changing seasons and their length govern this pear tree's life and set the vital rhythm for local flora and fauna

with the blanket's total height, nevertheless holds 80 per cent of all its weight and just about all its water vapour.

Air in the troposphere is colder and heavier, its molecules more densely packed. That is why it varies in thickness according to temperature. In this planetary melting pot, the world's weather is made. At the equator and over deserts and oceans, temperatures reach 40°C (104°F). In these regions, hot air soars, creating fierce tropical updraughts. At the poles, where temperatures sometimes drop to -70°C (-94°F), the air is heavier. Enormous volumes of dry, cold air fall earthwards. Furious winds, howling across the icy wastes, launch them at awesome speeds towards the equator. Even though nearly 20 000 km (12 400 miles) separates Earth's coldest and hottest regions, heat carried on the winds is transferred constantly from one to the other.

A final factor influencing our weather is the Earth's make-up of great mountain chains, sweeping plains, oceans and lakes. Water is slow to heat up and takes longer to cool down. That is why people living near the sea or beside a vast lake enjoy cooler summers and warmer winters. Warm currents, such as the Atlantic's Gulf Stream, protect many places from winter's fiercest blasts. Similarly, mountain barriers block the passage of chill winds, shielding some regions from snow and ice. These great ranges often cause benign rains to fall on one side of the barrier, and send dry, scorching winds to the other.

However it comes, weather is perhaps the greatest influence on our lives. We haven't yet learned to control it, but a range of meteorological instruments, plus photographs from artificial satellites and space probes, now give us a constant overall view, forewarning us sometimes of dangerous hurricanes and advancing tropical storms. Every year brings a greater understanding of the weather's mysteries, a gradual uncovering of its secrets.

Flood, drought and tornado can be forecast but rarely avoided. Floods struck Manila, the Philippine capital, in September 1990. The drought killed Australian sheep and cattle, a too-common calamity. And the tornado, one of many that occur in southeastern USA, hit Edmonton, Kentucky. Luckily, our skill at predicting such disasters is slowly improving

*A **pile of plates** is an apt expression for the impressive swirl of lenticular clouds rising over Antarctica. They occur when the atmosphere has alternate layers of moist and dry air. The patchy build-up of stratus clouds across a North American sky (inset) could bring rain or snow*

Why do clouds form in the sky?

Three main ingredients make up our daily weather – warmth, wind and clouds. To measure warmth and wind, we need instruments. But everybody knows that when giant black clouds cover the sky rain may fall at any minute. That fact was known to the first people who ever looked up at the skies.

Why clouds form and why rain falls are more puzzling matters, which still keep meteorologists busy. Precise answers are possibly the key to more accurate weather prediction and even to a distant goal of weather control or modification.

Not until 1830 was a scientific reason found for cloud formation. Then, American meteorologist James Espy linked convection currents, formed by rising air, with the condensation of water vapour in the atmosphere.

On warm days, the Earth gathers the Sun's heat. Some surfaces absorb heat more rapidly than others. Hard soil warms up more quickly than loose, crumbly soil; lakes and oceans warm up slowly, but retain their heat longer. When they have absorbed as much heat as they can, these surfaces radiate it back into the atmosphere, warming the air.

When air warms up, it expands and rises. The atmosphere tries constantly to equalise the pressures within it. So, when warm air rises, cooler air replaces it. All air holds molecules of water vapour. As they are heated, they move more quickly. While they are fast moving – warm – they can cram tightly into a space and still keep whirling. That is why warm air can hold more water vapour.

If the air cools, as it does when it rises, the molecules of water vapour slow down. If they strike particles of dust or other molecules of water vapour, they may join forces – condense. One group builds with another.

High in our atmosphere, many millions of particles swarm in the air. They come in many forms: as dust, swept up sometimes from degraded land; as carbon, billowing skywards in the smoke of forest fires, car exhausts, factories and power stations; and, perhaps most numerous of all, as salt from the world's oceans. To these particles, called condensation nuclei, water-vapour molecules tend to cling as tiny droplets of water. Invisible water vapour, a gas, has condensed to become visible as a cloud.

The droplets that make up the cloud are so small that they float on air. When they grow bigger, they reach a point where the air will no longer support them, and they fall as rain.

Why is snow so light and feathery?

Most rain starts its journey as snow. What happens inside a raincloud to cause rain to fall puzzled meteorologists until the mid-1930s. Why, they asked, should molecules of water vapour suddenly leave a cloud, and drift down, sometimes almost as a mist and at other times as a drenching torrent?

About sixty years ago, Tor Bergeron, a Swede, decided that some kind of catalyst was at work. A catalyst is a substance that triggers a chemical process without itself being changed. Even in warm weather, clouds at high altitudes hold some ice crystals. Bergeron knew that ice crystals, for complex reasons, make small drops of water evaporate. Their water vapour freezes on the crystals, and the crystals grow steadily bigger.

Strangely, droplets of pure water held in a cloud do not freeze at 0°C (32°F), the normal freezing point of water. The drops are so small that they get colder and colder, and may remain liquid at temperatures as low as -40°C (-40°F). Suddenly, in the presence of just a few ice crystals, they rush to form snow. Each flake that falls may come from a million tiny supercooled droplets of water which, as ice crystals, link up in a lacy network. Each flake holds more air than snow, which is why snowflakes sometimes drift so daintily to the ground. This accounts also for

*A **snow crystal**, when magnified, shows its characteristic six-sided structure*

the lightness of freshly fallen snow. Snow is a poor conductor of heat. In modest falls, it provides excellent protection for plants, trapping the Earth's warmth beneath a light and feathery blanket.

For snow to reach the ground, the air must be below freezing point. It rarely is, so the snow usually thaws on the way down and falls as rain. Or, according to air temperatures, some of it thaws and some doesn't, producing the mixture of rain and snow that we call sleet.

Hail is the product of thunderclouds, which may be up to 16 km (10 miles) high. Ice crystals are swept up and down by the fierce convection currents inside these thunderheads. Caught in an updraught, droplets of rain freeze. As they fall inside the cloud, their surface melts. Driven upwards again, they add more ice, until they become heavy enough to fall earthwards. A freshly fallen hailstone, sliced in half, shows layers of concentric rings, the story of its turbulent birth.

Why do we sometimes get fogs?

A key to the formation of dew, fog and clouds is what is known as the dew point – the temperature at which water vapour in a given sample of air starts to condense. This depends on how much water vapour the sample holds and also on the quality of the air. Water vapour condenses more readily in polluted air; filtered air, free of dust particles, will hold much more water as vapour.

Fog is low-level cloud, sometimes at ground level. Usually it forms at night. It may be caused when warm air, laden with water vapour, strikes cool areas of land. More often, it is seen in low-lying areas … swirling up from rivers, in valleys, over marshy land. All these are places where the air naturally has more water vapour, gathered as water evaporates in the warmth of the day. At night, the cool

Thousands died in London's heavy smog of 1953, and many people wore masks to beat the poisonous mixture of smoke and fog

air, which is heavier, flows downhill. At a certain temperature – the dew point – the invisible water vapour condenses into tiny, swirling droplets of water. If it strikes a suitable surface, such as a particle of dust or smoke or a lock of your hair, the condensing vapour may form large drops of water, the kind seen hanging during fog from fence rails and window ledges.

As inhabitants of many big cities know, fogs may be less frequent and not so thick these days. That is because fewer homes burn coal fires or, if they do, they use smokeless fuel. When fog blankets the city, it no longer traps the discharge of a million or more chimneys. Also, because the air in some cities is cleaner, water vapour is less likely to condense as fog.

EXPLODING THE MYTHS ABOUT RAINFALL

Battlegrounds in World War I soon became fields of mud. Many soldiers believed that heavy gunfire inevitably brought heavy rain

Many theorists have tried to explain what causes clouds to release their rain. The Greek academic Plutarch blamed wars: he noted that rain often follows a big battle. The belief passed on, so that Napoleon's armies and those of World War I were certain that heavy gunfire brought the deluges that turned their battlefields into seas of mud.

Just before World War I, American cornflakes magnate Charles W. Post decided to test the theory. At intervals over several years, he bombed clouds in the sky at Battle Creek, Michigan, with dynamite. It rained. While Post and his supporters cheered his success, news came in of widespread rain, all the way from the west coast to the Great Lakes.

In recent times, atomic-weapons tests were frequently blamed for adverse weather. But perhaps the most unusual explanation came in 1903 in the early days of radio. The London *Evening News* reported: 'The latest theory to account for the continued wet is that the wireless telegraphy operations of Signor Marconi are responsible.'

Why do we get thunderstorms?

Thunderstorms are brought by giant, cumulonimbus clouds, which usually develop after spells of hot, dry weather. The clouds are easily recognised by their size and anvil-like shape.

These clouds build up in a kind of atmospheric leapfrog. Pockets of air, warmed by the ground, rise higher into the sky. Others join them, rising one above another. As each parcel cools in the higher altitude, it falls, then warms up and rises again. Some meteorologists describe this as a battle between air of different temperatures, a battle that continues sometimes more than 16 km (10 miles) into the sky. Inside these thunderclouds

*A **lightning bolt** delivers about 125 million volts of electricity. It travels so fast that it is impossible for the human eye to see that it actually moves upwards from the ground*

faster than sound – 300 000 km (186 000 miles) a second, compared with 0.3 km (⅕ mile) a second – lightning reaches us before the thunder. If the lightning flash is followed swiftly by a thunderclap, the storm centre is close, which is why the thunder can be frighteningly loud. Some people calculate the storm's rough distance in kilometres by dividing by three the number of seconds between the flash and the thunder (in miles, divide by five).

Why does grass under a tree stay frost free?

Even in a hard frost, the ground beneath trees is often frost free. This is because the tree acts like an electric fire, and gives off infrared rays.

It may seem strange that a cold tree, bare of leaves, should give off heat. But so does everything, in a variety of waves of different frequencies: radio waves, microwaves, infrared rays and even visible light. A tree's microwaves are too weak to cook anything and its light is far too weak to see. If our eyes could distinguish infrared rays, the whole tree would be lit up. And so would most things on Earth, because their strongest radiation is in the infrared region. Military technology makes use of this. Night-vision equipment, which sees infrared emissions, can turn the blackest night into a ghostly kind of daylight.

Just as the tree sends out infrared heat to the grass, so the grass sends it back to the tree in a mutual exchange of warmth. Open grassland emits infrared rays, but with no trees to return them, not enough heat is generated to ward off the frost.

***Beating Jack Frost** is a centuries-old struggle. Illustrator George Cruikshank shows one family's answer in the 1850s*

is tremendous turbulence. Parachutists trapped in them have suffered terrifying ordeals, rising and falling helplessly like human hailstones inside a giant tumbling box. As the millions of water droplets whirl furiously around, they turn repeatedly from water to hail and back again. In the process they generate electrical energy, much as pulling off a shirt or our movements within a car build up significant charges of static.

While the icy particles remain within the cloud they all keep either a positive or negative electrical charge. If the particles within a thundercloud are positively charged, they will attract those that are negatively charged in a neighbouring cloud. The result is an explosive flash of lightning of enormous energy. A bolt of lightning is made up of channels of pulsing electrical energy 5 cm (2 in) across. Each bolt may be anything from 60 m to 30 km (66 yd to 19 miles) long. These flashes zip through the air at 145 000 km (90 000 miles) a second, so fast that it is impossible to see that the bolt actually travels from the ground to the clouds.

Every second, forty bolts of lightning strike the ground – well over three million a day. Even though 75 per cent of a bolt's energy vanishes in heat, each still delivers 125 million volts of electricity. A typical thunderstorm releases as much force as a dozen Hiroshima bombs, and records show that some 45 000 thunderstorms occur every day. Along its scorching path through the sky, the lightning heats the air, which expands at supersonic speed, causing the crashes we recognise as thunder.

Why do we see lightning before we hear thunder? The two are released together but, because light travels so much

Water, the maverick molecule

Every second of every day *some 2800 cu m (100 000 cu ft) of water flows over Niagara's Horseshoe Falls, one of the world's great spectacles*

Why don't we run out of water?

When the water supply runs out, as it does frequently in many parts of our planet, other places may experience unwanted floods. The events are not directly linked – in fact, rarely are – but they are part of a natural mechanism that has operated relentlessly for hundreds of millions of years.

The process resembles that of a massive steam engine in perpetual motion. Rain falls from the clouds, feeds rivers and oceans, evaporates from the sea, and is deposited again on the land and in the oceans. Since the first clouds dropped their first showers, Earth's original supply of water has barely changed. Like it or not, the water you drink today may have come from a Roman bath 2000 years ago.

Scientists have estimated that our oceans, lakes, rivers and icefields hold some 14 000 million cu km (330 million cu miles) of water. Another 8.4 million cu km (200 000 cu miles) are stored underground, and large amounts as water vapour in the atmosphere. Most of that water is locked in place. At any time, only a tiny fraction is in circulation in what is known as the hydrologic cycle. That doesn't mean that we are constantly using the same water. Eventually, in this gigantic waterpump powered by heat from the Sun, every drop of water will find its way into the system.

Can we rest confident that our water supply is more than ample for our needs? Of course not. Year by year we use more water. Since World War II, demand has far outstripped supply. Rivers that used to flow strongly have diminished in width and length, because water has been taken out of them for agricultural, industrial or drinking purposes. As well, irrigation schemes have saturated once-potable water with salt. To take the salt out of water, as is done now in many places, is expensive and consumes energy.

Our needs are for bountiful fresh water handily distributed. As we know, water falls regularly where it isn't wanted, and fails to fall where it is. Just under 3 per cent of the world's water is fresh. The rest is salty, held in the oceans. Every year, about 420 000 cu km (10 000 cu miles) of water evaporates into the air; some 90 per cent of that falls back into the sea as rain.

Most of the rain that doesn't fall in the oceans finds its way into rivers that flow into the sea. Where rain falls on land, the distribution is far from even. Average annual rainfall varies from 11 770 mm (463 in) at Tutunendo, Colombia, the world's wettest spot, to amounts elsewhere that are barely measurable.

If we are to enjoy abundant water at any time, our resources need careful management and constant vigilance from us to protect them against pollution.

Why do our seas and oceans have tides?

As the Moon cruises in orbit round the Earth, its gravitational force pulls at our landmasses and oceans. At the same time, Earth's gravity – more powerful than that of its satellite – keeps the Moon in check, like a dog on leash, and stops it from flying off into space.

The Moon's pull moves our mountains and even raises a tiny but measurable tide

The world's highest tides *rise in Canada's Bay of Fundy, which separates New Brunswick and Nova Scotia. The difference between low tide (left) and high is sometimes as much as 15 m (50 ft)*

The Moon's gravity makes oceans bulge, causing daily tides. Spring tides occur when the Sun and Moon are in line and neap tides when they form a right angle

in the Earth's crust. Also, it shifts our seas and oceans, constantly drawing them towards it and raising the water level in places by several metres. The effect is much like that of a giant vacuum cleaner on a carpet, lifting a hump as it passes.

The massive force exerted by the Moon causes a tidal bulge, a heaping up of the oceans. The peak of the bulge brings a high tide. As the Earth revolves and vast new areas come under the Moon's influence, the tidal bulge moves slowly on, creating high tides in one region and low tides in another. A low tide occurs about a quarter of the Earth's circumference ahead of the Moon's path and another about the same distance behind, provided of course that there are oceans there.

The Moon's path over the Earth is complicated by a variety of factors, and tides are affected considerably by an ocean's contours. For example, the Mediterranean Sea, which is almost land-locked, has virtually no tides; the Gulf of Mexico has only one high tide a day.

Oddly, a tidal bulge occurs also some 13 000 km (8000 miles) distant on the far side of the Earth. The Moon's gravitational influence there is about 7 per cent weaker than on the nearer side, but the Earth's centrifugal force, acting like that of a giant and fast-spinning fairground roundabout, throws the ocean outwards. This brings high and low tides to that part of the world. If that were not so, there would be only one high tide and one low tide during each daily spin of the Earth. But as you know, if you are beside the sea, high and low tides are usually about six hours apart, with two of each per day.

Even without the Moon's influence, our oceans and seas would still have tides, but

they would be significantly smaller. The Sun's gravitational pull also exerts an influence on the Earth. The force, though much stronger at its source than that of the Moon, has less effect, because the Sun is much farther away.

The tides caused by the Sun may strengthen or diminish those caused by the Moon. When the Sun and Moon are in line – at times of a full Moon and new Moon – their gravitational forces act together, creating an extra-strong pull that brings us exceptionally high tides. We call them spring tides, even though they are not confined to the spring. When the Sun and Moon form a right angle with the Earth, during the Moon's first and last quarters, the Sun's pull makes itself felt to give us lower, neap tides.

Why do oceans have waves?

Waves are walls of water, the energy of the wind transferred to the sea. It takes only the slightest wind to set waves in motion, as you can see on a small pond. In the world's great oceans, such as the Pacific, fierce storms drive waves across vast distances until, up to 10 m (33 ft) high, they finally break on islands or go roaring across beaches.

If you watch a wave, you might be deceived into thinking that the water itself is moving. The sea, after all, races back and forth on an ocean beach, clearly a sign of moving water. In fact, the water moves very little, as all surfers know. It takes skill to catch a wave – to tap into its energy. Beginners, who fail to time their takeoff correctly, are left riding their boards in roughly the same spot, as the wave passes beneath them and heads for the shore. Floating objects also are rarely caught by a wave, unless blown suddenly by the wind. Sea birds, too, stay where they are. As a wave passes, they ride over it. Seals and dolphins dive beneath the approaching arc, as do surfers paddling out from the shore, knowing that this will avoid the incoming force.

The water itself revolves like a wheel of energy, barely noticeable except near the shore, where it chisels away at rocks, churns the sand and explodes in foam as each wave ends its journey.

A surfer speeds along the curved face of a breaking wave, powered by its energy. Wind waves every day generate a force equal to that in a 50-megaton hydrogen bomb

Why is the sea salty?

If no more rain fell and the oceans dried up, there would be enough salt left to cover the world's continents with a layer 150 m (490 ft) thick. On average, about 3 to 5 per cent of the seas around us is salt. The Dead Sea, the saltiest body of water in the world – and, at 400 m (1300 ft) below sea level, the lowest point on the face of the Earth – holds at least 25 per cent salt, making it impossible for swimmers to sink. This happens because the salty water has a much higher density than the swimmers' bodies. In fact, the water is so dense that skindivers find it difficult to stay below the surface unless they carry a belt full of weights.

The oceans and salt lakes get their salt by dissolving it from the rocks in their beds and receiving it from feeder streams and rivers. As seas evaporate, the salt level builds up. Fresh water, falling as rain on adjacent land, seeps through the soil, dissolving more salt, which eventually reaches the rivers and the seas.

If salt were the only chemical transferred to water in this way, it would not be a problem. Unfortunately, in areas of intensive agriculture, fertilisers and pesticides also drain into the rivers and seas, with serious long-term effects on marine life. Also, in some irrigation areas, the repeated watering of the same land with river water builds up salt and other minerals in the soil, eventually poisoning it or the water table below.

*A **mountain of ice** floats in Antarctic seas. If water behaved like other substances, which become more dense as they freeze, icebergs would sink and most water would be ice*

Why does water freeze?

We all know that in wintry weather puddles are coated with ice, and ponds freeze solid enough sometimes to allow us to skate on them. But why, when the temperature is lowered, does water harden in this way? Why doesn't it react as it does when the temperature rises – turning into a gas and gradually vanishing into the air through evaporation?

Imagine a large group of unruly children racing about in a school playground, with a teacher anxious to restore order. The teacher gives a signal to walk, not run. She knows that only by slowing down can the children form orderly lines.

A picture of molecules in water would be similar. If the water is cooled, the molecules slow down. In time, the molecules, like the children in the playground, move so slowly that they can link up in an orderly way. They start to build a strong, three-dimensional structure in which each molecule joins four others.

The structure, which we call ice, is actually identical in arrangement to that of a diamond. Ice is really a diamond made of oxygen and hydrogen, instead of carbon. Diamonds, the hardest natural substance, are stronger because carbon atoms have stronger bonds than those in water molecules.

Ice doesn't form at temperatures above 0°C (32°F), because the water molecules, even at 3°C (37°F), are moving too fast. Even if the water is actually freezing, some evaporation takes place. Just as one or two children in the playground will never stay in line, some water molecules are always moving faster than average, and have the energy to escape into the atmosphere.

Why doesn't running water freeze?

Take a look at a fast-flowing river in the depths of winter. Its banks may be snow-covered and its edges lined with ice, but at its heart the river still flows strongly.

There are three reasons why the river doesn't turn into solid ice. First, fast-flowing water has more air dissolved in it; this lowers its freezing point. So would anything else dissolved in it, such as salt. That is why the sea takes longer to freeze, and why salt is sprinkled on roads to stop them becoming icy.

Secondly, running water tends to break up ice crystals as they form. Thus, stagnant water at a river's edge will freeze first. A third reason is that water flows because it has energy, usually from gravitational force or maybe from a propeller or paddle. This stirring or agitation can be used to heat water: if you stir vigorously, the water will warm up – but it takes a great deal of work. Water falling down a steep cascade will probably be slightly warmer than water in a nearby rock pool. In extreme cold, you won't need to test that theory with a thermometer. Almost certainly, you will see that the pool is already frozen over.

*A **river in winter** won't turn into solid ice if it flows strongly. Its energy warms it up*

CLOSE-KNIT BAND OF REBELS

A description of water and its properties sounds like the preamble to a riddle. What is commonplace yet extraordinary ... vanishes but never completely disappears ... may be hard or soft, visible or invisible? It supports life and destroys it. Gentle as a mist, it can level mountains and grind rocks to powder.

To explain water's rebellious nature, we need to understand its structure. Water, as shown by its chemical formula of H_2O, is a compound of two atoms of hydrogen to one of oxygen. Together, the atoms form a molecule, the smallest unit to which a compound can be reduced without losing its identity.

Hydrogen and oxygen readily combine to form water. Strike a match in their presence, and they will turn to water. Once formed, the water molecule is extremely strong. Much energy is needed to break it apart – and precisely the same amount of energy is released when water is formed.

The hydrogen and oxygen atoms are bound by a powerful link known as a covalent bond. In a band or shell around the centre, or nucleus, of the hydrogen atom is a single electron, but there is room for two.

Similarly, the oxygen atom has six electrons, but could accommodate eight. The vacant spaces are quickly filled in a kind of room-share arrangement: electrons from two hydrogen atoms join the oxygen molecule; two electrons from the oxygen atom mingle with those of the hydrogen atoms. When the vacancies are filled, the three atoms acquire strength and stability.

The water molecule is lopsided, with the two hydrogen atoms sitting on one side of the oxygen atom. One side, hydrogen, has a positive electrical charge, and the oxygen is negatively charged. This makes the molecule act like the electrical equivalent of a bar magnet. If you have tried to put two bar magnets together, you will know that, if you turn them one way, they will join up swiftly; turn one magnet round and the pair will fly apart. Water molecules behave in similar fashion.

Water's lopsidedness and its electrical charges result in its molecules linking up in distinctive patterns, and explain why water has so many maverick qualities. For a liquid composed of such small molecules, it boils at an extremely high temperature. Also, water expands when it freezes: most other liquids do the opposite.

When water freezes, each molecule connects with four others, and this group joins others similarly constructed. The attraction is electrical – the molecules tend to pull like magnets – and is what scientists call a hydrogen bond. This force acts like a molecular superglue, and gives water some of its strange but wonderful qualities.

Water's molecules have two atoms of hydrogen and one of oxygen. These molecules link up in patterns to form water in its three states – gas when heated (top), a liquid (centre) and solid ice

Why does ice form from the top down?

Have you ever wondered why there is ice on the surface of a puddle instead of at the bottom? Or why sometimes, when you collect milk on a frosty day, ice has formed in the neck of the container but not lower down?

It's lucky for all of us that ice behaves in this fashion. Were it not so – if water acted in the same way as other liquids that freeze – much of our water would be almost completely frozen. Ice would form on a river- or seabed, and build its way to the surface. The only available water might be a thin layer where the summer Sun had melted the ice.

Between 0°C (32°F) and 4°C (39°F), water acts strangely. At freezing point, the molecules in ice are widely spaced, making their structure lighter. If its temperature rises, the crystalline pattern breaks down. Some molecules, however, cling together in pairs. They are no longer ice crystals, but they are lighter and more widely spaced than molecules in warmer water. At 4°C (39°F) the water molecules are as tightly packed as they will ever be. They move at random, without any structure. At higher temperatures, water behaves like a normal liquid. Its molecules speed up and collide. This increases the distance between them, so that the water expands.

As a pond freezes, a dance takes place between different layers of water. The surface cools first and, because it is denser and heavier, sinks to the bottom. Now, the new top layer cools and sinks. After a while, the whole pond is at 4°C (39°F), and the water is as dense as it will ever be. When the top layer is cooled further – say to 3°C (37°F) – it stays on top, because it is lighter than the water underneath. Eventually, staying where it is, it turns into ice, floating with considerable buoyancy on the water below.

The freezing process now slows down, because the ice insulates the water from the frosty air. That is why ponds rarely freeze solid, killing the fish. It is also why, if you are anxious to skate, you need to exercise patience. As all pond skaters know, from the first sign of ice to having a layer 5 cm (2 in) thick, safe for skating, may take a frustratingly long time.

Temperatures fell dramatically across Europe from 1450 to 1850, and created a Little Ice Age. The severity of the 1812 winter helped destroy Napoleon's huge army in its retreat from Moscow. Dutch artist Hendrick Avercamp paints a typical winter scene in an early seventeenth-century town

Why does water take so long to boil?

The saying that a watched pot never boils probably came first from somebody who was amazed at how long it takes to heat just a small quantity of water. Touch the underside of the kettle and you will find it extremely hot, but the water inside may still be quite cold.

This ability of water to absorb heat without itself varying much in temperature makes it a useful cooling agent – in some car radiators and at power stations, for example. Large bodies of water, such as vast lakes and our oceans, keep the surrounding land cool in summer and warmer in winter. Waterless deserts, by comparison, may be fiercely hot in summer and bitterly cold in winter.

A substance warms up when its molecules are induced into vigorous motion. Applying heat does this, and some molecules react more swiftly than others. In liquid form, water molecules link up in an irregular way, whirling around almost like partners in an old-time dance, each group

joining others before moving on. These links between one group and another are known by scientists as hydrogen bonds, and are quite strong.

We should be glad of that. If the hydrogen bonds were weaker, it would be easier to break water molecules apart, and water would boil more easily – at Arctic temperatures or below. Our bountiful supplies of water would swiftly boil away.

Why does water bubble when it boils?

We have all at some time watched a saucepan of water heating on the stove. An early sign of its getting hot is that tiny air bubbles begin gradually to stream towards the surface.

Water holds dissolved air, but the warmer it is the less air it can hold. That is why, on a hot day, fish in a pond become listless, or you may see them near the surface, gasping for air.

As water heats up, more and more of its dissolved air rises to the surface. But the real bubbling starts when the water

The water boils, but it may not be hot. In a vacuum, cold water will bubble furiously

reaches boiling point (100°C or 212°F at sea level). At this temperature, bubbles of hot water vapour can form in the water, with enough pressure to overcome that of the atmosphere. Before that, the vapour lacked the push to form bubbles: it drifted gently from the surface of the water in what we commonly call steam.

Even cold water gives off vapour. That is why it slowly evaporates. Also, it can be made to boil, if you give it the advantage of reducing the atmospheric pressure on it. A glass of cold water placed in a vacuum will boil merrily. And, high on a mountain, where atmospheric pressure is lower than at sea level, water boils at a lower temperature – just 70°C (158°F) on the summit of Mt Everest.

Why does water feel wet?

Sometimes water feels wet and at other times it doesn't. Put your arm into a bath of water, try not to move, and you may have difficulty in detecting what we commonly describe as wetness. If the water is at body temperature, you may have even more trouble. Put a drop of water into the palm of your hand, and again you will have a problem in feeling its wetness.

When we say that water is wet, usually we are describing an oft-experienced sensation that comes as water evaporates. Water is low in viscosity – that is, it flows easily. When you spill some on your

clothes, it spreads out quickly because of its low viscosity and its capillary action, its ability to climb through the tiny tubes and pores in the fabric. Because it disperses in this way, it evaporates more easily, taking heat from your body to do so. Thus, if you get wet, you will get colder. You will feel wet until the water has evaporated.

Why do so many substances dissolve in water?

Water doesn't dissolve everything, but it tries very hard to do so. About half the world's chemical substances are found dissolved in water.

Sometimes, that is a major problem. For example, by-products of heavy metals discharged as industrial waste may pollute drinking water or, by poisoning fish, get into the food chain. On the other hand, our survival and that of all plants and animals depends on water's ability to dissolve a range of substances that give nourishment. If you put fertiliser on your onion bed, the onions receive it via their roots only when it is dissolved in water.

One reason why water is such a good solvent is because many substances have important similarities in their molecular structure to that of water. When water meets such substances its molecules behave like police controlling a disorderly mob. If, for instance, you put sugar into your cup of coffee (which is of course mainly water), the water molecules will break into a group of sugar molecules, and stop them joining forces with the rest. The two kinds of molecules will interact, the sugar forming strong hydrogen bonds with the water, so that the sugar becomes part water (or coffee) and the water becomes syrupy.

Water also dissolves other substances, such as salts and metals, through a process called ionic bonding. The atoms of table salt, for example, are held together by opposite electrical charges. These charged atoms are called ions. Water molecules, whose hydrogen atoms are positively charged and its oxygen atoms negatively charged, disrupt this attraction, and force the atoms of salt apart, thus dissolving it.

Ethanol – the kind of alcohol found in beer, wine, whisky and other spirits – is, like sugar, a good mixer. It, too, forms strong hydrogen bonds with water. If it didn't, the alcohol would float on top of the drink. Nobody would ask for whisky and water, because the two wouldn't mix.

Why don't oil and water mix?

Spill many liquids such as vinegar, wine or fruit juice into a bowl of water, and they mix readily with it. Drop in some oil of any kind and, no matter how much you stir the bowl, the oil will soon float on the surface. The anomaly rarely troubles us in our everyday lives, but it is clearly of major importance in, say, clearing up an oil spill from a tanker.

At the heart of the problem lies the peculiar behaviour of the water molecules, which gives them a strong attraction for one another but not much for the molecules in oil. Oil molecules are built differently. In scientific terms, they are non-polar – that is, they don't have negative and positive ends – and are not attracted electrically to water molecules. The water molecules cling closely together and the oil molecules, like a shunned minority group, are left outside the fence, unable to mingle.

It is possible to break down that fence by using an emulsifier. This modifies both the water and the oil, so that they can 'wet' each other. Many skin-care creams, which need to combine both substances, are emulsions of oil and water.

Oil from a supertanker washes up on France's Brittany coast in 1978. Ten years later, scientists said that fish were still not breeding normally

Breaking into the sound barrier

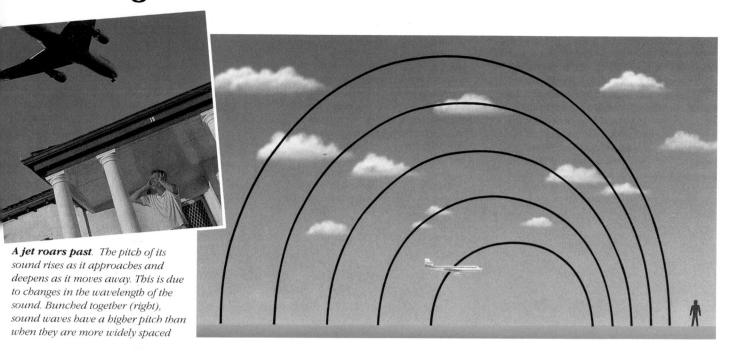

A jet roars past. *The pitch of its sound rises as it approaches and deepens as it moves away. This is due to changes in the wavelength of the sound. Bunched together (right), sound waves have a higher pitch than when they are more widely spaced*

Why does a moving sound change pitch?

An express train thunders down the track, the pitch of its sound rising noticeably as it approaches. As the train speeds past, the pitch changes dramatically, dropping several tones down the scale.

This switch in pitch comes from a subtle change in the distance between the sound waves sent out by the train. If the train were stationary, the pitch would remain constant as the sound waves radiated from it in all directions. A diagram of those waves would show them as evenly spaced spheres centred on the train.

When the train moves, the centre of each sound wave changes. The waves in front of the train bunch more closely together and those behind get farther apart. As the train gathers speed, this effect builds up. If you were standing beside the track as the train approached, more waves would reach you each second. Because the number of waves you hear each second – their frequency – determines the sound's pitch, you would hear it rise as the train got nearer. Conversely, when the train had passed, you would hear fewer waves and a sound of a lower pitch.

If you were in a fast-moving vehicle speeding towards a stationary noise-maker, the effect would be similar. First you would hear more sound waves per second and a higher pitch. As you moved away, the waves would overtake you less frequently, lowering the sound's pitch.

This curious change in the pitch of moving sounds is called the Doppler effect, after Austrian physicist Christian Johann Doppler, who first explained the phenomenon in 1842. Doppler had a locomotive draw a team of trumpeters along a track. As they sounded various notes, musicians with a perfect sense of pitch stood at the trackside and confirmed precisely how the notes changed pitch. The practical applications of the phenomenon include using ultrasonic sound to determine the blood flow within the body and, in refined sonar systems, to determine the speed and direction in which vessels are moving.

Why does sound penetrate walls?

We know that sound travels through air in much the same way as a wave travels through water, but it moves much faster – at about 1238 km/h (770 mph), depending on the temperature.

If sound needs a medium such as air, in which the molecules can pass the message along, how does it manage to move through a solid wall? It can do so only by making the wall itself oscillate slightly. If the wall does this, it activates the air molecules on its far side, and the sound moves on, maybe from your neighbour's apartment to yours.

Not all walls move easily. Thick and heavy walls have a lot of inertia – natural resistance to movement. It takes considerable force to get them moving. Sound of average volume, coming perhaps from your neighbour's television set, has enough force to move a lightweight wall. If it can, the sound will squeak through cracks and other openings, such as unsealed spaces around water and gas pipes. One way to insulate a room from noise without constructing thick walls is to use separate layers of lightweight material. Walls of two plasterboard layers each nailed to a different frame will move independently, and reduce the acoustic coupling between adjoining rooms.

This is why, in noisy cities, many homes now have double-glazed windows. The two panes of glass block the sound, when a single pane will not. Double-glazing will also keep out exterior cold or heat, if the panes of glass are at least 15 cm (6 in) apart and the window frames fit tightly.

What noise annoys? *Research shows we are more troubled by a neighbour's noise than by sound coming from anywhere else*

'What d'y' mean, stop that radio blaring? We ha' no radio on!'

SOUNDS THAT TAKE THE PLACE OF SIGHT

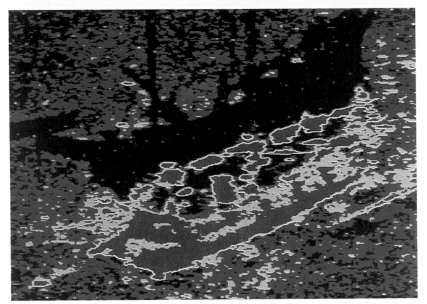

A piece of history is revealed as an ultrasonic scan outlines the wreck of a sailing ship. Echoes from high-frequency sound waves aimed at the ocean bed enable a computer to create a photograph. Coloured areas are caused by computer processing

Many animals, such as porpoises and bats, depend on their ability to detect echoes to guide their movements. They use sound as we use sight. Bats give out high-pitched squeaks, often at frequencies three times as high as those audible to our ears, and pick up the echoes from obstacles or from prey.

The high-pitched sounds made by bats have extremely short wavelengths, roughly 6 mm (¼ in) long. If they were any longer, small objects such as mosquitoes and moths would not reflect them. Scientists have shown just how efficient is a bat's echolocation system. In one test, they threw mealworms into the air at night, and bats caught 95 per cent of them. In another, bats avoided wires only 1 mm (0.04 in) in diameter.

Animals' use of sound as sight was adapted during World War II to hunt German U-boats. A variety of echolocation devices led eventually to sonar – sound navigation and ranging – techniques. Submarine hunters sent beams of high-frequency sound into the oceans, much as anti-aircraft teams swept the night skies with searchlights. By timing the echoes, hunters could determine a target's location.

Our ears hear sound waves ranging from 20 hertz to about 20 000 hertz. Those below our limit are known as infrasonic waves, and those above are called ultrasonic waves. Some spiders detect infrasonic waves, which are caused naturally mainly by earthquakes, and some respond to sounds with frequencies as high as 45 000 hertz.

Ultrasound has many practical uses. Because ultrasonic waves are not absorbed to any great extent by water, they are useful for mapping the ocean bed. Also, because they are high-frequency waves, they can be concentrated into beams so that they penetrate to great depths.

Another major use is as a diagnostic tool in medicine. Using a sonarlike technique, a gynaecologist can examine an unborn child for abnormalities. Ultrasonic waves enter a mother's body, without the need for surgery, and are harmless to the woman and her baby. These waves are used also in industry to detect flaws in metal.

Infrasound has few applications. Its main use is by geologists to determine the nature of the Earth's crust. Underground explosions generate infrasonic waves which behave differently according to whether, for example, they pass through solids or liquids. By setting off an explosion at one point and checking the speed at which infrasonic waves are received at others, geologists can map areas far below the Earth's surface.

Why doesn't sound travel as fast as light?

If you see a distant action – say, a ship hooting as it approaches harbour – you will notice a puff of steam coming from the siren before you hear the sound. Similarly, a flash of lightning always precedes a clap of thunder. In both events, the sound and light waves set off together, but light far outpaces the sound.

A sound wave travels by pushing and pulling atoms and molecules both closer together and farther apart. The particles bump back and forth, one against the other, much like people in a crowd. The wave's speed depends on how fast these particles can move or vibrate. The particles' speed depends on the density of the material and its springiness. That is why the speed of sound varies.

At sea level and at a temperature of 20°C (68°F), sound travels at 344 m (1128 ft) a second. In hydrogen, which is less dense than air, it moves nearly three times as fast. It travels faster through solids than through gases. Through steel

In an acoustic laboratory a scientist begins a se

The world's fastest passenger aircraft, the Concorde, cruises at about twice the speed of sound. It flies from London to New York in about three hours and fifty minutes. If it flew at the speed of light, it would complete the journey in a fraction of a second

it reaches a speed of about 5000 m (16 400 ft) a second; steel is dense, but its atoms are held tightly together. They don't need to vibrate much to pass on the sound wave. Temperature affects the speed. In freezing weather, because the molecules in the air move slowly, sound travels at only 331 m (1086 ft) a second; at 100°C (212°F), it goes some 43 m (141 ft) a second faster.

Light travels quite differently – as electromagnetic disturbances. It can move through a vacuum, which sound cannot. In empty space, these electromagnetic waves zip along at nearly 300 000 km (186 000 miles) a second. As far as we know, nothing can travel faster. When light passes through a transparent substance, such as glass, it slows down. That is because it is absorbed and then re-emitted an instant later by electrons it encounters along its path. Low-density materials, such as air and other gases, present only the slightest obstacle to its progress. Light flashes through them at close to its top speed.

Why are empty rooms so noisy?

Few things are quite so disturbing to our sense of wellbeing as loud noise. In some rooms, such as restaurants with shiny tiled floors, glass-topped tables and stainless-steel fittings, the noise level is inevitably high. Footsteps resound, knives clatter, and voices are raised to be heard. In other rooms, with carpets and soft furnishings, sounds seem to be swallowed up – and indeed they are. An empty room is noisier because it has no furnishings to swallow the sound.

A sound wave normally travels by causing a rhythmic vibration in molecules of air. When the wave hits a hard surface, it bounces back, setting the nearby air molecules into motion. The wave rebounds in a new direction.

Sound-absorbing materials stop the wave from bouncing back. These materials are usually very porous, with an open texture. When a sound wave strikes a surface of this kind, the vibrating air molecules collide against the inner surfaces of the material's pores. Each collision deprives the molecules of some of their energy, which doesn't vanish, but changes into heat. If the sound wave forces fibres in the material itself to vibrate, it loses even more energy and creates more heat. This heat is infinitesimal. The sound-absorber radiates it rapidly and silently into the surrounding air.

Why can't sound travel through a vacuum?

The precise nature of sound has puzzled people for centuries. Philosophers and scientists still debate whether sound exists even when nobody is present to hear it. If a great rock bounces down a mountainside, far from anybody's hearing, does it make a noise? And if it does, how indeed can that be proved?

Such a discussion rarely ends in agreement, because it depends on how sound

...sts. Sound-absorbing materials line all surfaces of the windowless room

is defined. Philosophers may say that sound exists only if it is heard; physicists usually take a more objective stance, arguing that sound is a form of energy that exists outside human experience.

Today, recorded messages constantly prove that sound energy is created when we are not present to hear the sound. But confusion about sound lives on. That is because sound is both cause and effect, and we tend to mix them up. On the one hand, sound is the forced vibration of atoms and molecules in a medium of some kind, such as the atmosphere or water. On the other, it is the sensation within the receiver, the reaction of the ear and the brain to those outside vibrations.

In elastic substances, such as gases, many liquids and most solids, the atoms and molecules are in constant motion. A sound, whether from a human voice or a clap of thunder, jolts one molecule into its neighbour. This sets up a chain reaction. As one molecule moves closer to its neighbour, the neighbour pushes it back but, at the same time, springs nearer to another molecule. This rhythmic, back-and-forth movement goes right through the medium, carrying the energy of the sound wave.

Normally, we hear sounds because they are conveyed by a sound wave passing through air. Withour air we would hear none of the sounds that are so familiar. A sound's volume depends on the energy of its waves. If we create a vacuum in, say, a large jar by removing all the air inside it, no sound can ever escape from the

*A **sound wave** travels by setting up a chain reaction. Energy causes one molecule to bump another, passing the force along. The air vibrates but does not otherwise move*

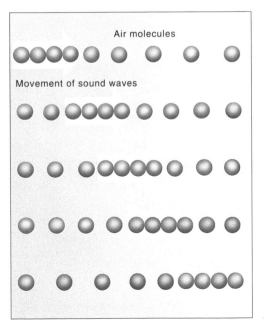

Air molecules

Movement of sound waves

*The **merest whisper** uttered in the whispering gallery of St Paul's Cathedral, London, can be heard on the far side of the gallery, 32 m (105 ft) away. The dome tends to focus the echoes, and their sound is reflected round the circular wall*

jar because there is nothing to convey that sound. In 1660, physicist Robert Boyle proved the point by suspending 'a watch with a good alarum' inside a vacuum. When the time came for the alarm to ring, his audience heard nothing.

Why do we occasionally hear echoes?

Many places in the world are renowned for their echoes, sounds repeated a short time after they are made. What makes these sites famous usually is the length of the gap between the original sound and its echo; in some valleys the sound echoes and re-echoes.

Sound waves are similar to other waves, and are subject to the same influences. If you shout in a valley, the sound is repeated because it strikes a hard surface and is reflected back to you, much in the way that light is reflected or a water wave bounces back from a river bank. If some of the sound strikes the opposite wall of the valley, we hear it again. The farther you are from these reflecting surfaces, the longer will be the gap between the sound and the echo. Because sound travels through dry air at about 344 m (1128 ft) a

second, a surface 17 m (56 ft) away will give an echo 0.1 seconds later. A really good echo may have a second's delay, showing that it comes from a reflector 172 m (188 yd) distant. Sounds echo and re-echo down a narrow valley, because if they are loud enough they bounce back and forth several times on the valley's walls.

In our everyday lives, we undoubtedly hear more echoes than we are aware of. At home and in city buildings we are often surrounded by a variety of hard, smooth and rigid surfaces that reflect sound perfectly.

Our ears retain a sound for about one-twentieth of a second after the sound ceases. If an echo comes back to us in less than that time, because the reflecting surface is close, the delay is too short for us to separate the echo from the original sound. For us to do so, the two must be separated by a brief period of silence. Without that, the reflected sound prolongs the original, creating what is known as reverberation.

This factor is of great concern to architects designing buildings, particularly concert halls, where sound quality is of prime importance. Because sound waves behave like other waves, architects sometimes assess the acoustics of a proposed building by making a cross-sectional model. This they test in a ripple tank, watching how water waves are reflected or absorbed by different surfaces. Frequently, plastic discs or other reflectants are suspended above or behind the platform of a concert hall to improve its sound quality.

As we all know, sometimes to our discomfort, sounds do not fade so quickly inside a building as they do in the open air. What is known as the time of reverberation measures the speed at which a sound diminishes to one-millionth of its original intensity. In a vast building, such as a cathedral, that is often as long as ten seconds. In a carpeted room with an array of soft furnishings it may be only a half-second or less.

A longer reverberation time gives music greater richness; a short period gives clarity to speech. That is why concert halls aren't always suitable places for staging plays and conferences.

Energy that lights up our lives

Why does light bend when it strikes water?

The ancient Greeks knew that light travels in straight lines. Euclid, as early as 300 BC, was aware that when light strikes a reflective surface such as a mirror it bounces off at an equal angle. That is why you cannot see yourself in a mirror except by standing directly in front of it.

Another phenomenon puzzled the Greeks. They noticed that a straight stick placed at an angle in water no longer seemed to be straight. Where it entered the water, it looked almost as though it were broken. The part of the stick below the water is still straight, but it is on a different line from that above water. You can see this oddity for yourself by placing a knitting needle or a pencil in a glass of water, and viewing it from the side.

It took many centuries from the time the Greeks first noticed this peculiarity for somebody to find a scientific explanation. In 1621, Dutch physicist Willebrord Snell discovered that light doesn't travel the same way in all transparent substances. The reason why a straight stick slanting into water seems to bend is that the light rays coming from the stick to the eyes change direction at the point where the water meets the air.

Snell tested his theory in different substances, and found that some bend light more than others. He discovered also that the distortion is greater according to the angle. A stick placed vertically in water doesn't appear to bend at all. The more it slants, the more it seems to bend. Snell used the term refraction to describe the way that different substances bend light.

Later that century, another Dutch physicist, Christian Huygens, explained the phenomenon. Already, French mathematician René Descartes had worked out a numerical scale – the refractive index – for the light-bending power of transparent substances. Huygens said that the refractive index of a substance indicated the speed at which light travelled through it. Light moved more slowly in some substances than in others. Another important point, discovered by Sir Isaac Newton, is that refraction varies with the colour of the light. Red and blue lights shining at the same angle into a thick piece of glass react differently. The red light bends less than the blue.

Why does wet sand look darker than dry sand?

When you walk at the water's edge on a sandy beach, you know at once how far the incoming waves are likely to reach. The wetter sand is firmer and darker.

Common sense disputes that this should be so. After all, the only difference between the wet and dry sand is that one has a coating of water. Why should a clear liquid make the sand so much darker?

The answer has nothing to do with the purity of the water. If you pour the purest, clearest water on to clean, dry sand, the result is the same. The water darkens the sand because it tends to hide the individual grains. They have less tendency to reflect the light into your eyes. Instead of being reflected, the light is absorbed. The more light that is absorbed, the darker

An optical illusion makes a pencil in water look broken. Water reduces the light's speed by 25 per cent, bending its rays

the sand appears. Conversely, the more light that is reflected, the lighter and whiter the sand will look. On a day of bright sunshine, it is the driest sand above the high-tide mark that dazzles the eyes, because it is reflecting more light than sand at the water's edge.

Water is not the only liquid that darkens sand. In fact, some clear liquids, such as benzene, will turn it even darker. This is because they have a refractivity, an ability to bend light rays, that is much closer to that of sand than is water's.

But please don't try to prove us right or wrong. Benzene is dangerous: it is flammable, poisonous and can cause cancer.

Wet and dry sand are clearly distinguishable on most beaches. Dry, white sand reflects more light, increasing the dangers of sunburn

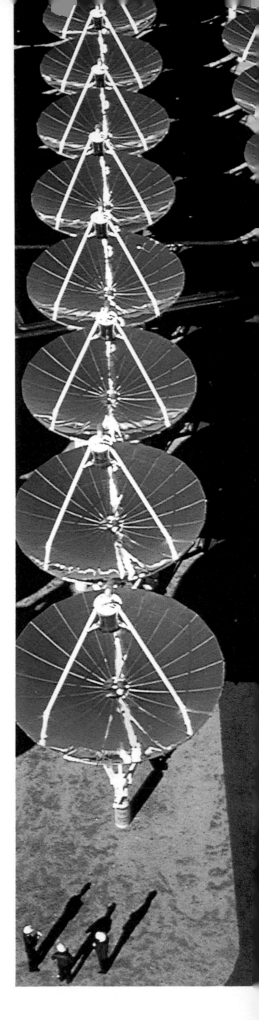

Why does broken glass cause fires?

Light travels only through transparent substances, and it moves through them at different speeds. The principle that some substances will bend light is an important one, used in all forms of lenses and in instruments such as telescopes.

A concave lens, which is thinner at its centre than at its edges, spreads light. A convex lens, which is thicker at the centre than at the edge, concentrates light onto a single point. This kind of lens is found in some flashlights. If it was of uniform thickness, all the light striking it, say from a flashlight bulb, would head straight on. The lamp would have no beam. The light comes from the bulb as a mass of parallel rays. The curve of the lens bends them so that, instead of going straight on, they converge. Other flashlights use a curved mirror behind a flat lens to make the light form a beam.

Just as a convex lens will concentrate light from a flashlight bulb, so it can be used to focus the Sun's rays onto a single point, concentrating their heat. Pieces of a broken bottle, especially the thickened glass from the base, will act like a lens. That is why on a hot day broken glass often causes fires.

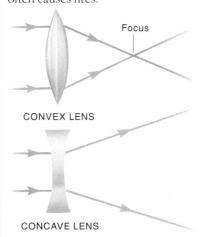

CONVEX LENS

CONCAVE LENS

The chief function of lenses is to refract light, or change the direction of its rays. A convex lens focuses them and a concave lens causes them to diverge

Why do some materials absorb light?

If you want to stay cooler on a hot sunny day, wear white. To our eyes, black clothes are black because they absorb so much light. White absorbs least of all. Light is a form of energy and, in absorbing it, clothes and materials of various colours convert light into heat. Usually, when atoms and molecules in opaque materials absorb light, the extra energy makes them vibrate more vigorously. You feel these vibrations as heat. Absorbed light isn't always converted into heat. Some materials eject electrons, if the light is of sufficiently high energy. Scientists know this as the photoelectric effect, which is used in the electric eye that opens shop doors and triggers burglar alarms.

The energy of light is linked to its wavelength. The shorter the wavelength, the higher is the light's energy. For example, blue light has more energy than red light of equal brightness.

In materials such as silicon, the electrons absorb light and become more mobile, making the material a better conductor of electricity. Silicon treated with certain impurities generates electricity, which is the basis of solar cells.

Why can light be turned into electricity?

We know that at the touch of a switch we can make electricity produce light, but the process can be reversed. All light, whether visible or invisible, is pure radiant energy. The energy reaching the Earth as sunlight is some 10 000 times the world's total fuel consumption.

Sunlight is a mixture of different light rays. The invisible infrared rays cause atoms and molecules to vibrate faster. This produces heat. Sunshine warms up the sea because some of the water's surface molecules absorb so much light energy that they vibrate right out of the liquid, evaporating as water vapour.

If we use an array of mirrors to concentrate the Sun's rays onto a water boiler, we can use its high-pressure steam to drive turbines and generate electricity. We are merely turning one form of energy into another. Similarly, plants use sunlight to make food. When we burn coal or oil to make electricity, we are in effect using up the sunshine stored by plants.

All those are indirect ways to turn light into electricity. Photovoltaic cells, which are seen these days on many house roofs in sunny parts of the world, use light more directly. So do spacecraft, which depend on solar cells for electricity.

Known also as solar batteries, the cells are made of two layers of silicon, one of which is impregnated with an element such as boron and the other usually with arsenic. The two layers interact. When light falls on them, electrons migrate from one layer to the other, producing electricity. To get usable power, many cells must be wired together.

Solar energy is in its infancy, but already has powered cars and aircraft. One idea is

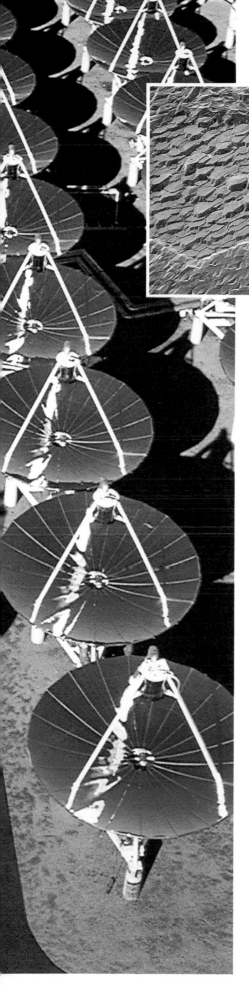

Farming sunshine, lines of solar dishes track the Sun to gather heat and generate electricity. An enlarged amorphous silicon cell (top) shows that its surface is made up of small crystals. The tiny Solar Eye is a new and highly efficient cell

to send solar-power satellites into space to collect energy nonstop and beam it back to Earth as microwaves. It is estimated that twenty-five satellites, each 65 sq km (25 sq miles) in area, could supply all America's electricity.

The problems of solar energy are now largely political. While electricity from fossil fuels remains inexpensive, scientific research into solar power is poorly funded. Meanwhile, fossil fuels are running out, and the added costs they bring in global warming and air pollution have yet to be counted.

Why is the sea blue?

All colour in the world comes from light. Without light, we would see no colour in the greenest grass, a peacock's feather, a bunch of flowers or a brilliant rainbow. Three factors determine the colours we see: the light itself, the material it falls on and the ability of the human eye to distinguish colours.

A beam of light appears to us to have no colour. Shine it through a prism, and it breaks down into a spread of colours resembling those in a rainbow. Indeed, that is why rainbows appear in the sky: a shower of raindrops acts to open up the full spectrum of light into all its different and wonderful wavelengths.

We see a ripe tomato as being bright red because its skin reflects the red light in the spectrum, and absorbs all other colours. Grass isn't in itself coloured green, nor are other objects in our world a myriad variety of colours. Their surface texture reflects light of a particular wavelength. That is why some objects appear to change colour if they are tilted towards or away from the light. A shiny fabric, for example, may look green from one angle and blue from another.

If the light source is changed, an object's colour may alter. A woman buying some curtains is wise to take them into the daylight: fluorescent store lights have more blue light; sunshine increases the amount of red in a fabric.

Travellers know that the seas appear to be dark green in some places and turquoise blue in others. The Mediterranean is renowned for its dark-blue colour. The sky and its reflection in the water account partly for the sea's colour. On grey and stormy days of heavy cloud, the water looks leaden.

When light strikes water, much is reflected, possibly causing glare. Of the light that penetrates the surface, some is absorbed; the rest is broken up and scattered back towards the surface. It is this scattering of light from beneath the surface that gives the sea its colour.

Different wavelengths of light penetrate to different depths. If the water is clear, the red and yellow wavelengths of light are soon absorbed, leaving only blue-green light to be scattered back. That is why clear seas appear bluer.

The time of year also affects the ocean's colour. If the water is rich in nutrients, as it may become through chemicals carried down by rivers, it may encourage spring and summer weed-growths. Fine particles suspended in the water will alter its colour. Blooms of algae, for example, can suddenly turn seas red.

A combination of red-brown seaweed and blue sky sometimes gives seas such as the Mediterranean a magenta or purple hue. Runoff from coastal rivers, bringing a range of different vegetable and mineral particles, may cause the sea to look red-brown on one day and almost yellow on another. And close to shore any light-coloured sand will make the water look blue-green rather than blue.

If you don't agree with a companion that the sea is a brilliant blue, the cause undoubtedly lies in your eyes. Our perception of colour varies according to how light-sensitive cells are distributed in the retina. What looks like dark blue to one person may be grey-blue to another.

THE ASTONISHING POWERS OF LIGHT

Wavelength (m)	Frequency (Hz)	
10^3	10^6	
10^2	10^7	Radio waves
10^1	10^8	
10^0	10^9	
10^{-1}	10^{10}	Microwaves
10^{-2}	10^{11}	
10^{-3}	10^{12}	
10^{-4}	10^{13}	Infrared waves
10^{-5}	10^{14}	
10^{-6}	10^{15}	
10^{-7}	10^{16}	Visible waves
10^{-8}	10^{17}	Ultraviolet waves
10^{-9}	10^{18}	
10^{-10}	10^{19}	X-rays
10^{-11}	10^{20}	
10^{-12}	10^{21}	
10^{-13}	10^{22}	Gamma rays
10^{-14}	10^{23}	
10^{-15}	10^{24}	
10^{-16}	10^{25}	

Light informs us about the complexity of the world, the vastness of space, the shape and colour of all the objects that surround us. But there is much more to light than ever meets the eye.

Light is pure energy radiating through space. This energy takes many forms, and all move through space as waves. These waves have a frequency and a wavelength. The frequency tells us how many peaks or troughs of the wave move past a fixed point in one second; the wavelength is the distance from one crest or trough to another.

Visible light is made up of all the colours that we see in the rainbow. Each of these colours has a separate range of wavelengths. When we see red, we are seeing light that has a wavelength of roughly 700 nanometres (a nanometre is one-thousand-millionth of a metre). The wavelength of violet light measures about 400 nanometres. All other visible colours fall between these two wavelengths.

Light with a longer wavelength than red – infrared rays – we cannot see. Nor can we see ultraviolet rays, which have a shorter wavelength than violet. But both are very important. Infrared rays, which you can feel as heat, have wavelengths from 700 nanometres to nearly a millimetre. From a millimetre to about 10 cm are microwaves, which we use in cooking, radar and many forms of communication, such as in the relaying of television signals between cities. Radio and television waves range in length from 3 cm to millions of metres. Special antennas enable us to detect all the different parts of this extensive range.

The rainbow hues of white light are revealed when a beam is split by a prism. Each of the colours has a different wavelength, with red the longest and violet the shortest. Visible light forms only a tiny part of the full electromagnetic spectrum, as can be seen from the wavelength chart on the left

Power lines carrying alternating electric current send out waves with a frequency of only 50 cycles a second but a wavelength of about 6 million km.

Ultraviolet light can kill germs, cause sunburn and make certain materials fluoresce. Known sometimes as 'black light', it causes some poster paints, clothing brighteners, minerals and phosphors to glow with visible light of different colours. It is used to create special effects in the theatre; everything is dark, but fluorescent objects that are suddenly bathed in ultraviolet light glow eerily.

X-rays, which have shorter wavelengths than ultraviolet rays, more easily penetrate the body's soft tissues than the bones, enabling us to detect fractures, where the rays pass through. Gamma rays, shorter still, can penetrate a metre-thick wall of concrete.

All these different forms of light move at the same speed of about 300 000 km (186 000 miles) a second. All are produced when an electrically charged particle, such as an electron or proton, is accelerated or made to vibrate. Each electrically charged particle is surrounded by an electric field – an area under its influence. When the particle's energy changes, so does its electric field. Changing the electric field at any point automatically creates a changing magnetic field. These changing fields are linked, increasing and decreasing in amplitude at the same rate, so that they behave like a wave.

These waves move through space as an electromagnetic disturbance. The rate at which the electromagnetic wave oscillates depends on how rapidly the particle vibrates or is accelerated. The faster the oscillations, the greater the wave's energy, which means that it has a greater frequency but a shorter wavelength.

The light that our eyes can see is just one wonderful slice of this vast and awesome flow of electromagnetic radiation, most of which comes from the Sun.

ALL ABOUT BODY & MIND

Medical scientists have rightly called the human body
the world's most amazing machine, an incredible creation that
outshines any invention of science fiction. Answers to those
puzzling questions about why we are what we are

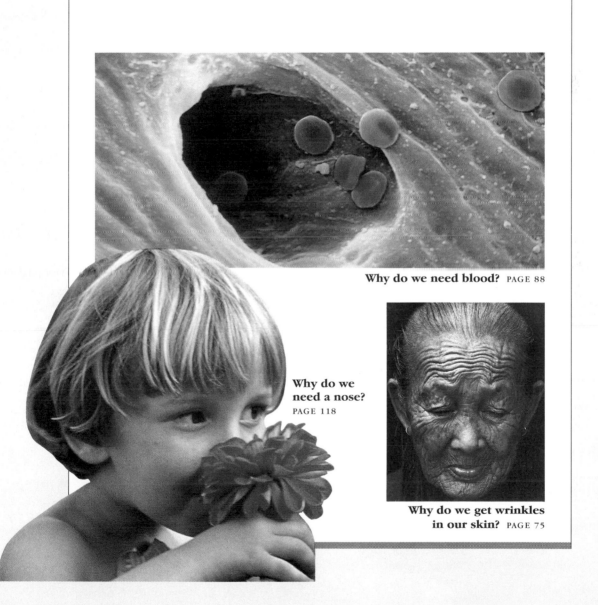

Why do we need blood? PAGE 88

**Why do we
need a nose?**
PAGE 118

**Why do we get wrinkles
in our skin?** PAGE 75

That fragile frontier, the skin

Why do some people have freckles?

If you have freckles, blame your ancestors. Almost certainly they are inherited. They first show up in childhood and, if you are going to have them, they have usually all appeared by your twenty-first birthday. Some adults get a few freckles later in life, particularly if they spend much time in the Sun, but these rarely cluster as normal freckles tend to do.

A comforting point about freckles is that it seems they do no harm. In many people, they add an attractive feature to the face. They are more common in fair and red-haired people, and always show more prominently after prolonged exposure to the Sun.

In most of us, sunshine increases the production of melanin, the pigment that tans our skin and protects it. Some fair-skinned people and most redheads don't tan in the Sun. Their pigment cells fail to respond, or do so unevenly. Instead of producing an even tan, the pigment collects irregularly in small dark spots. Even though freckles themselves are harmless, people who have them should

Fair-skinned redheads are more prone to freckles. There is no remedy. So-called freckle removers may damage the skin

take greater care out of doors. They should never go into the Sun without a hat, and guard themselves with sunscreens to avoid a tendency to burn.

Why do teenagers suffer from acne?

Few people in adolescence escape from the disfiguring pimples and blackheads known as acne. Because they often appear on the face, they always seem so much worse than they really are. If it's any comfort, the problem usually vanishes by adulthood, though a few people have some acne all their lives.

Acne is a companion of puberty, when increased hormone activity causes the sebaceous glands, which sit at the base of the hair follicles, to secrete more oil. That is why acne afflicts the face, forehead, chest and shoulders, areas with a high concentration of sebaceous glands.

The moisturising oil, or sebum, normally flows smoothly onto the skin through our pores. Sometimes, the pores become clogged, either through dirt, or because the sebaceous glands produce too much sebum. Bacteria multiply, often inflaming the site.

Time is usually the cure for acne, but some sensible practices can keep it in check and promote healing. Washing – no more than twice daily – will prevent it from spreading. Sunshine, but not overexposure, is beneficial. Doctors sometimes treat severe cases with antibiotics or they may prescribe retinoid drugs. Initially, for about six weeks, these may cause the skin to redden and peel. As the skin loosens, blocked pores open, relieving severe acne. These and other drugs prescribed for acne must be used with great care. Most important in treating acne is self-help. Diet in this case has no effect. Don't squeeze the spots, because this may leave permanent scars.

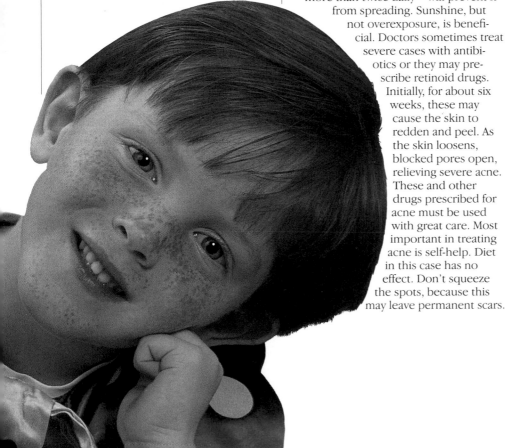

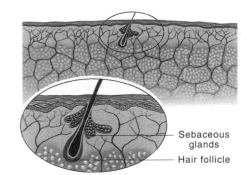
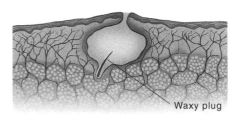
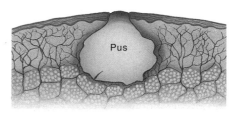
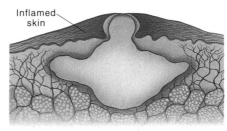

Sebaceous glands
Hair follicle
Waxy plug
Pus
Inflamed skin

Acne develops usually during puberty when more sebum is secreted from the sebaceous glands. Normally this passes through the hair follicles and oils the skin. An excess may form a plug and clog the pore. Then bacteria cause a pimple to form. The blackhead itself is not dirt but melanin produced naturally by the skin

Why does our skin sometimes itch?

Nothing is more common than an itch of some kind in the skin. Dozens of times a day, we touch our faces, rub our noses, scratch our heads, brush or dab the skin somewhere, all to remove some annoying irritation. And yet why we itch as we do is not yet fully understood.

Sometimes, as when a fly or insect buzzes in, the cause is obvious. But itching may come from an allergy, a medication, an infection, even an emotional upset. It is the most prominent factor in many skin diseases, but because you itch doesn't necessarily mean that your skin is infected. Even though it may be difficult to isolate the cause, the consequences are the same. Something stimulates small fibres – nerve endings – at or near the skin's surface to move. A message goes rapidly through the nervous system, which we respond to by rubbing or scratching. That act may remove the irritation or bring a moment of pain.

Many annoying itches can be prevented by daily care. Soaps often dry out the skin, making it itchy. Sufferers should substitute a mild cleansing lotion or use water alone, which most skin specialists say will keep the skin adequately clean.

Why do some people sweat so much?

We all sweat at times to cool ourselves down – during vigorous exercise, for example – and to cleanse the pores of the skin. Occasionally, in an emotional upset of some kind, we may break out into what is often called 'a cold sweat'. Perspiration of that kind is quite normal. Only when it becomes excessive and without apparent reason is there likely to be an underlying problem needing specialist attention.

People who perspire excessively suffer from what is known as hyperhidrosis. It may occur only in certain places, such as the armpits, the face or the palms, or it may be in all areas supplied by sweat glands. Any one of several factors may explain the condition – anxiety, an infection, clothing made from synthetic materials. Usually, it lasts during puberty and vanishes in early adulthood. Sufferers should be careful about their personal hygiene, and try using antiperspirants. If the condition is particularly troublesome, they should consult a doctor, who may prescribe helpful drugs.

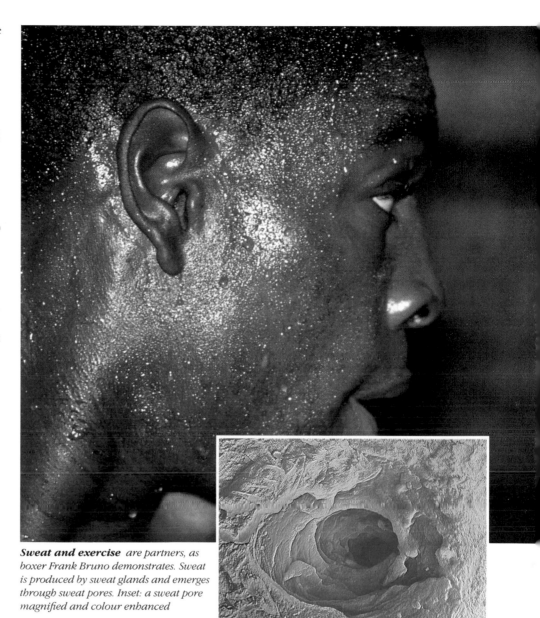

Sweat and exercise are partners, as boxer Frank Bruno demonstrates. Sweat is produced by sweat glands and emerges through sweat pores. Inset: a sweat pore magnified and colour enhanced

Why do we get cold sores when we don't have a cold?

What we know as cold sores – common but troublesome blisters that usually appear on our lips – are caused by a virus of the herpes family. Sometimes the sores erupt for no apparent reason, but usually it's not hard to find a cause.

Once the herpes virus first enters its victim, which may happen unnoticed or with flulike symptoms, it stays in the nerve cells of the face, waiting for something to jolt it into action. That need not be a cold. It commonly follows exposure to the Sun. It may come from stress, a fever, any kind of infection. The virus begins to grow, and within a day or two more sores appear.

Usually, the effects are mild. Within a week or so, the blisters dry up and the

sores vanish. The cold-sore virus is spread by contact, so sufferers should take care, because it is easily passed on to others.

The herpes virus that brings cold sores is sometimes confused with that causing genital herpes. The first, known as herpes simplex virus type 1, or HSV1, is indeed closely linked with the other, HSV2. Doctors say that some conditions caused by one type may also be caused by the other, and vice versa.

Genital herpes is spread by sexual contact with an infected person, and causes small blisters on the genitals. The blisters burst to leave small ulcers. This kind of herpes, like the other, cannot be cured. However, early treatment can reduce the severity of attacks. Women victims should have a cervical smear test at least once a year, because genital herpes may be linked with cervical cancer.

Why do we get wrinkles in our skin?

The skin is the body's largest organ, a complex combination of two layers made up of a variety of cells. It encloses and protects the rest of the body, and helps to keep it at an even temperature.

The outer layer, the epidermis, varies in thickness and is composed mainly of keratin, a protein made by some of its cells. Keratin is the major component of hair and nails, which are really extensions of the skin.

Beneath that outer layer is the dermis, which contains connective tissues and such structures as hair follicles, sebaceous glands, blood and lymph vessels, and nerves. The main constituent of the dermis is collagen, a substance making up about a third of the body's protein. Collagen gives the skin much of its elasticity, allowing it to stretch, twist, shake and shiver – and return smartly to its place.

As we get older, collagen loses some of its water. This process, known as polymerisation, stretches the collagen molecules into longer chains. It behaves then like elastic that has been too long in the Sun: it loses its snap and flexibility.

Below the dermis, cushioning the skin from bones or internal organs, is a layer of subcutaneous tissue, which holds a high proportion of fat. In time, the tissue loses fat and doesn't replace it. The cushion becomes thinner, and the skin sags. With some of its elasticity gone, the skin folds into a crease or wrinkle, increasing in depth as more fat vanishes from the subcutaneous layer.

Not all skin wrinkles come from age or sunlight. We all get wrinkles during a long swim or while taking a bath. Normally, the keratin in the epidermis waterproofs it and the body. If it didn't, we would soak up water like a sponge. During prolonged immersion, the outer layer of skin takes in some water, causing it to swell. Fortunately, the wrinkling is temporary. As we dry off with a towel, all those wrinkly creases soon vanish.

Wrinkles come faster *in skin that is exposed to sunshine and weather. To delay or prevent them, avoid too much tanning*

Why do fair-skinned people get more skin cancers?

As is evident in any summer holiday resort, fair-skinned people are more easily affected by the Sun. Without adequate protection, their skin soon reddens and peels. Sometimes it becomes swollen and tender. Such people are more prone to skin cancer, which is at its most severe among European immigrants to Australia and at its lowest levels in India.

Skin cancers are of three major kinds. Repeated bouts of sunburn or prolonged exposure to the Sun over many years may cause them in skin of any complexion.

Squamous-cell carcinoma is more common in elderly people, and usually shows up as a wartlike growth on the back of the hands, top of the head, face, ears, lips or neck. This form of skin cancer, which is usually not painful, responds well to treatment, if diagnosed quickly.

Malignant melanomas develop in moles or pigmented areas of skin. The mole or pigmented spot changes in size or colour, and may bleed or tingle. Urgent treatment is essential, because these cancers grow rapidly and spread throughout the body. The causes are uncertain, but studies show that malignant melanomas occur more frequently among fair-skinned people living in sunny climates.

Basal-cell carcinoma, known also as rodent ulcer, is a slow-growing tumour that may appear anywhere on the face, eyelids, neck, nose and ears. The cancer starts as a pearl-like pimple, and enlarges to a shiny nodule in which an ulcer forms. The tumour does not spread but, as with other skin cancers, early treatment gives the best chance of a successful cure.

Squamous-cell and basal-cell carcinomas are the most common of skin cancers, and are caused by chronic exposure to ultraviolet radiation. They are rarely found in dark-skinned races, and white people of darker complexion are less susceptible than those of fairer skin.

It is evident that hair colour and complexion are closely linked. Both depend on the type and distribution of melanin, a pigment that protects the skin against the Sun. Where the epidermis, the outer layer of skin, contains more melanin, as it does in darker-skinned races, it has greater protection against the harmful effects that come from ultraviolet radiation.

Though blacks rarely suffer from squamous-cell carcinoma, it is interesting to note that, when they do, tumours usually occur at the site of skin damage – on old scars or ulcers that have healed without the customary amount of pigment. Also, if

Holiday crowds *bask on a sunbaked beach in Spain. Few are taking guard against skin cancer by wearing hats or using sunshades*

blacks get malignant melanoma, which again is rare, the cancer will develop in lightly pigmented tissue, in places such as the sole of the foot, the palm, the mucous membrane.

All this doesn't mean we should keep out of the Sun. From it we get valuable supplies of vitamin D. But to avoid skin cancers we need to guard against excessive ultraviolet radiation. Note your local weather forecasts, if they give expected UV levels. Always wear adequate sunscreens on exposed skin, and never go into the Sun without a hat. Even on a cloudy day, you can suffer sunburn: 80 per cent of UV rays penetrate cloud. Burning rays are reflected from snow and water, so guard against them when skiing, boating or fishing.

A tanned skin will protect you against burning, but acquire your tan gradually. If you and your family enjoy swimming and surfing, use a water-repellent sunscreen, or renew your protection whenever you leave the water.

Hair today, gone tomorrow

Why don't women go bald?

Baldness in women may be more common than it seems. Most men make no attempt to hide their baldness, because they know that plenty of others will keep them company. Balding women are likely to feel more embarrassed, and hide their problem under a wig.

Nevertheless, baldness is rarer among women than among men, where it is caused principally by the male sex hormones, androgens, of which female bodies produce little. If women become bald, it is usually through disease, such as psoriasis, the use of chemotherapy to treat cancer, or from severe stress.

Hair loss may occur on ceasing to take contraceptive pills. Anaemia and lack of iron, due possibly to menstruation, also can have a severe effect on hair condition. Rarely does a woman's hair fall out to leave the scalp bare. Even in severe hair loss, which sometimes occurs after the menopause, the more usual pattern is an all-over thinning, again making the problem less noticeable to others.

Why do some men go bald?

'Grass doesn't grow on busy streets,' is the common reply of bald men to taunts about their shining pates. But despite claims that baldness results from too much thinking or from tight hats, dandruff, a dry scalp or an oily one, the naked truth is that most bald men can blame only one cause – heredity.

Find a bald man and you won't need to look far in the family photo album to find the source of his baldness. Sometimes the affliction skips a generation or two, but usually the condition is evident on one or other side of the family.

The average scalp produces some 100 000 hairs, each sprouting from a follicle supplied with nutrients at its bulb-like base. At any time, five out of six follicles grow hairs; the sixth is at rest. When a hair reaches maturity – shoulder length or longer, if left uncut – its follicle becomes dormant and the hair is shed. The average head loses about 100 hairs a day.

A man showing signs of male-pattern baldness, the kind due to heredity, sheds no more hair than anybody else: his dormant follicles become permanently and irreversibly inactive. Some drugs, and diseases such as shingles, psoriasis and ringworm, may cause excessive hair loss, but growth resumes when the basic problem is cured. This is not the case with male-pattern baldness.

The process may start as early as the teens, but usually begins in a man's mid-twenties, when the hair follicles produce excessive amounts of the enzyme, 5-alpha reductase. The male hormone, testosterone, combines to make dihydrotestosterone, the balding man's major foe. Under its spell, some follicles wither, producing thinner hairs and then just fine vellus, a kind of fuzz. Other follicles stop work for ever.

Centuries ago the link was discovered between male potency and hair loss. Aristotle and Hippocrates observed that eunuchs didn't go bald. And the castrati singers of seventeenth- and eighteenth-century opera – males castrated to prevent their voices breaking in adolescence – kept full heads of hair. Indeed, for the truly desperate, castration is the most effective way to ward off baldness. The notion persists that bald men are superbly virile, an idea that some are keen to perpetuate but which has no basis in fact.

Is there hope that baldness can be cured? Indeed, there is. One method – more camouflage than cure – is by hair transplant or 'punch graft'. Tufts or plugs of hair from the healthy fringe are surgically grafted into the wide open spaces. The average bald head needs about 250 plugs. New hair, sprouting from the crown, covers areas from which the plugs were taken. Another method, similar in style, is known as scalp reduction. Skin covering the crown is replaced by that from the hair-covered sides and neck.

New drugs also offer promise – at a price. A few years ago, 70 per cent of patients taking minoxidil, a drug that combats high blood pressure, reported a growth of new hair. The drug company, spotting a rich potential market, adapted minoxidil for external use. The treatment, however, is for younger men, whose baldness is recent – and it's a lifetime process. Stop using minoxidil and fall-out resumes.

More recently, thirty-two men tested an experimental drug, cyoctol, at the

Rays of hope for the hairless have shone from countless advertisements for wonder tonics. Baldness was no threat to New York state's Sutherland sisters, seen with their father in 1894. Their locks had a combined length of 11 m (36 ft)

University of California, Los Angeles. After a year, they had 12 per cent more hair. Without affecting a man's sexuality, the drug appears to block certain male sex hormones from interacting with hair-follicle cells.

Why does hair turn grey as we grow older?

For some of us, the first grey hairs appeared in our youth, even as early as fifteen. At thirty, about a quarter of the population has some tell-tale signs of the greying to come. Some 28 per cent of us will eventually have hair that is completely white. A few fortunate people will get no grey hairs at all.

If your parents or grandparents went grey, the chances are that you will do so at about the same age and in the same way. Caucasians have a fifty/fifty chance that half their hair will be grey or white at the age of fifty. Blacks begin to turn noticeably grey about six years later than whites, in their early forties.

But why should hair turn grey or white instead of, say, bright blue? Cells called melanocytes determine hair colour. By producing and mixing just two basic pigments, eumelanin and pheomelanin, these cells give human hair its wonderful range of colours. Eumelanin may tint each strand of hair any colour from the deepest black to the lightest brown; pheomelanin may turn it blonde, golden or red. The volume, shape, brightness and density of the pigments in each individual mix give your hair its distinctive look.

If melanocytes become less active, as they do in our twenties, new hairs growing from the hair follicles carry less of their original pigmentation, and emerge grey. When the melanocyte cells cease work, which they may do naturally according to your genes or when influenced by trauma or disease, your hair will grow without pigment, in the basic colour of its protein – snow white. Sometimes, because of the hair's normal colour, the growth of white hairs is hard to detect.

Redheads have some 90 000 hairs on their heads, brunettes about 108 000 and blondes 140 000. Half a blonde's hair could turn white before the overall effect was one of greyness. Scientists say that light-haired people are more likely to become completely grey.

Hair colour and quality, like complexion, is often a barometer of health. Severe trauma may prompt the growth of grey hair. And so may a range of diseases, such as influenza, diabetes, typhus, malaria, some forms of herpes and conditions such as malnutrition, hyperthyroidism and anaemia. People exposed to some kinds of radiation, whether by accident or in therapy, may go grey or lose their hair.

Can hair turn white overnight? Well, not quite so swiftly, but quickly enough to cause considerable distress. A person may be afflicted by alopecia areata, a disorder brought on often by stress. It may cause older, darker hairs to fall out in just a few

Youth and age are often shown by hair colour. The hair of a young girl, fair in childhood, may darken before finally going grey

days. If the victim already has a substantial scattering of grey or white hairs, the hair will indeed seem to have turned white overnight.

Can the grey-heads hope to see their hair regain its natural colour? Indeed they can unless baldness robs them of the little they've got. Recent research has found how to give hair new growth and even its original hues, when greyness results from disease. Anaemia sufferers, for instance, who were given vitamin B_{12}, found their hair gradually regaining its colour.

For some 40 per cent of women and 8 per cent of men who now use dyes, new products may offer a chance to impregnate their hair with natural melanin, adjusted to almost any shade.

But who says that grey hair is a sign of old age? Every society has outstanding examples to prove the adage that you can have snow on the roof and a blazing fire in the furnace.

Why is it said that fright will make the hair stand on end?

Countless stories of the macabre, illustrated in suitable fashion, tell how the hair of terrified victims has suddenly stood on end. The phenomenon appears to be authors' invention, perpetuated by tradition, because physicians deny that scalp hair will stand on end for any length of time, if at all.

Goose flesh, the phenomenon in which individual body hairs suddenly bristle through cold or fright, is the only verifiable example of human hair standing erect. In this sensation, a muscle called the arrector pili, a Latin term meaning 'erector of hair', pulls the hair follicle so that the hair within it stands upright. You will notice too that the skin takes on a pimply appearance, like that of a plucked goose, and a forest of fine hairs, suddenly stiffened, feels prickly to the touch.

Why can some people grow their hair longer than others?

Many factors affect hair growth. Malnutrition, disease and hormone imbalance may inhibit the normal growing pattern. The taking of steroid drugs will promote hair growth on the body, and may slow that on the scalp. Any abnormal shedding of hair should be checked by a doctor.

The failure of some people to grow their hair as long as they would wish is more likely to be due to heredity than to disease or drugs. Your genes decide most things about your body, including hair growth. People whose hair has a short growing cycle – say two years instead of six – can never grow it longer than about 30 cm (12 in). Then it will fall out, and the follicles will rest for a time before sprouting new hair.

Some people believe mistakenly that frequent cutting will increase hair growth. They are wrong. Hair is not like the shoots of a plant or tree, which may respond in this way. The hair you see is dead, and nothing can increase its vigour.

Why do some people have fine and curly hair?

Whether your hair is straight or curly depends on how the papillae – the hair roots – perform. If the follicles have a regular pattern of growth, your hair will be straight. If the growth is uneven, your hair will be curly. Two factors decide the texture of your hair: the diameter of the follicles and the amount of hard casing on each individual hair. If the follicles are small in diameter, the hair will be fine and sometimes difficult to control – in the wind, for example.

Each hair consists of a shell, known as the cuticle, and a softer, fibrous inner substance, the cortex. Fine hair has 40 per cent cuticle and 60 per cent cortex; coarse hair has only 10 per cent cuticle and 90 per cent cortex. Whether your hair is coarse or fine makes no difference to whether it will turn grey or leave you bald later in life.

Why does brushing make the hair shine?

Mothers used to instruct their daughters to brush the hair at least 100 times before going to bed, promising that they would wake in the morning with tresses shining brightly. Obedient girls were well rewarded: their hair did indeed take on an attractive sheen.

The reasons for this were once thought to be the polishing effect of the bristles, likened perhaps to that of a mild abrasive on metal. In fact, brushing stimulates oil glands in the scalp, making the hair more shiny; also it helps to remove dust and dandruff that might otherwise give the hair a duller appearance. But don't be overzealous. Trichologists warn that too much brushing, especially with a hard brush, will do more harm than good, thinning the hair and splitting the ends.

Why does hair become dull and dry in summer?

Most people like to spend more time out of doors in summer. Overexposure to the Sun will dry out not only the hair but the scalp beneath it. Swimming in the sea or

Sign of health and source of admiration, a fine head of hair needs regular brushing if it is to have and retain an attractive sheen. Gentle brushing stimulates oil glands in the scalp. Too much may split the ends of the hair

in chlorinated pools, followed by sunbathing, particularly on a windswept beach, all aggravate the condition.

If you want to safeguard your hair, and your skin, avoid too much sunbathing. Keep your hair covered as much as possible when in the Sun. Wear a bathing cap when swimming. Afterwards, and as soon as possible, wash your hair thoroughly in fresh water.

Several steps will improve the look of your hair if it is already damaged by too much Sun and salt water. Trim off the ends if they are split. Special conditioners and shampoos will tone up your appearance until new hair grows again.

Why don't we have more hair?

From birth, almost all of our skin has a fine covering of hair. It varies in diameter from 0.005 mm (0.0002 in) in the baby-hair known as lanugo to 0.2 mm (0.008 in) in the hairs in an average beard. Our body hair – vellus – is now almost invisible. That wasn't always so. Early humans

Hair is hardy, but sunshine and chlorine can easily ruin it. Swimmers should wear a cap

had a thick covering of hair over just about everything except their eyeballs, lips, palms and soles of their feet.

The hair served the same purpose as it does in other primates – warmth and protection. Over the ages, heated homes and a range of clothing have taken over those basic needs, and a thick mat of hair on the body and head is no longer essential. Our body hair has almost vanished and cranial hair has become much finer. The process is almost certain to continue. In fact, anthropologists predict with some certainty that future humans will have hairless domes but bigger skulls to accommodate larger brains.

Just as our hair is vanishing, so our bodies will change shape in response to how we use them. Jaws, for example, may recede, because our food needs less chewing. Molar teeth, used now for grinding, may diminish in size until they fail to appear, as has already happened to some wisdom teeth.

The current vogue for strenuous exercise may not be enough to offset changes in our general body structure. If that is so, many muscles will grow weaker, legs and arms more spindly and sticklike with less use and some parts, such as the small toe, may in time wither away.

MATTER OF LIFE AND DEATH

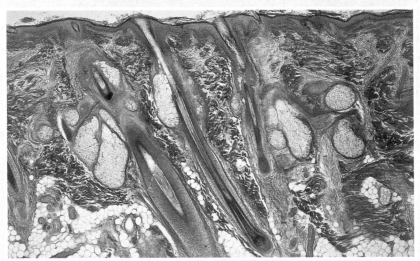

Microscopic view of your skin, showing three central hair follicles. The hair is rooted in a hair bulb. The white globules are sebaceous glands, which lubricate the hair

Though advertisements for hair tonics may urge you to 'Give New Life to Your Hair', all the hair you can see on your body is dead, and nothing will revive it. The only life is deep within the follicles that lie beneath the surface of your skin, where new hair cells are constantly formed.

Hair grows from almost all parts of your body. Some is so soft and fine that it is almost invisible. But fine or coarse, all hair grows in the same way and from the same kind of structure. Each strand emerges from a follicle nourished at its bulblike base, the papilla.

Growth takes three distinct phases. In the first, the anagen phase, new hair pushes out from the follicles at a rate, for scalp hair, of about 1 cm (nearly ½ in) a month. After a period of between two and six years, growth stops. The machine takes a rest, but not for long. A few weeks later comes the third, telogen phase, in which the hair separates from the papilla. The next anagen phase begins, and new hair pushes out the old. At any time, some 15 per cent of follicles on both the scalp and body are dormant.

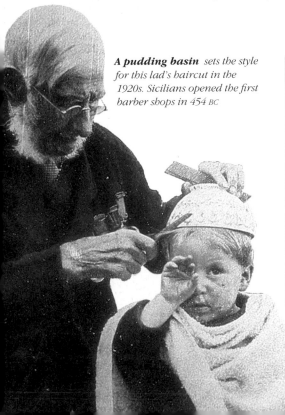

A pudding basin sets the style for this lad's haircut in the 1920s. Sicilians opened the first barber shops in 454 BC

Why doesn't a haircut hurt?

Almost your entire body is covered with hair, though much of it is so fine that it is barely visible. The hair grows from some five million follicles, of which about 100 000 are in the scalp. By the time each hair emerges from within a follicle, it is already dead and no amount of massage, hair tonic or wonder cure can revive it.

Scalp hair grows on average about 12 to 15 cm (5 to 6 in) a year. It keeps getting longer, even though it is dead, because the older, dead hair cells are pushed out by the new hair growth. Cut the dead hair and it doesn't hurt, but pull hair from the roots and you may cry out with pain.

Every time you brush or comb your hair, you may remove as many as 100 hairs. Unless the loss is excessive, this is no cause for worry. The hairs come from roots that are in their resting phase.

Why does hair grow darker as we age?

It's not unusual to hear a dark-haired adult exclaim, 'Believe it or not, but I had fair hair as a child.' Snowy-haired children rarely keep that colouring throughout life. Many teenage blondes later become brown- or even red-haired, and may puzzle why their hair has changed in this way.

Hair colour is determined by a pigment called melanin, produced by the melanocyte cells at the base of the hair follicle. For most of us, our hair grows gradually darker as the melanocyte cells become more active during our adolescence and late teens. In our early twenties, the process slows, but in some people darkening of the hair may continue for twenty more years, with blondes growing browner and redheads turning auburn.

Why are some of us hairier than others?

Anthropologists have made many attempts to devise a satisfactory division of the world's population into racial groups, using characteristics such as skin colour and type of hair to separate the different units. One difficulty is that characteristics overlap: every group will have some people who do not conform.

Some racial groups are hairier than others. Africans have more hair than native Americans or people of Chinese descent. People of Mediterranean background are naturally hairier as a rule than Scandinavians. Normal variations within these groups may be further accentuated by mixed breeding. In the United States, Canada and Australia, countries populated largely by immigrants, marriage between people of different nationalities is commonplace, leading to a greater diversity of physical characteristics within the group.

An excess of hair – hirsutism – is rarely regarded as abnormal. It causes no problems in men. How much hair a man or woman should have is largely dictated by fashion. Hirsutism may be genetic, or it may be traced to glandular irregularities, the taking of steroid drugs or to the menopause. A woman who is excessively hairy may doubt her femininity, but can be reassured that almost always the growth is natural and easily remedied. A few facial hairs are easily removed with tweezers – they will regrow in about six weeks – or may be permanently destroyed by electrolysis. Shaving with an electric razor is the easiest solution. Contrary to common belief, shaving has no effect on either the rate or thickness of new hair growth.

Abundant hair *or no hair at all, it depends entirely on a person's genes. A trio from Mandalay, Burma, shows how likenesses of many kinds can run in a family. Excessive hairiness is usually genetic. Shaving the hair makes no difference to its speed of growth or its thickness*

Exploring the miracle of sight

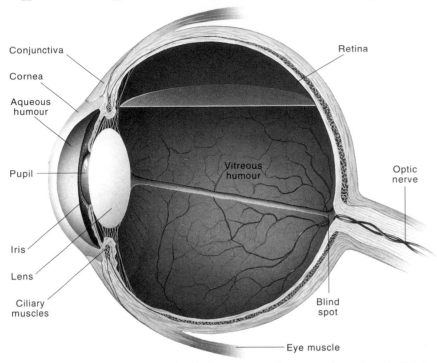

Anatomy of an eye shows it to be one of the body's most complex organs. A man's eye is slightly bigger than a woman's. A newborn baby has rounder eyes than an adult

Labels: Conjunctiva · Cornea · Aqueous humour · Pupil · Iris · Lens · Ciliary muscles · Retina · Vitreous humour · Optic nerve · Blind spot · Eye muscle

Why do we get spots in our field of vision?

If you look at a clear blue sky or a white background, you may see grey spots drifting across your vision. When you move your eyes rapidly, the spots move quite swiftly. When you try to focus on them, they appear to float slowly across the eyeball. That is why these moving shadows, cast on the retina, are usually known as floaters.

They are a minor nuisance, but fortunately are normal and quite harmless. The shadows come from tiny bits of tissue or debris in the vitreous humour, a jellylike and transparent part of the eye which lies behind the lens.

Some people who suddenly notice floaters in their field of vision believe they have a detached retina. If the spots appear in a cloudlike mass and are accompanied by flashing lights or dramatic sparks, that may indeed be so. Anybody with these symptoms should see an ophthalmologist as soon as possible.

The retina is a light-sensitive membrane lining the inside of the back of the eye. In many ways it resembles the film in a camera. The cornea and the lens cast images on to the retina. Special nerve cells convert light into impulses that are carried via the optic nerve to the brain. Some parts of the retina are bound tightly to the eye; others are held in place mainly by the pressure of fluid.

A severe blow to the eye or head can pull the retina away from the back of the eye. More often, a detached retina follows a tear or split in the retina. This may come through degeneration, which often makes the membrane thinner. Short-sighted people and those who have had cataract surgery commonly suffer the condition. A detached retina causes no pain, and sometimes a victim may be unaware of it until a dark curtain obscures vision in the affected eye. Fortunately, surgery for a detached retina today has a high rate of success but, as with many afflictions, swift attention improves a victim's chances.

Why do eye drops give patients a startled look?

People leaving an eye specialist's rooms sometimes have great difficulty in focusing if they emerge into bright sunlight. 'You look like a startled rabbit,' is a common if unkind comment.

Not all drops give the eyes that shocked appearance, but some used by doctors before examining patients' eyes enlarge the pupils and temporarily paralyse them. Normally, pupils adjust like an automatic camera's lens to admit just the right amount of light. If the light is bright, the pupils contract; if it is dim, they expand.

The eye specialist uses an instrument called an ophthalmoscope to examine the inside of the eye and particularly the retina, the membrane on which images are focused. The ophthalmoscope's bright light shining directly into the eye would automatically make the pupils contract, closing the windows through which the specialist wants to look.

To keep the pupils as wide open as possible the doctor puts in a few drops of tropicamide or cyclopentolate, stopping for a short time the pupils' natural reaction to light.

Sometimes, after an eye examination, you may find your eyelids stained orange. This is because your doctor, in checking for abrasions and ulcers, has inserted a few drops of a harmless orange dye known as fluorescein. The stain turns conjunctival ulcers yellow; if you have any corneal abrasions or ulcers they appear green under white light, but ultraviolet light makes them brilliantly fluorescent.

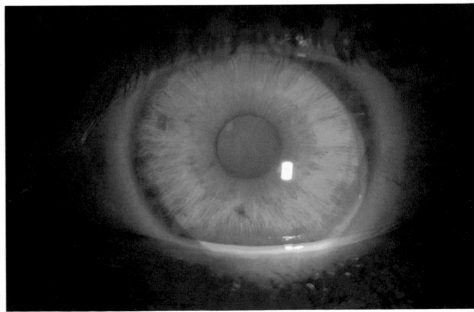

Dye in an eye helps an ophthalmologist check for abrasions. The orange fluorescein dye glows green under ultraviolet light. In this healthy eye only the margins fluoresce

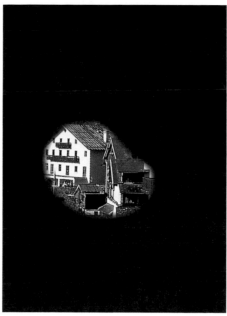

A camera view of a town (left) is what a healthy eye should see, clear vision all round, without turning the head. A glaucoma victim, who lacks peripheral vision, gets only a partial image

forty and rises to about 10 per cent in those over the age of seventy.

A less common form, acute – or closed angle – glaucoma, gives some warning. A victim may feel sick, have severe pain in the eye and foggy vision. It is an emergency requiring instant attention which, after the immediate eyeball pressure is under control, usually involves surgery.

Chronic simple glaucoma is usually kept in check quite successfully with eye drops, but the treatment – usually just one or two drops a day in one or both eyes – has to continue for life. Where medicines fail, an eye surgeon may try to relieve the pressure within the eye by opening the blocked drainage channel or creating a bypass for the fluid.

Why do some people suffer from glaucoma?

Pressure of fluid within our eyeballs keeps them in shape, and ensures that our vision is not distorted. Sometimes, for one or more reasons, that pressure builds up. This damages small blood vessels that feed the fibres of the optic nerve with oxygen and glucose, soon harming the delicate fibres themselves.

The condition is known as glaucoma, and few eye disorders are more dangerous. Its particular menace is that it steals a victim's sight by stealth: the first sign of

trouble may be partial or advanced blindness, and by then it is already too late. Only a regular examination, in which a doctor checks the pressure within each eye, will identify the disorder and avoid serious damage to the sight.

Why some people get glaucoma and others do not is uncertain. The most common form, known as chronic simple, or open angle, glaucoma, tends to run in families. Anybody with a family history of glaucoma should take a routine test once a year. So should those aged forty and over, because chronic simple glaucoma is more prevalent among older people. It is found in some 2 per cent of people over

Why do we need to blink?

Most of us blink about fifteen times a minute. We do that sometimes to protect the eye. Much of the eye is guarded inside its socket, a bony cavity padded with fat, and that, in turn, is shielded by the skull. But when your eyes, the body's most delicate sensors, are wide open, about one-tenth of their total surface is fully exposed to the atmosphere, to winds and possibly to dust.

The eyes need constant lubrication. Also, their front portion, which gathers light, must be kept crystal clear for good vision. Blinking serves this double purpose. The eyelids snap shut and flip open again, coating each eye with a film of tears, rinsing away fine debris, to clean and lubricate the surface. Frequently, we

FINDING THE BLIND SPOTS IN YOUR EYES

Ballplayers often excuse an error by saying that the action took place in their blind spot. In a fast-moving game such as tennis this can sometimes happen. At a crucial moment, the ball vanishes from sight for a split second, long enough to cost the point – and certainly to provide a good excuse.

We all have blind spots in our eyes, and you can easily find them with the aid of the two coloured tennis balls below. Close or cover your left eye. If you look at the red ball with your right eye as you move the page towards you, the yellow ball will vanish. Continue to move the page, and the yellow ball will reappear. Similarly, you can find the blind spot in your other eye.

As you moved the page, the image of the ball fell on a small, oval-shaped area in the retina where the optic nerve

leads to the brain. The image is not registered because, unlike other parts of the retina, the spot has no light receptors, nerves that are sensitive to light. It's useful to know about your blind spot. If a blind spot occurs elsewhere in your eye, you should immediately see your doctor.

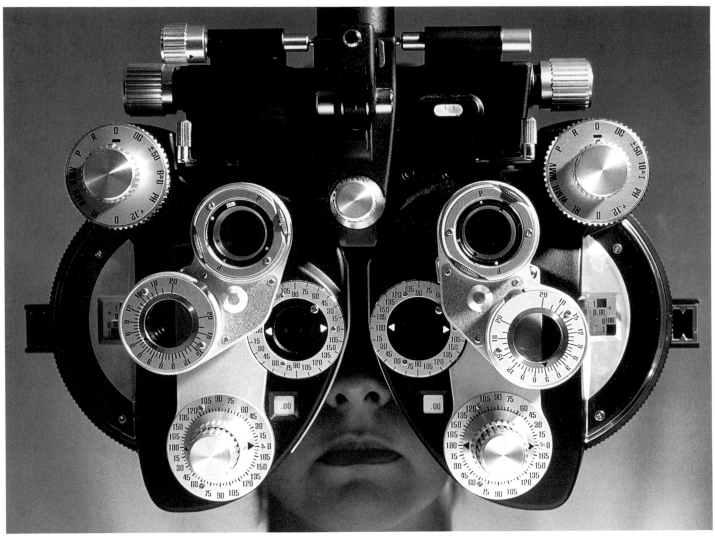

A routine test *on this woman's eyes demands examination by a phoropter, or refractor head, which has an array of lenses*

blink for other reasons, such as to guard our eyes against a sudden blow. Loud noises may make us blink and so may anxiety. Using hidden cameras, infrared lights and other specialised equipment, scientists have studied the eye reactions of people in many different circumstances, such as at meetings, driving in traffic and under various kinds of stress. Their findings show that we blink less when we are alert. Someone reading a novel blinks about six times a minute, but people in conversation blink twice as often. Car drivers blink less in city streets, when they need to concentrate more closely, than when out on the open road.

When we are bored, we blink for longer. In one experiment, people were asked to listen to a protracted and deliberately boring series of tones. As the test went on, the duration of each blink increased by more than 30 per cent.

Nervousness makes us blink more frequently. That is why TV newsreaders are coached to blink normally. This gives them an appearance of calm control. Lawyers say that witnesses under cross-examination blink more frequently than those facing more friendly questioning. And if politicians blink too often in a television interview, it's usually interpreted as a sure sign of tension. When George Bush and Michael Dukakis engaged in a TV debate in October 1988, Dukakis averaged seventy-five blinks a minute to Bush's sixty-seven.

Why aren't cataracts so feared as they were?

A few years ago, cataracts were a major cause of blindness, particularly in those over the age of sixty. In this disorder, delicate protein fibres within the lens slowly change their nature, turning the lens cloudy, much in the way that an egg white goes milky as it cooks. Sufferers can still detect light, but their vision loses its clarity. They see vague shapes, almost as though they were looking through a frosted window.

Cataracts, the clouding-over of the lens, usually affect both eyes and one more than the other. They are so common in elderly people that almost everybody over the age of sixty-five has some minor sign, usually at the edge of the lens, which doesn't greatly trouble the vision. Like aching backs and arthritic joints, cataracts are part of growing old. Fortunately, they are painless.

The other good news for victims is that in recent years eye surgeons have made enormous progress in treating cataracts. The operation, which takes one of several forms according to the condition of the lenses, lasts about an hour. The success rate is high – about 95 per cent. One technique, using a freezing probe, removes the whole lens. In another, the opaque part is drawn out by suction. In a third, a high-speed vibrator breaks up the cataract so that it can be withdrawn through a hollow needle. Because the operation destroys part of the lens, a replacement is needed before the patient can see clearly again. Sometimes, the ophthalmologist prescribes thick glasses or contact lenses. In other cases, a permanent plastic lens is implanted in the eye.

If this is intended, the surgeon makes a precise calculation before the operation to decide what power of lens will restore normal vision. This involves measuring the curvature of the cornea, the front part of the eye's tougher shell, and the length of the eye. Age is not a factor in cataract surgery, but the patient's health may determine which technique is used. Surgeons have successfully used plastic-lens implants to restore the sight of 100-year-old patients.

Why do we sometimes get eyestrain?

No matter how much you read, watch television, or work long hours in poor light, it's unlikely that you will damage your eyes. Ophthalmologists say you cannot strain your eyes by overuse, or by not wearing your glasses. Nor will it ruin your children's eyes if they try to read in a poor light. That doesn't mean we should make a habit of abusing our eyes. Good lighting helps to avoid the vague aches we call eyestrain.

The eyeballs are held in place by six delicate muscles which, like other body muscles, can suffer fatigue, giving you in fact a form of headache. But this is not necessarily the cause of the discomfort you sometimes feel in your eyes. This may come from soreness of the eyelid membranes, caused by drinking too much alcohol, smoking, or spending too long in a smoky atmosphere. Infection, such as conjunctivitis, also may sometimes be to blame.

If the tired feeling persists, you should see a specialist. A recurrent ache in or near the eyes could signify a serious problem, or indicate a need for glasses.

Why are some people colour-blind?

We recognise colour because we have special receptors behind the retina at the back of the eye. Light enters the lens, passes through the whole of the retina, and strikes these receptors, which are divided into rods and cones.

Colour perception depends mainly on the cones, which are of three kinds, each containing different colour-sensitive pigments. One responds best to red (long wavelength) light, another to green (intermediate) and the rest to blue (short). These correspond to the primary colours in an artist's paintbox. All the colours we see – between 120 and 150 hues – result from the combined stimulation of these cones, a mixing of the primary colours in the eye's palette.

The lack of one kind of cone brings a failure to see a particular colour. Total colour blindness, in which everything appears in shades of grey, is extremely rare. What we call colour blindness is usually an inability to distinguish red from green. It can be caused by injury to the optic nerve and retina, but most people inherit it. It affects about 8 per cent of white European males and less than 1 per cent of females; it is less prevalent among Asians and even rarer among blacks. Women who are not themselves colour-blind may pass the defect to some of their children.

In a severe case, somebody with green blindness has difficulty distinguishing oranges, greens, brown and pale reds. Those with a red deficiency never see brilliant reds; all reds are duller.

Until they are tested, which may be when applying for a job where colour differentiation is important, many people never know that they are colour-blind. A common test uses plates combining red, green, orange and brown dots. People who are colour-blind see different numerals displayed in the plates from those

seen by people with normal vision. Colour blindness has no cure, but a special contact lens can help victims distinguish red-green colours. The lens is worn only in one eye. It does not restore normal colour vision, but makes green appear darker than red, enabling the wearer to spot the difference.

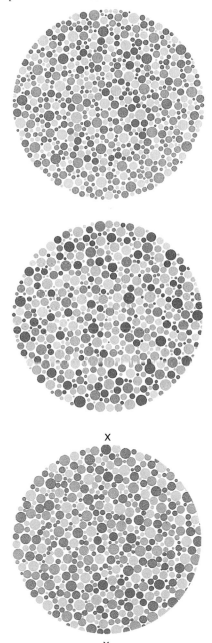

Colour blindness is usually detected by tests with coloured plates viewed in natural daylight. In the top plate, people with normal vision see a figure 8; those with red-green defect see 3; the totally colour-blind cannot see a numeral. In the middle plate, the normal see 16; those with colour defects see no numeral or a wrong one. In the bottom plate, the colour-blind cannot see a line winding its way from one X to the other

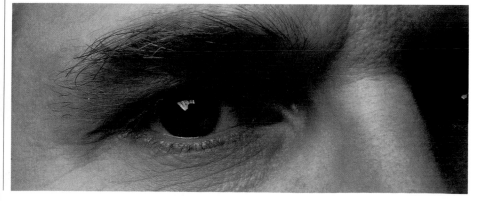

A sore eye is rarely a sign of serious problems, but pinpointing the cause may be difficult

Why are so many corneal-transplant operations performed?

Without much fanfare, corneal-transplant operations have restored clear sight to hundreds of thousands of people worldwide. The procedure, the most common form of organ transplant, is now routine, even at some small, country hospitals.

Corneal transplants replace the cornea, the eye's protective window through which light passes to the lens and onto the retina. For good vision the cornea must remain absolutely clear and in perfect shape. But it is among the body's most sensitive tissues, and is easily damaged by infection, dirt, a chemical burn or other accident.

One reason why corneal transplants, or grafts, are performed so regularly is their success. About 90 per cent are effective. For the first time, they provide a cure for severe keratoconus, an inherited condition in which the cornea becomes misshapen, distorting the vision. Another factor is that disorders requiring the operation are now more common. Some result from our current lifestyle – for example, greater participation in sports carrying risk of eye damage. Overuse of contact lenses, usually against doctor's orders, also may be to blame.

In performing corneal transplants, surgeons first need a cornea from a deceased donor, which they obtain from an eye bank. The donated cornea may replace the whole of a patient's defective cornea or just a part. In the more common operation, known as penetrating keratoplasty, a surgeon replaces the full thickness of the cornea; in another technique, lamellar keratoplasty, just a slice of the cornea is exchanged.

The surgeon works through a high-powered microscope, and removes part of the cornea he intends to replace. Usually, it is a disc between 5 and 10 mm wide (⅕ to ⅖ in). He cuts a slightly larger disc from the donor cornea, and sews it in place, using nylon thread finer than a

*A **corneal transplant** is today a speedy and commonplace operation, done in several stages. First, using an instrument like a tiny biscuit cutter, the surgeon removes the damaged cornea, completing the work with a pair of corneal scissors. The donor corneal button is held in place (3) with a few stitches before a continuous suture secures the graft. Now, the surgeon is keen to ensure that the tension is even and that the graft's shape is not distorted. Finally, an injection of fluid prevents the iris and lens from sticking to the newly grafted cornea*

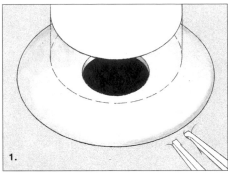

1.

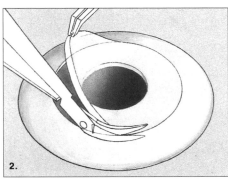

2.

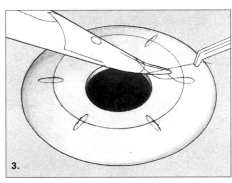

3.

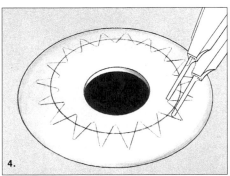

4.

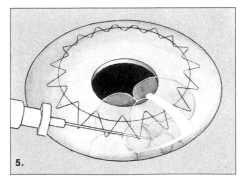

5.

human hair. The operation is soon over, taking usually about an hour.

A day or two later, when their bandages are removed, patients can see, but cannot focus. Good eyesight comes back gradually over a few months. The stitches are left in place for about a year to allow the cornea, which lacks blood vessels, time to heal completely.

Many people ask why a donor cornea is rarely rejected, as other donated organs frequently are. Because a healthy cornea has no blood vessels, white blood cells, which cause rejection, rarely get a chance to react.

Why does eyesight deteriorate with age?

It's not unusual to see a middle-aged person holding a book at arm's length in order to read the print, or struggling for some time to thread a needle. Both are signs of presbyopia, difficulty in focusing the eyes on close objects.

As we grow older, the lenses in our eyes lose their elasticity and ability to focus for near and distant vision. Most people notice this at about the age of forty, particularly when reading. The print becomes a little fuzzy and, instead of accommodating with our eyes, we tend to move the book or newspaper a little farther away. Before long, the focus becomes set at a more or less constant distance.

Some people find that they become near-sighted as they grow older. They see things clearly close at hand, but distant objects are blurred. The condition is known as myopia, which comes from

Newborn babies are far-sighted. For the first three to six months, they can see distant objects but not those close at hand

Greek words meaning 'to close the eye'. Myopic people develop the habit of half closing the eyes, which gives them sharper vision. In myopia, the eyeball becomes too long from front to back, so that light from distant objects comes to a focal point before it reaches the retina. Instead of casting a sharp image, objects appear blurry. Near-sighted people often find that as they age they don't need glasses for reading.

Far-sighted people have the opposite problem. Their eyeballs are too short from front to back. They see distant objects well, but the focal point of those nearby is behind the retina. Babies are born far-sighted. For three to six months their eyes don't focus on close objects, and then for months they may wander individually instead of working together.

Why do we have different eye colours?

Beautiful eyes are one of the most attractive features of a face, and their colour plays an important part. Colour in eyes comes from the iris, which lies behind the cornea and in front of the lens. In the centre of the iris is the pupil, an opening that admits light to the eye. The iris is made up of collagen, a tough fibrous protein found also in tendons and the body's connective tissues. Muscle fibres in the iris help it to expand or contract, controlling the amount of light going though the pupil.

Whether the iris is brown, blue or green depends on a pigment called melanin, which determines also skin and hair colour. Somebody with a large amount of melanin will have brown or hazel eyes; a person with less melanin will have blue or light green eyes.

How much melanin you have depends entirely on your parents. Two brown-eyed parents will usually have a brown-eyed child. Blue-eyed parents will almost always have blue-eyed offspring. When one parent has brown eyes and the other blue, the children are usually brown-eyed. Brown eyes are a stronger hereditary trait, which explains why a vast majority of the world's people have brown eyes.

In rare cases, the eyes are neither brown, blue or green but pink. This is due to albinism, a genetic disorder that inhibits the production of melanin. A victim's skin and hair may be snowy white, and the eyes at birth almost transparent. Later they darken a little. Victims suffer a number of eye problems, particularly squint, short-sightedness and intolerance of bright light. Fortunately, severe albinism affects only one person in 20 000.

PICTURES THAT FOOL THE EYE AND MIND

Optical illusions are not just deceptions of the eye but also of the brain. The eye feeds information to the brain, and the brain cannot decide what to make of it. That is because the information is contradictory. When we look at a landscape picture in an art gallery, we are deceived. The artist's use of perspective makes us believe we are seeing a three-dimensional scene, just like that in the real world, even though the picture is on a flat canvas.

Sometimes artists play tricks, so that we cannot make up our minds whether to look at a picture in one way or another. At first we may see a picture in only one way. Suddenly, a second aspect shows itself. Once that happens, the brain checks and rechecks in its efforts to resolve the problem. Even though we know we are seeing an illusion, we insist on seeing it.

Illusions affect not only what we see. How we react is often determined by what we expect. For example, if you believe a suitcase to be full, you apply appropriate strength to lift it; if the case is empty, your arm shoots upwards.

Psychologists say that our reactions to illusions are healthy, provided we are not deceived into an accident. When rival possibilities confront us, we search for a solution. Solving problems quickly, as we need to do many thousands of times a day, is essential for our safety and survival.

Bizarre illustrations can puzzle the brain, forcing it to wrong conclusions. Nothing in the waterfall lithograph by M. C. Escher is illogical, but the more we study it and the perplexing triangle (inset), the more baffling they become

A relentless army of couriers

Why do we need blood?

The liquid that runs through the body's 95 000 km (60 000 miles) of blood vessels is an ever-moving supply train carrying a vast and relentless force of workers who labour nonstop. A single drop of blood holds more than 250 million separate cells, each with a job to do. Blood makes up about 7 per cent of an average adult's body weight, a volume of between 3.5 and 5 litres (6 and 8½ UK pints; 7½ and 10½ US pints) – a mighty workforce indeed, which is being replenished at a rate of three million new cells every second.

We need blood to nourish our bodies with proteins, glucose, salts and vitamins. Most of these are carried in plasma, which constitutes about 55 per cent of blood. Plasma, a straw-coloured fluid, is 95 per cent water, with about as much salt as there is in seawater. That is why blood tastes salty. Also, plasma contains varying levels of nutrients and proteins. Plasma oils the works, ensuring that in a healthy body the blood flows freely.

Most of blood's other 45 per cent is made up of red blood cells, which outnumber the third constituent, white cells, by about 700 to 1. Red cells, or erythrocytes, are composed mainly of haemoglobin, a protein found in all animals, from insects and worms, to birds, fish and mammals. Their redness depends on how much oxygen this iron-charged pigment carries.

An average blood cell holds some 350 million haemoglobin molecules, which are made from haem and globin in the bone marrow. The red army's job is to gather oxygen, which it does with great efficiency: each haemoglobin molecule can carry four molecules of oxygen. Body tissues need oxygen when their cells burn glucose and other fuels to make energy.

Carbon dioxide is a by-product of this reaction. After delivering their oxygen, the haemoglobin molecules don't cruise back empty. The now not-so-red molecules transport carbon dioxide to the lungs, which expel it. All this hard labour finally wears out the red cells, which in a four-month life complete some 300 000 circuits of the body's transport system.

Their workforce comrades, the white cells, are in effect the body's defence force. And, like any efficient army, they are grouped into units. One destroys enemy invaders, such as harmful bacteria. Another group acts as scavengers, quietly removing dead cells. Other units pounce on poisons, nullifying their venom. The white cells are born in many places – in the bone marrow, the lymph nodes, the thymus and the spleen. If you have ever wondered why we have tonsils, white

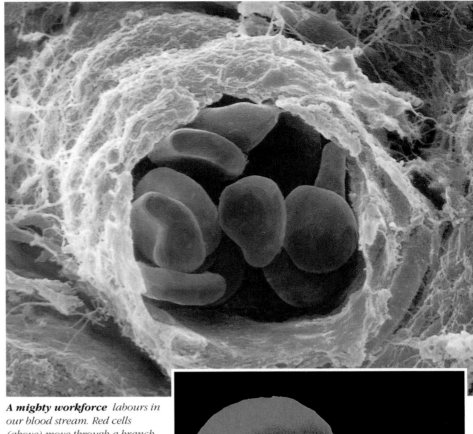

*A **mighty workforce** labours in our blood stream. Red cells (above) move through a branch of an artery. Right: a red cell, a white cell and a waferlike blood platelet. All are shown greatly magnified and in false colour. In carrying oxygen to all parts of the body, a red cell travels some 15 km (9.3 miles) a day*

blood cells are a good reason. Some of them come from there.

In 1952, haematologist Jean Dausset discovered the substance in white blood cells that fights infection. Known as human leukocyte antigen (HLA), its components can be arranged in 150 million different ways. Other ingredients of our blood – the red and white corpuscles, the enzymes and platelets – show similar variations. The range is so vast that, apart from identical twins, no two human beings have the same blood patterns.

Despite these variations, your blood is likely to resemble that of your relations. A specialist could take one drop, and tell you a considerable amount about your family history, your food preferences and perhaps even about where you live. If

your diet lacks green vegetables, your blood will have less folic acid. People living in the rarefied atmosphere of high altitudes need more oxygen. For that reason their blood may have twice as many red corpuscles as that of people living beside the sea.

At high altitudes, the air is cleaner. People breathing it don't need blood organisms that protect against diseases prevalent at sea level. That is why, when some people move from the mountains to the coast, they may suddenly become ill. A famous example is of Bolivian Indians who in the 1930s left their high-plateaux homelands to fight in lowland jungles of the Gran Chaco. Though impressive in physique, most of them soon sickened and died.

Why do some people suffer from blood pressure?

We all have blood pressure of a kind. If we didn't, blood wouldn't flow from the heart and through the arteries. This pressure has two forms. When the heart contracts, blood reaches its highest – systolic – pressure. When the heart relaxes between beats, the pressure falls to its lowest – diastolic – phase.

Your doctor measures these pressures in millimetres of mercury (mm/Hg) with an instrument known as a sphygmomanometer. Average pressure for a healthy young adult is about 110 mm/Hg systolic and 75 mm/Hg diastolic, which is usually expressed as 110/75.

Many factors may cause the pressure to be much higher. Exercise is one, because the heart needs to pump harder to supply more oxygen. Age is another but quite normal factor. A healthy sixty-year-old may have blood pressure of 130/90.

When people complain of blood pressure, they are talking about what doctors call hypertension – constant abnormally high pressure, which can cause life-threatening heart attacks and strokes. High pressure may force a weak spot in a blood vessel to balloon out and burst, releasing blood into surrounding tissue. Frequently, this is fatal.

To reduce blood pressure calls usually for changes in lifestyle. Hypertension affects up to 20 per cent of adults. Sometimes this has no obvious underlying cause. But many victims can lessen the risks by reducing their weight. Too much weight puts an extra burden on the heart. If these victims smoke, they should stop. Also, they should try to avoid stress which, like nicotine, constricts the blood vessels and forces the heart to work so much harder.

Everybody concerned about high blood pressure – now or later – should adopt a sensible diet. One rich in milk, cream, cheese, eggs and fatty meats, all sources of cholesterol, should be avoided.

Why is blood classified into groups?

For centuries beliefs persisted that some people, according to race or lineage, had superior blood. Members of the same families and races had the same blood type, it was said, but for reasons not explained some blood was purer.

When transfusions were first tried seriously in the seventeenth century, some succeeded, but others failed inexplicably, killing so many patients that in France, Italy and England the practice was banned. In 1900, Austrian pathologist Karl Landsteiner found the key to the doctors' dilemma. He mixed blood taken from several different people, and discovered that some blood types were compatible and others were not.

His research led to a theory that all blood would divide into four groups – A, B, AB and O. In general, transfusion works safely only within each group (except that all groups are compatible with O, and AB is compatible with everything). Ever since, blood has been broadly grouped in this way.

Marker proteins on the surface of red blood cells distinguish each group. These markers, known as antigens, equip cells to provoke an immune response to such threats as disease-carrying bacteria. In group A, red blood cells carry antigen A and the plasma has a protein called antibody b. Group B blood has antigen B and antibody a. Group AB has both antigens but no antibody. Group O has neither of the antigens but both antibodies.

World War I confirmed Landsteiner's ideas, and brought an end to theories about the superiority of some blood types. In 1915, during the Gallipoli and Macedonian campaigns, British and French doctors used Anamites, Senegalese and Indians as blood donors to save the lives of wounded British and French soldiers. Provided the transfusions came from compatible blood types, they were successful. Where the donor came from really didn't matter at all.

Some forty years later, Landsteiner, who was awarded a Nobel Prize for his life-saving research, discovered the rhesus (Rh) factor in blood, a system he first identified in rhesus monkeys. About 85 per cent of people are Rh positive. They have blood containing D antigen, one of the body's safeguards against disease. About 15 per cent are Rh-negative; their blood lacks this factor. Both of these rhesus factors are inherited traits and usually make little difference to a person's life.

The rhesus factor is extremely important in pregnancy. A pregnant woman who is Rh-negative may have a baby who is Rh-positive. As a reaction she may form antibodies against the baby's blood. When the baby is born, the mother is given special antibodies. This ensures that, if she has subsequent pregnancies of Rh-positive children, her blood does not give

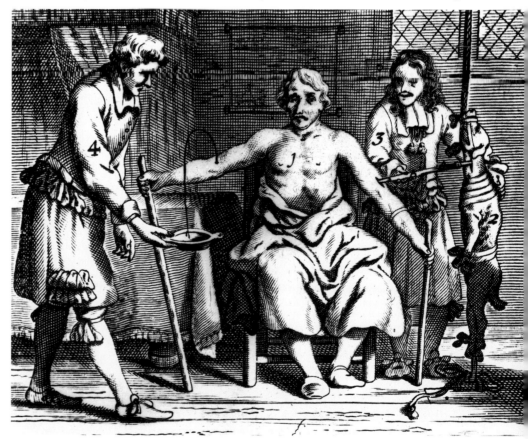

Blood transfusions *were first given in the Middle Ages. Surgeons in the late seventeenth century used them, sometimes from dogs, to ensure that a patient had the correct amount of blood. After a patient died, Jean Baptiste Denis, physician to Louis XIV, was charged with murder. He was cleared, but transfusions were then banned in many parts of Europe*

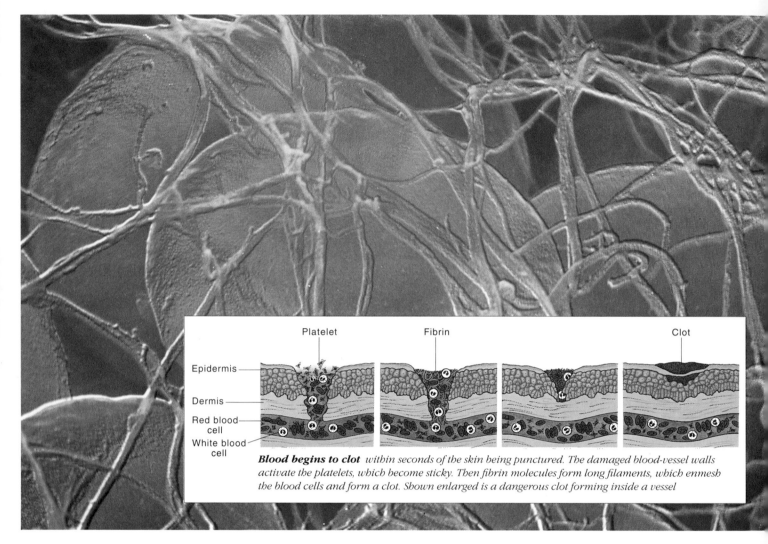

Blood begins to clot *within seconds of the skin being punctured. The damaged blood-vessel walls activate the platelets, which become sticky. Then fibrin molecules form long filaments, which enmesh the blood cells and form a clot. Shown enlarged is a dangerous clot forming inside a vessel*

Labels on figure: Platelet, Fibrin, Clot, Epidermis, Dermis, Red blood cell, White blood cell

them haemolytic disease, which would destroy their red blood cells.

In addition to his work on blood groups, Landsteiner discovered that the blood of all humans – like our fingerprints – is unique. That is why genetic finger-printing, a technique in modern criminal investigation, may positively identify a suspect from the slightest trace of blood.

Why does blood clot?

If you have normal blood and suffer a cut, tiny cells known as thrombocytes, or platelets, come to your rescue. These disclike cells, the smallest in the blood stream, clump together within seconds to seal off the wound. But first they need something, such as the feel of a damaged blood-vessel wall, to jolt them into action.

The first platelets to detect a hole in the blood-vessel wall become sticky, so that they can fasten on to the sides of the gap. As they do so, they change shape, becoming spiky globes that help them lock to-gether. Signals go out to other platelets to

help fill the breach. Every drop of blood usually holds about fifteen million platelets, so extra help is never far off. If the wound is not serious, this emergency force soon has everything under control. Normality returns almost without your knowing that it has been interrupted.

A final stage in the closing off of a wound is coagulation, the hardening of blood to form a tight seal. In a complex series of stages, known as the coagulation cascade, the blood produces a stringy protein called fibrin, the main component of all blood clots. Inactive molecules in the plasma suddenly become active, one triggering another in a remarkable chain reaction. Within seconds, one active mol-ecule may convert some 30 000 others.

Deficiencies in the blood may cause it to flow sluggishly or to clot unnecessarily. Other defects, such as a shortage of platelets, may stop it from clotting, caus-ing haemophilia. Doctors test the blood's ability to clot by pricking the skin, usually of the ear or forearm, and seeing how long it takes for the bleeding to stop. Three to eight minutes is the average.

Why do arteries become clogged?

Our arteries do the vital job of distribut-ing blood pumped by the heart. Basically, they are pliable tubes, cunningly con-structed in three layers to provide a smooth, lightweight pipeline that will withstand the constant, second-by-second pressure of the heart's pumping. That pressure may vary considerably. Most of the time you may hardly notice your heart beating; at other times, as when you exer-cise, it responds with a powerful thump.

Beneath a tough and fibrous outer casing, arteries have a thicker but elastic middle layer, with a smooth inner lining to make the blood flow more easily. Like any working surface, the lining is easily damaged. For many reasons, such as high blood pressure, smoking, family history and possibly stress, the lining thickens, narrowing the artery.

Cholesterol, which is made by the liver and used to produce new cells and some hormones, may be another factor. A diet

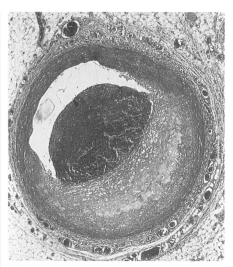

*A **heart attack** in the making, seen in a section of a coronary artery. The vessel is almost blocked by plaque (pink) and a haemorrhage (red) that has caused a clot*

rich in dairy foods, eggs and meat raises the cholesterol level. Even though frequent reports question whether cholesterol is a serious danger to health, doctors insist that a high blood cholesterol level increases the risk of coronary artery disease or of a stroke.

Damaged areas of the arteries develop raised patches, known as plaques. These consist of fatty deposits and such debris as decaying muscle cells and fibrous tissue. In addition, two types of blood cells contribute to the build-up: large white cells – macrophages – and clumps of platelets, the blood's smallest cells, whose normal job is to help blood to coagulate in sealing wounds.

As we get older, plaques get more numerous and thicker. Some areas accumulate calcium, and turn into a hard, chalky mass, choking the arteries. Narrow arteries make the job of delivering an adequate blood supply more difficult. At tight spots restricted by plaque, blood clots develop and sometimes break away, drifting through the blood stream to cause blockages elsewhere.

Because the heart and blood are so vital, any diseases of the system are serious. Atherosclerosis, the thickening of the arterial wall, is a major killer in most developed countries. In Britain, it heads the list of fatal diseases. Diseases of the arteries don't confine their effects to the cardiovascular system. Reduced blood flow to the intestines, the legs and the kidneys also may cause serious problems.

Arterial disease isn't inevitable, nor does it attack only the elderly. It is strongly linked to unhealthy lifestyles – fatty diets, smoking, lack of exercise. By countering these, all of us have a good chance of beating this killer.

SUDDENLY, BLOOD-SUCKERS ARE BACK IN FASHION

If you have ever been attacked by a blood-sucking leech, you will know that a surprising and possibly disturbing element is that only after the parasite released its hold did you realise you were its victim.

Since Roman times, physicians have used the leech's ability to draw blood painlessly. Until well into the nineteenth century, it was thought that many illnesses were caused by 'bad blood', and that the most effective treatment was to reduce its volume. The cure often proved worse than the complaint. Some patients were bled white, killing them.

British and French doctors were leading advocates of leeching. After about 1820, Britain exhausted its supply of native leeches, and had to import replacements. At that time, chemists and barbers sold leeches for home use, and many families kept their own as part of the household first-aid kit. Unpleasant as it might seem, a leech applied to a black eye or other disfiguring bruise can be a swift cure.

Leeches are worms found in water throughout the world and on land in tropical forests. Not all leeches depend on blood for food, but all will latch on to a vertebrate animal if given the chance.

Once it finds its victim, a leech grips swiftly with its suckers. Retractable jaws inside the sucker surrounding the mouth soon break the skin. A proboscis, similar to a mosquito's, draws off the blood. A feed may last from ten minutes to more than an hour, during which the leech changes its threadlike shape to something looking more like a fat slug.

When it is satisfied, it falls away, leaving a human victim with an itchy wound that may continue to bleed for several hours. This – and the painless nature of the blood-sucking – is due to an anticlotting substance called hirudin, which the leech injects with its saliva.

Leeching lost fashion in the 1860s, except in some parts of Europe and Asia, but researchers remained interested in the anticlotting properties of leech saliva. Now, extracts of hirudin are used to treat people at risk of a blockage in their blood circulation.

Since the 1980s, some surgeons have used live leeches, because of a discovery that leech saliva not only thins the blood but dilates veins. Surgeons attempting to rejoin tiny veins in accident victims or to repair surface blood vessels in delicate cosmetic operations sometimes apply leeches to open these channels wider.

If, after swimming or during a country walk, you find a leech clinging to you, a lighted match, alcohol, vinegar or salt will induce it to relax its hold. Pull it off gently to prevent its sucker and proboscis breaking away and possibly causing infection. A styptic pencil will help to stop the bleeding.

*A **cure-all remedy** in times past was to apply leeches to suck out the blood. Most households kept a supply on hand. In 1837, one London hospital used 96 000 leeches on 50 557 patients*

Little workaholic that rules your life

Forget the songs and the car stickers that equate the heart with love. The organ that beats in every breast has nothing to do with emotions, though it often reacts to them. The heart is a phenomenal workhorse, a pump that beats continuously and regularly, about seventy times a minute, every hour of the day and night, for perhaps as long as a century. It is the hardest working muscle in your body, and generates enough power in a day to drive a truck 32 km (20 miles).

Every week it contracts about 700 000 times, in an average life span more than 2500 million times. It drives hard – and it needs to. It operates a delivery service that never stops, sending life-sustaining blood charged with oxygen and nutrients through hundreds of kilometres of the body's vessels and bringing it back to dispose of wastes. What other machine gives such reliable service with so little care and attention?

For all its power, the heart is quite small – a muscle not much bigger than a closed fist. And for all its importance, most of us know little about it. We tend, for example, to think of it as a single organ, when in fact it is really two pumps, each with two chambers.

Ask somebody to place a hand on the heart, and almost certainly he or she will indicate the left side of the body. The heart is almost in the centre of the chest, with a little more of it to the left than to the right. One reason why we believe it to be on the left is because that is where we feel its beat more clearly. Another mistaken idea, encouraged by car stickers and St Valentine cards, is about the heart's shape. More accurately, the symbol for the heart should be a pear.

Mistaken ideas about the heart and its functions have a long history. Until the seventeenth century, doctors believed that the liver produced blood, and the heart delivered it once only to various reservoirs in the body. In 1553, Michael Servetus was burned as a heretic for declaring – quite correctly – that blood moves from the right side of the heart to the left via the lungs. His fate undoubtedly deterred other physicians from speaking out, and perpetuated fallacies about the heart's role.

The heart works like most pumps, with valves to make sure that the blood flows through it in only one direction. But unlike many water pumps, which work continuously, the heart pumps and then relaxes. Its sequence is controlled by electrical impulses from the heart's in-built pacemaker, the sinuatrial

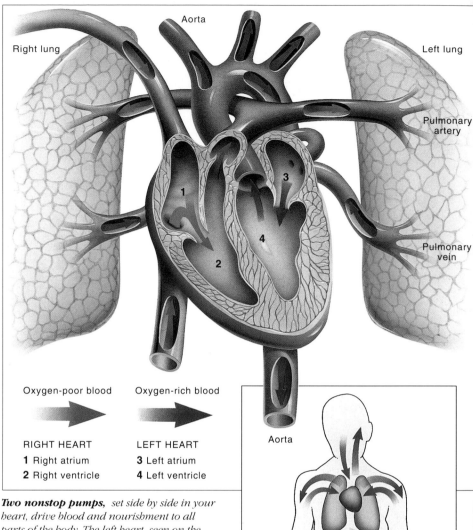

Oxygen-poor blood →

RIGHT HEART
1 Right atrium
2 Right ventricle

Oxygen-rich blood →

LEFT HEART
3 Left atrium
4 Left ventricle

Two nonstop pumps, set side by side in your heart, drive blood and nourishment to all parts of the body. The left heart, seen on the right in the diagram, takes oxygen-rich blood from the lungs and pumps it via the arteries. Blood returns through the veins to the right heart, which sends it into the lungs to be recharged with oxygen

node, which is situated at the top of the right atrium, one of its chambers.

In three precise phases the heart draws in blood and pumps it out. These three phases are called diastole, atrial systole and ventricular systole, and in a healthy heart are finely tuned. At each stroke, the volume of blood pumped by the two sides of the heart must be perfectly matched, even though the force required to drive it through the lungs to be oxygenated is less than that to circulate it to the rest of the body.

The heart is cunningly designed to cope with this delivery problem and avoid a build-up of blood in one place and a shortage in another. The heart's left side contracts with greater force than the right. That is why the heart is

shaped as it is, with more muscular bulk on its left side.

No matter whether your heart beats at 200 times a minute, as it may do if you exercise strenuously, or at a mere third of that when you rest, it must maintain its precise rhythm. Also, it must cope with wide variations in its output. When you exercise, your muscles demand more oxygen. To deliver it, the heart pumps more blood, as much as 50 litres (11 UKgal; 13 USgal) a minute, com-

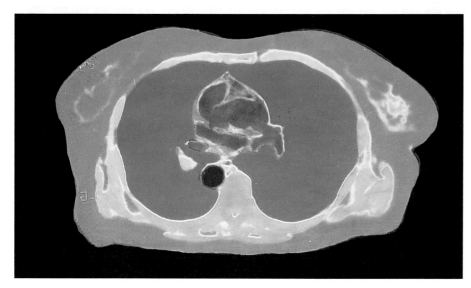

The heart beats almost in the centre of the chest, as seen in this computed tomography X-ray scan. The false colours show the aorta (red), the heart (orange) and the lungs (blue)

pared with about 6 litres (1.3 UKgal; 1.6 USgal) when it is at rest.

These changes in pace and output are achieved in two ways. Because it pushes out more blood, the heart also receives more. An increase in its intake produces an automatic increase in output. In addition, a nucleus of nerve cells located in the brain stem watches over the heart from what is known as the cardiac centre. These nerve cells are part of the body's automatic nervous system, which monitors a number of essential functions without your having to worry about them. If you are at rest, the heart rate automatically slows. If you exercise, a release of two hormones, adrenaline and noradrenaline, increases the heart rate and the force of its contraction.

A key measure of a heart's efficiency is its cardiac output, the amount of blood it pumps in a given time. This depends on how fast the heart beats and the volume of blood ejected with each contraction. On average, cardiac output is about 4.5 litres (1 UKgal; 1.2 USgal) a minute – a staggering 8 tonnes a day.

The heart is a tough muscle of a special kind, unlike any other in the body and perfect in design. Despite our command of technology, we have not yet made an artificial heart that compares in performance with the natural organ.

For all its efficiency and resilience, the heart is susceptible to disease. So, of course, is the rest of the body. The essential difference is that the heart plays such a vital role. If it stops beating for as little as four minutes, its owner may die or suffer irreversible brain damage.

That is why heart disease is such a killer. Today, it is the number one cause

of death, accounting for about one-third of all fatalities in adults, with a rising toll in both the developed and developing countries. Many of these deaths are premature, adults aged forty to sixty, with men of this group four times more likely to die than women.

Because so much premature heart disease is directly related to our lifestyle and is preventable, a worldwide campaign aims to teach people how to safeguard their hearts. The education program shows pleasing results. The United States, for example, has cut deaths from coronary heart disease by a third.

If you have a healthy heart and want to keep it, here are some everyday rules that will help you.

Do not smoke. The more you smoke, the greater the risk not only to your heart and cardiovascular system but to your lungs and brain. Even if you have smoked heavily for thirty years, it's not too late to benefit by stopping.

Watch your diet. Ask your doctor to check your cholesterol level. If it's high, cut down on fatty meats, eggs and rich dairy foods. Go for low fat and high fibre. It will reduce your weight – easing the strain on your heart – and improve your appearance.

Exercise sensibly. Leave the car at home and walk whenever you can – to the shops, up and down stairs. Forget all those heavy lunches. Have a light, healthy snack and take a walk.

Relax. Stress and tension, anxiety and conflict may all contribute to higher blood pressure. Vary your week with some truly relaxing leisure. Play games for enjoyment, not to satisfy a driving desire to win. If you are seriously troubled, take some relaxation therapy.

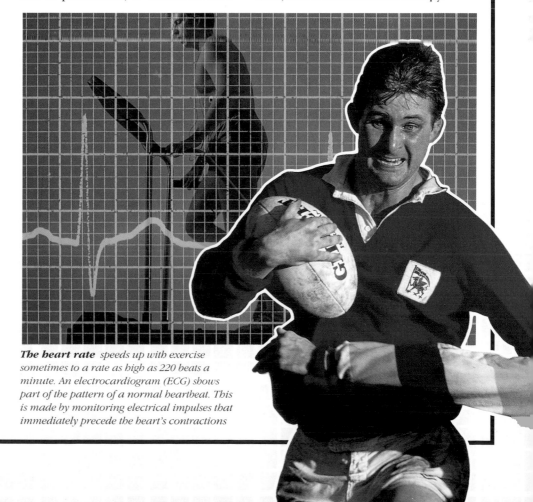

The heart rate speeds up with exercise sometimes to a rate as high as 220 beats a minute. An electrocardiogram (ECG) shows part of the pattern of a normal heartbeat. This is made by monitoring electrical impulses that immediately precede the heart's contractions

The battle to save your smile

Why do we get holes in our teeth?

Dentists say that our teeth are generally healthier today than they have ever been. Some youngsters in industrialised countries reach maturity without having a tooth cavity filled. Better dental hygiene is one reason; the fluoridation of water is another; and the addition of fluoride to toothpaste is a useful factor.

Plaque, the sticky mixture of food, saliva and bacteria that forms on the teeth, is the main cause of dental caries, or decay. The bacteria, which are of a kind found only in the mouth, feed on sugars and starches in food lodging in crevices and grooves, and create an acid that attacks the enamel. Once a small hole develops, the decay moves into the next layer, the dentine, and eventually into the tooth's central pulp.

Usually, the initial attack passes unnoticed. Not until a cavity has opened, exposing the nerve, do we feel any pain. Sweet, hot or very cold food often triggers toothache, the first sign of a problem. To cure it, the dentist removes the decayed section of the tooth, and fills the hole. Sound oral hygiene and regular dental inspections are the best preventive steps, and they should start early. Children should eat sweet, sticky foods only at mealtimes, and get into the habit of brushing the teeth thoroughly immediately afterwards.

Bottles of sweet liquids should never be given to babies as comforters. The practice is a common cause of early tooth decay, encouraged sometimes by a belief that a child's primary teeth aren't important. They are – and they need careful protection. Children's first teeth should be brushed gently with a soft brush as soon as they appear. Before that, the gums should be cleaned with a piece of damp cloth or gauze.

Why do our gums sometimes bleed?

Gums that bleed when you brush your teeth may be a first sign of gingivitis, or inflammation of the gums. This is one of a number of microbial infections that dentists group together as periodontal disease. Two out of three young adults have some sign of it, possibly without knowing.

In recent years dentists have paid more attention to periodontal disease, which may affect not just the gums but the deeper tooth-supporting structure, because in adults over the age of thirty-five this is the major cause of tooth loss. The

The agony of toothache once called on a range of simple household remedies, from putting drops in the ear, rubbing the tooth with tobacco ash or, as shown in an American wood engraving of last century (left), tying the jaw in a scarf. When these failed, the aching tooth was pulled out, either in the home or by the local doctor, barber or blacksmith, who sometimes used the crudest of tools. An engraving by Timothy Bobbin shows a tooth-drawer at work with pincers in 1810

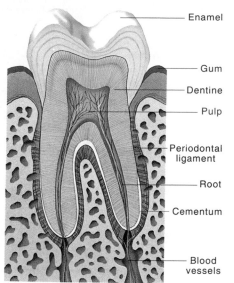

All teeth are complex structures of hard dentine and enamel, enclosing an inner pulpy core, plus blood vessels and nerves

Enamel

Gum

Dentine

Pulp

Periodontal ligament

Root

Cementum

Blood vessels

A PERFECT SET OF TOOLS FOR CUTTING AND GRINDING

Most of us cut the first of our primary or baby teeth at six months of age and the rest of the set during the next two or three years. Those twenty teeth are replaced gradually from about the age of six by our permanent teeth.

These, thirty-two in number, are divided into eight incisors, the chisel-shaped teeth at the front of the mouth, which are designed for cutting; four canines, the longest teeth, made for tearing food apart; eight premolars, or bicuspids, which have a grinding action; and twelve molars, the back teeth, which are also grinders. The molars include the wisdom teeth, the last to appear – if they do so. Some people never get them.

All teeth have the same basic structure. At the heart of each tooth is pulp-like matter containing blood vessels and nerves. This is enclosed in a hard substance known as dentine. The tooth is locked into the gum by its roots, which fit into sockets in the jawbone and are covered by cementum, a bony and sensitive material. Tying the cementum to the gums and the jaw is the periodontal ligament, which has an important additional function of absorbing shock as our teeth bang and grind together when we chew.

Enamel, the hardest substance in the body, covers the exposed areas of our teeth. But, for all its durability, it isn't designed for sugar-rich diets. Residues of these foods ferment as they break down, producing an acid that slowly erodes the enamel. Healthy teeth are an invaluable asset, affecting not only our enjoyment of food but our appearance and self-confidence.

teeth may be quite healthy, but the disease loosens them. Eventually, with nothing to hold them securely in their place, they fall out.

The various forms of the disease are nearly all caused by bacteria and our failure to remove them at least once a day from our teeth and gums. Dense microbial deposits called plaque build up along the gum-line. Sometimes this is difficult to detect. The plaque infects the gums, which swell. Deep pockets form between the teeth and gums. These hold more plaque and cause more inflammation. Swollen gums bleed quite easily, even when cleaned with a soft toothbrush.

If the initial inflammation is ignored, the infection spreads deeper, and in time the tooth wobbles in its socket. Some quite healthy people are more prone to the disease than others. So are those suffering from diabetes, anaemia and nutritional deficiencies. Periodontal disease may be triggered by puberty, pregnancy, the menopause and the taking of oral contraceptives.

Thorough professional cleaning can stabilise the disease, but advanced cases often need surgery. The dentist reshapes the gums so that in daily brushing the patient can reach all areas effectively. But essentially the job of keeping the teeth clean and the gums healthy is a matter of sound dental hygiene at home.

This may entail a range of measures, especially thorough brushing, and particularly between the teeth, to remove plaque. Your dentist will advise you about

Bacteria on teeth cause many of our dental problems. In this false-colour micrograph, the bacteria appear as red rods, enlarged about 1000 times, on a background of a yellow tooth. Gum disease, caused by microbial deposits, is a major reason for tooth loss in adults

mouthwashes that may help. Also, you can check your efficiency by occasional use of tablets or drops that stain the plaque you haven't removed. This will show you where your brush isn't reaching. Dental floss, toothpicks and rubber tips all help to keep the bacteria at bay.

Why don't dentists use X-rays more often?

A few years ago, some dentists X-rayed a patient's teeth annually. Because X-rays often reveal hidden problems, it seemed a sensible practice.

Just as chest X-rays are no longer given routinely by mobile units, dental X-rays are also less common. X-rays carry some risk from radiation, and medical practitioners in all fields try to limit their use.

A new electronic dental X-ray system, undergoing tests in the United States, may cut much of that danger. By providing images of teeth on a computer screen, it aims to give dentists a faster and safer screening technique. It reduces radiation to a half or third of that in conventional X-rays. In the computerised system, a small electronic sensor replaces the film. X-rays strike the sensor, which is linked to a personal computer, giving the dentist images within seconds. By using the live display or a recording, the dentist can explain to a patient precisely what needs to be done.

Why do some people have such beautiful white teeth?

It's certainly true that some people have whiter teeth than others but, just as nobody has white skin, nobody has white teeth. The colours of our teeth are varying hues of yellow, brown and grey. Like our individual skin colours, they are also largely hereditary.

Teeth become darker with age, because the red pulp at the heart of each tooth, which gives them their brightness, recedes towards the root. As it does so, it is replaced by dentine, the hard tissue surrounding a tooth's inner pulp. This tissue, known as secondary dentine, is darker and less translucent than the tooth's original dentine, which lies just below the outer shell of enamel.

Over the years, excessive brushing with a hard brush and abrasive toothpaste will gradually wear away the enamel. When this happens, the dentine shows through the enamel as yellow patches, reducing a tooth's whiteness.

Often, white lines or spots occur, caused by abnormalities during the teeth's development. Our first teeth begin to form before we are born – between three and six months. Permanent teeth, excluding wisdom teeth, develop in our first four years. For both sets of teeth,

A bright smile usually *depends on showing a healthy set of teeth. That is why many dentists today are concerned about saving not only the essential function of teeth but also their appearance. An attractive smile undoubtedly has an all-round, lifelong influence*

calcium and phosphorus crystals, carried in the blood supply, make up about 70 per cent of dentine and 95 per cent of enamel. Too little or too much of these crystals may discolour the teeth. Today, if the blemishes are severe, cosmetic treatment can blend the white areas into the rest of the tooth.

The most common forms of discoloration come from our food and drink and from smoking. Tea and coffee stain the teeth brown. So do liquids containing iron, such as some medicines. Tetracycline, an antibiotic drug, can make teeth yellow, brown or blue-violet, if it is taken during their development.

Similarly, excessive amounts of fluoride ingested while the teeth are forming may mottle the enamel, a condition known as fluorosis. This may occur through giving a child too many fluoride tablets. Toothpastes claiming to make teeth whiter can restore them only to their natural colour.

At present, the only way to lighten the natural colour is by bleaching. To do this, dentists use strong bleaching agents, sometimes combined with heat or ultraviolet light. Less severe cases may be treated at home with a special dental bleaching kit. Dentists can mask the natural colour of teeth by covering them with veneers of porcelain or resin, or by fixing crowns of a lighter colour.

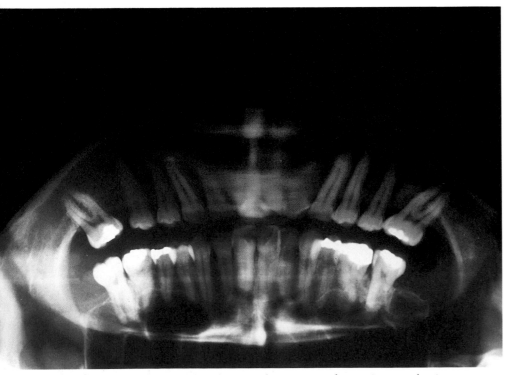

*A **dental X-ray** shows all the teeth and surrounding structure (but not in true colour) on one film. Taken with a special camera, which swings from one side of the jaw to the other, the picture enables the dentist to find impacted teeth, cysts, fractures and tumours. Bright areas are fillings*

Inner mysteries of the ear

Why is the ear divided into three parts?

Many of us tend to think of the ear as being merely the outside flap, the visible part that is a combination of skin and cartilage. The ear is one of the body's most complex organs – and the earflap is its least essential part. In fact, if you lost it through accident, your hearing would be little affected. Compared with the swivelling ear flaps of such animals as hares and cats, our ear flaps do an indifferent job and even poorer when hidden by hair.

The vital parts of the ear, those responsible for hearing and balance, lie within the skull. They are marvels of miniaturisation. The middle ear has an amplifying system of three linked bones, the ossicles, set inside a chamber so small that four or five drops of water would fill it. The inner ear, not much bigger than a pea, has as many circuits as the telephone systems of some cities.

You hear something when sound waves strike the eardrum, causing it to vibrate. Each minute inward movement of the drum sets up a reaction in the ossicles. These bones are named according to their shapes. The malleus, or hammer, takes up the eardrum's rhythm, and transfers the message to the incus (anvil). The incus passes on the vibrations to the stapes (stirrup).

The inner ear is among the best protected parts of the body, and it needs to be. It helps us to maintain our balance, and houses the cochlea, which converts sound waves into nerve impulses, the language of the brain.

The cochlea, which looks like the shell of a small snail, is a truly remarkable device. It has some 20 000 hairlike cells which react to sound. Some are narrow and stiff, and are activated by higher-pitched tones; others, wider and more flexible, pick up sounds of deeper pitch. As these sensory cells vibrate, they create impulses for the acoustic nerve to carry messages to the brain.

Why do we sometimes hear bells ringing in our ears?

From time to time, we all get strange noises in one or both of our ears. We hear a ringing, buzzing, whistling, rumbling or hissing, but it's created inside the head not in the world outside. Usually, the noise disappears as rapidly as it arrived. Doctors trace these brief episodes to many sources: a build-up of earwax, drugs such as aspirin and quinine, sudden loud

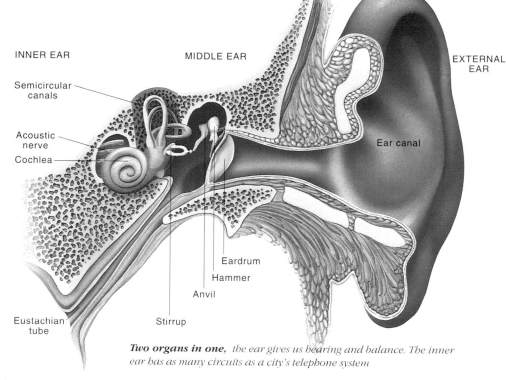

INNER EAR   MIDDLE EAR   EXTERNAL EAR

Semicircular canals
Acoustic nerve
Cochlea
Eustachian tube
Stirrup
Anvil
Hammer
Eardrum
Ear canal

Two organs in one, the ear gives us hearing and balance. The inner ear has as many circuits as a city's telephone system

noise. As soon as the effects of these wear off, normal hearing is restored.

Many people never get rid of this disorder, known as tinnitus. It may be so severe that it completely upsets their lives. For some reason, the acoustic nerve sends continuous impulses to the brain that aren't produced by normal sound vibrations. Often no cause is found, but we know that it may stem from a fault somewhere in the ear, in the acoustic nerve itself or in the brain.

A frequent cause is exposure to constant noise, generally at work. Tinnitus may come also from otosclerosis, bone deterioration in the middle ear, from anaemia, diabetes, some allergies and high blood pressure. In rare cases a tumour pressing on a blood vessel in the head is to blame. Often the disorder is a sign of approaching deafness.

If the cause can be found, treatment is often successful. Some people learn to live with tinnitus by using radio headphones, a cassette player or similar device to block out the annoyance.

Anybody suffering mild tinnitus – ear noises that persist for more than a day or two – should see an ear specialist. The disorder could be a symptom of a serious problem in the ears or elsewhere in the body.

Why do people go deaf?

Total deafness is fortunately very rare, and the luckless sufferers are usually among the one in 1000 who are born that way. Partial deafness creeps up on most of us as we get older. Those who become

hard of hearing earlier in their lives are usually the victims of disease, such as middle-ear infection, or accident.

Whatever its cause, hearing loss has two forms: conductive deafness and nerve deafness. In conductive deafness, damage to the eardrum or other parts of the hearing mechanism in the middle ear prevents the transmission of sound to the inner ear. Sometimes the cause is simply a build-up of earwax, or an infection has generated fluid in the middle ear. In these

Beethoven's deafness was a blessing for music-lovers. He gave up his career as a pianist and concentrated on composition

A DELICATE MATTER OF BALANCE

Tightrope-walker Blondin *crosses Niagara in 1859. Later he did it blindfolded*

Our ears play an important part in helping us to stay upright without toppling over, but they aren't our only control mechanism. Balance is a complex process, demanding a constant flow of signals to and from the brain. If, for example, we trip and fall sideways, an immediate reaction is to shoot out an arm on the opposite side of the body to provide a counterweight. A tightrope walker demonstrates these finely tuned controls working to perfection.

Three sources feed information to the brain about the body's position. The eyes convey visual data. Sensory receptors in the skin, muscles and joints report on the position and movement of various parts of the body. And delicate sensors in the inner ear stimulate nerve impulses to inform the brain about head movements. Any ear disorder, especially in the inner ear, is likely to upset our balance. In the labyrinth, the inner ear has three semicircular chambers filled with fluid. As the head moves, so do these fluids, shifting the hairlike sensors, which immediately alert the brain. Sensor cells in the cochlea, a spiral-shaped part of the inner ear that changes sound vibrations into nerve impulses, also help us maintain balance.

cases, the trouble is often easily remedied. Conductive deafness in young children is extremely common, affecting in some countries about 25 per cent of those starting school. If it is diagnosed quickly, the chances of a cure are good.

Injury to the inner ear or to the acoustic nerve, which carries sound impulses to the brain, are major reasons for nerve deafness. Damage of this kind occurs frequently before birth, possibly because the mother had rubella, or German measles, during the first three months of her pregnancy. It may also happen through injury during birth.

Later in life, a number of diseases – encephalitis, Ménière's disease and some viral infections – may damage the cochlea and other delicate mechanisms in the inner ear, causing nerve deafness. The acoustic nerve often degenerates through age. One sign of the disorder is that high sounds are less audible than low sounds.

Hearing tests quickly detect which kind of deafness is causing hearing loss. One

rough guide is that people with conductive deafness often speak more quietly, because their own voices sound loud to them. Those with nerve deafness tend to shout, because their own voices otherwise seem faint.

Why do we sometimes get earache?

Pain in the ear is one of the most frequent and distressing childhood ailments, as many sleepless parents know. Infection of the middle ear – acute otitis media – is its most common cause in adults and children. A severe, stabbing pain, high temperature and some hearing loss may precede a rupture of the eardrum and the release of fluid.

Sometimes, infection strikes the outer ear canal, inflaming it and even causing a particularly painful abscess or boil.

More rarely, a form of herpes blisters the canal, causing earache for long after

all signs of the infection have cleared up.

Not all earache results from ear trouble. Because the same nerves supply the ear and adjacent areas, pain in an ear can be a sign of tooth problems, a throat infection or a disorder of the jaw or neck muscles. A cold, flu, scarlet fever, mumps and measles may all trigger an earache. Because the ear, nose and throat are closely connected, it's easy for viruses and bacteria to move through the ear's Eustachian tube to settle in the middle ear, where they multiply. The mucous membrane lining the middle ear tries to defend itself by producing fluids. Pressure builds up, bringing pain and temporary hearing loss.

Persistent earache, like any other constant pain, should not be ignored. Ear infections can result in mastoiditis, meningitis and sometimes a brain abscess. Fortunately, if attention is swift, these complications today are rare.

Why does air travel affect the ears?

Many activities make the ears pop. If you ride to the top of a skyscraper or down a deep mine shaft, you will need to swallow several times to correct a bulging sensation within the eardrums. Similarly, when you fly, particularly in an unpressurised cabin, or ski fast downhill, you may suffer that same discomfort inside your ears.

All these activities have something in common. Whenever you travel fast up or down, you are suddenly changing the air pressure on your eardrums. Air pressure as you climb is lower than that on the ground; below the surface it gets steadily higher. If you go up, the air inside your middle ear is still at the higher pressure of ground level; it presses the eardrums out. If you go down, the air outside forces the eardrum inwards.

Normally, the pressure inside and outside your ear is the same, maintained by the Eustachian tube, which links the middle ear and the throat. If you climb a mountain, you will inevitably swallow many times. This opens a valve at the end of the Eustachian tube, admitting or releasing air to equalise the pressures inside and out. When we travel more quickly up or down, we don't always remember to do this until the eardrums tell us.

This discomfort in the ears is known as barotrauma. Usually, it wears off quite quickly, especially if you swallow or yawn a few times. A danger arises because of the close links between the throat and the ears. If you have a heavy cold, your ears could suffer some damage. In any case, for the sake of your own health and that of other passengers, you would be wiser not travelling until you are well.

Probing the brain's secret life

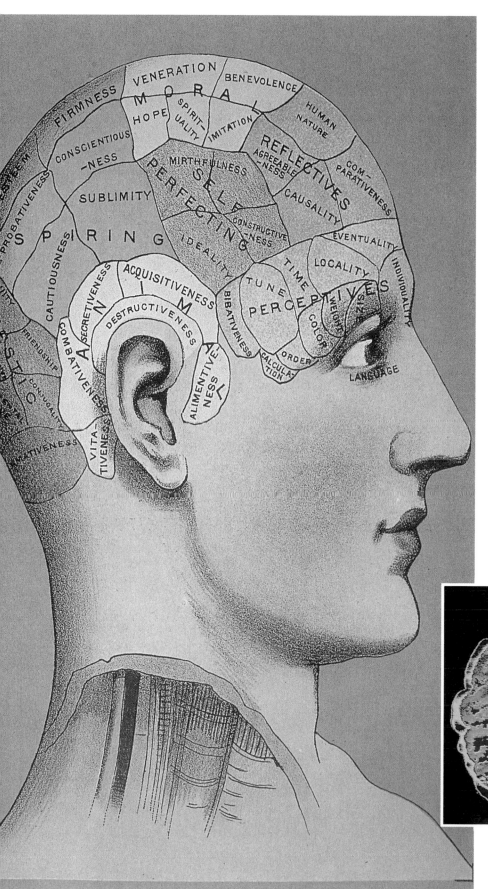

Why is the brain so remarkable?

Of all our organs, the brain distinguishes us as human beings. Our limbs, eyes, ears, lungs – all other parts in our system – are not remarkable when compared with those of animals. Most birds have far better eyesight; many wild beasts can outrun us. But no other creatures have our ability to reason, to judge, to create, to make and appreciate music and poetry.

As Hippocrates, the Greek father of medicine, once observed, 'From the brain and the brain only arise our pleasures, joys, laughter and jests, as well as our sorrows, pains, griefs and fears.' The brain is indeed the master organ, controlling all other organs and systems in our bodies.

Many people have likened the brain to a computer. A computer processes information one step at a time, after it has been programmed, or instructed, to do so. No computer can reject its program decide, indeed, that it doesn't want to work. Computers cannot laugh and no computer has ever fallen in love.

If, by some strange chance, we had never seen a computer and had found one on the Moon, we would soon have unravelled its mysteries, awesome as they might seem. Nothing yet found in the Universe compares with the complexity of the human brain, which remains the last great biological frontier.

Every second of our lives, the brain sends and receives some fifty million messages. It controls our thoughts and emotions, stores our memories, and directs every voluntary and involuntary move we make. Without our brains we

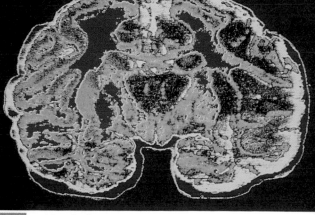

The skull's shape *has no bearing on the brain's function, as a last-century diagram suggests. By a technique known as magnetic resonance imaging (inset), specialists can test the reactions of different areas of the brain and detect psychiatric disorders*

could not breathe, process our food, get rid of wastes.

How, precisely, it works – what in the brain does what – we are only now beginning to discover. In the remaining years of what former US President George Bush declared the 'Decade of the Brain', neuroscientists hope to plot with the precision of the finest mapmakers the millions of micro-contours of this uncharted world. The voyage of discovery is enormously challenging. Inside the brain are some 100 000 million cells, or neurons. From each one comes a baffling maze of perhaps another 100 000 fibres. The mapmakers' job is to identify how – when we retrieve a fact from our memory store, for example – which pieces in the puzzle come into play.

The cartographers are not by any means starting from scratch. Already, scientists have found many ways to explore some of the brain's geography. In the past, they examined the brains of dead people who had been paralysed by a stroke or had suffered some neurological problem. In doing so, specialists often found a tumour or other abnormality.

In recent years, they have looked at patients with various brain lesions, or scars, and noted how they lacked certain abilities. Similarly, surgeons have given electrical stimulation to conscious patients during brain surgery. By such means, we have gradually pinpointed areas of the brain that seem to control specific functions.

Scanning devices such as CAT, for computerised-axial tomography, have already given us superb pictures of a healthy brain's structure. Into play now come several other technologies designed to track the electrical, magnetic and chemical power by which the brain conveys its messages.

By means of PET, positron emission tomography, researchers can discover which brain cells work in certain tasks. Active cells consume more glucose, the body's fuel. Volunteers are injected with radioactive glucose, then tested in various ways. A PET scanner tracks the passage of glucose to see which brain cells are demanding fuel. The scanner reports areas of heightened activity to a computer, which produces maps of the neural hot spots. Similar scanners peering into the skull can track the brain's blood flow and record its multitude of magnetic and electrical impulses.

When the mapmaking is complete we will have opened windows into the mysterious contours of the brain. That itself will be a remarkable achievement, but nothing compared with the awesome nature of the brain itself which, after all, is masterminding its own exploration.

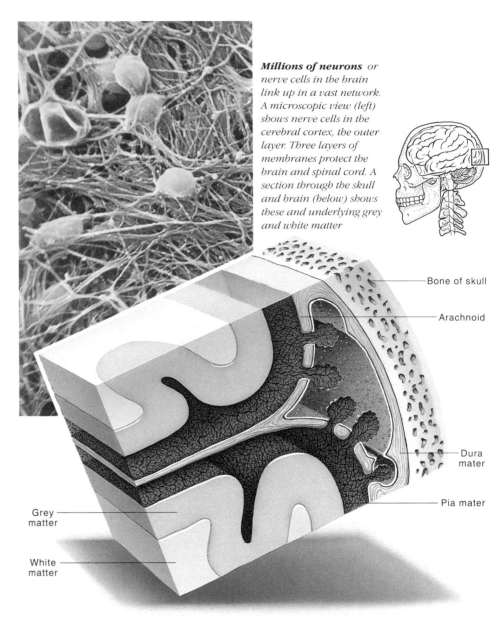

Millions of neurons or *nerve cells in the brain link up in a vast network. A microscopic view (left) shows nerve cells in the cerebral cortex, the outer layer. Three layers of membranes protect the brain and spinal cord. A section through the skull and brain (below) shows these and underlying grey and white matter*

Bone of skull

Arachnoid

Dura mater

Pia mater

Grey matter

White matter

Why is the brain often described as grey matter?

If you were to join a team of surgeons performing a brain operation, you would see them first drill a tiny hole into the skull. Then, with a powerful saw, they would remove a portion of bone. Through the opening, you might expect to get your first glimpse of the brain. In fact, your initial view would be of what is called the dura mater, the tough leathery outer layer of the meninges, the three strong membranes that cover and protect the brain and the spinal cord.

Then, when the surgeon cuts into the dura, cauterises the bleeding vessels and peels back the dural flap, you would see a glistening grey-white substance pulsating gently. This outer layer of the brain is

known as the cortex, a term applied also to the outer layer of other organs, such as the kidneys and adrenal glands. That of the brain is just 3 mm (⅛ in) thick and holds thousands of millions of nerve cells arranged in six layers. The cortex is the site of the brain's higher functions, the area concerned with thought, sensations and movement.

Amid a variety of technical terms used in detailed diagrams of the brain's structure – corpus callosum, sulcus, gyrus, ganglia and others – you will find the cortex described, even in specialist literature, as grey matter. Beneath the grey matter of the cortex lies white matter, tracts of thin nerve-cell fibres, which project like tails. These tracts link various areas of the grey matter to one another and to nerve centres elsewhere in the brain and the brain stem.

Why does the brain need oxygen?

Most people who have studied first aid know that, if breathing stops, it's essential to restart it quickly. Frequently, when somebody is saved from suffocation, for example, breathing restarts but not soon enough. The victim survives and suffers irreparable brain damage. Of all the body's organs, the brain cannot normally survive for more than four or five minutes without oxygen carried to it by the blood.

Other organs are not so delicate. Today, in what has become quite a commonplace operation, microsurgeons reattach fingers, hands and complete limbs that have been severed sometimes hours before. Provided the severed part is well preserved – usually it is wrapped in plastic and packed in ice to ensure this – it will eventually recover its functions.

The brain, however, consists of millions of cells, which are constantly active, while we are awake and asleep. The average blood cell has 350 million haemoglobin molecules, each holding four molecules of oxygen. The oxygen helps to provide energy for the chemical reactions of all living cells. If the ever-active brain cells are starved of oxygen, they perish. Because the brain cells are closely linked and interact, when some cells die others are doomed.

Until quite recently, doctors believed that oxygen starvation for just a few minutes would inevitably cause irreparable damage to the brain. A succession of freak survivals, cases in which swimmers were saved from drowning after being apparently dead for half an hour or more, made them revise their theories.

Nearly all these survivals were in cold water. Neurosurgeons know that cold stimulates a reflex action which slows the body's metabolism. In some operations, the body temperature is deliberately reduced for this reason. In the swimmers' case, cold water on their faces triggered the mammalian reflex, as it is known. Their metabolism slowed down, so that the brain and other vital organs needed less oxygen.

As specialists have observed, the brain begins to idle. When this happens, areas of the body such as the limbs give up their oxygen supply so that it can go where it is most wanted. Lifesavers and others should take note that, once the victim's face is out of the water, the mammalian reflex stops. That is why it is essential to start resuscitation immediately.

Why can amputees still feel the limbs they have lost?

Unfortunate people who have lost a limb or even a finger will tell you that they sometimes feel as though the missing part is still there. Some say that they notice this sensation more on a cold day than a warm one.

During World War I, in which many thousands of young men were maimed, it was believed that the sensations of 'phantom limbs' came from the damaged ends of nerves. Sometimes, when army surgeons performed an amputation, they cauterised the nerve ends in the stump of the limb in an effort to kill this unpleasant, lasting and often painful sensation. Such remedies were always unsuccessful. Brain surgeons today know that, if they

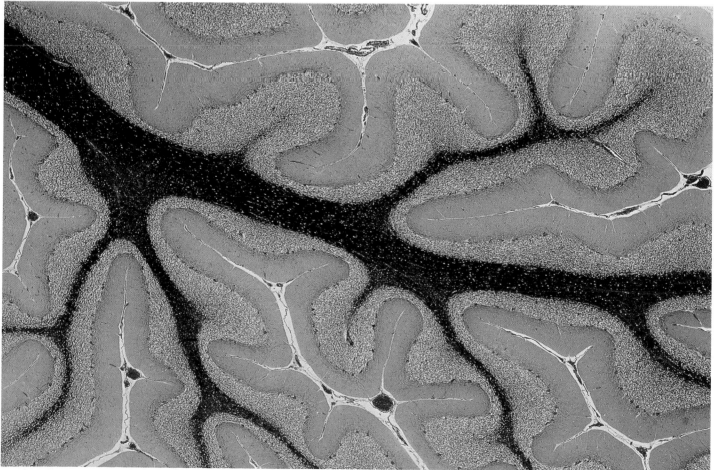

Many everyday actions such as walking a straight line and touching the nose are controlled by the cerebellum, shown here in a micrograph. The cerebellum has a distinctive arrangement of brain cells. A person with a damaged cerebellum cannot do simple things and may seem to be drunk

open the skull and lightly touch the middle of the brain's parietal lobe with a needle, the patient will experience a tingling sensation in a limb. As the needle is moved, similar feelings occur in other parts. It is almost as though the brain's surface carries a sketch plan of the body. The only way to kill the sensation of phantom limbs would be to deal with it at the source – in the brain itself.

Why do tumours attack the brain?

The brain is no more prone to tumours than are the body's other main organs, but when abnormal growths attack the brain they are often difficult to counter.

Not all brain tumours are malignant; in fact, about half, known as primary growths, are benign. But they are all serious. The brain is a compact organ, encased within the skull and without much room to move. If that weren't so, the brain would be under repeated and excessive stress, particularly when we engage in sports and other vigorous activities. A tumour growing in or on the brain causes pressure; brain tissue may be compressed against other tissue, against the various layers of the meningeal membrane or against the skull itself.

At first, a victim may suffer mild headaches. These often become rapidly more severe. Vision may become blurry in one or both eyes, leading to blindness. Sometimes, hearing and sense of smell are lost or change radically. Anybody suffering constant headaches should see a doctor immediately.

A doctor told of these symptoms will give the patient a series of tests, usually of the reflexes and muscles. The doctor can test, but without the benefit of modern diagnostic devices that are available usually only in hospitals he cannot peer into

*A **brain tumour** in a sixteen-year-old girl shows up in computed tomography (CT) scan as a round, blue mass. CT scanning has revolutionised the diagnosis of brain tumours*

the brain. If a tumour is suspected, the patient will need specialist help. In recent years, new techniques, such as magnetic resonance imaging (MRI), have revolutionised examinations of the brain and other organs. An MRI brain scan produces sharp, cross-sectional images that pinpoint abnormalities that would otherwise go undetected.

Once specialists have located a tumour they will decide whether or not it can be removed. In many cases, it can. Two basic problems occur: one is whether the tumour is accessible and can be removed without damaging the brain; the other is whether the tumour is benign or malignant, which nobody can tell for certain until the growth is removed and tested.

Benign growths are usually more clearly defined, and the chances of their successful removal are much higher, especially when on the brain's outer surface. Cancerous growths often extend far into the brain's tissues, and the outlook in these

cases is less hopeful: fewer than one in five patients survive for a year after the diagnosis of this kind of cancer.

Even when growths are inaccessible, methods exist to shrink them. In one, a computer-guided laser needle vaporises the tumour. Others bombard a growth with radiation or antitumour chemicals. Serious as brain tumours undoubtedly are, victims can take hope. Areas of the brain that yesterday were beyond the bounds of surgery have now become routinely accessible.

Why do we talk about brainwaves?

When scientists confirmed some sixty years ago that the brain generates electrical impulses, the term 'brainwave' came into the language. It became common then, as it is now, for somebody to exclaim on getting a bright idea, 'I've had a

***Brainwaves** in their different forms can be detected and recorded. They differ according to our activity but, even when we sleep, the brain is continually at work*

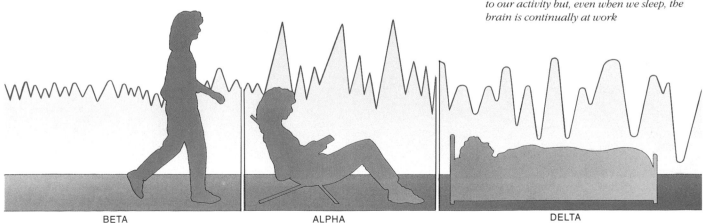

BETA   ALPHA   DELTA

EMERGENCY SIGNALS THAT SWITCH OFF THE BRAIN

It's a common sight at a football match to see a player suffer a severe blow to the head and wander for several minutes in a daze. Spectators remark that the player 'has no idea where he is', and that may indeed be so. He has suffered concussion. According to the blow's severity, it may be mild, with not much more than a view of flashing stars and lights before the eyes, or it may be long lasting.

Severe concussion may cause unconsciousness accompanied by memory loss, or amnesia. The footballer may not recall the injury itself or details of the game. Usually, a bout of amnesia doesn't last long. In any case, somebody suffering a severe head blow should see a doctor to remove doubts about a possible fracture. If amnesia persists for a week or more, specialist help is essential. It could be a sign of serious brain damage.

The brain has an impressive array of defences. It is the body's best-protected organ. First, it is guarded by the skull, the bony skeleton of the head. The skull is extremely strong. That is why most broken skulls are what is known as closed, or simple, fractures, in which the broken pieces stay in place. Depressed fractures, in which the pieces are displaced, are more serious, because fragments may pierce the brain's outer covering. Fortunately, they are more rare.

Inside the skull, the entire brain and the spinal cord are guarded, like delicate instruments in transit, in several layers of packaging. Outside comes the tough and leathery dura mater. Beneath that are two other strong membranes, the arachnoid and pia mater, which are cushioned in fluid.

Despite these safeguards, if the brain receives a severe blow, its regions concerned with memory may be temporarily or permanently damaged. Until normal service resumes, a victim may be unable to store new information.

Amnesia is caused not only by blows but by Alzheimer's disease, encephalitis, strokes and brain tumours. Heavy and persistent drinking also affects the memory, as does the process of growing older.

*A **boxer winces** with pain. The brain is well protected, but permanent damage may result from repeated severe blows*

brainwave'. The brain gives off electrical impulses all the time – not just to applaud brilliance. The heart, too, generates electrical currents, and its output is much stronger than signals from the brain. Specialists record both kinds when studying disorders.

The brain's electrical impulses can be detected and measured by an electroencephalograph, or EEG. The patient has several small electrodes attached to the unshaven scalp. These are connected to instruments that measure and amplify the brain's impulses in a series of painless tests, taking usually about an hour. First, the patient is at rest, eyes open and then closed. Next, reactions are measured while looking at a bright, flashing light. Sometimes, the brain's impulses are recorded while the patient sleeps. An advanced version of the EEG is known as BEAM, for brain electrical activity mapping. With each system, a moving graph records the brainwaves' patterns.

According to their frequency, brainwaves may form a mixture of two to four patterns. When you are relaxed and awake, but with your eyes closed, your brain gives off alpha waves. Beta waves produce a busier pattern, and come when you are active. If tests are performed while you are asleep or anaesthetised (or, in rare circumstances, suffering from severe brain damage), the graph will show a wider-spaced, more regular pattern of delta waves. A similar but more concentrated grouping is made by theta waves, the dominant brainwaves of young children; in adults, they are sometimes a sign of abnormality.

Why does alcohol affect the brain?

Most evidence shows that if alcohol is taken in moderate quantities it does no serious harm to the body. In fact, some studies show that one or two drinks a day could benefit your heart, lowering the risk of coronary heart disease.

Many researchers are reluctant to accept these findings until they are more fully investigated, and point quite rightly to the proven serious damage that alcohol is known to do to many vital organs in the body. It is clearly linked to diseases such as cirrhosis of the liver and to high blood pressure. It is an important factor in thousands of road deaths and industrial accidents, and has costly fallout in a link with domestic violence, hooliganism, marriage breakdown and child abuse.

Alcohol is a drug that acts as a depressant on the central nervous system, lowering its activity. This results in less anxiety, a more relaxed attitude and greater confidence, which is why alcohol fuels so many social functions.

Many people believe that alcohol improves their efficiency. Because they feel more confident, they believe they are more competent. Tests show that any such feelings are illusory. It doesn't take more than one drink to affect our mental and physical skills, particularly those such as driving, which demand good coordination and a sharp mind.

Alcohol acts quickly because it crosses the brain's protective system, known as the blood–brain barrier. The brain depends on a controlled and consistent environment. Many foreign and mildly poisonous substances daily enter the blood stream. If these got into the brain, they would damage it severely. Because

of the blood–brain barrier, chemicals composed of large molecules cannot move from the blood to the brain as they do in many other organs.

These organs have tiny and porous blood vessels. The brain's blood cells are linked so tightly that they are almost fused together. They will keep out large and harmful molecules, but they need to admit the small molecules of oxygen. In doing so, they cannot prevent entry to other substances with small molecules. Alcohol is one of these. If it had larger molecules, it wouldn't get into the brain. It wouldn't relax us and it's almost certain that we wouldn't drink it.

Why do strokes vary in their effects?

A stroke cuts off the blood supply to part of the brain, depriving some tissues of oxygen and nutrients, and swiftly killing them. This may happen through any of

three basic causes. In about half of all strokes, a blood clot builds up on the wall of an artery in the brain, eventually blocking the blood supply. This is known as a cerebral thrombosis. A blood clot swept into an artery, a cerebral embolism, causes another 35 per cent. The rest result when the wall of a blood vessel weakens and expands into a balloonlike mass, known as an aneurysm. This ruptures, causing bleeding within the brain.

Because a stroke damages a specific area of the brain, functions controlled by those brain cells are lost. In one person this may cause a speech impediment, in another sudden blindness, in others paralysis or weakness on one side of the body. The brain is divided into two hemispheres, left and right. If a stroke kills tissue in the left hemisphere, movement on the right side of the body may be affected. A stroke often causes this one-sided paralysis, or hemiplegia.

Sometimes, a stroke's effects last less than a day. Doctors call this a transient ischaemic attack – a TIA. For any victim, it should come as an urgent warning, a signal that must never be ignored.

Strokes are a major killer in developed countries. Often, high blood pressure and atherosclerosis, a narrowing of the arteries, are to blame. Stress, smoking, poor diet and lack of exercise – an unhealthy lifestyle – are usually the original villains.

Why do we get headaches?

From time to time, all of us suffer a headache. Usually, we have a good idea of its cause. We have had a late night, we've drunk too much at a party, we have spent too long in a smoke-filled or badly ventilated room. Perhaps we have worked too hard and too long, straining our eyes to decipher small print, or we have stared for hours at a television screen.

Headaches are associated with the brain, because that's where the pain seems to be. But it's not your brain that is aching. The brain signals trouble in other parts of the body, but it cannot register and tell you about trouble in its own structure. It lacks the sensory nerves to do so. Even when a surgeon cuts into brain tissue, the patient rarely feels pain.

Sensory nerves exist in and around the brain's tissues, membranes and blood cells. Your head throbs, but the trouble isn't necessarily there. What you have is referred pain – the kind that you feel in one place when the problem is somewhere else. Sciatica is a good example. Your backbone pinches the sciatic nerve, but you feel the pain in your legs.

Your headache may come one day from the muscles of the neck, another time

Like a red balloon, a brain aneurysm, shows up in an angiograph. To obtain the image, a special injection is given in an artery, so that the vessel and any flaws will appear in an X-ray

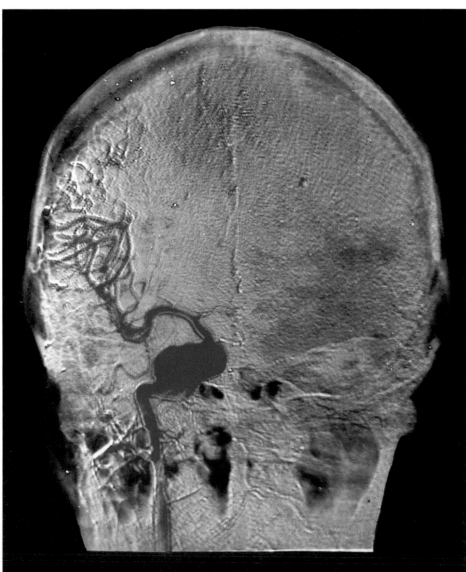

The misery of a headache, as seen by George Cruikshank in an etching of 1819. Some specialists claim that about 70 per cent of all headaches are due to food allergies, with milk, wheat and eggs the main culprits. Migraine headaches cause most grief, and some attacks may last for days

from those in the face or scalp. When muscles are under strain, they will give you a tension headache; if blood vessels dilate, stretching their nerve endings, you may get a vascular headache. Any form of stress that tightens the muscles can bring on a headache. So too, of course, can infection. For many of us, a headache is the first sign of impending flu.

Fortunately, headaches are rarely a sign of serious trouble. And, thanks to aspirin, we can cure them ourselves without visiting the doctor.

Why do doctors tap our knees?

Sometimes when we go into the cold, we shiver uncontrollably. The action is automatic. We don't decide to shiver: like many of our movements shivering is an inborn reflex, which happens without any conscious command.

When the doctor taps your knee with a rubber hammer, he is testing another inborn reflex controlled by the automatic nervous system. The blow stretches a thigh muscle tendon, sending a signal to the spinal cord. It sends back a message that contracts the muscle and jerks the leg upwards. The whole process from start to finish is known as a reflex arc.

If your leg doesn't respond, it may indicate some damage to your nervous

system. The doctor would probably recommend a full neurological examination, in which all or many of your reflexes would be thoroughly tested.

Other reflex tests, which often accompany the knee-tap, include shining a bright light in your eyes to see whether the pupils contract, and irritating the soles of your feet to see if you react by making the toes curl.

When a baby grasps your finger or any other object placed in its palm, it is using what is known as a primitive reflex. If you touch a baby's cheek near the corner of its mouth, it will turn its head and suck your finger, a movement that, when it is feeding, automatically enables it to find the mother's nipple. These are two of several reflex actions performed usually only during the first few months of life. At

some stage in human evolution, these movements were probably necessary for a baby's survival.

Primitive reflex actions indicate that a baby has a healthy nervous system. But if a child continues to show these reflexes after three or four months, a parent should seek specialist advice. The child may be showing a sign of brain damage.

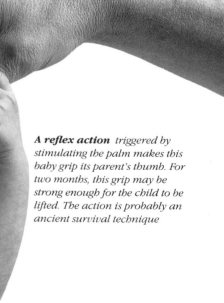

A reflex action triggered by stimulating the palm makes this baby grip its parent's thumb. For two months, this grip may be strong enough for the child to be lifted. The action is probably an ancient survival technique

Getting down to the bare bones

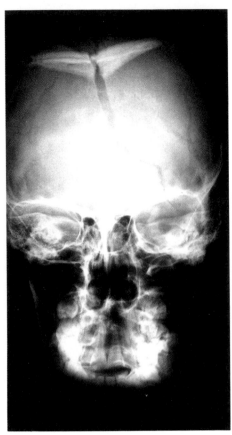

*A **violent blow**, possibly from a hammer or heavy club, caused this severe depression fracture of the skull, revealed by X-ray*

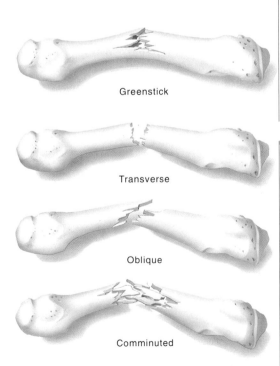

Greenstick

Transverse

Oblique

Comminuted

***Broken bones** are classified by shape. Those in a child will usually knit in just a few weeks, an elderly person's in several months. Arms usually mend more quickly than legs*

Why are some fractures simple and others compound?

A bone fractures for the same reason that anything breaks: the force applied to it is more than it can stand. Sometimes the break is straight across the bone, the broken ends stay more or less in place, and the ends don't penetrate the skin. This is known as a simple fracture. In a compound fracture, one or both ends of the broken bone break through the skin, opening the wound to possible infection.

Within these two classes are several types of fracture. They are classified by their shape, which is usually determined by the kind of force applied in the break. A fierce blow, such as in a car accident, may shatter the bone into several pieces, causing what is known as a comminuted fracture. A sharp, direct blow or constant stress, as from running, may bring a transverse fracture, a straight break that leaves the broken ends out of line. Children sometimes suffer greenstick fractures. A bone bends, breaking only its outer surface – like a green twig that fails to snap cleanly into two pieces.

Because bones start to mend immediately, it is important to get the broken ends together and correctly aligned as soon as possible. Correct first-aid treatment is essential. If the injured person cannot walk, an ambulance and competent medical help should be summoned. Until that arrives, a victim should be moved as little as possible – and not at all if a spinal injury is suspected. No food or drinks should be given in case a general anaesthetic is needed in hospital.

Why do so many of us suffer from backache?

If you get pains in your back, join the world's biggest club! Back problems bring occasional or constant misery to about 80 per cent of the world's population, and for many reasons the toll of victims is steadily rising. In Britain, for example, the number certified by doctors as being unfit for work through back pain has doubled in the past five years.

Even though medical science has made enormous progress in curing many serious ailments, doctors confess that their efforts to ease the world's aching backs have so far had little success.

Back pain is not a disease but a symptom. What makes it so difficult to cure is that, in 90 per cent of cases, it is impossible to pinpoint the cause. In the remainder, the reason for the pain is clearly evident. It comes usually from an injury to the spine or to the muscles supporting it. As a result, one of the discs separating the vertebrae may be dislodged slightly, so that it presses on a nerve.

If this happens in the neck, pain may be felt in the arms. More frequently it occurs in the lower back, causing a variety of aches – at the site, in the buttocks or in the sciatic nerve, which extends down the legs and into the toes. In older people, lower back pain often arises from osteoarthritis of the spine.

Where the cause is evident, doctors have a high success rate, usually by manipulation, physiotherapy or surgery. Some advise rest, warm baths and mild analgesics, such as aspirin. Others argue

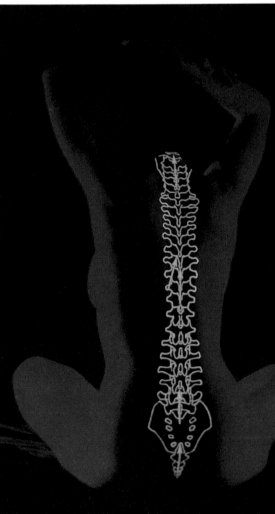

*A **spinal X-ray** is usually the first test that a doctor uses to find the cause of back pain, an increasing problem*

NEW WAYS TO MEND BROKEN BONES

Broken bones mend only if they have an adequate blood supply. For this reason a few of the body's bones will never mend if they break. Sometimes, a broken bone needs encouragement to heal. That is one reason why surgeons graft onto a broken bone a piece of bone taken from another part of the body, usually from the hip or ribs.

The graft, secured with screws or wires, provides a protein that stimulates new growth. Eventually the graft itself dies, but it provides a framework on which new bone can grow. Similarly, when bones have degenerated, surgeons sometimes implant an artificial material, a kind of ceramic, to form a base for natural bone.

The ceramic has one problem: it is not porous, so the new bone has to grow round the implant instead of inside it, which would be more desirable. Now scientists have discovered a natural implant material that is porous, with a structure closely matching that of human bone. It comes from the skeletons of sea creatures – urchins, coral and some algae.

The skeletons are made of calcium carbonate, which would break down in the human body, but they can be converted into chemically stable calcium phosphate. Also, they provide moulds from which to cast an improved form of artificial implants.

Serious fractures, such as this broken head of the thigh bone, or femur, may one day be remedied by an injection of bone-growing compounds. Pins, shown in red, secure the broken head to the long thigh bone

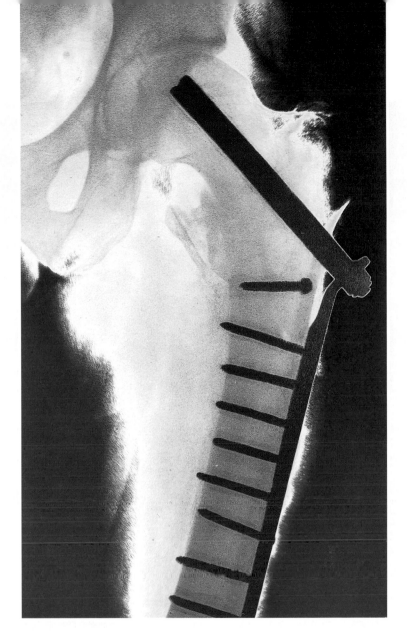

---

that lack of progress in curing backache calls for a more radical treatment – not too much rest and a lot of exercise.

Without doubt, victims of back pain can do much for themselves by getting fit, adopting a healthy, weight-reducing diet and being more active. As some doctors say, exercise may hurt a bit at first, but in the long run it seems to offer more hope of keeping backache under control.

The advice applies not only to those who already have back pain. If you are free of it, you can defend yourself against an attack by getting into shape and learning to use your body properly. Good posture at all times is a major safeguard. It's essential also to learn how to lift. Never bend over to lift heavy objects. Get close to them, slowly bend your knees, keeping your back straight. Let your legs take the strain, not your backbone.

Swimming is a good remedial exercise. If you do breaststroke, glide forward with your face in the water. This avoids arching your back and aggravating the pain.

Why do doctors sometimes take X-rays of sprains?

If you twist your ankle severely, or fall and wrench your wrist, it's likely you will tear some ligaments. These ligaments – the term comes from a Latin word meaning a bond – tie bones into a joint. They can stretch, as they do constantly in normal use, but not too far, nor too suddenly. That is why all those taking part in athletics and sports should first do a few gentle stretching exercises.

Doctors take X-rays when patients complain of a sprain, because the injuries often turn out to be fractures. Ankle sprains are the most common, caused usually by turning over a foot, so that most of the weight falls on to the ankle. Blood rushes to the injury. Synovial fluid, which lubricates the joint, may escape from its capsule. Very quickly, the ankle swells, turning black and blue. The best treatment for a sprain is first to reduce

the swelling with an ice pack. Rest is essential, preferably with the limb raised higher than the head. A firm bandage helps to restrict movement and subsequent pain. Once the swelling subsides, gentle exercise is usually beneficial.

Agony is not necessarily a reliable guide to the severity of a sprain. Perversely, slight sprains in which the ligaments are strained but not torn, sometimes hurt and swell more.

Why do so many people suffer from arthritis?

There is no single disease called arthritis. A reason why so many people say they have arthritis is undoubtedly because collectively they are talking about a number of diseases, which they put under one convenient heading.

Arthritis comes in at least six guises, and includes others, such as gout, which are not always recognised as part of the

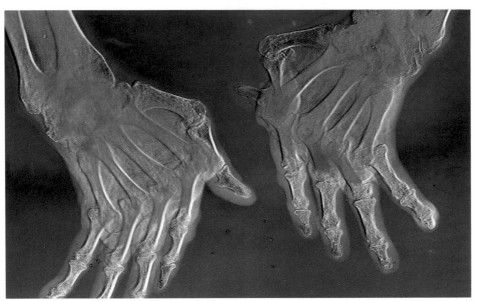

Severe rheumatoid arthritis shows itself in the X-rayed hands of a long-term victim. Some specialists believe that the disease may sometimes be triggered by anxiety and depression

Why do bones get brittle with age?

As we grow older, our bones become thinner. By the age of seventy our total skeleton may have only two-thirds of the density it had in its prime. Calcium is a key factor in bone strength, but the body calls on it also to help blood clot and to make nerves and muscles work efficiently.

For several reasons, the body's calcium supplies fall off as we age. Sometimes, older people pay less attention to their diet, ignoring their needs for calcium, which comes mainly from dairy foods, eggs, leafy vegetables and citrus fruits. As well, they get less exercise; regular, brisk walking – at least three hour-long walks a week – helps to maintain bone density.

To absorb calcium efficiently, the body needs vitamin D. That is why, when doctors recommend calcium tablets, they prescribe also cod-liver oil or some other rich source of the vitamin. Ultraviolet rays in sunshine enable us to make our own vitamin D. Because older people tend to spend more time indoors, they miss out also on this bone-maintenance factor.

When the body runs short of calcium, it draws on stocks held in the bones. That is why bones become thinner and sometimes more porous, a condition known as osteoporosis. The disorder is more common among women, particularly after the menopause. At this time they cease to produce oestrogen, the hormone that helps to form and maintain healthy bones. In the United States, oestrogen-replacement therapy has halved the rate of osteoporosis in older women.

family. The two commonest forms are osteoarthritis, a localised breakdown of one or more joints; and rheumatoid arthritis, a widespread disease affecting many joints and perhaps some body tissues, all at the same time.

Osteoarthritis, which tends to develop later in life, is often painful and debilitating. It results usually from wear and tear, particularly in the weight-carrying joints of the hip, spine and knees. It shows up also in the knobby, gnarled hands of people who have done years of heavy manual work. Loss of cartilage, which cushions healthy joints, causes bone ends to rub together, swelling the area.

So far, doctors have found no way to prevent osteoarthritis. Its effects can be minimised by rest, combined with moderate exercise, such as swimming, in which the body is supported by water. Weight reduction helps to ease the strain on the spine, hips and legs.

Rheumatoid arthritis, no less painful, sometimes strikes quite suddenly, affecting younger people and more women than men. Inflammation starts the problem. The synovial membrane lining the joint becomes raw, and swells. The inflammation spreads to the cartilage and other connective tissue. Unfortunately, it doesn't stop there. In severe cases, rheumatoid arthritis reaches the arteries, internal organs, the neck, shoulders and even the eyes.

Evidence suggests that the disorder runs in families. The course of the disease is often quite difficult to predict, because symptoms flare up suddenly and often vanish for years without evident cause. Effective management of persistent rheumatoid arthritis calls for a carefully

integrated program of therapeutic exercises, warm compresses, relaxation and appropriate medication.

The third most common form of arthritis, known as ankylosing spondylitis, is an inflammatory disorder of the spine. In general, it strikes young men in their twenties and thirties, who may have inherited a susceptibility to the disease. Doctors believe that a bowel infection sometimes triggers the initial inflammation, which affects tissues tying the vertebrae together. Treatment aims at keeping the spine flexible. If it is delayed, the entire spine may stiffen, causing the victim to have a permanent stoop.

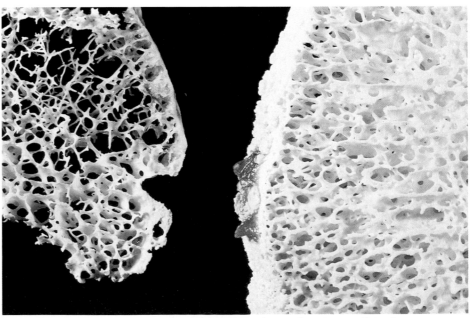

Lack of calcium may weaken bones, causing them to become lacy in a condition known as osteoporosis (left). Older women are at risk and may need to supplement their diets

Dire diseases and minor ailments

Sneezes spread diseases *over a considerable area. Each sneeze contains some 5000 droplets which, unless stopped by a handkerchief, can travel rapidly across a room*

colds, and give out more viruses. Among all the countermeasures, two hold out promise. The drug interferon, which the body produces naturally in response to viral infections, has had some success in preventing colds and reducing their severity; and synthetic antigens, which trigger an immune response, also have proved effective in tests.

Until science finds an answer, if it ever does, we can all take some sensible precautions. Regular handwashing prevents the transfer of germs. So does isolation. We'd all have fewer colds if those who got them kept clear of others, and always masked their coughs and sneezes.

Why do we sneeze if we look at the Sun?

Any irritation in the nasal passages usually brings on a sneeze. The irritant may be dust or pepper, or a kind of pollen to which a person may be allergic. Occasionally, the nose becomes blocked by mucus, and the body reacts involuntarily to clear it. A sneeze forces air from the nose and mouth, and with luck gets rid of whatever is causing the annoyance.

If we look up at the Sun, the increased intensity of the light reaching our eyes causes a high-frequency electrical signal to run through the optical nerves. The nasal nerves, which are close by, pick up some of this electrical impulse. They send a signal to the brain, which triggers the same response as would an irritation in the nasal cavity. The result: a sneeze.

Why is flu more dangerous than a cold?

Flu, more properly called influenza, is a disease caused by three basic viruses, known as A, B and C. In general, an infection from type A is more severe than B, and B is more debilitating than C. People with a C-type infection may believe they have only a cold: the two illnesses are almost impossible to distinguish.

Whenever we get a dose of flu, our bodies develop antibodies that protect us against that particular virus for life. One dose of C-type flu means we will never get another, because this virus is stable. Unfortunately, A and B types produce new strains of virus, which can penetrate our immune defences. And some of these invaders are extremely virulent.

The A type is particularly dangerous, because it constantly changes its form. The Spanish flu pandemic that began in 1918, the last year of World War I, killed an estimated twenty million people worldwide. The outbreaks of Asian flu

Why can't we cure the common cold?

Year by year over the centuries no ailment has caused such general misery as the common cold. Certainly, at times more devastating diseases have hit the human race, but for sheer persistence and nuisance value the cold outstrips all other afflictions. Studies show that schoolchildren may get ten colds a year; young adults, particularly parents, average two or three.

Countless weapons have been used to defend humanity against the cold. The Greeks tried blood-letting. The Roman historian Pliny the Younger advocated kissing the hairy muzzle of a mouse. For more than forty years, from 1946 to 1990, relays of volunteers endured ten days' isolation in the Common Cold Unit in Wiltshire, England, willingly catching colds in bids to help scientists find an answer. The unit shut down for lack of funds before they did.

In all these efforts, we have won a few battles. We know that we aren't fighting

just one cunning guerrilla but an elusive army. That is, without doubt, the prime reason for our failure to win the war. Common colds are caused by any one of almost 200 viruses, which attack the mucous membranes lining the nose and throat. Soon, the nose runs, the throat gets sore and the head may ache.

A cold virus spreads usually by water vapour in the breath. That's why we tend to get more colds in winter when we are shut inside, and why those mixing with others are more regular victims than those living or working alone. Hand-to-hand contact spreads cold germs, which may be picked up too from door handles, hand towels and other contaminated objects. The British unit discovered that cold doesn't start colds. Volunteers given wet feet, hosed with cold water or left in draughty corridors got no more colds than those kept warm and cosy.

Evidence shows that as we grow older we become immune to a wide variety of viruses that may give us colds. For that reason, children have more colds than adults, and some elderly adults suffer no colds at all. Introverts get more severe

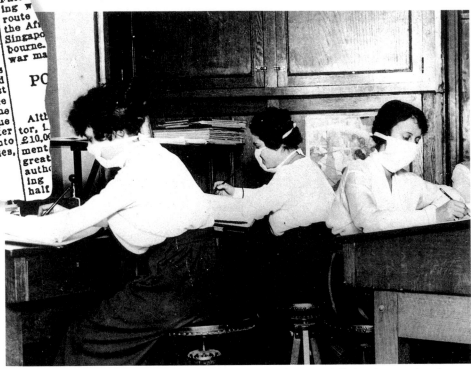

INFLUENZA'S HEAVY TOLL.

The Medical Research Committee reports that since the armistice influenza has killed more young people than the total lives lost on the battlefields. The British insurance companies lost many millions sterling, and the country lost much more in the economic value of the victims. The committee urges greater financial assistance to enable research into the causes of cancer, influenza, measles, mumps, and scarlet fever.

COAL-TRIMMERS' HIGH

in 1957 and Hong Kong flu in 1968 also were A-type infections. The B-type virus changes less often, but alters enough to cause trouble.

Flu is more dangerous than a cold because the A and B types pack some extra punches. One is their ability to bring crushing fatigue. As well, they induce fevers reaching to 40°C (104°F) and higher. The very young, the elderly and those with heart or respiratory problems are especially at risk.

More people died *in the influenza pandemic of 1918–19 than were killed in the preceding four years of World War I. Flu deaths totalled more than twenty million, twice those of the war. Women clerks in New York wore masks for protection, as did many workers worldwide*

Why is German measles so dangerous in pregnancy?

German measles, or rubella, is a mild disease when compared with measles. Many children get it and don't even know. The diseases are similar because they both cause a rash and a fever, but there the comparisons end. Measles is a dangerous disease; German measles is not – except when a woman contracts it in the first four months of her pregnancy. The earlier she gets rubella, the greater the danger to her child. Records show that miscarriage is a great possibility.

If rubella affects the child, the infant may suffer any one of a range of severe birth defects, known as rubella syndrome. Deafness is the most likely. Heart disease, brain damage, eye defects and bone problems are others. About one-fifth of affected children live only a few years.

Rubella is a viral disease, and is not easily detected, because several illnesses produce similar symptoms. Only laboratory tests can diagnose rubella with any certainty. Anybody with suspected rubella has a duty to avoid contact with other people until the disease is identified.

In many countries, vaccination programs provide long-lasting immunity, as does infection. Rubella doesn't strike the same person twice. A woman who plans to become pregnant but has not had rubella should seek immunisation. A pregnant woman who believes she has contracted the disease should consult her doctor immediately.

Why do stones form in the kidneys and bladder?

Most stones that grow in our kidneys, ureter and bladder are so small that they move harmlessly from our bodies. Others, 25 mm (1 in) or more in diameter, can bring intense pain. Even tiny stones sometimes cause agonising discomfort because they may be very sharp.

Some people, because of their lifestyle and diet, are troubled particularly by stones. Those who become regularly dehydrated by doing hard physical work,

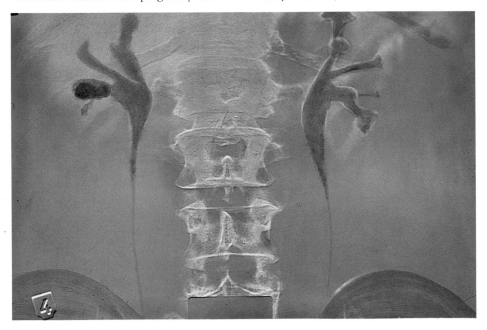

A kidney stone *shows up as an orange mass on the left of this X-ray image, which is obtained by giving the patient a special injection. Kidney stones can be painful, but new techniques remove them without surgery*

or who live in a tropical climate, are likely victims. Everywhere, the chances of men getting stones are estimated to be three times those of women. Large stones, which in the bladder may weigh as much as 1.5 kg (3.3 lb), often take years to develop; others form within a few weeks.

In most cases, doctors cannot identify a specific cause, but they can point to common factors. Stones occur more frequently during summer months, probably because more fluid is lost as sweat, and the urine becomes more concentrated. People who drink more water – eight large glasses is recommended as a daily intake – tend to get fewer stones.

Kidney stones are made up of calcium oxalate and/or phosphate. Calcium is part of a healthy diet, abundant in dairy foods and citrus fruits. Oxalate occurs naturally in urine, but rhubarb, spinach, leafy vegetables, chocolate and coffee, all of which are high in oxalic acid, may increase its level in the body.

Fortunately, modern techniques, ranging from lasers to shock waves, can dissolve or remove stones without the need for open surgery.

Why does too much laughter give us hiccups?

Doctors say it isn't laughter that causes hiccups but more probably the feasting that goes with the fun. Too much food and drink may irritate the diaphragm, a sheetlike muscle separating the chest and the abdomen. The victim loses control of the diaphragm, which contracts suddenly and causes a rapid closure of the vocal chords. The result is a loud and sometimes embarrassing *hic*.

Many attacks of hiccups (or hiccoughs) have no identifiable cause. Unless they are frequent or persistent, they are of no concern. In rare cases, hiccups may last for years. An American, Charles Osborne of Anthon, Iowa, is on record as the world's longest and most unfortunate victim. He started to hiccup in 1922 at forty *hics* a minute and continued for sixty-nine years.

Inevitably to every person who gets hiccups comes a variety of suggested cures. Holding the breath has a sound medical basis. Carbon dioxide, which we exhale when we breathe, inhibits hiccups. By holding the breath we build up carbon dioxide in our system. Most other successful remedies, such as breathing in and out of a paper bag, employ the same principle. Never use a plastic bag in this way. To do so is dangerous, especially for children.

Why are athletes banned if they take steroids?

Steroid drugs resemble hormones produced normally in the body. Anabolic steroids, those taken by some sportsmen and women, copy the effects of testosterone, the male sex hormone. In addition to stimulating male sexual development, testosterone promotes bone and muscle growth.

Some sports competitors – especially

Bodybuilders sometimes take steroid drugs to increase their muscle development. Hard training, particularly with heavy weights, rapidly builds muscle and strength. But the taking of steroids also imperils health

weightlifters and athletes in field events such as the shot put and hammer throw – took anabolic steroids to boost their strength and to speed recovery from injury. The drugs were widely abused, with great risks to health, because they can have serious side effects. Abuse of steroids damages the liver and the adrenal glands, and renders men impotent and infertile. Women who dose themselves with these male sex hormones become more masculine; their voices deepen, hair grows excessively on the body but may vanish from the scalp.

Sports administrators outlawed steroids basically for two reasons. Competitors who use them put their health seriously at risk. Also they are taking an unfair advantage, one that can be matched only by rivals who are prepared to imperil their own health.

Why do drivers fall asleep at the wheel?

It's difficult to prove, but worldwide research suggests that thousands of people die every year because drivers fall asleep. Researchers base their hunches partly on the number of accidents involving only one driver. The car hits a tree or the central barrier or runs over an embankment, with no skidmarks on the road. A feature of many unexplained accidents is that they happen on straight roads and in good conditions.

A report published in 1988 concluded that 13 per cent of America's 50 000 annual road deaths result from sleeping drivers. British studies show that, between 4 am and 6 am, a driver is about ten times as likely to nod off and crash as

Drivers falling asleep cause thousands of accidents every year. Doctors say that all motorists should beware of driving in the early morning and early afternoon, times when our body clock tells us to sleep. Stop, Revive and Survive is a wise message

at any other time of day. Late afternoon is another danger period.

Your inner clock, which automatically controls many body functions, urges you to sleep twice a day – at night and in the early afternoon. The desire for an afternoon nap is not brought on by eating lunch, but drinking alcohol may increase it. In many societies, people quite sensibly take a siesta: it's not an indulgence but a natural response.

Many sleep-related accidents involve truck drivers. In most countries, the law restricts the number of hours they may drive. But it doesn't control the times of day at which they drive and, even if it wanted to, it cannot insist that they get sound sleep. Researchers give this picture of a typical sleep-related accident. A truck driver rises in the early morning, helps to load his vehicle, and sets off three or four hours later. He drives for three or four hours, delivers his load, and waits while the truck is reloaded. He drives for two hours and rests for two hours. He completes his driving time and at 10 pm – sixteen hours after going to his depot that day – sleeps in his truck in an offroad bay. He wakes not when he wants to but when other truck drivers take to the road. Unable to sleep any longer, he drives off, planning to finish early and head for home. In those danger hours of the early morning, he falls asleep at the wheel.

Truck drivers aren't the only sleepy drivers. If the same law controlled all drivers, many would be in breach of it. Any motorist who drives for too long and after too little rest is at risk. Motorways combine two hazards: they are built for high speeds and their monotony encourages drowsiness. Once drowsiness sets in, a driver's eyes will eventually close, no matter how wide the windows are open and how loudly the radio plays.

The lesson for us all is never to drive for too long without taking an adequate break. Share the driving if you can. Avoid those danger times, especially if you haven't had a good night's sleep.

Why does car travel make some people sick?

The symptoms are familiar enough. You are driving your car and, after thirty minutes or so, a passenger feels dizzy, complains of a headache and nausea. At first, you may think your companion has food poisoning, but the malady is motion sickness, and it may linger on throughout the journey, sometimes without any vomiting.

Doctors are puzzled about why some people are so susceptible and others are never affected. Drivers are less likely to feel sick, but back-seat passengers, particularly children, are more frequent victims than those in front.

Researchers have discovered that motion sickness is caused by a temporary disturbance in what is known as the vestibular membranous labyrinth. This is part of the intricate series of structures of the inner ear, and helps to maintain the body's equilibrium. If the labyrinth becomes overloaded with information from the eyes and other senses, it can trigger a sudden desire to vomit. A few other factors, particularly anxiety about the possibility of an attack, also may play a part.

Most sailors and small-boat fishermen know that seasickness, which is similar to car sickness and occurs even on gentle seas, can sometimes be avoided by regularly switching the vision from sea to horizon, to objects at short range and those farther off.

That probably explains why car drivers aren't usually affected and why back-seat passengers often are. Those in the back seat have less opportunity for changing their view. If the front seats are occupied, other passengers may see only through the side windows, where the scenery flashes past and the brain's labyrinth has more information to process. Those in front have a panoramic, more stable and slower-moving scene.

Motion sickness was a major problem during World War II. Seaborne troops landing on beaches would sometimes be too sick to fight. Researchers developed a successful drug based on atropine but, like some remedies available now, it often caused intense drowsiness.

If you are taking a long car journey and suffer motion sickness, ask your doctor to prescribe a suitable medicine. Sit in the front seat. Stop once an hour to stretch your legs and breathe the outside air. Wear warm clothes. Keep a window slightly open. Do not try to read. If you are travelling with children, seat them where they can look out of a window.

From time to time, devices are marketed to counteract motion sickness. Some motorists suspend a leather or plastic strap beneath the car, and swear that it counteracts nausea. Many sailors wear an elastic band round the wrist; two metal balls on the band press on acupuncture points, supposedly preventing seasickness on the roughest oceans.

Researchers can find no sound reason to promote such aids – except the proven one that, if you believe they will work, they undoubtedly will. Optimism for yourself and other passengers is a sound approach. Car sickness is by no means inevitable.

Motion sickness poses a major problem for astronauts, because the inner ear relies on gravity to give us our sense of up and down. In the Vomit Comet, a simulator that includes a space shower, American trainee astronauts experience weightlessness, or zero-gravity, for about thirty seconds

Winning the fight against cancer

Of all the diseases that may afflict us, none is more feared than cancer. In the past two decades medical science has made enormous progress in unravelling the mysteries of cancer and in treating it. And yet, even though a patient's chances of surviving are greater today than they have ever been, the death toll from cancer continues to rise. It is much higher than it was forty years ago.

That, strangely, is a sign of our improving health. Life expectancy today is higher. Many diseases that in the past were often fatal – cholera, malaria, poliomyelitis, typhoid, pneumonia – no longer hold such dangers in the world's developed countries. Because more of us are living longer, we expose ourselves in our sixties and seventies to attack from heart disease and strokes, today's major killers, and to any of the wide variety of cancers.

Most people fear cancer more than they do a heart attack or a stroke, because they mistakenly believe that death is inevitable. Certainly, the death rate from cancer is still high, accounting for at least 20 per cent of deaths in the United States, in Britain and many parts of Europe. But about 40 per cent of the million Americans and the 220 000 Britons who are diagnosed each year as having cancer get early treatment and live for many years after it; many of them are fully cured.

One reason why cancer is so feared is because it takes so many forms. It is not one disease but more than 100, all having a common factor. Most people know that there are two forms of tumour, or abnormal growth of tissue. One is benign and grows slowly. Its main distinction is that, once formed, it stays where

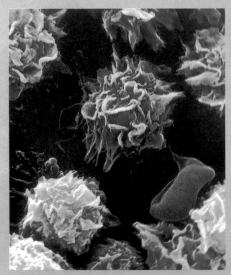

Tell-tale signs of hairy-cell leukaemia show in a blood test. The crinkly balls are diseased lymphocytes, a type of white blood cell that is important in the body's immune system

it is. In all cancers, malignant tumours sometimes grow rapidly, and they spread, affecting not only healthy tissues nearby but often invading vital parts of the body, such as the lungs, breasts and stomach. Sometimes, they do this by what doctors call metastasis. Cancer cells break away from the original growth, and travel in the blood stream. Or they may invade the lymphatic system which, among a range of jobs, defends us against bacteria. Once into either of these two conveyors the errant cells may attack parts of the body far from the original site.

Why this happens is not fully understood, but it may be because of a predisposition, an inherited susceptibility, to the disease. That doesn't mean that cancer itself is inherited. Because one of your relatives had cancer is no reason for believing that you will inevitably get it.

All of us have some 50 000 or more separate genes that determine every facet of our make-up. It seems that some of these – perhaps no more than 100 – begin to malfunction. These genes, known as oncogenes, control cell growth and multiplication. Suddenly, some cells grow abnormally and multiply uncontrollably. Eventually there's no room for normal cells alongside these mavericks. The normal cells get crowded out and replaced. If that happens swiftly, the attack is severe. Usually, it occurs more slowly and gives early warning signs.

From our increasing knowledge of the disease we know that a trigger of some kind can in some circumstances propel the wayward cells into action. These triggers, known as carcinogens, do not necessarily cause the disease, and that is one of its puzzles. For example, tobacco smoke is a recognised carcinogen, but everybody knows a heavy smoker who survives to old age without getting lung cancer. On the other hand, for every defiant, elderly smoker there are dozens who have had their lives cut

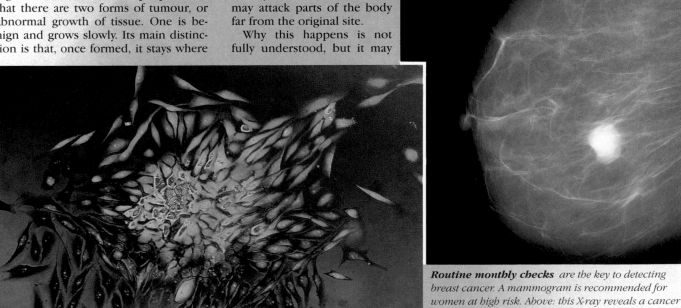

Routine monthly checks are the key to detecting breast cancer. A mammogram is recommended for women at high risk. Above: this X-ray reveals a cancer as a small white circle. A culture of breast-cancer cells (left) shows them gradually spreading outwards

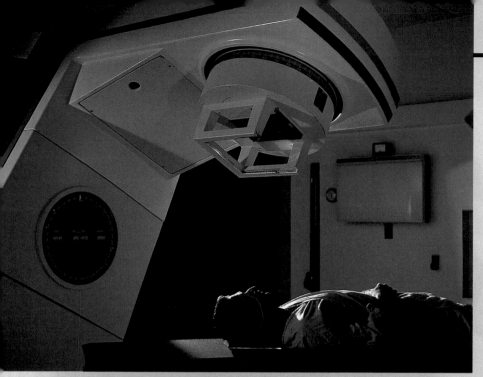

A remarkable weapon in the fight against cancer uses energy that can cause cancer. A linear accelerator treats a cancer patient by radiotherapy. The treatment tries to ensure that maximum damage is done to the cancer, while minimising the risk to healthy tissues

short. Doctors say that genetic make-up, which is inherited, explains why a carcinogen sets off cancer in some people but not in others.

As research continues, medical scientists identify more cancer triggers. We know that radioactive chemicals are high on the list, as the grim evidence from Chernobyl continues to tell us. So are other forms of radiation, such as from X-rays and the Sun. The list includes chemicals found in pesticides, industrial waste, car exhausts, building materials such as asbestos and fibreglass wool, and processed foods.

Sexual behaviour affects a woman's chances of getting cervical cancer: the more partners, the higher the risk. And having children while relatively young seems to reduce the chances of breast cancer. Chronic irritation may be another trigger. For example, ill-fitting dentures are blamed for some mouth and lip cancers.

Because, as each year goes by, we can point to an increasing list of cancer triggers, our defences against this range of diseases constantly grow. We know that smoking is a major cause (not only of cancer but of cardiovascular diseases also). About 30 per cent of all cancer victims are smokers.

If the smoker is also a heavy drinker, the risk rises not only for lung cancer but other cancers. Tests show that such a person is forty-four times more likely to get cancer of the oesophagus than somebody who drinks the same amount but smokes ten or fewer cigarettes a day. Smoking carries lung-cancer dangers not only for the smoker. Studies show that nonsmokers are forced every day to breathe a dangerous cocktail of chemicals in areas polluted by tobacco smoke. Around the world it is believed that thousands of nonsmokers die from cancer caused by passive smoking, the inhalation of tobacco smoke. Thus, banning smoking in public places and encouraging smokers to stop are two clear-cut ways to reduce cancer.

Sound diet is another. Studies suggest that food – too much of some things and too little of others – is a contributing factor in 35 per cent of all fatal cancers. Because the range of foods and food additives is so vast, it is almost impossible to pinpoint specific culprits. However, fatty meats, oils and dairy products appear to increase the risk of cancer in the breast, the stomach and colon. The intake of all preserved foods – smoked, pickled and salted – also should be limited.

More positively, some foods seem to offer protection. Fibre-rich foods, such as whole-grain cereals, fruits and vegetables, insure against bowel cancer. People who get plenty of vitamins A and C, which are abundant in spinach, capsicums, Brussels sprouts and broccoli, appear to get fewer cancers of the respiratory and digestive systems.

We know, too, that the incidence of skin cancers rises with increasing exposure to the Sun. About 20 per cent of residents in Queensland, Australia, will suffer some form of skin cancer by the age of seventy-five, the world's highest incidence. Residents in the southeastern and southwestern United States run them a close second. Sensible precautions – wearing a hat, using effective sunscreens, less sunbathing – will undoubtedly cut the toll.

Prevention is clearly the most sensible course. But cancers range so widely that many cannot be avoided. The second smart strategy is early detection. Screening tests for cervical, breast and intestinal cancers, for example, have now significantly reduced the death rate from these diseases.

Cancer gives many warning signs. Sudden loss of weight, sores or ulcers that fail to heal within a normal time, recurrent hoarseness, persistent pain of any kind, a lump or swelling, any discharge of blood … all these are signals that should send a victim to a doctor.

Today, almost half of all cancers can be cured completely. The range of treatments grows constantly wider and more effective. But improved therapy gets its best chance when coupled with early detection. In using that defence and in taking intelligent preventive measures, all of us are our own best doctors.

Constant exposure to radioactivity in her work gave Marie Curie leukaemia from which she died. Her research brought the world invaluable tools for treating cancer

Why is exercise essential to good health?

One remarkable change in recent years is that millions of people worldwide spend several hours a week in vigorous exercise. Ask any jogger the reason for running a considerable distance, come rain or shine, and the answer almost certainly will be: 'It makes me feel so good.'

Exercise of this kind, which makes the heart and lungs work harder, undoubtedly has a euphoric effect – provided, of course, that the program has a doctor's approval. Jogging, cycling, swimming and fast walking, all of which work the heart and lungs, are known as aerobic exercises. They force the cardiovascular system to deliver more blood and oxygen to feed the increased needs of the muscles. The heart eventually becomes more efficient, delivering more blood and oxygen with each stroke.

A slow heart rate is often a sign of long-term athletic activity. A world-class runner may have a heart beat as low as forty strokes a minute, less than half the average. If the heart beats more slowly and more efficiently, wear and tear on it and the arteries are clearly reduced. As disorders of the cardiovascular system head the list of fatal diseases in many countries, any move to cut their toll is beneficial. Because the heart pumps harder during

exercise, the blood surges through the arteries. This, say some doctors, discourages plaque, a substance that coats the artery walls, hindering the blood flow and often causing heart attacks. Exercise may stimulate the brain to release endorphins, painkillers with a similar structure to morphine. As well as their analgesic effect, endorphins are believed to help control stress and mood. This may explain why so many people feel better mentally after a work-out: it isn't, as cynics claim, an overdose of superiority complex.

Exercise helps to build bones and improves the muscles. Stronger bones ward off the dangers of the degenerative condition known as osteoporosis. A larger muscle is more efficient, more flexible and produces more energy. Better muscles help us to work with less fatigue.

A range of other exercises – isometric, isotonic and isokinetic – strengthen the muscles and make the body more supple.

Why is Aids such a worldwide threat?

Aids, an acronym for acquired immune deficiency syndrome, was first recognised in 1981. Medical scientists at the Centers for Disease Control in Atlanta, Georgia, USA, investigated reports of a rare lung infection, first seen among homosexual men in Los Angeles and later among

others in New York. Their illness resulted from an organism that had already caused pneumonia in people whose natural immune system, which guards us against disease, had failed to function.

In the following years a range of what are called opportunistic infections was reported. These infections are of a kind that do not normally trouble people with efficient immune systems. The victims were not all homosexuals; they included people injecting drugs into their veins, and haemophiliacs who had received blood transfusions. Scientists deduced that the disease was transmitted not only by sexual activity but also by exchanging blood. Within a few months of each other in 1983 and 1984, French and American researchers identified a virus that was later named HIV, for human immuno-deficiency virus.

We know now that a twenty-five-year-old former sailor who died mysteriously in Manchester, England, in 1959 was the first recorded Aids victim. Puzzled doctors preserved tissue from his kidney, bone marrow and spleen. In 1990, analysis showed that he had died of Aids. Already, the disease has claimed half a million victims in a total of 168 countries.

The HIV virus attacks a white blood cell that is essential in controlling our defence mechanism against disease. Not everybody who is infected by HIV gets Aids. In some, the virus lies dormant; others suffer slight fevers, weight loss, a vague feeling of being 'off colour'. The unfortunate victims in whom the virus causes Aids may get any of a variety of infections and cancers. Anybody losing weight unexplainedly or whose lymph glands swell may have HIV. A test for HIV involves checking the blood for antibodies to the virus. A positive result is always re-checked. A negative test does not necessarily rule out HIV: it may mean that it is too early to tell. If the suspected victim is in a high-risk group, another test will be held within about six months.

One reason why Aids is such a worldwide health danger is that medical scientists have not yet found a cure or produced a vaccine. Another is that HIV spreads in so many ways. For personal safety and to encourage compassion for the thousands of victims, we should all try to understand the disease.

HIV is transmitted in eight basic ways. Some 80 per cent of recorded cases arose from homosexual or bisexual activity. Another 8 per cent of victims received infected blood in transfusions. An additional 2 per cent were drug users who shared needles. Recently, Aids has increased significantly among heterosexual men and women. This has resulted in some infected women passing the disease

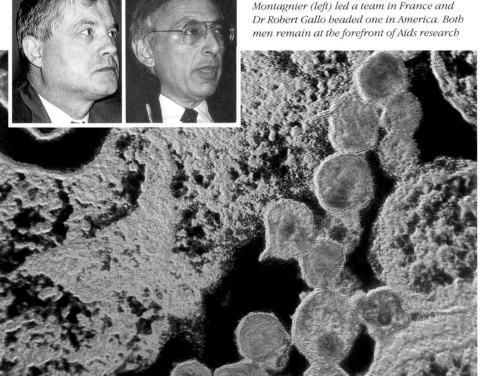

Two teams discovered the HIV virus, shown magnified in orange below. Professor Luc Montagnier (left) led a team in France and Dr Robert Gallo headed one in America. Both men remain at the forefront of Aids research

BATTLERS WHO BEAT DISEASE

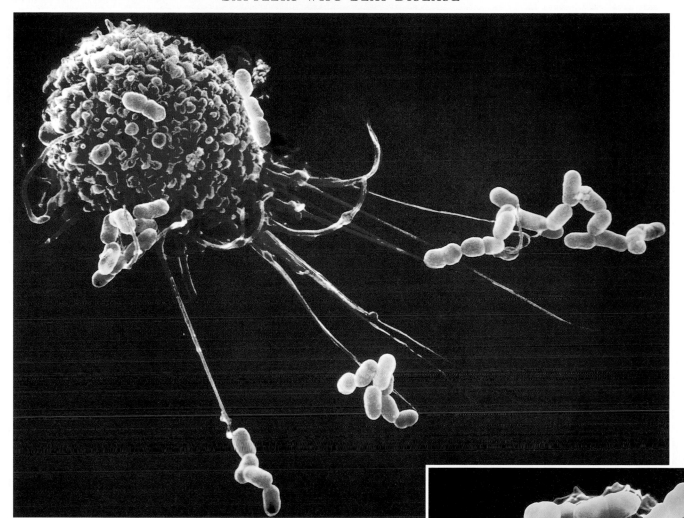

The brain and the body's immune system, which protects us against disease, are closely linked. An American team of researchers discovered this in 1984 through a remarkable series of laboratory experiments in which mice were taught how to strengthen their immune defences.

First, the mice were injected with a drug to enhance the activity of their natural killer cells, the immune system's warriors that deal with unwanted foreign invaders, such as viruses. Simultaneously, the mice were exposed to the smell of camphor. Later, when the mice smelled camphor but were not drugged they bolstered their immune defences.

Other researchers found that the brain and immune system communicate through hormones called thymosins and other factors in the blood. The importance of the work is that it uncovers the mechanism of something that doctors have long known, but could not explain: why people who refuse to give in to disease enhance considerably their prospects for eventual recovery.

It may show also why others are illness-prone. Mental stress plays havoc with immune systems. Blood tests of students during exam week showed that their ability to make interferon, a natural protein that counters viral infection, declined drastically. A study of 117 victims of malignant melanomas recorded that forty of them were given identical medical prognoses. In just over two years, twenty of these had died. All had shown more distress, dejection and anxiety about their malignancy than the twenty who lived.

Warning signals *in the body's natural defence system trigger a macrophage, part of our immune system, to act. The cell extends several pseudopods to engulf and digest any debris washing into the blood stream. Two steps in an attack on bacteria are shown, with (inset) their final absorption*

to their babies. In rare cases, people have contracted HIV or Aids by accident – for example, through treading on an infected needle.

Just as it is important to know how HIV is transmitted, it is necessary to know how it is not. Shaking hands with a sufferer will not give you Aids. Nor will kissing without exchanging saliva. Aids cannot be caught from toilet seats, or by sharing eating and drinking utensils. In most countries today, doctors taking blood or giving transfusions are well aware of the need for sterile implements.

Until scientists find a cure or a vaccine, prevention is the best safeguard against Aids. In that, safe-sex techniques head the list.

Why do we need a nose?

Of all the body's sense organs, the nose gets the scantiest regard. We worry about our eyes and ears – indeed, millions of people seek attention for them – but we tend to take our noses for granted. Eyes, ears and lips are the stuff of poetry: the nose is kept to the grindstone.

Maybe all that is because the nose causes so little trouble, and functions almost perfectly long after we are wearing glasses and perhaps a hearing aid. Every day, the average nose cleans and conditions about 15 cu m (530 cu ft) of air, enough to fill a small room. Whether the day is freezing cold or fiercely hot, this neat little air conditioner delivers air at about the same temperature of 35°C (95°F) and suitably humidified, about 80 per cent saturated.

Office air conditioners are notorious for supplying bacteria-laden air. Our nostrils

*A **perfume tester** assesses some of the 4000 odours that humans can readily detect*

When Father snores, everybody in the family goes sleepless, according to a cartoon from early this century. Surveys show that one person in five snores, and most snorers are men

screen out impurities before they can reach the lungs. That is why doctors and wise parents urge children to develop the habit of breathing through the nose and not the mouth. The nose filters air in a two-part process. First, a barrier of stiff hairs just inside the nose traps larger particles of grit and pollen. If the invader is particularly offensive, it may be ejected forcibly by triggering a sneeze.

Anything that beats the first defences meets a tougher enemy, the mucous membrane, which acts like a kind of fly-paper. To provide moisture for the air and a sticky mucus to coat the membrane, the nose secretes nearly a litre (about a quart) of moisture a day. The sticky mucus catches the bacteria, and kills them with an enzyme called lysozyme. This same agent protects our eyes from infection and makes breast milk so safe for infants.

To keep the flypaper fresh and sticky, the nose produces a fresh batch of mucus every twenty minutes. An army of microscopic brooms – fine hairs known as cilia – poke through the mucus coating and, with up to 1000 strokes a minute, sweep the old mucus to the throat. The debris goes into the stomach, where digestive juices destroy most of the bacteria.

Normally, the cilia keep the mucus moving at about 6 mm (¼ in) a minute. Smoking and drinking alcohol to excess will slow down the flow, weakening the body's defences against airborne disease.

In addition to its major role as an air conditioner, the nose gives the voice resonance. And it identifies a smell – on average, about 4000 different scents. A really sensitive nose, developed often by somebody born blind and deaf, can detect some 10 000 separate odours.

Why do so many people snore in their sleep?

The first thing a man learns after he is married, says an unknown wit, is that he snores. For all the disharmony it brings, snoring is surprisingly a neglected problem. Millions snore, and millions more are forced to listen. The snores of one man registered 87 decibels, twice as loud as normal conversation and equivalent to having a pneumatic drill operating all night in the street outside.

People who snore sleep with their mouths open. An obstruction in the nasal passages or in the throat, caused perhaps by a cold or an allergy, is sometimes to blame. More often, snoring starts through sleeping on the back.

In this position, the lower jaw drops open. Also, the tongue no longer lies flat in the mouth, but partially closes the windpipe. In breathing through the mouth, the intake of air vibrates the soft palate and the uvula, the fleshy muscle that hangs like a pendulum in the back of the throat. In the past, doctors cured severe cases of snoring by amputating the uvula.

If you are concerned about your snoring, sew something, such as a tennis ball, to your pyjamas to make it uncomfortable to sleep on your back. Two exercises can help: before going to sleep, clench a pencil between your teeth for ten minutes; press your tongue firmly against your lower teeth for about two minutes. Both exercises are aimed at keeping your mouth shut.

If you are worried about your partner's snoring, try ear plugs or separate rooms.

The stuff of our wildest dreams

Why do we have dreams and nightmares?

Nothing in our lives is stranger than the fantasies created in our dreams. Some of them are delightful, with all the joy and romance that have inspired poets since ancient times. We wake up sorry to find that we have been dreaming.

Other dreams are so bizarre that we are baffled: people appear who have been out of our thoughts for years; other characters are a composite of two or more acquaintances; decades become muddled; we do things we would never dare to do in real life.

Another kind of dream solves a problem. We see where a lost object is located. We get the answer to a tricky office matter or to some difficulty in arrangement or design. The solution comes in a miraculous flash of wisdom – and we remember it gratefully when we wake up.

In other dreams we find ourselves in hopeless situations: doors are shut fast, never to open; trains depart when we are desperate to catch them; we try to run, but our legs won't function. One degree farther and an unpleasant dream becomes a nightmare, from which a victim may wake in fright, trembling with terror.

Psychoanalyst Sigmund Freud, who gave us the first comprehensive study of dreams, believed that some dreams are a form of wish-fulfilment, closely related to the deep emotional reactions of infancy. A person's dreams revealed repressed feelings and thoughts, presented often in a disguised form.

Many psychologists today say that dreams are an extension of daytime consciousness, a process in which the ideas, feelings and mental impressions absorbed from a variety of sources during our waking hours are sorted out. Strange and inexplicable events take place in dreams because the conscious and awake mind of the day is sleeping: actions that the conscious mind would control in its waking hours are left to run freely.

Some true nightmares, experienced once or more a year by about half the population, may stem from infancy, and are vague in detail. Others are created by

Terrifying bats and vampires *surround the dreamer in Goya's etching* Fantastic Vision (The sleep of reason produces monsters). *Dreams can come at any time during sleep, but the phase known as rapid eye movement (REM) produces most dreams. In the graph of sleep cycles below, the upper horizontal bar shows the times when dreams occur. The second bar shows periods of rapid eye movement. We need REM and non-REM sleep, and catch up on one or the other if deprived*

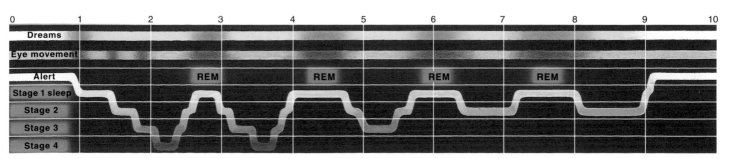

real and devastating experiences involving the dreamer, such as a car crash, fire or the death of a close relative. Studies have shown that certain personality types, particularly those doing creative work, may be more nightmare-prone than others.

Research using electroencephalography has divided our sleep into phases. By recording the brain's electrical impulses, we know that dreams take place during rapid eye movement (REM) sleep, which occurs four or five times a night and may last each time for up to twenty minutes.

During REM, the brain is extremely active. People woken during an REM phase often report quite vivid dreams, remembering them in great detail. This may explain why we recall some dreams and not others. Those remembered probably occur in an REM phase close to our normal waking time.

Babies spend more time in REM sleep. So do people who have suffered a head injury. Medical scientists say that this may indicate that REM sleep plays an important part in promoting brain activity. In the first few years of life, the impressions made on a baby and recorded during REM sleep may set up the patterns that dictate the child's personality.

By tracking brain activity during our sleep, some researchers believe they can pinpoint the exact location of the mind or 'psyche'. They place it within the limbic system, which is located in a semicircle in the middle of the brain. They say that this region acts as the brain's executive office, deciding which events should be filed away in the memory and which should be forgotten. The dream process, they suggest, is essential for these structures within the brain to function efficiently.

Why are men more aggressive than women?

Behaviour is difficult to measure, but many scientists – male and female – agree about certain differences between the sexes. They say that girls are superior at reading and understanding difficult material, and they speak more fluently. Boys are generally better at mathematics. They shine at such skills as reading maps and finding their way out of mazes – and they are without doubt more aggressive both physically and verbally. That doesn't mean, of course, that any one boy is better at maths than any particular girl, or that he is necessarily more aggressive. Scientists are talking about the average.

Psychologists Eleanor Maccoby and Carol Jacklin analysed more than 2000 separate studies to provide considerable evidence of standard differences in boys' and girls' behaviour. Others searched for

Aggression flares in a dispute between a team manager and a baseball umpire. Psychologists say that sports stars and successful people tend to be more aggressive

a biological explanation. Many scientists say that male aggression stems from androgen hormones, which trigger male secondary sexual characteristics, such as muscle bulk in the chest and shoulders, deepening of the voice, and the growth of hair on the chest and face. Among these androgens is the hormone testosterone. One study of male juvenile delinquents showed that the most aggressive had the highest levels of testosterone.

Aggression in men may come from prehistoric times, when only adept fighters were likely to survive. To scientists who argue that the biological evidence is inconclusive, anthropologists point out that in cultures worldwide men are the hunters and killers. It's rare for women to go to war. If similarities exist between otherwise different societies, behavioural scientists say they are likely to stem from biological, not environmental, factors.

Why is laughter said to be the best medicine?

Without doubt, the mind has an enormous influence over our health. Doctors' casebooks are full of examples of patients whose illness appears to stem from general depression. A healthy person receives bad news, is understandably upset, and before long complains of being 'run down'. One British study shows that chronic illness among the unemployed is six times as high as among those at work.

The body responds to mental stress by producing more cortisol and adrenaline. These hormones are designed, among

other functions, to increase the heart rate and blood pressure, improving our performance so that we can cope more efficiently. Too much stress overstimulates hormone production so that, instead of improving our efficiency, we become less able to cope. That is why some people faced with a life-threatening crisis find themselves unable to act sensibly.

Laughter triggers nerves in the brain to start a chain of reactions. The body's endocrine system secretes natural painkillers and tranquillisers. Other substances aid digestion, and the arteries relax to improve the blood flow. No doctor would claim that laughter will cure all ailments, but there is no doubt that a good laugh does us all a power of good.

Why do we blush with embarrassment?

Blushing is a complex reaction for which psychologists have a wide variety of explanations. The two certain facts are that animals don't blush, and people don't blush in private. Another is that the harder you try to stop yourself blushing, the more your face will redden. Blushing is an involuntary reaction, dictated by the mind – but a part of the mind over which you have no control. Tiny blood vessels that supply the face and surrounding areas suddenly widen, allowing more blood than usual to flow through. The cheeks and sometimes the ears and neck become flushed.

For what is a minor peculiarity of the human race, Charles Darwin spent an extraordinary amount of time seeking an explanation. Women blush more than men, and Darwin was keen to discover how far below the neck their blushes went. A medical authority and friend, Sir James Paget, told him that in 'women who blush intensely on the face, ears, nape of the neck, the blush does not commonly extend any lower down the body'.

Darwin noted that children too young to understand the finer points of behaviour never blush; nor do the mentally defective. From these and other observations, he concluded that people who blush are not to be trusted 'as he or she has violated the mores of the group or has committed some crime'.

We know now that some people blush in an instinctive reaction when they commit what they believe is a faux pas or, indeed, when they have done nothing wrong. For example, many people of great modesty are embarrassed by praise. The possibility is that they are shy: they prefer to be swallowed up in a crowd instead of being singled out from it.

Experts argue about blushing's significance. Says Dr Murray Blimes of Berkeley, California, 'The striking thing about blushing is its implicit mixed signals. A blush is a funny mixture of wanting to hide and at the same time wanting to attract someone. Blushers want to hide, but the blush draws attention to themselves.'

A consoling fact for adolescents is that, like acne, a tendency to excessive blushing usually vanishes with age.

Why are some people left-handed?

Nobody is quite sure what causes left-handedness, but almost certainly it is partly inherited. Ultrasound studies of three-month-old foetuses show that already they have a bias towards using one hand rather than the other. But heredity alone cannot explain left-handedness. Some 84 per cent of left-handed people are the offspring of two right-handed parents. And in about 12 per cent of genetically identical twins, one will be left-handed, the other right-handed.

Other research indicates that left-handedness may be caused by minor brain damage. This suggestion is based on the fact that some 20 per cent of all twins are left-handed – about twice the average – caused possibly by overcrowding before birth.

The greatest puzzle is perhaps not why some people are left-handed, but why so few are. In other species, such as chimpanzees, roughly half prefer one paw to the other. To unravel the puzzles of left-handedness, scientists are studying

the body's central nervous system and what they call its crossed laterality – how the right hand is controlled by the brain's left side, and vice versa.

In 95 per cent of right-handers, the speech–language centre is in the brain's left side. But only 15 per cent of left-handers have this crossed laterality; some 70 per cent of them have their speech–language centre on the left, and the rest have it in both hemispheres.

Research scientists say that left-handedness carries considerable dangers. Apart from the more obvious ones of battling through an unfair world where most things are designed for right-handers, left-handers face a significantly higher risk of schizophrenia, phobias and manic-depression. One study shows that they are three times more likely to commit suicide. Also, they appear to be twice as

prone to diabetes, rheumatoid arthritis and myasthenia gravis.

The bright side is that left-handers appear to be more intelligent. Mensa, the society whose membership is confined to people with a high IQ, estimates that 20 per cent of its members are left-handed, twice the proportion of lefties in the population. As further evidence, some famous figures in history were left-handed: Alexander the Great, Julius

Famous left-handers *include Charles Chaplin, Joan of Arc, Paul McCartney and Napoleon Bonaparte. In centuries past, a prejudice existed against all left-handed people, possibly because they were clearly different. Left-handedness was linked with witches and the Devil. Today doctors say that it may shorten a person's life*

Caesar, Charlemagne, Joan of Arc and Napoleon Bonaparte.

Handedness is not a simple matter of one hand or the other. Many of us are more nearly ambidextrous than we realise. A simple test may reveal this. Take a large piece of paper, and pick up a pencil in each hand. Sign your name slowly with your right hand, copying the movements – but in reverse – with your left, so that each hand moves away from the centre towards the sides of the paper. After a little practice, you may be surprised to find, when you hold up your left-hand signature to a mirror, that it closely resembles your normal hand.

Why is yawning contagious?

The scene: a crowded room in the late evening. Suddenly, one person yawns. Before long, others follow suit, accusing the first to yawn of having started the mass display of tiredness and boredom.

We have all had experiences of that kind, yet many researchers dispute that yawning is contagious. A likely explanation is that when one yawn follows another it becomes the subject of comment and impresses the memory. If it happens frequently enough, we believe, without any statistical basis, that one yawn has induced another. We come to similar conclusions about many other everyday events: lifts always go up when you want to go down; if you join a supermarket queue, the checker will start to cash up

or the machine will break down; four or five buses that you don't want to catch will arrive before one going your way.

Yawning is an involuntary act that may be brought on by tiredness or boredom. The mouth opens wide and admits a slow, deep breath, followed by an equally long expulsion of carbon dioxide. The heart rate speeds up a little, and the eyes may start to water. The purpose of yawning is unknown, but theories suggest that it is induced by a high level of carbon dioxide in the blood. By taking a deep breath and exhaling, we increase the blood's oxygen, livening ourselves up.

Another theory to explain why one yawn follows another is that the yawns come when we are all feeling drowsy. If we are crowded together in a stuffy room, we are all likely to need more oxygen; if it is also late evening, most of us are tired and keen to get to bed. One person's yawn may suggest to others that they should do the same. If we are yawning through boredom, our subconscious is perhaps signalling for the meeting to end.

Why do we remember faces, but forget names?

The experience is common to most of us and is often intensely embarrassing. We meet a man we recognise, but we can't remember his name. Or we know him well, but can't recall his wife's name – and hope that we don't have to introduce the couple to somebody else.

Sometimes, we remember absurd details about a person whose name we forget, such as the kind of car he drives, or that she likes Bach. And usually the harder we try to remember, the more elusive the name becomes. Panic, as many exam entrants know, can prevent the recollection of elementary facts. Conversely, high emotion is undoubtedly a memory aid. Most people can recall precisely what they were doing when President Kennedy was assassinated. And psychologists say that most first-year university students more easily recall love affairs of that time than specifics of their studies.

The fact that we can remember one face among so many is in itself remarkable. Most of us would have no difficulty in recognising several thousand people, but it seems that the process of identification works in reverse. Shown a photograph of, say, John McEnroe,

Boredom or stress may often induce a yawn. The reaction isn't confined to humans. Monkeys and apes do it too

the first response might be: 'He's a tennis player – the one who's always arguing with umpires.' And then, if we can recall it, would come the name.

For some reason, it appears that the brain stores information about names in a separate compartment. To unlock that store, we have first to go through others.

People suffering brain damage sometimes lose certain functions. One man was able to divide a pile of photographs into groups of famous and unfamiliar people, but he had the greatest difficulty in naming any of them. In similar tests, nobody has yet found a patient who could name people, but not identify them in some other way, adding perhaps an occupation or a person's nationality.

Why on the average do women live longer than men?

In most parts of the world, whether life expectancy at birth is a mere thirty-five years, as in some developing countries, or about eighty years, as in Japan, women live about five years longer than men. The one exception is India. Life expectancy there is about forty-six for men and forty-three for women.

The longer a person lives, the greater becomes the life expectancy. For example, a healthy seventy-year-old can reasonably expect to live for another fifteen years. Even though life expectancy at birth varies considerably in different countries, for forty-year-olds it is much the same.

Doctors point to several reasons why women generally live longer. At birth, girl babies are usually stronger, and women are believed to have better resistance to heart disease. As well as having what may be basic genetic factors in their favour, women tend to lead less dangerous lives.

Men customarily take more risks. Many of their jobs, in construction, mining and heavy engineering, are hazardous. Around the home, men are more likely to climb ladders, hang out of windows to paint them, and do heavy work in the garden. More men drive cars and motorcycles.

More men are full-time workers, and possibly do shiftwork, which affects their health. They retire later. With some exceptions, they form the combat units in war. Also, until recent times, many more men than women smoked, resulting often in premature deaths from lung cancer and other diseases. Since more women took up smoking, the differences in life expectancy between the sexes have narrowed.

An important factor that has increased life expectancy for women in this century is that in many countries childbirth is no longer a major killer of young women and their babies.

PUZZLES OF FOOD & DRINK

Never before has our daily diet been under closer scrutiny.
Never have we shown such concern for its healthful values, or
welcomed so gladly exotic dishes from afar. An appetising
menu of mysteries excites the taste buds

Why do Italians eat pasta? PAGE 128

Why do we associate curry with India?
PAGE 125

Why are there so many different varieties of wine?
PAGE 138

A menu of facts and fallacies

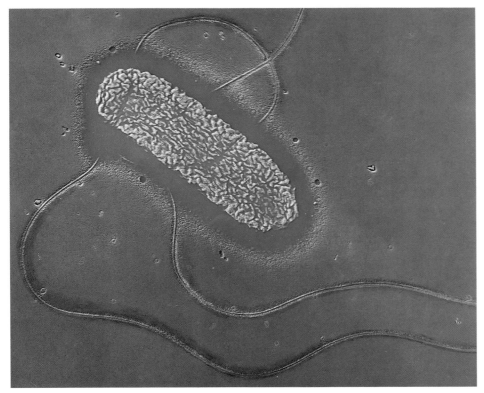

Food poisoning in the making – a magnified view of the Salmonella enteritidis *bacterium*

Why does an airtight container keep food fresher?

Some foodstuffs are spoiled by their own enzymes, and many are attacked by the oxygen in the air. Oxygen commonly reacts with fats, causing the rancid taste and smell of stale fats and oils. Its action is assisted by enzymes and by the ultraviolet rays in sunlight. An airtight container helps to preserve food by preventing oxygen from reaching it, except for the oxygen in the little air left in the container, which may react with fats and other components.

Oxygen reacts also with some chemicals produced by fungi, yeasts, bacteria and other microorganisms. These chemicals themselves may alter the taste, odour or colour of food. At low population levels most microorganisms do little harm, but they can multiply rapidly. Some bacteria can double their numbers every twenty minutes, one individual giving rise to a million in seven hours. Colonies of millions of microbes discolour the surface of food with fuzzy or slimy patches, especially when humidity increases the moisture content. An airtight container preserves food by excluding moisture-laden air and airborne microbes. The air is full of spores of moulds and other fungi, which quickly settle on any uncovered food. Mould will even grow on acid pickles if there is enough air.

An airtight container also prevents drying out of foods that taste better when moist, such as breads and cakes. Also, it keeps insects out of food. These can excrete wastes, secrete chemicals that make the food digestible to them but unpalatable to us, lay eggs, and even build cocoons and other structures.

Despite all this, food kept in airtight containers deteriorates eventually. A container cannot prevent natural metabolic reactions that use up sugar, inactivate enzymes that cause ripening and other changes, or halt the activity of organisms that are already in the food.

Why does freezing preserve food?

Frozen food made its mark on commerce in 1878, when frozen meat was shipped from Buenos Aires to Le Havre in France. Native Americans in icy Labrador already knew that freezing preserved food. When they caught fish in winter, it froze immediately and was fresh to eat when it finally thawed out months later. An American fur trader, Clarence Birdseye, observed this during 1912–15, and in 1924 he set up a company to produce quickly frozen food. In 1930 the company, under new ownership, began to market Birds Eye frozen vegetables, fruits, fish and meats.

Freezing brings the microorganisms and enzyme processes that spoil food to a standstill. Almost all chemical processes in living things are slowed at temperatures below the freezing point of water. By -10°C (14°F) few organisms can function. Food-spoiling fungi, bacteria and other microbes are unable to reproduce. The time that frozen foodstuffs will keep varies. At one extreme, the flesh of mammoths, frozen in Siberian ice for 20 000 years, was found to be edible.

Flavour is changed by freezing, but cryogenic freezing preserves the flavour of meat, shellfish and bread better than conventional methods. This process, which also freezes corpses for possible future revival, employs odourless, tasteless liquid nitrogen, cooled to near absolute zero, -273°C (-459.6°F).

Another method, freeze-drying, produces lightweight food which can be reconstituted by adding boiling water. The food is frozen between refrigerated plates in a vacuum chamber. When it is frozen hard, the plates are heated and the ice in the food is slowly converted directly into water vapour, which is pumped from the chamber. Freeze-drying works best with small items such as peas. As peas

A major aid in keeping food fresh came with the electric fridge, a Swedish invention of 1923. Shown here is an American one of a decade later

mature, their natural sugars change to starch, making them harder and less sweet. Within two or three hours of harvesting, they are blanched in boiling water or steam to inactivate any enzymes, and frozen rapidly.

Why do we associate curry with India?

Curries, delicate or fiery, are not confined to Indian cooking. They are found in wonderful variety throughout Asia, and have spread from there to the cuisine of every continent.

The use of curry spices is thousands of years old. A 3700-year-old Babylonian clay tablet records in cuneiform script what is believed to be the first-ever recipe – for braised turnips cooked with curry spices as a companion for kid stew. The epic Indian Sanskrit poem, the *Ramayana*, which dates from about 300 BC, mentions a meat pilaf cooked with pepper, saffron, mace and raw mango powder.

Even though curries are not peculiar to India, there are several reasons why we associate them particularly with that country. Our word curry comes from a Tamil word, *kari*, meaning sauce. Also, many important curry spices – cardamom, saffron and turmeric, for example – come from India, the world's major producer of spices. The British occupation of India and the need to keep and replenish an army there until India and Pakistan

Spices galore *await buyers in a Bombay market. Once prized like gold, spices have changed the course of history. Today, they underpin the economies of many Eastern countries and are common ingredients in everyday dishes served worldwide*

were given their independence in 1947 made Britons more familiar with many aspects of Indian life than with those of other Asian countries. Into the English language came a variety of words of Indian origin – such as bungalow, kedgeree and verandah – some of which also passed into other languages.

Why aren't lamb sausages as popular as those of beef and pork?

In some countries – Greece and Turkey, particularly – butchers have made lamb sausages for centuries, and they are an important and routine part of the diet. In others, where pork is not eaten for religious reasons, lamb sausages are also quite common.

The prejudice elsewhere against lamb as sausage meat has several causes: boneless lamb is often too expensive; lamb tends to be more chewy than ground pork or beef; lamb lacks the natural gelatin of other meats, so that a lamb sausage may be more crumbly in texture. Also, say some butchers, sausages are often made from trimmings. Those of lamb often have too much fat, and do not make such good sausage meat as those from pork or beef. If other meats, such as pork, are added to lamb, their flavour dominates, so that a sausage made from a mixture is not easily marketed.

Why do bad eggs float on water?

A reliable test of an egg's freshness is to put it into a bowl of water. If it floats, don't eat it. Its buoyancy is due to gas of one kind or another trapped inside the egg. Most eggs sold for human consumption are unfertilised. If one of these floats, it is because the egg has started to decompose, replacing its yolk and albumen with hydrogen sulphide – rotten-egg gas.

A fertilised egg will float soon after incubation has started. As the developing chick feeds and grows, it takes in oxygen through its blood vessels and exhales carbon dioxide. An eggshell is extremely porous, allowing both these gases to pass through. During incubation, an egg also loses water through its shell, which reduces its weight; if too much water is lost, the chick dehydrates and dies. In many species, air replaces the lost water, forming an air sac inside the egg. Just before it hatches, the chick forces its beak into this sac, and takes its first breaths of air through its nostrils.

SOME LIKE IT HOT

Chillies, cayenne pepper, chilli pepper or powder, paprika and hot red pepper come from one or more of the several varieties of the capsicum pepper, which was one of the taste surprises from the New World brought to Europe by the Spanish in the sixteenth century.

What is it in these peppers that gives the mouth sensations of heat? The answer is a powerful chemical, the alkaloid capsaicin. Capsaicin has several components that affect areas of the mouth and throat differently, ranging from a rapid sharp pungency to a longer lasting, less intense bite. The proportion of these components present in different varieties of peppers may give them their different sensory mouthprints.

About 90 per cent of the 'hot' ingredient resides in the white part of the capsicum to which the seeds are attached, with the rest of the capsaicin located in the seeds and the fruit. So for a mild dish add only the outsides of the whole pepper, but if you want your mouth to explore the limits of its hot threshold the inside edge of the chilli is the way to go.

That fiery flavour in chillies comes from capsaicin, a substance used also in antimugger sprays

125

Temptation comes in many guises, according to the chocolate-maker's art. Some scientists say that chocolate contains a stimulant that heightens sensations

Why is chocolate so popular?

In 1519, the Spanish conquistador Hernán Cortés saw a drink called *choco-latl* served in golden cups to Montezuma, the godlike ruler of the Aztecs. Cortés also saw how the drink was prepared from cacao beans, and when he returned to Spain in 1528 he took a supply with him. Christopher Columbus had sent some cacao beans to Spain in 1502 but, the secret of their preparation being unknown, they aroused no interest. The drink made from Cortés's beans was bitter, but when it was sweetened with sugar it became popular among the Spanish nobility. They managed to keep the expensive beverage a court secret until 1606, when it reached Italy. It became popular in France after a Spanish princess married the French king in 1615.

A Frenchman began selling chocolate bars in London in 1657, and in about 1700 someone in England improved chocolate by adding milk to it. However, chocolate was enjoyed almost exclusively as a drink until the nineteenth century because heavy duties made it expensive. In 1847, the English firm of Fry and Sons (which later merged with Cadbury's) began to mass-produce chocolate bars. M. D. Peter in Switzerland began making milk chocolate on a commercial scale in 1875.

The flavour that makes chocolate so appealing is the result of elaborate processes and numerous additives. More than 3000 years ago in Central America, the Maya and other peoples began to

cultivate the cacao tree. On its trunk it produces big hard pods which each contain between twenty and sixty beans.

The beans are fermented, dried in the Sun, broken into small nibs and ground up. This produces a liquor that solidifies into a block. It comprises lightly flavoured, yellowish cocoa butter finely mixed with strongly flavoured, brown cocoa solids – carbohydrates, protein and minerals. Chocolate tastes bitter in this pure form, which is called unsweetened chocolate or cooking chocolate.

This is not the same as 'bitter' eating chocolate, which may contain up to 40 per cent sugar. In sweet chocolate there may be as much as 70 per cent. Drinking chocolate, which was improved by Conrad van Houten in the Netherlands, also is sweetened with sugar.

Drinking chocolate is made by pressing much of the cocoa butter out of unsweetened chocolate and pulverising the dry cake that results. Cocoa is drinking chocolate treated with an alkali to turn the fats into soaps, which allows easier blending with milk.

Eating chocolate is enriched by returning up to 35 per cent cocoa butter. As much as 22 per cent milk solids are added to make milk chocolate. These additions dilute the bitterness of unsweetened chocolate. The flavour blends well with others such as honey, coffee, almond extract and, especially, vanilla, which was a particular favourite of the Aztecs.

The final mixture is grainy, but grinding, stirring and kneading reduce it to the velvety smoothness that is so pleasing in the mouth. Cocoa butter melts below

body temperature, which explains why chocolate readily liquefies in the mouth. As the sweet liquid diffuses over the taste buds on the tongue, some of the cocoa butter and other additives evaporate and carry complex aromas to the nose. It is the nose rather than the tongue that makes a more discriminating and sensitive contribution to the overall perception of flavour.

Chocolate contains a little caffeine and a related chemical, theobromine, which stimulate the nervous system. It is easily digestible and holds useful amounts of vitamin E, phosphorus, calcium, and iron. It is very high in sugar, saturated fat and energy value – 100 grams (3½ oz) of chocolate contains 2205 kilojoules (525 Cals). The sugar promotes growth of bacteria that live in the plaque on teeth. These produce acids and toxins that attack tooth enamel and the gums.

Why are some foods more fattening than others?

A man of average build expends 6000 to 7000 kilojoules (1450 to 1700 Cals) of energy a day just in maintaining his basal metabolic rate, to keep the heart pumping, the lungs breathing and the digestion working. If he is moderately active, he uses up a total of about 11 550 kJ (2750 Cals) a day. Most kilojoules are used to keep the body warm. Because women usually have more body fat to retain heat and they generally weigh less than men, they use less energy. The daily energy expenditure of a young woman of average build is about 8400 kJ (2000 Cals). Active people usually stay slimmer because they burn more energy than the inactive.

Any excess energy is converted to fat and stored within the body. If this continues, obesity results. Generally, people in the Western world have too much fuel and too little activity. In most countries, the chief sources of food energy are carbohydrates – sugars, starches and alcohol – and fats, the most concentrated source. Fats yield 37 kJ (9 Cals) per gram, compared with 16 kJ (4 Cals) per gram from carbohydrates and 17 kJ (4 Cals) per gram from proteins. Total removal of fat from the diet, however, entails risk of depletion of vitamins, especially the fat-soluble A, D and E groups. These cannot be manufactured in the body and are readily obtained only from fats.

Proteins in foods such as meat, eggs and cheese provide the raw materials the body needs for growth and for repair of worn tissues. The body is in a constant state of renewal, endlessly disassembling and reassembling itself. The lining of the small intestine, for example, is replaced every forty-eight hours; platelet cells in the blood live for about 120 days; some of the ligaments and protective tissues around the major joints are replaced over perhaps a decade.

Unless proteins and carbohydrates are taken together, the essential amino acids will be burned for energy instead of being

Too much food and little exercise explain why many people soon become overweight

utilised for cell building and repair. Proteins are metabolised in the body only with the aid of vitamins and minerals. Vitamins are crucial in the enormously complicated chemical reactions that maintain the health of various organs and tissues within the body. Many of the body's molecular processes also require minerals, or trace elements, such as calcium in bones and teeth and iron in the blood stream.

Fats, carbohydrates, protein, trace elements and vitamins are all vital in the diet, and health, longevity and resistance to disease rely on a proper balance of them. Maintaining the right weight depends on not eating too much of the foods that are disproportionately high in kilojoules – the fattening foods. Most fast foods are high in kilojoules and fat. For instance, dipping a piece of fish in batter and deep-frying it inflates its energy value by as much as four times.

Why do cakes and bread rise as they cook?

It was probably an Egyptian baker who, some 4000 years ago, discovered how to make bread rise, and we have been baking bread and cakes that are full of empty space ever since. A close look at the inside of a loaf of bread or a piece of cake will show you that it is full of holes. It is the formation of these holes before and during baking that makes the dough and batter rise and become light and porous.

The main way to make these holes is to mix a leavening agent evenly with the bread or cake ingredients before baking. Yeast, a type of fungus, is the leavening agent used in almost all breads. Baking powder, which is a mixture of sodium bicarbonate and an organic acid such as cream

Bubbles of gas give bread its open, spongy texture. Alcohol produced by fermenting dough causes that fresh-baked smell

of tartar, is added to most cakes and quick breads (such as corn bread) to make them rise. Both agents produce carbon-dioxide gas, which forces aside the dough to make the holes.

Yeast ferments (decomposes) sugars in the flour to form carbon dioxide and alcohol. You can see the dough rise during the fermentation period before baking. The heat of the oven kills the yeast but expands the carbon-dioxide gas to finish the rising process. Baking changes the structure of the proteins and starches in the mixture, causing the bread to set round the bubbles of gas, while the small amount of alcohol produced during fermentation evaporates and contributes to the fresh-baked smell. Partly because of the slower leavening action and a more elastic dough, yeast breads are larger in volume and have a lighter texture than chemically leavened quick breads.

Quick breads and cakes don't require a fermentation period before baking, because the chemicals in baking powder begin to produce gas as soon as they are moistened. This enables a cook to put the dough or batter into the oven as soon as all the ingredients are mixed. The resulting texture is coarser and more crumbly than that of yeast-leavened breads.

But some mixtures will rise without the aid of yeast or baking powder. Cakes that include a lot of egg white have air trapped in the beaten mixture. The heat of the oven causes the air to expand, which gives the cake its desired volume and texture. Surprisingly, even unleavened flat breads rise a little during baking, due to the expansion of steam generated by heating the water in the mixture.

Why do Italians eat pasta?

The Italian word *pasta* means simply a dough made from cereal flour and a liquid. In this sense, pasta has been known for 10 000 years, but the origins of dough worked into small shapes as a foodstuff are obscure. In Italy there are two basic kinds of pasta. The kind sold in packets is *pasta secca* (dried pasta) made from *semola*, the flour of durum wheat, also called hard wheat. *Pasta secca* is made by an industrial process which entails drying the pasta for forty to eighty hours, according to the shape. There is a multitude of shapes, including spaghetti (little strings), fusilli (spirals), vermicelli (little worms), elliche (helixes) and penne (pens).

Pasta secca was made solely with *semola* and water until recent times. Now it is sometimes coloured with vegetable dyes such as spinach or beetroot juice, and sometimes egg is added, as in *pasta fresca* (fresh pasta). This is often made at home with eggs and the finely ground flour of bread wheat. In home-made *pasta fresca* highly refined, finely ground durum-wheat flour called *semolino* – which is quite different from semolina – is sometimes used, alone or mixed with bread flour. *Pasta fresca* is mainly cut into ribbons of various dimensions, such as tagliatelle, used in sheets in lasagne or wrapped around fillings in such forms as ravioli and tortellini.

Some archaeologists believe wall paintings indicate that the Etruscans, who preceded the Romans in central Italy, made lasagna or tagliatelle. But if Etruscans used pasta, the secret of its making did not endure; certainly, the Romans did not eat it.

There are signs that pasta existed in China from the end of the first century AD. The story that Marco Polo introduced pasta to Italy when he returned to Venice from China in 1295 is now discounted, because pasta was already known in Italy. A document of 1279 records *pasta secca* at Genoa, in northern Italy.

Some authorities say that pasta originated in Genoa. Others put its origin in Sicily, theorising that pasta reached the

island with Arab invaders in the ninth century. Pasta may have been invented in the Middle East or central Asia and developed by the Chinese and Italians in their own distinctive ways.

The Sicilians introduced *pasta secca* to Naples, where it became widely popular in the early nineteenth century, with the advent of large-scale industrial production. The Sicilians called it *maccheroni*, and in southern Italy this word still means *pasta secca* made without eggs. In the rest of the country, where pasta was not widely eaten until the twentieth century, it means tubular pasta, short or long. The English word macaroni refers only to short tubular pasta.

Pasta remains secondary to rice and maize in much of northern Italy. Durum wheat grows less well in the north than in the centre and south, where most *pasta secca* is manufactured. The industry developed particularly on the Campania coast near Naples, where the climate is good for drying pasta.

Perfect pasta comes in a myriad variety of shapes and colours. Some of the finest pastas are made in the home or restaurant kitchen. Though Italy is the home of pasta, its true origins may be in the East

Why are tomatoes eaten as vegetables, not fruit?

The botanist and the cook use two entirely different systems of classification. Botanically, a fruit is any part of the plant that develops from an ovary. For the botanist, this settles the matter: the tomato is a fruit. But cooks are interested in flavour and nutrition, not in definitions. Tomatoes taste savoury rather than sweet, so tomatoes are commonly regarded as vegetables.

We eat them raw, grilled, stuffed and baked, in soups, sauces and in casseroles with all kinds of meats. Other fruits commonly found in the vegetable section of the produce market are chillies, cucumbers, avocados and squash.

Tomatoes come from the Andes region and were first brought back to Europe in the sixteenth century by Spanish explorers. The name comes from the Mexican word *tomatl*, but the French called them 'love apples'. Italians, probably looking at some early yellow varieties, called them 'apples of gold'.

For centuries in Europe, tomatoes were regarded as poisonous, and were grown mainly for their attractive colour in the garden. In England they were believed to cause gout and cancer, among other evils. There was an exception. The earliest known printed reference to cooking them is, not surprisingly, Italian. In Venice in 1544 it was recommended that tomatoes be eaten 'fried in oil with salt and pepper'. Clearly, the fruit-that-is-a-vegetable was already poised to claim its starring role in Italian cooking.

Today the average American eats about 14.5 kg (32 lb) of tomatoes a year, mostly in the form of ketchup, chilli sauce and other processed foods.

Why do we eat three meals a day?

The human body needs food to fuel the processes that keep it alive and warm and to provide the energy to move and work. Long before the body's energy reserves are depleted the brain sends out signals that lead to feelings of hunger in the stomach. Most of us begin to feel hungry about four to five hours after we have last eaten. This points to a need for a three-meal day.

The body's natural needs are not easily disentangled from social influences in patterns of mealtimes. These have varied widely over the centuries, and still do. Occupations dictate mealtimes. The needs of the manual worker, the farmer, the office worker and the actor, for example, are all different.

Three meals a day has not always been the rule. Benito Mussolini once referred to the British as a 'five-meals-a-day' people. A French writer in the 1950s noted that New Zealanders liked a cup of tea and a biscuit before breakfast, between meals and before bedtime. They ate seven meals a day, he admiringly declared. Small frequent meals, dietitians seem to agree, are better than large infrequent meals, at which overeating is more likely. It has been found that people who are obese commonly eat most of their daily food in the evening.

The evening meal is the main meal of the day in many countries, especially in the English-speaking world, but it has not always been so. In the Middle Ages, the main meal – and main social occasion – of the day for the leisured classes commonly began about 11 am and lasted several hours. During the fifteenth and sixteenth centuries, the main meal began a long, gradual shift towards the evening.

OLD FOODS FROM THE ANDES

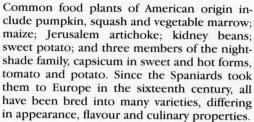

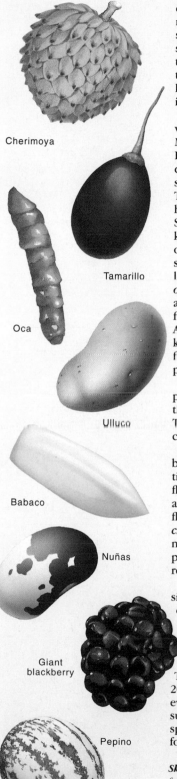

Cherimoya

Tamarillo

Oca

Ulluco

Babaco

Nuñas

Giant blackberry

Pepino

Common food plants of American origin include pumpkin, squash and vegetable marrow; maize; Jerusalem artichoke; kidney beans; sweet potato; and three members of the nightshade family, capsicum in sweet and hot forms, tomato and potato. Since the Spaniards took them to Europe in the sixteenth century, all have been bred into many varieties, differing in appearance, flavour and culinary properties.

The potato was a staple food of the Incas, whose empire stretched along the Andes Mountains, encompassing most of present-day Peru, Ecuador and Bolivia. The Spanish conquerors of the Incas accepted the potato but suppressed cultivation of many other plants. These foods survive in the Andean uplands, however. Some have even been grown beyond South America but have not been widely marketed. For example, the *tamarillo*, a member of the nightshade family with dark red, egg-shaped, sharp-flavoured, nutritious fruit has long been appreciated in New Zealand. So has *oca*, a species of *Oxalis* with pink tubers. They are acid when fresh, but age gives their white, floury flesh a flavour that reminds some of figs. Another Andean tuber is *ulluco*. After frost has killed its leaves, the tubers are lifted. Their flesh is lemon-yellow in colour, like young potato in flavour and sticky in texture.

At high altitudes, where water boils at a temperature too low to cook beans, the people of the Andes drop *nuñas* beans into hot oil. Their seed coats pop open, exposing a soft centre with a flavour like roasted peanut.

Fruits of the Incas' region include a giant blackberry and the *babaco*, a five-sided relative of the papaya, with waxy yellow skin. Its flesh is yellow and tastes of papaya, pineapple and strawberries. Pineapple and strawberry flavours also blend in the creamy flesh of the *cherimoya*. Mark Twain said it was 'deliciousness itself'. This lowland fruit looks like a plump, green pine cone, as does the closely related custard apple.

Another attractive fruit winning a place outside its native Peru is the *pepino*, sometimes called a tree melon. Its delicate flavour combines lemon, pineapple and melon.

All these plants of the Andes have excited scientists and growers with their potential for development and further exploitation. They are among the very few plants – about 200 of the 380 000 known species – that have ever been exploited for human food in any sustained or systematic way. A mere twenty species provide 90 per cent of today's global food supply.

Skilful farmers, *the Incas cultivated about eighty food crops, far more than were grown in Europe or Asia. Only recently have some of their foods become widely marketed overseas*

Cereal grains: the most widely used foods of all

Three kinds of grass seeds supply the world's people with more than half of their food. Wheat, rice and maize are all eaten directly or fed to animals that are slaughtered for human consumption. Some other grasses with edible seeds also make important contributions to human nutrition. These include oats, rye, barley, millet and sorghum. All the grasses that we eat are called cereals, after Ceres, the Roman goddess of agriculture.

Inside the husk of all cereal seeds, dry starchy endosperm surrounds the germ, or embryo, which is the seed itself. When the germ sprouts, enzymes start to break the starch down into maltose sugar and sticky substances called dextrins. The proportions of the seed's three components are about 2 per cent germ, 13 per cent husk and 85 per cent starch. The moisture content is low, so cereal seeds are built to resist spoilage.

At least 9000 years ago, hunter-gatherer peoples in the Euphrates valley in the Middle East discovered that carefully stored grass seeds would remain edible almost indefinitely. Among the seeds they harvested was a primitive species of wheat, and at least 6000 years ago they began to cultivate it. The species most widely used as food in the developed world now is bread wheat *Triticum vulgare*. It has a high content of gluten, a complex protein which has a useful property: it becomes elastic when water is added to it.

When wheaten flour is made into a dough with water and yeast or some other leavening, the resulting mild fermentation produces carbon dioxide. The elastic gluten expands and traps bubbles of the gas within the dough. Strong flour, high in gluten, makes bread of spongy texture and ample volume. Weak flour, lower in gluten, is better for biscuits, cakes and pastries.

More wheat is grown than any other cereal grain – some 600 million tonnes a year on about 230 million hectares (570 million acres) of land. It grows best in temperate climates with an annual rainfall of 300 to 900 mm (12 to 36 in) a year. High-protein hard wheat, used for making dried pasta, grows in dry conditions. Buckwheat, which provides flour that is favoured for breakfast pancakes in the United States, is not strictly a cereal, but is used as one.

Wild rice, eaten by native Americans, is a grass seed, but it is not related to rice, the staple food of about half the world's population. In India, rice was being cultivated by about 3000 BC. Needing abundant water and sunshine, rice grows best in places where it can be irrigated. Seedlings twenty-five to fifty days old are transplanted from nursery beds into fields filled with 50 to 100 mm (2 to 4 in) of water to mature. Rice lacks

gluten, vitamins A, C and B_{12} and contains less protein, fats and fibre than most other cereals.

Maize is lower in food value than other cereals and it contains no gluten. It was the mainstay of the Aztec, Maya and other ancient American civilisations. Evidence of maize production dates back 7000 years. The modern maize plant is a hybrid developed from several related strains, one of which may have been a plant called teosinte, from an Aztec term meaning 'god's ear of corn'. It is widely known in Mexico as *madre de maiz* (mother of maize). Maize is second to wheat in total production. The United States, producing about 200 million tonnes annually, supplies almost half the world crop. A great deal is fed to livestock.

Yield and climatic conditions, influenced by local dietary preferences, dictate which cereal grains are grown in a region. Barley, for example, can be grown in colder climates and on poorer soils than wheat. It was used for breadmaking before wheat, but it has insufficient gluten to make leavened bread. Most barley grown today is used in animal feed and in brewing, for which it is sprouted to make malt.

The staple bread grain of northern Europe until the mid-nineteenth century was rye, which tolerates cold and grows nearer the poles than any other cereal. It has some gluten and makes dense leavened bread. Oats, cultivated since the Bronze Age, contain no gluten but are nutritious. Apart from the oats made into breakfast cereals, most are

CEREAL COMPOSITION AND NUTRITIONAL VALUE
(per 100 grams; 3½ oz)

CEREAL	WATER %	PROTEIN %	FATS %	SUGARS %	FIBRE %	ENERGY VALUE Cals	ENERGY VALUE kJ
Oats	13.0	13.0	7.5	63.7	1.4	374	1566
Durum wheat	11.5	13.0	2.9	70.8	3.3	361	1511
Soft wheat	12.0	12.3	2.6	71.5	2.8	359	1503
Maize (corn)	12.5	9.2	3.3	73.0	2.2	363	1520
Pearled barley	12.2	10.5	1.4	74.0	0.7	347	1453
Polished rice	12.9	7.0	0.6	77.9	0.2	345	1444
Rye	13.7	11.6	1.7	71.1	2.1	346	1449

Oats

Maize (corn)   Soft wheat   Rye   Barley   Durum wheat   Rice

*A **momentous step** in history came with the cultivation of cereals. In China's Guizhou-Guangxi Province (left), farmers grow rice on irrigated terraces. An engraving of 1853 shows how native Americans guarded their cornfields against crows. And in 1859, Vincent van Gogh painted what was then a customary scene, a reaper in a wheatfield*

fed to livestock. Oats grow best in cold, wet places, while sorghum tolerates extremely hot and arid conditions. Various cereal grasses with small grains, known as millet, produce a crop in poor soil. Millet is mostly ground and made into unleavened bread or it is boiled and eaten as porridge.

Cereals have been cooked in water and served hot as gruel or porridge for centuries. There was no ready-made breakfast cereal until 1829, when Sylvester Graham, a Connecticut clergyman with extreme views on food and health, gave the world a dry biscuit called the Graham cracker. Graham later advocated unrefined whole-wheat flour, which is still called Graham flour in the United States.

Another religious figure, Mother Ellen Harmon White of the Adventist Church, founded a health-reform institute in Michigan in 1866. It became the Battle Creek Sanitarium under the management of Dr John Harvey Kellogg, who prescribed vegetarian diets for his patients and investigated healthy yet appetising meals. Kellogg's treatments seemed ineffective to an inventor and salesman named C. W. Post. He left Battle Creek and sought a cure under a doctor with different views. His health restored, Post also began to create new foods. From a recipe developed by a New York State doctor in 1863, he devised Grape Nuts. In 1897, he put them on the market against Shredded Wheat, invented in 1892 by Henry Perky, an enterprising lawyer from Denver, Colorado.

A further challenge came from Battle Creek, where Kellogg in 1898 had begun to serve a new breakfast food called

Corn Flakes. Eight years later, his brother William began commercial production. Cornflakes are made by cooking the husks and hard endosperm of maize grains with water and flavourings. When cooled, these grits are rolled flat and finally dried at high temperature.

Ready-made breakfast cereals boomed in the 1950s when marketers began to appeal to children by putting cartoon characters on cereal packets and prizes inside. Parents were enticed with advertising that emphasised nutritional enrichment and convenience, and with competitions for prizes. Then came specially flavoured, extra-sweetened and unusually shaped cereals, some of them nutritionally dubious because they contained more sugar than grain. Awareness of nutrition has recently brought a return to cereals that have less processing and more of the natural grain.

*A **new cereal story** began with the marketing of Shredded Wheat in 1892. It soon had a host of rivals. Breakfast cereals changed for ever how most Western families start their day*

CHEESE.

1 — Gorgonzola. 2 — Double Gloucester. 3 — Koboko. 4 — Parmesan. 5 — Dutch. 6 — Roquefort.
7 — Schabzieger. 8 — Dunragit. 9 — York Cream. 10 — Port du Salut. 11 — Cheddar.
12 — Pommel. 13 — Camembert. 14 — Mainzer. 15 — Cheshire. 16 — Stilton. 17 — Cream
Bondon. 18 — Gruyère. 19 — Wiltshire Loaf. 20 — Cheddar Loaf.

Say cheese and the list is almost endless. French gastronome Anthelme Brillat-Savarin once wrote that 'a dinner without cheese is like a beautiful woman with only one eye'

milk's coagulation can be hastened by warming it gently.

Most important are the bacteria that give every cheese its character. Young cheese becomes sweeter as bacteria feed upon its lactic acids. Bacteria also break down the casein, adding to the flavour. Some cheeses are 'surface-ripened' by the deliberate introduction of certain bacteria or moulds. Complex chemical processes change the surface casein into other compounds, forming a rind. This acts as a barrier to air and moisture, with subtle effects on ripening. Camembert and Brie are examples of such cheeses. In Camembert, oxygen-dependent moulds grow on the surface, and enzymes from them diffuse through the interior and ripen it.

Green moulds are introduced to form a growth that follows natural cracks in the curds, ripening the cheese internally and producing the distinctive flavours of Roquefort, Stilton, Gorgonzola and other blue-vein cheeses.

Large cheeses are ripened only by bacteria and enzymes. In many kinds the rind is washed, scraped, oiled or waxed to halt mould. Nowadays, large cheeses are often wrapped in moisture-proof film to prevent rind forming. Long, gradual ripening tends to produce harder, more aromatic and stronger-flavoured cheeses than those ripened swiftly.

Why does jelly set?

Jelly, called Jell-O in the United States, is set when it is at room temperature, about 20°C (68°F) or below, but above freezing. Warm it to about 27°C (81°F) and it gradually reverts to a watery mixture. Cool it

Why do some cheeses have rinds?

The first cheese was made, an ancient legend says, when an Arab traveller carried milk in a pouch made from a sheep's stomach. Rennet in the pouch and the heat of the Sun combined to separate the milk into curds and whey. Curds, drained of whey, are the simplest form of cheese – cottage cheese – and the basis of all types. There are countless cheeses, but only about eighteen distinct types, determined by the procedures of curdling the milk, cutting, stirring, heating, draining, pressing and salting the curd and ripening the cheese. Milk, usually from cows, sheep or goats, is soured naturally or treated with rennet or lactic acid so that protein coagulates and forms a curd of casein. Acid curds result in crumbly, porous cheeses and rennet curds in firmer, more elastic cheeses. The

and it thickens until it sets again. This behaviour is determined by a special gel-making ingredient in the jelly mixture. The usual gelling agent in jelly is gelatin, which is made from collagen, a fibrous protein found in all connective tissues in the body.

When animal skin or bone is boiled in water, the collagen strands separate and react with water to become gelatin. As little as 1 per cent dissolved in water will make a gel. Gelatin contains millions of long chains of protein that separate into tiny filaments when they are mixed with warm water.

Each filament attracts water molecules to itself along its length. This reduces the number of water molecules free to flow through the mixture. As the mixture cools, the water-rich filaments begin to bump into one another and intertwine. Eventually, the remaining water becomes confined within a thicket of protein filaments and the mixture thickens into a gel.

Besides its use in jelly and other moulded desserts, gelatin stabilises foams and emulsions in foods such as marshmallows and ice cream. It has many applications outside its use in food. For example, it also binds the light-sensitive chemicals in place in photographic film, and is used in pharmaceuticals and glue.

Before industrial gelatin was available, cooks had either to make their own gelatin by boiling up bones or to use isinglass, a kind of gelatin obtained from the swim bladders of fish. Gelatin is only one of the gelling and thickening agents used in foods. Starch is used to thicken sauces and to make confectionery such as Turkish delight. Pectin, obtained from fruit, sets natural fruit jellies, binds fruit preserves and confectionery and is used increasingly in the pharmaceutical and textile industries.

Carrageen and agar-agar, obtained from red seaweeds, set to firm jellies. Agar-agar is used in a wide range of foods, including desserts, ice cream, sauces and canned soup. It also solidifies the nutrient solution in which bacterial cultures are grown for scientific study.

Starch, pectin, agar-agar and carrageen are types of sugars formed into long molecular chains. Also called complex carbohydrates or polysaccharides, they are excellent sources of food energy. Because gelatin lacks an essential amino acid, its high protein content cannot be used by the body.

A decorative mould has turned an otherwise lacklustre jelly into an enticing dish. It stays set with an attractive wobble because of a complex series of chemical reactions

Why is soup served at the start of a meal?

Soup and bread were often the whole meal for peasants in medieval Europe. Many homes had a pot into which anything available was tossed, and a soup or stew could be maintained for months. In those days, food was either boiled or roasted, over an open fire or in a brick oven. The iron stove did not appear until the 1860s.

In a medieval banquet, soups were great dishes of meat or fish boiled with vegetables, into which diners plunged their spoons in turn. Many dishes were produced at once and guests sent servants to procure their choice of food. By the eighteenth century, dishes had been grouped into three courses. Soups appeared with fish and other light dishes in the first course, preceding the main course of poultry and large cuts of meat. Soup was associated with military meals in the field, and during Napoleon's campaigns it became suddenly fashionable at dinners in France.

In the nineteenth century, old-style table service was replaced by *service à la russe*. Waiters took dishes from the sideboard by turn and offered them to the guests. This gave fewer dishes in a course but more courses. Soup was regarded as indispensable for the first course. As an English writer in 1877 explained: 'People often sit down to a late dinner faint and irritable; and those who have observed how quickly a little liquid nourishment acts as a restorative will never be content to dispense with soup as the best of preliminaries at dinner.'

Why is garlic said to be good for you?

A close relative of the common onion, garlic is a member of the lily family, native to Asia and the Mediterranean region. It is mentioned in ancient Chinese, Indian, Greek, Assyrian, Egyptian and Hebrew writings. Nearly 3000 years before the birth of Christ, garlic was at the heart of what seems to have been the first labour dispute in history. Slaves working on the Egyptian pyramids had their rations cut and went on strike in protest. Garlic has figured in myth and superstition – perhaps most famously for its alleged value as an amulet to ward off vampires.

For at least 5000 years, garlic has been prized for its medicinal properties, some of which have been confirmed by modern Western research. Its volatile oils contain several complex sulphur compounds, and it has been shown to be a potent antibiotic and antiseptic. Many people find it

Bowls of soup for the farmer's wedding are carried on a door removed from its hinges. A detail from a sixteenth-century painting by Flemish artist Pieter Brueghel the Elder

Magical powers *were once attributed to garlic. Until modern times it was trusted as a charm to deter evil spirits*

beneficial as a defence against colds, for nausea or diarrhoea and to soothe a sore throat. There is some evidence, too, that it can bring down cholesterol levels and reduce high blood pressure.

Why does some corn pop?

There are several different types of corn (also called maize) but only the kinds with the strongest kernels will pop. To be strong, a kernel needs stiff yellow insides. Underneath the kernel's skin is the carotene-coloured endosperm which serves as food for the whitish corn embryo, called the germ.

The endosperm consists of protein, starch, sugar and water. The strongest endosperms contain the most protein and the least sugar, and the best poppers also have a moisture content of between 11 and 14 per cent.

When the kernel is heated quickly, the water in the endosperm first partly cooks the starch granules. Then, as the temperature inside the kernel reaches boiling point, the water vaporises to steam and expands rapidly in volume. The strong interlocking protein surrounding the starch and the dispersed water resists this expansion until the pressure is too great. Then, in an explosive instant, the steam bursts the tough kernel open. This sudden release of pressure causes the entire endosperm to expand. The steam escapes to leave behind a hot dry fluffy mass of popcorn.

The variety of corn appropriately called 'pop' has the right proportion of protein

to starch to explode rather than sizzle. Even then, not every corn kernel will pop fully or at all. If the skin is damaged, much of the steam will escape without building up a popping pressure. If the kernels have absorbed or lost water during storage, their poppability may suffer.

One consolation for those who like popcorn is that it isn't fattening. Plain popcorn contains useful dietary fibre and is low in kilojoules.

Why do onions make your eyes water?

The strong smell of fresh onions comes from the sulphur-rich oil they contain. Cutting or peeling an onion releases this oil, which readily evaporates and soon reaches the eyes.

This sulphurous and acidic oil irritates nerve endings in the conjunctiva, the transparent tissue that covers the eye and the underside of the eyelids. An instinctive reaction is for the sensitised nerves to send signals which stimulate the lacrimal (tear) gland in each eye to produce extra tear fluid. Tears then wash over the eye to flush out the chemical irritant.

Our eyes are always being watered by up to a quarter of a teaspoon a day of secretions to keep our eyes moist and to wash away foreign particles and bacteria. In normal circumstances all the fluid is drained away by the tear ducts. When tears are secreted faster than they can be drained, the excess tears flow out of the eye and run down the face. Use a mirror to see the tear duct in each eye. The duct is near the nose on the ridge of the lower eyelid. You will see what looks like a tiny hole or depression on the side that rests against the eye.

If you want to peel onions without tears, keep the onions under water as you cut them. The water will capture most of the juices of the oil and you'll finish the job without shedding tears.

Why do we add salt to our food?

Saltiness is generally ranked with sweetness, sourness, bitterness and acidity as a basic taste sensation, experienced on the tongue. Saltiness and sweetness are the most distinctive tastes, and humans have craved both since early times. In ancient Rome, soldiers were partly paid for their services with a *salarium* of salt – hence the word 'salary'.

Thousands of years ago, the Chinese began to obtain salt by evaporating seawater in wide pans over heat. On average, a litre of seawater contains 35 grams of

salt (a pint contains ⅝ oz). Sea salt, evaporated either artificially or naturally in bays, forms brittle flakes. Rock salt, extracted from deposits in land once covered by sea, comes in hard crystalline lumps.

Salt, judiciously added, enhances other flavours. It also has preservative powers, which placed it at the centre of the seasonal battle for survival in agricultural societies. From China to Europe, salt-cured sausage and bacon have added variety to the winter diet. Before the Reformation, Christians throughout Europe ate salted fish during the meatless fast of Lent and on Fridays.

Now refrigeration preserves foods more simply and salted products have lost their place as staples. We eat salami, bacon, ham, anchovies, kippers, olives, some cheeses, potato crisps and preserved vegetables for gastronomic merit rather than out of seasonal necessity. As appetisers or garnishes they provide the valued hint of saltiness.

We need salt also to maintain sound health. In the fluid surrounding the thousands of millions of cells that make up our bodies, the main conductors of electricity are sodium and chlorine. These elements constitute common salt – sodium chloride. Salt is vital in maintaining the body's water content, but excessive consumption of it has been linked to high blood pressure. Dieticians say that we get ample salt naturally in our diet without adding more.

Why are some kinds of honey light in colour and others dark?

Beekeepers will tell you that, if you know the nectar, you know the honey. The different kinds of nectar, gathered worldwide from a multitude of flowering plants, trees and shrubs, give honey its distinctive colours, flavours and aromas. One source will provide what graders call water-white honey; another produced by bees in the same locality but feeding on different plants may be dark brown. Food analysts can establish a honey's origin quite easily by identifying its pollens.

Honey ranges in colour from the almost colourless through shades of yellow, amber and brown. Graders, using an instrument known as a Pfund colour grader, give honey one of at least seven classifications. Other instruments give the honey's moisture content, which determines how well it will keep, and whether it will flow easily or be granulated.

The nectar of clover, of which there are more than a dozen kinds, usually makes the lightest coloured honey. Amber honey comes from such sources as the poplar,

Honey's colour varies according to the many kinds of nectar gathered by bees

eucalypts, magnolia, goldenrod and marigold. Heather honeys, which are strongly flavoured and command a high price, are notable for their dark colour. So is buckwheat honey, produced in the United States and some parts of Europe. In France, buckwheat honey is prized by bakers, who for centuries have used it to produce a special kind of bread, despite beekeepers' efforts to persuade them that other dark honeys are just as good.

Why are truffles always so expensive?

To the biologist, a truffle is an edible subterranean fungus belonging to the genus *Tuberof*, the order Tuberales, class Ascomycetes. Several species occur across much of the northern hemisphere, but to the gourmet, only two matter: the so-called white truffle, *T. magnatum*, and the even more exalted black truffle, *T. melanosporum*. The first is most abundant in northern Italy, the second in southern France.

Truffles are globular in shape, brown or black in colour, with a rough and warty surface. They thrive best in open woodland, usually close to the roots of trees, especially oaks. Because they grow underground – often at depths of 30 cm (12 in) or more – they are very hard to find. If they lie close to the surface, the trained eye can sometimes detect a telltale bulging. Some humans can smell the distinctive odour of truffles even through the covering of soil. But the traditional, and still the most efficient, method is to use a specially trained animal to sniff them out,

usually a pig in France, a dog in Italy. Truffles can sometimes be persuaded to grow if matured truffles and spores are reburied in specially planted oak woods, but a plantation does not begin to yield for at least five years, and reaches its maximum perhaps a decade later.

The high price of truffles is largely a matter of limited and erratic supply, the difficulty of cultivation and the necessity for hand gathering. An exquisite flavour reinforces their luxury status.

They are best eaten fresh, straight from the ground, although France now cans and exports a third of its crop. The renowned French chef Escoffier said of them: 'They should be prepared in a very simple fashion, since they have no need of refinement to be perfect.'

No surer way has yet been devised of finding truffles (right) than by using a sow. Truffles produce a musky chemical found in a male pig's saliva, which induces a female to mate

Those many cups of kindness

Why are fizzy drinks fizzy?

When first poured into a glass, most soft drinks fizz so actively that wet bubbles fly off the surface of the liquid into the air. The leaping fizz and the bubbles in the body of the liquid are all from carbon-dioxide gas escaping from the water in the drink.

In a process called carbonation the gas is mixed with the water at high pressures and cold temperatures, conditions at which water can dissolve more gas. A graphic proof that water can hold more gas at cold temperatures is to compare what happens when you open a warm and a cold bottle or can of carbonated soft drink. You've probably learned from experience that the warm one makes a frothy mess. A very cold drink will make only a brief sound of escaping gas when it is opened.

If you want the cold container to be-have like a warm one, give it a good shak-ing. This mixes in extra amounts of gas from the head space above the liquid. This gas is more than the water can nor-mally dissolve, and a sudden release of pressure will cause the gas to rush out, taking a lot of liquid with it. The best thing to do with a jolted container is to leave it in the refrigerator for a time; eventually, any excess gas will leave the liquid and return to the head space.

Champagne needs no added carbon dioxide: it is self-carbonating. The wines of the Champagne region of northeastern France were known and enjoyed by the Romans, but they were still wines, with-out the famous bubble and sparkle of champagne. These wines were extremely popular during the seventeenth century. Once he had tried them, Louis XIV is said never to have drunk any others. During his reign, growers discovered that they could produce an almost-white wine from black grapes if they gathered the grapes soon after dawn and stopped harvesting before the Sun caused the grapes to fer-ment. The wine had a rosy tint, known as *oeil-de-perdrix* (partridge's eye), and within a few months began to effervesce.

Experiments showed that the chalky soil of the region played a part, and that the wines of Champagne, made from black and white grapes, have a natural tendency to retain some sugar after their first fermentation. Winter halts a second fermentation, but warmer weather in-duces it. Winemakers call this twice-fer-mented wine *saute bouchon* (jumping cork) because the stoppers often popped out of the bottles.

In 1668, a Benedictine monk, Dom Pierre Pérignon, became cellar master at the Abbey of Hautvillers. He succeeded in controlling this second fermentation, speeding it up or slowing it down at will. His principles are followed today. First the still wine is assessed for its sugar content. Old wine to which cane sugar has been added is blended in. A good sparkle comes from wine containing about 25 grams of sugar per litre (½ oz per pint). Too little sugar brings no sparkle; too much may explode the bottles. As yeasts digest the sugar added to the liquid they produce carbon-dioxide gas which builds up to a substantial pressure in the con-fined space. Dom Pérignon made spark-ling wine of such quality that champagne was often known as *vin de Pérignon*.

Beer can be a self-carbonating bever-age, but it sometimes receives help from the brewer. The second fermentation of beer happens in large vats and far less carbon-dioxide pressure than in cham-pagne is allowed to develop. With tradi-tional brewing methods, undesirable odours that build up are vented off by opening the container briefly. Newer methods involve artificially carbonating the beer to purge it of these odours, a process sometimes followed by adding extract of hops for flavouring. Carbon dioxide plays a role here too: liquid car-bon dioxide is used to dissolve the flavour from hops. When the carbon dioxide is evaporated away, the liquid flavoured essence remains.

Sometimes the Earth does its own car-bonating. Gases released from volcanic

Sparkling champagne may gush from bottles in a gradually ascending range of sizes: a quarter, half-bottle, bottle, magnum, jeroboam, rehoboam and a methuselah

Champagne's secret is discovered by Dom Pierre Pérignon, depicted in a French journal. Inset: bottles of champagne are aged after the wine has undergone a second fermentation

Why don't champagne bottles burst?

Home-brewers and ginger-beer makers know the perils of fermentation. Without due care, bottles may blow their corks or explode as the gas pressure builds up.

That, indeed, was an early problem of champagne production. Corks replaced ill-fitting wooden bungs as a way of keeping the wine's sparkle. The Benedictine monk Dom Pérignon introduced corks to the Champagne region of northeastern France in the seventeenth century. Some say that the idea came from England, where they were already in use, others that Dom Pérignon copied Spanish pilgrims, who sealed their gourds with cork. Until that time, wooden staples wrapped in oil-soaked hemp stoppered the bottles and kept the bubbles from escaping. But as winemakers grew more skilful at producing bubbles more bottles burst. At one time the loss was as high as 80 per cent.

Then, after the Napoleonic Wars, a druggist named François de Châlons

is why, if you watch bubbles rising from one spot in your glass, you will see that they gradually get farther apart. However, the faster a bubble tries to rise, the greater the drag force on it from the surrounding liquid. If you have ever tried pushing your hand or a paddle through water, you will know that the faster you push the harder it becomes. So it is with the bubble. The drag force acts like a speed cop: bubbles of a certain size can rise so fast and no faster.

activity may dissolve in ground water to give naturally fizzy waters. Minerals also may dissolve in the water, but many commercially available mineral waters are artificially mineralised and carbonated.

So whether your bubbles come from yeast, the Earth, dry ice or a canister of gas you can thank carbon dioxide for the tangy taste of your drink as well as the tickle under your nose.

Why do bubbles in champagne get bigger as they rise?

Next time you have a glass of champagne – or, indeed, any fizzy drink – watch the bubbles. As they rise, they grow bigger, floating upwards like little balloons, because the carbon-dioxide gas inside them is lighter than the liquid. Once a bubble forms, it collects more of the carbon dioxide dissolved in the drink, and continues to grow.

Not only does each bubble grow, but it gathers more buoyant force, which tends to speed its ascent the higher it goes. This

CHEERS! THE DRINK FOR SPECIAL OCCASIONS

Champagne was once drunk almost exclusively by the aristocracy. The Industrial Revolution of the nineteenth century created a fast-growing group of manufacturers, and brought wealth to people who had never had it before. Because of its touch of class, champagne became the drink for the special occasion – to open a new factory, launch a ship, toast a bride, mark a christening.

Charles-Camille Heidsieck, founder of the Heidsieck champagne company, was an enthusiastic promoter of champagne as the drink to have when celebrating. He travelled much of the world in the mid-nineteenth century extolling the many virtues of champagne, and soon became known as 'Champagne Charlie'. A popular song of the same name ensured even more promotion for the bubbly wine and its tireless advocate.

The instant effervescent sparkle of champagne seemed to suit it ideally to joyful times, and its delicacy made it acceptable at any hour. It has remained a favourite ever since. It needs little promotion, so it escapes the high costs of advertising that beset many of its rivals. But top-quality champagne is expensive to make. The grapes are costly and the wine needs the skill of highly paid experts to bring it to perfection. A major factor, however, is time. Fine champagnes are aged in the bottle for at least six years before the grower can begin to recoup his initial costs.

Even supposing costs could be reduced, would the price be allowed to fall? Many in the industry believe that champagne's price helps to maintain its allure. Who, after all, would want to mark a special occasion with something as cheap, say, as a bottle of beer?

No other wine can rival champagne's touch of class, as this advertisement of 1897 is keen to stress

found a way to assess the amount of sugar in the wine and to gauge how effervescent it would be. He knew that the sugar produced carbon dioxide, which remains dissolved in the wine. He found that he could control not only the amount of gas but also the wine's sweetness. From his work come the classifications used today to indicate the dryness or sweetness of a wine: brut, sec, demi-sec and sweet.

Champagne has a pressure five to six times that of the normal atmosphere – far too great for a normal bottle to resist. After the pioneer work of François de Châlons, champagne was put into stronger bottles, capable of retaining the sparkle without bursting.

Why does beer foam look white when the liquid is amber?

The colour of beer or of any translucent liquid depends on how much of it you look through. A single drop of beer looks colourless. A glass of it may, according to the brew, appear to be an amber yellow or dark brown. Beer that is yellow in a tumbler would look red in a barrel-sized container of clear glass.

The froth or head on a glass of beer looks white because each bubble consists of carbon-dioxide gas inside a minute quantity of beer. The light reaching your eye passes through insufficient beer to turn yellow. In other words, it doesn't have time to change colour.

You may notice a similar phenomenon with water. A single drop of water is quite clear; so should a glass of it be, if the supply is pure. However, if you look through a tube of water several metres long, it has a tinge of blue. The longer the tube, the darker the shade of blue. If you went deep into the ocean, you would find it gradually getting darker. Eventually you would be in total darkness: the water above would have absorbed all the light. In an ocean of beer, the light would change from yellow to red, then from dark red to black. But the foam of beer and that on the sea look equally white because the light from each has passed through too little liquid.

Why does salt make beer bubble?

Take a pinch of salt, sprinkle it into a glass of beer, and immediately you will see bubbles forming along the path of each falling grain of salt. The bubbles have nothing to do with any chemical reaction between the beer and the salt – as you can easily prove by dropping in grains of a substance that doesn't dissolve.

The bubbles come from carbon dioxide dissolved in the beer at about twice atmospheric pressure. They won't form in the beer without some inducement. They need something to cling to – what scientists call a 'nucleation site'. If your glass is flawed in some way, or the beer contains a speck of cork or other impurity, bubbles will form at the site. The principle applies equally to all kinds of carbonated drinks. You may have noticed that, in glasses designed with a pebblelike finish, bubbles will stream from each nodule in the glass.

If you want to experiment, sprinkle some clean sand into the beer. As the grains fall, they will collect bubbles. Unlike the salt, which dissolves in the beer, the sand collects at the bottom of the glass and continues to send up bubbles.

Without some inducement, the dissolved carbon dioxide doesn't have the energy to start a bubble – in other words, to push aside a tiny volume of beer and fill the space with gas. Once a bubble gets started at a nucleation site, more carbon dioxide comes to the party, pushing into the bubble and expanding it. It's just like blowing up a balloon: the hardest part always is in getting it started.

Beer, glorious beer by the litre mugful is served at the annual Oktoberfest held in Munich. The festival once lasted only a day, but now goes on for sixteen

Wine tasters assess the vintages at a trade fair in London. Skilful judges rely more on the nose than on the tongue. Memory of how great wines taste is also important when comparing the merits of one wine with another

Why are there so many different varieties of wine?

The juice of many fruits can be fermented to produce an alcoholic drink by the reaction of sugar with yeast. Many such drinks are referred to as brandies. The term wine generally refers to beverages produced from a single genus of plants, the grapes *Vitis*, especially the species *V. vinifera*. Wines have been known from at least the time of the ancient Minoans, Greeks and Etruscans, and probably a great deal longer.

Although grapes come in two basic types, red and white, each has hundreds of varieties. And the grape differs from most other fruits in the extraordinary range of colour, flavour and aroma produced by differences in the variety used. Grapes vary also according to the climate, topography and soil in which they are grown, plus such variations in technique as the time of harvesting, length of ageing, and so on. This range results in the many types of wine on the market today. Under certain circumstances, the fermentation process produces excess carbon dioxide, imparting a sparkling quality to the wine and producing further possibilities for variation. Total world production of wine approaches 40 000 million bottles annually.

Why are red wines served at room temperature and white wines chilled?

Within ordinary limits, the temperature at which food or beverages are served often makes little difference to their food value, but usually makes a great deal of difference to our enjoyment of them. This is especially true of substances with complex and subtle flavours, and applies particularly in wine.

Our sense of taste is far less subtle than our sense of smell. We use smell to reinforce taste much more than we're generally aware – which is why we can neither smell nor taste with a bad head cold. Warm substances release their aromas more readily than cool substances. The greater the subtlety and complexity of the flavours, the more important the temperature factor.

Red wine's higher molecular weight means that it gives off vapour less readily than white wine. In general, the more solid and substantial the wine, the more

the release of the full range of its aroma and bouquet depends on gentle warmth. On the other hand, the lighter and sweeter the wine, the more it profits from being served slightly chilled. Personal taste plays a large role, but 'room temperature' is usually taken to mean around 15 to 20°C (60 to 70°F). Above this range, the subtle aromas of the wine may be masked by those given off by the alcohol itself as it vaporises.

Why are whiskies and other spirits aged?

Alcoholic beverages fall naturally into two groups, fermented and distilled. Fermented beverages include wines and beers, whereas gin, vodka, rum and whiskies are familiar examples of those that are distilled.

Fermentation is part of the natural process by which plant materials decompose: carbohydrates and sugars react with yeast to form simpler substances, including ethyl alcohol. The resulting solution can be concentrated by distillation. This process exploits the different boiling

points of water and ethyl alcohol – water boils at 100°C (212°F) at sea level, ethyl alcohol at only 78.5°C (173.3°F). If the solution is heated in a device commonly known as a still, the alcohol vaporises before the water, and can therefore be collected separately.

People around the world have been brewing alcoholic drinks, using the fermentation process, for thousands of years. The plants used as a basis vary from place to place, but the essential process remains the same.

Distillation is a much younger art, perfected only in the last few centuries. Purity of ingredients and careful technique are imperative: not for nothing was the rough and ready substitute, palmed off on native Americans by early explorers in barter, referred to as 'firewater'.

Distillation does not in itself yield an attractive drink, as pure ethyl alcohol is odourless, tasteless and colourless. Vodka is an exception because it is traditionally distilled to such a state. So is gin, which gains its characteristic flavour by being redistilled in the presence of juniper berries and other carefully selected herbs and spices. Liqueurs evolved partly

The luck of the Irish was to invent whisky, but the Scots made it a world-famous drink associated chiefly with Scotland. At a distillery in the Hebrides a centuries-old process flourishes

through attempts to moderate the potent ethyl alcohol by adding various kinds of fruit, herbs and spices.

Early distilled alcoholic beverages, including whisky, were produced mainly for medicinal purposes; only later were they given their modern status as popular drinks.

Whisky has been produced in the Scottish Highlands for centuries, the technique probably brought by early missionary monks from Ireland. The name whisky was adopted into English from the Gaelic *uisge beatha*, replacing the earlier *aqua vitae*, the Latin phrase of the same meaning (literally, 'water of life'). The earliest recorded reference to whisky appears in the Exchequer Rolls for 1494: 'Eight bolls of malt to Friar Cor wherewith to make Aquavitae.'

According to British law, a liquor may not be sold as Scotch unless it has been 'matured in warehouse in cask for a period of at least three years'. Impurities in the distilled liquor are known as congeners, which produce a harsh, sharp flavour. These influences can be mellowed by a very carefully controlled ageing process in wooden casks (preferably recently emptied sherry casks). The wood and liquor interact in a series of complex chemical reactions to generate colour, bouquet and flavour.

Scotch whiskies are usually aged for at least five years, some for eight years and some for twelve years.

Why are some people addicted to tea and coffee?

Coffee and tea have distinctive flavours that many people find very pleasant, but taste alone does not account for some people's dependence on frequent cups from early morning to late at night. Heavy tea and coffee drinkers seek the increased alertness or clearer thinking they experience after drinking a cup of either brew. The 'wake-me-up' properties of tea and coffee can become addictive.

The chemical in both coffee and tea that stimulates our nervous system is caffeine, which is also found naturally in cacao beans, used to make chocolate, and kola nuts, used in cola-flavoured soft drinks. Caffeine is added to some non-cola drinks and a range of pharmaceuticals. Tea also contains a small amount of a related and more potent stimulant, theophylline.

Once caffeine is absorbed into the blood stream it can reach all parts of the body, and causes a variety of effects. It makes the heart pump more blood, but it decreases the blood flow to the brain by constricting blood vessels there. Perhaps it compensates for this by stimulating the cerebral cortex, the outer part of the brain, to give us a more alert feeling.

Too much caffeine can cause irritability, nervousness, jumpiness, irregular heartbeat, headaches, insomnia and other unpleasant symptoms. But attempts to link caffeine to various types of cancer have been inconclusive. Even so, it's wise to watch your caffeine intake. Keep in mind that a can of soft drink may contain as much caffeine as a cup of tea and from a half to a fifth of that in a cup of strong, brewed coffee.

Those who are addicted to the flavour but not the caffeine of coffee and tea can use decaffeinated products which provide the taste without the jolt.

Coffee houses prospered in colonial America and more so after the Boston Tea Party revolt over harsh taxes on tea

Why does milk go sour?

Humans consume the milk of many other species of mammals, including asses, camels, goats, horses, water buffalo, sheep, zebu cattle and dairy cattle. The milks of these species vary greatly in composition. Dairy cow's milk consists of water plus 4.8 per cent lactose (milk sugar), 3.3 per cent proteins, 3.3 to 5 per cent fat according to the breed of cow, and a variety of vitamins and minerals.

The gentle milkmaid bends to her task in this illuminated English manuscript of c. 1250. From the earliest times milk has been a symbol of wealth

Many bacteria inhabit raw milk and thrive on it. They convert lactose into lactic acid, gradually making the milk taste sour as they multiply. The acid-forming bacteria are destroyed, along with any disease-carrying organisms, when milk is pasteurised. This involves heating it to about 70°C (160°F) for fifteen seconds and then rapidly cooling it to 4°C (39°F). Pasteurised milk keeps for four or five days in a refrigerator before surviving bacteria act on the protein and fat and it becomes bitter. Ultraheat treatment (UHT) destroys more microorganisms than pasteurisation. Milk is heated to about 140°C (284°F) for two or three seconds. Unopened UHT products can be kept for several months.

Microorganisms are deliberately employed in some milk products, including sour cream. This is not naturally soured but the result of adding a bacterial culture which thickens cream and gives it a slightly sour, nutty taste. Mixing sour cream or cultured buttermilk with fresh cream provides *crème fraîche*. Buttermilk, originally the liquid remaining after naturally soured cream had been churned into butter, is now usually made by adding a culture to pasteurised skim milk. This makes it creamy in consistency and mildly acidic in flavour.

Special bacteria are added to warm milk to make yoghurt. They break down lactose, releasing lactic acid, which coagulates the milk into a curd.

RIDDLES IN EVERYDAY LIFE

In the home, street and workplace, astonishing things occur before our eyes. For keen observers and inquiring minds, science shows its face in everything, from the car to the kitchen sink

Why did we ever start wearing clothes? PAGE 142

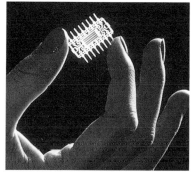

Why are computers so much smaller now? PAGE 172

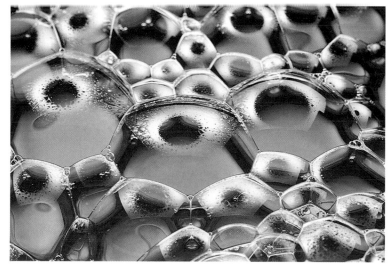

Why is it sometimes difficult to get a lather with soap? PAGE 165

From hair shirts to high fashion

Stepping out in style, *these young men of a West African nomadic tribe, the Wodaabe, parade in their Geerewol festival. They aim to show their beauty, charisma and charm in a bid to attract a wife. Marriageable women and tribal elders appraise the men's talents*

Why did we ever start wearing clothes?

Nineteenth-century British philosopher Thomas Carlyle asserted that 'The first purpose of clothes was not warmth or decency – but ornament.' Most of us accept that our far-distant ancestors were apelike creatures, covered in fur for warmth and protection. If Carlyle was right, we might ask what induced the earliest humans to decorate their hair-covered bodies and what they found so appealing.

It is almost certain that Carlyle was wrong. *Homo erectus*, who emerged some 1.5 million years ago and survived until about 500 000 BC, spread north and south from warm tropical regions. He used fire, possibly discovered accidentally from bushfires triggered by lightning, to warm himself and perhaps used it for cooking. This helped the steady advance into colder regions.

Between 200 000 and 120 000 years ago, the successors of *Homo erectus* pushed still farther north into barren areas on the edge of regions affected by the last but one of the great Ice Ages. To survive here needed more than the warmth of fire. Neanderthal people took to lighting fires in caves and rock shelters and almost certainly fashioned primitive clothes from skins.

Modern man, *Homo sapiens sapiens*, had spread from Europe and Asia into Australia and New Guinea by about 50 000 years ago. Whether these people wore clothes or not seems to have depended largely on their need for protection – against the weather and enemies.

Modesty probably played little part. Certainly, it isn't an innate human characteristic. Children have to be taught to cover themselves, and customs ruling which parts of the body may be exposed and which must be covered vary widely from society to society. Among the Suya Indians of Brazil, for instance, women go naked – but would be horrified to be seen without their wooden mouth and ear plugs.

Clothing can be a form of decoration or a symbol of success. Fashion began as a way of showing differences between social groups or classes. It made apparent who were masters and who were servants. Clothing can communicate also specific information, such as an unmarried or widowed state, the nature of an occupation or of a religion.

Why are most clothes sold 'off the peg'?

Although many people still make their own clothes or have them made, most of us welcome the convenience and cheapness of buying clothes 'off the peg'. The era of ready-made clothes, worn for a season and discarded the next, is quite recent. Until the late 1700s, people relied on their own skill with a needle or that of a family member or professional. For all but the wealthy, the variety of fabrics was limited. High prices meant that clothes had to last a long time.

Machinery developed in the Industrial Revolution led to more fabrics being produced faster and more cheaply than ever before. In the eighteenth century, cotton from the American colonies toppled wool from the dominant position it had enjoyed for centuries. Three inventions then caused a revolution in the British cotton processing industry: Kay's flying shuttle in 1733; Hargreave's spinning jenny in 1766; and Crompton's mule in 1779. The flying shuttle allowed one weaver to produce at far greater speeds by cutting out the awkward passing of the shuttle bearing the yarn from one hand to the other. This led to greater demand for yarn. The spinning jenny and Crompton's mule, which could be harnessed to steam or water power, reproduced mechanically the actions of the hand spinner.

By 1850, Britain's 750 000 powered looms led the world with their output of mass-produced fabrics. Other countries had lagged behind, but in the second half of the century mechanisation was introduced on a wider scale. The price of richer fabrics dropped, and fashionable garments were brought within the reach of ordinary people.

In the United States, the mass production of fabric was accelerated by Eli Whitney's invention in 1794 of the cotton gin, an ingenious device for cleaning cotton. This enabled the seed to be separated from the raw fibre at a rate fifty times that of a manual worker. The cotton gin transformed the American South into a prosperous society based on cotton-growing, and increased the demand for slave labour. Between 1815 and 1830 the American cotton trade boomed, growing by more than 1000 per cent.

As the nineteenth century progressed, more mechanisation meant more efficient techniques for mass production of garments. The sewing machine, invented at the beginning of the century and in widespread industrial use by the 1850s, drastically cut manufacturing times. At the same time, new, less formal styles that could be produced without traditional tailoring skills became fashionable.

Department stores emerged in the late nineteenth century and stocked these ready-made garments. Along with these changes and maybe hastened by them came a relaxation of rigid dress rules. Today, the specialist seamstress finds work for such one-off items as wedding dresses, and the tailor-made suit is in many places a luxury.

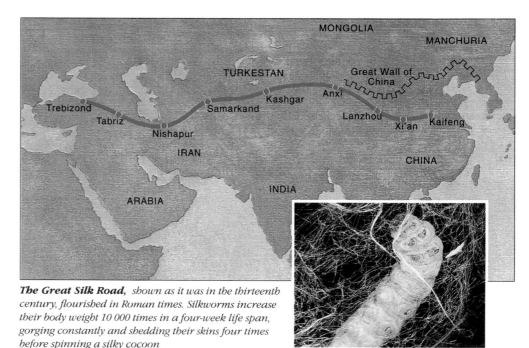

The Great Silk Road, shown as it was in the thirteenth century, flourished in Roman times. Silkworms increase their body weight 10 000 times in a four-week life span, gorging constantly and shedding their skins four times before spinning a silky cocoon

Why is silk so expensive?

Silk is a protein secretion made by spiders and many insects. The silk is extruded through tubes in the body and drawn out through minute holes. As these threads, from two to six in number, are pulled out by the insect, they congeal to form a stronger thread. This thread is used to form webs or cocoons.

Although a variety of creatures yield silk, none except the mulberry silkworm, the larvae of the moth *Bombyx mori*, produces a silk that can be spun profitably. Spider silk, for instance, is of exquisite quality and has often been used to make small items of clothing as a novelty. But the small quantity of silk spiders produce, together with the difficulty of farming them, has made it impractical to use spider silk commercially.

Commercial silkworms feed on the leaves of the white mulberry tree. After they spin their cocoons, they are killed. If the insects were allowed to mature they would make their way out of the cocoons and so spoil them. (Some silkworms are, of course, allowed to mature into moths for breeding purposes.) The cocoon is usually steamed or soaked in hot water to kill the silkworm inside. The process also softens the protein gum holding the threads together.

Each cocoon is unravelled by hand. The processor must first find the loose end, which can require much manual dexterity. A single thread unwound from a cocoon is about 1.6 km (1 mile) long. The threads from several cocoons are then reeled and spun into thicker thread for weaving into cloth. Cocoons that cannot be successfully unravelled are chopped up and spun into a still beautiful but coarser material.

Silk was carried from China through central Asia to the eastern Mediterranean from before the time of Christ until the mid-fifteenth century along the ancient Silk Road, so named because silk formed the main trade between East and West. The Chinese kept the secrets of silk manufacture until some silkworm eggs were smuggled by monks to Europe in the sixth century.

Silk manufacturing industries were eventually established in many places, notably Japan and the Lombardy region of northern Italy where mulberry trees flourish. Today, the greatest manufacturers of raw silk remain China, Japan and Italy, and the techniques involved in its

Mass production brought off-the-peg clothes at cheaper prices. A coloured engraving depicts a workroom in Douglas & Sherwood's skirt factory, New York, in the mid-nineteenth century

processing tend to be handed down from one generation to another.

Rarity and beauty have made silk a cherished material for centuries. The romantic story of silk weaving dates back to the Chinese Empress Xi Lingshi. She, it is said, discovered the secret of making silk by accident in the year 2640 BC, when she tried to discover what was eating her husband's mulberry trees. References to silk are found in the annals of the Han dynasty (206 BC to AD 221) when silk fabrics made up most of the trade with the Graeco-Roman world.

Silk was the favoured dress fabric of the Roman nobility during the time of Julius Caesar; later, the Romans passed laws forbidding certain classes of people from wearing silk garments. Subsequently, others copied the ban. In Spain, a law first passed in 1234 restricted the use of silk, and a legal handbook published in England in 1675 advises that: 'If one hath not in land a hundred pound, he cannot use … damask, silk, chamlet, taffay, in gowns, coats, outermost garments.'

Silk is still a fabric for the relatively well heeled, if not by royal edict then by simple economics. World production of silk is small, about 50 000 tonnes a year, and the finest silk fibres fetch high prices.

Why are some shoes deliberately ill-fitting?

A visitor from outer space could be forgiven, on looking in a shoeshop window, for assuming that most human feet come to a point in the middle, and that left and right feet are exactly the same. Clearly, our feet are neither symmetrical nor shaped like an arrow. Yet, over the centuries, vanity, fashion and custom have conspired to dictate sometimes bizarre and frequently unhealthy shoe shapes for both men and women. Practicality has rarely been a priority. In twelfth-century Europe, fashionable women wore *poulaines*, long and tapering shoes that must have compressed all but the narrowest feet. The same shoe fashion returned with even greater impact two centuries later and remained popular until about the middle of the 1400s. Historians find the fashion particularly interesting because the Church denounced it as lewd and provocative.

Small feet for men and women have often been thought desirable. Petrarch, the fourteenth-century Italian poet, is supposed to have gone almost lame from wearing too-small shoes in order to 'display to his Laura a neat foot'. Deformation of the

foot was taken to its extreme in China. For 1000 years, women endured foot-binding in the name of beauty. With tiny, hobbled feet that made walking an agony, Chinese women were much more likely to find a husband. Small feet were also an indication of status, implying the lack of a need to work. Foot-binding was banned when the Manchu dynasty was overthrown in 1911.

Modern women echo the hobbled walk of the Chinese in their use of high heels, which thrust the centre of balance forward unnaturally. High heels have been in and out of Western fashion since they first appeared towards the end of the seventeenth century. Men's boots had high heels until the mid-nineteenth century, as a heel helped to keep feet comfortably in stirrups for horse-riding. One explanation for the continued popularity of high heels among women is that such uncomfortable shoes enforce a hobbled gait, which is considered by some to be erotic. As a result, studies of American women show that they have four times as many problems with their feet as American men. Their most common foot problem is 'hammer toes', caused when arrow-shaped shoes crush the toes, forcing them to curl under.

There are signs, however, that women are beginning to insist on comfort and practicality in shoe design, as witnessed by the comparatively recent popularity of female athletic shoes and brogues. Perhaps the human foot, shod sensibly, will be allowed to keep its natural shape.

Why do so many men still wear a tie?

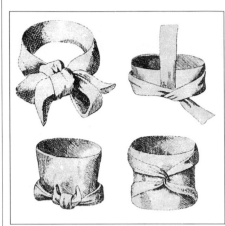

A man's reputation once depended on how stylishly he tied his cravat. Here are just four of thirty-two different modes of the Romantic period, from a definitive book on what was considered an essential art

Even though they serve no obvious purpose, neckties have been fashionable for at least 2000 years. Egyptian sculptures dating from the third century BC show the ancient pharaohs wearing broad jewelled neckbands. Extravagant neckwear, for both males and females, reached the height of absurdity with the elaborate ruffed collars of the late sixteenth century.

In the 1600s, a type of scarf worn knotted at the front was made popular by

Those giant boots weren't made for walking but to give Elton John something to sing about in the movie Tommy. *The high-heeled shoes, designed by Charles Jourdan in the 1930s, helped bring him fame*

Hallmarks of a dandy were a high neck-stock, pouter pigeon chest and tight trousers. Fashion leader 'Beau' Brummell argued for plainer clothes to replace the elaborate dress of the early 1800s

Croatian mercenaries serving in France. The French called it a *cravate* after *Hvat*, Serbo-Croatian for Croat. A cravat was fashionable throughout Europe until about 1710, when men adopted the neck-stock, a broad band of linen or cambric which was sometimes stiffened with card-board, worn buckled around the neck. A narrow black tie called a solitaire was another occasional fashion of the time.

During the nineteenth century, cravats and ties (which resembled bow ties) assumed great importance, and pamphlets of the day gave strict instructions as to how to achieve the perfect knot. In 1828, H. le Blanc published a definitive book entitled *The Art of Tying the Cravat*. By the middle of the century, the necktie as we recognise it was being worn.

Despite relaxing dress standards, a tie is still a required item of clothing for the serious businessman and is firmly associated with neatness, sobriety and conventionality. The business suit imposes a rigid and to some eyes rather sombre uniform, but the necktie provides an outlet for displaying individual taste. Often it adds a touch of colour and even flamboyance.

And who could deny the importance of the old school tie? This, whether it belongs to a school or club, gives the wearer an instant badge of belonging, a feeling of exclusivity and camaraderie with fellows.

Why are men's fashions less colourful than women's?

For centuries, men's fashions were as elaborate and colourful as women's – sometimes even more so. The change to dark, plain clothes for men started in England in the middle of the eighteenth century. The newly prevailing idea that fancy clothing was somehow effeminate was linked to a national mood of seriousness and introspection. Cosmopolitan courtiers were attacked as being frivolous, and elaborate male clothing became associated with foreign culture, specifically with the so-called moral corruption of the French court: a fashionably dressed man on the streets of London was open to attack as a 'French dog'. The new masculine ideal was the sensibly dressed English country gentleman.

Oddly enough, 'Beau' Brummell and his fellow dandies epitomised not the previously colourful fashionable male but the new, coldly correct style. Their elegant manner of dressing emphasised cut, discretion and simplicity.

With the development of the modern bureaucratic state came even greater uniformity in clothing, leading eventually to the adoption throughout the Western world of a sober business uniform.

Why did the idea of women wearing trousers take so long to be accepted?

Any woman who has tried to run in a tight skirt or ride a bicycle in a short skirt knows that women wear trousers for comfort and ease of movement. Trousers are, however, a recent addition to the female wardrobe. Throughout most of recorded history, some sort of dress or skirt was the rule for women. But by the mid-nineteenth century this fashion went to extremes. Women were tightly laced into corsets to emphasise preposterously – and dangerously – tiny waists. Skirts ballooned into crinolines, which had to be supported by cages of horsehair or metal and made normal movement extremely difficult.

In reaction, an American feminist, Amelia Bloomer, designed a knee-length skirt to be worn over baggy pants. She was inspired by traditional Turkish costume. She introduced the outfit in 1851 in her newspaper the *Lily*, but it never caught on. In fact, women who dared to wear the costume were severely criticised, mainly for looking too masculine. Critics thought that women who wore these bloomers, as they came to be called, might start to behave like men. Since most of the women who supported bloomers were also members of the burgeoning women's rights movement, this seemed a definite threat. Amelia Bloomer's attempts to introduce the fashion to Europe were met not only with ridicule but with outright hostility.

It wasn't until the end of the nineteenth century that trousers were more widely worn by women, and even then only as a cycling outfit. Cycling became the rage of the 1890s and the craze for the sport launched the new male and female costume of knickerbockers. When women began riding horses astride rather than side-saddle in the 1880s, the divided skirt became fashionable in the United States. By the 1920s, some women were wearing riding breeches. But

Cycling women brought new fashions and a hint of liberation

the major liberator of women's dress was war. When, during two world wars, women were called upon to work in factories and other previously male-only workplaces, many adopted uniforms or overalls that were practical rather than decorative. The vogue included trousers – or slacks, as they were sometimes called – for rough work. Perhaps women were expected to return to domestic pursuits and more feminine attire when the men came home, but the new-found freedom of wearing trousers was difficult to abandon. So women continued to wear shorts and slacks for comfort and convenience, with differing degrees of acceptance by the community at large. Today, there are few Western countries where slacks aren't part of everyday fashion for women. But, strangely, women in some occupations and places are still required to wear a skirt or a dress.

Why are white clothes cooler than dark clothes?

Light is a form of energy. White objects reflect virtually all of the light that reaches them. Black objects absorb almost all of this same energy. No wonder that people wearing black clothes usually feel hotter in summer than those dressed in white. Any fabric dark enough to absorb a high percentage of the Sun's energy will be noticeably warmer than a pale fabric of similar construction, and this heat is transmitted to the wearer.

Strangely, tribal groups who live in the North African deserts have traditionally worn dark clothes. These are, however, very loose-fitting, and allow a good flow of cooling air between the wearer and the garment.

Why are jeans so popular?

Levi's boast that their jeans are so tough that horses couldn't rip apart the fabric. Their tag reinforces the claim

The blue jeans first made by Levi Strauss for American miners and cowboys in the 1870s are now worn worldwide by everyone from students to grandmothers.

As work clothes, jeans immediately became popular because of their strength and durability. Strauss and his partner Jacob Davis patented a unique method of riveting pocket corners and seams to prevent the fabric from tearing under stress, and the fabric itself, *serge de Nîmes* (denim), was a particularly hard-wearing cotton twill. But it was not until the 1950s, with the image projected by such actors as James Dean and Marlon Brando, that blue jeans became the uniform of the young and the rebellious.

Far from being a passing fad, the fashion for blue jeans shows no sign of waning, and jeans are no longer solely inexpensive gear for teenagers. Jeans come in mini versions for children, in pricey styles by famous fashion houses, and in almost endless variety, plain or decorated, pre-shrunk and pre-faded. New lifestyles, with more travel and outdoor activities, have kicked the fashion along.

Why does wool shrink?

Wool shrinks for two reasons. Firstly, it is a naturally springy fibre and the forces of knitting or weaving stretch it out of place. But wool has a tendency to want to recover its original size; this is called relaxation shrinkage. The second reason for wool's shrinkage is related to

A tight veil guards this Tuareg tribesman against desert sand and winds. A Moslem, he is one of a tribe in which men, not women, cover their faces from puberty onwards

the make-up of its fibres. Each individual wool fibre is covered in microscopic overlapping scales, and when these are heated and agitated (for instance, in a washing machine) the fibres coil and become locked together. This is the principle behind felt making. Once this felting takes place, it is impossible to separate the fibres and stretch the garment back to its original shape without causing severe damage. Modern research has discovered plastic coatings which cover these scales and prevent tangling, felting and shrinkage from taking place. But even wool clothes proclaimed as being pre-shrunk require special care in laundering.

Why is wool warmer than cotton?

The springiness that causes wool to coil and contract contributes also to its bulkiness and warmth. Air becomes trapped between the springy fibres, and creates an insulation layer. The same bulk of cotton would be just as warm, but cotton lacks resilience and tends to mat down, losing its warmth. Imagine a blanket made of cotton wool. It would be fluffy when you went to bed, but by morning the fibres would be flattened and much of the warmth lost. A cloth's texture depends

Natural fibres compared. Cotton's (left) are fine but irregular. The thicker fibres of merino wool are durable and trap air

on the type and spacing of the yarns in the weaving. Smooth, tightly twisted yarns form a fabric with fewer air spaces surrounding the fibres and the surface of the cloth. Raising the ends of loose fibres, through finishing processes such as brushing, increases the number of fibre ends capable of forming an insulation layer. Fuzzy yarns thus create an outer fur of projecting ends that entrap warm, still air. This is why fuzzy fabrics, such as flannelette and velour, feel warmer to the touch than a smooth fabric such as satin.

Why are so many clothing fashions directed at young people?

For much of history, children and young people were either dressed as mini-adults or wore special clothes, dictated by adults, thought to be suitable for their needs and activities. It was only after World War II that young people living in industrialised countries began to establish their own styles and tastes. Today, they form one of the fashion industry's largest and most profitable markets.

This could not have happened until young people had money to spend as they pleased. In the 1950s, economic stability produced a sense of optimism. The poverty of the Great Depression and the deprivations of the war years seemed far away. Booming industry brought a greater demand for labour and a much higher rate of pay for young people. For the first time, they formed a separate market, and clothing manufacturers were quick to cater for it.

During the 1960s, the influence of young people on fashion became so strong that it was seen as their preserve. Mary Quant started the trend in London in 1955, soon followed by other designers who opened boutiques in Carnaby Street and the Kings Road. The Swinging Sixties had begun. These shops were exclusively for young people and had a distinctive style and atmosphere, very different from fuddy-duddy fashion emporiums of old.

Many fashions for youth, such as the punk and hippy styles, evolved as a means of challenging accepted standards. And often, through mass production and media promotion, they were absorbed by the mainstream fashion industry.

Why do men's clothes button on the right, women's on the left?

Many theories attempt to explain why men and women button clothes on different sides. One says that a man could adjust his buttons with his left hand while his right hand was kept free to grasp a sword. Women traditionally carry children in their left arm, and use their right hand to unbutton, especially when breast-feeding. Another theory is that during the thirteenth century, when French courtiers wore clothes fastened with many buttons, ladies' maids, standing in front of their mistresses, would have found it much easier to button from right to left. For right-handed noblemen, dressing and

The Punk Look *started in London in the late 1970s as a protest by jobless teenagers. It became a fashion for youth of all classes*

undressing without assistance, the reverse was easier. In some groups, however, the custom is reversed: male Hasidic Jews, for example, button right over left, a difference derived from a Biblical injunction to the Israelites to mark themselves off from unbelievers.

Why have parades become an essential part of the fashion industry?

Paris has been considered the fashion capital of the world for hundreds of years, and the very name conjures visions of lavish fashion parades. The very first Parisian *haute couture* house was founded by an expatriate Englishman, Charles Frederick Worth, in 1858. He had the idea of preparing an entire season's designs at once, to show to prospective customers.

The tradition of showing seasonal collections by having a fashion parade began with the 1900 Great Universal Exhibition in Paris, which showcased merchandise from all over the world. Several countries took pavilions, and thousands flocked to see its unique displays. None created greater interest than its fashion section, in which designers, including the house of Worth, showed their clothes in a revolu-

tionary new way: on models in everyday settings. The president of the fashion section, Madame Paquin, showed herself dressed in her own designs, sitting at her own dressing table. The first couturière to have her styles sold abroad, Paquin regularly sent ten mannequins dressed in identical costumes to the races or the casino when she wanted to launch new styles.

Since 1900, buyers from all over the world have regularly attended the elaborate seasonal parades of the various French fashion salons. Parades have become a useful way of displaying new styles to a number of potential buyers at the same time. A complex system has now developed between overseas buyers, press reporters and photographers, who between them carry the new styles from the show-rooms to the general public in a carefully planned progression.

On the catwalk, *a model displays fashions by Italian designer Angelo Tarlazzi. His cashmere knitwear is widely acclaimed*

The beguiling behaviour of pets

Fidelity and obedience *are rarely more clearly demonstrated than in a sheepdog's devoted service to its master. Dogs have herded and guarded sheep for more than 10 000 years*

Why do dogs and cats wave their tails?

Social predators need a rich vocabulary of gestures to communicate mood and intent to other members of the pack, to reinforce group cohesion and to coordinate their activities in the hunt. Many of these gestures, such as facial expression, operate at short range. In communication over greater distances other kinds of signals are needed. Dogs employ many tail signals. Held straight, extending the line of the spine, the tail expresses aggression; tucked between the hind legs it conveys submission; waved from side to side it shows friendliness.

The tail language of the cat is much less expressive on the whole. Being a more solitary animal, the cat has less need of a complex tail vocabulary. When a cat is threatened it will make itself seem as large as possible by arching its back and erecting its tail, poker stiff, the

Why are dogs more faithful than cats?

Dogs and cats are predators, and life is seldom easy for animals that prey upon others. Most predators often go hungry. Any minor ailment or injury can make the difference between a kill and a bungled attack.

Predators have evolved behaviours that can improve the odds in their favour. Wolves and other wild dogs hunt in packs, cooperating in the chase and sharing the spoils. No matter how bad the conditions, all members of the group are unlikely to be unsuccessful at any given time. One will surely catch something, and a small share of something is better than nothing.

The wild cat, on the other hand, is a solitary hunter. It survives by acquiring a close familiarity with its home range, learning by experience where the hunting is likely to be best under any particular circumstances. The domestic cat retains this advantage by remaining faithful to its home. The dog, in contrast, is a social animal, attached to its fellows in the wild and to humans in domestication.

Solitary by nature, *cats constantly reveal facets of their wild origins. The arched back of this Abyssinian sorrel cat shows fear and uncertainty. A tail waving rapidly from side to side is a clear expression of a cat's annoyance and possible aggression*

tip often quivering with tension. If you tease or play with a cat when it is not in the mood, it sometimes shows its displeasure by lashing its tail, an expression of its internal conflict and anxiety. The signal, often misinterpreted as anger, can be roughly translated as: 'If you don't stop what you're doing, I'll be forced to do something desperate.' This feline tail gesture seems to be uncommon in wild cats, simply because it is seldom needed. If they encounter humans, their usual reaction is to slink silently away.

Why do dogs and cats eat grass?

The ancestor of today's dog was almost certainly a predator but also a carrion-eating scavenger and even, on occasion, a fruit-eater. The modern dog will still eat a variety of non-meat foods without any obvious ill effect. The cat is markedly more confined to a carnivorous diet.

Both cats and dogs quite often nibble grass, weeds or leaves, essentially for much the same reason that humans now and then feel the need for an aspirin, an antacid, a laxative or a vitamin pill. Nibbling vegetation is not always a sign that the animal is ailing, however. Something more subtle than a simple purge seems to be needed sometimes. Often, a dog or cat will nibble vegetation in a manner very different from its normal eating habits, delicately sniffing and rejecting several leaves or blades of grass before selecting one, almost as though it is searching for a particular bouquet.

Many wild animals vary their diet from time to time, often in very precise ways, responding to some awareness of a slight deficiency. For example, elephants and other plant-eating animals sometimes travel great distances to congregate at salt licks, where mineral salts are exposed.

Why do cats purr?

Most of the smaller members of the cat family purr, but the larger members, such as lions and tigers, do not. It is not entirely clear how a cat purrs. The noise emanates not from the voice box, or larynx, but from somewhere deep in the chest. Mother cats purr to their kittens when about to suckle them. The kittens gather around as though in response to a call, and the purring normally stops when the kittens settle down to feed. Why a female cat purrs at other times or why a male cat purrs is unclear. To most of us, the sound is the very essence of contentment, but cats also purr when they are agitated and unsettled.

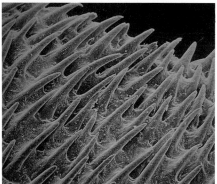

Abrasive barbs run down the centre of the cat's long and flexible tongue. They carry no taste buds, but enable the cat to scrape flesh from bones, and help it to clean its fur. The barbs point backwards to make sure that live prey is securely held. A cat tastes food with the tip, sides and base of its tongue

Why do cats have such rough tongues?

The almost universal primary purpose of an animal's tongue is to manipulate food in the mouth. The cat's tongue, which is unusually rough because of numerous tiny, hardened nodules, is very handy also for rasping the last scrap of flesh from bones and for cleaning the coat.

Cats need efficient grooming equipment because they are solitary animals and must groom themselves. Social animals, such as dogs, often groom one another. Dogs' tongues have evolved as cooling systems. As a dog pants, its sloppy, lolling tongue exposes a copious flow of saliva, which evaporates rapidly, cooling the blood stream.

Why do cats always find their way home?

Writers and naturalists have commented for centuries on the cat's homing abilities. Many a cat owner has taken the family pet with the household to a new home, only to have it promptly disappear and show up at its old home some time later. This

has given rise to folk restraints of doubtful use such as smearing the cat's paws with butter, or snipping off the tip of its tail and burying it beside the new front door.

Cats have home ranges to which they are strongly attached and they dislike disruption of their routines. A cat that is forcibly removed from its home range will often attempt to return.

Some cat owners have tried systematically to find out more about this homing instinct. In one series of experiments, a cat was taken from her kittens and put into a cage nearly 2 km (about 1 mile) away. From an observation spot some 30 m (100 ft) away, she was freed by remote control and watched. She promptly turned and set off in the direction of home. Eight hours later, she was back with her kittens. The experiment was repeated several times and at various distances up to 5 km (3 miles). In one test the cat was even taken away from home under anaesthetic. Each time she found her way back. Finally, she was taken about 26 km (16 miles) away, but this apparently tested her homing ability too severely, and she was never seen again.

In more rigorous tests in Germany, cats were placed in sacks, transported various distances from home and then released at the centre of a maze. Each cat was fitted with a collar attached to a string which unreeled from a spool at the centre of the maze, recording the cat's route. Most cats wasted no time in exploring their surroundings; they seemed easily to find the most direct way out of the maze and the direction of home. From then, however, the results were hardly impressive: the success rate was only about 60 per cent within a radius of 5 km (3 miles) and no better than chance at greater distances.

There are also persistent reports of cats employing homing ability in reverse: a family leaves a cat behind when moving, only to have it rejoin them months later. The owners of a two-year-old American tomcat named Pooh moved about 300 km (190 miles) from Newnan, Georgia, to Wellford, South Carolina. Some four months later Pooh was reported to have rejoined the family. There was no clue as to how he managed to find them.

Even more remarkable was a cat named Sugar, which took fourteen months to track down its owners after they moved some 2400 km (1500 miles) from California to Oklahoma. They confirmed Sugar's identity from its deformed hip joint. In such cases the cat that turns up is not always the one that was left behind. Owners doubtless exaggerate resemblances between cats. The evidence is almost always anecdotal, and it would seem to be extremely difficult to design any reliable test of the phenomenon.

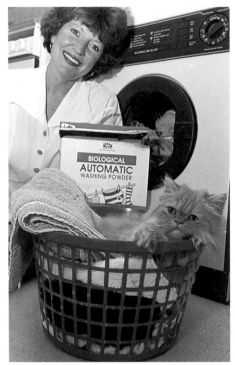

Supercat Rodney survived a full cycle in a washing machine, including a spin dry. The rare resilience of cats may explain why they have been regarded as gods and witches

Why do cats have nine lives?

Most animals need to be more alert than humans. No animal can afford to be inattentive if it is to evade predators, and predators themselves survive by outwitting their prey. Among domestic animals, the cat is most reliant upon alertness, inheriting from its ancestor the quick wits and instant reflexes that characterise the wild cat. Even the dog, the only other carnivore widely kept as a pet, seldom maintains quite the same razor-sharp alertness; its forte is stamina, plus cooperation with its fellows, canine and human.

The cat's combination of caution, agility and swift reaction to emergency has become part of our folklore. The myth prevails that, if there is a way of surviving, the cat somehow will find it whenever its life is threatened.

Why are tortoiseshell cats usually female?

Your cat looks as it does because of its genes. Eight genes in combination control almost all variations in the colour and pattern of the fur of domestic cats. All domestic cats carry the gene for the tabby pattern of their ancestor, the wild cat.

Pigmentation in cats' hairs is either black-brown or orange. The orange gene occurs on the X sex chromosome, and is therefore said to be sex-linked. Males have a single X chromosome, and can be orange or not. Females carry two X chromosomes, and may be both orange and black-brown. This gives them their tortoiseshell, or marmalade, pattern. Male tortoiseshell cats are extremely rare and almost always sterile.

Whether the tabby pattern shows depends upon the so-called agouti effect. If the coat of a grey tabby cat is closely examined it will be seen that all its hairs are black, but in the grey regions each hair has a broad, variable band of reduced pigmentation between root and tip. This agouti effect is genetically determined, as are the white patches that are often combined with the tortoiseshell pattern. A pure white cat is the result of the dominant white gene. Other genes produce faded colours such as grey, and control fur length and those distinctive dark 'points' – nose, ears, tail and feet – so important to breeders of Siamese cats.

Why do cats always land on their feet?

A cat called Sabrina fell thirty-two storeys from a New York skyscraper and limped away with a collapsed lung and a chipped tooth. City cats, which spend so much time on roofs and ledges, often fall several storeys onto a hard surface and escape without significant injury.

One reason why cats survive falls that would kill humans is that they weigh much less. This gives them a lower terminal velocity. As they fall, they reach a point where their acceleration due to gravity is balanced and offset by air resistance.

High-speed photographs show that in falls from exceptional heights, cats extend all four legs sideways, as do gliding mammals. This exposes a greater area to the cushion of air below and gives a cat greater control over its fall.

Humans tumble uncontrollably in free fall, but cats fall the right way up. A sensory system that acts like a gyroscope reports changes in the body's orientation to the central nervous system. A falling cat senses at once that it is upside down and responds instantly by twisting its agile body to position itself for a safer landing. It hits the ground with feet flexed to absorb shock and extended to spread the impact. Shock is further reduced because muscles rather than ligaments join and surround many bones in a cat's body.

Skydivers supreme, cats have an in-built mechanism that enables them to adjust their position during a sudden tumble. Agility, a lithe body and springy muscles do the rest

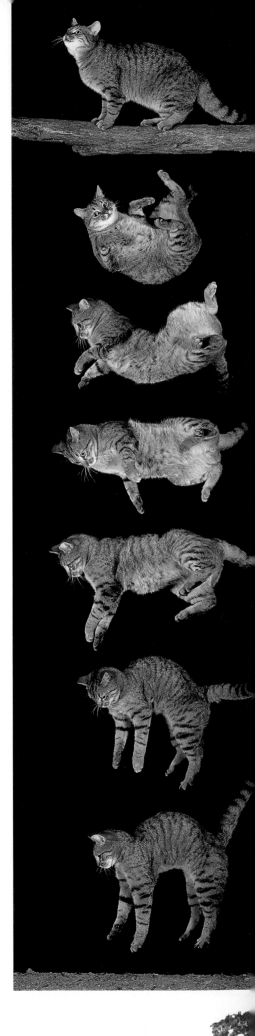

SATISFYING THAT PASSION FOR PETS

Keeping pets is one of the great common denominators of our society. The United States has some 45 million of the world's 160 million dogs, France about 9 million and Britain 6 million. In industrialised countries, one household in four has either a dog or a cat and perhaps a budgerigar, goldfish or rabbit, too.

The passion for keeping pets began in prehistoric times, when our early ancestors probably tamed the offspring of wolves. In that moment, some 20 000 years ago, the pattern was set not only for keeping pets but for changing their appearance and nature. Today, the world has about 400 different breeds of dog. All came from the same original species.

After domesticating the dog, more for its use than companionship, early humans put goats, cattle, sheep, pigs and horses into service. Ancient Egyptians worshipped cats as gods, and 300 000 mummified cats were found in one tomb.

Dogs and cats long reigned supreme as pet owners' favourites. But changing lifestyles, in which more women work and more people live in flats, have also affected pets. When families can't keep dogs or cats, they often have fish or birds. The budgerigar, domesticated just over a century ago, is now said to be the world's most popular pet.

Affluence has fed the desire to be different and extended the variety of the pets we keep. The list includes anything from black panthers to pythons and crocodiles to tarantulas. The world trade in smuggled animals depends on a willingness to pay high prices for exotic pets.

Pets help us to relax and enable millions of people to conquer loneliness. Recently, medical researchers have found that pet ownership can be the main factor in extending somebody's life. In one study of coronary heart disease, 28 per cent of pet-less patients died within a year, compared to only 6 per cent of those who had pets. Mentally handicapped children, psychiatric patients and those seeking a cure from drug addiction benefit particularly when pets are used in their therapy. In many countries, people regularly take their dogs to hospitals, so that patients can play with them and hasten a recovery.

There's really no limit *to what people will keep as pets – anything from lizards to a goose or a cougar to an alligator. The passion often brings considerable benefits to health, provided of course that a potential killer doesn't break loose*

Why do dogs bury bones?

In the wild, many predators kill prey that is bigger than they can consume at one meal. Wherever there are predators, scavengers usually follow – jackals, vultures or other animals that feed on carrion – quick to find and polish off the remnants of a kill. Some, in fact, seldom wait for the prey to be abandoned, but move in and seize it. Hyenas, for example, are much stronger than cheetahs and quickly take most of their kills.

Many predators attempt to hide the kill somewhere safe for a later meal. Leopards usually haul their prey up into a tree to eat at leisure. Predators that cannot climb trees or those in treeless open country bury their prey. Foxes and jackals occasionally bury surplus food, as does the domestic dog.

Bones of contention *develop a puppy's ability to fend for itself and bring out natural traits from its predatory past*

Why are there so many breeds of dog?

The origins of the domestication of dogs are lost in time, but most researchers have concluded that the wolf was probably the wild ancestor of the domestic dog. It's likely that wolves scavenged for food scraps around the camps of early humans. They were perhaps tolerated at first, and then encouraged because of their alertness and vigorous response to marauding predators and other threats in the night.

As the relationship strengthened, the ancestral dog's role probably extended gradually from guard to companion on hunting excursions. Wolves are social animals that hunt in a pack, coordinating their efforts in finding, chasing and bringing down prey. The dog's natural willingness and ability to respond to the demands of the chase strengthened its developing bond with humans. When a wolf transferred its allegiance from its pack to humans it became domesticated, but there was little real change in its function.

Virtually all breeds of dog were first established as specialists in particular tasks, their usefulness founded on the stamina, cooperation and group fidelity shown in their ancestral packs. In the 1800s came a new leisure activity, the showing of dogs. Today, there are about 400 distinct breeds of dog, recognised by kennel clubs and registries around the world.

Almost all breeds are the result of the development

It's hard to believe *that the wild ancestor of our 400 different breeds of dog, some of which are depicted here, was probably the wolf. The shar pei (left) is one of the world's rarest breeds. Its bristly coat gives it a Chinese name for sharkskin or sandpaper*

of instinctive skills in guarding or hunting. Pointers and setters indicate quarry for the hunter; retrievers fetch it once it has been shot down; hounds of various kinds track down and corner prey which the oncoming hunter can despatch upon arrival. Greyhounds sprint after quarry in open country, while terriers force their way into burrows to flush it out. Dobermans guard property. Collies and other working dogs control livestock. Huskies haul sleds. The demands of fashion and the show ring have extended the development of breeds, but even toy dogs such as chihuahuas, poodles and Pekinese have been bred and maintained partly because of their value as intelligent burglar alarms.

Why do budgies talk?

Songs and calls are important to birds. Many species rely on vocalisation to form pairs or to establish and maintain territory. Birds acquire their vocabularies in one of two ways, though occasionally both are involved.

In some species songs and calls are innate. For example, foster parents of other species raise cuckoos, which make cuckoo sounds when mature. Even when individuals of species with innate songs and calls are reared in isolation in the laboratory, with no chance of hearing other birds, they utter the sounds appropriate to their species when they reach maturity. In other species, such as the skylark, young birds must learn their songs by contact with others. This can be demonstrated in the laboratory by having a chick raised by foster parents of a different species. When adult, its songs and calls will be those of its foster parents and it will not respond to the vocalisations of its own species.

When birds of the species that ordinarily learn by mimicking their parents are carefully reared and cared for as pets, some can be trained to mimic human speech, sometimes with remarkable fidelity. The budgie is an especially apt pupil because it has other characteristics that combine to reinforce its natural tendency to mimicry. Like many parrots, it is highly intelligent, compared to most other birds. It is curious and strongly sociable, often forming a strong bond with its owner. The talking pet budgie makes sounds that resemble human speech, but does not use those sounds to convey ideas or feelings, which is what we normally mean by the word 'talk'.

The abilities of birds to think and learn are still under investigation. A scientist, Irene Pepperberg, has trained an African grey parrot called Alex to communicate in simple sentences in standard English. This bird has shown cognitive abilities previously recognised only in humans and in chimpanzees trained in language.

Despite much research into sound production in humans and other animals, the reasons why some birds can mimic human speech while others cannot, remain to some extent mysterious.

Why do budgerigars come in so many different colours?

In the wild in Australia the budgerigar is mainly green, with yellow and black bars on its head, back and wings. The familiar household budgie, however, has long had stable strains of white, yellow, green and blue birds, as well as a host of rarer and quite delicate colour combinations.

Colour effects in birds have three different causes, operating in isolation or in combination. Iridescence is caused by peculiarities in the microscopic structure of the feathers in some birds. When light hits the feathers, they act like a prism, giving the rainbow effect of spilt oil on a rainy street.

The second cause is chemical. Yellows and reds, for example, generally arise from a group of pigments known as carotinoids, while blacks and browns result from melanins. Melanin, controlled by a simple genetic structure, gives budgies their dark bars.

Blue colouring has another cause. It arises from exactly the same process that makes the sky blue – a phenomenon known as Tindall scattering. Microscopic bubbles in the structure of the feather scatter light in such a way that the blue component is reflected back to the observer; all other colours are absorbed. No blue pigment is known to exist in birds.

The effects of pigmentation and Tindall scattering often combine in various ways. The green component in budgies, for example, results from yellow pigment overlying blue structural colour, again with a fairly simple genetic basis.

Many of the attributes of an animal are the effects of hundreds or even thousands of genes operating in combination. But characteristics such as colour and pattern often hinge on the effects of only one gene. This means that it often takes only a few generations of selective breeding to isolate and maintain the factors involved in different colour combinations. Breeders of domestic budgies have long been able to remove the melanin to yield a plain green bird, the blue to form yellow strains, the yellow to form blue and all factors to yield white.

Budgies in the wild flock to a waterhole. The natural bird, a parakeet, is mainly green. Birds of a different colour were first bred in Belgium late last century

Handy carrybags are readily available in a hamster's cheeks. When filled with food to be stored for winter, they double the width of the head and shoulders

Why do hamsters have cheek pouches?

Wild hamsters spend the scorching summers on the steppes of central Eurasia in gathering seeds and leaves and carrying them off to their burrows, where they store them for the bitterly cold winter. They boost their rate of foraging by cramming food into their baggy cheeks, thereby minimising time spent in journeys to and from the burrow. Many other rodents also carry food in cheek pouches and many animals store food. For example, a small European songbird called the marsh tit hides food in the morning for retrieval later the same day.

Why do horses need shoes?

Horses walk on the tips of their toes. On each foot there is one toe, broadened at the tip and surrounded by a hoof, a structure corresponding to the nails and claws in other animals. Like a fingernail, a hoof is dead tissue and has no nerve endings. In the centre of the foot a soft pad of tissue called the frog serves as a cushion, absorbing the impact of the hoof on the ground. The horse's heel is raised well off the ground. This arrangement is more than adequate for domestic horses running free in fields. But when a horse carries the load of a rider or a pack, the

heavier impact on the ground may inflame the frogs and eventually lame the animal. An iron horseshoe nailed to the hoof reinforces it and keeps the frog from contact with the ground.

Why do rabbits have buck teeth?

Over the aeons, plants have evolved many subtle protections for their leaves, the vital organs by which they make food. Adaptations that protect plants from grazing or browsing animals include toxic or unpalatable chemical substances, needle-sharp spines and thorns, and hard, abrasive silicon compounds deposited in leaves and stems. These compounds wear away the teeth of animals that habitually eat them, to such an extent that some individuals die of starvation because their teeth are ground down to uselessness.

This danger does not threaten rabbits, hares or rodents, however. Their front teeth grow continuously throughout life. The upper teeth protrude from the jaw at an angle that allows them to grind on the lower teeth. This maintains sharp, chisel-like edges which are ideal for shearing grass stems. So sharp and strong are these teeth that some rodents have been known to gnaw through glass.

The rate at which teeth wear must always match the rate at which they grow. If the upper and lower teeth fail to meet for any reason, nothing can halt their growth, and eventually the animal dies. That is why veterinarians recommend giving pet rabbits plenty of green twigs to nibble on.

Soft food such as lettuce and carrots encourages a rabbit's teeth to grow. All pet rabbits need to nibble on something hard

Bubbles of air help to give this tank of tropical fish a healthy environment

Why do tropical fish tanks need aerators?

Like almost every animal big enough to be visible to the naked eye, fish breathe oxygen. Land animals extract oxygen from the air with their lungs; fish take it from water with their gills.

Turbulence puts air into water. That is why oxygen levels are high in rushing mountain streams and low in deep, stagnant pools. The amount of oxygen that water can hold varies inversely with temperature. The colder the water, the more oxygen it has dissolved in it; the warmer it is, the less oxygen it holds. A hot day sometimes makes the water in a pool so warm and deficient in oxygen that the fish gasp at the surface.

Tropical aquarium fish can survive only in warm water, which is naturally low in dissolved oxygen. Using an aerator to pump oxygen into the water keeps the fish alive and enables the tank to hold more fish.

Why do white mice have red eyes?

Animals gain their colouring by a complex process in many stages. They produce pigment within their bodies – exactly where depends on the species – transport it through the tissues and deposit it in the skin and other boundary tissues. At any stage of this complex process something can go wrong, so that the individual ends up white instead of the normal colour of its species.

This phenomenon, known as albinism, is perhaps most familiar in white rats and mice. In extreme albinism, the defect lies within the pigment-making process itself, not at any later stage of transport or deposition. This means that an animal has no pigment anywhere. Its eyes have only semitransparent tissues to screen from view the blood vessels of the iris and retina. That is why true albinos have red eyes. Often, such eyes are very sensitive and easily distressed by strong sunlight.

Marvels of science at your service

Why do we sometimes see ghostly images on TV?

Two images of a head, slightly offset from each other, may appear on your television screen. The extra head or other unwanted duplicate images are called ghosts. They occur when your receiver picks up more than one signal from the same television channel.

Most television stations send their signals through the air. A transmitter at the station produces a TV signal from separate audio and video – sound and picture – signals. The TV signal goes to an antenna, which sends it out in all directions. The signal reaches your home's receiving antenna by the shortest path, which is generally the line of sight between your antenna and that at the station. Circuits inside your TV set separate the sound and visual signals.

All is well, provided your antenna receives only one signal. But the station's signal may bounce off tall buildings or hills and arrive at your antenna slightly after the direct signal. The delay is usually only a few millionths of a second or less, but it is enough to create a ghosting on your screen. The longer the delay, the more likely that you will be troubled by more than one image.

Ghosts appear to the right of the main image because of the way the image is formed on the screen. For each picture frame, the electron beam in the picture tube starts at the top right corner of the screen as you look at it and scans across to the other side, its intensity changing as it moves. Then the beam is turned off and repositioned lower, and another line is scanned. The strength of the signal received by the set controls the intensity of the electron beam.

It takes the beam about fifty millionths of a second to scan each line, so a reflected signal coming in a few millionths of a second after the main signal will affect the intensity of the beam a few centimetres farther along in its scan. Line by line, the duplicate image is formed fractions of a second after the main image. Sometimes, the reflected signal is stronger than that coming directly to your antenna. If that is so, it will form the stronger image and the direct signal will appear as a ghost to its left.

Television signals reflect strongly from aircraft. If you live near an airport or under a flight path, you're probably familiar with intermittent wavering ghosts caused by reflections from the metal surfaces of aircraft. There is no cure for reflections from these flying mirrors. But when ghosts persistently haunt one or more channels, try to improve reception by rotating your antenna and, if it's outdoors, increasing its height. A more directional antenna may reduce the influence of reflected signals, but this may not provide equally good reception of all stations if they are broadcast from widely separated antennas.

Why do fluorescent tubes last so much longer than ordinary light bulbs?

A standard light bulb produces light by incandescence. Each time you switch on the light, electric current flows through the thin tungsten filament, heating it to about 2600°C (4700°F). At this white heat, the filament glows with light and its tungsten atoms vibrate so quickly that some are knocked right out of the wire. The atoms condense on the inside of the glass, gradually darkening it slightly. Tungsten slowly evaporates from the filament, but it does so unevenly. In places the filament gets thinner. A thinner filament offers more resistance to the flow of electricity. The thin spots become hotter and tungsten atoms evaporate even faster. In time, usually after about 1000 hours of lighting, you hear the characteristic pop of a filament failure.

A filament limits the lifetime of a fluorescent light also, but for different reasons. A fluorescent tube is coated inside with phosphors, chemicals that absorb invisible ultraviolet light and radiate visible light. This is a relatively cool process because the tube's two filaments, or electrodes, need to be heated only enough to give off electrons and not light. The electrons carry the electric current between the ends of the tube, which is filled with a gas containing mercury. On their way, the electrons bump into mercury atoms, causing mercury electrons to jump from their usual orbits. As the mercury electrons return to their normal state, they give off ultraviolet light, which activates the phosphors to produce visible light.

The filaments of fluorescent tubes run at much lower temperatures than those of incandescent bulbs, so they last about eight times longer. Ageing filaments in a fluorescent tube don't break, but gradually they stop giving off enough electrons to strike an arc in the vapour filling the tube. This causes old tubes to flicker.

Even new filaments need to heat for a moment, which is why conventional fluorescent tubes do not light up immediately. You can buy instant-start and rapid-start tubes, but they are more expensive. More compact and electrically efficient fluorescent lights also have been developed. All need less-frequent replacement and use less electricity than incandescent bulbs in producing the same amount of light.

Electric lamps *first shone in an invention by England's Joseph Swan in 1878 and another (left) by America's Thomas Edison in 1879. A fluorescent bulb (below left) burns for 8000 hours, an incandescent bulb (centre) for 1000 hours and an electronic E-Lamp for more than ten years*

Why do we sometimes hear static during radio broadcasts?

Discharges of electrical sparks – from lightning, for instance, or from the electric motors in some appliances – produce a burst of radio interference, especially if you're tuned to an AM station. FM broadcasts are rarely affected. The reason for this lies in how radio signals are broadcast and received.

Sounds travel in waves of a particular frequency and amplitude. Frequency is a measure of the number of waves that are transmitted per second, and is measured in hertz. Amplitude is the height of the waves. Radio programs are broadcast by combining sound information, such as a newsreader's voice, with another wave known as a carrier wave. This process is called modulation.

There are two ways of doing this: amplitude modulation (AM) and frequency modulation (FM). Each radio station transmits its carrier wave at a specific frequency – between 525 and 1605 kilohertz for AM stations and between 87 and 108 megahertz for FM stations.

In AM radio, the frequency of the carrier wave remains constant, but the sound information is used to change its amplitude. A radio receiver tuned to the frequency of a station picks up its carrier wave and extracts and amplifies only the amplitude information.

In FM radio, the sound information is used to change the frequency of the carrier wave slightly; the amplitude is unchanged. An FM receiver extracts and amplifies only the frequency information that varies from the frequency of the unmodulated carrier wave.

Electrical sparks radiate radio waves in a wide range of frequencies. These random waves combine with a modulated carrier wave to change its amplitude. The modulated wave's frequency is rarely affected, and this is why static is seldom heard in FM broadcasts. To an AM radio receiver, however, the amplitude changes seem the same as sound information, so the irritating crackle of static is amplified along with the information signal.

Why don't transistor radios need aerials?

You may believe, as you carry a transistor radio about the house or outdoors, that it is doing a wonderful job without an aerial. It is fooling you. Whether your transistor is tuned to FM or AM, it is using an aerial.

FM radio signals are best picked up by an antenna that is about 1.5 m (5 ft) long and fairly straight. Many FM radios contain a telescopic aerial that can be pulled out to do the job. In some mains-powered radios, the FM aerial is actually in the power cord. Others, such as some clock radios, have a small piece of wire hanging from the back that serves as an aerial. Many small portable FM radios, especially those without a built-in loudspeaker, have none of these devices. This is because the leads to the earphones are the right length to pick up FM waves.

The leads carry the electrical signal from the radio's audio amplifier to the tiny speakers in the earpieces, and take the incoming FM signal into the radio's receiving circuit. The two electrical signals are so different that the speakers and circuits respond to the correct one. The leads sometimes receive the signal more strongly in one direction than another, especially in areas where the radio signal is rather weak.

A transistor radio that seems to have no AM aerial always has one inside. It consists of a coil of wire wrapped around a small iron-containing core. Small AM antennas are also directional and when properly designed can extract a lot of power from the radio beam. You can find the best alignment by turning the radio in different directions and listening to whether the station sounds stronger or, in FM, receives clearer stereo.

Why have compact discs superseded vinyl discs?

The surface of a vinyl record contains a continuous spiral wavy groove in which the diamond stylus of the record player rides. Undulations in the width and depth of the groove carry the sound information. As the record turns, the stylus vibrates from side to side and up and down, producing a stream of electrical signals that are boosted in the amplifier and fed to the loudspeakers.

The sound information of a compact disc (CD) is also arranged in a spiral but not as a groove. The spiral has a series of about 1000 million tiny pits of different lengths, with smooth surfaces between them. A thin laser beam focuses on the smooth surface, which reflects more light than the pits. As the disc spins rapidly, a sensor monitors the reflected light and detects each change in level. A small computer in the CD player recognises the changing information, smooths it and converts it into electrical signals. These are amplified for the loudspeakers.

The pitted layer of a CD is protected by a clear coating. The disc is not affected by spilled liquids, shallow scratches, slight warping or dust, and it does not wear out. Compact discs deliver up to seventy-four minutes of accurate sound. By comparison, vinyl discs hold less than an hour of music and require great care. The slightest speck of dirt in the groove causes a click. And at every playing, the stylus slightly deforms the groove; the quality of the sound gradually deteriorates.

The proportion of new recordings issued as vinyl discs constantly diminishes as CDs gain favour and become cheaper. Already, however, the CD itself is under challenge from two new recording formats: the mini disc (MD), which is a smaller compact disc, and the digital compact cassette (DCC).

Audio-frequency waves

Carrier waves

Amplitude modulation (AM)

Frequency modulation (FM)

Radio transmissions *combine two kinds of electric vibrations. Sound entering a microphone generates audio-frequency waves which are combined with a carrier. The carrier is modulated for transmission over long (AM) or short (FM) ranges. Pocket transistor radios, such as that made by Sony in 1957, brought a revolution to radio communications*

In the groove, a diamond stylus (greatly magnified) travels over a vinyl record. Initially cleaned, the needle is already encrusted with dirt

Why don't microwave ovens heat food containers?

Put a meal in a microwave oven and minutes later you'll be sitting down to eat. The food will be steaming hot, but its container will be warm at best.

Microwaves, like X-rays, radio waves, visible light and ultraviolet and infrared rays, are a type of electromagnetic radiation. They are invisible and vibrate between 1000 million and 300 000 million times a second.

In a conventional oven, heat reaches the food mainly as infrared radiation and flows slowly from the surface into the interior by conduction. Infrared radiation doesn't penetrate far below the surface. Microwaves penetrate food to a depth of about 35 mm (1½ in), and conduction carries the heat both into the interior and outward to the surface. This makes cooking much faster.

Your microwave oven operates at a frequency of about 2450 megahertz. This means that every second, the microwaves vibrate 2450 million times, constantly changing from negative to positive. Microwaves are absorbed particularly strongly by water molecules and molecules similar to them. Like a bar magnet, these molecules have positive and negative ends. The rapidly alternating electromagnetic field of the microwaves pushes and pulls these poles, causing the molecules to vibrate at the same rate. Friction between the vibrating molecules generates heat.

Food containers are usually made of glass, ceramics, paper or plastics. All of these substances, except for a few plastics, contain no water or other polar molecules. Only heat conducted from the food makes them warm. An exception is Melamine, a plastic used in dinnerware, which absorbs microwaves and can become very hot. Metal reflects microwaves, so food in a covered metal container will not heat up.

Metal containers and metallised trims or glazes on non-metal containers may cause damaging electrical sparks (arcing) in a microwave oven. Aluminium foil can be used sparingly without causing arcing. Use of the correct materials ensures that the microwaves heat the food not the container, and don't cause a damaging display of lightning.

Why doesn't electricity spill from unused sockets?

Most metals, such as the copper in the electrical wiring in your home, are good conductors of electrical energy because their electrons are free to flow. Electrical energy is restrained by insulators, materials whose electrons are not free to wander from atom to atom. Air is a good insulator. It is so good that it conducts electricity only under the pressure of the extremely high voltages – between 100 million and 1000 million volts – that build up in thunderclouds. At these voltages, electrons are torn from the atoms in the air. A conducting pathway of free negatively charged electrons and positively charged atoms allows the electric discharge to flow. Then we see lightning.

Depending on where you live, the electrical voltage in your home is anything from 110 to 240 volts. That's high enough to give you a shock, but it's a million times too low to overcome the insulation of the air inside and outside an electrical socket. The electricity can't flow, let alone spill into the room, unless you bridge the holes in the socket with a conductor. This is what you do when you plug in an appliance and turn it on.

Why does water swirl down a plughole?

The water in your sink or bath has a gentle swirl in one direction or the other. When you pull out the plug, the swirl gets bigger and is visible. Watch a champion

*A **skater spins**. Moving her arms in or out determines how fast she revolves. As water leaves a washbasin, it swirls similarly*

ice-skater, and you will see something similar. The skater spins, arms extended. Then, as the arms are drawn in, the spin gets gradually faster.

The gentle swirls in the water may be induced in several ways: by the initial flow from the tap; by the action of washing; by small air currents moving over the water; by minor currents caused by temperature differences; and even by the way you pull the plug. The combination of all these forces will be stronger one way or the other. Whichever it is will decide the direction of the vortex or miniature whirlpool forming at the plughole.

A long-disputed question is whether the Earth's rotation governs the direction of the vortex. If this were true, water would always go down a plughole with an anticlockwise swirl in the northern hemisphere and clockwise in the southern hemisphere.

Scientists in the United States, Britain and Australia have conducted experiments to resolve the dispute. They say that it takes up to twenty hours before stray currents die down in a bowl of water kept in carefully controlled conditions. If the temperature is not steady, air currents form above the surface, setting up others in the water. Once all these factors are removed, the force of the Earth's rotation can be seen. Then, and only then, will your bath water depart down the plughole in an orderly, predictable manner.

Why do water pipes burst in a freeze-up?

Chemically, water is unique. In many ways it defies the rules. Nearly all other substances contract as they are cooled: as a gas they are lighter than as a liquid, and as a liquid they weigh less than as a solid. Water behaves itself in the change from gas to liquid, and continues to shrink in volume, thus growing heavier, until it gets close to freezing point. Suddenly, at 4°C (39°F), it rebels. As cooling continues, it

grows in volume, so that its solid form weighs less than its liquid.

When water freezes, its molecules group into the form of a tetrahedron, with four triangular faces. Each water molecule links up with four others, which in turn join others. The result is a solid but lightweight crystal, in which the water molecules are more widely spaced than when freely moving in the liquid. That is why water expands when it freezes. In fact, it gains about 9 per cent in volume. And it generates considerable force, sufficient to shatter pipes, as many luckless homeowners know.

Why do drains have U-bends?

An array of pipes carries water into and out of our homes. A glance under the kitchen and laundry sinks will show you a few of them. You will see that the waste pipes are much wider than the water pipes. Also, just below the sink outlet, each waste pipe twists to form a bend shaped like the letter U.

The U-bend provides an essential and cunning barrier between the sink and the drain or sewer pipe into which waste water flows. When you pull the sink-plug, water flows through the U-bend to the drain. When the flow stops, some water is trapped within each arm of the U. Without such barriers, foul-smelling gases from the drain and sewer pipe would flow up the waste pipes and into your kitchen, bathroom and laundry. Also, insects and vermin would use the pipes as an easy way into your home.

As you may have experienced, a U-bend can become clogged with hair, dirt and grease. Usually, it is easily cleared with a rubber suction cup. Some U-bends have a plug that unscrews to free any blockage. If you need to remove the plug, place a bucket to catch the water held in the U-bend. With the water gone, you will get immediate proof from the drain below of why your waste pipe has that bend.

Why do spiders appear in the bath?

Spiders don't climb up the drain pipe. If they did, they would have to swim through the water that fills the U-bend. They enter the bathroom through the window, a crack in the wall or floor, or a bath overflow pipe connected directly to the air outside the house. Once in the bath or hand basin, the spider cannot climb the steep, slippery sides. If you attempt to wash a spider down the plughole, it instinctively curls up its legs, trapping an air bubble beneath its body. If the spider manages to avoid being swept past the U-bend, the air bubble carries it to the surface. Then it may climb up the pipe and back into the bathtub or basin.

Why do magnifying glasses make things look bigger?

*A **magnifying glass** bends light rays, making close objects larger and sharper*

A faraway lamp post does not look as high as one nearby. If lines were stretched from the top and bottom of the distant post to the centre of your eye, they would meet at a narrow angle. Lines from the nearby post would meet at a much wider angle. Move closer to the distant post and its top and bottom seem farther apart and the angle between the lines widens.

The lines correspond to the rays of light reflected from the posts to your eyes. A narrow angle of light rays forms a small image on the retina at the back of your eye. A wider angle forms a correspondingly larger image.

A magnifying lens makes an object appear bigger by changing the angle at which light meets the optical centre of the lens of the eye. The convex shape of the magnifying lens bends parallel rays of light that pass through it so that they converge at a wide angle on a point called the focal point. When this point coincides with the eye's optical centre, the image is in focus and the object on the other side of the magnifying glass looks bigger.

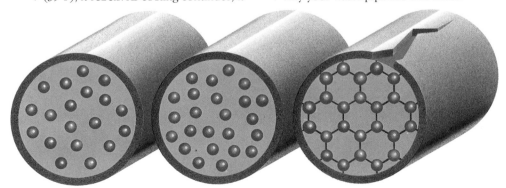

Water acts strangely *at different temperatures. At 16°C (60°F), left, its molecules are widely spaced and move randomly. At 4°C (39°F), they pack at their tightest, reducing the water's volume. When water forms ice, it expands as the molecules move farther apart to form crystals*

Why do mirrors reflect?

Few materials make their own light, but most reflect some of the light that falls on them. When you look at an object, it is light reflected from its surface that gives your eyes information about the object's colour, its shape, texture and other visual characteristics.

Under a microscope most surfaces, no matter how flat they seem, appear rough, made up of many randomly arranged complex shapes. This jumble of tiny reflecting surfaces scatters light in random directions. The reflecting surface of most objects is too uneven to allow you to see a reflected image of the source of light. Even the seemingly smooth pages of this book, for example, will not let you see the actual light you are reading by.

Flat mirrors, however, have smooth surfaces and can reflect the incoming light in so regular a way that all its patterns are preserved. This allows you to see a clear and undistorted reflected image of where the light is coming from.

If the surface of the mirror is curved, the clarity of the image is preserved but its shape is changed. Light strikes and reflects from a surface at the same angle to the perpendicular. On a curved surface the angle between incoming light rays and the perpendicular varies from place to place and the image is distorted.

When you look closely in most mirrors you will see two reflections of yourself, one strong and clear and the other faint. The main reflection comes from the silvery metal coating on the back of the glass and the faint one from the front surface of the glass. A silvery backing reflects almost all the light falling on it. Other coatings, used for special effects, absorb some colours of light to give the mirror a golden or other hue.

Fairground fun *often includes testing the bizarre effects produced by distorting mirrors. The first mirrors of 2000 BC were polished obsidian. Mirrors of glass were luxuries in Queen Elizabeth's England. When the queen began to age, she banned mirrors from her court*

Why is marble cold to the touch?

Even when they are all at the same temperature, marble feels colder to the touch than wood, and shiny metal feels even colder. When you touch any material that is colder than your skin it draws heat away from you and cools the skin. Nerve endings in the skin detect this change in temperature and send the brain information which is interpreted as a cool sensation. The faster that heat is drawn away from the skin, the colder the sensation.

How fast or slow heat flows through a material at a given temperature depends upon how well the material conducts heat. That is determined by how closely the molecules in the substance are packed together. The closer the particles, the faster that heat passes from one to another. Marble is a better heat conductor than wood. It draws heat away from your skin faster, cooling it down more quickly, and your brain says marble feels colder than wood. Metal takes the heat away faster, causing an even colder feeling.

Heat flow depends also on the difference between the temperatures of materials. The greater the temperature difference, the faster the flow of heat from the warmer material to the colder.

Harnessing the power of nothing

A perfect vacuum contains nothing, not even a single atom. The nearest approach to a perfect vacuum in the natural world is the vast emptiness of space surrounding our planet. Gravity holds our atmosphere in place, and we live in an ocean of air which presses on us with considerable force.

In 1657, the mayor of the German town of Magdeburg, Otto von Guericke, graphically demonstrated the pressure of the atmosphere. He fitted together two copper bowls to make a hollow sphere, then pumped out the air, forming a vacuum. The bowls were held in

An idea lay idle for a decade before James Watt (below) developed his steam engine. This led to Richard Trevethick's steam locomotive which in 1808 gave joy rides in London

place only by atmospheric pressure, but horse teams could not pull them apart.

Thirty-six years later, French physicist Denis Papin found another way of creating a vacuum (the word comes from the Latin *vacuus*, meaning empty). He boiled a little water in a small brass cylinder containing a piston. Steam drove the piston to the top of the cylinder, where a catch retained it. When the cylinder cooled, the steam condensed into water, leaving a partial vacuum in the cylinder. The catch was released, and atmospheric pressure drove the piston into the cylinder with great force.

In 1712, English toolsmith Thomas Newcomen put the vacuum principle to work in a steam engine for pumping water from mines. He connected a pump to one end of a see-sawing beam and fixed a piston, housed in a cylinder, to the other. Steam was piped into the cylinder, raising the piston. Newcomen cooled the cylinder with a spray of cold water, forming a partial vacuum inside. Atmospheric pressure forced the piston back into the cylinder, lifting the pump rod at the other end of the beam and with it a quantity of water. Newcomen's atmospheric engine was superseded within seventy years by James Watt's steam engine. This also needed the creation of a vacuum, but the piston was driven down by low-pressure steam instead of by atmospheric pressure.

Since the eighteenth century, inventors have found many other ways of exploiting a vacuum. Air is removed from incandescent light bulbs

Teams of horses struggled in vain to separate two spheres from which physicist Otto von Guericke had removed the air. In 1640, he invented a vacuum pump and later made weather forecasts with a barometer

so that gases won't react with the hot filament. Similarly, television picture tubes are airless to enable the picture-forming beam of electrons to flow from the back of the tube to the screen without hitting a barrier of air molecules.

Two other household devices that harness the power of nothing in ingenious ways are the vacuum flask and the vacuum cleaner.

Studying low-temperature phenomena in the 1890s, the British chemist and physicist Sir James Dewar needed a container for liquid oxygen. Oxygen remains liquid only at temperatures below its boiling point of -183°C (-297°F). In 1892, Dewar invented the vacuum flask to keep oxygen cold and liquid. Today, the vacuum flask is a common household appliance. Tea and coffee stay hot in a vacuum flask because little of their heat can escape. Cold drinks stay cold because outside heat can't get into the flask to warm them up. Heat is transferred in three ways:

Convection. As gases and liquids are heated they expand, becoming less dense. When the heat comes from beneath, the cooler, denser molecules sink and the warmer, less dense molecules rise. You can see this convective motion in water heated in a pan. Gases convect heat very well, as all glider and hang-glider enthusiasts know. Warm air rising from the ground carries them skywards.

Radiation. Very hot materials such as filaments in light bulbs radiate visible light. Cooler substances give off invisible infrared radiation, which we can sense as heat. Radiation is the fastest method of heat transfer, because it allows heat energy to travel at the speed of light through empty space and transparent substances. Like light, radiated heat can be reflected.

Conduction. When heat flows through a substance, it does so molecule by molecule. Conduction is quickest through metals and slowest through gases.

Vacuum flasks are designed to counter each of these methods of heat transfer. Flask linings are made of glass because it is only an average heat conductor. Also, it is a strong and easily moulded material, and doesn't react with food. The flask has twin glass walls with a vacuum between them so that air cannot convect heat from one wall to the other. The glass walls are silver-coated, like a mirror, to reflect back any heat radiating from its contents. The only way for a vacuum flask to lose heat or gain it is by conduction through a narrow path of molecules at the neck, where the walls are connected. And in an efficient flask, which keeps its contents hot or cold for several hours, it does this very slowly.

Dewar's invention became known as Dewar's flask, but he didn't patent it. In 1902, Reinhold Burger, a German manufacturer, adapted the flask for domestic use. Two years later, he added a protective metal casing and gave the flask the brand name Thermos (Greek for heat). Today, the casing is usually plastic. Some vacuum flasks have wide mouths to accommodate chunkier foods such as stews, but they are less efficient.

In 1901, Hubert Cecil Booth, an English engineer, was unimpressed by a demonstration of a cleaning machine that blew dust into a container. He thought that sucking would be a better way of removing the dust and dirt from carpets, curtains, furniture and other household surfaces, and he invented a machine to do the job. He named his device a vacuum suction cleaner and formed the Vacuum Cleaner Company to provide a cleaning service.

Booth's original device was driven by a petrol-powered electric motor and went through the streets on a horse-drawn cart. Long hoses connected to the air pump and to the dirt-collecting canister snaked up from the street through the windows of rooms to be cleaned. At first, wealthy families or institutions paid for the vacuum-cleaning

*A **vacuum flask** stays hot or cold by blocking the transfer of heat between the flask contents and the flask. A silver coating on the flask walls reduces the transfer of heat through radiation. A vacuum in the flask walls stops heat leaking by conduction or convection. In a coffee cup (lower inset) heat can escape freely*

service, but within a few years domestic vacuum cleaners, smaller but still bulky, were on the market. In 1908, the Hoover Company in the United States sold the first convenient and affordable electric vacuum cleaner for home use. It was an instant success, and soon many companies made their own versions. All

vacuum cleaners work in essentially the same way. An internal electric motor turns a fan at high speed. The fan draws air plus dirt through the cleaning nozzle and along the hose. Inside the machine, a bag or canister and perhaps a final filter extracts the grime, and discharges air into the room. When the cleaner is switched on, air rushes through the hose at a lower pressure than the air outside the machine. The 'vacuum' in the name refers to this reduction in pressure, but this isn't what lifts the dirt. It is the constant flow of air into the nozzle, pushed by the greater air pressure in the room, that picks up loose dust particles. The airstream carries them along the hose.

Attachments make vacuum cleaners more effective and versatile. Some machines have rotating brushes and other agitating devices to loosen the dust. Some, with an attachment fitted to the exhaust outlet, can blow as well as they suck, and are useful for paint-spraying and similar jobs.

*The **cleaning revolution** arrived in 1901 when Hubert Booth's vacuum cleaner toured city streets. In 1904, he marketed domestic models. Then America produced the Hoover*

Why does ironing remove wrinkles from clothes?

For those who hate to iron, the bad news is that nearly all fabrics are capable of becoming wrinkled, creased or otherwise crumpled. Some fabrics are treated during manufacture to be 'crease-resistant' or 'durable-press' and need little or no ironing after washing. Most of these treatments blend a special heat-setting nylon fibre with cotton or other fibre and add a shape-retaining resin. In this way, smooth areas of the fabric stay smooth. Trousers keep their intentional creases, and the pleats remain in skirts during wear and usually after repeated washing.

In untreated fabric, pressure and heat applied to random folds can form unwanted creases. This happens when you sit or recline and particularly if your clothes are loose fitting, allowing them to crease more easily. Even the weight of clothes tangled in a hot tumble dryer or in a hamper can cause wrinkles in fabrics. The threads in the weave are stretched around the folds and may slip past one another. Sometimes they bunch up unevenly, or the fibres are bent too sharply to return to their original shape when the pressure is removed.

Ironing applies heat and pressure to the fabric once more. The heat at first

Heated irons became common appliances in the eighteenth century. Called sadirons, because sad also means heavy, they were used in pairs, one always heating over the fire

relaxes the fibres and the weave. Pressure from the iron and the arm encourages the threads to slip back into place. Fibres in the threads conform to the surface of the ironing board and the sole of the iron. Heat and pressure lock the fabric into its former shape – at least temporarily. Moistening the fabric with steam or a mist of water softens the fibres even more and lubricates the threads, making them move past one another more easily. Sometimes, hanging up a fabric in a steamy bathroom is enough to relax the fibres so that the material's weight removes the wrinkles.

Why does a sponge soak up water?

Spill some water and an instant remedy is to mop it up with a cloth or a sponge. But why don't we reach for, say, a piece of metal or wood? We know from experience that highly porous materials, such as a sponge, a towel or blotting paper, will soak up water quickly and that solid substances won't.

Among water's bag of tricks is capillary action, its ability to climb. You can see this for yourself by inserting the tip of a fine glass tube into a tumbler of water. The level of water in the tube will be higher than that in the tumbler. If you use several tubes of different diameters, you will see that the finer the tube, the higher the water climbs.

Water behaves in this way, say scientists, because its molecules will bind themselves to many other substances, particularly those containing oxygen. The oxygen draws the hydrogen in the surface molecules of the water, and these climb higher, drawing a rope of molecules behind them. The ascent halts only when the weight of the raised water balances the capillary forces.

A sponge or a piece of blotting paper is a mass of tiny tubes, and water will invade them, unassisted. If you squeeze the sponge, you employ an additional force. As the sponge expands to regain its shape, it draws water into its tubes, almost as though it were sucking through a bunch of straws. Then, when the sponge is fully expanded, capillary action draws in even more water.

If water lacked its talent for climbing, plants and trees would probably die. Their root hairs take up water through a process known as osmosis, but capillary action helps to circulate it and dissolved nutrients to the branches, stems and leaves. In trees, water can rise to a height of 30 or 40 m (100 or 130 ft) by capillary action.

Why does boiling water turn into steam?

Next time you boil a kettle, study the jet of steam. As it emerges from the spout, it is barely visible. As it disperses into the kitchen, you can see it quite clearly.

Steam, the gas produced when water boils, is invisible. What most of us call steam is in fact water vapour, a mixture of air and minute particles of water.

Water doesn't need to boil to give off vapour. We see it rising from our bath water, yet none of us would take a bath in boiling water. What you see is a collection of fast-moving molecules that have escaped from your bath water and, indeed, left it a little cooler. You can see these molecules because the atmospheric conditions – the temperature and humidity – in your bathroom are just right. Similarly, on a cold morning, the steam in your breath becomes visible even though it is much too cool to scald anything. The frosty air turns the normally invisible steam back into water vapour.

As water is heated in the kettle, the forces holding its molecules together begin to lose their grip. The faster-moving molecules escape from the liquid and mix with the air as water vapour. As the water gets hotter, pockets of fast-moving molecules form bubbles of steam that rise and break through the surface. Sometimes, the steam building up inside can't escape swiftly enough through the spout. Its force raises the kettle's lid, clear evidence of steam power.

If you turn off the heat, the water cools because most of its fast-moving – 'hot' – molecules have escaped. The water will continue to boil only if you keep adding heat. Then the boiling and bubbling go on until the pot runs dry.

Why do kettles become lined with scale?

Tap water is seldom pure. Water-supply agencies add chemicals during treatment. Water itself dissolves chemicals from pipes, from the air when it falls as rain, and from the land over which it flows. In particular, water dissolves sulphates and carbonates of calcium or magnesium from soil. These calcium and magnesium salts are the chemicals that make the water hard, form scale in kettles and steam

Steam power was the driving force of the Industrial Revolution and for generations of locomotives. Hero of Alexandria made a machine to use steam in about AD 100, but he and others regarded it only as an amusing toy. The idea lay dormant for centuries

Masses of flowers appear to bloom in crystals of calcium carbonate lining a kettle. The crystals form the scaly deposit, sometimes known as fur, deposited by boiling hard water

Why do pressure cookers cook so quickly?

In 1682, the council of the Royal Society in London ate a meal cooked in the world's first pressure cooker. This was the New Digester, invented by Denis Papin, a French physicist working in London. Water was boiled in a cast-iron container with a tight-fitting lid which trapped the steam inside. As more and more steam formed, the pressure increased. The boiling point of water rises with pressure. Papin's invention allowed the water to boil at 130°C (266°F), instead of its normal 100°C (212°F), before safety valves came into operation. Food exposed to the superheated steam cooked in a quarter of the usual time.

Solid foods cook because heat applied to the surface flows slowly into the interior by conduction from molecule to molecule. The rate of heat flow depends

irons, and build up in hot-water pipes and around holes in shower heads.

When you boil the kettle, some of the magnesium and calcium salts dissolved in the water form crystals at its hottest parts and attach themselves to the metal. Any salts in the water become more concentrated as it evaporates. When you top up the kettle you add salts to water in which they are already concentrated. Eventually, the water becomes saturated with salts and they crystallise. Repeated topping up and boiling results in a thicker coating of scale inside the kettle than if you empty the kettle and refill it with fresh water each time you boil it.

Scale is a poor conductor of heat, and the more thickly it lines a kettle the more energy is needed to heat the water. A minor benefit is that scale protects the metal parts of the kettle from corrosion, so a thin lining of chemical fur is not altogether undesirable.

Why does washing dry on a freezing day?

It isn't a waste of time to hang washing outdoors on an ice-cold dry day. The clothes may not be completely dry before they freeze, but even when they are frozen stiff they will continue to dry, provided the air isn't saturated with water vapour. On a cold day air can't hold as much water vapour as on a warm day, but

it can still hold some, even when the temperature is below freezing point. The water vapour isn't frozen out of the air. Even ice evaporates if the surrounding air is dry. This principle is used commercially in freeze-drying coffee and other foods.

High-pressure cooking which cooks food faster was invented in 1679 by Denis Papin, a French physicist. His cookers worked at three times the pressure used in today's models. The idea lapsed for a century, then was used in canning and bottling food

DISHING UP THE DIRT

It's easy to hold a dry bar of soap in a dry hand. But add a little water and the soap becomes slippery. The forces that cause this slipperiness also enable soap and other detergents to remove dirt. Soap is composed of long molecules which behave differently at each end. One end loves water, the other hates it. At any point where soapy water comes into contact with a surface, the soap molecules' water-hating ends point towards that other surface – air, as in foam; to solids, such as in clothes in the wash; or liquids such as oil. They are particularly attracted to fatty substances.

The water-loving, or hydrophilic, ends try to dissolve in water and they point towards the water molecules. But the hydrophilic ends also slightly repel one another, unlike water molecules, which attract one another. It is this attraction that produces surface tension. The attraction that water molecules have for each other is counteracted by the mutual repulsion of the soap molecules as they form a film at the surface of the water. This lowers the surface tension, in effect making the water wetter. Water normally forms beads on oily, water-repellent surfaces such as your skin, but soapy water flows more readily. It coats even the ridges of the fingerprints, producing an overall film of slippery liquid between your skin and whatever you try to hold. And as you hold the wet soap, more of it dissolves in the water, its surface becoming softer and even smoother.

When soapy water is agitated, by hand or machine, the pull of the water on one end of

Washday magic *shows in micrographs of a cotton shirt before (left) and after washing. Detergent has removed all grease and dirt. Modern detergents developed from research in Germany during World War I, when scientists sought substitutes for soap. The first detergents, marketed in the United States in the 1950s, were too complex for bacteria to break down. Sewer ponds became masses of foam, which carried into rivers, lakes and oceans*

the soap molecule is matched by the pull of oily substances on the other end. Often, an oily material is more attracted to the oil-loving hydrophobic end of the soap molecule than to the surface to which it is attached. As the edges of the oily patch slowly lift with the tug of the moving soapy water, the oil-loving ends of more soap molecules can slip underneath. Soon more of the oily blob lifts and it starts to break up into smaller particles.

The soap molecules surround each particle of dirt. Their oil-loving ends attack the particle, while their water-loving ends seek the water. This is what keeps the particles of dirt suspended as scum until they are rinsed away.

But soap can't dissolve and dislodge everything. Some dirt adheres too strongly to fabric for soap to make any impact. Some layers of grease may be too thick for soap to break up quickly. Abrasives can be added to scour into the grime. These work by exposing more dirty surfaces for the soap to grip and prise away.

on the difference in temperature between two points, so the hotter that the food's surface becomes, the faster that heat will flow into it. The hotter the water surrounding the food, the hotter its surface and the shorter the cooking time.

Pressure cooking puts food on the table more quickly and saves energy, but it has lost some popularity because of competition from convenience foods and the microwave oven. Microwaves cook food extremely fast, but they cannot boil water at a higher temperature than the pressure of the surrounding air allows. At high altitudes, where water boils at a lower temperature, it is impossible with normal cooking methods to get piping-hot food. Also, cooking takes much longer. In such places, the pressure cooker remains a valued appliance and energy saver.

Why is it sometimes difficult to get a lather with soap?

If your tap water comes from a reservoir or well, it has probably travelled a long way. On its journey it has dissolved small amounts of a variety of chemicals from rocks, soils, vegetation, animal wastes and pipes. Tap water's chemical make-up depends upon the composition and solubility of the materials along the water's path and upon the chemicals added or removed during treatment.

The chemicals that remain in the water determine whether soap lathers in it. If it doesn't, the main chemical culprits are calcium and magnesium. Their presence

as salts and ions makes water hard. When you wash in hard water, soap chemically reacts with calcium and magnesium, producing the bathtub ring, the floating scum in the washbowl and other insoluble residues.

Before you can work up a satisfying lather, you have to dissolve enough soap to use all the calcium and magnesium dissolved in the water. And then you may have to rinse a lot of scummy residue off your skin. Some waterworks beat the problem of excessively hard water by treating their supply with slaked lime or soda ash. Elsewhere, many householders use a domestic water softener.

Synthetic laundry and dishwashing detergents have made hard water less of a problem. These contain chemicals that react with calcium and magnesium. In so

Rainbow hues *in a soap bubble are caused by its surface reflecting light. Soap deters water molecules from forming drops, creating instead a film. Air turns the film into bubbles*

doing, they form soluble compounds which rinse out with the water.

If you have a plentiful supply of clean rainwater you can wash everything with soap and have plenty of suds. There is virtually no calcium or magnesium in the atmosphere, so rainwater is chemically very soft, even though it may contain physically hard particles of dust or soot.

Why are some stains difficult to remove?

Laundry detergents contain substances that will loosen, dissolve, disperse and bleach most dirt particles and staining substances during a single washing-machine cycle. But some stains resist

Obstinate stains, *such as those from blood, grass, egg and other foods, defy our efforts to remove them because they contain glue-like proteins. Modern detergents have enzymes designed to attack the proteins and release the stains from the fabric*

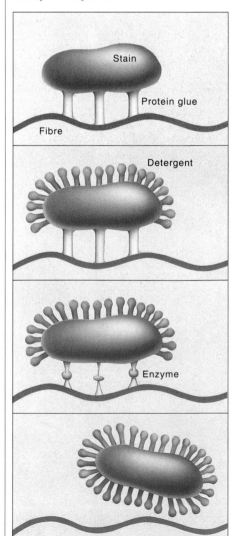

normal chemical and mechanical on-slaughts. In many cases, these substances are made from protein, such as milk, egg or blood. All are insoluble in water, attach strongly to clothing fibres and are not penetrated by normal detergent.

In the 1960s and 1970s, enzymes that could dissolve protein were added to laundry detergents. These are known as biological detergents because the stains they remove come from living things. For a time, biological detergents were withdrawn from sale because they caused allergic reactions in detergent-factory workers. The problem was overcome by encapsulating the enzymes in granules of a substance that dissolves in the wash – releasing the stain-digesting ingredient.

When added to the wash, most detergents turn the water alkaline, but some stains, such as rust, can be removed only when the water is acidic. One way to get rid of rust is to soak the stain in lemon juice, which is about 7 per cent citric acid, and then apply steam until the stain disappears. Fatty stains, such as chocolate and butter, can be dissolved by a newly developed enzyme called lipase. Bleach oxidises many difficult stains, but if it is strong it may remove colour from fabric and weaken the fibre.

Some stain-removing chemicals interfere with one another when mixed together. This incompatibility probably explains why the world still waits for the perfect detergent, one that will remove stains and leave the fabric like new.

Why does detergent make white clothes whiter?

Most white fabrics turn gradually yellow with age. To fight this natural process, many detergents contain what are known by their manufacturers as optical and chemical bleaches.

Optical bleaches, commonly called fabric brighteners or fluorescers, work by absorbing invisible ultraviolet light and emitting visible blue light. This counteracts any yellow in the fabric and produces white. In daylight, the light emitted from white fabric washed with optical bleach makes it appear brighter and 'whiter than white'. And in a dark room bathed only in ultraviolet light, optical bleach will make clothes glow eerily with an effect reminiscent of ghost scenes in a theatre.

Chemical bleaches brighten your whites by removing stains. They do this by either adding oxygen or chlorine to the chemicals that make up the stains (an oxidising bleach), or removing oxygen from the stains

Under disco lights dancers' clothes show as a blur of of pink, blue and stark white. Invisible ultraviolet light, used in some discos, makes clothes washed in detergent glow eerily

(a reducing bleach). These chemical reactions turn many colouring, stain-making agents into colourless chemicals. Laundry detergent usually contains just enough bleach to remove many stains without at the same time removing the dyes from normally colour-fast clothing.

Why do refrigerators and freezers frost up?

If you could keep the door shut all the time, your refrigerator would stay free of frost and your fuel bills would be lower. Every time the refrigerator door is opened, warm air moves in, carrying water vapour. This condenses on the colder surfaces, usually the coils of the freezer compartment, and turns to ice.

The air in the kitchen may be more humid than in the rest of the house because much water vapour is released during cooking and washing-up. Even if the humidity in the kitchen is a comfortable 50 per cent and the temperature is 20°C (68°F), every cubic metre of air holds about 9 grams (⅓ oz) of water vapour. This condenses to 9 millilitres of water, enough to half fill an egg cup. When that air is cooled to 4°C (39°F) in the refrigerator, it can carry only about 6 grams (⅕ oz) of water vapour per cubic metre. The rest condenses.

In a separate freezer the temperature is lower, perhaps -10°C (14°F). At this temperature, a cubic metre of air can carry only 2 grams (1/16 oz) of water vapour. A separate freezer also frosts up faster than a refrigerator because its door is often open for several minutes. It usually takes much longer to find something among items stacked in a freezer than it does in a well-arranged refrigerator. It's sensible to store food in a planned fashion in your refrigerator and freezer, so that the door is open for the shortest possible time, even if you have an automatic defrost system. An automatic defroster works by heating the coils sufficiently to melt the ice on them. The meltwater drains off, usually into a tray beneath the appliance. But heating the coils uses more power.

Proud pioneers of a modern boon, the electric fridge, were Swedish engineers Baltzar von Platen (left) and Carl Munters. Both worked for Electrolux, and are seen at a demonstration of their invention in 1923

Money, jewels and riches galore

Why do we use paper and metal currency?

The earliest form of trade was barter, the exchange of one object for another. A farmer might swap a wagon-load of wheat for a cow, for example.

It is difficult to become rich by barter, and the system has practical limits. The farmer with the wheat will be thwarted if no one has cows to trade that day. Of course, the farmer might be willing to part with his wheat in return for another trader's written promise to supply the cows at some future date. Such a transaction, strictly speaking, is no longer barter. It employs, in primitive form, a medium of exchange.

Early societies used a variety of objects as media of exchange. For example, one gourd might be swapped for three seashells, which could later be swapped for two fishes. The medium of exchange, the seashell, is lighter to carry, easier to count and more durable than either gourds or fishes. And the fact that society accepts the value of the seashell as a standard makes difficult transactions easier to arbitrate. Acceptance of a medium of exchange also paves the way for the entrance of the independent trader, or intermediary, whose presence makes society more complex.

Needs for standardisation, portability and enduring value eventually resulted in the first metal coins, in China about 3000 years ago. The earliest Chinese coins were small metal representations of everyday objects such as spades and knives. Coins as we know them today began to circulate in China, Egypt and Assyria, between 700 and 500 BC. They were made of metal of standard consistency and weight; the shekel, used in Middle Eastern countries, took its name from a unit of weight. By stamping coins with a seal or insignia, a local ruler guaranteed that they could be exchanged for goods. Coins became legally acceptable for the payment of debts.

Throughout the ages, rulers have lacked the means to pay the soldiers who enforced their territorial aspirations. Centuries ago a system arose of rewarding soldiers with paper vouchers, which could be exchanged for cash. Kublai Khan was probably the first to issue large amounts of paper money, when he occupied China in the thirteenth century. Marco Polo, who visited Kublai Khan's court in 1275, reported that the possessor of a damaged voucher could take it to the central mint and be issued with a brand new note on paying a surcharge of 3 per cent. The penalty for counterfeiting was death, and any informant was entitled to the criminal's entire property and a substantial reward from the state.

In Europe, bank notes were first issued in Sweden in 1661, but they did not become a familiar medium of exchange in most countries until the 1880s. Their significance has differed from place to place and changed over the years. In many countries, a currency note was in effect an IOU which the bank promised to

exchange for gold of the equivalent value on the bearer's demand. Great Britain and the United States backed their bank notes with gold until the 1930s. No country now issues bank notes that have more than token value. Similarly, coins no longer contain precious metals.

Why is gold so valuable?

Gold has been regarded as the ultimate precious metal since the days of ancient Egypt, and probably long before. Gold is rare but some other metals are rarer, and harder to extract. In Egypt, silver was much scarcer and more difficult to mine than gold.

The ancients appreciated the fact that gold does not tarnish, corrode or dissolve. They could find nothing to attack it. Gold is extremely inert and forms chemical compounds only under special circumstances. It conducts electricity almost as well as copper and, because it does not corrode, is even more useful than other metals in electronics.

Gold is also easily worked. It is so ductile that a mere 15 grams (about ½ oz) can be drawn through a conical hole in a metal die to form 30 km (nearly 20 miles)

Tons of money was clearly an ambition for inhabitants of Yap, in the northwest Pacific. The money discs, some of them 4 m (13 ft) across, were hewn from coral stone on the island of Palau and moved by raft or canoe. The stones are still valued but no longer used as currency

All that glisters *is gold in these stacks at New York's Federal Reserve Bank, which holds the world's biggest store. A nugget of 285.8 kg (630 lb), the largest ever, was mined at Hill End, Australia, in 1872. It is photographed with the mine's proud manager and part-owner, Bernard Holtermann, after whom it is named*

Why is dry-cleaning so called?

Washing clothes in water is risky. Woollen fabrics often shrink and become matted, and others, such as silk, may wrinkle. Some dyes may bleed. These risks were inescapable until a French dyer, Jean-Baptiste Jolly, discovered that camphene, a type of turpentine, would remove dirt. He opened the world's first dry-cleaning business in Paris in 1855.

Some enthusiastic marketer of the process invented the term dry-cleaning. It is a misnomer, because clothes do become wet, although not in water. They are agitated in a fluid that dissolves and removes dirt. Spinning removes the solvent, and then, depending on the type of fabric, the garment is either tumbled in warm air or hung in a drying cabinet for any remaining fluid to vaporise before pressing. The result should be clean clothing with no smell of solvent.

The principal cleaning liquids are white spirit, made from petroleum, and a chlorinated hydrocarbon, perchloroethylene. These are particularly effective solvents of fats and oils. They do not damage fabrics when used properly, but they can dissolve buttons and sequins made from polystyrene, sponge-rubber shoulder pads and some cements used to attach reinforcing, backing material or decoration.

Often, special detergents are added to the cleaning fluids to enable them to wet surfaces better and speed the release of dirt. These detergents are also able to absorb a small amount of water, which is needed to dissolve water-soluble substances. The amount is carefully controlled to prevent the problems caused by washing the garment in water.

Why do we wear jewellery?

The human desire to embellish the body is ancient and universal. Prehistoric rock paintings show hunters adorned with the teeth and claws of animals. Tribal peoples on occasion still wear decorations, from simple shells and feathers to complex neck rings and breastplates.

Decorations made from precious materials identify the wearer as a person of exceptional status. In Europe, fine fabrics, furs and jewellery were indicators of rank by the late Middle Ages. Some classes of people were even forbidden to wear certain precious stones, under sumptuary laws passed in Italy, France, Spain and England. Bejewelled opulence peaked in late sixteenth-century France, where Gabrielle d'Estrées, mistress of Henry IV, wore a court dress so loaded with gold, silver and precious stones that, it was said, she could hardly move.

In the nineteenth century, mass production made jewellery available to a wider public. Jewellers devised a galaxy of designs. Women wore brooches, necklaces, earrings and hatpins. Men ornamented their clothing with tiepins, cufflinks, watch chains and fobs. Both sexes wore rings. Jewellery is less fashionable today but remains a potent status symbol.

Smiles flash, jewels gleam *as film stars Elizabeth Taylor (left) and Raquel Welch sport their finery. In 1972, Richard Burton gave Taylor a $1.1 million diamond ring. On display in New York and Chicago, it attracted crowds of 10 000 a day*

of fine wire. It is so malleable that 15 grams can be beaten into a sheet about 15 sq m (160 sq ft) in extent, so thin that it becomes almost transparent, with a faint greenish tinge. A thin film of gold, which reflects 90 per cent of infrared radiation, reduces heat transmission in visors for spacesuits and plate glass for skyscrapers.

In its pure state, gold is so soft that it loses shape in everyday use and is difficult to use as jewellery. It is usually hardened by alloying it with some other metal such as silver, palladium or platinum. The purity of gold is expressed in carats (karats in the United States), each equal to one twenty-fourth part. At 24 carats gold is pure, whereas 18-carat gold contains 25 per cent of other metal.

Gold often occurs naturally in essentially pure form. It is sometimes found virtually lying on the ground, though its abundance in the Earth's crust is estimated at only 0.005 parts per million. All the gold ever mined may amount to a little more than 100 000 tonnes, or about enough to make a cube with sides measuring roughly 18 m (about 60 ft). The hoard is enlarged at the rate of some 2000 tonnes a year. In spite of its rarity and utility, however, gold is perhaps so valuable largely because we believe it is.

Why do women wear cosmetics?

Women and men have used cosmetics since ancient times. Archaeologists have found them in Egyptian tombs dating from 3500 BC. We know now that, when Greeks powdered their faces to present themselves as pale beauties and Romans rouged their cheeks, some of them were ultimately paralysed and others probably paid with their lives. The face powder, used until the nineteenth century, was based on white lead; the rouge was red lead. Both are lethal poisons. Another deadly poison, mercuric chloride, was a common ingredient of rouge in the seventeenth century. In the fifteenth and sixteenth centuries, women put drops of belladonna ('beautiful woman' in Italian) in their eyes to make them sparkle. This practice led to blindness.

Despite such horrors, the use of cosmetics persisted, particularly among the wealthy. In 1770, a Bill put before the British Parliament sought to classify as a witch any woman who would 'betray into matrimony any of His Majesty's subjects, by … scents, paints, cosmetic washes, artificial teeth, false hair … high-heeled shoes, [or] bolstered hips'. This attitude to cosmetics has emerged every now and again, perhaps because of association with Jezebel, the painted and despised woman of the Bible.

In the 1920s, the huge popularity of motion pictures gave rise to widespread

Fashionable ladies in Japan once had traditional make-up styles that used white face paint and rouge. At times they gilded the lower lip, shaved their eyebrows and painted in new ones of their own design

use of cosmetics, based on film actors' make-up. In the middle of the twentieth century, the pallid look lost popularity and a suntanned appearance, which once would have denoted a lowly outdoor worker, became fashionable. Recently, growing awareness of the Sun's power to cause skin cancer has made many people cover up with clothes and sunscreens, restoring a pale skin to favour.

Why do we put stamps on letters?

Until the mid-nineteenth century, mail was carried by couriers, messengers and private postal services. The Assyrian, Persian and Roman empires had postal systems, but issued no stamps. Marco Polo was amazed to discover that Kublai Khan's China had a postal service using 300 000 horses. Fifteenth-century France and England delivered mail by courier. Henry VIII's postmasters were innkeepers who supplied horses to couriers.

In all these services, the recipient paid on delivery. Street posting boxes first appeared in Paris in 1653, but messengers, fearing for their jobs, dropped mice into the boxes to eat the mail.

The postal system that has spread throughout the world was suggested in 1837 by Rowland Hill, a British social reformer. In *Post Office Reform: Its Importance and Practicability*, he advocated a rate of postal charges based on a package's weight, not the distance it travelled. The sender, not the recipient, would pay the cost by buying an adhesive stamp.

In May 1840, the British Post Office issued the first official stamps. Collectors now call them the Penny Black and the Twopenny Blue. They were for internal use, so the name of the country did not appear on them, and it never has. The United Kingdom is the only country that does not identify its postage stamps with its name.

With the development of rail and ocean transport and the growth in literacy in the nineteenth century, the volume of mail between countries increased. In 1875, the General Postal Union (later the Universal Postal Union) established international postal cooperation. Member countries agreed to treat mail from another country as they did their own. In 1969, however, reform was necessary to ensure that mail posted in one country for delivery in another did not impose undue charges on the receiving country. Postage stamps on overseas mail therefore pay the postal system not just of the sender's country but also of the recipient's.

The United States has the world's biggest postal service, handling some 165 000 million letters and packages annually. The Swiss are the greatest senders of mail – an average 655 pieces per person a year.

The world's first postage stamp, known as the Penny Black, was issued in Britain in May 1840. Some people thought it was undignified and even an act of treason to lick the back of the queen's head

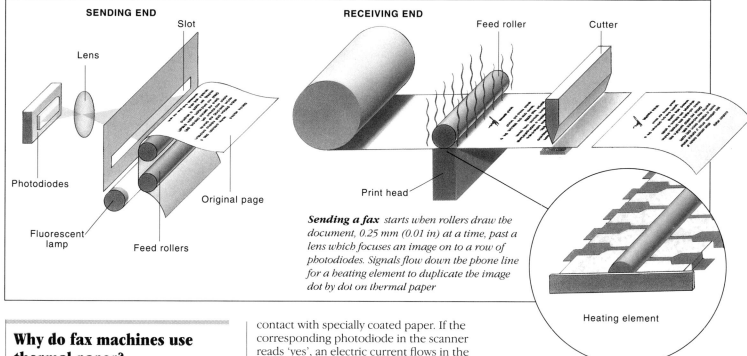

SENDING END

Lens

Slot

Photodiodes

Fluorescent lamp

Feed rollers

Original page

RECEIVING END

Feed roller

Cutter

Print head

Heating element

Sending a fax starts when rollers draw the document, 0.25 mm (0.01 in) at a time, past a lens which focuses an image on to a row of photodiodes. Signals flow down the phone line for a heating element to duplicate the image dot by dot on thermal paper

Why do fax machines use thermal paper?

A Scot named Alexander Bain proposed sending images by electricity in 1842. But it wasn't until the 1920s that facsimile machines became widely used, mainly in newspaper offices for sending photographs. Sending a fax became an everyday event only after technological improvements in the 1970s.

A modern fax machine scans a document, reduces it to a stream of digits, sends them by telephone to another fax machine, which transforms the numbers into a facsimile of the original.

The heart of a fax machine is the photodiode, a device that emits a small electrical charge when light falls upon it. It can be very small, very cheap and very sensitive. A typical office or home fax machine contains 1728 photodiodes, arranged in a row like beads on a string.

A roller draws the document, 0.25 mm (0.01 in) at a time, past a lens, which focuses an image of the page onto the row of photodiodes. Each photodiode responds to a tiny area of the paper, releasing an electrical signal if it is light (plain white paper), no signal if it is dark (part of a printed letter or some other mark on the paper). The resulting list of 1728 'yes' or 'no' (1 or 0) values is fed down the telephone line. Then the document is advanced for the photodiodes to scan the next 0.25 mm. The number 1728 and the distance 0.25 mm are related to a resolution of 100 dots per inch across and down the paper, a standard for ordinary office machines for some years.

At the receiving end, a corresponding array of 1728 fine parallel wires is held in contact with specially coated paper. If the corresponding photodiode in the scanner reads 'yes', an electric current flows in the wire. It generates a tiny surge of heat, burning the coating on the paper at that point and turning it black. By the end of the scanning process a copy of the original document has been burned, dot by dot, into the paper.

Many small devices, such as hand-held calculators, use heat printing to deliver a print-out. This system makes for a printer that is cheaper and much more compact than the bulky and complicated machinery in most office photocopiers. The fax machine's reliance on thermal paper is troublesome and expensive, but plain-paper processes, including laser printing, are on the way.

Why don't photocopying machines need ink?

The ordinary office photocopier uses a process known as xerography, a term derived from ancient Greek words meaning 'dry writing'. It works by a kind of electrical photography.

At the photocopier's heart is a rotating metal drum coated with material that conducts electricity if light shines upon it. In darkness the drum rotates past a thin wire carrying a high-voltage electric charge. This induces a charge of static electricity in the drum. A brilliant light shines on the document to be copied and a mirror projects its image onto the drum. Where the document is white – unprinted paper – light strikes the drum and removes the static charge.

The drum remains charged in the areas, corresponding to the black parts of the original, where no light strikes it. A fine black powder called toner, carrying the opposite electrical charge, is attracted to the charged areas of the drum. The toner is then transferred to a sheet of paper and fused to it by a heated roller. You can feel some of this heat on the photocopy as it emerges from the machine.

The photocopier was patented in 1938, first marketed in 1947 – by Xerox in the United States – and came into wide use in the 1960s. Modern photocopiers can copy continuous-tone documents such as photographs, copy in colour, copy onto both sides of the paper and make enlarged or reduced copies. Colour photocopiers reproduce images so accurately that they are used to forge bank notes.

Why is there sometimes an echo during long-distance telephone calls?

Like cars on a suburban street, calls in a local telephone network travel by a two-way path. Cars going in different directions share the same road; calls travelling from sender to receiver use the same set of wires. Long-distance calls link two local networks and, like cars on a freeway, must always travel along quite separate paths for each direction.

At the end of a freeway, traffic is directed onto two-way streets by a roundabout or other intersection. During long-distance calls, a circuit called a hybrid acts in a similar way, transforming the separate send and receive paths into a two-way path on the same set of wires. But a small proportion of the incoming signal can leak through and appear as an outgoing signal, returning as an echo. Often this does not matter because the echo arrives too quickly to be noticed, but on a long circuit the cumulative time delay is significant and the returning signal is only too apparent and disturbing.

Echo is particularly noticeable when the signal travels via satellite. An orbiting satellite is 36 700 km (22 800 miles) from Earth, and a radio wave, travelling at the speed of light, takes 0.3 seconds to arrive. This up-link signal is amplified by a transponder on the satellite. It is then transmitted to Earth at a different frequency in the down-link, which takes another 0.3 seconds. The whole transmission takes 0.6 seconds. Any echo takes precisely the same time to return, and you hear your last word 1.2 seconds after you uttered it.

Telecommunications engineers combat the problem with an echo canceller, a device that compares the incoming and outgoing signals. When it detects a match, it creates an electronic mirror image of the incoming signal and dovetails it to the outgoing signal. This cancels out the echo.

The world's telephone services amount to an enormous network of cables and wires enmeshing the globe, though all the links are no longer of metal. Fibre-optic cable, in which light pulses through strands of glass the thickness of a human hair, is increasingly used.

As well as this mass of cables, our world depends on invisible links, by microwave radio and by satellite. The first telecommunications satellite, Telstar, launched for American Telephone and Telegraph in 1962, could handle twelve simultaneous telephone conversations between North America and Europe. Intelsat 1, launched in 1965, could carry one television channel or 240 telephone links across the Atlantic. Intelsat 5, placed in orbit fifteen years later, had a capacity of two television channels plus 12 000 telephone links. Improvement in capacity and efficiency continues in more recent satellites.

Why do we eat with knives, forks and spoons?

Many foods are intended to be eaten with no implements other than those that nature gave us – our fingers. In India and many other countries people prefer to eat with the fingers. When we want to eat hot food, stews and soups, however, we clearly need more than our fingers. At least 3000 years ago the Chinese devised chopsticks as heatproof extensions of the

A knife and fork of 1698. Knives were once the only cutlery. Because they could serve also as weapons, strict rules grew up about their use – the first table manners

forefinger and thumb. Their use at the table instead of knives has been said to reflect the superiority of the scholar over the warrior in Chinese society.

The earliest known knives, sharp-pointed blades shaped from flint more than 25 000 years ago, were cutting tools and weapons. The Egyptians and later the Romans ate with small ornamental metal knives. The Latin word for knife, *culter*, is the origin of the term cutlery. The Romans also had spoons – which superseded snail shells and seashells – but until the mid-seventeenth century, spoons were employed for preparing rather than consuming food.

Two-pronged forks were in use in Italy in the eleventh century for eating fruit without staining the fingers, but they did not replace knives as an implement for spearing other food until the 1500s. The use of forks gradually spread north of the Alps until by the early seventeenth century they had become commonplace in Britain. Forks gained a third prong about 200 years later.

Four-pronged forks followed in the 1880s as the cutlers of Sheffield and other manufacturing centres devised an array of shapes and sizes of cutlery. They provided special knives, forks and spoons for every kind of food, spurring the development of elaborate formal table settings. Until stainless steel was invented in Britain in 1913 – it became popular decades later – cutlery required constant polishing to prevent rusting or tarnishing.

Why are computers so much smaller now?

Between 1950 and 1990, the overall performance of computers improved by about a million times. The fastest electronic computer in production today, the Cray-2, is capable of 250 million calculations a second. Early computers performed only a few dozen calculations a second, although they filled entire rooms and devoured huge quantities of electricity. Now, a fully functional computer can easily be carried in a briefcase and uses little more power than a hair dryer.

Since ancient times people have used a variety of mechanical data-manipulating devices. The abacus originated in China 5000 years ago. But true computers are a twentieth-century invention. The first general-purpose electronic computer was built in 1946 at the University of

Pennsylvania, and called ENIAC (Electronic Numeral Integrator and Calculator). It weighed 30 tonnes, occupied 85 cu m (3000 cu ft) and used 150 kW of electricity. The development of the transistor in 1948 and the integrated circuit in 1962 made smaller and more efficient computers possible. The first minicomputer, Digital Equipment Corporation's PDP-8, appeared in 1965.

The transistor, a tiny solid-state amplifying and switching device, replaced bulky, fragile thermionic valves. Comparison of a 1930s radio, housed often in a heavy wooden cabinet, and today's pocket transistor sets shows what a far-reaching difference that made.

In an integrated computer circuit, microscopic transistors, other components and circuitry are built into a tiny wafer of material, generally silicon. There are no wires. Design and manufacturing techniques are now so advanced that millions of individual components can be incorporated into a single tiny chip. Reducing the size of a circuit lessens its power requirements and makes the system faster and more efficient.

But as integrated circuits become ever smaller, their microscopic components are brought closer and closer together and an electrical effect that can be ignored at ordinary scales soon becomes increasingly troublesome. An electrical current in one conductor induces an electrical current in any nearby conductor. When these effects cannot be controlled, the circuit cannot be made smaller. Some designers feel that without a significant advance in technology, integrated circuits may be reaching a minimum size.

Why does this symbol signify a query?

Our system of punctuation came to us from classical Greek and Latin, where its chief purpose was not to assist comprehension but to guide those reading aloud. Different marks showed the reader how to stress syllables, and where to pause and draw breath to maintain the metre in a line of poetry.

In Latin, a query was indicated by the word *questio* placed at the end of the sentence. The laborious task of handwriting books was made easier by abbreviating many words, and *questio* was shortened to QO. Since QO could be mistaken for other abbreviations, scribes began to place the Q above the O. Before long, the Q deteriorated into a squiggle and the O became a dot.

By the ninth century AD, the *punctus interrogativus* was one of the markings used to aid the singing of Gregorian chants, the free and melodic chanting of sacred texts. The sign resembled our modern question mark, but tilted slightly to the right. It indicated a pause and a rising inflection of the voice.

The development of printing in the fifteenth century produced a need for standard punctuation. In 1566, Aldo Manuzio published the first book to give the principles of punctuation. His *Orthographiae Ratio* (System of Orthography) included the full stop, comma, colon, semicolon and question mark. By 1660, writers and printers were also using the exclamation mark, quotation marks and the dash. These symbols were widely adopted throughout Europe, although still mainly as a guide to elocution.

The practice of silent reading spread as a result of printing, and it made punctuation marks particularly important in the English language. Lacking many of the grammatical inflections of other languages – in which, for example, nouns change their form to indicate case – English needed punctuation to clarify the meaning of printed passages. In other languages punctuation marks served to enforce rhetoric. In English they strengthened the syntax of the written language so that, in scholarship and literature, it gradually took over from Latin.

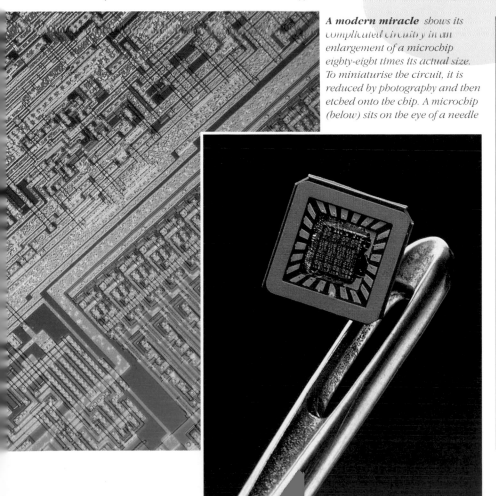

A modern miracle shows its complicated circuitry in an enlargement of a microchip eighty-eight times its actual size. To miniaturise the circuit, it is reduced by photography and then etched onto the chip. A microchip (below) sits on the eye of a needle

Why are typewriter and computer keyboards arranged as they are?

The Qwerty keyboard (named for the first six letters of the top row) is far from ideal. A well-designed keyboard would see the six most commonly used letters in English – E, T, A, O, I and N – located on the most accessible second, or home, row; only the A appears on the Qwerty home row. And in this right-handed world, just over half of all keystrokes on the Qwerty board require the left hand.

Our keyboards owe their layout to Christopher Latham Sholes, a printer of Milwaukee, Wisconsin. In 1866, he teamed up with Carlos Glidden, an amateur inventor, to design a typing machine based on a page-numbering apparatus. In 1873, the small-arms manufacturers E. Remington and Sons of Ilion, New York, agreed to make the machine, and next year the first typewriter appeared on the American market.

Sholes's early machines were very different from their modern descendants. Crudely built, they jammed easily, especially when typed quickly. Keys struck the paper not from the front but from beneath, so that a typist could not see what

Typewriter keyboards *have had many different layouts since the machines were invented. The Hammond of 1895 was popular and efficient. It developed finally into the Varityper, used in the printing trade*

was typed. This meant that it was possible to type for some time without noticing that the type-bars had collided and jammed. The solution was to slow down the typist by putting commonly used characters far apart. You can still see remnants of Sholes's initial alphabetical layout in the modern machine's second line, which is arranged ASDFGHJKL.

Some claim that preventing jamming was not the only intention in designing the QWERTYUIOP line. From these keys even a one-finger typist can tap out the word TYPEWRITER. This would have been a boon for the Remington salesmen who demonstrated the new machines in the 1870s. Mark Twain bought one, and became the first author to send a typewritten book manuscript to a publisher.

The Sholes keyboard has many detractors and alternatives have been proposed. In 1936, August Dvořák, cousin of the composer Antonin, invented a keyboard that put the most common letters on the home row. Another alternative is a boomerang-shaped keyboard designed to reduce strain on the wrists and hands. But the Sholes keyboard remains the most popular, probably because it's too familiar to change. With all its idiosyncrasies it has allowed typists to reach speeds of 176 words a minute on a manual typewriter and 216 words a minute on an electric machine.

Why do we read and write from left to right?

The twenty-six–letter Roman alphabet used in modern English became fixed in the Middle Ages, but its origins can be traced back thousands of years. Its earliest forerunner was an alphabet devised by the Phoenicians, Semitic-speaking people who lived on the eastern shores of the Mediterranean Sea, principally in what is now Lebanon. The Phoenician alphabet advanced from the picture-writing of ancient Egypt and other earlier societies by representing consonants with signs, beginning *alef, bet, gimel*. Vowels were not written.

Between 1000 and 900 BC, the Greeks adapted the script of their Phoenician trading partners to represent their own language. One Greek innovation was to use six of the Semitic signs to represent vowels. The first letter, *alef*, became *alpha*, which is transliterated in the Roman alphabet as A.

The Phoenicians wrote from right to left, as in Hebrew, Arabic and many present-day Asian languages. The earliest Greek inscriptions also read from right to left. The Greeks then adopted a style known as *boustrophedon* (turning as in ploughing with oxen), in which they wrote from left to right and from right to left on alternate lines.

At some time around 500 BC, for reasons that are uncertain, they started to write exclusively from left to right, perhaps because it was easier to move the newly introduced split-reed pen in this direction. The Etruscans in Italy took Greek as the model for their own alphabet, from which came the ancient twenty-three–letter Roman alphabet. The letters J, U and W were added in medieval times.

Why don't ballpoint pens constantly dry up?

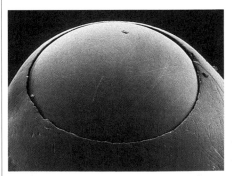

Working tip *of a ballpoint pen is actually a precision-ground metal ball which turns smoothly to transfer fast-drying ink onto paper*

Imprisoned in a socket at the tip of a ballpoint pen is a tiny sphere of metal. It is usually made of mild or stainless steel and is sometimes pitted to give a better grip on the writing surface. Tiny ridges in the socket help the flow of ink. When you write with a ballpoint pen, the ball rolls in ink from a reservoir in the body of the pen and carries it to the paper.

The ink flows smoothly over the ball because it has a buttery consistency derived from an oil base. The oil also helps to reduce volatility, so that ballpoint-pen

Egyptian hieroglyphic	Proto-Sinaitic script	North Semitic (Phoenician)	Hebrew	Greek (with local variations)	Latin
(ox)		(alef)		(alpha)	A
(building, house)		(bet)		(beta)	B
(head)		(resh)		(rho)	R
(eye)		(ayin)		(omikron)	O
(fence)		(he)		(epsilon)	E

Our alphabet evolved, *as did the Greek, Cyrillic, Hebrew and Arabic, mainly from a North Semitic script that developed along the eastern Mediterranean in the second millenium BC. This script possibly came from ancient Egyptian hieroglyphs that represented entire objects. Thus, our letter A is believed to have had its origins in the Egyptian hieroglyph for an ox*

Moment of history at Versailles as Louis XVI presides on May 5, 1789, at the opening of the Estates General. Two months later, the Paris mob stormed the Bastille. The revolution had begun

ink is much less likely to dry in the reservoir than inks based on water or alcohol, which are used in fountain pens. A vent in the ballpoint pen allows air to bleed in to replace used ink; otherwise the resulting near-vacuum would restrict ink flow.

The principle of the ballpoint pen was known as far back as the 1880s, but the first practical device was developed in the 1930s by Laszlo Biro, a Hungarian journalist, and his brother Georg, a chemist. In the 1940s, the pen was marketed under their family name, and ballpoint pens are known as biros to this day in many English-speaking countries.

Why do we refer to 'left' and 'right' in politics?

In 1788, France had a huge national debt, and an excessive number of privileged people were paying far less than their fair share of taxes. There was such turmoil that King Louis XVI called a meeting of a representative national body that had not met since 1614, the Estates General.

It consisted of 300 representatives of the First Estate (the clergy), 300 of the Second Estate (the nobility) and 600 of the Third Estate (the commoners). When the assembly met at Versailles in May 1789, the custom of seating honoured guests on the host's right was followed. The nobility and clergy sat on the king's right and the commoners on his left. In June 1789, the king recognised the Third Estate

as a National Assembly. In the new assembly, the more revolutionary members sat on the left of the speaker's rostrum, and the less fervent on the right.

'Left' and 'right' became shorthand descriptions for the various factions in French politics. Despite political and social problems, France was then the undisputed cultural and intellectual centre of Europe and the terms became commonly used in many countries to mean radical and conservative respectively. The terms are still used, sometimes obscurely. Whereas 'left-wing' once described people with socialist or communist beliefs, die-hard communists in the former Soviet Union are frequently described as right-wingers, because they commonly express what advocates of a new order regard as conservative and reactionary political views.

Why are some newspapers called tabloids?

Digests of information and opinion have existed since a handwritten gazette called the *Acta Diurna* (Daily Events) was prominently displayed in Rome more than 2000 years ago. Printed news sheets appeared in the sixteenth century and in 1609 the first regular newspaper, a weekly, was published in Germany. Newspapers were aimed at the moneyed and propertied elite until the nineteenth century, when a huge increase in literacy throughout the Western world brought a market for popular journals.

Publishers in New York City began to aim for readers among the urban workers. Joseph Pulitzer, publisher of the *World*, introduced a more vigorous and popular style of journalism in the 1880s. The new approach paid off, and the paper's circulation rose rapidly from 15 000 to 250 000 in just three years.

All newspapers were printed on paper of broadsheet size, about 58 by 38 cm (23 by 15 in), until 1903, when Alfred Harmsworth, later Lord Northcliffe, started the *Daily Mirror* in London. Turning the type sideways enabled presses to print two smaller pages

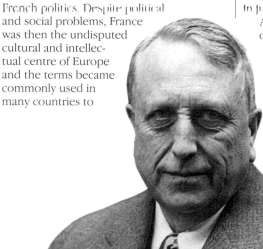

Sensational journalism was the aim of US publisher and magnate William Randolph Hearst. Inset is the first edition of America's first tabloid newspaper, a fierce competitor later of Hearst's own tabloid, the Daily Mirror

on a broadsheet, giving readers a newspaper that was easier to handle, particularly on crowded buses and trains. Taking its cue from New York, the *Mirror* had snappier prose, more and shorter stories, bigger headlines in bolder type and large photographs. Harmsworth called this new, condensed style of newspaper a tabloid, borrowing a word that had been initially a brand name for concentrated medicinal tablets and then a term for a compressed form or dose of anything. The first American tabloid was the New York *Daily News*, which was launched in 1919. It took the new form of journalism to extremes of sensationalism.

The British tabloids of the 1980s and 1990s, relentlessly concentrating on sex, scandal and sensation, have made tabloid synonymous with yellow press. This term, denoting sensationalism, came from a cartoon character. William Randolph Hearst bought the New York *Morning Journal* in 1895. In the following year, he launched a Sunday comic supplement starring the Yellow Kid, a bald-headed Asian boy in a nightgown, who had first appeared in the *World*'s comic supplement. Pithy comments emblazoned on the Yellow Kid's nightgown, coupled with bold headlines and sensational reporting all combined to bring the *Morning Journal* the derogatory epithet.

IT'S MORE PROBABLE THAN YOU THINK...

Have you ever wondered, when waiting for the elevator, or lift, on an intermediate floor of a multistorey building, why the first car to arrive is inevitably going up when you are in a desperate hurry to go down?

You might think that on any given floor, a car going up will be just as likely to arrive as one going down. But in fact, if you're waiting on a lower floor, most cars are likely to be above you. So the first to arrive will probably be going down. Similarly, if you're on an upper floor, most of the cars are likely to be below you and the first to arrive is therefore likely to be going up.

Knowing the number of cars and the number of floors in the building, you could, as you waited, calculate the probability of the wrong car arriving first. Assigning a numerical value to a possible outcome of an unpredictable event uses the principle of probability, which was first investigated in the mid-seventeenth century by two French mathematicians, Blaise Pascal and Pierre de Fermat. Their work arose from a question raised with Pascal by a gambler, and gamblers have pondered its consequences ever since.

A peculiarity of the laws of probability is known as the birthday paradox. There are twenty-three people in a room. What is the probability that at least two of them were born on the same day of the same month? The odds against such a coincidence may seem high but, in fact, they are about even.

The chance that the birthdays of any two persons won't match is 364 out of 365. The first person has a birthday on one of the 365 days in the year, so there are 364 days on which the second person may have a different birthday. If the birthdays of these two don't match, the chance that a third person's birthday won't match either of theirs is 363 out of 365. The chance that none of the three birthdays will match can be worked out this way: 364/365 x 363/365.

The chance that a fourth person's birthday won't match any of the first three is 362 out of 365. To work out the probability of any number of birthdays matching, multiply all the fractions together – that is, 364/365 x 363/365 x 362/365 x ... and so on. If you have twenty-three people, that probability falls below 50 per cent, with a slightly better than even chance that two have the same birthday. The more people, the greater likelihood that two birthdays match. With fifty people, the chance is 97 per cent.

The chances of having an acquaintance in common with a complete stranger from

Breaking the bank *is the dream of every roulette gambler and many devise systems to do so. In the long run, all must fail because payouts are calculated to favour the casino*

another part of the country, or even from overseas, are greater than you think. Rapidly expanding personal, postal and electronic communication with friends, relatives and colleagues ties us into networks far more extensive than our forbears ever had.

An American psychologist, funded by Harvard University, once tested the extent of networks of people in Wichita, Kansas. Names were picked at random. Each person was given a letter addressed to a woman named Alice in Cambridge, Massachusetts, and asked to send it to the acquaintance they thought most likely to know her. The idea was that recipients would then send the letters on to one of their acquaintances, and the chain would continue until a letter reached Alice, 2250 km (1400 miles) away.

Only four days passed before Alice, the wife of a divinity student, received one of the letters. A Wichita farmer had given it to a minister he knew. The minister sent it to a friend, another minister, in Cambridge. That friend knew Alice personally and gave her the letter. There were only two links in the chain between the farmer and Alice. In the entire study, the number of intermediate links ranged from two to ten, with a median of five. When people were asked how many links they thought such a chain would have, most guessed about a hundred.

The dice fall, *as they have for centuries. The earliest dice yet discovered, found in India and Iraq, date from 3000 BC*

Broadening the mind about travel

Why do we rely on petrol to fuel our cars?

It's a frequent and intelligent query: why do we rely so heavily on petrol? That reliance gives many countries crippling oil bills. Also, as petrol supplies run out, we need to find alternative fuels. Why haven't we done so? The quick answer is that we have. Common alternatives are alcohol and three kinds of gas: butane, propane and methane.

Cars have run on alcohol for many years. Racing cars, such as those in the Indianapolis 500, use wood alcohol (methanol) as fuel. Methanol-powered trucks collect the garbage in Tokyo and Osaka. Over 80 per cent of cars run on grain alcohol (ethanol) in Brazil, which has a major program to make cheap alcohol from sugar cane. Both methanol and ethanol have a high octane rating, and are excellent fuels. Their chief drawback is that they are expensive to produce.

Meanwhile, the search goes on for an economic way to make alcohol in large quantities from a crop of some kind. This, if successful, offers many benefits. The net greenhouse effect is zero, because each new crop absorbs the carbon dioxide released in burning alcohol from a previous crop. Farmers, hard pressed in many countries, would get a new and major source of revenue. And because virtually every country could produce its own fuel, dependence on Middle East oil supplies would be a thing of the past.

Alcohol can be made cheaply from coal, oil and natural gas. Any move to do so on a major scale has clear disadvantages in depleting our reserves of fossil fuels and adding more carbon dioxide to the planet's greenhouse blanket. Similar objections are raised about the use of gas to fuel cars. Already, because liquefied petroleum gas (LPG) is cheaper, drivers in many countries have converted their cars to run on LPG as well as petrol. Some 10 per cent of New Zealand's cars run this way. Experts predict that by the year 2000, LPG will make up about 20 per cent of American fuel consumption. LPG, which is either butane or propane, or a mixture of both, is produced in refining crude oil. Supplies depend therefore on those of oil. Both butane and propane liquefy readily at workable temperatures and pressures, making them useful fuels.

Natural gas, found in gas fields in the ground, is largely methane, which as marsh gas causes will-o'-the-wisps. It burns cleanly in petrol engines, producing about 20 per cent less carbon dioxide than petrol, but stays liquid only at very low temperatures (about -250°C; -418°F) and extremely high pressures. It is usually

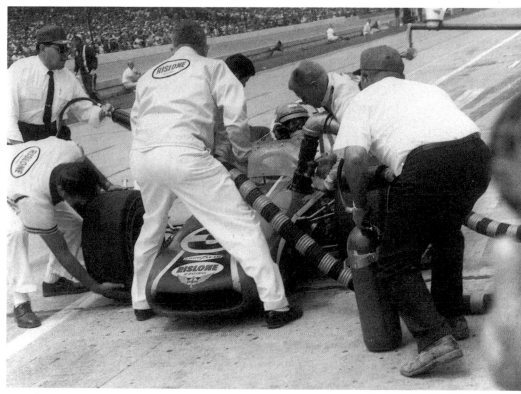

It's all action *as a team refuels a racing car in the Indianapolis-500. All cars in the race run on methanol, or wood alcohol, a petrol substitute usually produced from methane*

stored as compressed natural gas (CNG), but needs a large, strong tank to hold it in quantity. For this reason, its use may stay confined to large vehicles, such as trucks and buses. Worldwide, about half a million such vehicles run on CNG.

Why does some petrol contain lead?

If you don't know the history, it may seem irresponsible to put lead into petrol. Nowadays, lead is clearly recognised as a poison. To burn it in any form and release fumes into the atmosphere is particularly dangerous to children, inflaming the brain's nervous tissue and resulting in some cases in mental subnormality.

Why was it ever done? Adding lead to petrol makes it burn well in a high-efficiency engine. In internal combustion engines, a mixture of fuel and air is compressed before it is ignited. The more that the pistons compress the mixture – the higher the engine's compression ratio – the greater the engine's efficiency and the greater the power of the car.

When auto-engineers confronted the problems of designing engines with higher compression ratios, they found a practical difficulty. High-compression engines need a special grade of fuel, one with a high-octane rating. Lower-grade petrols burn too fast, which makes the

engine 'ping' or 'knock', putting it under considerable strain.

The choice of car fuel raises a series of dilemmas. We can burn expensive petrol efficiently or cheaper petrol less efficiently. If we add lead to low-octane petrol, it has an almost magical effect, transforming it into a fuel that behaves like its expensive superiors. At no great cost, it seemed, we had inexpensive fuel burning well in a powerful engine.

Later, with the exhausts of some 500 million vehicles worldwide puffing lead fumes into the air, we discovered that the community faced a much bigger bill in atmospheric pollution and health costs. Most developed countries have acted to phase out the use of lead in petrol. Today, more cars use unleaded fuel. They have lower compression ratios, so that their engines won't ping and knock. But again there is a price. Cars using unleaded petrol have less efficient engines, which burn more fuel. They are not puffing poisonous lead into the air, but they are adding more carbon dioxide, a greenhouse gas.

To put lead into petrol, oil companies add a liquid, lead tetraethyl. This can escape into the atmosphere by evaporation. The fumes are highly toxic, and can cause symptoms resembling those of psychosis. In extreme cases, victims go mad. If you use leaded petrol for cleaning or degreasing, beware of the hazards.

Traffic and fumes build up in a Bangkok street. Fewer cars in developing countries burn leadless petrol. The long-term results are serious, causing heart attacks and brain damage

Why does leadless petrol cause such a smell?

The experience is unforgettable. You are standing at a bus stop and suddenly you get the smell of something like an old-time stink-bomb, a whiff of rotten eggs. Or you are driving uphill behind other cars – and there is that smell again. You have heard that the cause is unleaded petrol, but what precisely causes the smell? And what can we do about it?

There are two culprits, and they work together: the car's catalytic converter and sulphur in the petrol. Without a catalytic converter, the vehicle's exhaust fumes would have a high proportion of carbon monoxide, which in concentration is a deadly gas. The catalytic converter, an antipollution device mounted in the exhaust system near the manifold, changes the carbon monoxide into carbon dioxide, eliminates unburned hydrocarbons, and gets rid of oxides of nitrogen that cause photochemical smog.

All petrol, leaded and unleaded, contains sulphur, which occurs naturally in crude oil and is difficult for refiners to remove completely. While dealing with carbon monoxide, the catalytic converter turns the sulphur into hydrogen sulphide, the same gas that occurs in rotten eggs.

It may seem strange that, though petrol-burning vehicles have been on the roads for decades, we have never had to endure this smell before. That's because vehicles using leaded petrol don't have catalytic converters: the lead in the petrol would quickly destroy them. Automotive engineers have solutions, but all carry a price. To abolish catalytic converters would increase pollution. Even so, the conversion of carbon monoxide into carbon dioxide has questionable benefits: we are putting more carbon dioxide, a greenhouse gas, into the atmosphere, with possibly serious long-term consequences.

We could ban the sale of petrol containing sulphur. To produce sulphur-free petrol, oil companies would need to install expensive new equipment at their refineries. Everybody would pay the price of dearer petrol.

We could improve car engines so that catalytic converters don't produce hydrogen sulphide. This, too, is theoretically possible. You may have noticed that the rotten-egg smell isn't there all the time. That is because the catalytic converter makes hydrogen sulphide only when the vehicle is 'running rich' – that is, burning a fuel mixture with a high petrol content. This usually occurs when accelerating. We could design cars to run well on a leaner mixture, avoiding production of hydrogen sulphide. Manufacturers say that this would make vehicles more expensive.

Alternatively, we could invent a catalytic converter that doesn't produce hydrogen sulphide. Again, we're talking about making dearer cars.

The good news in all this is that hydrogen sulphide may be a stinker, but in small doses isn't a health hazard. It is certainly preferable to fumes containing highly toxic lead.

Why do car batteries sometimes need water?

You may have noticed that pump hands rarely offer these days to top up your car battery. All part of a general fall-off in service, you may think. After all, in the past when customers were given some attention, the battery was checked and water added almost every time your tank was filled with petrol.

Blame poor service if you like, but the reason is more likely to be that you have a modern 'maintenance-free' battery. An old-style battery needs topping up with water not, as you might have thought, because liquid has evaporated, but because the battery is 'gassing'. Every time you start your car (or when absentmindedly you leave on the lights) the battery loses some of its stored electricity. When you restart the engine, the battery is recharged. That process in an old-type battery breaks down the water into its constituent elements, hydrogen and oxygen, slightly increasing the internal pressure. These gases leak out, and the level of the liquid drops.

Older car batteries have lead plates to which 10 per cent antimony was added for strength. The antimony causes gassing while the battery is charged. Later batteries have little antimony (instead using calcium, another strengthening metal), and normally do not gas. If you have a low-maintenance battery that is losing its electrolyte – needs topping up – it is a sign of a fault in either the generator or regulator. It means that the battery is being recharged at higher than 15 volts.

Why does a car battery go flat?

The cylindrical, single-cell batteries you put into a flashlight or transistor radio gradually lose power. The light goes dim, the radio becomes inaudible. Unless they are of a special kind, these dry-cell batteries cannot be recharged.

Your car has a wet-cell battery of a kind that many years ago was used in most homes to provide low-voltage power in early radio receivers. As their power runs down, they can be recharged.

Most car batteries have six cells, each producing about 2 volts of electricity. In each cell, positive and negative plates (electrodes) alternate; the positive electrodes are filled with lead dioxide, the negative ones with spongy lead. All the electrodes are immersed in a conducting fluid, an electrolyte – usually two-thirds distilled water and one-third sulphuric acid. Chemical reactions between the electrodes and the electrolyte produce electrical energy. The process starts when an electrical circuit is completed between the terminals connected to each cell, for example when headlights are switched on. The lead dioxide of the positive electrode begins to dissolve slowly in the electrolyte. Its atoms start to break up, releasing positive ions into the liquid, and electrons into the wiring of the car's circuitry at the negative terminal. The spongy lead of the negative electrode does not dissolve as much, but it loses electrons to positive ions in the electrolyte. The constant flow of electrons from the positive electrode through the circuit to make up the deficiency in the negative electrode forms the electric current.

These chemical reactions also cause both sets of electrodes to turn into lead sulphate, and turn the sulphuric acid into water. When the engine is running, the car's generator feeds current back into the battery and the chemical process is reversed, restoring the plates and maintaining the strength of the sulphuric acid.

If you leave your car unused for a time, you may find you cannot restart the engine. This is because the chemical reactions between electrodes and electrolyte go on, very gradually, even without any demand on the battery. Without the engine being run to make the generator do its work, the battery will go flat.

Why do cars need gears?

The first mass-produced cars came on to the road nearly a century ago. We might think that, with all the brainpower the industry commands, some bright inventor would by now have found a way to get rid of gears. Even automatic cars seem sometimes to hesitate, as if they are unsure quite what to do. And millions of drivers worldwide choose to drive vehicles with a manual gear change, despite the occasional stall and gnashing of cogs.

A car engine's fundamental design requires it to have gears. You may have heard that word 'torque', beloved of motor-car advertisers. Torque, measured in Newton-metres, is the twisting force produced by the engine to turn the car

A car's power reaches the wheels via the transmission system. When the gears are engaged, they relate the speed of the engine to that of the propeller shaft by one toothed wheel driving another. The low gear shown revolves three times to turn a driven gear once, making it easier to get that tough, initial movement

wheels. The more torque on the wheels, the faster the car accelerates.

More effort is needed to get the car moving over the first few metres in its lowest gear than to keep it zipping along in top gear. The engine can't produce much torque until it runs quite fast. At low engine speeds, the torque is weak. At higher speeds, the torque builds up. Most engines get into their stride only when turning at 2000 to 3000 revolutions per minute. At those speeds, the engine produces its maximum torque. Go a bit faster and the torque lessens.

If a car had no gears, its acceleration would depend on how fast it was going. You would have plenty of acceleration only when the car moved fast enough for the engine to exert real torque. Gears in a car can be compared to levers and pulleys. Just as a lever or a pulley allows you to shift great weights with less effort, so the low gear you engage to set your car going lets the engine turn over fast but move the car slowly.

Without a meshing of minds to produce a new kind of engine, it looks as though gears are here to stay.

Why are traffic lights red and green?

Long before roads needed traffic lights, signals controlled railway trains. The earliest nineteenth century railway signalling systems involved a ball and what looked like a canvas kite. Hauled to the top of a post, the kite indicated danger and the ball meant 'all clear ahead'.

From 1841, semaphore was widely used: a signal arm in a horizontal position ordered a driver to stop; lowered to 45 degrees it urged him to proceed with caution; and pointing vertically skywards it showed that the track ahead was all clear. Signals were painted red, the colour thought most likely to attract a driver's attention.

At night, oil lamps were added to the signal poles. A red light signified 'stop' and white 'carry on'. About 1872, an additional yellow lamp told drivers to proceed with caution to the next signal and await further instructions. In 1893, green lights replaced the white to avoid the confusion caused to train drivers by the spread of street and house lighting.

When railway signals were electrified late in the nineteenth century, the standard code became a red light for stop, amber for caution and green for go. The colours were used later in electric lights controlling road traffic. Cleveland, Ohio, installed the world's first automatic traffic lights in 1914. Europe's first appeared in France in 1923.

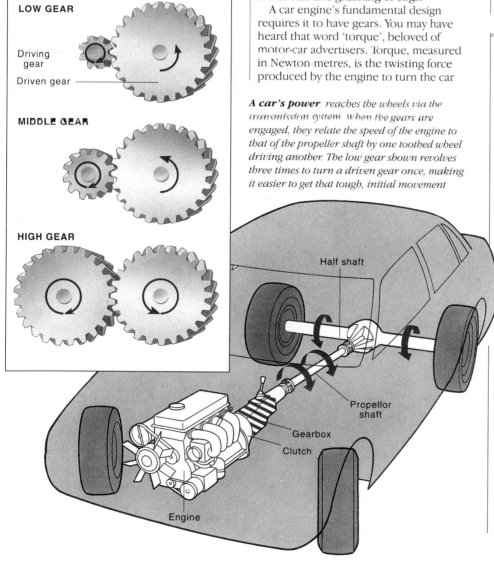

LOW GEAR

Driving gear

Driven gear

MIDDLE GEAR

HIGH GEAR

Half shaft

Propellor shaft

Gearbox

Clutch

Engine

Why do we seal our roads with tar?

Tarmacadam, popularly known as Tarmac, has surfaced roads and highways for nearly a century and a half. It takes its name from John Loudon McAdam, a Scot who revolutionised our ways of building roads. But McAdam didn't invent Tarmacadam. That came in 1854, eighteen years after his death.

E. P. Hooley, a British surveyor, noticed that a barrel of tar spilled by accident had solidified to a hard and smooth surface. Hooley decided that a layer of tar added to McAdam's roads would give them a waterproof bond, lengthen their life, and make travel smoother and faster.

Until 1815, when McAdam's technique was first used for rebuilding England's roads, nothing much had changed since Roman times. Roads were in such a poor state that mail coaches dawdled along at not much more than walking pace, and in wet weather frequently became bogged down in mud.

McAdam developed a technique for road building in which first came a thick layer of broken stones, each about 50 mm (2 in) in diameter. Then roadmen laid a layer of smaller stones that was rolled down and interlocked with the base material. Finally came a dressing of pebbles, which traffic would reduce to dust, filling the gaps. More traffic gradually solidified the surface.

The Scotsman's roads almost doubled the speed of coaches. Tarmac reduced the number of potholes, and paved the way for our high-speed journeys of today.

Why do racing cars have smooth tyres?

Watching a racing car roar through a tight bend, you could be excused for thinking that it must have wonderful treads on its tyres. You would be wrong. Racing-car tyres are quite smooth, with no pattern of treads to help them grip the road.

Cars have tyres for two purposes. By acting as cushions they help to absorb the shocks of travelling on bumpy roads. Also, they give the car a good grip on a surface that may be wet and slippery. Thin cuts (known as sipes) in the rubber act as sponges, soaking up road water; revolving at speed, patterns in the treads squirt the water behind. Designers calculate that, on a wet road, the treads on each tyre move

Built for speed, *the wide tyre of a racing car gets more surface grip. That of a normal car copes better with wet roads*

some 5 litres (about 1 gal) of water every second to ensure a safe grip.

Because racing cars usually compete on dry roads – torrential rain sometimes causes the cancellation of grand-prix events – teams choose treadless tyres, called slicks. These, plus their extra width, give maximum possible contact with the track. If heavy rain falls during the race, pit crews fit treaded tyres. Sometimes, a decision is delayed, and the driver finds he loses control. A film of water builds up in front of the slicks, lifting them off the road. The car skates ahead in a manner known as aquaplaning, and the driver may be lucky to avoid a high-speed collision.

Why can you get an electric shock from your car?

It is a dry day, and you are wearing a nylon jacket and rubber-soled shoes. You slide briskly across your car seat, hop out and, as you reach to close the door – *crackle*! A spark jumps from your hand to the car. Your hand tingles and may even hurt. What happened?

As you slid across the seat, you built up a charge of static electricity. The phenomenon, which makes some garments crackle as you take them off and sparks fly from your hair when you comb it, was observed long before electricity was understood and harnessed. People with abnormally dry skin may generate up to 30 000 volts, making them a hazard in such places as explosives factories and petroleum refineries.

No wonder that you don't need to slide much in your car seat to turn yourself into a kind of human powerhouse, with a load of electricity waiting to escape. And that's what it did when you touched the car door. The electrons in your body took the chance to spread themselves over the much larger surface

Modern road-building *owes much to John Loudon McAdam (inset) who rebuilt roads in Britain from 1815 onwards. Higher speeds and heavier vehicles brought the need for constant repairs, such as those (inset below) by a New York team early this century. Today, concrete makes highways more durable. Road trains can complete some 300 m (330 yd) of road a day*

SO MANY CARS, SO LITTLE SPACE

As motorists caught in a traffic jam frequently observe: 'There are too many cars on the road.' And, as travellers know, the roads in some countries are more jammed than in others.

But how bad are the world's traffic jams? And what would happen if, in some terrifying emergency, all the cars in any one country headed on to the road at the same time?

To get some idea of the problem, we need only divide the total length of a nation's roads by its total vehicles. Italy, which already has some of the world's biggest traffic bottlenecks, would have a nationwide jam. If its 25.5 million vehicles were evenly spread, which in an emergency would be a miracle, each would have less than 12 m (39 ft) of space. Britain, with nearly 25 million vehicles but a bigger road network, would be slightly better off. Each would occupy 14 m (46 ft) of roadway.

Even America's great network of highways and roads would be jammed, with one vehicle for every 33 m (108 ft). The United States has the world's longest network of roads, totalling some 6.23 million km (3.87 million miles). But the nation's continuing love affair with the automobile gives it some 186.5 million vehicles, three times as many as Japan and, on average, one vehicle for every 1.3 people. Because of Americans' reliance on private cars instead of public transport, the ratio of automobiles is much higher – 77 per cent – than in many other countries, and those cars get more use. The average American drives more than 12 500 km (7800 miles) a year, more than twice the distance of Britons and Canadians.

In the wide open spaces of Australia, the prospect is a little rosier. Its 9.4 million vehicles each have 91 m (298 ft) of road

Jammed-up streets have long been with us, as shown by this Chicago scene of 1905. But traffic jams have a bright side. Studies indicate that the worse they get, the faster we are likely to create cities that don't depend on cars

space, if they manage to escape from the cities to enjoy it. Ireland is one of the few places in the Western world where the driver has plenty of freedom. Lucky Irish motorists each have 111 m (364 ft) of road to call their own.

of the car. There they linger, because the insulating barrier of the car's rubber tyres prevents them from escaping to the even larger body of the Earth.

Several factors decide what kind of shock you get, or indeed whether you get one at all. The state of your car tyres plays an important role. New tyres are better insulators than worn ones, because they have less contact with the ground. Wet weather breaks down this insulation. In dry weather, you will build up a charge and tend to keep it. If your clothes are good insulators, as are most synthetics, your static electricity will increase; the same clothes, freshly laundered, are better insulators than when they are dirty. Rubber or synthetic soles on your shoes also improve your insulation; leather soles let your charge of

It's quite shocking, as this man finds when touching a science-museum's machine designed to produce static electricity

electricity leak harmlessly into the ground as you step out of the car.

Of course, you could avoid these shocks by driving only in wet weather and when wearing leather sandals and grimy cotton clothes. A more practical remedy is to treat your car seats with an antistatic spray. Better still might be to remember to grip the car's metal doorframe before you step out. This gives the electrons the chance to spread in the way they prefer to be, as far from one another as possible. Once they are happy – and they move almost instantly – you are safe. You are still carrying a charge but a smaller one, exactly compatible with that on the car body, eliminating any chance of shock.

Why in some countries do we drive on the left and in others on the right?

When Pope Boniface VIII reiterated in AD 1300 that 'all roads lead to Rome', he told pilgrims to keep to the left – and set a pattern that causes worldwide controversy today. Pilgrims invariably walked on the left-hand side of the road, but the pope's edict gave the custom almost the force of law, and for centuries appeared to settle the rights and wrongs of travel.

The rule we apply today – that, for safety's sake, pedestrians should face oncoming traffic – was apparently not considered necessary for the pilgrims of the time. Already, horsemen usually rode on the left-hand side. Most riders find it more natural to mount from the left, and mounting blocks were set on the left-hand side of the road to help them do so.

Mounting from the left was more convenient also for most swordsmen, the 90 per cent who wielded their weapons with the right hand. The sword, worn on the left by right-handed swordsmen, didn't impede the swing into the saddle. Also, when passing a stranger, it seemed safer to do so on the left, making it easier for a right-hander to use a sword or lance to ward off any surprise attack.

Passing on the left became the custom in most countries, and it carried over to the days of horse-drawn carts and carriages. During the French Revolution, Robespierre, architect of the Reign of Terror, ordered the citizens of Paris to drive on the right, apparently as a gesture of defiance against the Catholic Church. A few years later, Napoleon Bonaparte commanded his military columns and supply wagons to keep to the right. Napoleon was left-handed, and argued that it was natural to travel on the right. To avoid collisions, other traffic was forced to use that side of the road.

Britain was isolated from these influences, but argument flared. Early in the nineteenth century, writer and orator Henry Erskine declared emphatically,

The rule of the road is a paradox quite,
Both in riding and driving along;
If you keep to the left, you are sure
*   to be right,*
If you keep to the right you are wrong.

Vehicle design reinforced Britain's practice of keeping left. British freight wagons, unlike those in use in Europe and America, had a driver's seat. This was placed on the right, so that most drivers – right-handers – could urge on the horse team without getting the whip snarled in or

The changing face *of Stockholm's traffic showed clearly in 1967, when Sweden joined the rest of mainland Europe by driving on the right. Good order was quickly restored*

deflected by the wagon load behind. Seated on the right, drivers preferred to pass to the left of oncoming wagons, making it easier to judge clearance on narrow roads.

Territories in Britain's empire inherited the same rules. In the early 1800s, Singapore and Hong Kong were ordered to keep left. In 1859, the Japanese, then great admirers of most things British, chose to follow suit. China and the Philippines copied their neighbours, except that in 1946 China switched to the right. Nevertheless, in much of Asia today, all vehicles keep left.

Why America, once colonised by the British, drives on the right is a matter of controversy. Whatever practice was followed by the British in occupation set no long-term pattern. Today's rules probably originated in the late eighteenth century

with the use of large freight wagons drawn by six or eight horses hitched in pairs. Among these were the Conestoga wagons of the eastern United States, the forerunners of the prairie schooners of the American West.

These wagons, designed to haul wheat from Pennsylvania's Conestoga Valley to nearby cities, had no driver's seat. They followed the practice common in Europe of the driver controlling the team by sitting astride the rear horse on the left-hand side. When two wagons met on a typical narrow and potholed road, it was easier to keep to the right. Each driver then had a better view of the clearance.

Today, of at least 230 independently administered countries and territories, only about a quarter drive on the left. Three of the world's most populous countries – China, the United States and the former USSR – drive on the right. In Europe, only Britain, Ireland and Malta drive on the left.

In recent times, drivers in Sweden, Iceland, Burma, Nigeria and Bahrain have had to switch from left to right. Those in Okinawa and East Timor have gone from right to left.

Closer ties with Europe have put Britain under renewed pressure for a shift to the right. It was felt, too, that the Channel Tunnel might force a change. Would traffic follow the British or European rules? The dilemma was neatly solved: cars and trucks go by train. Meanwhile, British drivers show little inclination for change, and non-driving taxpayers are even more reluctant to meet the enormous costs that a switch-over would inevitably bring.

Why does an idling car cause more air pollution?

The emissions from the exhaust pipe of a typical petrol engine contain at least 100 chemicals, some of which contribute to photochemical smog, the dirty haze that hangs like a blanket over many of the world's major cities.

Car engines produce energy by burning petrol mixed with air. In a cold car, or one made cooler by idling, the fuel is not fully vaporised or distributed evenly to the cylinders, and more unburned fuel, with all its polluting chemicals, is released into the air. The effect is intensified in an out-of-tune car. All modern cars are fitted with a catalytic converter, a device designed to remove many hazardous substances that would otherwise be released with exhaust gases. The converter works most effectively when the car is warm and running with the correct fuel–air ratio. When the

engine idles, the temperature of the exhaust gases falls, and the catalyst removes only the hydrocarbons that are easily oxidised.

Another factor is our confined city streets. Idling cars intensify air pollution in traffic jams where there is less flow of air to disperse the emissions. The problem may be eased within a few years when car manufacturers introduce engines that turn themselves off when they have been idling for a time.

Motorists can help to cut pollution by keeping their cars in good tune and warming them up as quickly as possible when first started. Make sure that the cooling system thermostat is operating correctly to assist with a rapid warm-up. In congested city traffic, switch off the engine if you are forced to halt for more than a few minutes.

Why are windows in ships called portholes?

When ships were propelled by oars, their sides were especially vulnerable. Damage inflicted on the oars or oarsmen crippled the ship. The essence of naval tactics was to ram and board the opponent, and to do that ships sailed abreast in standard battle formation.

In the sixteenth century the development of heavy cannon revolutionised naval warfare. A ship could sail alongside another and open fire with a row of guns, but many cannon on deck made a ship unstable. To beat the problem, James Baker, shipwright to Henry VIII of England, mounted multiple rows of heavy guns below decks. He cut holes in the sides of a ship and shielded the openings

Porthole portraits for a couple on the British warship HMS Hood, *which was sunk in 1941. Unlike the first portholes, those on the* Hood *were not built for guns*

against sea and weather with hinged flaps of stout wood. These were called gun ports, from the Latin *porta* (a door). The first ship with gun ports was probably Henry VIII's ill-fated flagship, *Mary Rose*. She foundered while leaving Portsmouth to engage the French fleet in 1545, and was not raised until 1982.

Designers of multidecked cargo and passenger ships saw an advantage in having hinged windows in the hulls, and copied the idea of gun ports. Lacking guns, they were known first as ports and then as portholes.

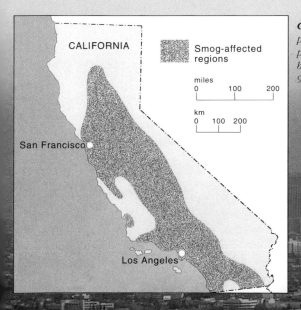

California breaks records for vehicle ownership, petrol consumption and levels of photochemical smog. Los Angeles is regularly blanketed in a brown haze, caused by pollutants reacting to sunlight. The map shows how vast an area of the state is affected by air pollution. But change is on the way. Recent plans aim to reduce hydrocarbons by 90 per cent, improve public transport and generally discourage the use of cars

CALIFORNIA

Smog-affected regions

miles
0   100   200

km
0 100 200

San Francisco

Los Angeles

Why are the sides of a ship called port and starboard?

The earliest sea-going ships were propelled chiefly by oars. Ships needed so many oarsmen that there was little room for cargo. This in turn brought a demand for better sails.

At first, ships were guided by two long oars, one on each side of the stern. The Vikings' superb longships had sails and oars, and were steered by a single long oar. A horizontal tiller was fixed to its shaft for easy manipulation by the helmsman. For unknown reasons, this oar was mounted on the right-hand side of the stern, looking towards the bow. In Old English the right-hand side of the vessel came to be called the *steorbord* (steering side). From this comes starboard.

The left-hand side of a vessel was once known as the *laddeborde* (loading side). In time this, because of its natural association with starboard, became larboard. The terms were easily confused, with potentially disastrous results, and larboard gave way to port. The Royal Navy forbade larboard in 1844, and the United States Navy did so two years later. Port probably comes originally from port-side, the side of the ship moored to the landing place.

Why is a ship's speed expressed in knots?

The earliest method of estimating a ship's speed through water was probably to time how long a floating object took to pass from stem to stern. A refinement was to tie knots in a line, spacing them at equal distances, and tie it to an object called the log.

As the ship left the log behind, a mariner paid out line, called the logline. For a standard period, measured usually by sand in an hourglass, he counted the passing knots, which determined the vessel's speed. In the days of navigation by dead reckoning, establishing position by direction and distance, this was a vital routine measurement, recorded daily in the ship's logbook.

The knot came to be defined as a speed of one nautical mile an hour. The nautical mile was originally defined as a sixtieth of one degree at the equator, or one 21 600th of the Earth's circumference. This is a variable distance because the Earth is not a perfect sphere, and eventually the nautical mile was set at 6076.12 ft (1.852 km). A speed of 10 knots is therefore equal to 18.52 km/h. Mariners, with whom tradition dies hard, still express a ship's speed in knots, a system often used also for aircraft.

After the crash US officials recover black boxes, painted orange, from the wreck of a Colombian Boeing 707. The aircraft crashed on its approach to New York. The devices are keys to explaining air disasters

Why do aircraft have a black box?

The black box, frequently mentioned in news of an air disaster, plays no part in making an aircraft fly. Its only function is to help investigators discover the cause of a crash – and maybe prevent others.

In a passenger aircraft, there are actually two black boxes. One contains the flight-data recorder, which registers the aircraft's speed, direction, altitude and other information throughout the flight. The other, the cockpit-voice recorder, contains an endless loop of tape, similar to that in an answering machine. This runs continuously, recording conversations for the previous thirty, or sometimes sixty, minutes. Each recorder is packed separately within a crashproof and fireproof metal shell. This is almost always painted bright yellow or orange for ease of finding in wreckage.

As it is painted orange, why call it a black box? The term is not confined to aircraft, but is used also in industry. Engineers and technicians refer to any device not essential to the functioning of a system as a black box.

Why do aircraft have only two wings?

The two wings that characterise virtually all modern aircraft make up a single surface, say aeronautical engineers. They classify such aircraft as monoplanes. In the early days of flight, most aircraft were biplanes, with two wings on each side, or triplanes, with three. The quest to give aircraft a greater lifting surface resulted even in some aircraft having more than three pairs of wings. But multiple wings caused more drag. To hold the flimsy canvas-over-wood contraption together, early aircraft needed a forest of stays and spars. These and the extra wings slowed down the aircraft and raised its fuel consumption. Early multiwinged aircraft were so frail and unreliable that more than a third of all air casualties during World War I were caused by accident or aircraft failure, not enemy action.

To give them lift, monoplanes needed more efficient engines, with a higher power-to-weight ratio. Powerful engines had to be housed in more substantial aircraft, so designers turned to light metals, such as aluminium and alloys. Metal construction encouraged more streamlined design. Aircraft with two wings soon dominated the skies.

The Red Baron, Manfred von Richthofen, flew the Fokker Dr. I triplane during World War I. The Sopwith Pup biplane is one of the most renowned aircraft of that era

UP, UP AND FINALLY AWAY

The ancient Greeks told a story about Icarus, a youth imprisoned in Crete with his father Daedalus. The pair escaped by fixing feathers to their arms with wax and jumping from their prison tower. Daedalus flew soberly and steadily to freedom in Sicily, but Icarus, exulting in his ability to fly with the eagles, soared high and close to the Sun. Its heat melted the wax, the feathers fell off, and Icarus plummeted to his death in the Aegean Sea.

The legend of Icarus, with its vision of human flight, inspired inventors, engineers and dreamers, including Leonardo da Vinci, who toyed in his notebooks with various kinds of gliders and helicopters. The first to realise the vision were two Frenchmen who made a free flight on November 21, 1783, in a hot-air balloon devised by Joseph and Etienne Montgolfier. British inventor Sir George Cayley experimented with gliders, and in 1849 sent a ten-year-old boy aloft to make the first piloted glider flight. Three years later, a French engineer, Henri Giffard, flew a steam-powered, hydrogen-filled airship.

A young farmer in New Zealand, Richard Pearse, designed a powered aircraft and flew it in March 1903, but he had no control over his machine and crashed after just 45 m (50 yd). It was Orville Wright who made the first fully controlled flight in a heavier-than-air machine. He piloted Flyer I over sand dunes at Kill Devil Hills, North Carolina, for twelve seconds on December 17, 1903.

Nine decades after the flight of the aircraft designed by Orville Wright and his brother Wilbur, humans fly by means as diverse as jet-propelled back-packs, hang-gliders, pedal-powered aircraft and the supersonic Concorde airliner, which can outpace a rifle bullet. Supersonic flight has not, however, become the standard. Mass travel is dominated by huge airliners such as the Boeing 747 jumbo jet, which carries some 500 people at 980 km/h (608 mph) for distances up to 10 000 km (about 6000 miles).

Designers are planning airliners bigger than the Boeing 747, the largest version of which is about 71 m (233 ft) long and has a wingspan of 65 m (213 ft). One plan is for a 600-passenger plane, 85 m (279 ft) long with a wingspan of 60 m (197 ft), which will have a range of 13 000 km (8000 miles). Another is for a giant carrying 1000 passengers on three decks.

Bigger aircraft create problems in handling passengers and baggage, but fewer aircraft would reduce congestion in the air and on the tarmac. Airports, which now sprawl over vast areas near our cities, could be smaller if passenger aircraft, like helicopters and some military jets, took off and landed without runways.

Eccentric ideas played a key part in conquering the air. French pioneer Clément Ader put a steam engine into his novel plane (right) of 1897. Ten years later, Jacob Ellehammer made a flight in his triplane (inset above). In 1908, Count d'Ecquevilley, a Frenchman, tried to launch a strange aircraft that had twelve linked wings but no tail

Why do passenger jets fly so high?

Most modern long-range passenger jet aircraft cruise at an altitude of about 10 000 m (33 000 ft). By doing so, they avoid many of the storms and much of the turbulence of lower levels, giving travellers a safe and comfortable flight. As well, the engines function most efficiently in the high, thinner air, which also offers less resistance to the plane's motion. This means that a plane can fly farther and faster on a given quantity of fuel. The benefits of hoisting the aircraft and its load of passengers, baggage and fuel to a high altitude far outweigh the costs. In general, an aircraft's optimum altitude is one that gives the best compromise between going up and going forward.

Many other considerations limit an aircraft's ideal cruising altitude, speed and range. They include the size, shape and configuration of the aircraft's wing. For example, planes with wings suited to flying far and fast usually must make long, speedy landings.

Why are disposable lighters dangerous in aircraft?

People take extraordinary things onto aircraft. A passenger's baggage in Britain in 1983 held 144 quarter-litre bottles of nitric acid. A passenger flying from London to Pakistan had a small pressure-stove on which, in mid-flight, he began to cook his family a meal. Two passengers on another flight carried 960 disposable cigarette lighters in their hand baggage and had 163 in their suitcases.

Disposable lighters are among many everyday devices that are usually safe and reliable, but can malfunction dangerously in an aircraft in flight. Lighters contain highly flammable gas under pressure. In some circumstances, cabin temperatures may reach 55°C (131°F), which expands the gas and may cause or worsen a leak. Constant vibration may agitate the mechanism sufficiently to ignite the leaking gas. If the cabin's pressure system fails at high altitude, the lighter may explode, with catastrophic consequences. Vibration can ignite book matches, so they are forbidden in baggage. Aerosol cans contain gas under pressure and may explode in flight.

In the past thirty years, passenger jet aircraft have had more than fifty in-flight cabin fires, about half of them fatal. In the three worst, a total of more than 1000 lives were lost. In all three cases many passengers died after the pilot had successfully landed the aircraft.

Acrobats of the air, the renowned Red Arrows team of Britain's Royal Air Force, are just as proficient at flying upside down in tight formation as they are at performing their high-speed feats the right way up. Today, all military pilots train in aerobatics

Why can aircraft fly upside down?

Without wings, aircraft can't lift themselves off the ground. In cross-section, wings are rounder and thicker at the front (the leading edge), and taper to a sharp edge at the back (the trailing edge). As a plane moves along the tarmac to take off, air travelling over the curved top surface of the wing has farther to go than the air under the flatter undersurface. The top air has to travel faster, while air underneath travels more slowly, becoming compressed. The higher pressure underneath combined with the lower pressure above creates lift. This, together with the forward thrust generated by the engine, allows the plane to take off.

The aircraft rises and continues to do so while the leading edge of the wing is higher than the trailing edge. The pilot makes sure of this by controlling the lift on the tailplane. This is done by adjusting the elevators, the two horizontal 'hinges' on the plane's tail.

If the wings enable an aircraft to rise into the sky, we might wonder why, if it flies upside down, it doesn't fall into the ground. Indeed it would, if the pilot kept the fuselage at its normal angle – more or less parallel to the ground. This would result in the wings' leading edge being lower than their trailing edge. The wings would then have what is known as 'negative lift'. That is, air pressure would be greater above the wing than below, forcing the plane lower. The pilot counteracts this in upside-down flight by allowing the tailplane to drop, or in the case of large aircraft, by adjusting the wing flaps.

If you see a stunt pilot flying upside down, you will notice that, although the plane's fuselage is tilted at a similar angle to that on takeoff, the aircraft is maintaining level flight. You may notice too that the flight looks laboured. It works, but experts in aerodynamics will tell you that it is for stunts and emergencies only. As a means of travel it is very inefficient.

Railways for people arrived with the Rocket, *the epoch-making steam locomotive built by George Stephenson and his son Robert. In 1829, it outpaced all rivals to become the chosen model for the Liverpool and Manchester Railway, heralding the age of passenger trains*

Why did diesel and electric engines oust steam power?

Until the late nineteenth century, only the steam engine provided enough power to pull the heavy load of a long line of railway wagons or carriages. The first challenge to steam came from electricity. The electric motor delivers the enormous torque, or turning power, needed to move heavy rolling stock quickly from a standing start to a steady speed. Also, it is quiet, reliable, easier and cheaper to maintain than the steam engine. It produces no noxious fumes, although the power station may do so.

In 1881, only eight years after the invention of a practical electric motor, the world's first electric railway, 2.4 km (1½ miles) long, opened in Berlin. Within two years Britain also had electric trains, and in 1895 the Baltimore and Ohio Railroad electrified a main line in the United States. In 1902, an electric train on an experimental line in Germany reached 210 km/h (130 mph), a remarkable speed for the time.

During the first few decades of this century, Europe saw widespread electrification of its railways, especially on shorter lines where revenue from heavy traffic offset the high initial costs. Steam trains survived in large countries such as Argentina, Australia, Russia and the United States. There, vast distances and less traffic tended to make electrification of railways uneconomic.

In 1892, German engineer Rudolf Diesel improved the compression-ignition engine invented earlier in Britain. Conventional internal-combustion engines use sparking plugs to ignite their fuel. A diesel engine compresses air, producing heat sufficient to explode an intake of fuel. For twenty years, little use was found for diesel engines except to generate electricity and to power ships. Then in 1912, the Diesel-Klose-Sulzer company designed a diesel locomotive, but it was suitable only for light work, such as shunting empty rolling stock. Steady improvement brought a major innovation with the diesel-electric locomotive, which runs on electricity generated by an onboard diesel engine. A regular diesel-electric train ran between Hamburg and Berlin in 1932, and a similar service started in the United States two years later.

After World War II, the shift to diesel locomotives gained pace. Diesel locomotives require fewer crew, and are easier to fuel and operate than steam engines. Britain, which had an efficient steam system fuelled by local coal, was conspicuously slower to follow the trend, but even there diesel had replaced most steam locomotives by the 1960s.

Why are there so many different railway gauges?

Before British ironworks first used steam locomotives in the early 1800s, it was common for horses to draw heavy loads in wagons mounted on rails. These rails were often spaced 4 ft 8 in (1422 mm) apart, the width between the wheels on many road carts. For unknown reasons, Robert Stephenson, son of railway pioneer George Stephenson, increased the space by half an inch. This measurement (1435 mm) came to be accepted as standard gauge worldwide.

In the nineteenth century, roads between towns and even major cities were poor or non-existent. Railways offered a lucrative link, and railway companies rushed to lay tracks, sometimes of different gauges from those of their rivals. Wide tracks cost more to build than narrow tracks, but they are more stable, give a more comfortable ride, and can carry higher and wider loads.

Some countries ended up with three gauges or more, ranging from 1676 mm (5 ft 6 in) in parts of India to 762 mm (2 ft 6 in) on some minor lines in the Australian colony of Victoria. At one time in Australia, passengers had to change trains six times to travel from Brisbane on the east coast to Perth on the west. Today, India, Australia and Argentina still have three gauges.

Three different gauges combine in one line at Gladstone, South Australia. Trains from other areas can all use the track

FEASTS, CUSTOMS & STRANGE BELIEFS

In a variety of ways, many of which are so habitual that we rarely question them, ancient conventions guide our actions. They decide our dress, our manners and celebrations, ruling our lives from the first days to the last

Why are black cats both lucky and unlucky?
PAGE 208

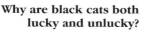

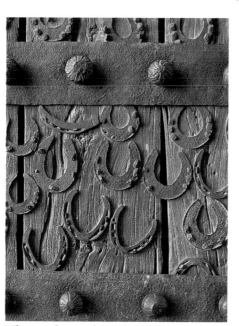

Why are horseshoes hung over doors? PAGE 212

Why do brides wear white?
PAGE 207

A special blend of magic

Why do we celebrate Christmas?

If the question offends or the answer seems obvious, read on. For in many Christian countries during the sixteenth century, Christmas as a season of festivity almost vanished, and in England and America a century later citizens celebrated under threat of punishment.

Confusion about the origins of Christmas arises because it is difficult to say precisely when the festival, as we know it, began. A feast with a semblance of Christmas, Sacaea, was celebrated thousands of years before Christ's birth. In 2000 BC, in what is now Iraq, a five-day festival with exchanges of gifts, the performance of plays, accompanied by processions and merrymaking, marked the death of winter and heralded the New Year.

It is likely that those beliefs from the East spread into central Europe to influence the festivals already observed there, most of which marked seasonal changes and the growing and harvesting of crops. In the depths of winter, for example, people lit bonfires in the hope of reviving the dying Sun and bringing warmth to the ground. Also, they decorated their homes with evergreens – holly and firs – to show dormant seeds and lifeless plants that all was not dead. When the Sun eventually shone again, they rejoiced in their success and no doubt vowed to repeat the magic for ever after.

Further north, along the Baltic and in Scandinavia, a winter festival known as the Yule honoured the gods Odin and Thor. Great logs blazed, minstrels sang, famous legends were recounted, and villagers drank lustily from horns of mead.

In the Roman Empire, a week-long orgy of feasting and wild revelry, the Saturnalia, was held in mid-December, when the Sun was approaching its lowest. The winter solstice – the turning point of the year, when the length of the day began to increase – was marked by a sacred day called Dies Natalis Invicti Solis (Birthday of the Unconquered Sun). During the Saturnalia, the Romans decked their houses with laurels and greenery; friends exchanged presents; the army rested; criminals were spared from execution; and slaves were as good as their masters, free to do and say what they liked. It was a season of general rejoicing, with good will to all men.

The Persians, too, burned fires at the winter solstice. Their feast revered Mithras, the god of light and guardian against evil. Soldiers and traders spread the worship of Mithras to Europe, where for a time the belief rivalled Christianity.

No precise date is known for the birth

*The **birth of Christ**, as painted in the fifteenth century by an unknown Spanish artist. For nearly 2000 years argument has persisted about whether revelry and feasting should celebrate the Nativity. Cromwell's ban on festivities brought riots to many English cities*

of Christ, but it is certain that He was born late in the reign of Herod the Great, king of Judaea until his death in what we now call 4 BC. For centuries after His death, several different dates, from April to December, were proposed for the celebration of Christmas. January 6, believed to mark Christ's baptism, was widely observed as Christmas Day, and still is in some countries by Orthodox Christians.

By the middle of the fourth century, December 25 had become the accepted date of Christmas Day in the Western Roman Empire, confirming a date that Roman Christians had already marked for some two centuries as a solemn feast. In the late fourth century, Church leaders in Rome proclaimed that the Feast of Epiphany, a twelve-day period from December 25 to January 6, should be both a festive and sacred occasion.

In time, Christians almost everywhere accepted December 25 as Christmas Day, a date coinciding roughly with celebrations for the winter solstice, Yule and Saturnalia. Also, a Jewish feast – the

dedication of the Temple, or Hanukah – was held in mid-December.

Many attempts were made to separate the overindulgence and merrymaking of pagan feasts from Christian observance of the Nativity. The Greek writer Origen, a devout Christian, declared in about the year 200 that it was sinful to celebrate Christ's birthday 'as though he were a King Pharaoh'. But throughout the Middle Ages, among the noblemen and their attendants, the revelry continued, with feasting at its heart. In Tudor England, the Christmas banquet, which included many customs carried over from heathen times, usually lasted from midday until late in the evening.

When Christians in Europe broke away from the Catholic Church during the Reformation, many old customs were suppressed. All forms of colourful display, such as processions, decorations and plays, were banned. Little remained of Christmas as it had once been.

In England after the Civil War, Oliver Cromwell and the Puritans outlawed

Christmas celebrations as heathen, and town criers warned citizens not to celebrate in any way. It was work as usual. Shops and markets stayed open. Parliament itself sat on Christmas Day to set an example to the nation. Christmas Day was designated a fast day. Soldiers even searched the kitchens and ovens of London homes and carried off any meat they found being cooked for the traditional feast. The edict brought rioting in many cities, but the spirit of Christmas was soon duly extinguished.

The same situation had prevailed in the New World since 1621, when a law passed by Governor Bradford of the Plymouth Colony prohibited Christmas observance. Another law, in 1659, pronounced: 'Whosoever shall be found observing any such days as Christmas … either by forbearing of labour, feasting or any other way … shall pay five shillings as a fine to the country.'

When the English monarchy was restored under Charles II in 1660, old customs returned, but for many years the Puritan influence lived on. It was not until the late Victorian period that the feasting and merrymaking of earlier times regained their place in the English Christmas. Worldwide, the Church in general took a pragmatic stance. Unable to ban the pagan excesses that had become part of the celebration, it endeavoured to rid them of their undesirable features, and welcomed the refurbished rites into Christmas rejoicing as if they were sacred.

The old-time Christmas customs survived, and new ones were added. Christmas became, as we know it today, a magical mixture of Christian devotion and pagan pleasures, a festival that survives through popular demand.

Why do we have Christmas trees?

Legend has it that in ages past a child seeking shelter on a bitter winter's night knocked at a forest hut. A woodcutter and his wife took in the child and fed him. Overnight, the boy turned into an angel – the Christ child – dressed in gold. As a reward for the couple's kindness, the child broke a twig from a fir tree, and told them to plant it, promising that each Christmas it would bear fruit. And so it did, a crop of golden apples and silver nuts, the first Christmas tree. Of all its symbols, nothing expresses the magic of Christmas more fully than a fir tree ablaze with light, shimmering with frost, real or artificial, and crowned with a star. But the custom has been popular worldwide

*A **touch of joy** is captured in many lands by a well-decorated Christmas tree. The custom spread worldwide from Germany, promoted last century by British royalty*

for quite a short time. Originating in Germany, the Christmas tree spread overseas during the nineteenth century. The custom's growth in popularity was sometimes boosted by royalty. In Britain, for example, Prince Albert, Queen Victoria's husband, had a tree sent from his native Germany in 1841 for the family celebration at Windsor Castle. Before long, the now-familiar sight of giant Christmas trees in public places and more modest ones in shops and homes was widespread.

Why do we honour Santa Claus?

The jovial figure of Santa Claus, or Father Christmas, embodies a mass of legends going back some 1600 years to a certain Nicholas, bishop of the Roman-ruled city of Myra in Asia Minor. In a general persecution of Christians, Emperor Diocletian imprisoned him. Later, Constantine the Great set him free. He died in about the year 326, and was renowned for his piety and gentleness, his gifts to the poor and

for his love of children; in 1087 his remains were taken to the Church of San Nicola in Bari, Italy.

For the next 500 years, St Nicholas was revered by adults and children throughout Europe. Russia and Greece adopted him as their patron saint. Many hundreds of churches in numerous countries were named after him – over 400 in England alone. Sailors and travellers, particularly, prayed to him, because he was said to help them endure storms at sea and to save lives. Dutch vessels often had his statue as a figurehead, and Russian and Greek ships habitually carried his image in the forecastle to ward off danger.

With Dutch seamen went stories of St Nicholas's benevolence and generosity. On December 6, St Nicholas Day, worthy Dutch children received presents, brought, it was said, by a bearded saint astride a white horse, who also carried birch rods to beat the mischief-makers.

How did St Nicholas become Santa Claus? The name comes originally from the Latin, Sanctus Nicolaus, which the Dutch called Sinterklaas. But why did this saintly figure of staid demeanour become the jolly, red-robed, ho-ho-ho character of current tradition? The most likely explanation again rests partly with the Dutch – but in the New World. It is said that Dutch settlers going to New Amsterdam, now New York City, sailed on a ship that carried an image of a pipe-smoking St Nicholas, wearing breeches and wide-brimmed hat. Later, Dutch parades in New York at Christmas time always featured St Nicholas, his character changing inevitably at the whim of his creators.

In 1809, the American writer and publisher, Washington Irving, depicted a chuckling Santa riding through the sky in a wagon, smoking a pipe. Building on this image, Clement Clarke Moore, the son of the bishop of New York, published in 1823 a wildly popular poem, ''Twas the

***Ho-ho-ho, it's Santa** bringing a call for children to rejoice, whether in Australia's sunbaked outback or amid the ice and snow of a European winter*

Night Before Christmas'. The poem depicted a chubby St Nick riding with his eight flying reindeer, squeezing down chimneys and filling up children's stockings with toys. Finally, in 1863, *Harper's Illustrated Weekly* published a cartoon in which Santa appeared as we know him today, complete with long white beard and fur-trimmed coat.

Why is turkey traditional Christmas fare?

Turkeys were unknown in Europe until the Spanish introduced them from the New World. When Hernán Cortés conquered Mexico in 1521, the invaders found that the local population had already domesticated the bird that we know as the turkey. Ten years later, the first turkey farms were thriving in Europe. In many countries, a common sight was of farmers and their families walking their fattened turkey flocks to the nearest market town. In England, the introduced bird was often confused with a guinea fowl, which was known at the time as a turkey, because it was believed that the bird came from Turkey. Gradually, the newcomer from the New World took over the guinea fowl's other name.

The popularity of turkey at Christmas time is undoubtedly due to the bird's superior bulk when compared with its rivals in the poultry world. The turkey fattens more easily and economically than a goose, for example, which eats more

food for meat produced than any other bird. When Christmas dinner was indisputably the feast of the year – as it was until recent times – the turkey, weighing 10 kg (22 lb) or more, was unmatched as a provider of hot roast meat on one day and cold meat on days to follow.

And why do Americans eat turkey at Thanksgiving? When the Pilgrim Fathers celebrated their first Thanksgiving Day, in 1621, Indians brought them wild turkeys. The turkeys eaten in America today are not descendants of local birds, however, but of domesticated Mexican turkeys. English settlers took their offspring back to the American colonies.

Why do we sing Christmas carols?

The first Christmas songs, written in Latin and solemn in tone, were probably composed in the fourth century, when the Roman Church made the festival a holiday. But carols date back to pagan times. The Greeks used them in plays, and Romans sang them during the Saturnalia.

Barbarians from northern Europe brought the Roman Empire to an end, but Christianity survived and spread. So did the custom of ring dancing, in which lively songs accompanied the dance movements. The Roman legions had introduced these dances to many parts of Europe and Asia Minor during their occupation. The word 'carol' came to mean both the ring dance and the song, and later, just the song itself.

For centuries, the Church banned carols because of their heathen associations. A remarkable service conducted in the thirteenth century by St Francis of Assisi is said to have introduced carols into Christmas rejoicing. As a way of taking the Christmas message to all the people, St Francis borrowed some animals from

A feast of turkey came to us from Mexico. The Pilgrim Fathers had one on the first Thanksgiving Day, depicted by artist Jennie Brownscombe

Happy tidings in the form of Christmas carols were once banned as heathen. In Victorian times, as shown in this book illustration, they enabled poor children to raise money

friendly farmers, decorated a cave near Grecchio, northeast of Rome, to resemble a stable, and placed a statue of the infant Jesus in a manger filled with hay. On Christmas Eve, St Francis held a midnight mass at the cave, for which friars wrote and sang joyful songs in commemoration of the song the angels sang when they appeared to the shepherds at Bethlehem. This is believed to be the first re-creation of the Nativity scene, ubiquitous in our modern Christmas, and the first recital of carols with a sacred theme.

Medieval mystery plays, which were usually dramatised Bible stories plus pageantry and song, produced new carols, and strolling bards added more. The carol flourished until the Protestant Reformation of the sixteenth century, when Puritanism gave Christmas in many parts of Europe an ascetic tone.

After the English Civil War, Christmas carols almost vanished. Only a few early English carols, such as 'The First Nowell', still survive. 'The Boar's Head Carol', centuries old, is another rarity, but is still sung each Christmas at Queen's College, Oxford, as the roast head of a boar is carried into the hall.

Despite its demise, the carol re-emerged in various forms in England, France and Germany just over a century ago, possibly because of the growing commercialism of Christmas. Most of the carols we sing today date from Victorian times, but imaginative choirmasters and musicians are helping to preserve ancient melodies, while new carols by modern composers, spread across the world by radio and television, are a welcome addition to our heritage of the old.

Greetings by mail began in Britain. J. C. Horsley's card of 1843, one of the first, was condemned for encouraging drinking

Why is a boar's head a Christmas symbol?

Glance in the butcher's window at Christmas and you may well see as its centrepiece a pig's head with an apple or orange in its mouth and perhaps sprigs of rosemary in its ears. The custom dates back to ancient times, when a wild boar was sacrificed to Frey, the Norse god of fertility. The fruit represented the Sun and rosemary the return of summer.

In England, the tradition is linked also with legend. A wild boar is said to have attacked a student of Queen's College, Oxford, on Christmas Day. With no time to draw his sword, the student choked the boar by stuffing a copy of Aristotle's works down its throat – certain to kill anything, say derisive scholars. He severed the head to retrieve the book, and bore the trophy in triumph to the college. Ever since, the college has served roast boar's head as a Christmas feast.

Fertility and sunshine are represented in a dish of roast boar's head. In ancient times, a wild boar was sacrificed to the Norse god, Frey. The pig's mouth often holds an apple, its ears some sprigs of rosemary

Why do we send Christmas cards?

The Penny Post, introduced in Britain by Rowland Hill in 1837, undoubtedly spurred a custom that has now become universal. Before that event, only the wealthy could afford the cost of sending any form of greeting by mail. Christmas cards were unknown until the 1840s. English artist William Edgley produced what may have been the first in 1842 or 1848 – the date is disputed. His card is now in London's Victoria and Albert Museum.

In 1843, J. C. Horsley, an artist commissioned by Sir Henry Cole, designed a lithograph bearing the greeting, 'A Merry Christmas and a Happy New Year to you'. Three scenes illustrated the spirit of Christmas. One showed a family raising a toast in greeting, and others 'feeding the hungry' and 'clothing the naked'. A thousand cards sold for a shilling each – and Christmas cards in all their many forms were launched upon the world.

Why do so many of them feature robin redbreast? The robin was regarded in many countries as sacred, and an ancient British rhyme goes: 'Little Cock Robin and Little Jenny Wren are God's almighty cock and hen.' Also, the robin's fearless nature brings it close to houses to feed in the hungry winter months, making it a conspicuous Christmas companion.

Why do we observe Boxing Day?

Boxing Day, December 26, is also the Feast of St Stephen, the first Christian martyr, and inevitably his day became linked with Christmas. There are many explanations for the origin of the name Boxing Day.

In medieval times, it was the day on which priests emptied church alms-boxes of money given by parishioners at Christmas, and distributed it to the poor. In prosperous homes, servants opened boxes that held tips saved during the year. In workshops, apprentices kept their Christmas tips in special boxes, and delayed opening them until all hope of further donations had gone.

Boxing Day was, and in some places still is, the time for giving a tip – a 'Christmas box' – to reward a faithful tradesman.

Why do we eat plum pudding and mince pies?

Plum pudding became a Christmas dish in England in the late seventeenth century, when the festival returned after its prohibition by Oliver Cromwell. The pudding replaced plum porridge, a once-popular, semi-liquid dish that was served with the first course and eaten with a spoon. This dish often contained prunes – dried plums – and thus came to be known as plum pudding. Prunes were later replaced largely by raisins.

In an ages-old tradition, many people put coins and lucky charms – a ring and a thimble – into the pudding. Finding the coin is said to bring good fortune in the coming year; the ring heralds a wedding and the thimble a happy (but unmarried) life. In many homes, when the pudding is mixed, family members are invited to stir and wish. The practice is believed to come from witchcraft, with the witch stirring a cauldron while casting a spell.

The Christmas mince pies eaten today bear little resemblance to those first eaten in England. When soldiers returned from crusading wars in the Holy Land, they brought back many spices, particularly cinnamon, cloves, ginger and nutmeg. These, introduced into English cooking, were used in meat dishes served throughout the year. At Christmas time, the pie was fashioned to resemble a manger, and talented pastrycooks sometimes also sculpted a figure of Jesus. Over the centuries, the ingredients changed. Fruit peel and raisins replaced meat, and the pies were made circular. Good luck in the coming year was ensured by eating a pie on each of the twelve days of Christmas.

Why is holly used in Christmas decorations?

Holly, found in most countries of the world in one or more of its many varieties, was used in ancient times to decorate homes in winter. Often it symbolised immortality, and gave comfort to primitive people by showing that, though all around them the world seemed dead, here were clear signs of life.

Later, as Christian and pagan customs became inextricably mixed, holly leaves were seen by many to represent Christ's crown of thorns and the red berries His blood. These are symbols of Easter not Christmas, but it seems likely that, because the berries would normally be past their best at Eastertide in Europe, their use in celebrating the Nativity was accepted. One legend holds that as shepherds visited the infant child in the manger a lamb was pricked by holly and its blood froze as red berries.

Holly figured also in ancient Yule festivities, features of which, such as the burning of a Yule log, still survive today in some parts of Europe. In Yuletide songs and customs, holly was sometimes understood to represent the male and ivy the female; if holly arrived first in a house, then the males would dominate throughout the ensuing year.

In medieval England, holly was believed to have curative powers, particularly in treating rheumatism and fevers. A holly bush, it was said, would protect travellers lost in a storm. A sprig of holly taken into the house would guard it against evil spirits. If the holly came from church decorations, happiness would bless the house throughout the year.

Why do we give Christmas presents?

The Romans gave gifts at their Saturnalia. St Nicholas, the benevolent forerunner of our Santa Claus, is said to have handed presents to well-behaved children. And the Three Wise Men, the Magi, carried gifts of gold, frankincense and myrrh to the infant Jesus.

In every country where Christmas is celebrated, the giving of presents is an inseparable part of the feast – though not always at the same time or on the same

*A **harvest of holly** goes homeward in a ritual dating back to earliest times. Once a pagan symbol of life, holly was later associated with Christ's crown of thorns and the berries with His blood*

day. In many countries where St Nicholas Day (December 6) is celebrated, children receive presents then and on Christmas Day. In others, such as Italy, gifts are given at Epiphany (January 6), the day of Christ's baptism and when the Magi arrived in Bethlehem. Like so many other seasonal traditions, it is difficult to say whether that of Christmas gifts has pagan or Christian origins.

Why do we kiss beneath the mistletoe?

Hanging up mistletoe at Christmas, like so many of today's festive customs, dates back far beyond the birth of Christ. Throughout Europe, ancient peoples invested this parasitic shrub with magical properties. The Druids, in particular, worshipped mistletoe as a universal healer and fertility symbol.

In England during the Middle Ages, mistletoe was believed to guard against witchcraft and was said to bring good luck. A piece of mistletoe hanging over the doorway was a sign of welcome to visitors. To kiss beneath it was a pledge of enduring friendship.

One custom demands that every male who kisses beneath the mistletoe should pluck a berry; when all the berries have gone, the kissing must cease. Some people still hold to the old tradition of burning mistletoe on Twelfth Night, designed to ensure that single girls who had kissed under it would indeed get married.

It is unusual to see mistletoe decorating a church or church hall, though many

Christians are not sure why. The reason again goes back through the ages: because of the powerful pagan cult surrounding the Druids, their holy plant was excluded from all forms of Christian worship. Some Christian traditions hold, however, that mistletoe was once a tree and that Christ's cross was made from its wood. This, they say, gives mistletoe its curative properties.

Why do we light candles at Christmas?

Old customs die and, like smouldering embers, spring suddenly to life again. From the earliest times, light has signified comfort and joy, and darkness the fear of the unknown. Ancient peoples, aware of the changing seasons, lit fires to encourage the return of spring. Romans, during their Saturnalia, decked their homes with lighted candles and greenery. Long before the birth of Christ, Jews marked their winning of religious freedom by holding an eight-day Festival of Lights. Primitive peoples took blazing brands into their fields in the hope that the hot ashes would inspire growth. And when Hallowe'en fires, deemed to comfort souls in purgatory, were extinguished in many countries by the Reformation, new bonfire parties were quick to replace them.

In early Christian times, Pope Gelasius proclaimed Candlemas, February 2, as the day for blessing candles in church; it is also the feast of thanksgiving for the Purification of the Virgin Mary, and commemorates Jesus's Presentation in the Temple, when Simeon heralded him as 'a light to lighten the Gentiles'.

From these origins came the medieval custom of burning a mammoth Christmas

candle whose light, it was hoped, would glow until Twelfth Night. When we put candles or fairy lights on a Christmas tree today, we are following traditions of ancient Rome, or those passed on from Martin Luther, whose tree glowed with lighted tapers.

Wherever Christmas is celebrated, candles glow – to light up the tree, add a feeling of warmth to outdoor carol singing or, as in homes in Ireland, to shine into the cold darkness and beckon wanderers to food and shelter.

Comfort and joy *amid winter's darkness come from lighting Christmas candles. The custom first began in ancient Rome*

Why do we wear party hats?

When you put on a colourful party hat or wear one from a cracker at the Christmas table, you are doing as the Romans did at their annual Saturnalia. Pointed hats, the badge of freed men, were donned by slaves, allowed during the festival to behave like their masters. Colourful hats, bizarrely shaped and accompanied sometimes by a mask, were worn by Roman revellers in street processions.

THE MAN WHO CHANGED CHRISTMAS

By the early nineteenth century, Christmas was no longer a festive event in the lives of many people. In Britain, it had still not recovered from its banning by the Puritans, an edict long since revoked but still lingering in its sombre effects. Christmas was a one-day holiday, generally regarded as a time for quiet pursuits. In many American homes, too, it was a solemn feast, without much sign of its current jollity and show of benevolence.

So why do we celebrate with such gusto today? It may be a cynical view, but it is often said that Charles Dickens invented our modern Christmas. That is an exaggeration, but it is true that the novelist gave new life to a festival that seemed to be fading away.

In 1843, Dickens wrote *A Christmas Carol*, the first of a series of annual Christmas books that were aimed, he said, 'to awaken loving and forebearing thoughts'. In his stories, Dickens combined a rousing celebration of the old merrymaking Christmas with the idea of Christmas as an occasion that united families in a spirit of charity and love. He depicted Christ-

Thousands cheered *Charles Dickens when he gave readings of his Christmas stories. He helped to revive the season's true joy*

mas as being warm and cosy for some and miserably cold and hungry for others. Constantly troubled by the poverty, injustice and divisions in society, he saw his Christmas stories as a means of bringing the depressed working classes out of the cold and into the warm embrace of the nation.

His public readings, which he first gave in 1853, attracted enthusiastic audiences. In Birmingham, 2000 working people, admitted at a reduced price at his request, cheered a three-hour reading of *A Christmas Carol*, interpreting it as the work of a man who understood and spoke out for them. When Queen Victoria, too, asked to hear Dickens read the story of Scrooge and Tiny Tim, it seemed that the nation was truly united in a spirit of goodwill.

Internationally, Dickens's stories were just as successful. *A Christmas Carol* is said to have had such an influence on one American factory owner that he added a day to his workers' holidays.

Dickens is said to have fashioned not only the style of our modern Christmas but the myth – in Britain, if not elsewhere – that the typical Christmas is white. Climatologists say that in Dickens's childhood there were eight white Christmases in a row, which undoubtedly influenced the way that he, followed by millions of Christmas cards, portrayed the British Christmas. But only two or three times this century has snow fallen 'deep and crisp and even' over most of Britain on Christmas Day.

Holy festivals and pagan deeds

Why do we greet the New Year with noise?

It's a custom that has spread from Europe to many parts of the world. The clock ticks away the seconds of the dying year and suddenly, on the last stroke of midnight, the waiting crowds let out a cacophony of sound. Voices shout, bells ring, car horns and factory hooters blast away, all in a concerted bid to make as much noise as possible.

'Ring out the old, ring in the new' is a comparatively recent explanation of a superstition that has figured in New Year celebrations since pagan times. For centuries, in the Scottish Highlands, villagers carrying sticks and dried cowhides surrounded one another's houses each New Year's Eve. As midnight came, they thrashed the walls with clubs and beat their sticks against the cowhides, chanting and shouting as loudly as they could. It was a rite designed to drive out the fairies, demons and spirits of the old year.

The same ritual – a superstitious clearing of the air to give the New Year a fair chance to bring good fortune – has been handed on, though possibly few revellers today understand why they are called upon to make such a racket at midnight.

Why is 'first-footing' a New Year custom?

Ancient beliefs assert that what happens in the first few moments of the year decides everything for the next twelve months. That is why, in a superstition that probably started with the Scots, whoever

All hands linked in a symbolic ring, a family dances to greet the year 1873. Tradition rules that actions in those first minutes after midnight set the year's pattern

is the first to cross a threshold on New Year's Day is believed to bring the household much or little luck.

The reasons why the ideal first-footer should be tall and dark are lost in time, but the tradition breaks a general rule. Almost without exception, black objects – even black cats, which are deemed by some to be unlucky – carry evil omens. In many homes, a fair first-footer would be most unwelcome. A widower promises bad luck, possibly tragedy, and a redhead imminent disaster. Indeed, in years gone by, some superstitious families considered a good first-footer to be so essential that they hired one to enter the house as the New Year arrived, rather than risk many months of misfortune.

Usually, first-footers carry a lump of coal, a gift to ensure that the home will always be warm and friendly. At one time, they also gave the head of the family a coin and a piece of bread, symbolising wealth and ample food. For good luck in the year ahead, something must come into a house before anything is taken out.

First-footing is one of many traditions linked with those opening moments of the year. Another, still observed in some parts of Europe and America, is to open a Bible at random and, without looking, point to a spot on the page. The passage is believed to indicate in some way what the year holds in store. Some families invite the first-footer to perform the custom, then reward him with the last drink from a bottle, another New Year good-luck custom – and a generous one if it's the only bottle in the house.

Good luck or bad? A last-century scene in Edinburgh shows first-footers bent on taking a year's good fortune to their friends

Why do we give Valentines?

No festival in the calendar has become more commercialised than February 14, St Valentine's Day, and many customs associated with it have disappeared. For example, it was once almost obligatory for lovers to fashion their own Valentine cards and to compose their own greetings. And the senders kept their anonymity. Today, Valentine cards are sold by the million, and in many countries sweethearts proclaim their passion in newspaper advertisements.

Historians argue about who really was St Valentine. Some say that he was a young priest, jailed by the Romans on February 14, AD 269, for helping Christians. In prison, he restored the sight of the jailer's daughter, who fell in love with him before he was killed. Another legend is that a young priest defied an edict of the Emperor Claudius by conducting weddings for several soldiers. Marriage, the Emperor had decreed, ruined the spirit of fighting men and for them was banned. The priest was executed, and became the patron saint of lovers. Other accounts hold that a handsome Roman, awaiting execution, fell in love with his jailer's blind daughter. Before he died, he sent her a love letter, signed, 'From your Valentine' – his name. Seven Christian saints and martyrs named Valentine have February 14 as their day.

Most classical scholars trace St Valentine's Day back to the early Roman festival of Lupercalia, a lovers' feast to welcome the return of spring. At this feast began the custom of holding a ballot, a lottery of love, into which went the names of unmarried young women, to be drawn in turn by an equal number of eligible young men. For the following year, the pairs took part in courtship.

As with many other pagan rites, the Church tried either to abolish them or to give them Christian significance. One move, in the lovers' ballot, was to substitute the names of saints for those of young women. Those taking part in the ballot were expected, on drawing a saint's name, to follow his example during the ensuing year.

The Valentine tradition survived in Britain, despite the chaos that followed the withdrawal of the Roman legions. Until a century ago, it was still traditional to draw lots on St Valentine's Eve. Into one bag, for the men, went slips of paper bearing the names of young ladies; into another went the names of young men. If any person took out the same name three times, it was a strong omen of the couple's marriage.

It was customary, too, for a young man who had good luck in the draw to back up his fortune with an appropriate gift. A pair of gloves expressed his intention

Home-made, *as most Valentines usually were, this one is typical of the elaborate greetings fashionable early last century*

to ask for the lady's hand. Along with ballots came heart-shaped greetings and, later, elaborate home-made Valentine cards. A long-running belief, still commonly held in this century, was that the

first unmarried person of the opposite sex seen on February 14 was the beholder's Valentine for the year and possible future partner. To avoid the fate of encountering an unwanted partner, sweethearts sometimes contrived ways of meeting each other blindfold.

February 14 is said by some to be the day on which birds choose their mates. In Britain and America a superstition holds that the first bird seen by a girl on that day will decide what kind of man she will marry. A goldfinch or yellow bird indicates wealth; a blackbird symbolises a clergyman; a sparrow that she will find lasting love in a country cottage.

Why do we eat pancakes on Shrove Tuesday?

Shrove Tuesday, the last day before the austerity of Lent, was once in some countries a day for schoolboy pranks. Teachers were stopped from entering schools. If they did get in, they were expected to take part in the day's fun and games,

Frypans in hand *and pancakes ready for tossing, women compete in a Shrove Tuesday race held every year at Olney in England*

which often included cock-fighting. The day, known sometimes as Goody Tuesday, was also one for great feasting, the last chance before the forty-day period of Lenten abstinence. Pancakes made a convenient way of using stores of fat, particularly beef and mutton dripping, which were forbidden on Ash Wednesday and after. Often, pancakes were cooked at monastery gates and distributed to the poor. In some parts of Britain, the feast was always signalled by the ringing of a bell, which became known locally as the Pancake Bell.

The Pancake Bell also summoned families to church for their 'shriving' or confession. Some households gave their pancakes rich fillings in preparation for hours of waiting in church. Ringers of the Pancake Bell were traditionally entitled to a gift of pancakes, provided these were eaten before eight in the evening, when a curfew came down on all merriment and, in medieval times, all fires and lights were put out.

Why is April the First a day for fools?

The origins of April Fools' Day are uncertain, but without doubt they are linked to a time when the year was deemed to begin in late March or early April. In many cultures, the New Year is a time for pranks and merriment.

Some historians find traces of our April Fool tradition in Greek and Roman mythology. Demeter, searching for her daughter Persephone, who had been carried off by Pluto, heard the girl's screams echoing through a valley. She followed the screams, on what may be interpreted as a fool's quest, but never found more than their echo. Anthropologists compare our custom to that of India's Huli Festival, held on March 31, in which it is traditional to trick people by sending them on useless quests.

Even though such customs go back to ancient times, our April Fools' Day is probably of more recent origin. In 1564, the French decided that January 1, not March 25, should start the year. Until that time, it had been customary to give New-Year gifts in late March, which often coincided with Easter's Holy Week. When the calendar changed, Church and government officials decided that April 1 should replace the old festival. A tradition grew of playing pranks on this day. One explanation for this is that calendar changes annoyed French citizens, who decided to take it out on officials by sending them on false errands. Another is that April 1 became a day for visiting friends and possibly for taking small gifts, all with the intent of creating confusion about what was really New Year's Day.

Whatever its origins, the tradition of playing pranks on April 1 has spread to many countries and beyond the realm of children. Today, many newspapers and radio and TV stations join in the fun by staging elaborate and often highly amusing hoaxes.

Playing pranks on April the First is not confined to children. Today, newspapers and TV stations often join in the fun with elaborate hoaxes to fool the public

Why do we play games at Hallowe'en?

Hallowe'en, the last day of October, was once a pagan feast of the dead, a time when the Druids honoured Saman, the lord of death. On that one day of the year, the dead were said to come to life. Ghosts and goblins were everywhere, and witches freely spread their fearful predictions. Who on such a night would dare to go to bed?

Once a time to strike terror into the bravest hearts, Hallowe'en has gradually become a festival of fun, particularly for the young. Games of 'trick or treat', bonfire parties, gruesome disguises, spooky lanterns, all have links with ancient times.

As with those of so many feasts, Hallowe'en customs today are drawn from many sources. Clearly, many of them come directly from the All Souls' Feast of the Druids, in which good and bad souls of the dead wandered in search of some new abode. Many practices go back farther. The lighting of bonfires, for example, may come from the worship of Baal, the Syrian Sun god, or from other end-of-summer feasts in which fire symbolised the Sun. Another link may be with the Roman festival to Pomona, the goddess of fruits, which was held on November 1 to store fruits and nuts for winter.

When the Romans occupied Britain, their customs became mixed with those surviving from the Druids and others. To Hallowe'en fears of ghosts and goblins were added rituals of eating fruit and roasting nuts on all-night bonfires. Villagers sat or slept there until dawn, too scared to return to their spirit-infested homes. A range of Hallowe'en superstitions involving apples and nuts grew up. If a girl ate an apple before a mirror on that night, it was said she would see the face of her future husband. Another belief was in the power of apples to drive away evil spirits. Walnuts or chestnuts thrown into a fire could give clues to the future. And so, it was believed, could cabbages. Blindfolded girls and boys would tear them out by the roots. A well-grown cabbage was an omen

Spooky lanterns and pointed hats are drawn from witchcraft. Hallowe'en celebrates a time when evil spirits wandered at large

of a healthy partner. In time, fun replaced fear. Lively children, seeking the delight of scaring adults out of their wits, made a mockery of superstition. They disguised themselves as ghosts, goblins and witches – and demonstrated that Hallowe'en spooks never strike back.

Why isn't Easter a fixed date?

The point is often made that, if we can establish December 25 as the day for celebrating Christ's birth, why can't we set a date for Easter, the commemoration of His Resurrection? In some years, the clamour to have a fixed date becomes louder, because Easter is either very early or very late. In fact, in Western countries the feast can occur at any weekend between March 22 and April 25.

Originally, Easter had nothing to do with the Christian calendar. Our word for the festival comes from Eastre or Ostâra, the goddess of spring among Germanic tribes of northern Europe. Pagan tribes rejoiced at the coming of spring, which is why many of our Easter customs, such as the giving of eggs, have pagan not Christian origins.

Many Europeans take their word for Easter from the Hebrew word *Pesach*, which means Passover. The French, for example, call the festival *Pâques* and the Italians *Pasqua*. Jews celebrate the Passover, an eight-day festival, to commemorate their flight from slavery in Egypt. Easter is associated with the Jewish Passover, because Christ was arrested, tried and crucified at that time. The Jewish calendar is based on lunar (not solar) months, and the Passover always begins on the day of the first full Moon after March 21, the northern spring equinox.

Easter's date fluctuates, because it is linked with the Passover. For centuries, the date has caused argument and doubt even among leaders of various churches. Early Christians celebrated Easter during the Passover. Later, clerics wanted to give Easter's holy days special significance, and tried to separate them from the Jewish festival. In AD 325, the Council of Nicaea ruled that Easter, the day marking Christ's Resurrection, would always be a Sunday but *after* the start of the Passover.

Because some churches use different calendars, Easter's date may vary from country to country by a matter of weeks. According to the Gregorian calendar, which most of us follow, Easter Day is the first Sunday after the first full Moon on or after March 21. If there is a full Moon on Sunday, March 21, Easter is the following Sunday.

However, the Eastern Orthodox Churches, strongest in eastern Europe and the eastern Mediterranean, use the Julian calendar to decide when Easter falls. (For fixed feasts, such as Christmas, they follow the Gregorian calendar.) The Orthodox Easter can occur up to five weeks after the Western.

Church leaders have tried many times to solve the problems caused by this movable feast. An obvious solution would be to fix the date, but Easter could then fall in the middle of the week. In 1963, the Roman Catholic Church recommended a set date, but none of the other denominations agreed with the suggestion.

Another, more sweeping, proposal is for the world to have a new calendar by which, year in and year out, any date would fall on the same day of the week. By this system, Easter would always be Sunday, April 8, about midway between its current extremes. To many people, that sounds like a perfect compromise, but to the world's decision-makers the idea has all the appeal of a stale hot cross bun.

Stained glass in an English church depicts the Resurrection of Christ. The window – in All Hallows at Allerton, Liverpool – was designed by Sir Edward Burne-Jones

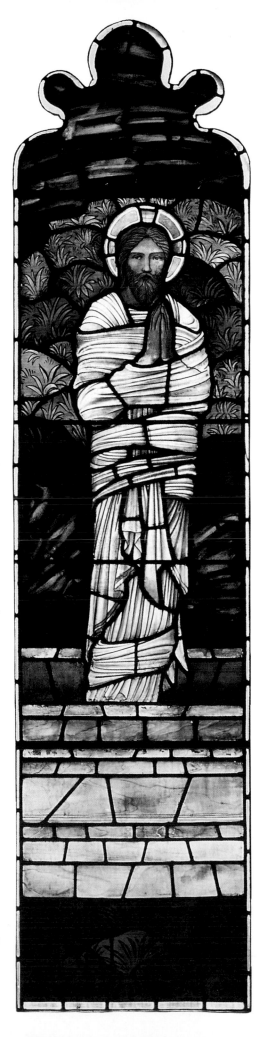

Why do we give eggs at Easter?

Just as pagan customs figure in our Christmas festival, so too they have become associated inextricably with Easter. Long before the beginnings of Christianity, Egyptians and Romans gave gifts of eggs as symbols of life. Easter was originally a pagan festival to celebrate the coming of spring, which marked the rebirth of life in plants, a time when many birds mated and produced young. The hen's egg, from which new life could spring, was a potent sign of regeneration. Often its shell was decorated with colours representing certain flowers and aimed at encouraging their regrowth.

Early Christians continued the custom of giving eggs, and gradually the practice was linked with Easter. The egg became an appropriate emblem of Christ's Resurrection, and shell decorations were adapted to have religious significance. Often, for example, eggs were painted or dyed red to represent the blood of Christ.

Almost everywhere in the Christian world, old rituals associated with spring continued alongside those of the holy feast. Anybody opening a boiled egg on Easter Day and finding two yolks was blessed, it was said, with a double stroke of luck. Ploughmen put an egg in the first

A greetings card from Germany, where the Easter bunny probably originated, has links with ancient and pagan beliefs

Why do we have an Easter bunny?

The rabbit, as a good-luck omen, is undoubtedly an impostor. It owes its magical significance to popular ignorance in confusing it with the hare, the true talisman of ancient times. Hares are born with their eyes open and are nocturnal. Because of this, the Egyptians made them sacred to the Moon. Later, ancient Britons gave the hare magical powers, using it in rites such as fortune-telling. Some villagers in Ireland refused to kill or eat hares, believing that they carried the souls of their grandparents.

Later, Germanic tribes who worshipped Eastre (or Ostâra), associated the fecund hare with her, their goddess of life and spring. Good children, they said, in an age-old form of bribery, would be rewarded with eggs laid by the Easter hare. Elsewhere in Europe, the more prevalent rabbit, which was often confused with the hare, took over as a good-luck symbol.

The rabbit's foot, frequently carried for luck, owes its existence to this confusion. In America, which had no hares, the rabbit was a convenient replacement for the hare as a talisman and as an Easter symbol. Confectioners boosted the rabbit's takeover by fashioning such popular Easter offerings as candy rabbits clutching hats filled with eggs.

In one country at least, the Easter bunny is under threat. Nobody in Australia disputes the rabbit's claims as a fertility symbol because, despite shotguns, poisons and myxomatosis, its

offspring by the million threaten constantly to ruin the nation's farmers. What is in doubt is whether this acknowledged pest should continue to woo children's affections. Moves are afoot to replace the bunny with a more deserving Easter symbol, such as the bilby. This long-eared bandicoot is an animal under threat – partly because the ubiquitous rabbit has invaded its territory in such force.

Decorated eggs are symbols of life and love. Some Christians believe that Mary dyed eggs to amuse the infant Jesus

ANCIENT FEAST OF THE DANCING SUN

Many good-luck beliefs associated with Easter are linked with pre-Christian rites of Sun worship. What is now Eastertide originally celebrated the coming of spring, when the Sun glowed with new warmth and brought fresh growth from trees and plants. The Church added to those rites, and gave the spring festival Christian significance.

Some 2500 years before Christ, Sun worship was the official religion of Egypt. In ancient Babylon, Assyria, Persia and Asia Minor, the Sun was a god. The Druids, also, worshipped the Sun. American Indians greet New Year's Day – like Easter a time of renewal – with Sun dances. A Gaelic custom is for a bride to walk three times round the church, following the Sun's course, before entering to meet her future spouse. People in many early cultures believed that the Sun's rays were the Sun god's hair. In winter, the hair was shorn; in the spring, at Easter, it grew again.

In some parts of the world, people still rise early on Easter Sunday to see the Sun rise, watching its reflection if possible in the waters of a tranquil pool or stream. According to an ancient superstition, this is the day when the Sun dances, and a lamb and flag appear in the centre of its disc. Again, even though this tradition undoubtedly goes back to earliest times, it is linked today with Christianity. Believers say that the angels who were at the Resurrection are dancing backwards and forwards before the Sun.

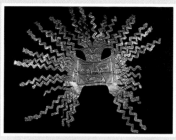

Sun worship *has dominated many cultures. For the Incas, the Sun god Inti (above right) was supreme, represented in temples by a golden disc with a human face. The Romans also gave their Sun god Apollo (above) a human face in this mosaic from Corinth, Greece. The Egyptian pharaoh Akhenaton replaced the worship of many gods with that of one god, Aten (right), a disc of the Sun. On the pharaoh's death, Egyptians reverted to the worship of several gods*

furrow they cut, believing it would boost their yields. In eastern Europe, farmers planted scarlet eggs to ward off storms.

In England, children received gifts of hard-boiled eggs, which they rolled down hillsides in an ancient game. In pagan times, the rolling egg was believed to imitate the Sun's movement as it returned after winter's darkness. The last egg to break supposedly brought good luck. Later, egg-rolling became part of the Christian festival, and was said to symbolise the stone rolling back from Christ's tomb. Egg-rolling is still popular in England and, until recently, was played every Easter on the lawns of the White House, home of the United States president.

Spanish conquistadors took chocolate to Europe after discovering it in Mexico in 1519. Before long, its use was widespread in cooking and for confectionery. In many countries, the chocolate egg – at first, small and solid – replaced the decorated hen's egg. Interestingly, many chocolate eggs today are embossed with sugar flowers, another link with our pagan past.

Why do we eat hot cross buns?

Traditionally, hot cross buns are eaten on Good Friday, but their origins, like many Eastertide and Christmas customs, go back to pagan times. Bread has long been

symbolic of good fortune. To pass it at the table is an expression of hope that the receiver might enjoy long life.

The baking of special bread, flavoured with spices, was part of pagan celebrations to greet the spring and worship the Sun. The ancient Greeks stamped their festival bread with a horned emblem in honour of Astarte, their goddess of love and fertility. The word 'bun' comes from *boun*, an ancient word for a sacred ox. Cakes stamped with horns became buns marked with a cross.

Because Christ and the disciples ate

Hot cross buns *are today inseparable from Easter, but cross-marked cakes were baked centuries before the birth of Christ*

unleavened bread at the Last Supper, bread came to have Christian significance. Buns of unleavened bread were baked at Eastertide, and many bakers marked them with a cross. Some historians say the cross represents the sign that Christ made over the bread before it was eaten; others claim that, because the buns are eaten only on Good Friday, the cross is in memory of His Crucifixion.

In time, the pagan custom of baking spiced bread joined the Christian practice of serving unleavened bread to recall the Last Supper. The pagan belief that bread brings good fortune explains why many people eat hot cross buns for luck, or say that the buns will cure stomach pains. Another superstition is that to hang a hot cross bun in a building will protect it from bad luck, particularly fire. Some inns kept a netful of buns suspended from the ceiling, adding a new bun each year.

A bun (or bread) made on Good Friday is said never to go mouldy, but baking is the only work blessed with luck on this day. Some gardeners believe that seeds sown on Good Friday will never grow. And laundrymen and women may refuse to wash clothes, fearing that when they hang them to dry they will become spotted with blood. Legend has it that a washerwoman waved a wet garment in Christ's face on his way to Calvary, supposedly exacting the rebuke: 'Cursed be everyone who hereafter shall wash on this day.'

Ancient rites for marital bliss

Marry in June *and life, it is said, will be one long honeymoon. The Romans consecrated the month to Juno, guardian of womanhood, who is depicted in this eighteenth-century painting*

Why is June a favourite month for weddings?

An old British saying is that one wedding makes many. And that is undoubtedly true in June, a month when all weddings are said to be guaranteed lifelong bliss. The belief dates from ancient times, a relic of Roman mythology.

The month is said to take its name from Juno, the goddess of youth, the faithful wife of Jupiter and guardian of womanhood from birth to death. The goddess ensured that a marriage in her month was blessed with happiness.

In many countries, particularly in the northern hemisphere, more marriages take place in June than in any other month. Mid-summer weather is one explanation; another is the survival of this ancient superstition, which seems to overpower beliefs about lucky days on which to wed. Saturday, the most popular day for a wedding, is also according to ancient beliefs regarded as the unluckiest.

If Saturday is the unluckiest day, a Saturday wedding in May must be instantly doomed. Fewer weddings are held in May, which is still regarded by many as the unluckiest month for marital vows. The goddess Maia, or Majesta, is said to have been the month's protector, but she was also the wife of Vulcan, god of fiery elements. A May marriage, some believed, would bring an unpleasantly fierce relationship. Others pointed to Maia's role as patroness of old people, asserting that June weddings were for young lovers and May for the elderly.

Are June weddings blessed with greater happiness? Divorce statistics don't support this. Proportionally, just as many June marriages break up as those made in any other month of the year.

Why do couples 'tie the knot'?

It's a fair bet that during the course of a couple's engagement somebody will remark that they are 'tying the knot'. Equally, it is unlikely that the person making the remark or those hearing it will have much idea of its origins.

The reference is to what was originally an ancient Babylonian custom, probably 3000 years old. At the marriage ceremony, friends of the couple would take a thread from the bride's clothes and one from the groom's and tie them together, a gesture symbolising the pair's eternal union.

The custom spread in various ways, and the tying or undoing of knots acquired many meanings. At some marriage services in medieval Britain, as the priest intoned, 'Whom God hath joined together let no man separate,' a needle-woman tied three knots in a piece of lace to ensure the couple's fidelity.

At ceremonies in the Scottish Hebrides, a groomsman took three threads, each of a different hue, tied three knots in each, and uttered what he believed were the most cruel disappointments of the nuptial bed. To avoid such calamity, the groom stood at the altar with his shoes untied. Elsewhere in Scotland, as late as the mid-nineteenth century, all knots on the bride's clothes – garters, shoelaces, petticoat strings – and on the groom's were untied immediately before the ceremony. Afterwards, the strings and laces were examined. If sorcerers wished to render the union childless, they had only to tie any cord with a special knot. The couple, it was believed, would then have no hope of raising a family.

At some Irish weddings a century ago, the tying of knots as the priest gave his benediction was thought to bring equally dire consequences. An ill-wisher repeated the benediction and, at the mention of each of the three sacred names of the Holy Trinity, tied a knot in a handkerchief or piece of string. Such an act, it was believed, would render the marriage childless for fifteen years, unless someone destroyed the curse by burning the handkerchief or knotted string.

Why do newlyweds take a 'honeymoon'?

When a bridegroom and his bride slip away – unnoticed, if they can – to start their honeymoon, they are repeating part of a barbarous practice of centuries past. In those days, a young man, usually aided by his best man, seized a wife by force, hiding her away and fighting off all attempts to recapture her. Later, having convinced his wife that he was the perfect husband, the pair would come out of hiding, and the young man would try to placate the bride's family by offering gifts.

Today, the wife is a willing partner in the getaway ploy, aiming merely to avoid the pranks that often upset the departure of newly wed couples. Many keep their destination secret, another link with past times of honeymoon hideaways.

The honeymoon custom started with the ancient Teutons, who lived in Jutland, northern Europe, until they migrated south in the second century BC. For a lunar month, or Moon, after their wedding, Teutonic newlyweds celebrated their union with mead, wine made from honey. This feast became known as a honeymoon, and later defined the custom of newlyweds taking a holiday immediately after marriage. Since then, the term has come into more general usage. Today it is often applied, somewhat cynically, to any period, particularly involving a new government, when harsh realities are temporarily suspended.

Why do we shower the couple with confetti?

It started, as did many of our festive customs, with the Romans, who tossed nuts, sweets or wheat over a home-going bride to ensure her fertility. In some parts of Germany today that custom continues, but guests give the bride nuts instead of throwing them. Elsewhere, well-wishers shower the bride with good-luck tokens of many kinds, particularly slippers, cakes and handfuls of rice.

Greek, Roman and Anglo-Saxon brides sometimes wore headbands of corn or wheat, another emblem of fertility, and in Saxon times brides walked down an aisle that was scattered with wheat and barley. From these customs came that of throwing wheat, not just at weddings but also at other ceremonies. A memoir of 1486 records that, on a visit to the west of England, King Henry VII was showered with wheat to bid him welcome.

Later, perhaps through Oriental influence or as an adaption of the Saxon ritual, rice – symbolic of fecundity – was substituted for wheat, and the custom was confined to weddings. In some parts of Europe during the Middle Ages, it was believed that male and female demons, lurking jealously, could replace the husband or wife in a marriage, and wreck the couple's happiness. Rice, thrown at the wedding as food for the spirits, would feed and placate them.

Towards the end of the nineteenth century, rice-throwing was common at weddings in many parts of Europe and America. Its introduction to Britain in the 1880s was condemned by many as 'a horrid modern fashion'. Ministers particularly deplored it, especially within their churches, even though that was where the English custom once started.

Soon, confetti – Italian for confectionery, such as tiny cakes and sweets – was thrown in addition to rice and in some regions replaced it. The cakes and sweets were often made in the shape of hearts, flowers and various good-luck symbols. Already, in parts of Europe and South America, multicoloured paper streamers were commonly thrown at carnival celebrations.

In time, paper imitations appeared of Italian confetti. Cheaper and more readily

Confetti or rice, *the custom once sought to ensure a bride's fertility and pacify demons*

available, it soon replaced the older symbols of rose petals, cakes and rice. Today, it is not unusual to see a bride and bridegroom showered with something cheaper still – the circular punchings from sheets of computer paper.

Just married *and the happy couple, adopting a style of their own, are assured of a fast getaway. Honeymoons started with the Teutons, who celebrated with mead*

Why does a bride have maids?

In ancient times, a bride and her maids might be almost indistinguishable. A bride chose bridesmaids who resembled her as closely as possible, and she and her maids would dress in similar costumes.

This contrived similarity in overall appearance was designed to confuse evil spirits, overcome with jealousy at the prospect of impending joy and good fortune. On the theory that numbers bring safety, and more so if you can't pick one from another, the bride surrounded herself with lookalikes.

In ancient Rome, marriages required ten witnesses, and some historians trace our custom of bridesmaids and groomsmen to Roman times. Later, bridesmaids and groomsmen served to defend a betrothed couple from attack. Until the Middle Ages, it was not unusual for a rival suitor and his aides to carry off the bride during the wedding ceremony.

By becoming a bridesmaid, a young woman draws her own set of good and bad omens. For her to stumble on her way to the altar is said to doom her chances of marriage. And superstition holds that to be a bridesmaid thrice ensures she will stay for ever single.

Mystics endowed the number three with both good and bad fortune. For a bridesmaid, it boded ill – unless she served as a bridesmaid at four more weddings. Seven, the days of the week, is a lucky number, linked with the changing phases of the Moon. For a seven-times bridesmaid any change, it is argued, must inevitably be for the better.

Why is wedding cake so symbolic?

Of all the elements that go to make up a marital feast, none has more significance than the wedding cake. No bride can be happily married, it is said, if she makes her own cake, because she will commit herself to a life of drudgery. Nor will she be happy unless she is the first to cut it – with her husband's sword, if he has one, or otherwise with the best knife in the house. As she does so, she should make a silent wish. The groom places his hand on hers, not to help cut the cake but to show that he is eager to share in her good fortune.

A piece of wedding cake can convey the bride's good luck to her friends. That's why guests are invited to take home a portion, and slices are mailed to absent friends. Traditionally, the cake should be given to an unmarried woman. There is a widespread superstition that, if she

*A **bride's maids** should be unflappable (even on the windiest day) advise manuals on wedding etiquette. In Victorian times, a bride often had a dozen maids to follow her up the aisle*

passes a small piece of it through a wedding ring, stores the cake in the foot of her left stocking, then sleeps with it under her pillow, she will see her future husband in her dreams. Another version insists that the groom should pass fragments of cake nine times through his bride's wedding ring before distributing them to unmarried girls at the feast. Such practices were common and even more elaborate earlier this century. A history of British folklore records that wedding cake sent to an unmarried woman must include some icing. The cake represents the future husband, the icing symbolises the bride. The girl should take the cake in her

were done, many believed the marriage would end in poverty. In Scotland, before the bride crossed the threshold of her new home, an oaten wedding cake was broken above her head. In England, the bride's head was covered with a cloth, and the groom broke a thin currant cake above her. Then he tossed the cake in the air for others to seize and follow various rituals that were said to guarantee their own good fortune.

Why do brides wear 'something old, something new'?

Although wedding ceremonies have changed considerably in their style and settings in recent years, many customs are still observed, even by brides with modern ideas and tastes. Most still keep to the centuries-old tradition of 'Something old, something new, Something borrowed, something blue.' An extra requirement, according to some English traditions, is 'And a sovereign (or a sixpence) in her shoe.'

This quintet of superstitions is believed to have originated in England, but many other cultures have similar customs. All come from a belief in the idea that one person's good luck can be readily handed on to another.

To wear something old, particularly a mother's wedding dress, is said to confer

*A **princess smiles** on a happy day. For her wedding in November 1947, Elizabeth, now Britain's reigning queen, wore a diamond tiara borrowed from her mother*

hands, get into bed backwards, saying the rhyme: 'I put this cake under my head, To dream of the living and not the dead, To dream of the man that I am to wed.' After intoning the verse, the girl must keep silent until falling asleep, with the cake under her pillow.

The wedding cake and rituals associated with it come to us from ancient Rome, where marriages were followed by

a feast at which symbolic dishes were served. A special cake, made from flour, salt and water, was broken over the bride's head, a sign of fertility and good fortune. Wedding guests were given pieces of the cake as lucky tokens.

The Roman custom of breaking the wedding cake over the bride was still followed last century at weddings in Scotland and the north of England. Unless this

good luck on the bride, though most modern brides put fashion first. An old garter from a happily married woman similarly passes on some of that person's good fortune. A borrowed item, such as a bridal veil from a blissful wife, also is said to bring happiness. When Princess Elizabeth, now Britain's reigning queen, married in 1947, she borrowed her mother's tiara. When her mother, then Lady Elizabeth Bowes-Lyon, married in 1923, she borrowed the old veil of *point de Flandres* lace worn by Queen Mary.

'Something blue' is often a bride's only departure from all-white attire. Upholders of tradition – or superstition – insist that the blue must be sky blue, the colour of the heavens, which symbolises trueness and fidelity. Some believe that to abide by the rule of having everything white the blue accessory should not be visible. That's why the old, borrowed and blue are sometimes combined in one item – a garter.

In many cultures, coins are a token of future prosperity. One British superstition is that on her wedding eve a bride should be dressed by her maids in her oldest sleeping attire. Another asserts that 'lucky is the bride who marries in old shoes'. If she has a coin, particularly a gold one, taped inside her shoe, she is walking her way to future wealth.

Why does a wedding end with a kiss for the bride?

A symbolic kiss today seals the marriage vows, but sometimes brings bridal tears

Many superstitions are associated with kissing which, among many peoples of the world, is not done only as a sign of love or affection. Often, a kiss is believed to bring luck, and evidence of such is not hard to find. Job-seekers kiss envelopes before mailing their applications; footballers blow kisses skywards after scoring a goal; before a horse-race punters kiss their betting slips.

The kiss as a sacred pledge, which is what it has come to signify when a groom kisses his bride, probably originated in Asia Minor. To show allegiance, men kissed a ruler's hand or the ground he walked on. Today, in the marriage service, when the minister says, 'You may kiss the bride,' he is in effect announcing the end of the service. The kiss is symbolic, sealing the wedding vows.

The kissing ceremony has had many variations over the centuries. At one time in Scotland, no bride would be happy unless the pastor gave her the first kiss. In other countries, it was customary for the bride to kiss all the men at her wedding. And to avoid misery during her married life, one custom insisted that a bride should break into tears when her husband lifted the bridal veil. Another held that a bride's tears would inevitably bring future misery.

Why do brides carry flowers?

Since ancient times, people in many parts of the world have given flowers an aura of magic, attributing to them the ability to influence many events and particularly future happiness. Children and young lovers still play 'Love me, love me not' games with dandelion clocks, and walkers pause during a country stroll to hunt for a four-leaved clover.

Flowers have always been associated with romance. In ancient Egypt, a gift of flowers was seen as one of good luck, a joyful sign of affection. In the East, flowers were thought to influence whether a young man would marry happily or not at all. Daisylike flowers that we call bachelor's buttons get the name from an Oriental custom that spread to Europe. Young men in love picked a flower with the dew still on it. If it remained bright and fresh after twenty-four hours in their pockets, the omen was for wedded bliss. Often, a man who found a shrivelled bloom remained a bachelor rather than risk having a life of misery.

Among ancient peoples, flowers symbolised sex and fertility, and became a natural part of the marriage ritual. Today, brides carry a floral bouquet in the hope of ensuring marital happiness. Usually, the bouquet contains roses, signs of love and of luck. Ribbons tying the bouquet also are symbolic, said to bring good wishes from the bride's friends.

As well as carrying a bouquet, brides often wear orange blossoms – real or

LIFTING A VEIL OF MYSTERY

Of all the customs still clinging to the marriage ceremony in times of equality and liberation, none is stranger than that of the bride wearing a veil. Brides have amended their marriage vows, many no longer promising to honour and obey, but few in formal weddings go to the altar without a veil.

This convention, still popularly accepted without a qualm, comes to us almost certainly from the East. Some say it is a symbol of the bride's submission. Others claim it is linked with Purdah, the Moslem and Hindu restriction in which women are covered from head to foot to screen them from the prying eyes of strangers. A bridegroom is the first to lift the veil on his new bride.

The veil has links too with sorcery, protecting the bride and her beauty against 'the evil eye' of possible ill-wishers.

A veiled bride follows a Roman custom revived in Europe last century

Twenty thousand couples *took their vows in this mass wedding conducted by the Rev. Moon of the Unification Church at the Olympic Stadium in Seoul. Brides and grooms were from Japan, South Korea and 138 other countries. Some partners met only two days before the ceremony*

artificial – in a crown above the veil, another custom coming from ages past. Historians trace this to the Saracens, and say it was introduced to Europe by soldiers returning from the Crusades. Orange blossom has for centuries been worn by brides in Mediterranean countries. Because the orange tree is an evergreen, it has become a symbol of unchanging affection and fidelity. The ancient Chinese believed the orange tree to be especially lucky because it bears flowers and fruit at the same time. Amid the white blossoms, symbolic of purity and chastity, was abundant fruit, undoubted proof of fertility.

The bride's happiness, like a lucky charm, can be passed on to her bridesmaids and friends. An old English saying advises nubile young ladies, 'Catch sprigs from a bride's bouquet and marry first.' The custom of a bride tossing her bouquet into a throng of well-wishers is more firmly established in the United States than in Europe, where the bride's aim may more often be to steal quietly away for her honeymoon. But wedding scenes in American films and on television will almost certainly ensure that a custom that has crossed the Atlantic will return. More brides will toss a well-aimed bouquet – to give hope to some other young woman of an early trip to the altar.

Sex and fertility are symbolised by the flowers in a bride's bouquet. Many believe the bouquet can carry her luck to others

Why do brides wear white?

Few events are more prone to omens and superstitions than the marriage ceremony, and nobody has greater need to be aware of them, if she cares at all, than the bride herself.

In formal weddings, an age-old rule is still observed that the bride should wear nothing coloured (except for something blue that is usually hidden). Brides wear white because this has been the tradition for centuries. White is said to signify the bride's purity, her innocence and candour. At one time, though rarely now, it indicated her acceptance of simple values. In ancient Greece, white was a symbol of joy. Greeks always wore white on feast days, and carried garlands of white flowers. Before wedding ceremonies, they painted their bodies white.

Many superstitions apply to coloured gowns, which nevertheless are traditional in some countries. 'Married in red, you'd better be dead … Married in yellow, you're ashamed of the fellow … Married in green, you're ashamed to be seen … Married in pink, your spirits will sink.'

Only white ('Married in white, you have chosen right') and blue ('your lover is true') escape this kind of criticism.

Our bizarre courtship of Lady Luck

Why are black cats said to be both lucky and unlucky?

Few animals are more surrounded by superstition and myth than the domestic cat. This may be in part a response to its nocturnal habits, its apparent ability to see in the dark and, when active, its supreme alertness. Few cat owners have not, at some time, watched their pet suddenly stiffen and gaze with uncanny intensity at a disturbance so subtle as to seem that nothing is there. No wonder our less educated forebears believed that cats were gifted with second sight, an ability to see ghosts or unspeakable things in the night.

The link between cats and religion, the occult and the supernatural can be traced back for several millennia and across a wide range of cultures. Cats are mentioned, for example, in the writings of both Confucius and Mohammed, and cats were held sacred in Thai temples from very early times. But the oldest link has its origins in the civilisation of ancient Egypt, several thousand years ago.

From contemporary records we know that the cat was a familiar domestic animal in Egypt by about 1500 BC, and perhaps much earlier. Cats gradually became part of the complex religious systems of Egypt; male cats acquired a link with the Sun god Ra and females with Bastet, goddess of motherhood and fertility. The ancient Egyptians believed that an eclipse of the Sun was a mighty battle between Ra and Apap, the god of night, in which Ra took the form of a giant cat. Killing a cat, even accidentally, was a far more heinous crime than murdering another human being.

When Egyptian civilisation finally fell to the Roman legions in 58 BC, the gods of Egypt vanished, but later some reappeared in another form. For example, Pasht, the Egyptian goddess of the Moon, became identified with the Roman goddess Diana, who often manifested herself as Hecate, a being who presided over evil magic in the underworld. Hecate was thought to become a black cat in her dreaded excursions from the underworld to the world of humans. Suddenly, the black cat, revered by the Egyptians, had become an animal to fear. In the chaotic aftermath of the fall of Rome, the cat was gradually established in European thought as a symbol of Satan.

Throughout the Dark Ages, it was firmly believed that demons disguised themselves as cats. From this evolved the conviction that cats were the necessary companions of witches. To carry out her mischief, a witch needed a familiar – a

Cats and the occult are linked in many cultures. In America and most of Europe, black cats are regarded as the embodiment of the Devil. In Britain, they are signs of good luck

spirit slave – a role ideally filled by a black cat. A witch's sorcery included the ability to assume any shape or guise, even that of a black cat.

The dilemma arose among those confronted by a black cat of whether they were seeing a bewitched animal capable of supernatural and malevolent deeds or the evil witch herself. Either way, it was regarded as an omen of impending doom. The persecution of cats was persistent and widespread: many festivals throughout Europe at Easter, Lent and other times involved the ritual torture and sacrifice of cats. A festival held for centuries in Paris was celebrated around bonfires fuelled by wicker cages full of cats. Says a remedy of 1602, 'To cure an ill caste by any Witch on any childe … roast the heart of a blacke cat and give to eat seven nights at bed.' And the head of a black cat – 'which hath not a spot of another colour in it' – when burned to powder was believed to cure blindness.

By the eighteenth century, however, an extraordinary ambivalence towards cats emerged, especially in England. Occult fears gave way to indulgence and acceptance, encouraged by the pragmatic interests of farmers and merchants, aware of

the cat's value in controlling rats and mice. The black cat became a symbol of good luck. Sailors' wives in the north of England kept black cats in the hope of ensuring their husbands' safety at sea. Football teams took black cats onto the field as mascots. Black cats became so valued that they were constantly stolen.

The wheel eventually turned full circle so that, in urban English homes, the domestic cat gained something of the status it had once enjoyed as a pampered deity in ancient Egyptian temples. The Dutch scholar Erasmus noted after a visit to England that, invited into an English home, he was expected to kiss all members of the household, including the cat.

Against such an ancient, rich and varied tapestry, it is perhaps not surprising that scattered and contrary remnants of folklore and superstition should survive to this day. For example, many miners believe it is unlucky to go down the pit if a black cat crosses their path. Some brides hope to see a black cat on their way to the church – and others don't. And according to Irish folklore, any cat is a demoniac creature. Its influence is nullified only by saying, when entering a house, 'God save all here, except the cat.'

Why is Friday the unluckiest day?

If all the superstitions were obeyed about the perils of doing anything on a Friday, it would be a day of total rest. Sailors believe it is unlucky to set sail on a Friday, avowing that 'A Friday's sail, Always fail.' Shipbuilders have refused to lay a keel or to launch a vessel, farmers to begin their harvest, travellers to make a journey. And workers at many trades have failed to finish Thursday jobs for fear of suffering ill luck by starting new tasks next day.

The superstition is centuries old and deep-rooted. It has various origins. Some historians trace it back to a belief, unconfirmed by the Bible, that Adam and Eve ate of the forbidden apple on a Friday, and were banished from the Garden of Eden on a Friday. Linked with that is Cain's murder of Abel, also said to have occurred on a Friday. Other traditional beliefs are that the Flood started on a Friday and that Jesus Christ was crucified on a Friday.

How the day was named is in dispute. Many say that it is derived from the names of two Norse gods – Freya, the goddess of love, and Frigga, wife of Odin.

Because it is associated with these gods, some people, such as the early Scandinavians, regarded Friday as lucky. And some Scots still do, choosing for instance to get married on a Friday. In the Islamic world, Friday is the Sabbath.

The coming of Christianity changed the attitudes of Norse and Teutonic peoples to the goddess Freya, who was banished by them as a witch. Friday became a day of sorcery, a time for witches to meet and plot their evil.

In many parts of the world, the idea of not starting new tasks on a Friday was broken by the executioner. Friday became known as 'hangman's day'. In places where the death sentence is still given – in the United States, for example – that is the day of execution and for some the unluckiest day of all.

Why do we shake hands as a greeting?

Our customary greeting after an introduction or on meeting a former acquaintance is to shake hands – and always, except in unusual circumstances – right hand clasping right hand. This practice, like many of good and bad manners, goes back to warrior days.

When two warriors met, they grasped each other's weapon hand in a gesture of peace and goodwill. By taking the acquaintance's right hand, a warrior could be certain that no weapon would be drawn; also, by neutralising his own weapon hand, he showed that he intended no treachery during the encounter.

Today, some people still regard it as bad manners to shake hands in gloves. That tradition, also, goes back to the days of chivalry. Knights removed their gauntlets to show trust in another's greeting and to indicate that they weren't about to deliver a blow with a mailed fist. From this tradition comes a convention that it is bad manners to wear gloves in the presence of royalty.

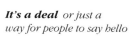

It's a deal *or just a way for people to say hello*

BEAUTY IN THE BATH BECAME A TOAST

In centuries past it was sometimes the custom to flavour a glass of wine on special occasions by adding a piece of spiced toast. Before long, drinking a person's health or that of a group became known as 'toasting'.

Later, in the reign of Britain's Charles I (1600–49), the term 'toast' was applied to much-admired people, particularly attractive women. According to one account, a celebrated English beauty was in the Cross Bath at the fashionable spa of Bath, Somerset. From among a crowd of admirers, a gallant stepped forth, took a glass of water from the bath, and proposed her health. Another young buck, befuddled with drink, prepared to join the lady in the bath, declaring that he didn't think much of the liquor she was in, but he really fancied the toast. Gentlemen in the throng dissuaded him, but from then on the idea of a fashionable belle being 'the toast of the town' has been with us right to this day.

Here's a toast *and the custom today is almost universal. The clinking of glasses is said to stop evil forces opposing the wish. To break a glass is an omen of death*

Why do we touch wood?

We've all had the feeling that things are sometimes going too well, that by over-confidence or idle boasting we may stretch our luck too far and bring some terrible retribution. An old proverb says, 'He who talks much of happiness, summons grief.'

The idea that joyful events in life may suddenly run in reverse and end in misfortune or tragedy is closely linked with the superstition of touching or knocking on wood. That action is so commonplace that we scarcely recognise it as superstition. Any statement that may be seen to tempt the fates is almost inevitably followed – and swiftly! – by a search for the nearest piece of wood.

The belief that touching wood will placate the evil spirits goes back to pagan times, when trees were held sacred as the abode of gods. These gods commanded the trees to spring into life and to lose their leaves. They chose some trees to be ever green, a sign of immortality. Touching a tree was a mark of respect to the gods, a request for a favour to be granted or thanks for one already given.

After the Crucifixion, pagan reverence was joined by a Christian belief that, because Christ died on a wooden cross, all wood was holy. Many people wore wooden crucifixes, touching them as a sign of penitence if they caught themselves gloating or making a rash statement of intent. They felt, too, that Christ had called upon them to lead humble lives. Lack of humility was not only tempting fate – it was a sin.

The super-superstitious aren't happy about touching just any piece of wood. If no living tree is at hand, they will try to find unpainted wood, touching or knocking upon it not once but three times.

It's interesting to note that touching wood for safety features in many children's hide-and-seek games. A player gets home, safe from capture, by touching base, usually a tree or wooden post.

Druid stones stand amid sacred trees in this drawing by contemporary artist Gordon Wain. In many early societies, trees were believed to be the abode of gods. For the Druids and throughout Europe, no tree was more revered than the oak. Newlyweds danced round the tree for luck

Why do we wear rings?

The Egyptians were probably the first to make rings. These were large, and women wore them as bracelets, one on each wrist. For the Egyptians, the circle represented eternity and unity. It was also a potent symbol in other cultures.

When the ancient Greeks conquered the Persians, they saw that leaders among the vanquished wore bracelets to show their standing. The Greeks took back the idea. They gave bracelets to their own distinguished soldiers to reward their valour, and made miniature bracelets to be worn as rings by Greek brides.

For centuries, the fourth finger of the left hand had had special significance. The Greeks and later the Romans called it the medicated finger, believing that a vein ran from it straight to the heart. This finger was always used to stir potions. As marriages were regarded as a matter of the heart, it was appropriate for the fourth finger of the left hand to carry the wedding ring. The Roman scholar Macrobius declared that with a ring on the medicated finger the sentiments of the heart could not escape.

The Jews copied the Roman use of the ring to seal the bond between a husband and wife, and from the Anglo-Saxons came our fashion for wedding rings of plain gold.

The belief that rings could have great curative powers persisted until recent times. It was customary on Good Friday in medieval England for the king to give silver coins to be made into rings to help 'them whyche hath the Crampe'. Early this century, it was not unusual for somebody who wanted to cure a severe affliction to collect a penny from thirty fellow parishioners as they entered a church on Sunday. The copper coins were exchanged for a silver half-crown, which was turned into a ring to be worn as a remedy, particularly for epileptic fits.

Why do polite men raise their hats?

Many of our current customs, what is regarded as good manners or bad, go back to the days of chivalry. When one knight encountered another on the road, he raised his visor, the metal strip on a helmet that protected the eyes, to show that the meeting was friendly. If a knight kept his visor down, it was a warning to prepare for battle.

When men swapped helmets for hats, touching or raising the hat, like touching the helmet to push up the visor, was recognised as a friendly – and therefore polite – gesture.

For a knight to take off his helmet showed that he trusted his host and was under his protection. That is why polite men today always remove their hats before walking indoors. With some notable exceptions, ladies never engaged in battle and thus were always to be trusted. Because they never wore helmets, they never needed to show respect by taking them off. In times past, a lady caused no offence by wearing a hat indoors, a convention that still applies today.

Why do we break a wishbone and wish?

When chicken was a once-a-year dish or meat for a special occasion, wishing on a wishbone was almost a ceremony in itself. Luck came in getting the bone in the first place and a touch of romance in choosing a partner to share in breaking it. One of the pair – whoever got the larger piece of the broken bone – had the greatest luck of all, the chance to make a wish that, in the best traditions of fairy tales, would certainly come true.

The popular custom of snapping wishbones goes back to ancient

Knights errant raised their visors as a token of peace. Hat-raising could be a sign of chivalry or, as some claim, of submission

times. Scholars say it was done centuries before the birth of Christ. Ancient people revered both the cock and the hen – the cock for announcing daybreak and the hen for providing eggs.

In the fourth century BC, the Etruscans of central Italy sacrificed fowl in calling upon one of their gods to foretell future events or to solve grave problems. The forked bone from the bird's breast, the furcula, was dried in the Sun. Later, two people broke it, exactly as we do now, and whoever got the larger piece made a wish. The Romans adopted the custom, taking it with them to many parts of Europe.

Two reasons are given why the ancients chose the furcula and not, say, a rib or

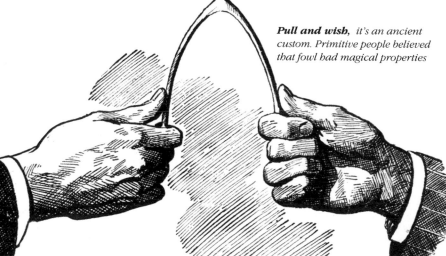

Pull and wish, it's an ancient custom. Primitive people believed that fowl had magical properties

wing in this ceremony. One says that the wishbone resembles the human crotch, which is symbolic of life. Another explanation is that the wishbone is shaped like another good-luck symbol, the horseshoe. But, as the wishbone ceremony probably predates the horseshoe, historians say this explanation is less likely.

People in many cultures have credited fowl with the ability to divine the future. A favourite game of the Etruscans was to mark out a circle with letters of the alphabet. Some corn was piled near each letter, and a fowl was released in the ring. Questions were asked, such as who would marry whom. Wherever the bird fed first gave a clue to the answer.

Why is an old boot a symbol of luck?

If a fisherman pulls out an old boot on the end of his line, he is not necessarily dismayed. He may believe that his luck will change, and he'll end the day by taking home a big bag of fish.

Today, the old boot or shoe as a lucky symbol is usually associated only with weddings. That came probably from the Anglo-Saxons. In their weddings, the bride's father handed one of her shoes to the husband, who showed his authority by touching her on the head or back of her neck with it. In a variant of the ritual the husband put the shoe at the foot of the marital bed, another sign of dominance. After some weddings it was customary for the girl's father to throw away one of her shoes to show that the bride was now in the care of another man.

In none of these wedding customs is the shoe seen as a lucky omen, but as a sign that the bride is leaving the authority of her parents. Sealing a bargain with a shoe was once a custom. When land was sold among the ancient Assyrians and Hebrews, the buyer received a shoe. Elsewhere, placing a pair of shoes on a piece of land was proof of ownership.

At some time, almost impossible to establish accurately, beliefs about good and bad luck associated with shoes became mixed with those symbolic of authority. In some cultures, shoes have long been linked with fertility, derived perhaps from their association with the foot, a phallic symbol. In other societies, it is believed that leather has the power to drive off evil spirits.

Some Indians put an upturned shoe on the roof of a new house to guarantee happiness for the occupants. Scots and Irish throw old shoes as a good-luck token at somebody starting a journey or a new venture. Sailors' wives in the north of England used to toss old shoes at departing ships, believing that this would ensure a safe voyage.

Some people believe that burning shoes brings bad luck, particularly sudden illness. Others say it will fend off disease and guarantee good fortune. According to one superstition of the Scottish Highlands, commonly quoted early this century, fairies were likely to abduct mothers and their babies from the childbed unless an old shoe was put in the fire. And an old Devonshire saying is: 'If you burn a boot on Christmas Eve, it will keep you in shoe leather all next year.'

Why are horseshoes hung over doors?

For a variety of reasons, a horseshoe is said to be lucky. Its shape resembles several symbols of good fortune – the half circle or crescent, the oval and the U. The iron from which it is made is linked to strength and power. And, among some early peoples, the horse itself was sacred.

The semicircle, coming from the circle travelled by the Sun, and the crescent appear as fertility and good-luck symbols in many cultures, ancient and modern. The U sign, derived possibly from the

*A **stout door** keeps out evil spirits and horseshoes guard against witches*

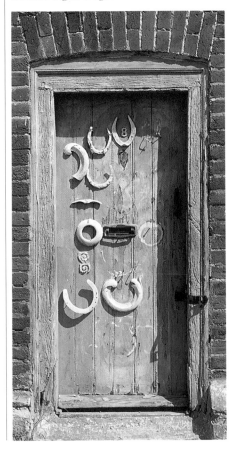

human crotch, symbolised motherhood or masculinity, according to whether its points were turned down or up. Often it was given horns to ward off evil spirits.

When horseshoes were first made by the Greeks, they were fastened to the hoofs by seven nails. The Babylonians and the Egyptians regarded seven as a magic symbol, and that idea continues today in the belief by many people that seven is a lucky number.

Combining all these signs of good fortune, the horseshoe was soon regarded as a potent device to bring luck or repel evil.

Attached to it are many other superstitions. A horseshoe must be found, not bought or given. To find one is a lucky omen, especially if the finder spits on it and casts it over the left shoulder. Its luck will last for as many years as the nails still in it. Bend one of those nails into a ring, and you will be spared from many diseases, particularly rheumatism.

In many cultures, the door has great significance. People believed that not only strangers but evil spirits would enter the house unless the door were suitably guarded. For this reason, many old buildings have figureheads of one kind or another, such as carved cherubs and deities, set in the arch above the door.

Horseshoes became a convenient and cheap replacement, ready in a trice to guard the doors of homes and outhouses. Many medieval books on witchcraft advise householders to nail a horseshoe to the door to protect themselves and to 'unbewitch' visitors (for it is no easy matter to detect a witch). Even though, in times gone by, the U symbol might effectively point up or down, a superstition about horseshoes is that, unless they are mounted upright like a cup, the luck they hold will swiftly spill away.

Why is it unlucky to spill salt?

Throughout history, salt has been symbolic of life. Even people with no real understanding of medicine know that it is essential for their wellbeing. They know, too, as we do, that it is a preservative. Well-salted foods resist decay, a blight that was seen among ancient peoples as evil worked by the Devil.

Salt, with its ability to fight evil, came to represent good. To spill it was, and still is, an omen of misfortune, likely to encourage the Devil in his attempts to undermine life. Few of us ever spill salt without taking the countermeasure of casting some over our left shoulder. This action, our forebears believed, would drive away the evil that always lurks on our left-hand (or sinister) side.

Why is thirteen an unlucky number?

No superstition is so strong or so widespread as the belief that thirteen is unlucky. From Argentina to New Zealand, and Scotland to Siberia, the numeral 13 brings shudders of foreboding.

Hotel guests refuse to take Room 13 (so hotels usually renumber them 12A or 14), hospital patients feel they are doomed if they find themselves in bed 13, and some home-buyers refuse to look at a house numbered 13 in a street. Office blocks commonly have no thirteenth

Betrayal and death soon followed the Last Supper of Jesus and the twelve apostles, shown here in a twelfth-century Norman mosaic. The events probably added strength to a fear of thirteen, which is said to come from Norse mythology

floor, many passenger aircraft have no Row 13, and only a brave hostess would seat 13 at dinner.

Triskaidekaphobia, fear of the number 13, is said to come from Norse mythology. Odin's son Balder, the god of peace and light, went to a banquet in Valhalla. Loki, god of discord, was an uninvited thirteenth guest. He tricked Hoder, the blind symbol of darkness, to shoot and kill Balder with an arrow of mistletoe.

The superstition gained pace after the Last Supper, when the 13 at the table included Judas. He was the first to quit the table, and later hanged himself. Another superstition decrees that, if 13 dine together, the first to leave will die before the year is out. At a dinner including royalty, the royal guests are always the first to rise from the table. For that reason, no royal dinner ever has a table of 13.

Friday, the unluckiest day of the week, has its own range of superstitions. When it comes as Black Friday, coinciding with the thirteenth day of a month, some people fear a double dose of disaster. Doctors and dentists say that many patients are reluctant to book appointments. On Friday the Thirteenth, removalists find that some householders are afraid to move.

One group of Americans in the Philadelphia Friday the Thirteenth Club sets out to defy the fates on that day by deliberately walking under ladders, spilling salt, breaking mirrors and opening umbrellas indoors. As cynics say, if they do that for long enough, bad luck will inevitably come their way.

If there is anything lucky about Friday the Thirteenth, it is that no year can have more than three Black Fridays and some have only one.

For the famous, superstition rules okay

History is studded with superstition. Ancient peoples believed that lightning and thunder were messages from the gods. Soothsayers and astrologers guided the planning of wars and the tactics of battle. Setbacks were blamed on star signs or evil influences. In medieval Europe, Joan of Arc's victories over the English were denounced as the work of a witch, rewarded by death at the stake. And early this century, Rasputin held influence at the Russian court because he seemed to have supernatural powers. Superstition has been, and still is, part of daily life, knowing no barriers of race or class.

It is said that Christopher Columbus and his crew, during their voyage to the New World in 1492, believed that sharks following their vessel were an omen of

*A **magician's advice** helped England's Queen Elizabeth I arrange the date for her coronation. John Dee's horoscopes also won him many favours in the queen's court*

disaster. During one particularly fierce storm, Columbus calmed his anxious men by tossing a pack of playing cards into the sea, a custom aimed at quelling the terrifying waves.

Soothsayers and oracles of one kind or another were never far from the courts of English royals, who were often swayed by superstition. King Henry VIII was convinced that Anne Boleyn's witchcraft had trapped him into falling in love. He had her beheaded. Elizabeth I retained a magician, John Dee, to help her plan her future. His magic stone rests in the British Museum.

When King Charles I stood trial after England's civil war, the head of his golden staff suddenly fell to the floor. The king, it is said, knew that he was doomed. Later, he was executed.

Samuel Johnson, the renowned English lexicographer, had the strange practice of never entering or leaving a building except with his right foot foremost. He believed that if he stepped in or out with his left foot he would bring down evil upon the occupiers. He touched every wooden post he passed, and never stepped on the cracks between paving stones.

Among composers, none was more superstitious than Mozart. He is said to have hesitated about accepting a commission to write his *Requiem*, because he feared it would result in his death. He died before it was finished.

Before embarking on a major campaign, Napoleon Bonaparte always sought advice from his clairvoyant, Madame Normand. Historians say he took special notice of dreams, believing that they foretold the future. Many times he claimed that the stars controlled all his actions and that his personal guiding star shone during his great victories. Napoleon attributed great significance to minor events, such as the stumbling of his horse, an omen of a military reversal, and a sudden brush with a black cat, which he saw as very unlucky. He dreamed of a black cat before the Battle of Waterloo – and suffered a massive defeat.

Britain's King Edward VII, who reigned from 1901 to 1910, was extremely superstitious, refusing ever to have either his bed turned or the

Minor mishaps, such as a stumble by his horse, were seen by Napoleon Bonaparte as bad omens. When his army crossed the Alps, Napoleon rode slowly on a mule and not even the guide knew his identity. Artist Jacques Louis David paints a more dashing picture

D-Day commander *Dwight Eisenhower kept a lucky gold coin in his pocket. Psychologists observe that age-old superstitions suddenly surface in wartime*

A lucky stick *went with Winston Churchill on most of his walks. When he visited bombed areas during World War II, he was often seen to stroke black cats*

The great dictators *often called on astrologers and fortune-tellers for guidance. When Italy surrendered in 1943, Hitler asked occultists to help find Mussolini. The Nazi swastika emblem was once a sign of luck*

linen replaced on a Friday. If you change your sheets on a Friday, says an old belief, the Devil has control of your dreams for a week.

When King Alphonso XIII of Spain visited Italy in 1923, several fatal accidents occurred among sailors while he was reviewing the Italian fleet. Later, a dam collapsed at Lake Gleno as the royal train passed. This caused no great surprise to superstitious Italians. What else could one expect from a thirteenth Alphonso? From then on they welcomed the monarch by rattling their keys to ward off his evil influence.

Dictators Benito Mussolini and Adolf Hitler were fanatically superstitious. Mussolini is said to have changed planes on the slightest whim, once because he feared that a fellow passenger had the evil eye. Hitler believed that the number seven had special powers, and he frequently asked for guidance from both astrologers and fortune-tellers. The Nazi

emblem, the swastika, is an ancient symbol, believed by some to have magical influence. Such was the Führer's acceptance of astrology that Allied intelligence officers consulted their own experts, hoping to anticipate how Hitler's horoscope might influence the war.

But superstition during World War II wasn't one-sided. Britain's prime minister, Winston Churchill, carried a 'lucky' walking stick and rarely failed to stroke a passing black cat – all to the delight of his onlookers. And Dwight Eisenhower, who later became US president, is said by some who knew him well to have shown many superstitious traits. As supreme commander of Allied Expeditionary Forces he launched the D-Day invasion of occupied Europe in June 1944. He is reported to have had great faith in a gold coin he carried in his pocket. Superstition ruled then and, touch wood, always will.

Evil eyes shine in a peacock's tail, according to ancient beliefs. The birds were removed from lawns at New York's United Nations building because they made some delegates uneasy

Why do some people fear peacocks?

An Indian saying, shared by Moslems and Hindus, claims that a peacock has the feathers of an angel, the Devil's voice and the walk of a thief. All the same, many Indians believe that to own a peacock is lucky, because its cry can warn them of impending evil.

In Japan and China, peacock feathers have been valued for centuries. The Chinese gave them to soldiers and civilians as a mark of distinction. Yet, in many parts of Europe and America, peacock feathers are associated with bad luck. North American Indians, who believe that people wearing feathers will take on the characteristics of the bird, won't use peacock plumes, because the bird has a vain, strutting walk and is greedy.

Most ill opinions about peacocks come from the idea that its brilliantly iridescent tail feathers carry an evil eye. Indeed, when a peacock spreads its tail in a canopy above its back, the shining eyes in the feathers have a hypnotic effect. In a profession renowned for superstitious beliefs, some actors refuse to have peacock feathers in a theatre or anywhere on a cinema set. In 1968, British actor Peter Bull lamented, 'Anything to do with peacocks is fatal … I put on a play called *Cage Me a Peacock*, which lost me every penny I had.'

He was unaware perhaps that, before World War I, Florenz Ziegfeld set out deliberately to challenge the taboo. In a New York musical called *Miss Innocence*, he dared to dress his wife, Anna Held, as a white peacock, and had a group of chorus girls in peacock feathers dance the 'peacock strut' – all without mishap.

Another reason for the peacock's mixed reputation is a Moslem belief that the peacock opened the gate of Paradise to the Devil, making it a bird never to be trusted. Also, in ancient times, peacock feathers as symbols of immortality were used at funerals to speed the deceased's passage to the place of eternal life. Perversely, from being linked with everlasting life, the feathers took on an association with death. Many people today refuse to have a peacock feather in the house.

Why is it unlucky to walk under a ladder?

Some people go to considerable trouble to avoid walking under a ladder, even making a detour by stepping onto a busy road with its greater dangers. Rationalists say that those who walk under ladders risk getting splashed with paint, or of having the ladder fall on them.

The superstition is usually explained by a reference to Christianity. The ladder, propped against a wall or a tree, forms the longest side of a triangle, which is symbolic of the Holy Trinity. To walk through the triangle desecrates that symbol, and shows an affinity with the Devil.

Several remedies are available to those who breach this triangle. Crossing the fingers, and keeping them crossed until seeing a dog, is one way to seek absolution. Another is to spit on a shoe and leave the spittle to dry. Some recommend making the sign of the *fico* (fig) by closing the fist, with the thumb poking out between the first and second fingers.

Certainly, ladder superstitions are associated with Christian belief, but they predate the birth of Jesus by many centuries. In an ancient Egyptian legend, Osiris, the Sun god, is constantly at war with Typhon, the spirit of darkness. After one victory, Typhon thrusts Osiris into the darkness of the grave. With two powerful charms, one a ladder and the other depicting a two-fingered V sign, Horus, the hawk-headed god of the rising Sun, helps his father climb out of the darkness. Lucky charms in the form of miniature ladders were found in Egyptian tombs, and some people still carry similar charms.

Some allegorical paintings show the soul mounting a ladder to climb from the grave, or taking a ladder to the pinnacle of eternal light. In the Bible, Jacob dreams of angels ascending and descending a ladder reaching to Heaven. Thus, the ladder became a sacred symbol, and was reinforced by its association with the Sacred Triangle, symbolic of life since ancient times. One early belief was that to walk under a ladder would shorten the stay of gods visiting Earth, and bring from them a terrible retribution.

Early pictures of the Crucifixion fuelled the idea that the ladder symbolised both good and evil. These depicted Satan, angry because Christ's death had saved humanity, standing beneath a ladder propped against the cross. The area under the ladder was Satan's domain; only a devil-worshipper would venture there. Making a sign of the cross by crossing the fingers would guarantee a safe passage, thwarting Satan from taking revenge. In some countries, ladders are associated

Sunshades and umbrellas *were once luxuries and status symbols. No ladies, such as these at a British garden party in 1903, would go without a parasol in days when a pale complexion was dignified and attractive. Coachmen saw umbrellas as a threat to their livelihood*

with criminals and death. Often, executioners made a gallows by propping a ladder against a tree. After the hanging, nobody walked beneath the ladder for fear of meeting the victim's ghost. In France, before the days of the guillotine, condemned men were forced first to walk under the ladder that took them to the scaffold. Whenever the executioner climbed up or down, he took the precaution of spitting several times between the rungs to make sure of warding off the condemned man's curses.

Jacob dreams of a ladder reaching to heaven. The illustration is from a German manuscript of the twelfth century

Why is it unlucky to open an umbrella indoors?

Umbrellas are fickle friends, and in times past they were even less reliable than they are today. Makers had great difficulty in devising a spring that allowed the umbrella to open gently: when the catch was released, the canopy and its supports were liable to rocket up the handle, trapping the user's fingers and injuring anybody standing nearby.

It was not merely unlucky to open an umbrella in the house, it was dangerous to people and property. Such accidents were often excused as bad luck, because nobody could be quite sure how the umbrella would behave or precisely how much space its open canopy would occupy. A taboo grew up about opening umbrellas indoors. From that developed another superstition – that it is particularly unlucky to lay an umbrella on a table and almost certain to provoke a quarrel.

Umbrellas of one kind or another have been in use for some 3000 years. The ancient Greeks carried them in processions, but as protection against the Sun not the rain. Among some Hindus, the umbrella was a sign of power. In other societies, umbrellas were used to guard kings and chieftains against evil spirits in the Sun's fierce rays.

Later, when many young ladies carried an umbrella (or parasol) and were under the watchful eyes of a chaperon, a new sign language evolved – the language of the umbrella. Dropping an umbrella once, like dropping a glove, gave the chance for a flirtatious word with an interesting male. Dropping it twice, like dropping two gloves, meant 'I love you.'

Why is it impolite to cross on the stairs?

The convention is still common but, like many practices, not so frequent as it once was. Two people meet on the stairs, one going up, the other going down. If one is a woman, the man may well step away. If he doesn't the woman may refuse to pass.

A refusal to pass another person on the stairs has become linked with manners, possibly because most stairways don't allow two people to cross without touching. Originally, it was held to be unlucky even to meet another person on the stairs. A century ago, house guests would wait in their rooms if they heard somebody using the stairs, rather than risk meeting them on the staircase.

The practice of not crossing on the stairs is probably linked with the belief that to stumble anywhere in a house is an evil omen. To do so first thing in the morning was said by the ancients to presage an unlucky day. In medieval times, for somebody to stumble while visiting a house was believed to be a sure sign of witchcraft.

A variety of countermeasures could negate the evil effects of one's own pratfalls. As a rhyme advises, 'Turning round three times about Will put all bad luck to rout.' Other recommended remedies are to snap the fingers instantly to scare off the evil spirits. Not all stumbles are considered unlucky. To stumble into a house is held by some to be propitious, perhaps resulting in our comment about people's successes that 'they just fell into it'.

Because an attempt to pass another person on the stairs is likely to cause a stumble, the practice attracted its own superstition. A stumble up was considered lucky, a happy omen for lovers, a stumble down unlucky (proved no doubt by a fall to the bottom). In any stumble caused by passing on the stairs one person was inevitably the loser. Anybody who heard a stumble on the stairs could bring good luck, it was said, by immediately shouting, 'Stumble up!'

To obey superstition, people trying to avoid passing on the stairs should back away – never turn around. According to some old-time beliefs, to turn on the stairs is to court ill luck. Some sages say that, if you walk upstairs and turn back before you get to the top, bad luck will certainly follow. Always complete the ascent or descent before retracing your steps – provided, of course, that nobody else is doing the same.

Why is a rabbit's foot a lucky charm?

In an age of scepticism, the rabbit's foot reigns supreme as the king of good-luck tokens. Among the $125 million that Americans spend each year on attempts to bring good fortune is the cost of some ten million rabbits' feet, about twice the number sold in Europe.

On the opening night of a play, some actors put on their make-up with a rabbit's foot. Well-wishers brush a rabbit's foot across the brow of a newborn baby. Rabbits' feet by the dozen appear on tables before play starts at bingo halls and whist drives. Sportsmen wear rabbit-foot charms on neck-chains.

And yet historians say that confusion with the hare has produced this belief in the rabbit's supernatural powers. In many pagan societies, the hare was revered. In Europe it was both feared and held sacred. As a nocturnal animal, it was sometimes seen only during bright moonlight, silhouetted against the skyline as it performed its magical dances.

In China, the Moon and the hare in combination symbolised power. In Britain, the hare was said to have an evil eye, whose glance could be countered only by possession of a hare's hind foot. When Boadicea fought the Romans, she is said to have carried a hare next to her

BIRTH OF A CUSTOM

The gun carriage bearing Queen Victoria's coffin rolls slowly through the streets of Windsor. Close to the castle, a new tradition was surprisingly born

The death of a queen in 1901 brought the birth of a British tradition. As Queen Victoria's funeral procession drew slowly up the hill towards Windsor Castle, horses pulling the gun carriage on which her coffin was mounted began to slip on the cobblestone roadway. Suddenly, some of the traces broke, and the gun carriage was in danger of rolling back down the hill.

With great presence of mind, a party of naval ratings who were in the procession and accompanying the carriage rushed forward to grasp the broken traces. Others steadied the carriage from behind. Between them, the two groups of naval men eased the carriage and its coffin up the hill to the castle. Since that time, it has become a custom at state funerals in Britain for the gun carriage bearing the coffin to be drawn by naval ratings.

breast to ensure luck in battle. The Aztecs believed that the hare had miraculous curative powers; a sure remedy for some diseases was to throw the animal's fur onto a fire, and sniff the fumes.

After St Augustine, the first Archbishop of Canterbury, had converted the Britons to Christianity in the sixth century, pagan symbols and practices were banned. Instead of worshipping the hare, many Britons carried a hare's foot, hidden in a pocket or a purse. Later, rabbits were introduced to Britain from Europe, probably after the Norman Conquest, and as

a bringer of good fortune, the rabbit's foot – more easily obtained – took over from the hare's.

Many people have asked why the foot and not an ear or a few whiskers should be the lucky token. The foot in many cultures is a symbol of potency. As the hare and the rabbit are two of nature's fastest-breeding mammals, it's not hard to understand why the foot of one should be thought to convey extraordinary powers. In all the demand for rabbit's-foot charms, the only being for which it brings no luck is the hapless animal itself.

Why is black the colour of mourning?

'Hung be the heavens with black,' says the opening line of *Henry VI*, lamenting the death of the previous and revered king. But Shakespeare was undoubtedly wrong. At the time of Henry V's funeral in 1422, white was usually the colour of mourning.

Funereal black comes to us from ancient Rome, where women wore black dresses known as *lugubria* to mourn their loved ones. Later, imperial decree declared that white was the colour of mourning, and it became so for several hundred years in many parts of Europe, particularly in France, Spain and England.

In 1498, Anne of Brittany wore black for the funeral of her husband, Charles VIII, and draped her coat of arms in black. It was the first black funeral since Roman times. The widow looked so stunning, it is said, that the new king, Louis XII, asked for her hand, and she became queen of France for a second time.

Aided by the day's fashion designers, the custom of wearing black for mourning returned, but with some exceptions. Mary, Queen of Scots, lamented the death of her husband, Lord Darnley, by wearing white, and became known as the White Queen. Kings of France mourned in purple, a colour that probably came originally from the purple garment that Roman soldiers put on Jesus when they mocked him before his death as the King of the Jews.

Sober black has become the colour not only of mourning but in many countries that of dignified dress for those past middle age. Originally, black was worn to scare away a dead person's ghost

Why do we wish upon a falling star?

Superstitions about stars are as old as humankind. When people first looked at the heavens, they believed them to be the dwelling place of gods. When Jesus was born, wise men claimed they had seen his star shining in the east, fostering the idea that bright stars indicated a birth. In early societies, people believed that each star was one person's soul. A shooting (or falling) star was a new baby: it fell to earth over the place where the child was born. A wish made while the star was falling would certainly come true.

Along with these superstitions came others that shooting stars were omens of death, many people believing that 'where there's a birth, there follows a death'. Until recent times it was almost inevitable that, among a group given news of a tragedy, somebody would claim to have had warning by seeing a shooting star.

Some historians say that wishing upon stars, fixed or falling, probably started as a kind of remedial action. If the stars were capable of bringing good or ill, wishing upon them was a safety factor, an acknowledgment of their power, for which the wisher would be rewarded.

However, to count the stars is generally held to be unlucky – unless you count nine stars on nine successive nights and wish. English children dared one another to risk death by counting a hundred stars. To point at stars is said by some to be sinful and even fatal. English countryfolk last century claimed that pointing at stars had brought instant death to many.

Following a star, the wise men took gifts to the infant Jesus, an event depicted in a book of Psalms, circa 1140

Why is it unlucky to break a mirror?

Almost inevitably, if somebody breaks a mirror, you'll hear the exclamation: 'That's seven years' bad luck!' Millions of people attach superstitions of one kind or another to mirrors, most of them believing that to break one will bring not only bad luck but a death in the family within the following year.

Unusual steps are taken to defeat the evil that is supposed to lurk in mirrors. Some parents turn them to the wall to prevent a baby from seeing itself before it is one year old: if it should, they say it will stutter; or it will grow no bigger; or it will die before the year is out. Many families cover a mirror if somebody dies, believing that the mirror will capture the dead person's soul and delay or prevent its journey to heaven. Some people refuse to have a bedroom mirror, or they reverse it before going to bed. They fear that, if their soul wanders during the night, the mirror will capture it, causing their death.

A European superstition asserts that it is courting tragedy to see yourself in a mirror by candlelight. Worldwide, many people cover mirrors during a thunderstorm, believing that it is unlucky to see reflected lightning. As a safeguard against ill luck, some brides remove a shoe or a glove before adjusting their wedding attire in front of a full-length mirror. According to ancient beliefs, it is unlucky for

All mirrors *encourage what our ancestors*
called the sin of vanity. Narcissus fell in
love with his own image and died, pining

a bride to try on her bridal clothes before
the wedding day, and inviting further
mishap if she sees herself fully dressed.

The ancient Egyptians and Romans had
mirrors of highly polished metal, but the
awesome, assumed powers of mirrors
originated long before the first mirror was
made. Mirror superstitions arose when
early humans first saw their reflections in
pools of water, and believed them to be
their spirits or souls, or some essential
living part of themselves, equally vulnerable to injury. To shatter the reflection
was to injure the other 'self'.

Mirrors brought vanity, which was regarded as a sin. The story of Narcissus,
who fell in love with his reflection in a
pool and died still pining, probably explains why generations of parents have
chided their children for spending too
much time in front of a mirror. The punishment, some promised, would be a visit
from the Devil.

In medieval Europe, mirrors were said
to have magical powers, useful in divina-
tion, essential equipment for magicians
and fortune-tellers. 'Mirror, mirror on the
wall, Who is the fairest one of all?' demands a fairy-tale witch, causing no surprise at all to readers down the ages.

To break a mirror would end its magic
powers, and bring revenge upon the
person whose image the mirror held. The
Romans, who believed that a person's life
was renewed every seven years, set a
timespan to the misfortune.

In company with these beliefs came
another – that mirrors were devices of the
gods. By causing one to break they prevented anybody from seeing a forthcom-
ing tragedy. From this arose the superstition that to break a mirror would result in
a relative's death.

Along with these fearful omens came a
range of counter-remedies. In the north

of England particularly, it is said that all
trouble may be averted if the broken
mirror is pounded into tiny fragments,
so that no piece can ever reflect anything
again. Some Americans believe that to
produce a five-dollar bill and make the
sign of the cross will grant instant immunity from the broken mirror's evil.

It might be thought that the weight of
superstition would affect the sales of
mirrors. There's no sign of that. It seems
that there's something of Narcissus in all
of us. We'll take any risk to get a good
look at ourselves.

Why do chefs
use dish-covers?

At many feasts and banquets, the chef's
special dish is usually delivered with some
ceremony. Often, it is wheeled into the
dining hall, concealed under a cover to
maintain the surprise. Then – presto! –
the cover is removed to reveal the *chef-
d'oeuvre* in all its magnificence.

Dish-covers serve to maintain surprise
and keep the dish hot, but that wasn't
their original function. When poisoning
was a convenient way to dispatch an un-
popular monarch, ill-lit corridors from the
kitchen to banqueting hall offered ample
opportunity to pop a fatal dose into the
royal dinner.

Before any food left the kitchen, it was
placed on a dish, and the cover was pad-
locked. At the table, the chef or household steward unlocked the cover and
tasted the food before it was served. If the
steward failed to supervise his staff, or
made too many enemies, he ran a high
risk of suffering a painful death.

*A **chef's special** revealed. Dish-covers once*
did more than merely conceal a surprise

Why do we throw coins
into wells and fountains?

It isn't surprising that water and coins
should figure in so many beliefs and
omens. Throughout history, water has
been a symbol of fertility, without which
nothing springs to life or regenerates. A
bowl of water was the ancient Egyptian
symbol for motherhood. And for pleasing
gods or devils, gypsies or beggars, money
understandably has always had an unfail-
ing magic of its own.

From ancient times to the present,
people have believed that water's cleansing powers can defeat disease and wash
away evil. In the earliest civilisations,
newborn babies were dipped in a lake or
river, a custom we still follow today in the
ritual of baptism.

Whenever a new spring burst from the
ground, it was the subject of worship and
awe, seen as a gift from the gods to cure
ills. Running water, cooler and fresher
than that in a stagnant pool, was believed
to be more therapeutic. Hot springs and
spa waters were the most beneficial of all.
Sick people flocked to them, sometimes
to be swiftly cured of their aches and
pains, as are some visitors to such health
resorts today.

Alongside water's multitude of magical
properties grew up a variety of practices
designed to please the gods who had
bestowed these benefits. Because water
was said to deter evil spirits, it was believed to be unlucky to throw away any
after nightfall – when those spirits were
most likely to be at large.

An English country superstition is that
boiled water should never be placed in a
bedroom. The Devil hates boiled water,
and will wreak vengeance on those sleeping there. On the other hand, a bowl of
unboiled water, taken preferably from a
spring and placed under the bed, will
keep away the evils of cramp during the
night. In some societies, a bride-to-be
took a ritual bath in a particular stream or
well as a safeguard against ill luck, particularly infertility, in her married life.

People in some cultures believed that
spirits lived in certain wells and springs,
and the water had extraordinary powers.
Many of these wells were later dedicated
to saints. In AD 77, Roman historian Pliny
the Elder recommended mixing equal
parts of water from three wells as a cure
for tertian fever.

In AD 200, an unknown Roman left a
Latin inscription on a lead tablet in a hot
spring at Bath, England. It addressed the
goddess Sulis: 'I curse him who has stolen
my hooded cloak, whether man or woman, slave or free, that the goddess Sulis
will not allow the thief sleep or children

until he has brought the cloak to the temple of her divinity.'

Chaucer's Pardoner suggests drinking a draught from a well before cockcrow so that 'beestes and stoor shall multiplie'. Irish and Scottish countryfolk sought out wells adjacent to oak trees or upright unhewn pieces of stone. They decorated the branches or stone with rags, which they spat on, believing that this ritual would protect themselves or their cattle against infection sent by the Druids.

From the time when they were first made, probably by the Lydians of Asia Minor centuries before Christ's birth, coins have understandably been lucky symbols. Today, it is common to see them on bracelets and chains. Brides sometimes put a coin in a shoe; many people refuse to part with a 'lucky' coin; others immediately turn over a piece of silver when they see a new Moon.

In the earliest societies, people believed that they would please the spirits who lived in a well, or had commanded a spring to flow, by dropping a gift into the water. Pliny the Younger records that a spring near Rome was 'clear and transparent, so that you are able to count the small coins thrown in it'.

As recently as a century ago, English villagers dropped pins (which carry their own range of superstitions) into wells to preserve themselves from being bewitched. Others, following an age-old tradition, dropped in a pebble, making a wish as the stone hit the water.

But today, in wells and fountains around the world, coins remain the favourite gift and particularly for the romantic and young at heart who hope to see their dreams come true.

Most famous fountain *in the world, Rome's Trevi Fountain, brings the city a harvest of coins. The belief lives on that water has a touch of magic*

Why do we set a table with napkins?

The practice of setting a dining table with napkins, or serviettes, goes back many centuries, and was common in polite society long before table forks came into everyday use. Forks were introduced into Britain and France in the seventeenth century. Until that time, napkins were considered essential for handling food and for cleaning the hands afterwards.

English writer Thomas Coryate saw forks in common use during a visit to Italy in 1611, and took one back from his travels. 'The Italians,' he wrote, 'cannot by any means endure to have flesh touched with their fingers, seeing all men's fingers are not alike clean.'

In fact, Italians started using forks in the eleventh century, because the wife of Dominico Silvio, the Venetian Doge, disliked eating with her fingers. She was given a golden fork, a small version of the large meat fork that was then commonly used in kitchens.

When Coryate copied the Italians, he was mocked, but dining with a fork soon became fashionable in England. Later in the seventeenth century, the Duke of Montausier introduced the table fork into France. The napkin kept its place on the table, because feasts of the past still had many dishes that were difficult to eat except with the fingers. Picking up meaty bones was not regarded then as impolite.

The napkin, like the knife and fork, attracted a superstition of its own. Some say that a guest, dining with friends for the first time, should never replace the napkin in its ring at the end of the meal. To fold it is regarded as a sign of folding up the friendship.

Diners once ate only with knives and their fingers. Then forks became fashionable, but napkins held their place in polite society

Swords crossed, *two sixteenth-century noblemen duel for their honour. Many of our current customs and sayings can be traced back to long-distant days of chivalry*

Why is it said to be bad manners to cross a knife and fork?

In countries where meals are customarily eaten with a knife and fork, it is usual to end a meal by placing these implements side by side. It is generally considered impolite to leave them crossed on the plate. Indeed, books on etiquette always emphasise this most strongly, but few of them say why.

Crossing a knife and fork has become a question of manners, but it was originally a matter of luck – bad luck – and among some superstitious people is still regarded as that.

After Christ's death, the placing of any objects to form a cross was seen as a reminder of His death, and became an omen of ill luck. In the eighteenth century, when knives and forks came into everyday use, diners were careful not to leave them crossed on the plate during or after a meal.

Crossed knives are more ominous. If left that way, say some people, the friendship of those at the table will certainly end. Even today, it is rare for knives to remain crossed for long on a table before somebody rearranges them. This superstition goes back to the time when the dagger was used both as a weapon and for eating. Because swords and daggers were crossed in a duel, to cross them at the table was regarded as a hostile act. Associated with a dagger were the assumed magical properties of its metal, iron, to turn the crossing of knives on a table into a real-life conflict.

Because of its many uses – in battle, in killing animals for food, in eating, as a tool – the knife attracted a range of superstitions. Its iron was said to give its owner protection against witches and evil spirits. Many Scots once believed that to sleep with a knife under the pillow would prevent fairies from carrying them off during their sleep.

In some countries, it is considered unlucky to hand somebody a knife. In others, a knife is never given as a present, because its cutting edge, an offensive weapon, 'will sever the friendship'. That is why, when receiving a knife or set of knives as a gift, some people, including Britain's Queen Elizabeth II, hand over a coin as a token payment.

Many superstitions are linked with the dropping of a knife. If the knife sticks in the ground – in effect, sheathing it – the belief is that good luck or friends will soon arrive. If the knife handle points in a particular direction, it indicates where the luck or visitors will come from. Many people say that to drop a knife or a pair of scissors will end a love affair. If the knife lands with its edge pointing upwards, expect bad luck, because the fairies will cut their feet.

KEEPING OURSELVES AMUSED

The wonderful world of art and entertainment has its own treasurehouse of lore and legend. Whether the action is on the stage, at a crowded stadium or amid a fairground's razzmatazz, behind it inevitably lies a fascinating story

Why did snooker suddenly soar in popularity? PAGE 258

Why are Fred and Ginger the world's best-known dance partners? PAGE 238

Why are roller coasters the most popular funfair ride? PAGE 240

Masterworks from the world of art

Why is Pablo Picasso the best-known modern painter?

Pablo Picasso was more famous during his lifetime than any other artist in history. His genius was recognised when he was in his teens; his reputation continued throughout his long working life and, if anything, grew more strongly after his death in 1973 at the age of ninety-two.

Picasso had not only a long career, spanning some seventy-eight years, but a prolific one. He produced some 13 500 paintings, 100 000 prints and engravings, 34 000 book illustrations and 300 sculptures and ceramics. In 1980, a Picasso exhibition filled all of New York's Metropolitan Museum of Modern Art. Two museums, one in Paris and one in Barcelona, are devoted exclusively to the artist. Almost every major art gallery in the world has at least one example of his work, and reprints, posters and postcards in abundance convey his mastery to art lovers in many countries who have little chance of ever seeing his originals.

As well as having enormous energy, Picasso was incredibly versatile. He was a painter, sculptor, ceramicist, book illustrator, lithographer, graphic artist and etcher. He acted also as stage designer for Diaghilev's Ballets Russes. His work and reputation were tested in many fields and won acclaim from an array of judges.

Picasso was in the vanguard of many innovative movements in art. His name was constantly linked with controversy, ensuring that he was known by the public at large. From his early paintings of street and café scenes in Montmartre, Picasso moved into what became renowned as his symbolist, or blue, period. In the first four years of the century, his subjects featured old age, poverty and social outcasts, painted in the distinctive, cold blues with which many still associate him. *Frugal Repast* and *La Vie* are two of his most famous pictures from this period.

In 1905, Picasso began his rose period, painting clowns, acrobats and little girls. Two years later, following Cezanne's theory that a form of geometry underlies all art, Picasso and Georges Braque settled on the cube as their geometric shape in a new movement known as cubism. Some of Picasso's best-known paintings date from this period.

Unlike many great artists who lived in poverty during their lifetime, Picasso earned huge sums from his work. It is said that, if he wanted to buy a house, all he had to do was to draw one: the picture would be worth more than the house.

Fame and wealth came to Pablo Picasso long before his death in 1973. He once said, 'I am only a public entertainer who understood his time'

WHEN PALETTES WERE LOADED WITH POISON

The paintbrushes used by artists today have come a long way from the feathers and leaves that were used in prehistoric times. The Egyptians painted with reeds, fraying their ends into fibres. The Greeks made the first animal-hair brushes, which gave their artists greater control in applying paints.

Oil painters, who want a stiffer brush, prefer those made from a hog's bristles. Watercolourists choose the more flexible camel hair or sable, though camel-hair brushes are in fact made from squirrel fur.

Before the fifteenth century, artists usually mixed their paints on shells. Then came the palette, a flat board that may vary from the kidney shape most often associated with artists to others that may be rectangular or ovoid. Irrespective of its shape, a feature of every palette, a French word meaning little shovel, is that it has a thumb hole, enabling the board to be held in one hand.

Blazing colour *is a noted feature of Vincent van Gogh's palette. The artist is seen at work here in a self-portrait*

Most oil painters, particularly those who sometimes apply their colours with a knife, prefer to use a palette made of mahogany, a hardwood that isn't easily chipped or cut. Artists normally mix their watercolours on an ivory or porcelain palette.

Nothing is more important than the choice of pigments and the sequence in which they are laid on the palette. The word has come to mean not only the board but the range of an artist's colours. Leonardo da Vinci is said to have had a restricted palette and Claude Monet a bright one.

The brilliant colours of some artists' palettes carried an unseen danger. They contained poisonous metals, including lead, mercury, cadmium, cobalt and arsenic. Pierre Auguste Renoir, who rolled his own cigarettes and smoked while he painted, developed chronic rheumatoid arthritis, caused by metal poisoning. His hands became rigid claws, and he could paint only by having the brush tied to his arm. Peter Paul Rubens, Raoul Dufy and Paul Klee, three other artists renowned for their use of bright colours, also were afflicted by rheumatic disease.

harder, a useful property whether the finished piece stands inside or out.

A sculptor starts on a massive block of stone by making a small wax or clay model – a *maquette* or *bozetto* – of the intended form. With an enlarging frame, the design is transferred to the stone, which is carved roughly to shape. Fine chisels, rasps and files give the final form, to which a tool called an abrader applies a smooth polish.

Marble takes a finer polish, but tends to break easily. That is why many marble sculptures have broken arms. It explains, too, why some are carved with a foot or leg resting against another object. Without support, thin marble ankles would break under the body's weight.

Unfinished but revealing, *Atlas is a guide to Michelangelo's technique, such as his manner of carving straight into the block instead of working evenly all round*

Why is marble used in so many sculptures?

Sculptors have worked in many types of rock and stone, but limestone, transformed into marble by pressure, heat and natural chemical changes, remains their first choice.

Marble has a wider range of colours than any other rock. It may be pure white or cream, pink, brown or black. Crystallised minerals within the marble produce its mottled and veined effects, making each piece unique in colour and pattern. The most famous marble is that used by Michelangelo – white Carrara, quarried at Massa, Santa and Pietrasanta in Tuscany. Many sculptors, however, prefer the warmer fleshlike tones of the marble used in one of the world's oldest surviving marble sculptures, Aphrodite of Cyrene, a work found in Libya in 1913 and dated between 100 BC and AD 400.

Most sculptors say that marble is a pleasure to carve. Ideally, it should be free of flaws that might cause cracking. Freshly quarried marble is easier to work, because exposure makes the surface

A protective shield of bullet-proof glass guards the Mona Lisa *from attack by vandals. The world's most-famous painting was stolen in 1911 as part of a fraud. Six copies were sold to Americans, each of whom believed that the painting on offer was Leonardo's original masterpiece. Police found the real* Mona Lisa *in Italy two years later*

Why are we fascinated by the *Mona Lisa*?

No painting in the world is more universally admired and discussed than Leonardo da Vinci's *Mona Lisa*. If proof were wanted, it is to be found in the Louvre in Paris. Of all its masterpieces, none consistently attracts such attention. Moreover, the painting is instantly recognised by millions of people worldwide who have never been to an art gallery.

Leonardo painted *Mona Lisa*, or *La Gioconda* as it is also known, probably between 1503 and 1506. Some doubt exists about the sitter for the portrait. Most art historians and other authorities say that almost certainly it was Mona Lisa Gherardini, who in 1495 was married to the Florentine nobleman Francesco del Giocondo, a rich silk merchant. She was then in her mid-twenties.

Mona Lisa's husband so disliked the painting that he is said to have refused to pay for it, and it stayed in the artist's possession. In 1516, François I invited Leonardo to France, where he died three years later. The *Mona Lisa* became part of the king's collection and is said to have decorated the royal bathroom. Apart from its exhibition abroad and when thieves took it to Italy in 1913, the *Mona Lisa* has remained in France. In 1963, when it went on show in Washington, it was insured for $100 million, the highest insurance value ever put on a work of art.

Art experts and connoisseurs have long debated why the *Mona Lisa* has won such fame and fortune. Undoubtedly, its appeal is largely subjective, dependent on what individual viewers feel, which accounts for much of the picture's continuing fascination. We may argue, for example, whether the subject is smiling or not. Subtle, dark pigments around the eyes and mouth give a strange sense of movement, while the arms and hands convey a sublime feeling of relaxation, in marked contrast to the rigidity of many portraits of the time.

Critics have called on a sweeping array of adjectives to describe the face – enigmatic, spiritual, serene, mysterious. What's more, the figure sits tranquilly before one of Leonardo's richest and strangest backgrounds, crossed by roads and bridges to nowhere. The fact that we try to read character into an immobile, two-dimensional painting, 77 by 53 cm (30 by 21 in), is a compliment to a great master, one who brought new life to the art of portraiture.

Why are some wall paintings called frescoes?

Murals and frescoes are wall paintings, but murals can be peeled or scraped off, leaving the wall intact. A fresco is an integral part of the wall, and can be removed only by chipping away the plaster.

The word *fresco* is Italian for fresh. In a fresco painting, the artist applies pure, powdered pigments onto freshly laid wet plaster. The pigments, usually mixed with a solution of lime, are absorbed into and fuse with the plaster to form a *fresco buon* or true fresco. An inferior and less durable fresco, a *fresco secco*, is painted on dry, slightly roughened plaster, which may later powder or peel.

Because the plastering of a wall for a fresco is in itself a skilled craft, many fresco painters work in a creative partnership with their plasterers. The first or *arriccio* layer of plaster is applied quite thickly to the whole wall, but the one or two finer *intonaco* layers cover only the amount of wall that can be painted in one day without drying.

By looking carefully at the plaster joins in old frescoes, we can see how many days they took to paint. We have only a vague date for the painting of Michelangelo's *Creation of Adam,* one of the magnificent frescoes on the ceiling of the Sistine Chapel. The whole of the massive work, with some 300 figures from the Old and New Testaments, was painted in four and a half years, from 1508 to 1512. But Adam, we can tell, took Michelangelo precisely three days, because one plaster seam runs through Adam's neck and another through the top of his legs.

Fresco painting gives no margin for error, and demands careful planning. Any mistake means that the wall must be replastered. After initial drawings, the artist creates a full-sized outline called a cartoon. A small spiked wheel, a *roulette*, is run over the outline to pierce it with dots. After the cartoon is positioned on the fresh plaster, the painter dusts or 'pounces' it with charcoal. When the cartoon is removed, the plaster carries a dotted outline of the proposed fresco. Some old frescoes still show their pounced dots.

Once the outline is on the wet plaster, the painter must work quickly to ensure that the pigments penetrate. As the plaster dries, they get a distinctive, bleached look, with colours less intense than those in murals. At the same time, a film of carbonate of lime forms on the fresco's

A fresco begins with the plasterer applying smooth layers of intonaco *plaster over a rougher layer of dry* arriccio

surface, giving the fresco lasting protection, provided the climate is dry.

The techniques of fresco were known to the ancient Greeks and Romans, to the Chinese and Indians. They were used more primitively in France by the cavemen of the Dordogne who, as early as 15 000 BC, rubbed pigments into the walls of the Lascaux caves to create their famous bison. Giotto's frescoes in the Arena Chapel at Padua, painted between about 1303 and 1305, are the oldest in Italy, which remains the fresco's true home. The combination of a dry climate, a grand style of architecture with vast walls and ceilings, plus a wealth of talented artists, gives Italy the right to name this unique art technique.

Michelangelo's masterpiece on the ceiling of the Vatican's Sistine Chapel took twelve years, from 1980 to 1992, to restore. As discoloured varnishes and centuries of dirt were removed, the awesome work shone with new light. An example is shown in the figure of one of the ignudi, male nudes, before and after restoration. Michelangelo spent four years on the frescoes, commissioned by Pope Julius II, who bullied him constantly. Reports say that the first viewers of the completed work were 'speechless with astonishment'

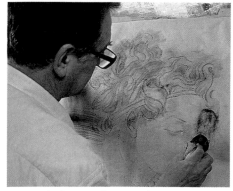

As a guide the artist fastens a drawing onto damp plaster, pricks holes in its outline and impregnates them with charcoal dust

An image shows on the still-damp wall as the sketch is removed. Charcoal dots are clearly visible on many famous frescoes

Fast and faultless must be the artist now to complete the work before the plaster dries. As it does so, the colours lighten

All for the sound of music

Why is the Stradivarius the world's most famous violin?

The chances of finding a genuine Stradivarius violin in a battered case in somebody's attic are about as remote as those of seeing a snowman in the Sahara. But, because the exact whereabouts are known of only 635 Stradivarius violins, hope – and forgeries – abound.

In 1666, when Antonio Stradivari first inscribed one of his violins, the practice was to use the maker's Latinised name. That is why the Stradivarius violin is better known than its maker. In all, from that first instrument to his last, made in 1737 when Stradivari was ninety-three years old, the Italian craftsman produced some 1100 violins, twelve violas and fifty cellos. Of the three great violin-making families of Cremona – the Amatis, the Stradivaris and the Guarneris – Antonio Stradivari is the acknowledged master.

No pictures survive of Stradivari, but contemporaries described him as tall, thin and 'rarely out of his working costume'. Stradivari worked on the ground floor of a three-storey house in Cremona's Piazza San Domenico. He used the building's flat roof to dry the varnished violins. Of his eleven children from two marriages, only two sons, Francesco and Omobono, became violin-makers.

Stradivari's home was pulled down in 1928, and the graveyard in which he was buried was totally destroyed some years later. A small museum in Cremona, a tombstone that he inscribed himself in 1730, plus 635 of his famous violins, are all that remains.

Musicians, instrument-makers, collectors, scientists and acoustics engineers have tried to analyse what makes Stradivari's violins so special. But neither the specialists nor Stradivari's own tools and templates in the museum at Cremona reveal the secret. Age is not a factor, because Stradivari's violins were renowned in his lifetime. Experts point to the wood, the varnish, the dimensions and shape of the instruments as key factors. But, just as a great composer uses basic ingredients to create a masterpiece, so Stradivari built violins in a way that has defied all attempts at imitation. The wood in a Stradivarius has a high silica content, perhaps because timber in Lombardy was floated downriver, absorbing minerals from the water. But other violin-makers in Cremona used similar wood – spruce and maple. Stradivari did not vary the basic design taught by the Amati family, where he was apprenticed, but he experimented with dimensions. In 1700, he reverted to a standard length of just under 14 in (35.5 cm), with a narrower width of 8 in (20.3 cm). Stradivari had an intuitive ability to gauge the tone

The great violins made by Stradivari are not exact replicas. The Mulgan (left), made in 1699, is slightly longer. Since Stradivari first made his violins, famous musicians such as Nigel Kennedy have delighted in playing them

of an instrument while he was building it, and made constant subtle adjustments. The wood in a good violin needs to be stiff to give the instrument power. But it needs also a high degree of damping, subtle use of varnish to soften and improve its tone. Too much damping diminishes the instrument's power; too little makes it loud and possibly harsh.

In Stradivari's violins the composition and colour of the varnish varies. His earlier instruments are golden-yellow, the later ones a distinctive soft orange-red. He is said to have written the formula in the family Bible, which has not survived.

Some violin-makers believe that his varnishes may have been water-based, binding them well to the wood without damping the sound too much. Others suspect that he mixed chitin, from insect wings, with linseed oil. Whatever were Stradivari's secrets, acoustical scientists are working to find them. In the end they may discover that the psychological impact of playing a Stradivarius makes great violinists just that much greater.

Four of Stradivari's brilliantly carved and inlaid violins were made for the court orchestra of King Amadeus II of Sardinia; three went to Philip V of Spain. His most famous violins, such as the Hellier, Mendelssohn and Hubermann, which are named after one-time owners, change hands for enormous sums. In 1990, the Mendelssohn fetched $1.7 million, a record price for a musical instrument.

The most famous of all, the Messiah or Messie, is in Oxford's Ashmolean Museum and is not for sale. Stradivari knew the supreme quality of this violin and would not part with it. It was sold in 1775 by his son Paolo.

Why do women sometimes sing male roles in opera?

The shorter and tighter the strings on a violin, the higher the notes. Vocal cords operate in the same way. Women – and boys before they reach puberty – have shorter and tighter vocal cords, enabling them to sing higher notes than can adult men, whose vocal cords are more relaxed.

In sixteenth-century Italy, papal decrees barred women from singing in church. This led to the castration of musically talented young boys before they reached puberty, ensuring that their vocal cords would not change. The first *castrato*, who combined the pure high notes of a boy's larynx with the large chest and lungs of an adult male, sang in the papal chapel in

The male soprano *Farinelli won fame and a fortune. In Madrid he sang nightly to cure King Philip V of melancholy*

1562. Later in that century, *castrati* sang in the Sistine Chapel.

The voices of the *castrati* were said to be pure, wide-ranging, powerful and moving. The rise of Italian opera in the seventeenth century gave them more dramatic roles in which to display their singing. Often, the leading, heroic parts in Italian opera at the time were written for *castrati*; adult males with normal voices played servants, priests and elderly men.

The most famous *castrati* earned wealth, prestige and fame. Baldassare Ferri served the courts of Warsaw, Stockholm and Vienna, and was created a Knight of St Mark. On his death in 1680, he left 600 000 crowns to charity. Fans mobbed Carlo Broschi (known as Farinelli) almost wherever he went.

In 1878, a decree by Pope Leo XIII ended the castration of boy singers, and created a problem for companies wishing to produce operas that included roles for *castrati*. In some operas the roles were rewritten for men; in others they are sung by women.

Why did Handel write the *Messiah*?

If George Frideric Handel's father had lived much longer, it is likely that the world would have lost a great composer. The father, a physician of Halle in Saxony, married for a second time at sixty, and George Frideric was a child of this marriage. Even though the young Handel showed exceptional talents as a musician, performing on the organ at the age of seven, his father wanted him to become a lawyer. A few years after his father's death, Handel turned full-time to music. In Italy, he wrote his first operas, and in 1710 went to London, where an intended short visit turned into a lifetime's stay.

In 1713, aged thirty-six, he wrote a work to celebrate Queen Anne's birthday

and received a pension of 200 pounds a year for life. He became, in effect, an unofficial Master of the Royal Music. George I doubled his pension and George II's coronation ceremony in 1727 included four Handel anthems. That same year, Handel became a naturalised Englishman and anglicised his name to George Frederick.

Handel realised that 'What the English like is something they can beat time to, something that hits them straight on the drum of the ear.' For almost thirty years he wrote operas that brought fashionable Londoners flocking to the theatres. But Handel's operas had a distinctly Italian flavour, and Italian opera suddenly went out of fashion.

His health failing, Handel was about to leave England for good, when the Lord Lieutenant of Ireland invited him to give a series of concerts in Dublin. While making plans for his visit, Handel wrote a new oratorio, the *Messiah*, in just twenty-three days, often foregoing sleep and food. When he completed the Hallelujah Chorus, he told an assistant, 'I did think I did see all Heaven before me – and the great God himself.' The oratorio's first performance, in Dublin on April 13, 1742, was for charity and was a spectacular success.

Handel was deeply religious, but his decision to write the *Messiah* and to concentrate on oratorio came as much from

the demise of opera. He saw oratorio as a form of opera meeting the spirit of the times, with stories from the scriptures set to music and performed by solo singers, chorus and orchestra. Because of its religious flavour, oratorio had another practical advantage: it could be performed during Lent, when theatres were closed.

The *Messiah* had its first London performance at Covent Garden, where George II became so excited during the Hallelujah Chorus that he leapt to his feet. His loyal subjects did the same, and a tradition was born for the audience to stand whenever this is played.

Handel, blind for the last seven years of his life, fainted during a performance of the *Messiah* in 1759, and never recovered. He was buried at Westminster Abbey, but his request for 'burial in a private manner' was ignored. Some 3000 mourners attended the funeral. On the twenty-fifth anniversary of his death, a commemorative performance of the *Messiah* included 95 violins, 26 violas, 21 cellos, 20 oboes, 12 trumpets, 4 sets of kettle drums and a chorus of 257 voices. At Handel festivals between 1857 and 1926, as many as 4000 performers took part.

This vastness of scale, not part of Handel's original concept, has made the *Messiah* one of Handel's best-known works. No Christmas or Easter goes by without a performance somewhere.

In his will *Handel gave a copy of the Messiah's score to the Foundling Hospital in London. The first performance benefited prisons, a hospital and an infirmary*

MUSICAL GENIUS THE WORLD FORGOT

Italian composer Gioacchino Rossini, born in Pesaro in 1792, was once the most famous composer in Europe. In his lifetime, kings courted him, and the public hummed and whistled his tunes. A century and a half later, most of his music was never heard.

At the age of thirty-seven, Rossini had written thirty-nine operas. One of them, *William Tell* had more than 500 performances at the Paris Opera during his lifetime. Suddenly, in 1829 he gave up composing operas, explaining that nobody could sing them any more. Rossini's operas demanded bel canto singing, a style calling for superb vocal technique. The singer often had to make swift but smooth leaps from note to note with ease and assurance, soaring and plummeting under perfect control.

A new breed of composers and singers spurned bel canto singing, and Rossini was suddenly out of fashion. When his orchestral works were performed, they were often appallingly mutilated, with some instrumental parts clumsily rescored to be played by different instruments. Rossini joked that he had decided to give up composing operas so that he could indulge in a favourite pastime, eating. He was a noted gourmet, and is said to be the only composer to have created a famous dish – tournedos Rossini, a rich combination of fillet steak, foie gras and truffles.

But already he had made a fortune. When he died in 1868, he left much of it to his native town, which established the Fondazione Rossini in his honour. In 1980, the foundation published the first critical edition of Rossini's complete works, and revealed to a new generation a composer of enormous versatility and force. The once-spurned Rossini emerged from the shadows to win new and deserved recognition as one of the great composers of all time.

Charming and affable, Rossini was a brilliant composer and a lavish host, famed for his dinners. In Paris, chefs sought his recipes

Why is a violinist the leader of an orchestra?

The ritual of modern symphony concerts is well established. The orchestra members take their seats, tune their instruments, and the audience settles into an expectant silence. On comes the leader, or concertmaster, to a burst of applause, to be followed soon by the orchestra's star, the conductor.

That wasn't always so. Only in the past 150 years have orchestras had a conductor, baton in hand, directing from a rostrum. Today's conductors are among the highest paid and without doubt the most revered of all musical performers. The demands on their skills are acknowledged to be more intense and more varied than those on other musicians.

Before the advent of conductors as we know them, orchestras were generally smaller, and composers often directed the playing of their own compositions from a keyboard instrument. Later, in the early eighteenth century, the make-up of the symphony orchestra changed, and stringed instruments became predominant. The principal first violinist took the role of director, or leader, dipping his instrument or waving his bow to give the first beat of each bar. Many chamber ensembles today follow that practice.

As orchestras grew in size and the musical repertoire expanded, the need came for a specialist who could direct the musicians and interpret the compositions. Significantly, many of the new-style conductors, such as Mendelssohn and Weber, were composers who had earlier directed orchestras playing their own music.

The large string sections of modern orchestras, which include thirty or more first and second violins, and the complexity of orchestration created a further need for a constant liaison between the conductor and this main body of the orchestra. The job fell naturally to the principal first violinist, who controls important technical aspects of his group's playing, such as how the bow should be used in a particular passage. He, like the principals in other sections of the orchestra, needs also to be a fine performer, able to play demanding solo parts as they occur in orchestral pieces.

How to play it is discussed during a rehearsal by conductor Sir Georg Solti and the leader of the London Philharmonic Orchestra. In a symphony orchestra, the leader, the principal first violinist, provides an essential link between the orchestra and its conductor

Wordsmiths weave their spells

Caricaturists delighted *in lampooning Joseph Pulitzer. In the 1880s he is shown expressing great dismay because a rival, New York's* Evening Sun, *'is getting a little too strong for my eyes'*

Why are Pulitzer prize-winners always American?

Whenever the annual Pulitzer prizes are announced, somebody somewhere is sure to object: 'But they are all Americans.'

They have to be. The will of Joseph Pulitzer, which set up the awards, stipulates that they may go only to American citizens. Pulitzer, born in Hungary in 1847, arrived in the United States as a seventeen-year-old immigrant. He left his adopted country two major legacies: he pioneered sensational journalism and bequeathed money for Pulitzer prizes.

His newspaper, the New York *World*, became the nation's biggest seller on a recipe of yellow-press stories about oppressed workers, the fat cats of big business and corrupt government officials. Pulitzer died in 1911, leaving $1.5 million in his will to start a School of Journalism at Columbia University. He also left $500 000, the income from which provides annual prizes for 'journalism, letters and music' and 'for the encouragement of public service, public morals … and the advancement of education.'

In the letters awards, juries recommend winners in the five categories of novel, play, poetry, history and biography. These recommendations go to an advisory board, which may accept or reject them and even substitute other choices. In 1917, the first year, the board made no awards for novel and play, deciding that the submissions were not up to standard. In 1948, it amended the novel category to embrace 'fiction in book form', so that James Michener's short-story collection, *Tales of the South Pacific*, could win.

The Pulitzer prize for fiction differs in many ways from other literary prizes, such as the Booker and the Nobel prize for literature. The prize is small – since 1988, just a fixed $3000 – compared with $900 000 for the Nobel laureate in 1992. The Pulitzer usually goes to popular and commercially successful novels. Recent winners include Alice Walker's *The Color Purple*, William Kennedy's *Ironweed* and Alison Lurie's *Foreign Affairs*, all of which were made into films. John Updike won in 1991 with *Rabbit at Rest*, exactly nine years after his award for *Rabbit Is Rich*.

Why is Agatha Christie called the queen of crime fiction?

On any scale, Agatha Christie is a phenomenon. Sales of her books, in 157 languages, exceed 300 million copies, making her not only the top-selling woman writer, but a writer who has outsold all except Shakespeare. She is one of few authors to have had a million copies of her work published on one day.

Agatha Mary Clarissa Miller was born in the English seaside resort of Torquay, Devonshire, in 1890, and wrote several books under the pseudonym Mary Westmacott. As Lady Mallowan, she died in 1976. But the world knows her as Agatha Christie; the surname came from her first husband, Archibald Christie.

Between her first novel, *The Mysterious Affair at Styles*, published in 1920, and her last, published posthumously in 1977, she wrote more than 110 titles. Agatha Christie's output was not phenomenal, but her success is prodigious.

Critics say that it stems from her brisk, often humorous, writing style, ingenious

Crime-fiction writer *Agatha Christie could turn out a best-seller in weeks. She devised many of her best plots in the bath*

IT ALL COMES 'TRIPPINGLY ON THE TONGUE'

Two Oscars *were won by Laurence Olivier's Hamlet – for his acting and for the film*

No other writer did more than Shakespeare to enrich the English language. And of all his plays none surpasses *Hamlet* in giving us a wealth of everyday expressions. One elderly woman who went to London to see the play for the first time was asked how she enjoyed it. 'Not at all,' she is said to have replied. 'It's too full of clichés.'

Most of us are familiar with such quotes from *Hamlet* as 'To be or not to be' and 'Alas! poor Yorick', but many of the play's lines and phrases we use unknowingly in our daily conversation. We 'set [things] right', sum up 'in a nutshell' and see in our 'mind's eye'. We are 'cruel only to be kind' and do many things 'more in sorrow than in anger'. We advise others 'neither a borrower nor a lender be' and warn against wandering down 'the primrose path'.

We joke that somebody has been 'hoist with his own petar' and comment that a rule is 'more honoured in the breach than in the observance'. We exclaim, 'That it should come to this!' We talk soberly about news that 'must give us pause', of the time when we have 'shuffled off this mortal coil'. Exuberant youngsters are 'flaming youth'; guilty parties 'protest too much'; and the innocent are 'pure as snow'. In health clubs, instructors mock iron-pumping young ladies with the gibe, 'Frailty, thy name is woman!' and the weight-conscious lament, 'O! that this too too solid flesh would melt'. About Shakespeare one fact seems sure: we 'shall not look upon his like again'.

---

plots that cleverly misdirect the reader and from her memorable main characters. Her Belgian detective, Hercule Poirot, appeared in the first of her sixty-seven detective novels. His death in a 1975 novel brought a page-one obituary in *The New York Times*. The elderly Miss Jane Marple made her debut in 1930 in *Murder in the Vicarage*. One of Christie's best-known novels, *The Murder of Roger Ackroyd*, is noted for the controversy that greeted its publication in 1926. It wasn't the butler who did it but the narrator.

Fifteen of her books were made into films. One short story, *Three Blind Mice*, prompted what became the longest-running play in theatrical history. *The Mousetrap* opened in London in 1952 and was still running more than forty years later.

Why is it said that Francis Bacon wrote Shakespeare's plays?

Scholars have credited not only Francis Bacon as being the true author of some or all of Shakespeare's thirty-seven plays. Over the years, the list has included John Donne, Ben Jonson, Walter Raleigh, the Earl of Southampton, Mary Queen of Scots and an Irish nun.

The rumour started in the nineteenth century that the talented Bacon, philosopher, statesman and essayist, was the real writer of the plays attributed to his contemporary. The story persisted for so long that many books on Shakespeare inevitably include a discussion of the Baconian Theory.

Scholars who support the theory point to Shakespeare's background. His father was at various times a glover, butcher and wool dealer. It is unlikely, goes the argument, that Shakespeare had the ability or education to write such brilliant plays. Class-conscious nobles and literati refused to believe that a provincial upstart could be England's greatest writer. They suggested that Francis Bacon, not wanting to be associated with such a lowly profession as play writing, paid Shakespeare to use his name.

Despite the gaps in our knowledge of Shakespeare's background, it is almost certain that he was educated at the free grammar school in Stratford-upon-Avon, where his father was a burgess. Young Will's education may have fitted him for writing his plays. Bacon's, by contrast, led to his writing mainly in Latin, then considered a superior language.

Proponents of the Baconian Theory don't explain how Bacon found time to write the plays. As Baron Verulam, he led a busy political life, latterly as Lord Chancellor. For all his reputed skills in deception, he failed to keep secret the corruption that led to his dismissal from office.

Today, few scholars pay much attention to the Baconian Theory, generally accepting that William Shakespeare wrote all thirty-seven plays attributed to him.

Why did Herman Melville name his whale Moby-Dick?

American novelist and poet Herman Melville spent much of his youth and early manhood at sea. Born in New York in 1819, Melville left school at thirteen after his father's death, and later joined a mailship's crew on the run to England.

In his early twenties he worked as a harpooner on the *Acushnet*, a whaler working the South Seas. Other whalers had reported encounters with a monster and terrifying whale, which became known as Mocha Dick, because it was often seen near the island of Mocha, off the coast of Chile.

Whether Melville himself saw Mocha is uncertain. He was a constant reader and it is likely that he read a magazine article in 1839 on 'Mocha Dick, or the White Whale of the Pacific'. Students puzzle over why he changed that whale's name to Moby-Dick. One explanation is that, in 1846, four years before his famous novel was published, Melville met Richard Tobias Green, a former South Seas shipmate. A familiar version of Green's first names was probably Dick Toby, from which Melville may have got Moby-Dick.

Spotlight on the stage

Why do we clap to show our enjoyment?

The Greeks expressed their approval of theatrical performances by cheering and clapping. The Romans snapped their fingers and clapped their hands, and waved the pointed ends of their togas, or brandished special strips distributed to audiences for the purpose.

By the seventeenth century, whistling, stamping and clapping were considered the correct way to applaud. The practice spread to church congregations for a time; when the clergy disapproved, coughing, nose blowing and humming became ways to applaud a lively sermon or a well-drilled choir.

Psychologists say that applause in any form satisfies the human need to express an opinion, and gives an audience a feeling of participation. Clapping both hands together to express approval possibly developed from clapping somebody on the back as a form of congratulation. Because audiences cannot clap actors on the back, they clap their hands instead. Clapping is a means also of expressing pent-up excitement or delight. Small children and chimpanzees are known to do so spontaneously.

Hiring professional clappers dates back to the Roman Empire. Nero paid some 5000 young *plausores* to applaud his public appearance. *Imbrex*, clapping with hollowed hands, and *testa*, clapping with flat hands, were rehearsed in advance.

Later came the ploy of scattering paid applauders – a *claque*, from a French word meaning 'to clap' – among the audience to encourage others to follow the example. The claque infiltrated New York theatres and the Metropolitan Opera House, and was common in European theatres earlier this century. In France, an agency called *Assurance de Succès Dramatique*, would for a fee ensure that the final curtain was greeted with approval or disapproval. Sometimes, rival claques appeared at the same performance, one clapping and cheering while the other hissed, jeered and booed.

Vaudeville stars were well equipped to become movie actors, and many comics such as Jimmy Durante (far right) and W. C. Fields won new fame. 'Schnozzle' Durante was noted for his piano-playing and jokes about his nose, Fields for his witty but caustic humour

Why are music-hall shows sometimes called vaudeville?

Vaudeville originated in France, where the term was first used in the fifteenth century for satiric songs and later for light musical plays performed by strolling players. By the nineteenth century, English music halls offered variety shows that included a program of light comedy and popular ballads.

In the United States, actor Tony Pastor took beer-hall variety acts, which played mainly to audiences of drunks and prostitutes, and cleaned them up for a New York variety theatre on 14th Street. His first vaudeville show, in 1881, had eight acts ranging from comedy and acrobatics to song and dance.

With a new clientele and classier performers, vaudeville was at its peak between 1890 and 1925. Many well-known film actors, such as W. C. Fields, Eddie Cantor and Jimmy Durante, made their mark in vaudeville. In 1932, only fifty years after the first performance, vaudeville acts began to be replaced by talkies at the Palace Theatre on Broadway. Vaudeville died out entirely soon after World War II, a victim of the new light entertainment of movies, radio and television.

The word vaudeville, French in origin, comes either from *voix de villes*, the voice or song of the city streets, or from Vau (or Val) de Vire, the Vire Valley in Normandy. Here, in the fifteenth century, Olivier Basselin wrote his first satiric songs poking fun at the English invaders. That, say some jesters, is why the English prefer the terms music hall or variety to describe this kind of entertainment.

Why is Punch the most celebrated of puppets?

The curtains open on the miniature stage of the collapsible booth, and the villain appears in all his gloating glory. Punch, hooknosed and humpbacked, is ready to evoke screams of outrage as he has done for centuries. In a time-tested plot, he confronts and usually outwits all figures of authority – priest, doctor, policeman and executioner. He tells lies constantly, beats his wife with a huge club, and never minds the baby without causing grievous bodily harm. His only friend is his faithful dog Toby, usually a terrier.

Punch has an ancestry going back to *commedia dell'arte*, improvised comedy that flourished in Italy from 1545 until the early eighteenth century. Characters included the *zanni*, a number of comic servants who helped or hindered as the plot demanded.

Among the *zanni* whose identities survived were Arlecchino (Harlequin) and Pulcinella, a humpbacked dolt. Pulcinella is important as the forerunner of the French buffoon Polichinelle, the German Kasperle and the English Punch.

As Samuel Pepys notes in his diary, visiting marionette shows first took Punch to England after the restoration of the monarchy in 1662. By stages, Punch became the character he is today. A resourceful showman gave him a wife, Joan, later renamed Judy. Another, speaking Punch's role with a squeaker or 'swazzle' in his mouth, produced the high-pitched voice that remains a traditional part of the act.

Punch's popularity waned during the 1800s, but a revival came by using glove puppets instead of stringed marionettes. This enabled the show to be done by one man and his dog. In 1962, Punch's 300th anniversary was celebrated in London by a service in St Paul's Church, Covent Garden. About fifty Punch-and-Judy showmen attended with their dogs.

Why is knockabout comedy called slapstick?

Much of the laughter in old-style comedy and farce comes from simulated acts of violence. Clowns are clubbed, a kick in the pants brings a headlong plunge, objects shatter on people's heads. Bodies are sponges for punishment. We laugh because we know that none of this violence is real.

Added sounds heighten the comic effect. A loud beat on the bass drum or the clang of a gong accompanies almost every blow. The device is ages old. In the Italian *commedia dell'arte* of the late sixteenth century, some players carried flexible cudgels. As blows were struck, these slapsticks, as they came to be known, gave off a loud cracking noise. Since then, all forms of boisterous comedy, with or without sound effects, have been referred to as slapstick.

Why do ballerinas wear tutus?

When Madame Marie Taglioni danced her most famous role in *La Sylphide* at the Paris Opera in 1832, she wore a new costume designed by Eugène Lamy. The high-waisted, empire-line dresses and Grecian robes previously worn by ballerinas restricted the movement of their arms and legs. Lamy's costume had a close-fitting bodice, which left the neck and shoulders bare; its calf-length skirt gave the dancer more freedom. The audience could now see the dancer's intricate steps and expressive arm movements.

The skirt, made of white tulle, resembled the stiff petticoat – *tutu* in French – worn under a crinoline. Theories that tutu came from a Melanesian word for a fringe of leaves on a totem or an Indian word for cotton weaving are unlikely.

When she first wore the tutu, Marie Taglioni was the world's best-known dancer. Filippo Taglioni, her father, choreographed *La*

The ethereal beauty of ballet dancer Marie Taglioni (below) captivated audiences in the 1830s. She was the first to wear the tutu, which was then calf-length. In time it was shortened (right) to show the whole leg

Sylphide for her; it was also the first ballet in which a ballerina danced on points.

In the 1880s, the bell-shaped and calf-length skirt of Lamy's romantic tutu was adapted to jut out horizontally just above the knee in a new classical tutu, worn for the first time by Italian ballerina Virginia Zucchi. Romantic and classical tutus are still worn today in performances of nineteenth-century ballets.

The modern tutu, made from multiple layers of tarlatan, tulle, silk or nylon, is much shorter and flimsier than earlier tutus. It leaves the whole leg free and visible, something that occurred with Marie Taglioni's tutu only when the skirt swirled up during energetic high jumps or lifts.

NEW STEPS TO SAVE THE GREAT BALLETS

In 1907, when Vaslav Nijinsky danced solo for the first time in public, his Russian audience went wild with delight. Nijinsky was then sixteen, and for the next decade he enjoyed the kind of success that others dream of. In the world's great ballet theatres he was revered for his expressive style, physical beauty and extraordinary combination of dancing skill and dramatic talent. Above all, his remarkable leaps, in which he seemed to defy gravity, left audiences gasping with admiration. He was said to go up like a rocket and come down like thistle-fluff.

Nijinsky choreographed four ballets during a career cut short in 1917 by schizophrenia, and three have disappeared. In his day, the only way to preserve a ballet was for it to be passed on from one generation of dancers to another, an inexact method because slight adaptations and alterations soon lost much of the original. If a ballet went out of fashion, it could disappear for ever. Nijinsky's insanity left him incapable of handing on his knowledge.

When he danced *L'après-midi d'un faune* in Paris in 1912, his mildly erotic choreography caused both shock and delight. The ballet vanished for years, but Dame Marie Rambert managed to recreate it, because she was one of the few who had seen it and had the skills to revive it.

Some Russian ballets escaped westwards during the revolution, because they were recorded in Stepanov notation, one of three ways to indicate a dancer's movements. In the United States, some 200 ballets are recorded in Labanotation, a complex but more precise method developed by Rudolf von Laban early this century. Labanotation uses three vertical lines, to the right and left of which are symbols representing the dancers' movements and positions. A third method, the Benesh system, invented by Rudolf Benesh in the 1950s, uses symbols to indicate the position of the head, arms, hands, feet and elbows. It is commonly used in Europe. A fault with all systems is that they take too much time to record and to understand. Recording one minute's ballet is about a six-hour job. Recently, film and video have

Nijinsky's great dancing *in* L'après-midi d'un faune *created uproar and joy. He is depicted in a 1912 design by artist Léon Bakst*

recorded dance movements, but these have technical problems. If the camera focuses closely on one dancer, it misses the broader action elsewhere on the stage. In a long shot, it may lose detailed movements and essential facial expressions.

Since the early 1980s, computer scientists have worked to develop recording programs using animated figures to simulate all the ingredients of a dancer's performance. Such programs require large computers, beyond the reach of most dance companies. But, just as computers of remarkable power are already in many homes, it seems certain that technology will soon help choreographers to preserve for all time their own individual artistry.

Why does the curtain 'rise' on a performance?

Even though theatre curtains may not rise these days on a performance – often they draw apart – we still talk about the curtain going up, and sometimes refer to the first item in any show as a curtain-raiser.

The curtain certainly did not rise in the Elizabethan theatre, because there was no curtain. Only after Charles II was restored to the throne in 1660 and Restoration theatre emerged in England was a curtain used in the proscenium arch in front of the stage. The prologue to the play was read in front of this curtain which then opened. It remained open until the end of the performance.

As scenes and acts ended, the audience gazed at an empty stage, or watched stage hands change the scenery, as happens today in many theatres that have no curtain or do not use one.

By the 1750s, the curtain fell to mark the end of the act and the beginning of an interval. Many theatres avoided this elaborate procedure by substituting an act-drop, a simple painted cloth.

In 1880, during a performance in London of *The Corsican Brothers*, a popular English adaptation of a French play, the curtain was used for the first time to hide scene changes. They were made so fast that the curtain was never closed for more than forty seconds. During the nineteenth century, a short and usually humorous one-act play, a curtain-raiser, was sometimes performed in front of the closed curtains to allow latecomers to find their seats before the main play began. For the same reason, later plays

rarely opened with action of any consequence, which explains why so many feature the maid dusting the living room.

The earliest theatre curtains were French valance in style; cords passed through rings at the back of the curtain, so that it rose vertically in a series of billowing folds. Today's curtains are in three styles, only one of which rises or flies straight up. Some open sideways, like most household curtains; others move both sideways and vertically to bunch at the top corners.

Increasingly, the fashion is to dispense with curtains and return to the style of Shakespeare's day. And in many theatres the doors close when the performance begins, locking out latecomers until an interval and allowing the cast to get immediately into the action without the need for any kind of curtain-raiser.

Movies for the millions

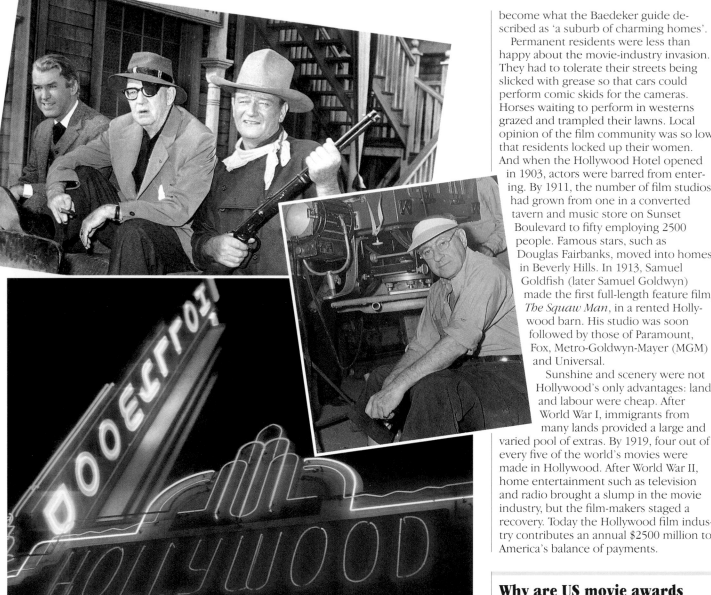

Actors and directors in the booming American film industry soon became household names. Few directors won greater fame than Cecil B. DeMille (inset) and John Ford, seen above flanked by actors John Wayne, a star of western movies, and James Stewart. Hollywood, too, became world famous, a synonym for filmland, with its name in lights as on this cinema in Hollywood Boulevard

become what the Baedeker guide described as 'a suburb of charming homes'.

Permanent residents were less than happy about the movie-industry invasion. They had to tolerate their streets being slicked with grease so that cars could perform comic skids for the cameras. Horses waiting to perform in westerns grazed and trampled their lawns. Local opinion of the film community was so low that residents locked up their women. And when the Hollywood Hotel opened in 1903, actors were barred from entering. By 1911, the number of film studios had grown from one in a converted tavern and music store on Sunset Boulevard to fifty employing 2500 people. Famous stars, such as Douglas Fairbanks, moved into homes in Beverly Hills. In 1913, Samuel Goldfish (later Samuel Goldwyn) made the first full-length feature film, *The Squaw Man*, in a rented Hollywood barn. His studio was soon followed by those of Paramount, Fox, Metro-Goldwyn-Mayer (MGM) and Universal.

Sunshine and scenery were not Hollywood's only advantages: land and labour were cheap. After World War I, immigrants from many lands provided a large and varied pool of extras. By 1919, four out of every five of the world's movies were made in Hollywood. After World War II, home entertainment such as television and radio brought a slump in the movie industry, but the film-makers staged a recovery. Today the Hollywood film industry contributes an annual $2500 million to America's balance of payments.

Why did Hollywood become the centre of the movie industry?

In 1887, when Daeida Wilcox suggested Hollywood as a name for the family's ranch, she could have had no idea of how the place would win worldwide fame. The 50-hectare (123-acre) ranch, just 13 km (8 miles) northwest of Los Angeles, was five days by train from New York, seemingly the natural centre for the new and burgeoning movie-picture industry. New York was the nation's financial centre. It was also its theatrical heart, although serious Broadway actors were at first reluctant to belittle themselves by appearing in what were called 'flickers'.

Early this century, New York–based movie companies occasionally filmed on location in the Hollywood region, where they had access to a wider variety of scenery, from mountains and valleys to deserts and coastlines. Photographic film of the time was a fraction of the speed of that used by movie cameramen today and demanded bright light. Southern California provided abundant sunshine.

Film-makers built a number of crude, outdoor sets close to the hills near Hollywood which, because of its proximity to downtown Los Angeles, had already

Why are US movie awards called Oscars?

When the US Academy of Motion Picture Arts and Sciences made its first awards for the outstanding achievements in cinema of 1927–28, the occasion had none of the show-biz pomp that accompanies it today. Since then, almost everything in the movie industry has changed, but Hollywood's token of excellence, a bronze-gilt statuette, 34 cm (13½ in) high, remains the same, but is even more coveted.

The figure was designed, according to some authorities, by MGM's senior art director, Cedric Gibbons, who sketched it on a tablecloth at a Hollywood banquet. The first awards were presented in May 1929. Argument continues about who first named the statuette an Oscar. Movie historians agree that the words 'just like my Uncle Oscar' were first uttered in 1931 by somebody in the film industry who took a close look at the figure. Some say

Smiles of triumph from Oscar winners Emma Thompson and Al Pacino, voted best actress and best actor in 1993. Pacino was successful at his sixth nomination

that Oscar was Oscar Pierce of Texas, uncle of one of the academy's executive secretaries. Others claim that Margaret Herrick, the academy's librarian, made the remark, referring to her own uncle. And many attribute the saying to actress Bette Davis or to film columnist Sidney

Skolsky. Whoever said it, the name stuck, and in 1966 became the title for a film, *The Oscar*, which had a cast of stars but won little acclaim from the critics.

The process for awarding Oscars has changed several times. Today, as in 1929, only academy members may nominate films and actors for awards, but the academy now has just over 5000 members, well over 100 times the original number. The Oscars are the oldest and most publicised of all film awards, and have the greatest impact on box-office success. *Ben Hur*, made for a second time in 1959, won eleven Oscars, one more than *Gone with the Wind*. These two films head the all-time list of winners.

The Oscar ceremonies have rarely escaped controversy. In 1937, Dudley Nichols, a member of the Screenwriters' Guild, made history by becoming the first winner to refuse his Oscar. The guild was at that time in dispute with the academy about labour relations. In later years, George C. Scott and Marlon Brando also refused to accept their awards.

What surprises many people is not those who have won awards but those who haven't. Edward G. Robinson was never nominated. Henry Fonda, nominated first in the 1940s, had to wait forty years before winning with his performance in *On Golden Pond*. Paul Newman was nominated, but did not win, for his role as 'Fast' Eddie in *The Hustler* (1961); twenty-five years later he played the same character in *The Color of Money* and won. But the Oscars list doesn't include two of the most famous stars of all time, Charles Chaplin and Greta Garbo. The academy honoured Chaplin late in his life with a special tribute at its Oscar ceremony.

Why have movie gimmicks rarely caught on?

Advertisements for the 1952 movie *Bwana Devil* promised filmgoers the sensation of having a lion in their laps. The movie, set in Africa, used a 3-D (for three-dimensional) technique, intended to give viewers the impression of being part of events on the screen, rather than looking in on them.

Three-dimensional movies were shot by two cameras, and the two separate films were projected simultaneously on to the screen. To unscramble the result, viewers entering a cinema were given special 3-D spectacles, which had one green lens and one red. The impression of watching an actual event, rather than a two-dimensional picture of one, was often realistic and alarming. When the 1953 movie *House of Wax* was shown, theatregoers ducked en masse as a ball was hit fiercely towards them.

Experiments with 3-D movies started as early as 1915, and *Power of Love*, made in 1922, was the first full-length feature of its kind. But it was the success of *Bwana Devil*, made thirty years later, that began the 3-D boom. In the year following its release, some forty 3-D movies were made. The bubble burst, however, and the gimmick quickly lost its mass appeal. Movie producers give several reasons for

Movies in 3-D were a short-lived fad but they gave a swift fortune to 3-D inventor Milton Gunzberg. As America's sole distributor of glasses essential for viewing 3-D films, he made a rapid $6.24 million, more than the profits of any 3-D movie

the technique's short-lived popularity. Projecting the two film strips needed precise synchronisation. If one film slipped even slightly behind, the effect was entirely ruined. Issuing plastic glasses to every viewer was an expense that film-makers and cinemas could not recoup even from larger audiences.

Three-dimensional films were just one of several experiments in the 1950s to meet competition from television. Drive-ins ('no babysitter needed'), colour films, the wide-screen techniques of Cinerama, Cinemascope and Panavision all suc-ceeded, but these weren't gimmicks. Smell-O-Vision undoubtedly was. It sent appropriate odours, such as that of bacon cooking on the stove, wafting through the theatre to give a movie hoped-for realism. Usually, such tricks brought unwanted laughs. Smell-O-Vision quickly joined 3-D on the movie-maker's scrapheap.

Nothing could stop the march of televi-sion, except its constant shortage of mate-rial. Learning from an old-time maxim that 'if you can't beat them, join them', Hollywood found new life by making movies for television.

Why are Fred and Ginger the world's best-known dance partners?

Fred Astaire and sister Adele were childhood vaudeville stars who became live Broadway per-formers. Adele, the elder, was said to be 'the talented one' and Fred her reliable partner. The pair danced together for some twenty years until Adele married Lord Charles Cavendish in 1932. Fred danced with Ginger Rogers for only six years in the 1930s, yet they are linked like peaches and cream in a way that Fred and Adele never were.

Ginger Rogers was not Fred's first screen partner. In his first film, *Danc-ing Lady*, made in 1933, he danced briefly with star Joan Crawford. And in *Flying Down to Rio*, also produced in 1933, he danced two numbers with leading lady Delores del Rio. But the hit of that movie was the pairing of Fred and Ginger in a Latin-American dance called 'The Carioca'. A new partnership was born. Ginger's earthy, rather brash ap-proach complemented Fred's genteel, refined style. Critics said that Fred, older by eleven years, gave Ginger some class and she gave him some sex appeal.

From 1934–37, they made two films a year, of which the best known are *Top Hat* and *Swing Time*. The magic of their seem-ingly effortless dancing – a mixture of

Fred and Ginger step it out for the last time in the 1949 film, The Barkleys of Broadway. *Critics say that* Shall We Dance?, *made in 1937, marked their peak. Rogers remains Astaire's best-known partner but for all their success he was not happy about her*

ballroom, ballet and tap – was backed by magnificent sets, plus music by George Gershwin and Irving Berlin. Their films were an ideal antidote to the Depression, and helped bring a revival in ballroom dancing. They were among few to make RKO Studios a profit at that time.

Most filmgoers believed that Fred and Ginger had the ideal partnership, but he was never really happy about it. They made their last film together in 1949, after which Fred danced with such stars as Judy Garland and Rita Hayworth. But screen historians and fans agree that no later combination matched that of Astaire and Rogers, a verdict reinforced by countless televised repeats of their films. Ginger stayed with RKO, and starred in several comedies and dramas. She never won an Oscar during her partnership with Fred Astaire, but was awarded one in 1940 for a dramatic, non-dancing role in *Kitty Foyle*.

Why did Walt Disney invent Mickey Mouse?

The great cartoonist and animator, Walt Disney, had a basic rule to guide his work. His unflagging optimism and faith in his own abilities urged him always to 'Think tomorrow'. The maxim got him through some of his greatest crises.

None was greater than when he took a trip from California to New York in the late 1920s to negotiate a new distribution contract for his cartoons starring Oswald the Rabbit. He discovered that the distributor owned all rights to the rabbit and had signed up Disney's key artists.

On the train ride home, Disney took his sketchpad to work out a new idea. Suddenly, he remembered a cheeky fieldmouse that had sat on his drawing board during his early days in Kansas City. He turned the mouse into a character, and named him Mortimer Mouse. Disney's wife Lilly objected strongly to the name Mortimer – 'a horrible name for a mouse'. So Walt suggested Mickey.

The friendly little mouse with the shy smile and buoyant spirit cheered Americans during the Depression and millions of moviegoers worldwide. It became the symbol for an international entertainment empire, which includes Disney World in Florida and Disneylands in California, Tokyo and near Paris.

Disney's faith in Mickey Mouse saw him through the character's two early failures in which the cartoons were silent. Thinking of tomorrow, he adapted his idea. He produced *Steamboat Willie*, the first

A cheeky fieldmouse inspired Walt Disney to create Mickey Mouse. Mickey's soundtrack was always spoken by Disney

animated talkie, in November 1928, and scored an enormous hit. That success spurred others. In 1937, he made *Snow White and the Seven Dwarfs*, the first feature-length cartoon. Nearly sixty years later, it remains one of the biggest money-earning movies of all time.

Another Disney maxim was always to strive for lasting quality. He refused to release a film until he was satisfied that it would stand the test of time. In 1938, he suspended production of *Pinocchio* because he said the film had no heart. 'Humour involves both laughter and tears,' he said. He made many expensive changes to the film which increased its cost to $2.6 million, about $1.1 million more than *Snow White*'s.

Why is Marilyn Monroe still so famous?

Marilyn Monroe died more than thirty years ago, but her spell lingers on.

Mann's Chinese Theatre in Los Angeles has a forecourt with the handprints, footprints and signatures of famous screen actors. The centrepiece, a golden-coloured block, features Marilyn's. Every day, young girls who never saw a Monroe film when she was alive, peer curiously at her footprints, and try to match their own handprints with hers.

Movie directors and critics have tried many times to explain Marilyn Monroe's extraordinary success in films and her lasting attraction. 'It wasn't her body, because there were many women just as

Marilyn Monroe's magic puzzled Dame Sybil Thorndike when the pair acted together in The Prince and the Showgirl. *Dame Sybil never discovered the secret of Marilyn's sparkle*

beautiful,' said director George Cukor. 'Her power came from her eyes and the way she looked at you.'

Billy Wilder, who directed many of her films, said that Marilyn Monroe had a superb ear for dialogue, particularly comedy. She delivered the most suggestive lines with a tone of sweet naivety, making them sound amusing and tender.

American poet Delmore Schwartz wrote, 'She can be understood only from one point of view.... Her poise and carriage have a true innocence.' Certainly, Marilyn Monroe for all her sex appeal was never vulgar or obscene.

Writer Maurice Zolotow, who knew Marilyn for many years, said that off screen she often passed unrecognised in the streets. On screen, she looked more powerful and entrancing than she ever did on the set. Dame Sybil Thorndike, who acted with Monroe in *The Prince and the Showgirl*, studied prints of Marilyn's films to try to discover why scenes that seemed quite flat on the set were unbelievably vibrant on the screen. She never managed to find the secret and nor did anybody else.

Monroe, born Norma Jean Baker in 1926, made only twenty-eight films, and in a dozen of those she was not the star. Of the rest, many have become classics. Millions of movie-watchers see her films reshown today on television, which is undoubtedly one reason for her lasting fame. But, unlike movies that wilt under such exposure, Monroe's gain more fans, seduced by her magic. Whatever lies behind her spell – beauty, innocence, comedy – it shows few signs of vanishing.

The things we do for fun

Why are fairground merry-go-rounds called carousels?

Over the years many words have changed their meaning. In doing so, few have travelled so far and for so long as carousel, which today means a merry-go-round and once meant a little war or a war game. The original little wars or war games were played by Arabic, Moorish and Turkish horsemen in the twelfth century. Opposing teams of highly skilled horsemen fought mock battles, hurling clay balls as they charged towards one another. The balls were strongly perfumed to give evidence of a hit. In other war games, horsemen lanced rings suspended between posts.

Brought to Europe by returning Crusaders, the sport became known in Italy as *carosello* and in France as *carrousel*. It was a popular court and military event, especially in France during the reign of Louis XIV, when extravagant tournaments were staged in the Place du Carrousel, a large square in Paris between the Tuileries and the Louvre.

In 1680, the French devised a mechanical device to train young nobles in the art of ring-spearing for the *carrousel*. Model horses were suspended by chains from arms radiating from a central pole. A mule tethered to the centre turned the pole, so that the horses and their riders revolved. As they did so, the young noblemen made practice thrusts with their lances through rings set on poles outside the perimeter of this primitive roundabout.

In the early nineteenth century, showmen added carousel rides to all the other fun of the fair. The first fairground carousels were turned by hand or by horse. Then came the steam engine, which gave the carousel and other fairground rides new life. Carousels became bigger and more elaborate, with three rows of horses galloping to the music of a pipe organ, while the engine puffed its unforgettable aroma of steam.

To international travellers, a carousel today is where they collect luggage at journey's end. But for those who have known great days at the fair, the word will surely revive memories of gaily painted prancing horses, laughing children and that unmistakable fairground music.

Why are roller coasters the world's most popular funfair ride?

Ever since the early nineteenth century, when the French first put wheeled cars on a track to imitate a Russian ice-slide, funfairs have worked hard to satisfy demands for higher, faster and more terrifying roller coasters. Frightening these may be, but across the world thrill-seeking patrons queue and pay for the joy of being scared almost to death.

Funfair owners can afford to invest millions of dollars in a new roller coaster, confident that riders will soon repay the

Built to thrill, roller coasters are getting higher and faster. The limit, say designers, is determined not by engineering but by what the human body can stand

investment. When the world's highest roller coaster opened in 1989 at Cedar Point, Ohio, more than 1.8 million people rode it during the first year. Another, planned to open in 1994 at Blackpool, England, will be 70 m (230 ft) high, 10 m (33 ft) higher than that in Ohio, and a guaranteed money-spinner.

The earliest roller coasters built up suspense with a slow but very steep ascent, followed by a fast, twisting run back to earth. Today's rides turn on the terror with a series of hurtling bends and stomach-churning loops. For the comfort of nervous riders, loops are usually teardrop-shaped, not circular, to minimise the chances of a car hurling itself off the rails.

On a roller-coaster ride, the laws of physics and anatomy join forces. The physical effects of this union give the rides their great attraction. In the steepest roller-coaster descents, the g-force exerted on the human body is, for a few seconds, equal to three times that of normal gravity. The effect is equivalent to accelerating from standstill to 134 km/h (83 mph) in one second.

The biggest roller coasters sit higher than a space shuttle waiting on the launch pad. But astronauts within the shuttle are strapped firmly into padded couches to withstand the g-forces inflicted during takeoff. On a roller-coaster ride the car is wide open; only a safety bar, gripped by white knuckles, gives any comfort.

The physical feeling of having left the stomach at the bottom of a fearsome loop is caused by the downward force exerted

Painted horses prance and music plays as the carousel gives another joy-filled ride. It's hard to believe that today's fairground fun began with war games and charging lancers

on the liver. That light-headed sense of weightlessness comes when blood rushes from the brain to the buttocks, legs and feet. Hoarse, dry throats are a guarantee that riders are getting their money's worth: the dryness comes from involuntary screams of fear.

On fast bends, roller-coaster cars reach speeds of about 110 km/h (68 mph). Wheels positioned in groups of three – one on the inside of the rail, one below and one above – ensure that the risk of a car flying off the rails or of metal fatigue in the track are minimal. Roller-coaster operators say that computerised controls, monitoring consoles and remote sensors to detect metal fatigue reduce the risk of accident to six in 100 million.

Why is a circus held in a ring?

In the Circus Maximus, the first and largest circus in the Roman world, gladiators, charioteers, wild beasts and hapless slaves were on show in a vast, oval arena 600 m (660 yd) long by 200 m (220 yd) wide. The fall of the Roman Empire saw an end to the enormous bloodshed of the Roman circus.

In the late eighteenth century, the circus – Latin for ring – emerged again as a form of entertainment. In 1768, Philip Astley developed the first modern circus at his riding school near Blackfriars, London. A former NCO in the Light Dragoons, the flamboyant Astley sat in full military uniform astride his horse and, with his sword, directed paying customers to their seats around the ring. Within the ring, Astley and his wife gave displays of trick riding, and soon discovered that standing bareback on a horse

The circus art of daredevil riding, as painted by Georges Seurat in 1891, started in Europe's equestrian schools. When fairs declined in the late eighteenth century, acrobats, jugglers and other entertainers joined the circus

Bring on the clowns for the annual service in London to Joseph Grimaldi (inset), one of the greatest clowns of all. Grimaldi's act left him crippled, and he made his farewell sitting in a chair on the stage

was easier if the horse cantered in a circle about 13 m (14 yd) in diameter.

Horses and their riders were the true stars of the early circuses, showing a mixture of skills that combined daredevil, acrobatic riding with superb training. Other acts were introduced later only to provide variety. As late as the first decades of this century, circus owners were still primarily horsemen.

Why do clowns wear make-up and baggy clothes?

Circus clowns adopted their distinctive make-up and clothes in imitation of the world-famous Joseph Grimaldi. As a child, Grimaldi played small parts in pantomimes. His mother was a dancer in the chorus line at London's Drury Lane Theatre, and his father was a former ballet master. At Drury Lane in 1800, Grimaldi, then twenty-one, played a clown for the first time. Over the next twenty years he became London's funniest and the world's best-known clown.

Grimaldi was the first to wear the brightly coloured baggy trousers, tufted hair and make-up that we associate today with circus clowns. But he appeared only in the theatre and never in a circus. His acrobatic act crippled him, and in 1823 he was forced to retire. He passed on a legacy that lasts to this day.

Before Grimaldi perfected his stylish and original performance, clowns were traditionally either ruddy-cheeked country yokels or stupid servants. Grimaldi gave the servant's livery bright patterns and gaily-coloured breeches. He made the breeches baggy to hide all the objects, usually food such as fish and sausages, that he pilfered as part of his act. He exaggerated his ruddy complexion by drawing red triangles on his cheeks, and gave his cockscomb haircut three gaudy and amusing tufts.

The white make-up used by clowns since the nineteenth century is now greasepaint, not the zinc oxide, lard and tincture of benzoin of Grimaldi's day. All clowns develop their own distinctive face, which they establish as theirs alone by painting it on an egg.

With their make-up and characteristic clothes, clowns remain the only act in a circus that needs no introduction from the ringmaster. Among them and within the circus, where clowns are commonly known as joeys, Joseph Grimaldi's legend lives on. Each year in London, circus clowns still gather to pay tribute to him at a traditional memorial service.

Pastimes full of pleasure

Why are playing cards divided into four suits?

The world had its first pack of cards between about 1000 and 1400 years ago. In China and Korea, ancient fortune-telling sticks marked with symbols became tokens in gambling games. The symbols were later painted onto long, narrow strips of oiled paper, the first playing cards. Korean cards had eight suits – man, fish, crow, pheasant, antelope, star, rabbit and horse. Chinese cards had only three, which were cash or *t'sin*, strings of cash or *sok* and many strings of cash or *man*.

Because playing cards were usually made of paper or cardboard, which quickly disintegrated, tracing their history is difficult. Much of what we know about them comes, surprisingly, from the covers of old books. Bookbinders in medieval Europe often used waste paper, including sheets of uncut playing cards, to bind their products.

From the French came the packs of fifty-two cards that are most commonly used today. These probably evolved from the numbered cards of the tarot deck. According to legend, in 1392 courtiers attempted to cheer up the gloomy Charles VI by commissioning Jacquemin Gringonneur to make three packs of cards. The artist painted what were probably tarot cards in many colours on a golden ground. The cards did nothing to improve the royal mood. Later that year, the king was declared insane, but historians can't say whether incessant games of cards caused his madness.

Arab traders, nomadic gypsies, returning Crusaders, conquering Moors and even Marco Polo are credited with bringing cards to Europe by the late fourteenth century. From these playing cards, three sets of emblems evolved, and all had four suits. In Italian–Spanish packs, the suits were swords, cups, coins or rosettes, and clubs or batons. Each suit had three royal cards – king, cavalier and knave.

Some historians believe these cards came originally from India, where playing cards showed a figure that is half Siva, the destroyer god, and half Devi, his wife. The four hands held a cup, a sword, a coin and a baton.

The four suits in German cards are said to be based on the four classes of society: hearts represented the Church, bells stood for the hawk bells of the nobility, leaves for the middle classes and acorns for the peasants. The royal cards were king, queen, upper-valet and under-valet.

In the mid-fifteenth century, French cards were divided into four suits: *piques* or pikes, *coeur* (hearts), *trèfle* (clubs) and *carreau* (diamonds). To the English, the French symbol of a pikestaff's tip looked like a spade. *Trèfle* comes from the French for trefoil, or clover; the clubs symbol resembles a clover leaf. *Carreau* or diamonds is based on the shape of paving stones found in some French churches. The French, too, divided the suits into two red and two black.

The court cards were originally named after figures of history, mythology and the Bible. The king of hearts, for example, was Charlemagne, while Argine was queen of clubs and Hector jack of diamonds. Later, the court cards lost their distinctive names and became king, queen and knave or jack, as they are known today. During the French Revolution, the guillotine came down on court cards: new cards were printed in which popular figures replaced those of the king, queen and jack.

Why does a boomerang come back?

For 15 000 years, Aboriginal Australians used boomerangs to kill animals, birds and lizards for food. The weapons, made from heavy wood, flew hard and straight, and didn't return to the thrower.

The Aboriginals discovered that other boomerangs, shaped roughly like a

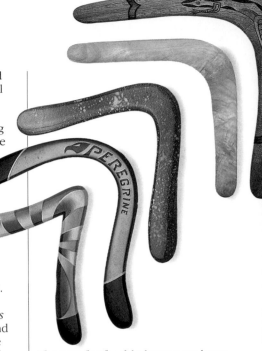

The comeback of the boomerang began when Aboriginals used them for fun, not as weapons. All these are non-traditional boomerangs made to throw in competitions

banana, would curve in flight; if fashioned and thrown correctly, they returned to their starting point. Throw and catch became an Aboriginal sport.

Boomerangs don't need to be banana-shaped to curve in flight. Pieces of wood assembled to form a T, V, X or Y also will perform in this way. The key factor is that each spoke or leg in the design must, in cross section, be curved on the top and flatter on the bottom. Shaped like this, it acts like an aircraft's wing.

When thrown properly, a returning boomerang flies at up to 100 km/h (about 60 mph). Also it spins swiftly, maybe a dozen times a second, so that its legs or wings give it lift. If held almost upright and thrown, a boomerang behaves like an aircraft and a gyroscope in one, performing complex flight patterns explained only by aerodynamics and physics.

In flight, a boomerang is unstable. Its spinning action means that, in a simple V-shaped boomerang, the right wing becomes in turn the left, but then moves in the opposite direction. When it is the right wing and is moving forward, it has more lift. This instability, with the right wing constantly having more lift than the left one, tilts the boomerang to the left.

The spinning action, like that of a top, drags the boomerang back to the horizontal. The result is that a boomerang thrown strongly by a right-handed person will at first shoot upwards, then flatten out. It will curve to the left before tipping slowly to the right. Swinging leftwards in a wide loop, it will arrive back at the thrower. If it has sufficient power and isn't stopped by the thrower, the boomerang will take an elaborate, figure-of-eight flight path.

Playing cards as we know them were designed by the French, who gave names to the court cards. Rachel was the queen of diamonds

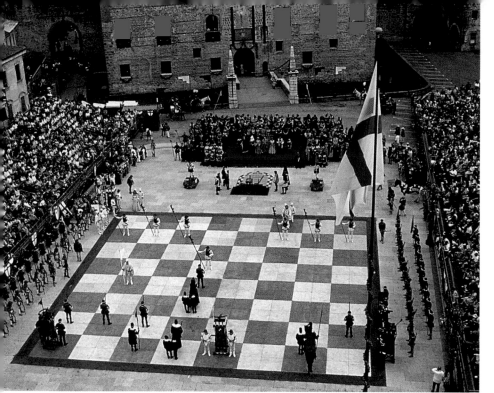

Chess is alive and well in Marostica, Italy, where every two years people act as chessmen. Knights ride horses, and page boys attend the kings and queens. The custom goes back to 1454, when two gentlemen, forbidden to fight a duel, played a chess match for the right to marry a local beauty

Why do we say 'checkmate' in chess?

In what was once the Soviet Union, some seven million people regularly play chess. They are following an ancient tradition. Two ancient figurines, believed to be chessmen, were found in Uzbekistan in 1972, and date back to AD 200.

Our game developed from the Indian war game of Chaturanga, meaning four corps, which were chariots, elephants, cavalry and infantry, the predecessors of rooks, bishops, knights and pawns. But the language of chess, including the term checkmate, is Persian. Historians say that chess was brought from Persia by the Arabs, and reached Europe in about the tenth century.

Despite its ancient origins, chess got international rules only in this century. As different European countries took up the game, they devised their own rules. When the chess champion of Lombardy met the Spanish champion in 1290, lawyers decided that the players should follow the rules of the country staging the match. François-André Philidor, a musician who in the eighteenth century became one of France's greatest chess champions, refused to abide by this ancient decision, and the move began for international rules.

In 1924, the Fédération Internationale des Echecs, the world governing body, set down rules that are now followed everywhere. Under these, a player must say *échec* or check when the opposing king is in a position where he could be captured. If the king cannot escape from the threat

he is checkmated, ending the game. The term checkmate has nothing to do with mating and more to do with dying. It comes from the Persian *shah mat*, meaning 'The king is dead.'

Why do teenagers dance in a disco?

The French word *discothèque*, meaning a record library, kept that meaning until September 1960. In that month, Chubby Checker had a hit record with *The Twist*, and the smart sets of New York, Paris and London took up a new dance craze. A Paris nightclub where café society gathered became the first discotheque. The owner installed loudspeakers, and hired a young man to choose and announce each record. The coolness of dancing without any physical contact to music from a human jukebox was an immediate success.

For a time the trend was confined to smart clubs, but by the late 1960s discotheques were operating at private parties. Pubs and clubs took the craze to larger groups. The record industry had a large and ready-made market for a different kind of music, dominated by a heavy bass rhythm designed for dancing rather than singing.

With the 1976 release of *Saturday Night Fever*, starring John Travolta, the discotheque had come of age, with its own music, dance style, dress code and a new set of teenage fans.

Why is Monopoly a worldwide winner?

Board games were played by the ancient Egyptians, and Roman emperor Nero was not only a fiddler but a high-stakes gambler at a form of backgammon. But, in the long history of board games, Monopoly is a hands-down winner.

Charles Darrow of Philadelphia, an unemployed heating equipment salesman, invented Monopoly in 1932, in the depths of the Great Depression. He tried to sell it to Parker Brothers, and the firm turned him down. Undaunted, Darrow had 5000 sets made and sold them all, proving that the game had considerable appeal. In 1935, Parker Brothers had second thoughts, and marketed the game on a national scale with phenomenal success, making Darrow a millionaire.

Since then, sales have reached about 100 million, with two million Monopoly sets sold every year. In most years, the output of Monopoly money has a face value exceeding that of notes issued by the US Treasury. What makes the game so popular? Psychologists say that it appeals to the tycoon lurking in all of us.

'Twist and shout' became the smart set's cry in the 1960s after Chubby Checker started a new dance craze

The greatest show on Earth

decided unanimously to restart the games. That year, Baron de Coubertin published his famous edict supporting 'the supreme importance of preserving the noble and chivalrous character of athletics against professionalism'.

The first games in Athens in 1896 drew enthusiastic crowds, but the Paris Olympics in 1900 were overshadowed by the Paris Exposition. For a festival desperate to capture public support, the revived Olympics had the clear disadvantage of occurring too rarely. De Coubertin had no intention of letting the flame die out.

In those early years he was supported by Father Henri-Martin Didon, Dominican

The high priest of Olympism was Baron Pierre de Coubertin who aimed at emulating the best that the ancient Greeks had to offer. The reborn Olympic Games in Athens in 1896 were an instant success

Why were the Olympic Games revived?

Frenchman Pierre de Fredy, better known as Baron de Coubertin, is usually credited with reviving the Olympic Games in modern form. In fact, moves to restart the Olympics had existed for at least two centuries. From 1612 until 1852, with a break during the Civil War, the Cotswold Olimpick Games were held in rural England. (They were revived in 1963.) In 1852, German archaeologist Ernst Curtius, who had worked with others on excavations at Olympia, site of the ancient games, suggested restarting the Olympics. But it took de Coubertin's zeal to give the movement real pace.

After visiting Rugby and Eton schools in England as a young man, de Coubertin advocated that French schoolchildren would gain more from physical sports than from studying Latin verse. As a result, schools introduced organised games and interschool competition. The government then turned to him to promote an international conference on physical education. De Coubertin took up the idea of reviving the Olympics, and preached it in London and the United States.

In 1894, seventy-nine delegates from thirteen countries attended the first International Olympic Congress in Paris, and

prior of Arceuil College, in Paris. He wanted all his pupils to practise sport, and gave them a maxim: *Citius, Altius, Fortius* (Faster, Higher, Stronger) which became the Olympic motto, used first at the Antwerp games in 1920.

In 1908, when the games were held in London, de Coubertin attended a service in St Paul's Cathedral to mark the fourth Olympiad. The Bishop of Pennsylvania preached a sermon about the value of competing in the Olympic Games. The message inspired de Coubertin, and he enlarged it: 'The important thing in the Olympic Games is not winning but to take part. The essential thing in life is not conquering but fighting well.'

Since 1932, scoreboards have displayed the words at ceremonies opening the games. The proclamation is at odds with the spirit of the ancient Olympics, where to win was everything. In recent times, as many have observed, competitors and nations are doing their best to revive the Greek tradition. De Coubertin was the

driving force to get the games restarted, capturing and enlarging a minor wave of interest. His enthusiasm and promotional instincts – he had a hand also in designing the Olympic flag – nurtured the movement through its early years, when it was in danger of petering out. Without his work, the Olympics would not be the mighty festival it is today.

Why is there doubt about the origins of the Olympics?

Many historians give the year we now reckon as 776 BC to be that in which the ancient Olympics were revived at Olympia, in the city-state of Elis.

The site had long been sacred to the god Zeus and a focus of religious worship. For centuries the Greeks had linked athletic achievement with religion, and the earliest games or festivals, dating back to 1000 BC or earlier, were dominated by religious ritual, such as sacrifices and acts of atonement. The twenty-third book of Homer's *Iliad* refers to a festival of games accompanying funeral rites.

Close study reveals no evidence that these festivals were suddenly discontinued and then restarted. What is certain is that athletic competition gradually became more important. By 776 BC, it was paramount. The only competitive event in those games was a great foot race of about 200 m (220 yd), won by Coroebus, a local cook, who was crowned with a

Hundreds of reporters, part of a total contingent of 15 000 journalists, watch the 1992 Barcelona games. Rights to televise the event fetched more than $600 million

wreath of wild olive. The leaves were said to have come from a tree brought back by Heracles from the mythical paradise of the Hyperboreans, and planted in the sacred grove near the Temple of Zeus at Olympia.

Archaeologists cast further doubt that the ancient games had a sudden rebirth in 776 BC. They know that an altar of Zeus and other monuments within the original stadium date back to the tenth century BC. Greek poets, too, tell of mighty contests held there. According to Pindar, Zeus fought on this site with his father Kronos for mastery of the world. But what is legend and what is truth is too difficult now to establish with certainty, and Coroebus remains the first Olympic victor.

The ancient games were held every four years until AD 393, when the Roman emperor Theodosius I banned them and other Greek festivals as pagan.

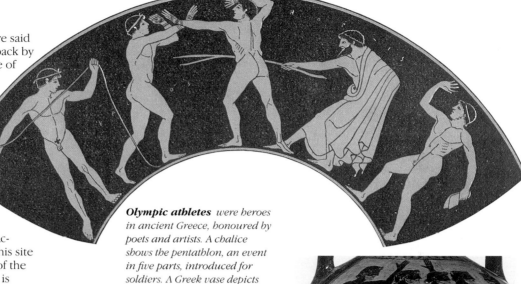

Olympic athletes were heroes in ancient Greece, honoured by poets and artists. A chalice shows the pentathlon, an event in five parts, introduced for soldiers. A Greek vase depicts competitors in a footrace

Why aren't the Olympics always held in Greece?

When the first International Olympic Congress decided in 1894 to revive the games, Baron de Coubertin wanted them to be held in Paris. De Coubertin, pioneer of the modern Olympic movement, was keen to restore not only the games but France's dwindling national prestige.

Delegates from twelve other countries had other plans. Supported later by twenty-one others, they were keen to follow the romantic notion of restarting the Olympics in Greece. The Greeks themselves were even keener, and had the revival date advanced from the proposed 1900 to 1896.

In fact, the Greeks were ill prepared and desperately short of money. Moves were made to transfer the first games to Hungary. De Coubertin, anxious to avoid a fiasco, went to Greece and rallied support. Funds were raised to restore a stadium built in 300 BC, and on Easter Sunday, 1896, the Olympics were reborn.

When the International Congress met in 1897 to plan the next Olympics, delegates wanted to hold them again in Greece. De Coubertin argued successfully that the 1900 games should go to Paris. Such an event, he said, should be truly international.

The French, busy with the Paris Exposition, showed little interest. The games, which included angling in the Seine and a cricket match between England and France, were a flop. Until they received their medals, some athletes believed that they were competing in a meet associated with the world fair.

The St Louis Olympics of 1904 weren't much better. Again, a world fair overshadowed the games. De Coubertin himself did not travel to the United States to attend the event, and France didn't send a team. Sensing an opportunity, the Greeks tried then to regain the right to hold the games. They suggested that, every four years from 1906, an interim games should be held in Greece. Twenty-two countries sent competitors to the Athens games of 1906, but the event was not recognised officially, and the idea was abandoned.

Since then, Greece has not held an Olympics, although it once looked likely that Athens would host the centenary games of 1996. Today, cities around the world bid fiercely for the prestige of staging a festival that television continues to boost in size and interest.

Why were the Olympics restricted to amateurs?

The once-strict rules that banned professional sportsmen from Olympic competition would have excluded the heroes of ancient Greece. Those athletes were not amateurs. They were supported for almost a year in training. They received only an olive wreath for victory, but were richly rewarded on their return home.

In recent times, the concept of amateurism has changed considerably. Many competitors sponsored in a variety of ways take part in the games when in the past they would have been banned.

The Olympic rules about amateurism probably came from Britain, where they were encouraged to exclude working people from competing against the aristocracy. The wealthy could train and compete without having to worry about money. To have had money prizes would have enabled others to enter on almost equal terms.

Baron de Coubertin, the Olympics pioneer, took many ideas from Britain. Also, he campaigned constantly to preserve athletics from any taint of professionalism. He believed in what he called 'a natural elite', and said that the wealthy had a sacred duty to act as patrons to those of natural ability who could not afford to be full-time athletes.

Why is the marathon measured in yards not metres?

Ever since the Olympic Games were revived in Athens in 1896, competitors have run, walked, swum, rowed and ridden over courses measured in metric distances. Had another city hosted the first modern games, the marathon might never have been an Olympic event and one that today, outside the Olympics, attracts thousands of runners worldwide.

The Greeks included the race to commemorate the heroic feat of Pheidippides after the battle of Marathon in 490 BC. He is said to have run nonstop from the battlefield to Athens, a distance of about 40 km (25 miles), to announce an Athenian victory over the Persian invaders. He died uttering, in Greek, the words, 'Greetings, we conquer.'

The Athens marathon of 1896 was the only track-and-field event won by a Greek, and he was rewarded among other things with free shaves for life. The race was so popular that the event was held at the next two Olympics, but the course varied slightly in length.

When London staged the games in 1908, organisers were briefed to hold a marathon of about 25 miles. They decided that the Princess of Wales, watched by the royal grandchildren, should start the race on the lawns at Windsor Castle and that it should finish at the White City stadium, a distance of 26 miles to the entrance. Another 385 yd was added, so that the race could finish in front of King Edward VII and Queen Alexandra in the royal box. Since then, 26 miles 385 yd (or 42.195 km) has become the standard marathon distance.

Had competitors in the 1908 marathon run 'about 25 miles', the Olympic Games would almost certainly have lost one of its most dramatic and debatable moments. First into the stadium was a little Italian pastrycook named Dorando Pietri. He should have turned left towards the finishing line, but was so dazed from heat exhaustion that he turned right. Officials

Far in front, *Dorando Pietri heads for the stadium and drama in the 1908 marathon in London. His courage won lasting fame*

and policemen guided him back. Several times he fell on the track, and eventually was helped over the line.

After much argument, the race was awarded to an American, John Hayes, who finished second, about 150 yd (140 m) behind. But in Olympic history, Dorando, the gallant loser, is more famous than the winner, and is still known affectionately by his first name.

SYMBOL THAT LINKS THE WORLD

During the ancient Olympics a sacred truce reigned. All wars in the Greek world ceased, the death penalty was suspended, and safety was guaranteed to all competitors. The terms of the truce were said to be inscribed in five rings on the sacred discus of King Iphitus of Elis who, in 884 BC, first declared the armistice on the advice of the Delphic oracle. The truce applied to all rituals and festivals, and later to the Olympic Games.

Baron de Coubertin visited the site of the ancient games in Greece in 1913. He went also to Delphi, which in ancient times was the sanctuary of Apollo and where five linked rings were said to have decorated the altar. De Coubertin, keen to promote the international theme of the modern Olympics, saw at once the value of the symbol in his campaign. 'These five rings,' he wrote, 'represent the five parts of the world won over to Olympism and ready to accept its bountiful rivalries.'

A flag was designed using the five interlaced rings, each one distinctively coloured – blue, yellow, black, green and red – and set against a white background. 'The six colours combined in this way,' said de Coubertin, 'represent those of every nation without exception.'

The flag was flown for the first time in Paris in June 1914 at a congress marking the Olympic movement's twentieth anniversary. Ironically, a few weeks later, the outbreak of World War I caused the cancellation of the Olympics scheduled for Berlin in 1916.

The modern Olympic movement adopted the emblem in 1920, because of its suggested origins and also because the five rings represent the world's five continents.

Five interlaced rings *in the Olympic flag symbolise the five continents. They have a link, too, with ancient Greece*

Why are the Olympics held every four years?

The origins of the ancient Olympics are obscure, but it is certain that from 776 BC, the date usually given for the first festival, they took place every four years for more than 1000 years. The games, held at Olympia in Greece, were of tremendous prestige. Prizewinners became heroes.

The period between the start of one festival and another was known as an Olympiad. In 300 BC, the Greeks acknowledged the festival's importance by dating all events according to the number of the Olympiad in which they occurred.

When the Olympics were revived in 1896, organisers turned to the ancient games for inspiration, and adopted the original four-year timetable. They have never succeeded, however, in following the ancient festival's major principal of suspending hostilities during the games. Instead, no Olympics have been held during two world wars.

Why was Adolf Hitler allowed to stage the games?

The International Olympic Committee chose Berlin as the venue for the 1936 games in 1932, more than a year before Adolf Hitler and the Nazis came to power. The organising committee for the Berlin Olympics held its first meeting six days before Hitler's accession. Shortly after, its president, Dr Theodor Lewald, was threatened with dismissal because one of his grandparents had been Jewish. Jews in many countries proposed a boycott of the games. In the United States, their bid nearly succeeded.

Attempts were made to hold an alternative People's Olympics in Barcelona. These were cancelled almost as they were due to begin, because in 1936 civil war broke out in Spain.

Fears that Hitler would use the Olympics as an international stage to promote Nazism were justified. Swastika flags flew, German spectators raised their arms in the Nazi salute, and fervent shouts of 'Heil Hitler!' greeted German athletes. The spectacle was seen not only inside the stadium. These were the first televised games: twenty-five Berlin theatres installed large screens to enable thousands unable to buy tickets for the stadium to view the events and ceremony.

The Führer's hopes that the Berlin games would demonstrate his claims of Aryan superiority were shattered. If the 1936 Olympics are linked with Hitler, they are remembered equally for the triumphs of Jesse Owens, one of the black athletes

Hitler salutes to open the Berlin games in 1936. Successful German athletes, such as broad jumper Lutz Long, also gave Nazi salutes. Jesse Owens, winner of four gold medals, had a different response

whom the Nazis despised as 'auxiliaries'. Owens won four gold medals, and set a record in the broad jump that lasted for twenty-four years.

In setting that record, Owens showed superb sportsmanship. When German favourite Lutz Long developed cramp, Owens massaged him until he was able to jump again. The gesture restored faith among many spectators in the true Olympic ideals.

Why were no Olympics held in wartime?

Unlike the era of ancient Greece, when hostilities were suspended so that the Olympics could be held in peace, this century has seen the games called off while the wars go on.

The 1916 games, scheduled for Berlin, were cancelled because of World War I. The United States, a major participant in all modern Olympics till then, was still at peace. But too many problems had to be overcome to stage any Olympics and too many nations would have been absent.

The 1940 Olympics were awarded to Japan – the winter games to Sapporo and the summer games to Tokyo. When Japan invaded China in July 1937, the winter Olympics were rescheduled for Garmisch-Partenkirchen, Germany, where they had been held in 1936. In September 1939, Germany invaded Poland, and the 1940 winter games were cancelled. The 1940 summer games, rescheduled for Helsinki, were cancelled when Soviet troops invaded Finland.

Strangely, one might think, for a movement claiming such high ideals, organisers have banned nations vanquished in war from competing in Olympics held soon after a major conflict. Austria, Bulgaria, Germany, Hungary and Turkey were not invited to the 1920 games in Antwerp. Those Olympics were held in Belgium to compensate that country for the grief inflicted on it during World War I. When the games were held in London in 1948, three years after the end of World War II, Germany and Japan did not compete. Nor did the USSR, one of the victors, which then had no affiliations with the International Olympic Committee.

Why didn't women compete in the first modern Olympics?

When the Olympic Games were restarted in Athens in 1896, organisers understandably had the ancient Olympics as a model. The ancient festival, in honour of Zeus, had a strong religious element. It was open only to men, who competed naked. With a few exceptions, women were barred even as spectators; any who broke that rule could be sentenced to death.

The first modern Olympics allowed women to watch, but still barred them from competition. Until the 1928 games in Amsterdam, women competed only at

Events for women were restricted in early Olympics. The first woman champion was Britain's Charlotte Cooper (inset) who won the tennis singles in 1900. Suzanne Lenglen of France won two gold medals in the 1920 games at Antwerp

such sports as golf, tennis, fencing and swimming; even in these the events were few. In Amsterdam, women athletes were offered Olympic track-and-field events for the first time.

Their five events included an 800-m race, and it caused great controversy. After the race several contestants collapsed. Hardened traditionalists seized on the outcome as evidence for banning women from the games. The president of the International Olympic Committee, Comte de Baillet-Latour, urged a return to the ancient custom of an all-male Olympics. Others said that, because of their frailty, women should have no races longer than 200 m.

Newspapers quoted doctors who said that women were not suited to feats of endurance, which made them 'old too soon'. Feminists pointed out that in men's races athletes often fainted from exhaustion. In fact, if they didn't do so, they were often accused of 'not putting everything into it'.

The diehards prevailed. As a result, the Olympic Games had no women's races longer than half-a-lap of the track – 200 m – until 1964, when Betty Cuthbert of Australia won the 400 m. The 1500 m was introduced at Munich in 1972, the 3000 m and marathon at Los Angeles in 1984. Longer races for women on the track have been complemented by those in the swimming pool, so that today there is essentially no great difference between the programs for men and women.

Why does a torch ceremony open the games?

During the ancient games, sacred fires burned in many shrines within the Olympic enclosure. Legend has it that during the five-day festival these were never allowed to go out.

The custom of having a relay of runners carry a blazing torch from the site of the ancient Olympics to that of a modern celebration began at the Berlin games in 1936. Lit by the Sun's rays amid the ruins of the Temple of Zeus at Olympia, the flame travelled some 3200 km (nearly 2000 miles) through seven countries. Finally, after almost 4000 runners had transferred the flame from one magnesium torch to another, it was carried into Berlin's Olympic Stadium, where it burned spectacularly in a marble fire-font throughout the games.

Those games are remembered now as Hitler's Olympics, because the Nazi leader tried to turn them into a show of German might and efficiency. The torch ceremony, accompanied by a ritual of trumpet fanfares and cannon fire, was part of the showmanship.

At subsequent Olympics, organisers decided to retain the ceremony, despite its Nazi overtones. The flame has burned brightly at every games bar one. At Montreal, Canada, on July 27, 1976, a cloudburst extinguished it, but the stadium was closed for a rest day. Only workmen were inside. A plumber named Pierre Bouchard, using his cigarette lighter and a rolled-up newspaper, had the honour of rekindling the flame.

A Royal and Ancient game

The eighteenth hole *of the world's most famous golf course is in full view of the St Andrews clubhouse. It is said that Mary Queen of Scots played golf here*

Why is St Andrews said to be the home of golf?

Ask any golfer where the game began, and the answer almost certainly will be St Andrews, Scotland. The Scots are reluctant to admit it, but it is doubtful whether golf is a Scottish game. And there is no doubt that St Andrews, in Fife, wasn't the first of Scotland's golf clubs.

Searching for a game's origins has obvious difficulties. Records are poor. Ancient illustrations of men wielding clubs to strike what looks like a ball are open to many interpretations. Is the game golf, croquet or hockey? A window dated 1350 in Gloucester Cathedral, England, shows a scene in which a man appears to be hitting a golf ball. Historians argue that the game could be *paganica*, a Roman pastime, or *cambuca*, a similar English game, or a Flemish game called *chole*. In *chole*, players hit the ball towards a succession of targets – a door, a tree, a pole – making the game clearly similar to golf.

Another influence may have been *jeu de mail*, originally an Italian mallet game. The French developed a cross-country version. They exported *jeu de mail* to England, where it was known as pall (or pull) mall. This game is said also to be the forerunner of billiards and croquet. The London street, Pall Mall, is where the game was once played.

Loenen aan de Vecht in northern Holland could claim to be golf's birthplace. There, on Boxing Day, 1297, townspeople played four 'holes' of *colf* over a course of about 4800 m (5250 yd) to commemorate the relief of Kronenburg Castle. The holes were in fact doors – in a windmill, a kitchen, a courthouse and the castle. The game of *colf* was played at some forty different places in Holland until, suddenly and mysteriously, it lost favour to a shorter version called *kolf*.

Scotland's earliest references to golf go back to 1457, when James II decreed that 'Fute ball and Golfe be utterly cryit doune'. He feared that the two sports kept young men from becoming good bowmen. But golf took hold. In 1552, the people of St Andrews were given the right to play on the local course, and in the 1580s two irreverent hackers were found guilty and fined for playing at Leith on the Sabbath 'in tyme of the sermonsis'.

The 1740s saw the opening shots in a battle for golf supremacy. The Honourable Company of Edinburgh Golfers, the world's oldest club, drew up the first rules and, in 1744, held the first championship, for a silver club given by the City of Edinburgh.

Ten years later, twenty-two noblemen and gentlemen, 'admirers of the ancient and healthful exercise of the Golf' formed the St Andrews Society of Golfers. In 1834, the society played a stroke better than any ever made on the course: it invited William IV to become patron. The king agreed, and allowed the society to rename itself the Royal and Ancient Golf Club of St Andrews. The stroke was brilliantly timed: the Honourable Company in Edinburgh at that moment had no course: any claims that it was golf's birthplace would have met with derision. The Honourable Company was stymied and unable to recover.

The R & A became golf's ruling body and remains so (with help from the United States Golf Association). Its jurisdiction goes beyond the planet. In February 1971, Captain Alan Shepard, commander of the Apollo 14 space mission, hit two shots with a six-iron on the Moon. The R & A sent a telegram of congratulations, and drew his attention to the rules: 'Before leaving a bunker, a player should carefully fill up and smooth over all holes and footprints made by him.'

Sports historians argue *whether the Dutch game of* colf, *shown in this French woodcut of 1497, was really a forerunner of golf. Players tried to hit a number of targets, such as doors in buildings, in the fewest strokes*

Carrying the clubs poses a problem that has brought ample solutions. Once, a caddie carried them loosely. Then came golf bags and motorised carts. Energy was saved for play

Why is a golfer allowed only fourteen clubs?

To see some golfers or their caddies labouring with so much equipment, it would seem they are ready for any contingency. Indeed, to restrict their load of clubs would appear to be a kindness.

Yet, in the 1930s, players sometimes set out with twenty-five clubs or more, carrying some for use perhaps only once in several rounds. They were ignoring the example of Francis Ouimet, who won the US Open in 1913 with only seven clubs.

In 1938, a new rule stipulated a maximum of fourteen clubs of any legitimate pattern. This was agreed to correspond with the choice of most professionals – eight irons, one or two wedges, a putter and three or four woods. Players who break the rule are penalised a maximum of two holes in match-play contests and four strokes in stroke play.

Some famous golfers have inadvertently broken the rule. In the 1976 World Series of Golf, American Johnny Miller played seventeen holes before discovering his son's cut-down putter in the bottom of his bag. It cost him four strokes. And Jack Nicklaus once found while playing the first hole of a competition that he had one club too many. Earlier in the day, he had practised with Australian David Graham, who used the same brand of clubs. Somehow, Nicklaus had picked up one of Graham's clubs.

A player who breaks a club may replace it, but not by borrowing on the course. The break must come by accident during play. Snapping a club across a knee, or hurling all fourteen into a lake in disgust, doesn't allow a player to send to the clubhouse for replacements.

Why does a golf ball swerve in flight?

As every golfer knows, but accepts only after bitter experience, the most difficult shot to hit is one that goes dead straight. Any deviation in the club's swing will send the ball swerving from left to right in what is politely called a 'fade' or from right to left in a 'draw'. Greater, uncontrolled swerves are known as a slice and a hook.

An unwritten law asserts that these quirks inevitably occur in the face of hazards: if there is water or dense scrub nearby, the ball will find it. Most players know which way their shots tend to swerve, and make allowances. Highly skilled players control the swerve to direct the ball round obstacles or to counteract adverse winds.

The phenomenon of swerve in flight was explained a century ago by British physicist Lord Rayleigh. He called it the Magnus effect, after Heinrich Gustav Magnus, a German scientist who had studied the subject.

When a golf ball spins, as it will always do on impact, it pulls air around itself in the direction of the spin. Air on one side

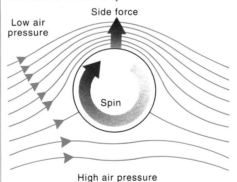

All golf shots make the ball spin, and skilful players use that factor to control the flight. Spin creates differences in the pressure of air around the ball, which will always tend to veer towards the zone of lower resistance

of the ball moves faster than on the other, and exerts less pressure. The ball will move in the direction of least pressure, where the air is moving faster, causing a deviation in flight. If the ball spins on a vertical axis, it will swerve sideways; if it spins on a horizontal axis, with backspin, it will rise moderately or sharply according to the speed of spin.

Golfers are not the only sportsmen who need to deal with the effects of a spinning ball. By gripping the ball in a variety of ways, baseball pitchers use the same principles to make the ball curve away from or towards the batter, or to dip suddenly. The faster the spin, the greater the curve. A ball spinning at up to thirty-eight

revolutions per second may curve some 600 mm (2 ft) in its 18-m (60-ft) journey to the plate.

Many tennis players have been fooled by a ball that seems certain to fall outside the court and suddenly drops in. The shot was probably hit cunningly with topspin. Soccer players, too, impart spin, particularly when shooting at goal, to make the ball swerve deceptively.

Slow bowlers in cricket spin the ball for two purposes: in flight, the spin helps the ball to 'drift' – move off its line; when the ball hits the ground, the spin causes it to change direction. Faster bowlers get curve or 'swing' without using spin, but the dynamics still apply. The seam on the ball and its initial polish or shine cause air to flow more quickly over one side. That is why bowlers polish one side of the ball on their trousers. The shine increases the air flow and reduces the pressure on that side, inducing the ball to swing away from or towards the batsman.

Atmosphere has a strong influence. Baseball pitchers and cricket bowlers know that the ball will move more in humid conditions. At high altitudes, such as at Denver, Colorado, pitchers have a tough time. The air is less dense and the ball will not curve so well.

Why do golf balls vary in size?

Under golf's official rules, drawn up jointly by the Royal and Ancient Golf Club of St Andrews and the United States Golf Association, balls must be no less than 1.68 in (42.672 mm) in diameter and 1.62 oz (45.927 grams) in weight.

That wasn't always so. Until 1988, golfers in Britain and many other countries played with a slightly smaller ball, diameter 1.62 in (41.148 mm). Americans played with the larger ball that is now used everywhere in competition golf. This difference in ball sizes mattered little where everybody used balls of the same size. But in international team contests, such as the Ryder Cup, a different ball was used according to where the matches were played.

The size difference, a mere 1.524 mm, may seem negligible, but international golfers argued that having to switch from one ball to another caused problems. The smaller ball travelled 5 per cent farther, which was perhaps an advantage when driving off the tee but not necessarily so when playing a short and tricky shot to the green. The British ball tended to spin faster, producing more swerve.

For many years Americans tried unsuccessfully to have bigger golf holes to match their bigger ball. But the Royal and Ancient Golf Club, which decreed in 1893 that a hole must be 4.25 in (107.95 mm) in diameter and at least 4 in deep, would not budge.

Newcomers to golf should beware that in some countries old stocks of smaller balls are occasionally offered for sale, sometimes with second-hand clubs and bags. They are permitted in social games, but not in competitions. A hole in one with a smaller ball won't win a prize.

Why are there eighteen holes on a full-sized golf course?

Golf took hold in Scotland in the 1650s at a dozen courses along the east coast. In 1744, the Honourable Company of Edinburgh Golfers, the world's oldest club, held the first-ever championship at Leith. The event was match play, decided hole by hole instead of by the number of strokes for the round, and was over a course of five holes – 414, 461, 426, 495

and 435 yd (about 400 to 450 m).

The Royal Aberdeen had fifteen holes; Montrose had twenty-five. St Andrews had twelve, ten of which were played twice, making a round of twenty-two. Early records show that good golfers went round the Old Course in about 120 strokes.

Fairways and greens serving more than one hole were a feature of St Andrews, so the club simplified the course layout, reducing the holes to eighteen. In 1764, the Royal and Ancient Golf Club stipulated that 'one round of the Links, or eighteen holes, is reckoned a match.' Other golf clubs accepted the need for a uniform game, and gradually adjusted their courses. On those with only six holes, players went round three times; on nine-hole courses they played twice, as they do today at many clubs worldwide.

An endless stream of cartoon jokes and golfing stories has come from the golf-club bar, often called the nineteenth hole. Since 1764, a round has been eighteen holes

BIG DRIVE FOR THE PERFECT BALL

Nothing has had greater influence on golf than the ball itself, which has changed many times in size and composition. The first golf balls were made of wood, and probably lasted until the early seventeenth century when a remarkable ball known as a 'feathery' came into use.

Because a skilled ballmaker could make only three or four balls a day, featheries were more expensive than clubs. Only the wealthy could afford to play. Featheries had an outer casing of hide, handstitched inside out, then reversed through a tiny slit to conceal the raised seam. The ballmaker inserted boiled breast feathers of chickens or geese, stuffing them so tightly that the finished ball, about the size of one today, held more than a top-hatful of feathers. An average golfer could drive a feathery about 180 yd (165 m), but one record hit was nearly twice that distance.

In 1848, gutta-percha, a rubberlike resin, was imported into Britain. The resin sets hard but softens in hot water, allowing it to be shaped by hand or in a mould. Golf balls made of gutta-percha, known as 'gutties', were cheaper and more durable. Players discovered that gutties scarred

inadvertently by iron clubs flew more accurately. Makers took to marking balls with a crisscross pattern or with their own emblems, from raised bumps to crescent moons.

Gutta-percha balls had one major flaw. They were so hard that they damaged wooden clubs. Coburn Haskell of Akron, Ohio, solved that problem in 1898 by inventing a ball filled with a great length of fine rubber, similar to that in elastic bands, wound tightly around a solid rubber core.

Since then, golfers have had a choice of at least 200 different balls, with cores of cork, lead, ball bearings and even mercury. Studies of laws governing a golf ball's flight will produce many changes yet, but it's unlikely that golfers will ever see the perfect ball – one that does precisely what they want.

Many kinds of ball have taxed golfers' skills. Featheries were first used nearly 400 years ago. The Haskell ball, with its heart of tightly wound rubber, was suddenly in demand when Sandy Herd used one to win the 1902 British Open. The balata ball has a water-filled core wrapped in rubber yarn

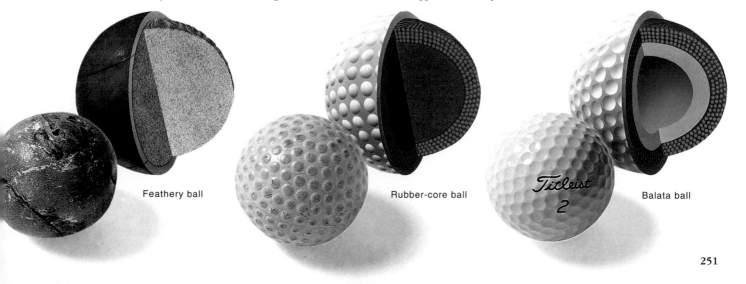

Feathery ball   Rubber-core ball   Balata ball

It's all eyes on the ball

Why is American football called gridiron?

It may seem hard to believe but, for much of the nineteenth century, American college students and those on the playing fields of England enjoyed similar kinds of football. The games bore little resemblance to any football played today, and the rules were roughly whatever the players decided.

Later in the century, American universities, like those in England, began to distil order from chaos. In 1867, Princeton drew up rules allowing twenty-five in a team. Together with Princeton, Rutgers College decided that players could not run with the ball; to score, they had to kick the ball, soccer style, under the bar and between the posts. In 1873, Yale played a team from England, the Eton Players, and as a result campaigned for eleven-a-side football.

A meeting at Princeton in November 1867 undoubtedly had a profound influence in giving America its own brand of football. Also, decisions made at the meeting helped put the United States among a minority of nations that don't play soccer as their major winter game.

At that meeting, Princeton adopted the rugby code. It decided to invite Harvard, Yale and Columbia to a convention to discuss the future of college football. Yale, represented by Walter Camp, was wedded to an eleven-a-side game, and by 1880 persuaded others to follow. No other form of rugby has so few players. More than anybody, Camp created the distinctive American game. He worked to have football played on a small field instead of, as it sometimes was, over a vast tract of open countryside.

In those early years, American football became something of a farce and, but for Camp, might never have survived. The team receiving the ball from the kickoff kept possession, and it was almost impossible under the rules for the opposition to deprive them of it. Whenever seriously threatened, a player would touch down behind his own goal line for 'a safety', then bring the ball out to the 25-yd (22-m) line, where the pattern began again. Games were decided not on points scored, but on how few 'safeties' a team had to concede.

The tedium of such tactics angered spectators. In 1882, Camp persuaded administrators to introduce a new rule of 'downs'. For every three touchdowns anywhere on the field, a team had to gain at least 5 yd (about 4 m) of its rival's territory, or surrender the ball where the third touchdown occurred. This rule forced an attacking team to kick the ball on the third 'down' unless it could gain 5 yd. Suddenly, the game was revitalised.

For the rule to work, the field had to be marked in 5-yd strips, making it resemble a gridiron, the metal frame once placed over the fire for cooking. Gridiron became the nickname for the playing field and for the game itself. Before the end of the century, it was a professional game, soon to be played nationwide.

Why is Edson Arantes do Nascimento known as Pelé?

Brazilian soccer player Edson Arantes do Nascimento is possibly the most famous of all the game's brightest stars – but the world knows him as Pelé, a name

American football has eleven players in a team, the least number of any game based on rugby. Some players spend only seconds on the field before being replaced by others from the total pool of forty-five players

whose origins he says go back to his early youth in the streets of his home city, Três Corações. Born in 1940 into a poor black family, he was called Dico for most of his childhood. When he began playing professional soccer, Brazilian fans soon gave him a nickname, as they do many other players. In his early teens, the young Edson shone at *pelada*, a street version of soccer, and it is believed that his skill at that game led friends to call him Pelé.

During his career, Pelé played 1363 matches and scored 1281 goals. He was a member of Brazil's teams that won the World Cup in 1958, 1962 and 1970. In 1975 he signed a three-year contract worth almost $4 million to play for New York Cosmos in the North American Soccer League. Some 76 000 fans, captivated by the Brazilian's spectacular skills, crowded Giants Stadium to see and cheer his farewell appearance.

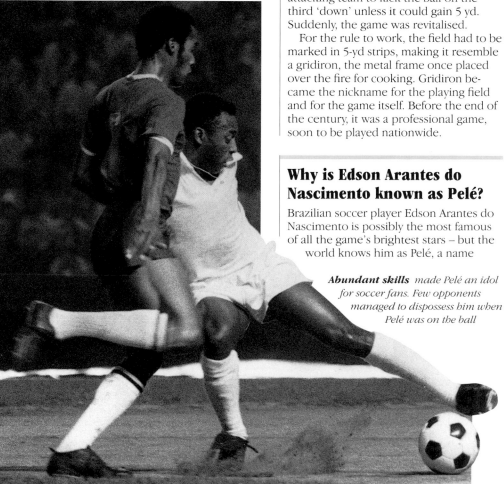

Abundant skills made Pelé an idol for soccer fans. Few opponents managed to dispossess him when Pelé was on the ball

Why are some footballs oval?

The earliest footballs were not round, nor were they oval. Just as the game itself at first had no set rules, the ball had no defined shape. Its size and shape were determined by whatever came from blowing up a pig's bladder by mouth. The bigger the bladder and the more powerful the lungs, the bigger the ball. The more irregular the bladder, the more perversely

the early nineteenth century, notably at Rugby School in England, handling the ball and running with it became an essential part of the game. So did what were called place kicks, attempts to kick a stationary ball from a set position through the goal posts and over a crossbar. Players discovered that an oval ball was better to pass and handle, and a place-kicker could get more lift and greater accuracy than with a round one.

Soon, an oval ball, kept roughly in shape by its leather covering, was in regular use at Rugby. William Gilbert, a local bootmaker who supplied the school's boots and footballs, became renowned for producing harder balls than his town rivals. At the Great Exhibition, held in London's Crystal Palace in 1851, Gilbert displayed two 'educational appliances', a round, leather-covered ball suitable for 'dribbling' and an ovoid ball for a game of carrying and handling.

H. J. Lindon also supplied balls to Rugby School, and his wife is said to have contracted a lung disease from blowing up so many pig's bladders. In 1862, Lindon produced an inflatable rubber bladder that ensured the ball would be both hard and regular in shape. He claimed to be the inventor of the rugby ball, but failed to patent his invention.

As football games became codified with set laws, they spread worldwide. Today, all the handling games, except Gaelic football, use oval balls but of different sizes; Gaelic football and association football, basically a kicking game, have round ones.

*At **Rugby School** in the 1870s football was a hurly-burly affair with at least twenty players in a team. Matches were decided by goals, worth only one point*

the ball behaved in play. Usually, the bladder was inflated by blowing through the inserted stem of a clay pipe. When this was removed, the hole in the bladder was stitched up. Often, a local shoemaker covered the bladder with leather strips, sewn together, to make it harder and more durable.

The earliest football games varied considerably from region to region. Most depended more on kicking the ball than on handling it, and players generally preferred a round ball, which could be controlled when kicking it on the ground. In

Why did rugby union become rugby league?

Late last century, players of rugby union in the north of England wanted their clubs to give them 'broken-time payments', a form of expenses, to cover wages lost while travelling to matches. The Rugby Union, dominated largely by southern clubs, refused, arguing that such payments would lead to abuses and make rugby a professional game. At a meeting in the George Hotel, at Huddersfield,

Yorkshire, in 1895, delegates from twenty clubs formed the Northern Rugby Football Union. Gradually, they changed the rugby rules to make what is now a distinctly different game. In 1906, they reduced the number of players in each team from fifteen to thirteen. Later, in 1922, the organisation's name was changed to the Northern Rugby League, and rugby league, with an elite of fully professional teams, became the name of the game.

Why in rugby games do players score a 'try'?

In some early forms of football, which varied considerably in their rules, players scored goals only by kicking the ball between two goal posts. But they couldn't attempt to do that until they had first crossed their opponents' goal line with the ball and touched it down. When they succeeded in doing so, supporters would shout 'a try … a try'. Their team would be entitled to a shot at goal and a chance of scoring.

Confusion arises sometimes because of the different uses of the word 'goal'. Rugby union has goals from free kicks or penalties, field (or dropped) goals, and goals that result when a try is converted into a goal by a successful kick. A goal from a converted try scores seven points, but the five points normally awarded for a try do not count. Rugby league has the same methods of scoring but different points values. In that game, a goal may be either a penalty goal or a successful kick at goal after a try; the four points for a try are counted, and tries, converted or not, are listed separately on the scoreboard.

It's a try for France in a rugby match against England in 1992. The move wins points and the right to try a kick at goal

A feast of games called football

Ask for a definition of football and, according to where you seek it, you could get any one of seven answers. Britain has three homespun football games. Australia has all those plus Australian Rules. Gaelic football flourishes in Ireland and nowhere else. The United States and Canada have their own forms of gridiron. For most of these games, handball might be a more appropriate name, for they are played as much with the hands as feet.

The reason why they are all called football is clear: they come from various football games played in Britain for countless years and given set rules there

All rugby fans revere William Webb Ellis as the boy who, at Rugby School in 1823, picked up the ball and ran. The report came from a former fellow pupil fifty-seven years later. Ellis, a vicar, died unaware that he was said to be the boy who invented rugby

about the middle of last century. Britain can claim to have organised the games and exported them, but football's origins are worldwide. Nobody can be sure where the first ball was kicked or passed by hand. Ancient civilisations had ball games requiring great skill. Forms of football played in China and Mexico allowed the ball to be propelled by the head or feet, with the object of directing it through holes in a curtain or rings on a wall. In Florence, Italy, a football game known as *calcio*, with twenty-seven players in each team, was popular in the

Soccer under lights when players were allowed to handle the ball. In 1870, handling was banned and the game changed for ever

sixteenth century. In Japan and some other Asian countries a game survives in which a bamboo ball is juggled with any part of the body except the hands.

The football played in medieval England was more like a battle across open countryside, which was often strewn afterwards with the dead and injured. Rival communities fought it out in lawless fashion, endeavouring to kick or carry a ball or other object across a boundary mark.

Every Shrove Tuesday, in Ashbourne, Derbyshire, a custom that goes back to medieval times is revived, with a contest between two halves of the town to kick a ball through goals nearly 5 km (3 miles) apart. Few goals are scored. Records show that forty-two similar games were played at Shrovetide in English towns and villages. After one particularly violent game in which a player died, these football contests were generally condemned as 'disgraceful to humanity and civilisation, subversive of good order and destructive of morals, properties and the very lives of inhabitants'.

Despite bans by several monarchs and the Church, football of a kind survived, though rarely with any set rules. By 1600, it was played openly at Cambridge University. As an undergraduate there, Oliver Cromwell was said to have been a footballer of great skill.

The Industrial Revolution, with its long factory hours and few holidays, almost killed football among the masses, but the game took root in England's public schools. Each developed its own rules. At Charterhouse, handling was banned. Eton invented its renowned Wall Game, with one goal (a small door) and the other (a tree) at opposite ends of a pitch about 6.5 m (6 yd) wide and lined on one side by a long wall. That game is still played annually and a goal is scored about once every two years. Harrow pioneered a game with eleven players in each team. Winchester boys played football without any goal posts; they scored points by kicking the ball over a goal line.

At Rugby, players could handle the ball but not run with it until, in 1823, William Webb Ellis won eternal fame by breaking that rule. He picked up the ball and ran, setting the basic pattern of all football's handling games. Webb Ellis gets the credit, but the evidence rests on the word of one man. Sports historians agree that, in a rough-and-tumble game involving 300 players, nobody can

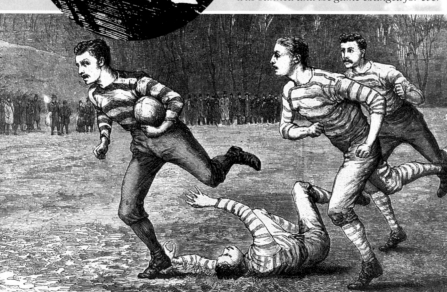

Running with the ball and never passing it forward made rugby a distinctive game. From it developed other football games in which the ball is handled more than it is kicked

Football chaos gave way late last century to order and variety as rules were laid down to decide how different games would be played. High leaps to catch the ball are an exciting feature of Australian Rules (far left). Heading the ball became a part of soccer (but dangerous play is penalised). In America, rugby football developed into gridiron with its own brand of sporting razzle-dazzle

be certain about what happened or who did what first.

Because so many different kinds of football existed, interschool games were impossible, and so were games between those who had left school. In 1848, fourteen Cambridge University students, from Eton and Shrewsbury schools, met to draw up rules of a game all could play. They decided to outlaw use of the hands, except to stop the ball in flight, and carrying the ball was barred. Players scored by kicking the ball between two flagposts and under a piece of string stretched between them. It was foul play to grab, trip or kick an opponent. The basics of association football were laid.

The first football club was formed at Sheffield in the north of England in the mid-1850s, and a dozen others sprang up in the region. Before long, though, neither rugby nor soccer as we know them existed, two kinds of football dominated: in one, carrying the ball was permitted; in the other, it was banned. Teams often debated before a match which rules would apply.

Then, on October 26, 1863, football changed for ever. Members of eleven London clubs met in a tavern to set up an association which would later draw up formal rules. Delegates argued over whether players were allowed to 'charge, hold, trip or hack' their opponents, but it was agreed that nobody should be held and hacked at the same time. The Rugbeians and Blackheath favoured hacking – stopping an opponent with the foot. When they lost this point, they left the association. In 1871, they helped to form the Rugby Union.

Paradoxically, the Football Association's first eight rules were basically those of rugby today. They allowed the ball to be handled; goals were scored by kicking the ball at any height between the posts; a touchdown, touching the ball after it had crossed the goal line, entitled a player to a shot at goal. Rule Nine stated that no player shall carry the ball. Those rules were later modified many times to produce the eleven-a-side game we know as soccer, in which handling the ball is almost entirely banned.

The Rugby Union devised a fifteen-a-side amateur game, played with an oval ball, in which handling predominates. In 1922, a dispute over players in the north of England being paid led to another form of football, Rugby League, a thirteen-a-side game.

British colonists took their rough-and-tumble football to North America. With the later importation of rugby, the game there developed into gridiron. In the 1850s, Irish soldiers introduced Gaelic football to Melbourne, Australia, where local cricketers seeking something to play in winter combined it with rugby to form their own eighteen-a-side Australian Rules. Today, that is the nation's most popular winter game, attracting crowds as big as any in the world.

Today's tennis goes hi-tech

Anyone for real tennis? *The game, a forerunner of lawn tennis, was first played in monastery cloisters in France during the eleventh century. There, it was and still is called* le jeu de paume, *or handball. When courts were specially built, they retained features of the cloisters, such as roofs and galleries*

Why does tennis have such unusual scoring?

A tennis game is usually over when one player has won four points. So why doesn't the umpire simply say, 'One-nil, two-nil, three-nil, game'?

Instead, as players and spectators know, the first point takes the score to fifteen, the second to thirty and the third to forty (when logically it should be forty-five). Failure to score is not called as nil but 'love'; if opponents reach forty points each (which is really three–three), the umpire calls 'deuce'.

Lawn tennis comes from the medieval French pastime of real, meaning royal, tennis, a racket-and-ball game played on an enclosed court and known also as court tennis. Another influence was the game of rackets, which is similar to the indoor game of squash.

In early games of lawn tennis, some players used the real-tennis scoring system: others scored rackets-style, a game being won, with some exceptions, by the player who first scored fifteen points or

'aces'. Later, real-tennis scoring became more general, and was adopted for the first Wimbledon Championships in 1877.

At least three explanations are given for the quirky scoring system. In real tennis, a clockface was used to denote the score, with one hand for each player's points. After the first rally (or rest, as it is called), the appropriate hand was moved a quarter of an hour to denote fifteen points. Originally, the score was called as fifteen, thirty, forty-five. Tennis historians agree that forty-five became corrupted to forty.

Another explanation is that in medieval times the score was recorded on a sextant, which has a dial that is one-sixth of a circle or 60 degrees. In a tennis game of four points, each was worth 15 degrees.

Other historians say that few real-tennis matches were played without wagers. The currency of the day was divided into sixty smaller units, and at the side of the court these were piled, fifteen high, for each of the four points in a game.

A player reaching forty-five points in real tennis needed to win one more to take the game. This, in medieval times, brought a cry of *una*. If both players or

sides reached forty-five, they needed two successive points – in Italian *due*, in French *deux* – for the game. In English, the latter call became deuce. Similarly, the call of 'love' is a believed to be a corruption of the French *l'oeuf*, or egg, which is shaped like the figure 0.

Why has tennis become so fast?

Eight years after retiring, former world tennis champion Björn Borg tried in 1991 to make a comeback. Playing an opponent ranked fifty-second in the world, Borg was outclassed. He won only five out of seventeen games.

Borg used the kind of wooden racket with which he had won sixty-two tournaments. His Spanish rival, Jordi Arrese, had a hi-tech, graphite racket which, for any proficient player, will send the ball 30 per cent faster. Also, the head of Arrese's racket was 35 per cent bigger in its strung area than that used by Borg.

Twenty years ago, top players used rackets made of laminated wood. The use of wood and aluminium in later designs restricted the size of a racket's head. If rackets were kept to a usable weight, from 340 to 400 grams (12 to 14 oz), a larger head soon buckled under stress of its stringing and the ball's impact.

In 1976, Howard Head, an American, invented a new-style racket with laminations of aluminium and fibreglass. This allowed the stringed area to be almost doubled. Other makers brought out rackets with even larger heads, so that in 1980 the International Tennis Federation limited the stringed area of rackets to 390 mm (15½ in) in length and 290 mm (11½ in) wide.

Scientific research showed that stiffer and lighter materials, such as graphite and fibreglass, give rackets more power. Also, the elasticity of looser strings enables a player to hit the ball harder than with a tightly strung racket. Physicists at the University of Pennsylvania showed that the speed at which a player can swing a racket, determined chiefly by the racket's weight, is all-important. Increasing the racket-head speed by a third propels the ball almost that much faster. Compared

Today's rackets, such as those made of graphite (left), enable players to hit balls harder and faster. A bigger head would have made the 1930s wooden racket too heavy, and it would also have quickly lost its shape

with those of a decade ago, some rackets now are 64 per cent bigger in surface area, more than twice as thick, yet weigh only 280 grams (10 oz), enabling even children to hit sizzling shots.

Many professional tennis players believe that the game is becoming too fast and that legislators will have to decide how rackets are designed. Others say that research on rackets should go on and that changes should be made in the game, possibly allowing only one service for each point and even raising the net.

Why are line judges needed in tennis matches?

As tennis fans know, whether the ball has bounced in or out is decided in major matches by the umpire and a team of line judges, positioned to watch every line on the court. But a match rarely goes by without a series of disputes, sometimes quite angry and penalised by fines for offending players.

That is perhaps not surprising, considering the difficulty of detecting precisely where a hard-hit tennis ball lands and the enormous sums at stake in modern tournaments. In tennis, a ball is in if it strikes a line. Some professional players hit balls at more than 200 km/h (120 mph), faster than the eye can clearly see.

On some shots, such as those going straight down a line, it is easier to tell where the ball strikes. In a service, the ball may travel the 23.77 m (78 ft) in less than 700 milliseconds. All the eye sees is a blur. Nobody, not the umpire in his chair above the court nor a line judge looking directly across the service line, can say with certainty whether a 'line ball' is truly in or marginally out.

These days, they don't have to rely solely on their eyesight. Courts worldwide where major matches are played have a magic eye keeping watch on controversial areas near the lines. One system used for many years is known as Cyclops, after the one-eyed Titans who forged thunderbolts for the Greek god Zeus.

This electronic line judge emits infrared rays, invisible to human eyes. A ball crossing an infrared beam sets off a signal showing that the shot is out. The service line, the most difficult to judge, is watched by a master ray. If the ball hits the line, even on its outermost edge, a yellow light shines on a screen at the umpire's chair, indicating that the service is in. A ball bouncing just outside the service court sets off a red light and a beeping sound. With all this electronic

wizardry, why are line judges necessary? Tennis officials say that Cyclops, though used widely since 1980, is not supported wholeheartedly by many major players, who complain that the system errs. Line judges are an extra insurance against error, perhaps by a faulty Cyclops.

But later systems may well see the demise of line judges. In one, known as Accu-Call, a mesh embedded in the court keeps track of the ball when it hits the court or the net. The ball itself has to be redesigned. Wires woven into its covering complete a circuit whenever the ball strikes the mesh. A console in front of the umpire helps him make difficult decisions. The system's fault is that moisture in a grass court may make it unreliable.

Another system undergoing extensive trials holds out more promise. Known as TEL, it relies on sensors embedded 25 mm (about an inch) below the lines. The sensors set up an electromagnetic field. Tennis balls are impregnated with iron powder, and their path is detected before they hit the court. If they pass the line, a loud beep indicates they are out. Tested in forty-five matches at the US Open in 1992, TEL registered 2596 calls; 301, about three in every set, disagreed with those of the line judges.

For the Olympic Games at Atlanta in 1996, as many as twelve systems are being checked. The winner will almost certainly not be the line judge.

Fiery outbursts made John McEnroe better known than the brilliance of his tennis. New technology may end such line-call disputes

More paths to sporting glory

Why did snooker suddenly soar in popularity?

For more than a decade until the late 1980s, a game that most people had never seen played and few could describe in any detail suddenly became popular among vast audiences across the world. The game's stars became household names, and many of them rapidly became sporting millionaires.

The reason was a British TV show called 'Pot Black'. Producers of 'Grandstand', a BBC sports program that showed an afternoon's horse-racing, were looking for ways to fill the gaps between races, or as a substitute if bad weather caused racing to be cancelled. Snooker, which uses coloured balls, had been shown without much success in the days of black-and-white television. With the advent of colour TV, the idea was revived.

In 1969, producer Phillip Lewis devised a snooker program that featured a single game – one frame, as it is known – between two professional players. Called 'Pot Black', because that is the game's top and sometimes final shot, the show became a winner in its own right, and had a peak of 15.6 million viewers in Britain alone. It was discontinued in 1986.

Why is a billiard table green?

Billiards comes from a fifteenth-century French game called *palle-maille*, which was played on grass or straw. When the first billiard tables were made, the surface was given the look of grass. Louis XIV is said to have had such a table.

Later, presumably to give their own tables some distinction or to boost sales, different makers in England sold billiard tables in a variety of colours. An orange table caused a violent dispute that probably settled for all time the colour of the felt covering on billiard tables.

On December 8, 1871, a man was charged at Plymouth with 'occasioning violent harm in the course of a melee'. The brawl started during a match on an orange table, in which one player accused the other of moving a ball. The lighting was bad, and the table's colour made a red ball more difficult to see. The magistrates found the man guilty, but imposed no punishment because they believed that the orange table was partly to blame. In a far-sighted decision they recommended that 'the cause of harmonious play would be advanced if tables were manufactured in standard green, giving strong contrast to the red of the ball'.

Why is there doubt about baseball's origins?

Controversy about the origins of baseball arises because of British claims, largely derisive, that baseball came from rounders, a children's game played in England for hundreds of years. Americans were convinced that baseball was as home-grown as corn-on-the-cob.

Americans took the matter seriously and, in 1907, sports-goods manufacturer Albert Spalding set up a commission to investigate the true origins of their national summer game. They found that baseball was born when Abner Doubleday, who later became a renowned Civil War soldier, laid out the first baseball diamond at Cooperstown, New York, in 1839. Understandably, the report set the citizens of Cooperstown agog. They built a baseball

Nothing happens slowly in baseball, a game that has spread from the United States to take root in Cuba (above) and Japan

stadium and museum, which became tourist attractions.

On the eve of baseball's centenary celebrations in 1939, the commission's inquiry and findings were denounced as a hoax. A researcher found that the commission's chairman, Abraham G. Mills, had been a close friend of Abner Doubleday's, and had probably invented the whole story. Doubleday, it seemed, had taken no interest in baseball and may not even have been in Cooperstown in 1839.

The search for baseball's origins went back to England, where records showed that a vicar in a Kent village objected in 1700 to children playing a game called base-ball on Sundays. The game was better known as rounders, and had existed since the Middle Ages.

Why do boxers wear gloves?

Early boxing matches were usually bare-knuckle outdoor contests, often fought to a finish, until one participant was beaten helpless or cried for mercy. It was sometimes difficult to control the fighters and even harder to manage the spectators.

In 1743, British fighter Jack Broughton, unbeaten for sixteen years, gave the sport

Large crowds gathered to watch billiards in France a century ago. The game's earliest mention was in France in 1429. A favourite with royalty, it was later played in Paris cafés

THAT'S THE NAME OF THE GAME!

Many of our sports and pastimes got their names in unusual ways. None, perhaps, is stranger than that of snooker, which is said to have come from an insult. In 1875, British army officers at Jabalpur, India, were bored playing billiards and took up a new game called pyramids, which used a number of red balls. Later, they devised a variation, adding balls of different colours until there were twenty-two on the table, the current number for snooker.

In the 1880s, Colonel Sir Neville Chamberlain (not the future British prime minister) introduced the game at the Ooty Club in Ootacamund. One evening, when a guest missed an easy shot, Sir Neville called him 'a snooker', a term used at the Royal Military Academy in London to describe first-year (and unschooled) cadets. The colonel, afraid that his guest might take offence, quickly added, 'We are all snookers when it comes to this game.' The name caused amusement, and caught on.

Badminton, the racket game of hitting a feather shuttlecock over a net, comes from a children's game known as battledore and shuttlecock. It is named after Badminton, a country estate in Gloucestershire, England, where the game was once played by the family and guests of the Duke of Beaufort. Like snooker, badminton became popular with British army officers in India in the 1870s. The modern rules were first drawn up in Karachi in 1877.

Skiing, our name for the most popular of winter sports, comes from *ski*, a Norwegian word that originally meant a splinter of wood. Such splinters were used as snowshoes and in shape resembled our modern skis. The earliest known ski was recovered from a Swedish peatbog and dates back to about 4500 BC.

Table-tennis was once, and sometimes still is, called ping-pong. An English engineer, James Gibb, helped to pioneer the sport, which was played in the 1880s with a cork ball. Later, Gibb introduced an American celluloid ball, called a Gossima, which made the game faster and more popular. In 1901, John Jacques, a British manufacturer of table-tennis equipment, renamed the game ping-pong, based on the sound of the celluloid ball striking one side of the table and then the other. Early this century, ping-pong enjoyed great popularity as a game played on home dining tables. Later, special standard-sized tables were marketed. A Ping-Pong Association was formed in Britain in 1922, and shortly after was renamed the Table Tennis Association.

***High-speed action** in table-tennis, recorded by stroboscope. Smashes from some players travel at up to 170 km/h (105 mph)*

respectability by bringing it inside, with standard rules and a roped-off ring. Young aristocrats were among the sport's most ardent followers, and often fancied their chances against star boxers of the day, backing themselves in bets with other bluebloods. They didn't, however, enjoy the prospect of getting their noses smashed. Broughton made the boxers wear padded gloves, known then as feather-bedders, to reduce the risk of damage to the good looks of some of his most valued clients.

The practice was reinforced in 1866 by the Marquess of Queensberry rules, which are basically those of modern boxing. Long after young aristocrats ceased demonstrating their prowess at 'the noble art of self-defence', boxing administrators passed rules stipulating wisely that all contestants should wear gloves to guard against excessive injury.

Why is curling known as 'the roaring game'?

Curling, sometimes referred to jocularly as bowls on ice, is believed to have originated in the Netherlands more than 400 years ago. The Scots popularised the game, and introduced it to Canada, from where it went to the United States.

The game is played usually between teams of four, who slide large, polished stones, weighing about 18 kg (40 lb) down an ice rink, with the aim of getting as close as possible to a fixed mark in the centre of a circle. The stones travel at speed, generating a low-pitched roaring noise, which accounts for the game's unofficial name.

***A low roar** goes up when a curling stone travels down the rink. Scots took the game to North America*

Hazardous jumps such as that at Valentine's Brook make England's Grand National course an awesome challenge. Many riders and horses have died in the race, bringing calls for its abolition

Why are horse-races over hurdles known as steeplechases?

Steeplechases such as the English Grand National, in which the man-made course has a series of obstacles including hedges, fences and water jumps, originated with horse-races held in the open country. These in turn probably developed from hunting sports.

As in point-to-point races, where the course is defined by certain landmarks, steeplechase competitors were guided by set marks. The races usually ended in a town or village, where the most prominent mark, often visible from far off, was the church steeple.

Riders in their final chase to the finish took their bearings from the steeple.

Why do racehorses share the same birthday?

In the northern hemisphere, a racehorse born on New Year's Eve becomes one year old next day, sharing the birthday with other thoroughbreds. In most of the southern hemisphere, all thoroughbreds become one year older on August 1.

The decision to give racehorses a shared birthday on January 1 was first made in Britain in 1834 in a move to implement a troublefree way of classifying

them for age racing. Races such as the Epsom Derby are for three-year-olds only.

Giving horses the same birthday is practical and makes cheating over a horse's age more difficult. To some extent it is unfair, because a horse born just before the birthday might have to race against horses nearly a year older. But no system would eliminate that. A race for three-year-olds decided on actual birthdays could still have almost a one-year difference between the youngest and oldest entrants.

In practice, breeders in both hemispheres keep the horses' birthdays in mind, and aim to produce new racing stock as soon after the dates as possible.

Why do high jumpers use the Fosbury Flop?

Most top-class high jumpers today have a method of jumping known as the Fosbury Flop. The technique resembles a dive in which the jumper clears the bar headfirst, twists onto the back, then flops the legs upwards. It is named after American high jumper Dick Fosbury, who used it in winning a gold medal at the 1968 Olympic Games in Mexico City.

Over many years since then, the flop has proved superior to other styles of high jumping, which is why it is now so fashionable. Ironically, other jumpers have used the flop to set world records, something that eluded Fosbury himself.

Why are Sumo wrestlers so fat?

In the early days of Sumo wrestling, a favourite sport of the Japanese and the first martial art, fights were often to the death. Many wrestlers ended their lives earlier than they would have wished.

Today, Japan has some 800 of these mountainous men, professional Sumo wrestlers who are revered as *rikishi* or, if they are of the greatest prowess, as *yokozuna*. Their clashes, as irresistible forces meet immovable objects, leave many spectators wondering how any human could survive such blows.

Bulk is crucial to Sumo wrestlers, some of whom weigh in at 135 kg (nearly 300 lb) and more. Konishiki, the heaviest-ever, was a mighty 252 kg (556 lb). To achieve such massive bulk, *rikishi* eat huge quantities of stew, enhanced with proteins and designed to enlarge their thighs and stomachs. The ideal shape for a Sumo wrestler would be like a giant bell with tree-trunk legs. Weight low down gives a *rikishi* a depressed centre of gravity. This makes him more difficult to push to the ground or out of the circle, 4.6 m (15 ft) in diameter, a winning manoeuvre.

When they retire from fighting, Sumo wrestlers slim rapidly. But years of bearing excess weight, which might be compared with an ordinary mortal carrying another human for life, exact a heavy price. On average, Sumo wrestlers die at the age of sixty-four; the average Japanese male has a life expectancy of seventy-five years, the world's highest.

Giants face off before a Sumo wrestling match. To breed future champions, wrestlers often marry the daughters of wrestlers

WONDERS IN THE WILD

Incredible in diversity and matchless in performance,
the planet's animals and plants are an endless source of joyful
surprise. From the tropics to the polar wastes, constant
battles are fought and compelling dramas unfold

Why don't snakes choke on their food? PAGE 298

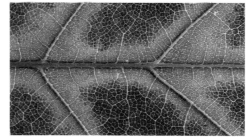

**Why do some trees lose their
leaves for winter?** PAGE 322

**Why are butterflies
more colourful
than moths?** PAGE 314

Lifestyles of the meek and the mighty

Why are most mammals drably coloured?

With a few exceptions, mammals are a lacklustre bunch. Their colouring is usually a shade of brown or grey, perfect to mingle with their background, but drab when compared with the brilliance of many birds and fish.

Land-dwelling mammals, whether predators or potential prey, find no advantage in drawing attention to themselves, and for obvious reasons. Early or late in the day, when they tend to be most at risk, their coats reflect about as much light as their typical surroundings.

Most mammals see colours only as variations of light intensity. The eyes of felines, for example, have many more rod cells than cone cells in the retina. Rods are better at detecting light, but cones pick up its colour.

A number of land mammals, such as zebras, are strongly marked – but not gaudily coloured – because they scatter to feed among other grazing animals. If danger threatens, their stripes give herd members swift identification, enabling them to group rapidly for protection.

Mammals with more colourful coats, such as the giant flying squirrels and small forest squirrels of tropical Asia, have some colour vision. So do lemurs, the small and lively primates of several kinds that are found mainly in Madagascar.

Monkeys are closest to human beings in their perception of colour. Some advertise not only their species but also their sex by vivid variations of hair and skin pigmentation. In others, colour can signal emotion. African mandrills, for example, have brightly coloured faces and buttock pads, which get even brighter when the animals are excited.

Why do camels have humps?

A widely held belief is that camels use their humps as water tanks, and that this enables these 'ships of the desert' to roam vast distances without the need to take a drink. But the most remarkable fact about camels is not how long they can go without water – after all, many animals never drink at all – but how they cope with extreme heat.

The humps of camels are not reservoirs of water but emergency stores of fat, to be drawn upon for energy when the animals can't get enough to eat.

The majority of mammals store surplus fat in a layer around the body. That layer acts as a blanket, holding in heat. Camels, living and working in the torrid conditions of the desert, need to shed heat freely. So, instead of having a fatty blanket around their bodies, they load their fat onto their backs – in two humps in the Bactrian camels of central Asia and a single hump in Arabian dromedaries.

Most warm-blooded creatures need to keep a stable temperature. To avoid overheating, they stay out of the Sun or lose heat by sweating, which costs body moisture. Excessive thickening of the blood through dehydration can be fatal.

Camels can't escape from the fierce heat of their environment. They allow their body temperature to rise with that of the air – from around 35°C (95°F) in the morning to above 40°C (104°F) later in the day. Then they sweat. But instead of losing moisture primarily from the blood stream, as with most mammals, camels lose water from the whole body evenly – body tissues as well as blood. In this way, a camel can lose up to 40 per cent of its body weight before its life is in danger. When it reaches an oasis and the chance of a drink, it may consume as much as 200 litres (44 UKgal; 53 USgal) of water in one long binge.

The one-humped camel, or dromedary, was once native to Arabia and North Africa and the lowlands of central Asia. The two-humped camel originated in territories farther to the north and east. For centuries, both kinds have been domesticated as beasts of burden, so that they have become as far removed from wild camels as today's cattle are from their ancestors. Some twenty years ago, a herd of strange wild animals – sleek, short-haired and light in body – was found in Mongolia. It took some time before researchers identified them as distant relatives of Bactrian camels.

Why don't female deer have antlers?

Animals usually have horns for defence. Antlers in most deer species aren't true armaments but emblems of male sexuality. They are sported like battle standards, inciting stags during the breeding season to show their worth in trials of strength. Though antlers crash together in bursts of fury, and rival stags wrestle in what appear to be fights to the death, the contestants are rarely harmed. When horns interlock, they are usually prevented by that action from piercing the flesh. To the winner goes control of a group of does; the loser retires, usually to fight again elsewhere.

Deer breed in the autumn or early winter. Afterwards, and for much of the year, the males curb their aggression. This is because their antlers won't stand up to a fight. In late winter or early spring the antlers become weak at the base and eventually break off.

Stags then feed greedily to rebuild their reserves of energy and their antlers. For a number of years, antlers regrow with more branches, signifying the wearer's increasing seniority.

As they sprout again they are coated with a sensitive layer of skin known as velvet. To go into battle with antlers covered in velvet would cause stags great distress, so for a time they live in peace with their rivals. Before the autumn mating seaon or rut, this velvet loses its blood

Brilliant colours *escape most mammals' eyes, but all primates have some colour vision. These macaws (left) are as seen by humans. New World monkeys get a less-colourful view (right)*

Horns clash as two red deer stags join a battle for supremacy. It may look like a fight to the death, but rivals are rarely hurt. Unlike horns of other animals, deer antlers are grown and cast aside each year

supply and dies, leaving insensate bone capable of absorbing mighty shocks without hurting its owner.

The horns of many other animals – cattle, buffalo, sheep, goats – are nourished through a hollow core, and have slow but almost lifelong growth. Usually they serve as weapons for both sexes, the females employing them particularly to defend their young. Often those of the males grow bigger because, like those of stags in the mating season, they are used in ritual contests.

Why aren't white rhinos white?

Africa has two kinds of rhinoceroses – black and white. Both kinds like to wallow in mud and, if they can, emerge from a pool with a thick coating of it. A layer of mud keeps a rhino cool and, more important, helps to ward off biting insects.

When their hides are clean, both species are the same dark grey. 'White' is a mistranslation of the Afrikaans word for wide, and refers to the shape of the mouth. The two kinds are better distinguished as hook-lipped (black) and square-lipped (white) rhinoceroses. Both have two horns, one behind the other. The larger horns of white rhinos are sometimes more than 1.5 m (5 ft) long, making them a valuable prize for poachers who sell the horn for use in traditional Oriental medicines.

Even though we tend to associate them only with Africa, rhinos are found also in parts of southern Asia. The Sumatran rhinoceros has two horns; the Indian, distinguished by its pleated skin that looks like armour plating, has only one. The other single-horned Asian rhino, the

Javan, is facing extinction, with perhaps as few as fifty individuals remaining.

All rhinos are normally peaceful grazers, and all are known for unprovoked acts of aggression. Their poor, long-range vision is to blame. Curious to find the source of a strange noise or unfamiliar smell, they approach with a lumbering gait. Their power and bulk – up to 4 tonnes in a white rhino – gives them a sense of security and overconfidence. Fearing the worst, because they can't readily identify a distant object, their heavy jog can turn without warning into a dangerous charge.

Square lips and two horns identify the African white rhino which, like all rhinos, is now under threat. To deter poachers, game wardens sometimes cut off the horns

Why do giraffes chew the cud?

Many grazing animals eat hastily and continuously, tearing up mouthfuls of grass and swallowing without chewing. The chewing comes later, after they have eaten their fill and are at rest.

Rumination – chewing the cud – is common to sheep and goats, deer, antelopes and giraffes, as well as to cattle.

They regurgitate their food, bringing the partially digested material – the cud – back into the mouth from a special compartment in the stomach called a rumen. Thanks to bacteria living in the rumen, the breaking down of indigestible cellulose, of which grass is largely composed, has already begun.

All these animals have stomachs consisting of four compartments. After bacteria have started their work, the reticulum, an offshoot of the rumen, assembles the grass into wads. These are regurgitated one by one into the mouth, and slowly chewed to pulp. When this food is swallowed it bypasses the rumen and goes into a third compartment, the omasum. Muscles there stir and reduce it further until finally it enters the abomasum, a stomach much like ours, where gastric juices enable the animals to complete the digestion in a conventional way.

This process allows ruminants to feed on coarse grasses and other plants that

*A **warm fur coat** enables the polar bear to defy the worst Arctic winter. It insulates the animal so perfectly that scientists using infrared sensors can detect no loss of body heat*

would otherwise be unusable. Rumination makes its possible also for an animal to feed very quickly; if danger suddenly threatens, the animal can escape to a safe place to rechew the food at leisure.

When calves and other young ruminants swallow milk, it goes straight to the abomasum, or rennet stomach, where it is curdled and digested. As cheesemakers know, rennet, a dried extract made from the lining of the fourth stomach of young calves, has an active constituent called rennin, a milk-coagulating enzyme. Rennin is used also to make junkets.

GRAZING

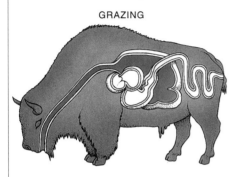

CHEWING THE CUD

Reticulum   Omasum
Abomasum   Rumen

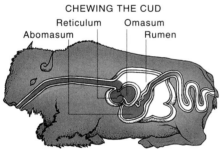

Chewing the cud gives some animals great benefits, but they need special stomachs. As they graze, undigested food goes to the rumen and the reticulum. Later, regurgitated food is rechewed before reaching the omasum and the equivalent of our stomach, the abomasum

Why don't polar bears hibernate?

When winter comes, the brown bears of northern Europe and the brown and black bears of North America tuck themselves up in snug dens and take a sleep. Polar bears, which live in a much more severe climate on the fringes of the Arctic Ocean, remain active all year round.

Diet makes the difference. Bears that hibernate are vegetarians: their food supplies die off in winter or disappear under the snow. Polar bears are carnivores, living mainly on seal flesh. Their sense of smell is so powerful that they can detect a dead seal 20 km (12 miles) away.

Male polar bears and non-breeding females put on weight in winter. Strong swimmers, they hunt for food mostly in the sea, spotting their prey from platforms of ice on which they walk with assurance on hairy, non-slip feet.

When the ice breaks up during the brief Arctic summer, polar bears move onto land. They hunt less often and lose weight. If they have to pursue their prey, they can move with impressive speed, fast enough for them to catch foxes, lemmings and water birds. Male polar bears grow 3 m (10 ft) tall and, at 600 kg (over 1300 lb), are about three times as heavy as the females. Zoo specimens have lived for forty years, about twice the normal life span of polar bears in the wild.

Polar bears' coats provide near-perfect insulation, making the animals well equipped to withstand the Arctic cold. The fur isn't waterproof like the coats of seals and otters. Instead, stiff hairs in the outer layer of fur provide a barrier against water and snow, ensuring that the woolly underwrap remains dry.

It's great to have a warm fur coat, but the temperature of Arctic air in winter drops down to around -50°C (-58°F), which could severely damage an animal's lungs. The polar bear survives because its snout is equipped with a heat-exchanging membrane. As the bear breathes the dry, freezing air, its intake is warmed and moistened. Exhaled breath returns heat and moisture to the membrane.

Why do elephants have big ears?

An elephant on the rampage is a fearsome beast. When its enormous ear flaps are spread wide like wings, the sight can terrify all in its path. But that isn't why elephants have big ears. Nor are they designed to flip away flies, useful as they are for that. They keep their owner cool.

Elephants' ears are thin-skinned and rich in blood vessels. The ears of some African elephants are nearly 2 m (6½ ft) long and almost as wide, much bigger than those of Indian elephants. When an African elephant waves its ear flaps, it can lower the temperature of the blood flowing within them by as much as 5°C (9°F).

Indian elephants are essentially creatures of shady forests. They don't have to endure the high temperatures that African elephants encounter on their sunburnt grasslands, so they don't need such large ears. Both species had a common ancestor, but have diverged in so many ways that it is easy now to pick one from the other. African elephants are considerably bigger, males reaching a height of 3.2 m (10½ ft) at the shoulder, about half a metre (20 in) higher than male Indian elephants. Both sexes of African elephants grow tusks; in Indian elephants only the males have them. African elephants are distinguished also by having arched foreheads – those of Indians are concave in shape – and two opposing triangular projections or lips at the tip of the trunk; Indian elephants have only one.

Why do elephants have trunks?

Most mammals feed by taking their mouths to the food. Human beings are among the exceptions: we, of course, take the food to our mouths. And so do elephants. If elephants didn't have trunks, they would need to get down on their knees to feed. Food high in trees would be out of reach.

Elephants grow taller, longer and heavier throughout their lives. At the age of thirty an African elephant may stand about 3 m (10 ft) tall and weigh more than 4 tonnes; the oldest bull elephants exceed 6 tonnes. A huge frame is a good defence against enemies, but doesn't lend itself to suppleness. Bending and stretching aren't easy. If an elephant lowers itself to its knees, it's a laborious process.

Originating as a smelling organ, the trunk evolved as a way around the problems caused by size and bulk. It makes it possible for the elephant to eat and drink while standing, the head held high enough to remain watchful. The use of the trunk to carry food and water to the mouth is unique among animals.

The trunk serves also to cool the body with jets of water or daubings of mud, and occasionally to condition the skin by rubbing in sand. Over the ages it has become a useful tool, able to move or tear down obstacles. More delicately, and with training, elephants can use their trunks to untie knotted ropes.

Another development made possible by the trunk has proved to be a doubtful blessing. Not having to take the mouth to the food has allowed elephants to grow huge upper incisor teeth. These are the ivory tusks for which they are hunted, in many places to extinction.

Why do face masks frighten tigers?

Among the great cats none has a more terrifying reputation than the tiger as a taker of human lives. Records over the centuries show a toll of many thousands of deaths a year. One notorious killer, known as the Champawat Tigress, alone accounted for at least 436 victims. People have never been part of a tiger's natural diet but, like most other great cats, these animals won't refuse an easy kill if one comes their way.

Nowhere is the tiger more feared than in the immense delta region where the Ganges and Brahmaputra rivers flow into the Bay of Bengal. There, in 1670, French

Man-eating tigers *usually attack from behind, so this Indian confuses them with a face mask on the back of his head*

traveller François Bernier described how man-eaters climbed aboard boats in search of victims. Today, the Sundarbans area has some 500 tigers, the largest known group in existence. Since 1987 scientists have found an effective way to safeguard people entering the forests and mangrove swamps of the region.

The extraordinary protective device is a plastic face mask worn on the back of the head. Tigers usually stalk and attack their prey from behind, but a worker wearing a face mask back to front seems to have no behind. Several thousand men who have worn these masks in the forest report that tigers have followed them, visibly confused – and have given up the hunt without moving in to attack. Remarkably, butterflies may have inspired the idea. To deter possible predators, such as birds, many butterflies and some other insects have large spots resembling eyes, which scare off their attackers.

Face masks are extremely successful, but a method has been devised to educate marauding tigers into believing that any attack on a human being will bring an unpleasant surprise. A tiger acting in a threatening manner may be lured towards a dummy of a forest worker. The dummy's clothes are impregnated with human scent, but its body is wired to car batteries to give the tiger a sharp electric shock.

These days, man-eating tigers are shot only as a last resort. Authorities determine whether an attack resulted from a surprise confrontation in which the tiger felt threatened and killed to defend itself. Also, they watch a female with cubs to see that she has adequate food, and isn't tempted to supplement her diet by a trip to the nearest village.

Spread like wings, *an African elephant's ears add a touch of terror to a fearsome sight. Their chief task is to cool the animal, which is why elephants in cooler climates have smaller ears*

SPOT THE SPOTS – AND START RUNNING

Cheetahs seem out of place on the African plains where most of them live. Unlike other cats, they hunt in full daylight and, against a background of dry grass and scrub, their strongly spotted coats give them little camouflage.

Rarely successful in stalking prey, cheetahs resort to an open approach that immediately puts such animals as small antelopes to flight. The cheetah's weapon is its pace and rapid acceleration, which make it the fastest of all mammals. When it fixes on its quarry, usually the slowest of a herd, it tries to run it down in one furious burst of speed that may reach 110 km/h (68 mph).

The cheetah's problem as a hunter is that it is no long-distance runner. It turns on the speed for about 500 m (550 yd) at the very most, a considerable distance for any animal, but not far enough if a fleet-footed prey gets away to a good start. On average, a chase lasts about twenty seconds, and only one in two succeeds.

No fossil remains of cheetahs have been found in Africa, suggesting that they were introduced there from Asia. Their name comes from a Hindi word *chita*, which means 'spotted one'. Because of their speed, cheetahs were kept in captivity by Asian potentates and used for the sport of coursing – running down wild animals.

Cheetahs rarely climb trees, and their blunt claws don't retract like those of typical cats. In these respects, along with their preference for daytime activity, cheetahs have more in common with dogs than with other cats.

Fastest animals afoot, cheetahs reach about 110 km/h (68 mph) in short bursts. But only half their pursuits bring a kill

Why are tigers striped and leopards spotted?

Swift in attack and awesome in their killing power, nature's five great cats – the lion, tiger, jaguar, leopard and snow leopard – lack the stamina to chase their prey over long distances. They prefer to lie in wait, usually near a waterhole or beside a well-used track. Alternatively, they stalk their quarry, moving with utmost stealth, slowly and patiently. Whichever tactic they choose, concealment is all-important. Their coats provide camouflage, and vary according to the animals' usual habitat.

Leopards, jaguars and ocelots live and hunt in forests. Their coats are usually clustered with dark spots on a yellowish background, and make them particularly difficult to distinguish in the broken light that penetrates foliage. The snow leopard, a magnificent animal with silky white fur and diffuse, darker spots, lives and hunts during winter in mountain forests. In summer it follows its prey – ibex, wild sheep, goats and ground-dwelling birds – into higher, treeless regions. Its colouring and the density of its markings may vary considerably to suit its surroundings.

Tigers live in a variety of regions, from tropical jungle to mangrove swamps and dry forests, but they emerge to patrol grassy woodland territories where they hunt aggressively. They prey chiefly on grazing animals such as buffalo and deer, and often kill more than they need.

Because their vision and sense of smell are poor, they hunt by ear. The tiger's stripes, running vertically and alternating between dark and tawny, merge perfectly into a background of tall grasses and shrubs, allowing it to get close to its prey with less chance of detection.

Lions have neither stripes nor spots. They have no need for them. Their unmarked sandy colouring conceals them well on the sunburnt, semi-arid African plains, where they often spend as much as twenty hours a day at rest. When they hunt, they usually rely on stealth, before making a short and rapid chase. Lionesses, which do most of the hunting, often work in groups, with one pair driving the prey towards others lying in wait.

Stealthy hunters need camouflage to mask them when stalking their prey. Spots enable leopards to merge with the background of the forest and stripes hide tigers on grassy plains

Why do cats' eyes shine at night?

Cats are very well adapted to hunting in dim conditions. Most of the forty or so species of the cat family, which range from lions and tigers to the little sand-dune cats of the Sahara Desert, have unusually large eyes for the size of their skulls. The eyes of some domestic cats are almost as big as ours, but their pupils will expand to an area about three times as large as those in human eyes.

Cats' eyes make double use of available light, leading to the belief that cats can see in complete darkness. Nothing can do that. But what cats and other nocturnal animals do very efficiently is to see much better than we can in low light.

Behind each retina of a cat's eyes is a layer of crystalline material known as guanin, which acts as a mirror. After light has passed once through the receptor cells of the retina, it is reflected back, giving the sensory cells a second chance to pick up an image. This is why cats' eyes shine in the dark.

This device makes a cat's eyes and those of many nocturnal hunters more sensitive to movement. But acuity – sharpness of vision – is diminished. The reflective layer, called the tapetum lucidum, increases the brightness of the image, but also blurs it.

Another distinctive feature of all cats' eyes, when compared with those of many other mammals, is that like ours they are set right at the front of the face. Some writers have speculated that it is this similarity in the positioning of the eyes that has contributed to our fascination with felines through the ages.

Eyes positioned at the front of the face improve stereoscopic – three-dimensional – vision, and give cats a more accurate assessment of distance. This ability is

Like a camera lens, *the pupil of a cat's eye controls how much light reaches the retina. Peering into the darkness, the leopard's pupils (above) open widely. To reduce glare, small cats' pupils become narrow slits, those of panthers dotlike apertures*

particularly important when they are making a short, sharp dash after prey. For these predators, success in the hunt depends on speed and precision.

Rare among mammals are the vertical slits in the pupils of smaller cats. Because mammals frequently hunt by day and sometimes in very bright sunshine, they need to limit the amount of light entering the pupil. Humans do this by half-closing their eyes and contracting the pupils. The vertical slits in a cat's eyes, with their much larger pupils, can shut out almost all of the light that might otherwise overwhelm the sensory cells.

What cats see by day is also poorly defined. If the prey stops moving, they are likely to lose sight of it. When hunting by day, cats undoubtedly rely on their sense of smell and excellent hearing. Experiments with house cats show that their hearing range is much greater than ours. They pick up sounds in frequencies as high as 60 to 70 kilohertz. Our highest is about 20 kilohertz.

Why do cats have needle-sharp claws?

As owners of domestic cats well know, a cat's claws are normally hidden inside its paws. Those of a dog are always exposed. House cats are no different in this respect from all other cats, with the single exception of the cheetah, which has blunt claws that don't retract.

Without their knifelike claws, lions and tigers would find it more difficult to hunt in their customary way, pouncing on the neck of a victim and clinging on to deliver the fatal bite. Climbing cats, such as the Latin American margay and the Asian clouded leopard, would not reach the treetops with such ease.

Cats withdraw their claws to keep them sharp. If they were constantly exposed, they would wear down, losing their savage points. When cats need to activate their claws, a springlike device shoots them out – with all the speed and menace

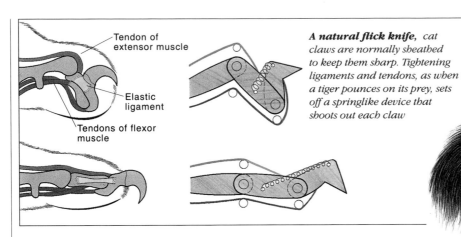

Tendon of
extensor muscle

Elastic
ligament

Tendons of flexor
muscle

*A **natural flick knife**,* cat claws are normally sheathed to keep them sharp. Tightening ligaments and tendons, as when a tiger pounces on its prey, sets off a springlike device that shoots out each claw

of a flick knife. An elastic ligament holds each claw within its sheath. When the ligaments are tightened, the claws are automatically uncovered.

Why do rats chew metal?

Rats and other rodents, such as mice, squirrels, porcupines, beavers and their various relatives, have front teeth that grow continuously and are self-sharpening. Pairs of long incisors on both jaws are hardened with enamel on only their forward face. As they are ground down by constant use, they become worn on their rear side, producing a bevelled cutting edge, much like that on a chisel.

Chisel-sharp teeth give these creatures an obvious advantage, provided the wear keeps pace with growth. If it doesn't, some teeth may become too long for a rodent to make an effective bite. In extreme circumstances, such as through paralysis or loss of an opposing tooth, an upper incisor could grow out of the mouth and curve backwards and up, piercing the throat and eventually the snout, and so locking the jaw shut.

That's why rats in particular, while amply fed on the soft foods they find in our garbage, must gnaw constantly on wood, plastic and even metal.

Why do lemmings leap into the sea?

A worldwide quiz about lemmings would without doubt produce one persistent belief. Many respondents would have difficulty in describing these creatures or in saying precisely where they live, but almost certainly a majority would state that lemmings commit suicide by plunging from clifftops into the ocean. The belief is fiction, given wide currency by fanciful film-makers and reinforced by our language. 'Lemminglike' has come to describe a course of thoughtless self-

destruction. For all that, scientists can find no evidence that lemmings deliberately kill themselves.

Lemmings are plant-eating, vole-like animals of two main, and similar, kinds. The Norway lemming, boldly patterned, lives in tundra and grassland in Scandinavia. The southern bog lemming ranges through the northeastern United States and southeastern Canada. Both kinds are prolific breeders – especially the Norway lemming, which produces up to thirteen young as often as every three weeks. Frequently, particularly in a warm spring when food is abundant, their populations rise dramatically. Adults then fight to the death for breeding territories, and females kill their neighbours' young.

Inevitably, food runs low and communities disperse, usually to face starvation somewhere else. Driven by famine, they swarm in vast numbers into new territories and often cross small streams and lakes. Without doubt, many fall into the sea – but by mishap not design.

When lemmings populate and perish, their lives aren't wasted. 'Lemming years', which occur about every three or four years, are boom times for stoats, snowy owls, Arctic foxes and bears, which move in to enjoy the feast.

Mayhem and murder may follow when Norway lemmings start mating. Adults fight to the death and kill others' young. But lemming numbers soar – until enemies move in

Why do skunks stink?

Annoy a skunk and you risk being sprayed with a vile-smelling liquid, squirted up to 3 m (10 ft) from two musk glands at the base of the animal's tail. The odour clings particularly to hair and woollen clothing, and efforts to wash it off seem to worsen the smell. The offensive components of skunk musk, six different compounds based on sulphur and hydrogen, react chemically with the proteins of animal fibres, increasing the smelly effect. Three of these chemicals have a delayed action, triggered by contact with water. A spraying with musk is disgusting but not harmful to humans. For animals that rely on their sense of smell to find food and identify others of their own species, the consequences are more serious and sometimes long lasting. So possible victims learn to recognise the skunk's warning, a show of

Beware if a skunk lifts its tail. It's a warning of offensive action

black-and-white fur, revealed when it raises its tail and prepares to shoot.

Skunks are members of the mustelid family, and are found in the Americas. Africa's musk-spraying mustelids – the striped weasel, the zorille, or striped polecat, and the ratel – also give warning in the same conspicuous colour contrast. And in a striking example of what biologists call convergent evolution, those same colours appear on a completely unrelated Australian marsupial, the notoriously smelly striped possum.

Why do we say 'as blind as a bat'?

Most bats are small insect-eaters that roost by day in total darkness. In flight, they avoid obstacles and catch prey by using a highly developed form of echo-location, similar to sonar systems employed by naval surface ships to detect

submarines. Through their mouths or nostrils, and at rapid speed, bats send out sounds ranging as high as 200 kilohertz far too high for our ears to hear – which sometimes last for only about one two-hundredths of a second. A bat calculates the distance between itself and solid objects by gauging how long it takes for sounds to bounce back from them.

Bats' reliance on this system has led some people to suppose that they are blind. In fact, insect-eating bats are merely very short-sighted. Their eyes are specialised for detecting moving prey at close range in the poorest light.

Fruit bats, much larger animals, are often called flying foxes. They live in warm climates and roost in trees. Their audible squeaking is not for navigation but to maintain contact within a group. At night, when they emerge to feed, fruit bats have good vision, and readily identify landmarks as they fly considerable distances to feed on favourite trees.

Why do bats hang upside down?

Of all the world's mammals – some 4300 species – only bats are capable of sustained flight. Over the ages, they evolved for flight to such an extent that their legs now lack the strength to support their

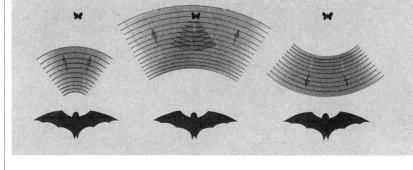

They're bats, but on the wing they are wizards of technology. As night hunters they use a sonar system to navigate, emitting high-pitched squeaks that bounce off their prey. The bats home in on the echoes

bodies. In order to fly, bats had to lose weight, and much of this came from their limbs, especially the hind pair. These remained long so that a bat could use them to support the tail membrane that helps it steer during flight.

The leg bones became so thin that no bats can walk. Instead, they drag their bodies along the ground, sometimes scuttling at surprising speed, in a way that avoids putting too much pressure on their delicate limbs.

And when they roost during the day, they lock their hind claws onto suitable toeholds and hang downwards, taking all weight off their legs. The load is borne effortlessly by stretched muscles and

tendons. Many people with spinal problems find relief in a similar way.

The wings of bats are membranes of skin stretched between the limbs. This expanse of naked skin is far greater than the surface area of a bat's furry body, so heat and moisture are readily lost. Flight itself demands a high cost in energy for all of the several hundred different kinds of bats. On their nightly excursions, they feed insatiably, many of them on fruit, others on insects and a few on birds, fish and frogs. In cool climates, while they rest during the day, bats have to cluster together in places that are constantly warm and humid. Where winters are severe, most species hibernate.

One giant leap can propel a large kangaroo, such as this adult red, about 10 m (33 ft). Its hind legs work like springs, enabling it to save energy and reach speeds of up to 65 km/h (40 mph)

Why do kangaroos hop?

Almost all the world's land animals move by walking or running. In that regard, humans are no different: usually we walk, but if we need to we run.

Kangaroos, of which there are some fifty species, are unique among marsupials – animals that carry their young in a pouch – because almost without exception they move by hopping. Research suggests that the larger kangaroos may be the only animals weighing more than 5 kg (11 lb) ever to have moved in this fashion.

Some researchers believe that the key to why they do so may be found eight million years ago in the process of their evolution. At that time, central Australia began to dry out and rainforests retracted to the coasts. Kangaroos were more successful than other animals in adapting to drier conditions. Animals of a similar weight to kangaroos use about one-third more energy when running at 15 km/h (9 mph) or more than do kangaroos hopping at the same speed. Kangaroos, therefore, had a considerable advantage when travelling long distances for food or in fleeing from carnivorous predators.

Large kangaroos can travel quite fast – up to 65 km/h (40 mph). Their well-developed hind legs, acting as powerful springs, generate remarkable force, propelling a large animal up to 10 m (33 ft) with each hop. As the kangaroo leaps forward, its stomach organs bounce backwards and forwards. This action helps the lungs to pump air in and out, sparing work in the muscles and saving on energy.

Scientists ask why other animals haven't developed similar ways of getting around. A key reason may be that they haven't had to, because their natural diet is richer or more readily available. Another theory is that large kangaroos evolved from smaller ancestors, and

inherited their basic body structure and ability to hop. Under pressure from other animals they might have restructured their bodies and developed as runners, but such competition was lacking.

As well, a kangaroo's anatomy is more suited to hopping, its pelvis particularly being able to withstand the strain that hopping imposes on it. Placental mammals need flexible pelvises in giving birth to large young. The kangaroo's pelvis requires no such flexibility, because the young at birth are tiny and immature.

Another explanation of why kangaroos hop may lie in the clumsy way that they move when they are not hurrying. Below 5 km/h (3 mph) they shuffle along in a pentapedal – five-footed – gait, using the tail as an extra leg. The animal balances on its forelimbs and tail, while the two hindlegs move forward in unison. This action uses a lot of energy, but hopping slowly would consume even more.

Why do we say 'as mad as a March hare'?

As a rule, hares lie low. By day, they rest in a form, or hollow in the ground, and are usually seen only when they are speeding away to escape a predator, such as a fox. Some hares are so anxious to hide themselves that they turn white in winter to merge with the snow.

In the spring hares seem to throw their customary caution to the wind. Suddenly they are seen prancing madly, chasing one another, and often lashing out with forepaws and hindlegs, as though they were fighting in a Thai boxing match.

At one time it was thought that this mating-time madness afflicted only the males, and that they were fighting one another to demonstrate supremacy. Zoologists now believe that the aggression comes from the female, which is larger than the male, and that she is repelling unwanted advances.

Hares have a long breeding season, stretching in the northern hemisphere from January to August. Because they are active in the early evening, their antics in the first two months of the year are cloaked in winter gloom. In the warmer weather of spring, when in times past more people were walking the fields during the evening, the hares' bizarre behaviour was more noticeable and became associated particularly with the month of March.

The March hare, noted for its whimsical behaviour, won worldwide renown as a character in Lewis Carroll's fantasy, Alice's Adventures in Wonderland. *Here, he attends the Hatter's mad tea party*

Oceans of marvellous mystery

Why do some fish fly?

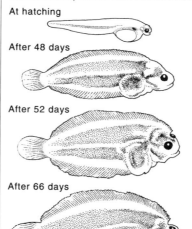

Nobody knew whether flying fish really flew when Thomas Berwick drew this one in 1822. We know now that most are graceful gliders

Fish have evolved a multitude of devices to ensure their survival. Camouflage makes many species difficult to detect. Streamlined bodies and smooth, close-fitting scales enable others to move more swiftly through the water.

High-speed hunters, such as bonito, marlin and tuna, developed powerful muscles along their backbones to enable them to whip their tails from side to side and propel themselves swiftly and tirelessly through the water. The fish they hunted, a rich variety that includes many surface-feeding species, needed to find their own answers to sudden raids by these marauders. If they couldn't outpace them they had to evade them.

Flying fish, of which as many as fifty species have been classified, have developed winglike pectoral fins; some kinds also have broad ventral fins, notable for their striking patterns. When startled, the fish hurl themselves from the water, spread their wings and glide at an average speed of about 56 km/h (35 mph).

Researchers have logged flights lasting thirteen seconds, during which the fish travel hundreds of metres to elude their pursuers. The fish usually fly close to the water, but passengers on many ocean liners have been startled by flying fish landing on decks up to 11 m (36 ft) above the tops of the waves.

For many years, argument continued about whether flying fish actually fly. To qualify as true, birdlike fliers, these fish would need to vibrate their wings, not keep them rigid for gliding. High-speed photography has ended the debate: most flying fish rarely flutter their wings, but

hold them steady. Some kinds of South American hatchet fish and an African freshwater species known as the butterfly fish really do fly, vibrating their wings on leaving the water.

Another trick picked up by the high-speed camera is that sometimes in their flight flying fish change their body angle so that their tails dip into the water. With a swift flick, they are airborne again, careering on in another, and possibly life-saving, glide.

Leaping in this way from the water may enable flying fish to escape seaborne predators, but it gives another enemy – sea birds – a better chance of a feast. Most flying fish live in the open ocean, where there are usually few birds. But those that put on their flying circus closer to shore always risk being snapped up in flight by the superior performers of the air.

Why are some fish flat?

Some 350 million years ago a new group of fish developed, lighter in weight than their ancestors. Over many thousands of years the heavy bones in their skeletons had been replaced with cartilage, a lighter and more elastic material. If you enjoy eating skate and similar fish, you'll know that they have no bones: scrape away the flesh from their winglike flaps and you find a dense mass of flexible cartilage.

Becoming lighter made swimming less arduous. But because these fish have no bladder to control the depth at which they swim, they have to keep moving to stop themselves sinking to the ocean floor. Sharks, which also have skeletons

made of cartilage, generally keep on the move. Most skates and rays, however, became adapted to life on the seabed, where their diet of crustaceans and molluscs is readily available.

For a life on the sea bottom it pays to be flat-bodied rather than tubular. When threatened, skates and rays wave their flaps and head swiftly away, whipping up a smoke screen of sand. Alternatively, their flatness enables them to lock onto the seabed, defying attempts to shift them and making it difficult for a predator to latch on to them with its mouth.

In time, bony fish such as the gurnard and the flounder copied this tactic of lying low. In doing so, they have lost their swim bladders – no longer needed because the fish stay put on the seabed.

To prepare for a low-down lifestyle, flounders and similar fish, such as plaice, sole and halibut, undergo an extraordinary transformation. When hatched, their young have an eye on each side of their bodies. Controlling their depth with a bladder, they swim in an upright position close to the surface.

Within weeks, the youngsters lose their swim bladders. One eye shifts around or through the head until it comes to rest close to the other, but retains its faculty to focus independently. The head and the mouth twist to a new position and the young flatties descend to make a fresh start, lying on one side on the seabed. The fins take on a new role. The pectoral fins are now almost useless and, as compensation, the dorsal and anal fins grow and spread until they form a fringe around most of the body. A flatfish relies on these and its tail for movement.

Finally, when they are settled on the ocean floor, most kinds of flatfish change colour to become superbly camouflaged on their upper sides. Viewed from above they are almost indistinguishable from the sand on which they lie. Their lower side, which is rarely seen, turns silvery white.

At hatching

After 48 days

After 52 days

After 66 days

By a nifty twist, a plaice develops in about twenty days from a fish with an eye on each side of its head to a flatfish with both eyes on top. Finally it changes colour to become almost invisible as it lies on the ocean bed

*A **brown bear's picnic** takes place on Alaska's Brooks River when sockeye salmon (right) run upstream to spawn. All salmon, except those that are landlocked, migrate to the sea. Then, guided possibly by taste or smell, they return to the rivers in which they were born*

Why do some fish migrate to the sea?

Most fish spend their entire lives in the waters in which they were born. A few others, notably salmon, eels and the Asian ayu, divide their time between fresh and salt water. Why and how they do so is still not fully understood. Migration is strongly linked to spawning, and to obey their instincts these fish take enormous risks and show amazing endurance.

One possible explanation for the migration of salmon is that they are essentially freshwater fish. Inadequate supplies of food and a lack of nutrients in their native streams, perhaps aggravated by flows of glacial silt, drove them farther and farther downstream. To survive, many were forced to live closer to the estuaries of these coastal rivers, where tides brought regular flushes of saline water. Eventually, salmon moved into the sea and now spend most of their lives there.

Because Atlantic and Pacific salmon have long been exploited for their commercial value, we know more about these than about other migratory fish. Every year thousands of salmon and their close relatives, various kinds of sea trout, return from the ocean to their native rivers.

Frequently, because the river levels are low, they must wait for rains to swell the flow. Then, with incredible persistence, they fight their way upstream, pitting their strength against fierce currents and leaping over waterfalls and cascades.

From the moment they enter the rivers they cease feeding. Fresh-run fish are fat, full of condition. When they reach the spawning redds – stretches of gravel where their parents mated – they are blackened and often emaciated. The males now suddenly change shape, developing hooked jaws and long fangs, and fight a furious battle to win a stretch of gravel. A successful male is joined by a female. The pair mate and bury their fertilised eggs beneath the stones, where they stay all winter before hatching in spring. Pacific salmon die after mating. So do many male Atlantic salmon; some, known as kelts, return to the sea. Studies show that female Atlantic salmon may make the journey two or three times.

Buried beneath the gravel, the fertilised egg develops first into a fish form known as an alevin, tiny and almost transparent. For about a month it feeds on its attached yolk-sac. Then it comes out of hiding and lives in the stream as a fry, foraging itself for food. The fry soon turns into a brown-blotched parr, which after about two years becomes a silvery smolt, ready for its seaward migration to the rich feeding grounds of the ocean.

Some salmon, known as grilse and weighing about 2 kg (4½ lb), for unknown reasons spend only a winter at sea before they develop a sexual urge. Then they head back to their birthplace to spawn and usually die.

Others, again for reasons we do not yet understand, stay in the sea for many years. One explanation for this may be that to complete the return journey to their native rivers they need greater reserves of strength. Many Atlantic salmon on their spawning run weigh 10 kg (22 lb) and more. One fish, the heaviest Atlantic salmon ever caught, weighed a remarkable 36 kg (79 lb) when it was taken from Norway's Tana River in 1928.

How do salmon find their native streams? Some scientists believe that in its homing instinct the fish is guided by taste or smell, remembering the distinctive flavour of a river's minerals and plants. Tests show that a salmon can detect substances diluted to one part in several million. Tagged fish that have their nostrils blocked wander off course.

Before the salmon can pick up the scent of its native river, it must first make a long sea voyage. Atlantic salmon spawning in Scotland travel from waters off Greenland. Researchers believe that salmon recognise distinctive sea currents, or they steer by magnetic influences or by the Sun and the stars.

Not all kinds of salmon migrate to the sea. Some, such as the kokanee, a relative of the Pacific sockeye, are landlocked. So are some Atlantic salmon introduced into lakes in Europe and North America. The American lake trout, a member of the salmon family, spawns on gravel beds in its lake home. Some lake-dwelling brown and rainbow trout make impressive runs into the feeder streams where they were born in order to spawn. On many world-renowned fishing lakes, such as Taupo, in the North Island of New Zealand, anglers group themselves side by side in what is sometimes called a 'picket fence' to snare trout on their upstream run.

Eels, too, show uncanny homing abilities – but in reverse. The closely related European and American eels leave rivers and ponds to breed in the Sargasso Sea, a vast area of the North Atlantic noted for its fields of thick weed. From their birth there, the young are swept on ocean currents northwards 1600 km (1000 miles) to America or northeastwards 5000 km (3000 miles) to Europe, where they enter streams and rivers. Some even find their way into small, landlocked ponds by slithering overland for short distances.

The eel's ability to sense the closeness of water is truly remarkable. Many a fishmonger, offering live eels for sale, has been startled to see them disappear from his slab, and vanish across the footway to freedom in the nearest drain.

Why do fish have scales?

Almost all the world's 25 000 species of fish have scales. And as anglers know, those on some fish are larger, thicker and tougher than on others.

The nature of a fish's scales can be a guide to its development: as a general rule, the more primitive the fish, the hornier and more armourlike are its scales. For example, those of the coelacanth, the fish that was once believed to have been extinct for seventy million years, are so rough and tough that they were used by Comoro Islanders as an abrasive, a substitute for sandpaper. Another primitive fish, the sturgeon, noted for its sharklike appearance and impressive size – those of the Black and Caspian seas exceed a tonne in weight – has rows of heavy and sharply pointed plates along its flanks. Sharks, on the other hand, have small scales, but each is armed with a sharp tip of dentine covered with enamel, and this gives the skin a prickly feel. At the other extreme from the coelacanth, the scales of eels are so minute and sunk so deeply into the skin that the fish appear to be scaleless.

A fish's scales are essentially an outer skeleton, a suit of armour developed as a safeguard against predators or in response to a harsh environment. For coastal and reef dwellers, subject to sudden swells and surges of current, scales need to be thick and tough to shield the fish from a battering against abrasive rocks and corals.

As you will know, if you have tried to exercise in a swimming pool, walking through water is much more strenuous than walking through air. That is because water is about 800 times as dense as air. Heavy, rough scales cause a drag, impeding movement. Fish such as trout, which need to make quick bursts of speed to capture food in fast-flowing streams, have smaller, thinner and more malleable scales. The speedsters of the ocean – marlin, tuna and mackerel – have fine and smoothly fitting scales to complement their streamlined bodies. To keep everything working like a well-oiled machine, special cells under the skin lubricate the outer body with mucus. Other fish, too, coat their scales with a slimy mucus for extra protection. That's why anglers who practise catch and release, as many now do, should wet their hands before picking up a fish and returning it to the water. Dry hands will remove the mucus, exposing the fish to possibly fatal attacks by fungi and bacteria.

Reptiles also have scales, but these serve a different function from fish's scales. Immersed as they must be for survival, fish are in no danger of drying out. Reptiles often are, and their scales serve to slow down dehydration. That is why some of these creatures can survive in some of the driest places on Earth.

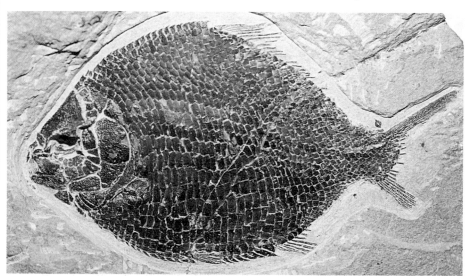

Scales from ancient times *show clearly on this fossil found on England's southwest coast. The fossil, about 200 million years old, is of a* Dapedium, *which probably lived among coral*

Old Fourlegs, the fossil that came to life

Three days before Christmas 1938, Marjorie Courtenay-Latimer received a telephone call that had her hurrying from her work. The young and enthusiastic curator of a newly formed museum at East London, South Africa, had told local fishermen of her interest in unusual fish. She urged them, if they ever caught one, to keep it and get in touch with her.

Now, Hendrik Goosen, captain of the trawler *Nerine*, had just such a fish. Returning from his usual run southwest of East London, he had decided on impulse to shoot his net off the Chalumna River mouth. There, a rocky ledge about 75 m (240 ft) deep borders a submarine shelf more than 180 m (600 ft) below. When Goosen hauled in his net, he found a fish unlike anything he had seen before. About 1.5 m (5 ft) long, it was bright blue, with an oily skin, and weighed nearly 60 kg (130 lb). It had fierce teeth and rough scales like armour plating. But its strangest feature was its limblike fins. Goosen thought it was some kind of sea lizard.

It was hot summer weather and, when Courtenay-Latimer got the fish back to her museum, its carcass was already reeking. She sketched it roughly, then sent it to the museum's taxidermist, who preserved it as well as he could. Courtenay-Latimer sought help in identifying the fish from J. L. B. Smith, professor of chemistry at Rhodes University College in Grahamstown, whose spare-time passion for fishing and fish had made him a leading South African authority. When Smith received Courtenay-Latimer's sketch and letter, he was astonished. As he wrote later, 'A bomb seemed to burst in my brain.'

Preposterous as the idea seemed, the professor believed that the fish might be a coelacanth (pronounced 'seel-uh-kanth'), which was thought to have become extinct some seventy million years earlier. Fossils of coelacanths had been found in rocks dating back nearly 400 million years. The fish are thought to be closely related to our earliest ancestors, from a time in the evolutionary chain when creatures first emerged from water to walk or crawl on land.

If this specimen was indeed a coelacanth, Smith calculated that the fish had survived for some thirty million generations. Yet he knew that to announce such a capture was sure to bring ridicule. How, he asked himself, was it possible for coelacanths to be swimming in the sea and for nobody in the scientific world to know about them?

Painstakingly, Smith dissected and analysed every scale, fin and bone of the museum's specimen, then tried to organise an expedition to capture another coelacanth. War had just broken out in Europe, and Smith's efforts to track down a fish got no official help. For years he and his wife, Margaret, trekked up and down the South African coast showing photographs of the peculiar fish to anglers and professional fishermen. He knew that the fish wasn't resident in local waters, but hoped to discover that the one caught by skipper Goosen had strayed southwards on the warm Mozambique current, as tropical species often did.

Later, the Smiths went to remote parts of Mozambique, where they distributed leaflets in English, Portuguese and French, offering a reward to anyone who caught a coelacanth. In 1952, fourteen years after the first coelacanth was landed, Smith received a telegram from Eric Hunt, a friend who owned a schooner. The message announced the capture of another coelacanth, at Domoni, on the island of Anjouan, one of the Comoros group in the Indian Ocean. The fish was about to be cut up in a market when a schoolteacher recognised it from the photograph in Smith's leaflet. Islanders customarily ate coelacanths – and used their skins as sandpaper. Hunt obtained the fish, and did his best to preserve it.

Smith had a considerable problem. The Comoros lay more than 2500 km (1550 miles) distant, and in those days there were no commercial flights; the only way to get there was by sea, a long and tedious voyage. If Smith wanted to see the fish before it disintegrated, he

A priceless cargo lies in the box beside Professor Smith's bed. On his historic return trip with a coelacanth, he guarded it day and night. Leaflets in three languages led to the fish's capture

PREMIO RECOMPENSE
£100 REWARD
COELACANTH

History was made when naturalist Marjorie Courtenay-Latimer saw the first coelacanth in a fisherman's catch. The fish, behind her, is now a museum showpiece

had to arrive within days. The persistent professor turned to South Africa's prime minister, Daniel Malan. Using all his skills, Smith convinced the prime minister that to bring back the coelacanth for positive identification was a matter of national importance.

Malan provided an army plane, and Smith flew to the Comoros to identify the fish. On the return flight, he refused to let its crate out of his sight. Whenever the plane made an overnight stop, he slept with the coelacanth's box beside him. Smith's years of obsessive patience, in which he'd resisted the scorn of scientists worldwide, were suddenly vindicated. He returned to Cape Town in triumph, unpacking the prize before his wife and an enthusiastic prime minister. The discovery made front-page news, and the fish with the strange name and bizarre appearance suddenly became an international celebrity. Smith identified it as a coelacanth of an entirely new kind, and named it *Latimeria chalumnae* in honour of Marjorie Courtenay-Latimer and the river mouth where the first fish was found.

In March 1987, Hans Fricke, a marine biologist and documentary film-maker with the Max Planck Institute, then in West Germany, headed a team of researchers working off the island of Grande Comore. Using a miniature submarine in extremely deep waters, they filmed coelacanths swimming in their natural environment. The films showed that coelacanths are capable of some surprising feats, such as standing on their heads for up to two minutes, swimming backwards and upside down. But, despite having four leglike fins, it seems that Old Fourlegs, as Smith dubbed the coelacanth, does not walk.

Fricke showed his films to Smith's widow, who had always hoped to see a coelacanth swimming in its natural environment. The films delighted her, and she declared, 'The circle of my life has closed.' She died of cancer three months later.

Smith's impressive work – perhaps the most exciting scientific discovery of the century – is perpetuated in that of the J. L. B. Smith Institute of Ichthyology at Rhodes University College, which continues to study and protect the coelacanths of the Comoros. A less happy sequel to his find is that a worldwide demand for coelacanth specimens from museums and scientists has put the remarkable fish in danger of extinction. Efforts to find other colonies continue, but have so far failed.

Locked in stone, *a coelacanth fossil is almost a carbon copy of today's living fish. Scientists have found coelacanth remains in rocks dating back 400 million years*

In the ocean depths, *a coelacanth explores an ancient lava flow. The fish props itself on its stalklike fins and sometimes stands on its head, but it has never been seen to walk*

Why do fish sometimes explode?

Many fish live in shallow water and experience no problems in moving gradually closer to the surface. Others, such as the redfish or ocean perch which live in water as deep as 400 m (1300 ft), suffer decompression injuries if they are suddenly brought to the surface in a fishing net or on the end of a line.

These fish, like many others, have a gas-filled swim bladder, which gives them buoyancy control. By adjusting its size, the fish can rest weightless and almost motionless in the water.

The system works well until a fish is suddenly pulled from the depths. When that happens, the fish is unable to reduce the amount of gas in its bladder quickly enough, and the bladder expands rapidly as the water pressure decreases. In extreme cases, the expansion is so great that the fish may explode; in others, the fish's shape is grossly distorted, so that its stomach is thrust from its mouth.

Fish don't need to live at such great depths for this to happen. A reduction in pressure – decompression – will injure those swimming in water only 10 m (33 ft) deep if the ascent is too rapid.

Some fish, such as sharks, don't have swim bladders. They avoid the problem of decompression, but they must beat their tails continuously or else sink to the bottom. Many sharks do in fact take a regular nap on the ocean floor.

Why do dolphins guide ships?

Many a legend, ancient and modern, has grown from the natural pleasure-seeking of dolphins and porpoises. Shipboard observers often see these delightful creatures hurrying to meet and keep pace with moving vessels. Where short trips are made regularly – by ferries, for example – dolphins habitually greet the same ships and seem to pilot them, leaping in and out of the water, chasing from bow to stern and crisscrossing from one side of the vessel to the other.

In reality, the dolphins are enjoying themselves. They have discovered that playing in the ship's bow-wave exerts unusual and enjoyable pressures on their bodies, much as sitting in a bubbling spa pool pleases ours.

The same sensuous sporting spirit attracts these creatures to boisterous surf. Many a board rider has found a school of dolphins sharing the fun at a favourite surfing spot. Swimmers tell tales of how, swept out to sea and exhausted, they were guided and nudged towards safer

Guardians of a god is how the Greek potter *Exekias depicted dolphins late in the sixth century* BC. *His black-figured cup shows Dionysius, the god of wine and ecstasy, sailing with a friendly escort*

water by dolphins. These people were lucky that their plight coincided with the animals' desire to move inshore.

Without doubt, dolphins and porpoises have an affinity with human beings. They seem to understand that we, too, do some things for fun. Wild dolphins and porpoises in a number of places around the world pay regular visits to congregate with swimmers at the water's edge.

They seem to be especially tolerant of children, often giving them rides on their backs. And when females return from their breeding grounds with new calves, they nudge them towards people they recognise, as if to introduce them to friends of the family.

Much of the brain capacity of dolphins and porpoises is devoted to navigation and underwater communication. They achieve the latter by a complex system of clicks and squeaks. Although they are supposed by many to be superintelligent, they are probably no more so than horses and dogs; certainly, they don't have the

GIVE A DOLPHIN A BAD NAME

Orcas, the biggest and fastest dolphins, are more often called killer whales. As well as fish, they eat warm-blooded prey: seals are their favourite food. Hunting in packs, these dolphins, which grow to 10 m (33 ft) long and weigh as much as 8 tonnes, will bite off the soft lips and tongues of whales many times larger than themselves. In polar regions, they often batter pack ice to try to dislodge seals or penguins. Because of that practice, they have acquired a reputation as man-eaters.

During Captain Scott's final Antarctic expedition of 1911, the world-famous photographer Herbert Ponting fled as eight orcas tried to break up the sheet of ice on which he was standing. Ponting later wrote that he believed the orcas had mistaken for seals two huskies tethered nearby, and that he 'had happened on the scene at an inopportune moment'. Nevertheless, the incident was misinterpreted as a direct attack on him.

Unsubstantiated reports from South Africa and the North American Arctic further built up the orcas' awesome reputation. Soon, the US Navy warned divers and polar explorers that orcas were among the most dangerous creatures they could encounter – ready to attack 'at every opportunity'. So far, scientists have found no evidence that orcas ever attack humans.

In a burst of frenzy a killer whale, or orca, lunges at sea lions on the Patagonian coast. No other whale is known to beach itself deliberately in this way. Usually, the sea lions panic and are soon caught. Whalers have used orcas to herd whales into bays, rewarding them with part of the kill

reasoning power of chimpanzees. But their playfulness and good memory make them easy to train in captivity.

The bottlenose dolphin, called a porpoise in the United States, is the species most commonly used in entertainment. Orcas, the black-and-white giants of the dolphin family, are more prized as performers because of their ability to execute tail-walks and spectacular leaps. Males grow to 10 m (33 ft) in length, compared with about 3.5 m (11½ ft) for a bottlenose dolphin, and because of their size are popularly confused with whales.

Why do some edible shellfish become poisonous?

Shellfish such as clams, mussels, oysters and scallops lead a life of retirement. Protected by their outer casing – two halves of shell, hinged to form a snug house – they settle down on the ocean bed or attach themselves to a rock. To feed, they open a gap in their shells and draw in water from which they trap microscopic particles of food in their filters.

All is well for these creatures, known as bivalve molluscs – and for those who enjoy eating them – if the water they live in is free of pollution. If, as sometimes happens, untreated sewage and toxic chemicals get into the water, the bivalves may absorb poisons and the viruses and bacteria of serious diseases.

But even in natural conditions, shellfish can become highly poisonous. Sometimes warm currents invade cool seas. When that happens, single-celled marine organisms called dinoflagellates, which float in incalculable numbers near the surface in every ocean, may suddenly multiply, turning the water red by day and more phosphorescent by night.

In 1947 and again in 1974, off the coast of Florida, one species was found in concentrations of about fifty million to a litre (about a quart). The toxin produced by this 'red tide' killed marine animals of many kinds. In lesser concentrations, it may render shellfish poisonous. Similar red tides sometimes appear in the southern Pacific and in the Atlantic off Spain and Portugal. Elsewhere in the world, other dinoflagellates sometimes turn the seas yellow. All these organisms, in sufficient numbers, can rapidly make fish and shellfish unfit to eat.

Commercial growers beat the problems of pollution by moving their oysters to tanks of purified water for a short period before sending the shellfish to market.

Why do whales beach themselves?

Shielded by thick blankets of blubber, whales thrive in the nutrient-rich waters of the world's coldest oceans. But every winter the spread of polar pack ice curtails their food supplies, and they set out on long journeys to traditional meeting grounds in warmer seas. Once there, females of breeding age give birth to their calves and mate again. The timing of these annual migrations and their routes

High and perilously dry, these whales became stranded on Australia's east coast. Some scientists believe that sunspots may affect the whales' ability to navigate

are highly predictable, whales following them from season to season. They apparently learn the routes in infancy and keep to them for lifetimes of up to fifty years.

Whales can see well in good light, and they navigate underwater by using, at times, a system of echolocation similar to that employed by bats to avoid obstacles and catch prey. Whales send out a succession of clicking sounds, and sense their surroundings by timing how long the echoes take to return.

Even so, the system is not faultless, and frequently whales lose their way. (They do not, as some people believe, commit suicide.) Individually or in groups, whales surge onto beaches. Incapable of swimming backwards, they are stranded, and death is inevitable unless people intervene to help them. If the whales don't perish first from overheating, the enormous mass of their bodies gradually crushes their lungs.

Beaching isn't a modern phenomenon, though it may seem to be so because considerable publicity sometimes accompanies a mass stranding of whales. The Greek philosopher Aristotle (384–322 BC) remarked on the mystery, and over the centuries many explanations have been offered. None carried much scientific weight until recent studies by British scientist Margaret Klinowska. She compared the known migration paths of pilot whales with patterns of varying magnetic force on the surface of the Earth. Regions of greater or lesser magnetic strength can be charted like a contour map. It quickly became apparent that the whales carried a memory of these patterns, generally finding their migration routes by following troughs of low magnetic strength.

The planet's magnetic field is disrupted periodically by a bombardment of energy from solar flares. These same flares are known as sunspots and often interfere with our own radio communications. Scientists theorised that, if magnetic storms occurred while whales were migrating, the mammals could be disoriented. Convincing evidence came from Australia in November 1991. Three days after the peak of a severe magnetic storm, 170 pilot whales beached themselves at Sandy Cape in western Tasmania. Geomagnetic measurements confirmed the development of a trough that ran parallel to the shore for some 50 km (31 miles), then swung inwards to the beach.

Why do crabs run sideways?

Crabs usually walk as we do, head turned forward, eyes to the front and looking. When we run, we increase the length of our stride. So does a crab. But the joints and muscles of its eight walking legs are modified so that they get their greatest extension with a simple swinging action, like a gate on a hinge, in and out from the side of its body.

This enables crabs to do something that is done by nothing else on legs – move to one side or the other, at top speed in either direction, without turning their bodies. What's more, they can move across the seabed or a sandy shore far more quickly than other crustaceans.

This unique running style evolved when crabs adopted their unusual shape. Their basic anatomy is much the same as that of lobsters and shrimps. But as crabs became flatter, so that they could squeeze under rocks to shelter, their protective shells, known as carapaces, grew not only shallower but much broader. A shell of this shape prevents full forward extension of their legs, so early crabs were clearly very poor runners, unable to evade birds and other predators. They solved the problem that may have threatened their survival by changing the direction in which their legs extended – sideways instead of forwards.

Anybody who has tried to catch crabs on a rocky shoreline knows that they have a quick turn of speed combined with ease of mobility, as well as the uncanny habit of looking one way and going the other.

Why don't seals get the bends?

If human divers ascend quickly from the high pressure of deep water, they suffer from decompression sickness, commonly known as the bends. They feel cramps, joint pains and paralysis; if the symptoms are not treated rapidly, the victims may die. Treatment consists of putting divers into a decompression chamber, in which the air pressure can be varied, so that they can gradually readjust from the high pressure of their workplace to that of the normal atmosphere.

Some seals dive to enormous depths. Meters attached to Weddell seals, among the deepest diving of all mammals, show that they descend sometimes to 600 m (about 2000 ft) and may stay underwater for more than an hour. Also, they ascend rapidly. So why don't they suffer the disorders of human divers?

It is true that seals have lungs similar to ours, but when they dive they don't rely entirely on oxygen stored in the lungs. Nor is the supply as continuous as that received by divers from their air tanks. Before diving, seals expel air. At a depth of about 40 m (130 ft), their lungs collapse. The seals depend then on oxygen from the blood, of which they have an ample supply: relative to weight, an elephant seal has about two and a half times as much blood as a human.

Champion divers such as the Weddell seal can descend to 600 m (about 2000 ft) and stay underwater for an hour or more

Why don't sea snakes drown?

No stranger in some tropical seas, an olive sea snake checks a visitor. It surfaces to breathe, but sleeps on the ocean bed

Sea snakes, like those on the land, breathe oxygen. But unlike land snakes, they can stay underwater for as long as two hours at a time without coming up for air. So what's the trick?

One of their lungs – the right one – extends almost the length of the body. Much of this lung is free of blood vessels, allowing it to be used as a storage tank. Sea snakes are hunters of fish, and they can travel about as fast as we can walk. When moving rapidly underwater, they soon burn up their oxygen store and need to call upon fresh supplies. These they get through a soft skin, which admits sea water from which they take about a fifth of their oxygen. Though the skin lets in sea water, it excludes the salt. One snag for the snake is that marine growths build up on its skin, blocking its auxiliary air supply. For this reason, it sheds its skin as often as every two weeks, compared with about three months for most land snakes.

Sea snakes can stay alive on land – in fact, some species hunt on mudflats – but they can't travel far. Their belly scales are too small and soft to provide traction. All of some sixty species live in the tropical Indian and western Pacific oceans. One, the pelagic or yellow-bellied sea snake, is found on the west coast of the Americas.

Naturalists have puzzled about why there are no sea snakes in the Atlantic. One theory is that these reptiles evolved after the African and American continents took up their present positions, denying the sea snakes a way of spreading farther through warm waters.

Why are jellyfish stings so severe?

Most jellyfish, of which there are thousands of different species, are harmless to humans. Many are passive predators that simply wait for shrimps and other small

crustaceans to blunder into their tentacles and become entrapped there. When we touch a jellyfish while swimming in the sea, we may feel a slight stickiness or at worst a prickly sensation.

Many jellyfish possess another weapon, which they use only when they feel severely threatened. Their tentacles are coated with capsules that can fire grasping hooks into their prey or exude a sticky fluid. If by accident the jellyfish gets its hooks into something much bigger than a shrimp – a fish or a human – the violent actions of its foe could tear the jellyfish apart. It then releases its shock blow, capsules loaded with powerful venoms. For a human, intense pain, followed by skin damage and severe illness, can result.

The stings of two kinds of coastal jellyfish can be fatal. Box jellyfish, found in waters off southeast Asia and northern Australia, have a four-cornered bell-like structure which carries bunches of long tentacles. They present a double danger: their venom is highly potent; also, because of the number and size of their tentacles, the poison can be delivered simultaneously to most of a victim's body. What's more, these jellyfish are almost translucent, which makes them extremely difficult to see in the water.

A full-grown chironex, the Australian box jellyfish, has as many as sixty tentacles. Extended for feeding, each is up to 3 m (10 ft) long. For a chironex, the combined length of the tentacles averages about 90 m (300 ft), and the stinging capsules number in the thousands of millions. Authorities disagree about the length of tentacle adhesion that, without

Jet propulsion enables this compass jellyfish, like all others, to travel the ocean. By opening and shutting its bell, it thrusts its way through the water

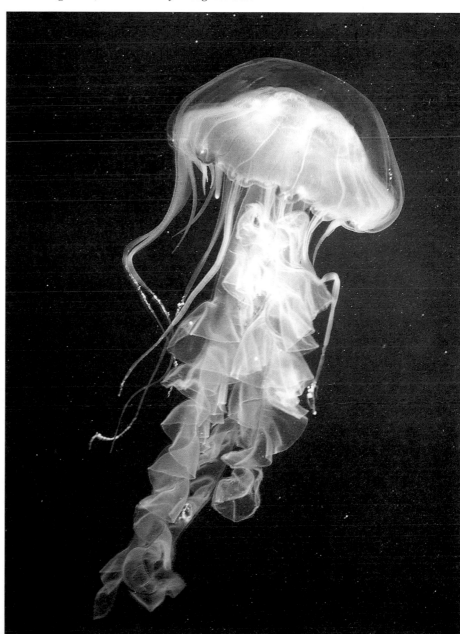

swift medical help, would result in a human death. Some say it could be less than 10 m (33 ft) for adults and considerably less for children.

Contrary to widespread belief, the world's best-known marine stinger, the Portuguese man-of-war or bluebottle, is not strictly speaking a jellyfish. Scientists call it a siphonophore. It's a drifting colony of as many as 1000 individual organisms, born from one egg but programmed to do different jobs. One group fills with gas to form a float; others help in reproduction; the rest, trailing tentacles up to 18 m (60 ft) long, are dedicated to feeding or stinging. A brush with these can bring a dose of poison almost as deadly as a cobra's. The Portuguese man-of-war, drifting in warm currents worldwide, was so named because it was thought to look like a medieval warship.

Why do squids squirt ink?

Unlike octopuses, which are generally quite harmless to humans, squids are capable of delivering a vicious bite. They use this bite in capturing food and in self-defence. Squids have been known to bite people, but only when provoked or threatened in some way.

Along with octopuses and cuttlefish, squids are known to marine biologists as cephalopods – from Greek words meaning 'head-foot' – because the animals' feet (the arms) are attached to their heads. They are firm and muscular creatures, with acutely sensitive nervous systems more highly developed than those of other molluscs. Millions of years ago they defended themselves from attack by retreating into a shell. Today, only two

types of cephalopods – the nautiluses of the southwest Pacific and the spirula, found mainly in parts of the Atlantic and Indian oceans – retain their shells.

Some other cephalopods, commonly known as cuttlefish, still produce part of their old shell internally. It consists of a substance that is soft and limy on one side with a hard casing on the other. This material is the cuttlebone sold in pet shops to encourage canaries and other birds to keep their beaks in trim.

Now that they can no longer hide in their shells, all cephalopods, except the nautiluses, have developed a new weapon to confuse an enemy. In an emergency, a special gland releases a pungent, black liquid – a kind of aquatic smoke screen – that clouds the water and befuddles any foe that might be tracking a squid by sight or smell.

Centuries ago, this liquid was collected from cuttlefish in the Indian Ocean. It was the original India ink, used particularly for marking cloth. The word 'sepia', which also applies to ink, is Latin for cuttlefish.

Why are people scared of octopuses?

Blame our fear of octopuses on French novelist Victor Hugo. In *Toilers of the Sea*, which he wrote in 1866, he described how the novel's narrator was shipwrecked and sucked into the huge maw of an octopus. Hugo was short on fact and long

A monster strikes – *but in fantasy only. No verified records exist of octopuses attacking people*

on terrifying imagery. The octopus is a shy, retiring creature, more interested in getting out of our way than in attacking us for a meal. In no way does it deserve its reputation as 'the devil fish'.

Certainly, the eight weaving tentacles of a large octopus are awesome, spreading across a circle almost 4 m (13 ft) in diameter, but most octopuses are less than a tenth of that size. The octopus has a comparatively small body and a tiny beak like a parrot's. Even when provoked it is reluctant to bite.

Could a large octopus drown a human by pulling him or her into the depths? Over the years there have been a number of accounts of such attacks, but experts have yet to verify even one. The idea of an octopus drowning a swimmer is mere fantasy, a by-product of horror movies in which rubber models are used as props.

In theory, the buoyancy of a man weighing 89 kg (196 lb) can be restrained by a pull of only 4.5 kg (10 lb) – but only if he doesn't resist. Octopuses sometimes mistake waving human limbs for those of their own kind, and probe with their arms to investigate. Any aggressive response usually sends them scurrying for cover in the nearest rocky recess.

The only truly dangerous octopus is so small that it would fit into a coffee mug, arms and all. Blue-ringed octopuses of two species, found in the South Pacific and Indian oceans, inject a potent, paralysing venom to subdue crabs and other small prey. They have bitten and killed people who have picked them up.

Nature's torpedoes, *squid are the ocean's fastest jet-propelled creatures. But they need to pump vast volumes of water to build up speed, and must swim constantly or they sink*

Why does coral lose its colour?

Many visitors to a coral reef are disappointed by what they see. Certainly, the intricate shapes and variety of the corals are eye-catching and memorable, but somehow they don't live up to the promise of the picture postcards.

That is because nearly all corals feed only at night. By day, their colourful feeding tentacles are withdrawn into saclike limestone casings. These casings, usually white or pale brown, are often sold for souvenirs in tourist shops. They, too, are lacklustre by comparison with the splendour of live, feeding coral – and for a good reason. The animals that produced them are dead and gone. All that remains is their limestone outer skeletons, which soon lose their colour when removed from the water. Brightly coloured souvenirs are dyed or painted.

The polyps that give living coral reefs their infinite variety of colours are tiny relatives of sea anemones and jellyfish. They are similarly equipped with sticky and stinging tentacles to capture the minute marine organisms that swim or drift over them.

Night diving, or viewing corals through a glass-bottomed boat equipped with a powerful light, reveals a picture more like those in the tourist brochures. Fully extruded for night-time feeding, the waving tentacles of different coral species, living in colonies side by side, can produce a glorious patchwork of colours, some vivid but most in delicate pastel shades.

The most colourful sight of all, for those lucky enough to see it, is the mass spawning of corals. About three to five days after the first full Moon of summer, the polyps release clouds of eggs and sperm. Brilliantly coloured in strong reds, yellows and blues, these float swiftly to the surface. Then they mingle and drift on the currents to produce what is often described as an underwater fireworks display or an upside-down snowstorm.

We don't yet know for certain why so many species spawn at once. It may be a survival strategy: predators are swamped by an overabundance of food, and can't possibly eat *all* the young corals.

Black coral, used for jewellery, comes from the flexible skeleton of a plantlike, soft coral that doesn't build reefs. Pink pieces of organ-pipe coral, sometimes found on beaches, come from another soft coral that is green before it dies.

Why do corals have such a range of colours? Marine scientists aren't certain. They believe that particular colours may attract some kinds of fish, which protect the coral from predators.

Lobophyllia coral

Branching coral

Tube coral

Sea-fan coral

Black coral

Fortresses on the seabed *provide homes for coral polyps. By day these tiny creatures retract into their limestone skeletons and at night emerge to feed. All photographs, except that of the prized black coral, show feeding polyps. Corals are carnivores, and catch food by extending tentacles armed with barbed darts which paralyse their microscopic prey. Then the corals haul in the helpless victims*

Flighty conquerors of inner space

Why do birds breed by laying eggs?

When animals reproduce, they nurture their young to varying stages of development within their own bodies. Some, such as turtles and a number of swans, ducks and gulls, are nearly self-sufficient at birth; others, humans among them, need extensive parental care.

To improve their flying ability, the reptiles that evolved over millions of years to become birds had to conquer weight problems. The females needed to unburden themselves of their young as soon as possible. Laying and hatching eggs provides a neat way of achieving that.

The egg, when fertilised, is a convenient, self-contained package: an embryo that develops into a chick, a yolk to supply its food, and some nourishing and shock-absorbing fluids, all encased in a shell of calcium. Two cords, the chalazae, control the position of the yolk and ovum within the shell; whether the egg is turned deliberately or accidentally, the embryo always stays on top of the yolk.

To lay eggs, a bird must find extra food, often as much as 40 per cent more. Also, the female needs more protein and must collect calcium – in the form of grit, bones and snails – for the eggshells. Incubating the eggs puts heavy demands on most adult birds. Even under their best care many eggs are lost by accident or to predators, and nestlings frequently die. Feeding a hungry brood also makes tremendous demands. Between them, a pair of blue tits fly about 1000 food-carrying trips to the nest each day.

All this work is necessary because female birds develop youngsters outside their bodies. If, like mammals, birds nourished their young within their bodies, they would not be able to fly. The increasing weight of the chick and the placenta would soon distort the delicate structure and balance of the bird's body – its light skeleton and aerodynamically designed wings – and so make flight impossible.

Some distant relatives of birds have stopped laying eggs. Many snakes and lizards bear their young fully formed and breathing, or in soft casings from which they hatch within hours.

Naturalists have looked for similar tendencies among flightless birds, particularly among species that haven't flown for millions of years. So far, they haven't found any. New Zealand's kiwi lays an egg that is nearly a quarter the weight of its

Like a spaceship, an egg gives a developing chick almost all it needs. When the oxygen runs out, it has to break free. Its beak has a hardened tip for cracking the shell

body and takes about eighty days to incubate. Even then, the chick lacks the independence displayed by the offspring of other flightless birds. Young ostriches, for example, feed themselves within a day or two of hatching.

Why don't two chicks hatch from a double-yolked egg?

Eggs with two yolks are rare, and it is very unusual for a double-yolked egg to produce one chick, let alone two. The presence of two yolks restricts the growth of the fertilised ovum contained in each yolk, so that generally neither reaches the hatching stage.

Multiple-yolked eggs are laid after a bird releases more than one yolk simultaneously into its egg-tube, or oviduct. In the bird's ovary yolks range from some about the size of a pinhead to those that are fully developed. Sometimes the funnel near the beginning of the oviduct fails to catch a yolk as it is released, and the bird lays an egg that has no yolk.

In chickens, double-yolked eggs usually come from old or very young hens. In older birds it may be a sign of serious problems in ovulation. Younger birds soon lose the habit, laying them with diminishing frequency. After about three months, these birds usually produce only normal eggs.

Nowadays, double-yolked eggs rarely make it onto supermarket shelves. One reason for this is that commercial hatcheries remove these and other deformed eggs from the production line. Eggs are 'candled' – examined under a strong light – before they are packed.

Why don't birds' eggs cook in the Sun?

Photographing an egg frying on the pavement has long been a newspaper stunt to demonstrate the intensity of a heatwave. If a hen's egg will cook in this way, it seems likely that other birds' eggs, particularly those laid on the ground, might do the same.

In fact, their shells keep them safe. Pale shells and the glossy surfaces of darker ones reflect too much light. Any absorbed heat spreads across the shell and radiates into the surrounding air. The heat entering an egg may kill it, but usually the incubating bird returns in time to keep it at a safe temperature.

Birds' eggs are incubated usually at temperatures of 33 to 35°C (92 to 95°F). The hatching time varies from about two weeks for smaller birds to two months or more for albatrosses.

Why do some birds lay so many eggs?

Most birds raise only one brood a year, others two or more in quick succession. But whether they hatch a single group of nestlings or several, the number of eggs in the clutch varies from one, in penguins and albatrosses, to a tit's half-dozen or more, and up to twenty for some partridges, ducks and rails.

There is no single reason for this. Researchers agree that the number of eggs in a clutch, multiplied by the number of clutches laid each year, is related to the annual death rate of each species. If that were not so, bird populations would fluctuate considerably. A small clutch of eggs, for example, may show that youngsters have a high rate of survival, that birds of the species enjoy long lives, or that they have few enemies.

Some birds lay a set number of eggs, which may be decided genetically. If eggs are smashed or stolen, the bird lays no more. Other birds replace lost eggs. When its newly laid egg was removed,

an American flicker – a woodpecker – laid seventy-one eggs in seventy-three days. Birds of this kind continue to lay until they complete a clutch. The right number, which the bird senses with her stomach skin, triggers a secretion of hormones that immediately shuts down egg production in the ovary.

Domestic poultry came originally from birds in this category of indeterminate layers. Given sufficient food, they lay indefinitely. One hen laid 361 eggs in 365 days; another laid 1515 eggs in eight years. The record is claimed for a domestic duck that failed to lay on only two days in a year.

The number of eggs laid varies among birds of the same species according to latitude. For example, horned larks in the central United States lay three eggs, those in southern Canada usually four, and those in the Arctic as many as six. Ornithologists say that birds living in warmer climates are more likely to raise their young, so they lay fewer eggs.

Food supply is another influence on clutch sizes, and some birds lay more eggs when food is abundant than when it

is scarce. In some years mice and lemmings breed prolifically. Hawks and owls, which feed on them, take the chance then to have bigger families. Scientists aren't sure what determines this – whether it is the sight of more food, the result of the birds being better fed, or whether the same climatic factors that urged the mice and lemmings to breed stimulated the birds into laying more eggs.

No wild birds lay more than one egg a day. (Battery fowl may do so under artificial lights, programmed to fool them that a new day has dawned.) Most birds lay daily until they have completed their clutch, but others space out their laying.

The female mallee fowl hatches her eggs in a compost heap made and tended by her mate. Depending on how well she feeds, she may lay as many as thirty-five eggs, with an interval of two days to two weeks between each. The eggs take seven weeks or more to hatch, and youngsters emerge from the mound fully independent. Throughout the incubation, the male mallee fowl acts as a stoker, opening or closing the mound to maintain an even heat of about 33°C (92°F).

*A **giant egg**, a quarter of the bird's body weight, is laid by the kiwi. Then she deserts her mate, who incubates it, which takes about eighty days*

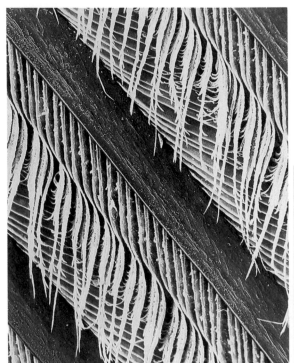

Superbly strong *yet super-light, all birds' feathers, like these of the European magpie, are natural marvels of engineering. Rows of tiny hooks and grooves link the filaments, so that they lock together to withstand air or open to let it pass through*

Why do birds have feathers?

Next time you find a flight feather from a bird's wing or tail – easily identified because it is longer and stiffer than the body feathers – examine it under a microscope. The effect is truly surprising. Each filament that branches from the quill, the central hollow shaft, is a mini-feather with its own fringing filaments criss-crossing those of its neighbours.

As anglers who tie their own fishing flies know, these filaments carry a multitude of tiny interlocking hooks, a million

or more to a single feather. During flight, they act in a similar way to those on a zip fastener, locking and unlocking each filament to its neighbours.

What other structure could be both as firm and as flexible – and as light – as a feather? Feathers provide superb insulation against winter cold, but are easily damaged. They need to be – and are – readily renewable: most birds have a complete change of wardrobe at least once every year. To assist a bird's safety or enhance its sex life, feathers come in just about any colour. They are wonderful products, all the more remarkable

perhaps because they evolved originally from the frayed scales of reptiles.

The number of feathers in a bird's plumage varies considerably from one species to another. One of the smallest birds in the world, the ruby-throated hummingbird, has about 900, a whistling swan more than 25 000. Birds usually have more feathers in winter.

Surprisingly, though feathers are extremely light, a bird's plumage may weigh more than twice as much as its skeleton. For example, a bald eagle's feathers weighed 670 grams (24 oz); its skeleton scaled only 272 grams (9½oz).

In flight, feathered wings are aerodynamically superior to the stretched skin of bats' wings, to the fragile membranes that enable insects to fly or to anything yet devised by humans. Watch a bird in flight and you'll see that even when its wings are not flapping it can soar through the air. This is because its wings have a natural curvature that gives the bird lift. When its wings make a downbeat – the power stroke – the feathers hold together to present a solid surface that acts like a paddle in water. On an upstroke the feathers open up, letting the air flow through. The primary feathers, located at the wing tips, bend during the power stroke, providing forward propulsion.

But such masterpieces of natural engineering require constant maintenance. Ruffled flight feathers need regular attention and rearrangement. That is why birds bathe themselves frequently in water and occasionally in dust, then perch somewhere to preen. Most birds have an oil-secreting preen gland near the base of the tail. Observe closely and you will see the

ANTING ANTICS

For all the marvellous benefits of having feathers, there is one great disadvantage: warm skin and a downy covering make a parasite's paradise. Birds control infestations of fleas, lice and mites by washing, sunbathing and pecking. As well, they appear to encourage counterattacks by other insects.

The best-known type of this behaviour is called anting, and has two forms. Some species squat, feathers spread, on ants' nests. Other birds may pick up individual ants with their beaks and place them among their feathers. The angry ants squirt formic acid, an excellent pesticide.

In addition, some birds deliberately provoke wasps to sting them. Sparrows bathe themselves in smoke from chimneys. Rooks and jays pick up lighted cigarette butts or hot twigs from smouldering fires and apply them to their feathers.

Scientists debate the purpose of these unusual activities, which may have little effect on an infestation of lice. One suggestion is that the birds are enjoying themselves – a birdworld equivalent of living for kicks. A touch of pain is said to drive some birds into an ecstatic frenzy.

Fine feathers *encourage fleas and lice, but this jay has an instant remedy. Angry ants spray it with formic acid, a strong pesticide*

bird rub its beak on the gland and then on its feathers. This keeps them supple and waterproof. Parrots, pigeons, herons and some other birds don't have preen glands. Instead, the fraying tips of some feathers crumble into a dust resembling talcum powder, which the birds use to keep their plumage in trim.

Why do ducks pluck their own feathers?

When a duck is ready to lay eggs, she lines her nest with feathers plucked from her own breast. She isn't just making herself more comfortable. Her feathers provide such efficient insulation that little body warmth is released. Like it or not, she must bare some of her skin to incubate her eggs.

Gannets and boobies solve this problem by putting their feet on their eggs. Penguins stand with an egg balanced between their feet and their bellies. Most other birds at nesting time – male and female, if both share the job of incubating the eggs – develop one or more 'brood patches'. Feathers drop out, fat breaks down and swollen blood vessels turn the skin a deep pink. Birds position these patches over their eggs, allowing a direct transfer of heat at blood temperature.

The brood feathers of ducks, swans and geese don't drop out. These birds make their own patches by baring their breasts. The small, soft feathers, known as down, grow back after the breeding season. Collected from nests or during the plucking of table birds, down has for centuries made luxurious stuffing for pillows, cushions, bed coverings and mattresses. Eiderdowns are so called because originally they were filled with the most valued down of all, that of Arctic eider ducks.

Why would a bird eat its own feathers?

Many birds use their feathers to line their nests. But not the great crested grebe. It eats them and even feeds them to its young, showing a distinct preference for soft feathers that are moulted year-round from its flanks.

The staple diet of grebes is fish, and every second day they eject through their mouths a large pellet or two of whatever remains in their stomachs. The pellet is made up largely of indigestible fish bones and scales, but it also includes gastric parasites that otherwise would invade the grebe's intestines in dangerous numbers. So why does it eat feathers? Scientists surmise that these give bulk to the pellet, making it easier to disgorge.

Robin redbreast produces young that have brown chests. This distinguishes the immature birds and helps to conceal them. After moulting they take on the adults' crimson hue

Why aren't birds handicapped when they shed their feathers?

Anybody who has used an old-fashioned feather duster knows that feathers are light and delicate, easily damaged by rough treatment. They get plenty of that in the wild. The wear and tear on a bird's plumage demands its regular replacement. Old feathers are pushed out by new ones growing from the same follicles.

Nearly all birds moult – replace their feathers – within a few weeks at a certain time of the year, usually late summer or autumn. Body feathers are shed only a few at a time, so that the bird doesn't suffer extreme exposure. To maintain balance when flying, wing feathers are replaced in pairs, one from each wing.

Penguins, which have to endure cold air on land and near-freezing waters when hunting for food, don't shed feathers in the same way as other birds: they pluck out the old feathers when new ones are fully grown, thus avoiding the patchy look – and cold spots – that are the usual signs of moulting.

Some waterfowl, such as European shelducks, black swans and species of rails and cranes, undergo a complete moult, and are the only birds to render themselves flightless in the process. They can afford to do so, because their habitat on lakes and swamps gives them sufficient protection. Shelducks start their moult towards the end of July. They retire to isolated sandbanks, where they find plenty of food and protection, and stay there for about two months until they have a new set of feathers.

As a rule, birds rarely moult while breeding or during migration. The need to fly – to collect food or to travel – would put too great a strain on depleted wings. Birds such as the European sparrowhawk are an exception. Because they spend most of their lives on the wing, time spent on the ground during the breeding season gives them their only chance to change their plumage. The female moults while incubating the eggs, and is fed by the male. After the chicks are hatched, the male moults. Some migrant birds, such as species of gulls and terns, have a two-stage moult, replacing some plumage before their journey and the rest after.

Moulting allows birds to vary their coloration, which usually becomes brighter, with more distinctive markings, as birds advance through juvenile and immature stages to sexual maturity.

Many species, such as the tanager of Central and South America, moult twice a year, changing their colours seasonally. Less striking for much of the year, they burst into vivid courtship colours in the breeding season.

Why aren't cuckoo chicks abandoned?

To see a small bird such as a wren striving to meet the demands of a ravenous baby cuckoo is something to evoke awe and pity. We wonder how the foster parent can cope, and why it ever fell for the ruse in the first place.

Birds raising young respond to two overriding commands: the cry of the chicks and the bright pink linings of their gaping mouths. No matter how often a mouth pops up, they toil to fill it with food. Even if the chick grows to twice the size of its foster parents and takes on a completely different appearance, the race to satisfy its growing appetite goes on. Sometimes the young monster becomes a kind of welfare case as other adult birds also strive to feed it. Meanwhile, the foster parents' own offspring, if they are still alive, are invariably neglected.

Not all cuckoos are parasites; many raise their own young. Nor are cuckoos

Two urgent commands make this warbler feed the cuckoo in her nest. One is the chick's cry, the other the sight of an open mouth

the only parasites of the bird world. This method of breeding is used by some species of ducks, honeyguides, cowbirds, weavers and finches.

Cuckoos that lay eggs in the nests of other birds, and dodge all parental responsibilities, sometimes take great trouble to ensure that the deception works. First, they find nesting birds whose eggs resemble their own. Many cuckoos, though closely related, lay eggs of strikingly different appearance; in Europe, this enables cuckoos to victimise about 130 other species. The common cuckoo lays a single egg in the nest of a small bird, such as the European robin. If it laid more, the young might not survive, because the host birds could never feed them. The egg is unusually small, just 2.5 per cent of the female's weight. The great spotted cuckoo chooses a different host – the magpie, a bird of roughly its own size – and lays a large egg, about 7 per cent of its body weight.

A chosen foster parent is carefully observed. After she has started laying, the male cuckoo draws her away by pretending to attack the nest. His mate slips in, quickly lays a single egg, and may carry off one from the original clutch. Because a

cuckoo's eggs must be laid in a hurry and often are dropped into a nest, they have unusually thick shells. Also, they hatch very quickly for such a large bird. This enables the young cuckoo to dominate the nest, or eliminate all competition.

Some cuckoo squabs have a sensitive hollow in their backs. For the first few days after hatching, this responds to pressure from any solid – usually an egg or rival hatchling. The cuckoo manoeuvres the object into position, braces its legs, and heaves until the weight vanishes over the side of the nest.

Other young cuckoos disguise themselves to resemble the hosts' genuine offspring. The Indian koel, a cuckoo, lays its egg in a crow's nest. Young koels of both sexes are as black as crows, but the females later become brown.

Interestingly, when they're ready to fend for themselves, fostered cuckoo chicks ignore everything they have seen and heard in the hosts' nests, except perhaps in one important respect. Females are believed to carry with them an image of the hosts' nest site or of the bird that raised them, so that when they return as adults they know which kind of nest to choose for their eggs.

Do-it-yourself artistry *rarely surpasses that of these builders and architects of the bird world. Clockwise from the left, our masters of craft are a bald eagle (photographed in Alaska), a northern gilded flicker (Mexico), a striated weaver (India), a paradise flycatcher (South Africa) and the European penduline tit. A nest may be built by a single bird in a day; others are the work of pairs over several months. Some birds, such as eagles, often use the same nest for many years. Golden eagles in Scotland built a nest some 4.5 m (15 ft) deep. Successive generations used it for forty-five years*

Why do birds build so many different kinds of nests?

Nothing is more remarkable in the bird world than the patience, ingenuity and skills that go into the building of nests. Some, often suspended from vines, are so small that a nesting bird hides them completely from view. Others are domed palaces into which the bird disappears to incubate the eggs. Some nests are cunningly camouflaged and concealed from predators. Others – like that of the South American ovenbird, which sets its nest on a fence post – resemble small fortresses and are highly visible.

Not all birds are architects and builders. The emperor penguin, for example, doesn't bother to have a nest. It holds its single egg on its feet, covering it with a flap of skin. The flamingo scrapes up a cone of mud. Gannets and gulls lay eggs among rocks on a cliff edge.

A bird in a hurry to lay may build its nest in a day or two. Birds living in gentle climates, where breeding may be more leisurely, sometimes work on the nest in pairs, spreading the job over a period of several months.

The enormous diversity in the location, size and shape of birds' nests and in the materials used in them has many explanations. First, a breeding bird needs more than its normal food supply – to make its eggs and to feed itself and its young. Usually it chooses a site close to readily available food. The nest needs protection from enemies. Given a chance, some birds, mammals and reptiles will eat the eggs, the young and the nesting adult. A bird may attempt to camouflage its nest with materials matching the surroundings. It may hide its nest among grasses or deep in a hole in a tree. It may fortify its nest by lining the entrance with thorny sticks. Some hole-nesting birds, such as the nuthatch, make access difficult for predators by plastering the entrance with mud to reduce its size.

Such devices often fail to defeat enemies, which may explain why some birds build relatively simple nests. A study of English blackbirds showed that only 14 per cent of nests raised young successfully; a similar study of Trinidad black-and-white manakins recorded a 19 per cent success rate.

But researchers point out that, among birds whose nests may be particularly vulnerable to attack, persistence pays off. Undaunted females may lay as many as five clutches of eggs in a season, hoping to rear at least one successful brood.

Why do starlings steal carrot tops?

Starlings and some other birds are sometimes seen snapping off fresh plant foliage to weave into their nests. For many years, the habit puzzled ornithologists. Did the birds want fresh, green material for camouflage? For insulation? Or perhaps to boost humidity inside the nest? None of these suggestions explained why starlings pecked the foliage from only certain plants, particularly carrots.

In 1990, Americans carrying out research into means of sensing different chemicals discovered that starlings develop a sharp sense of smell during the breeding season. Some scents, remembered perhaps from nestling days, have a special attraction.

Analysis suggested that substances yielding these scents were possibly pesticides. Tested against the blood-sucking mites that infest birds' nests, they proved to be not killers but powerful growth inhibitors, which stall the development of parasites during their larval stages. Removal of the greenery produced remarkable results: in just three weeks the average population of mites in a starling's nest soared from 8000 to 750 000.

Intrepid pioneers of the airways

Birds that travel to warmer climates in winter aren't eluding the cold. After all, their feathers provide perfect natural insulation, a shield against the harshest winter. Most species migrate because their food supply dies off or becomes buried deep under ice and snow.

Often, the shift is minor. Mountain-dwellers in temperate zones may move to lower ground. Birds such as the chaffinch, blackbird and European robin are known as partial migrants: some move and others do not. After a series of mild winters, more stay near their breeding grounds; after a severe winter, more tend to move, but not necessarily a vast distance.

By contrast, birds such as the willow warbler, some of which breed in Alaska, fly to Africa for the winter, a distance of 13 000 km (8000 miles). Arctic terns are the greatest travellers of all. In autumn, before their feeding waters freeze, they abandon breeding grounds near the Arctic Circle, and fly up to 18 000 km (11 000 miles) to the pack-ice fringes of Antarctica. Even though these terns are getting two summers a year, they actually enjoy the cold. They won't feed in

water warmer than 0°C (32°F), slightly above the sea's freezing point.

Food availability partly explains migration. But why do short-tailed shearwaters, fish-eaters that breed on the cooler coasts of New Zealand and southern Australia, make a round trip of 30 000 km (19 000 miles) to the Bering Sea and back every year? Their home waters don't freeze – in fact, they are not much colder in winter. Fish are, if

anything, more abundant. Yet the shearwaters forsake a life of ease to make a journey that in some years kills them, particularly young birds, in their thousands. A clue to their seemingly illogical behaviour may be that sites for their breeding burrows are limited and crowded. By clinging to a habit that no longer has a climatic cause, the birds are perhaps exercising unconsciously a kind of population control.

No doubt the migratory instincts of birds were reinforced in relatively recent times by the rigours of the ice ages. But the origins of their long-range travel probably go back farther. Early birds were in the air 150 million years ago. As major landmasses drifted apart and habitats became fragmented, birds able to span the widening gaps would have had better chances of survival.

Birds migrating in short stages over land seem to do so simply in response to weather changes. They retreat with the onset of severe weather, and are usually the first to return in the warmth

Three distinct patterns of migration are shown by the barnacle geese (in flight, top of page), the imperial shags at their nests and the dense cloud of yellow-headed blackbirds (right). Every year, the geese leave islands in the Arctic to fly south to the Netherlands and northern Britain. The shags of southern South America move only a short distance if winter is severe. The blackbirds of western North America tend to congregate, those in areas to the north and south joining non-movers at the centre

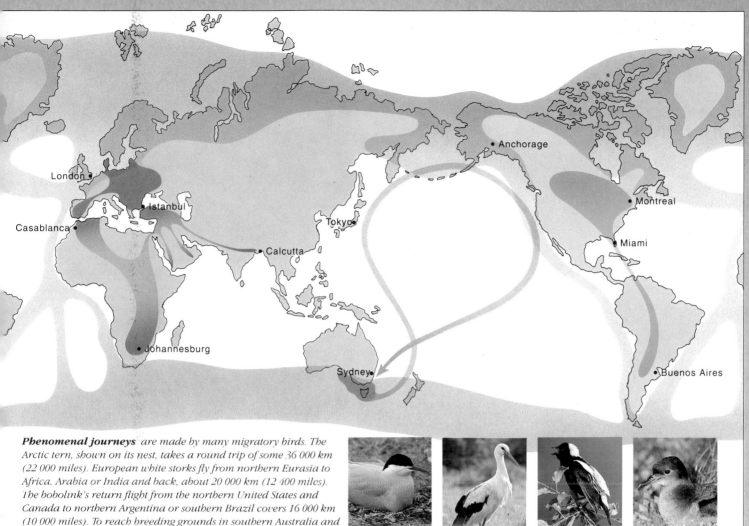

Phenomenal journeys *are made by many migratory birds. The Arctic tern, shown on its nest, takes a round trip of some 36 000 km (22 000 miles). European white storks fly from northern Eurasia to Africa, Arabia or India and back, about 20 000 km (12 400 miles). The bobolink's return flight from the northern United States and Canada to northern Argentina or southern Brazil covers 16 000 km (10 000 miles). To reach breeding grounds in southern Australia and return to the northern Pacific, short-tailed shearwaters travel a prodigious 30 000 km (19 000 miles)*

| Arctic tern | White stork | Bobolink | Shearwater |

of spring. But the marathon fliers start their journeys at about the same time every year, regardless of weather.

They seem to have an instinctive ability to measure the length of daylight. When it shortens to a particular point in autumn, they know it is time to go. The influence of these changing day lengths, known as photoperiodicity, may also be the spur for long-distance migrants to build up reserves of fat to fuel their awesome journeys.

The astonishing ability of birds to navigate accurately to far-distant places was recognised centuries ago. The Egyptians used pigeons to carry messages. At Roman chariot races, competitors were colour-coded; coloured cotton was tied to the legs of swallows to convey the results to distant punters, who waited near the birds' nests.

How birds find their way has puzzled scientists for centuries – and still does. Flocks migrating over land by day seem to rely on ground observation and the memory of their elders. Their routes follow major geographical features, and may include traditional resting places. But even these birds change their 'flyways' if the weather doesn't suit them.

Experiments show us that birds are guided in some way by the position of the Sun. They allow automatically for the Sun's daily movements and the seasonal changes in its angle with the Earth. Other tests prove that night fliers navigate by the stars. Released in a planetarium, hand-raised indigo buntings that had never seen the sky have oriented themselves, showing that some of their navigational instincts are inherited.

If, through storms or bad visibility, their usual methods fail, some birds switch to an in-built direction-finder, which apparently detects lines of force in the Earth's magnetic field. Between the skull and brain, pigeons have a tiny chain of crystals that react to magnetism. As a bird moves its head, the Earth's magnetic field causes the crystals to produce tiny electric currents, which give a pigeon its bearings. We know now that when bad weather coincides with solar storms, which send electrically charged protons into space, homing pigeons become seriously disoriented.

Some researchers suggest that birds have senses that the human mind cannot comprehend. How else can we explain their prodigious feats? To reach a distant airport, aircraft carry an imposing panel of instruments. To perform a similar journey, migratory birds, it seems, have maps, clocks, calendars, star charts and compasses, all in their heads. And in most cases, they are born with them.

When they head for the coasts of Alaska and Siberia, juvenile short-tailed shearwaters leave weeks later than their parents. Shining bronze cuckoos from New Zealand, which have never seen their parents and are raised by foster parents that don't migrate, know instinctively how to find the Solomon Islands, 4000 km (2500 miles) away.

To call somebody a birdbrain is surely a massive compliment.

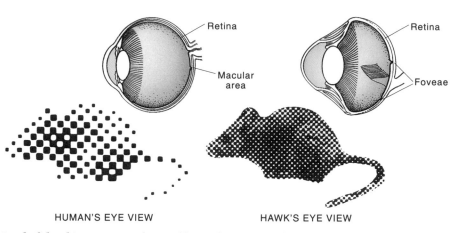

HUMAN'S EYE VIEW   HAWK'S EYE VIEW

Lord of the skies, an augur buzzard hovers for prey over the African savanna. Like all hawks, this high-flying bird has exceptional eyesight – not through some form of telescopic vision, but because of its eye structure. A hawk has about eight times the number of visual cells in its foveae as we have in the macular area of our eyes

Why do hawks see so well?

When we say that a sharp-eyed person has eyes like a hawk's, we are grossly exaggerating. No other animals can match the acute sight of birds in general, and hawks have the best sight of all.

Essential to vision is the retina, the light-sensitive membrane lining the back of the eye and on which images are cast by the cornea and lens. The clearest vision is obtained at a point known as the fovea, a small depression. In a bird's eye this is densely packed with far more visual cells than other creatures possess. And many birds, such as the hawk, have two foveae in each eye. Each of the hawk's foveae has as many as 1.5 million visual cells; in the macular area, the corresponding part of our eyes, we have about 200 000 visual cells.

In addition, a bird's fovea has convex sides, which magnify part of an image by as much as 30 per cent. A hawk sees distant objects, which we cannot identify, in about eight times as much detail as we do. The difference in resolution is much like that between two television sets, one with eight times as many scanning lines as the other.

Other birds, such as owls, have large, immobile eyes designed for gathering light. An owl can spot a mouse in what seems to us like darkness. For us to see the mouse we'd need light 100 times as bright. If the mouse moves, the owl needs no light at all: it can home in on the slightest rustle, aided by directional ear flaps that keep it on course.

Why are vultures bald?

Vultures, great scavengers of the bird world, feed by plunging their heads into rotting animal carcasses and piles of excrement. For that we should be thankful. If they didn't clean up this debris, germs and disease would spread.

To safeguard themselves against infection, vultures have developed bald pates; some species have lost their neck feathers too. Their bare skin exposes bacteria to deadly sunlight and dehydration. Vultures have a line of defence also against bacteria they swallow. Their digestive system destroys them. Unlike the excretions of other birds, which often encourage germs, those of vultures kill them. That is why vultures – and the African marabou stork, another carrion feeder – let their excrement plaster their legs and feet.

Vultures feed communally. As individual birds circle at great height, they look not only for dead animals on the ground but for other vultures descending to feed. Thus, a flock can cover a vast territory. On the African savannas, three or four different vulture species may feed together, each feasting on different parts of a big carcass ripped open by a lion or leopard. These birds will be joined by one or two other types with feathered necks. These pick up scraps.

Vultures are rightly valued as sanitation workers in many countries of the tropics. In ancient Egypt, the white vulture – also called Pharaoh's chicken – was held to be sacred. Parsee Indians erect open towers for their dead so that vultures can pick the skeletons clean.

*A **bare head** and mighty bill give this lappet-faced vulture its chief tools of trade to be a scavenger supreme*

Why would a wild bird seek human help?

Fluttering and chattering in the African savanna, the greater honeyguide begs to be followed. It wants a partner in crime. The ratel, a honey-loving badger, is its preferred accomplice, but a baboon or a human will do almost as well.

First fluttering to attract attention, the sparrow-sized bird zigzags ahead, then pauses to keep within sight of its aide, which it leads to a wild bees' nest. Lacking the strength to break open the nest, it watches its accomplice do that. As soon as it can, the honeyguide gorges on its favourite food, beeswax and bee larvae from the exposed honeycomb.

Specially developed stomach secretions make it one of the few creatures with the ability to digest wax. The greater honeyguide – ornithologists call it *Indicator indicator* – is also one of the rare birds for which a sense of smell is important.

Why do we call owls wise?

Wisdom in owls was no doubt suggested by their solemn, unwavering gaze. Most birds have one eye on each side of the head, a safety device that gives them vision front and rear. The owl has both eyes at the front.

It has a broad field of stereoscopic vision, which aids the detection of prey in poor light, but it cannot move its eyes because they are fixed in their sockets. If the object of its attention moves, the bird turns its head to follow.

Ancient religions frequently associated certain animals with particular gods. In Greek mythology the owl was revered as the companion of Athena, goddess of wisdom as well as of war. The owl became a symbol of the city state of Athens, appearing on coins of 525 BC. An old saying, originating in *The Birds*, a comedy written by Aristophanes, ridicules someone who supplies a commodity already abundant as 'carrying owls to Athens'. But not everybody associates owls with wisdom. To the nineteenth-century British writer Frederick Marryat an owl's fixed stare suggested stupor. He coined the expression 'drunk as owls'.

Why do some birds never get a chance in life?

If you believe that being born unlucky applies only to human beings, consider the miserable beginnings of some newly hatched birds.

Ducks, geese, swans and the majority of perching birds don't begin to incubate their eggs until the clutch is complete. Thus, even though the clutch may take a week or more to lay, all the chicks hatch at once and get roughly the same start in life.

Many other birds, however, particularly those that hunt live prey, start incubating as soon as the first egg is laid, often with fatal consequences for the last to hatch. Its bigger brothers and sisters will get most of the food and, if they are birds of prey, may eat any weaker siblings.

This type of incubation, known as asynchronous hatching, has a purpose. If food is scarce, the stronger survive. If all the chicks hatched at roughly the same time, they would compete equally, and the whole brood might perish.

Sibling murder is inevitable among brown and masked boobies that breed on the Great Barrier Reef off Australia's northeast coast. Most tropical sea birds lay only one egg; these boobies lay two. The first is about 10 per cent bigger, and hatches three to five days before the second. The later chick, if the first has survived, stands no chance. It is constantly attacked by its older nestmate and neglected by its parents. If not pushed out of the nest, it starves to death within a week. Only very rarely do researchers find a nest containing two chicks more than a couple of weeks old.

Overproduction of eggs and chicks is a survival strategy – an insurance against accidents, starvation and raids by predators – and a successful one. Compared with single-egg layers of the same species that breed at other locations, Australian boobies show a much higher rate of successful fledging. As well, a significant number of surviving youngsters come from back-up eggs.

Some species of seagulls lay eggs that are not intended to hatch. Their last egg in a clutch is smaller and different in colour and markings. If a predator raids the nest, the odd-egg-out, a clever decoy, is usually taken.

Eyes front and looking *makes the owl seem wise, and has made it a revered bird since ancient times. A Greek silver coin of 440 BC (inset) salutes the bird's imagined wisdom*

No other animals can survive an Antarctic winter as do these emperor penguins. One of the largest sea birds, their bulk helps them to conquer the cold

Why are there no penguins in the Arctic?

Some zoologists believe that penguins never flew, but that they evolved as super-swimmers. Instead of wings, they have scaly flippers. They feed entirely in the sea, hunting fish, squid and crustaceans. The two species of penguins that live on the fringes of the Antarctic continent feed all year round. In winter, they move to ice shelves that are within waddling distance of the unfrozen waters of the Southern Ocean, where food is abundant.

The north has no equivalent continent – only the Arctic Ocean, which freezes over. Flightless birds would soon starve there. Ice-free feeding grounds off northern coasts outside the Arctic Circle, such as those of northern Greenland and the Arctic islands of Canada, would suit penguins well. But even if such birds had evolved in these regions – and something vaguely similar existed there some eighty million years ago – they would not have survived the coming of big mammals. Bears and wolves would have wiped out shorebound colonies. And if, by chance, any had escaped, human hunters would probably have destroyed them.

In Antarctica, seals are the penguins' only serious enemies. Living space and food supplies are bountiful, and penguins living there have no need to spread far.

Penguins don't live only in cold regions. Some species are at home on temperate islands in the South Pacific. And a few hundred penguins live in the Galápagos Islands, right on the equator. Scientists believe that they arrived there by accident, after some birds were caught in the cold Humboldt Current, which sweeps up the western coast of South America.

Why don't penguins get frozen feet?

Nowadays, when people frequently venture into harsh, freezing environments, the effects of exposure to intense cold and persistent winds are more widely understood. Most skiers, trekkers and backpackers know that if they are exposed for too long to icy conditions they face the dangers of hypothermia. They would be aware also that, if they were unlucky enough to lose their boots and had to walk barefoot across ice, they would not survive for long.

Our blood vessels lie close to the surface of our skin. In an automatic response to life-threatening cold, blood circulation to our extremities shuts down; the supply concentrates around vital internal organs. We suffer frostbite, which usually starts in the hands and feet, because blood-starved tissue rapidly dies.

Penguins react to extreme cold in the opposite way. Their bodies are perfectly insulated. Short, fine feathers grow uniformly over their bodies and legs, forming a dense and waterproof coat that is much like fur. Under their skin, Antarctic species have a thick layer of oily fat, similar to blubber in whales and seals. And their feet are sheathed, like the feet of all birds, in scales of a hornlike material that has no blood vessels. A dutiful father penguin can stand on ice for weeks, incubating an egg by balancing it between his toes and a special flap of belly skin. While he does so, he starves. To stay alive, he converts fat to heat, which may cost him as much as 40 per cent of his body weight. But the blood pumped to his feet keeps them constantly warm.

Why don't birds have teeth?

In mastering the complexities of flight, birds had to sacrifice an ability to chew food. A weighty jaw, complete with teeth, would have made them, in aircraft terms, nose-heavy in the air. To counteract this,

A tough nut doesn't worry this king parrot whose bill can match almost any teeth

they developed beaks or bills of lightweight keratin, the same material as in their feathers and our nails.

Birds such as parrots have beaks of exceptional strength, able to crack nuts and hard seeds with ease. But however specialised beaks and bills have become, they remain essentially food-gathering tools. Birds don't chew food, as we do. They swallow it, and the gizzard, a muscular compartment of the stomach, breaks it down. Because the gizzard is situated between the wings, whether it is full or empty makes no great difference to the balance and trim of a bird's flight.

Acid in the gizzard dissolves soft food. Muscular contractions, aided by grit, grind up harder material. All seed-eating birds need to eat grit regularly. That is why people who keep canaries and budgerigars need to provide some for their pets. Bigger birds often swallow stones to aid their digestion. Hundreds of gizzard stones, measuring up to 10 cm (4 in) in diameter, have been found with the skeletons of the now extinct giant moas of New Zealand.

Why do many birds never fly?

Flying takes tremendous energy. Birds that migrate need to lay down stores of fat as fuel, because they may lose half their weight on the journey. Experiments show that the domestic fowl, which rarely flies, requires every day only about 4 per cent of its body weight in food, while a small flying bird, such as a tit, needs 30 per cent. If birds don't fly, they eat less – or, if their intake remains steady, in time the species grows bigger.

Scientists believe that, almost from the era in which feathered fliers evolved, some chose to stay on the ground wherever it seemed safe to do so. Today, many able fliers, such as the partridge, are reluctant to take to the air, even when frightened. They prefer to run, or they 'freeze' and hope that their camouflage will enable them to escape detection.

Maintaining the flying apparatus also calls for reliable food supplies. A bird's flight muscles alone may take up onesixth of its total weight. A flightless bird, therefore, would survive a shortage when a flier would not.

In birds that ceased to fly, the great muscles linking the breastbone and wings shrivelled. Wings became smaller. Flight feathers were adapted for other purposes. The cassowary, for example, grew bare quills like oversized knitting needles, and uses them in defence.

About sixty-five million years ago, many birds lost their ability to fly because they were no longer at risk on the ground. The

dinosaurs, which had originally chased their ancestors into the trees, had vanished. Flightless birds became ever bigger, and seized their chance to rule the land. For a few million years, no mammals were powerful enough to menace them.

When predatory mammals evolved and spread around the world, many of the smaller flightless birds succumbed. Giants such as the ostrich – up to 2.5 m (8 ft) tall and weighing 135 kg (300 lb) – survived

Tallest bird ever, Dinornis maximus *stood more than 3 m (10 ft) tall. One of a dozen kinds of moa in New Zealand, this flightless bird was hunted to extinction by 1800*

by learning to run fast, at speeds up to 64 km/h (40 mph).

In isolated lands not reached by predatory animals, some flightless birds held their ground until the arrival of human hunters. New Zealand, for example, is home to a flightless rail and a flightless parrot, as well as the famous kiwi. All three, alas, are becoming rare and are fighting for survival.

Why don't sleeping birds fall off their perches?

Those who wonder how birds can sleep on a tree's branches are puzzled, perhaps, because they know what happens to people who fall asleep while standing or sitting. Without support, they topple over.

Sleeping on a perch, even in a swaying tree, is as natural for many birds as resting in bed is for us. To stay secure, a perching bird has only to bend its legs. As it does so, its flexor muscles tighten the tendon that runs to its toes. The toes curl, locking the feet and claws firmly round the perch.

The same mechanism makes birds of prey such efficient killers. Feet extended, they swoop on their victims. The force of the impact bends their legs and automatically drives in their talons.

Sleeping birds sometimes need extra camouflage, especially if, like these tawny frogmouths, they doze by day. Under threat, they freeze – to resemble broken branches

Why do birds sing?

Delightful as it usually is to human ears, birdsong is primarily a declaration of territorial rights, conveying a threat of violence to intruders of the same species and sex. The songs are heard most persistently in the breeding season, and have a secondary purpose: they broadcast a come-hither message to the opposite sex.

Almost without exception, birds communicate by voice to maintain contact among flocks, between pairs or between parents and chicks. Many utter calls to advertise a food supply or to warn of a nearby enemy. Others use sound to help their breeding prospects. Most birds can produce two different sounds at once, and duets sung by single birds are common. The remarkable North American brown thrasher can sing four notes at once, overlapping one with others.

Some songs, which sound to us like a single continuous note, are in fact a complex series of sounds delivered at up to eighty a second. Not all bird calls are pleasant – the crowing of cocks, for example – and some may be frightening. The screaming of some owls at night sounds like a woman in torment.

The most vividly coloured or distinctively patterned birds tend not to sing. Their plumage serves to advertise their territorial claims and sexual readiness. And birds that breed in nesting colonies or live in close-knit flocks communicate by actions instead of song. They assert their rights through gestures, such as threat postures, dancing and bill-clapping, and court their mates by similar means.

The melodious song that pleases us most is likely to come from small, drably coloured birds that lead solitary lives in low shrubbery, in open fields and plains, or on forest floors. Observers are often surprised and disappointed to find that the plumage of the nightingale, perhaps the most renowned songbird of all, doesn't match the glory of its voice. Dull plumage serves to conceal these birds from their enemies. When their sexual instinct urges them to advertise, they pour out their song. Skylarks, which are well camouflaged on the ground, sing to draw attention as they soar high above their territories.

What we call the dawn chorus is a disorganised clamour produced by individual songbirds, all anxious to make themselves heard. And not all birds are early risers. A study of fifty-seven species in the New England region of the United States found that the earliest riser, the wood pewee, started singing about eighty minutes before sunrise; the downy woodpecker rose about an hour and a half

Poets extol *the nightingale's song, which may be heard day and night. French composer Olivier Messiaen, who used birdsong in his music, called the nightingale 'a great tenor'*

later. Singers at dusk – kookaburras, thrushes and robins, for example – are more rare; those that sing after dark are even rarer. We hear their songs more clearly and, if they are melodic, tend to appreciate them the most.

Not so the efforts of species that sing all day, monotonously repeating the same phrase. A dogged American researcher recorded one day's output by the notoriously tiresome red-eyed vireo or preacher bird, which made a total of 22 197 calls without the slightest variation.

Males of two Australian species of whistler, both day-long singers, can't abide competition from any source – it makes them whistle louder. Early settlers called them thunderbirds, because they seemed to be trying to drown out the noise of storms. These days, the birds compete also against the rumbling of high-flying jet aircraft.

Experiments show that basic song patterns are innate. Birds raised without any

contact with their own kind will start singing at the appropriate age, but their song will show some distinct abnormalities. Birds with more elaborate and varied songs perfect their performances in a kind of master class, learning from their

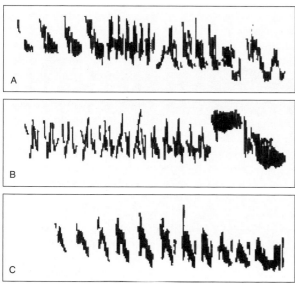

*A **chaffinch sings** to mark its territory. A sonagram of its song (A) shows a complex pattern that ends with a flourish. A young bird (B) gives out a series of chirping notes and attempts to imitate the flourish, a part that must be learned. A captive chaffinch, reared where it could not hear the songs of other birds, sings a vague song (C). An adult male has a song lasting about two and a half seconds, and repeats it about every ten seconds*

elders. It seems that some of these introduce their own vocal variations, which serve perhaps as a signature tune and distinguish them as individuals.

Birds that mimic others may do so to improve their food supplies by discouraging other species. But mimicry in some cases is hard to explain. There seems to be no biological reason, for example, for the Californian mockingbird to imitate the croaking of tree frogs.

Supreme among vocal mimics are the lyrebirds of Australia. Hidden in forest gullies, the males perform long-lasting medleys. The repertoire includes imitations of a dozen or more birds – not only songs but various hoots, screeches, gurglings and twitterings. These are interspersed sometimes with the snarls and screams of marsupial mammals.

Lyrebirds in one district may have different calls from those in another. Local sounds, such as the whistle of trains and even, it is said, the noise of chainsaws, are passed on to later generations. Workers in one forest in the early 1980s heard a lyrebird whistling what sounded like a few bars of a song. The snatch of melody was repeated on a national radio program. A listener identified it as the melody his brother had habitually whistled as he worked in the forest forty years earlier.

Why do hummingbirds fly backwards?

When they take to the air, birds perform a remarkable range of feats – soaring, diving, hovering, gliding – which, over the centuries, human ingenuity has found hard to match. But, except for hummingbirds, no birds can make a controlled flight backwards. Hummingbirds have unique, swivel-mounted wings that rotate through nearly 180 degrees at the shoulder. This enables them to hover, stationary, close to a flower. Heads up and bodies almost vertical, they beat their wings at up to eighty strokes a second, while their long beaks suck out the nectar. Feeding on the wing creates a problem: to extract its beak, the bird needs to fly backwards. A hummingbird does this by curling its tail forwards, which creates sufficient backward thrust to free its beak from the flower.

Other nectar-feeding birds, such as honeyeaters, perch close to the blossom, which conserves their energy. Hummingbirds, constantly on the wing, use their food at a furious rate – about thirty times as fast as a domestic fowl and more than twice as fast as other small and hyperactive birds, such as the wren. If hummingbirds slept normally, they would suffer night starvation. They survive the night only by going into a helpless torpor. By reducing their body temperature, they reduce the amount of energy they need to stay warm.

Some other tiny acrobats of the air, such as flycatchers, make split-second backward movements in flight, but these lack the steady control shown by hummingbirds. They cannot truly be described as flying backwards.

To avoid the need to fly backwards, birds have developed remarkable skills in steering. And some birds, such as swallows and martins, achieve this at high speed, because they have forked tails, which help them to make abrupt turns. A slight fold of one wing or a change in its angle will have a bird turning in a supertight circle, enabling it to reach its target without ever going into reverse.

*A **miniature marvel**, the hummingbird can hover stationary in flight, feed on the wing and fly backwards, a sequence shown below. Its wings beat so swiftly that they make a humming sound, which gives the bird its name*

Living relics of our ancient past

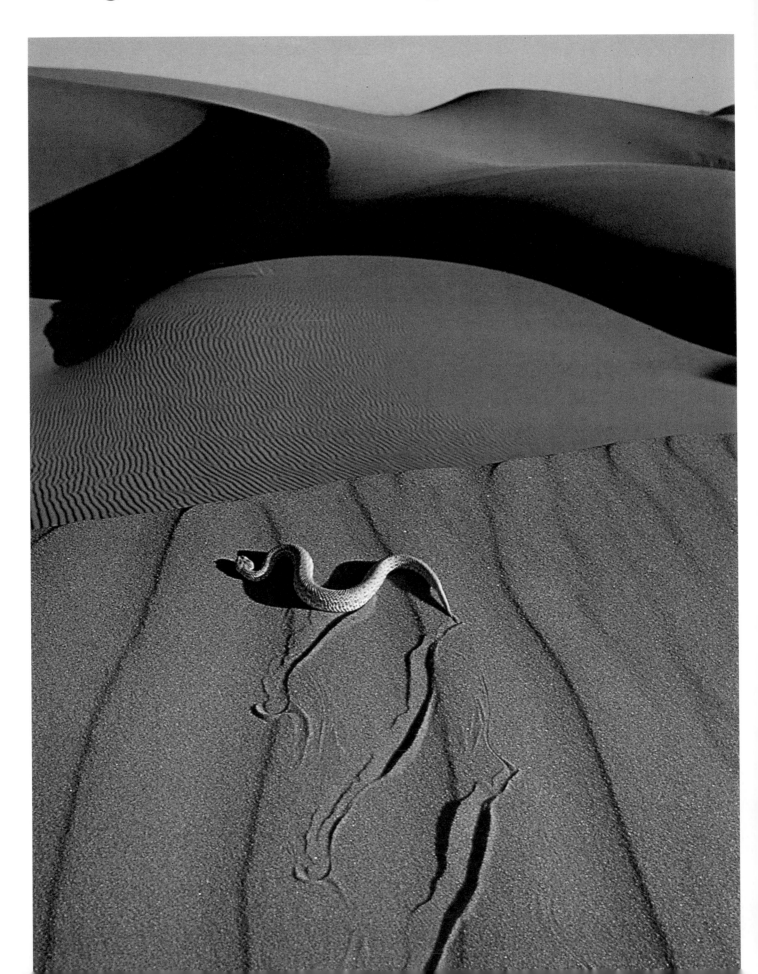

Why do snakes bite people?

Even though snakes can swallow prey much larger than themselves, humans are not part of their regular diet. Over the years, snakes have bitten thousands of people, but eaten very few.

Most snakes are not aggressive. At the slightest sign of trouble, which they detect as vibration of the ground, they usually retreat into hiding. But because snakes are well camouflaged and like to lie dormant in the Sun, they are easily surprised by walkers. Bites are generally received by people who tread on snakes accidentally, or foolishly goad them to strike. Using venom on targets too big to eat is wasteful for snakes, so biting is usually a last defence.

The most dangerous snakes are those that get stepped on most frequently. India's common cobra coexists with a vast human population, and regularly enters buildings. It kills about 10 000 people a year. Australia has eleven species more deadly than the cobras, but in general they live away from human habitations. In the United States, an average of ten people per year die from the bites of rattlesnakes and coral snakes – about 5 per cent of those who are bitten – and vipers kill a similar number in Europe.

Why don't snakes have legs?

Snakes and lizards are descended from the same four-legged stock. Most lizards have kept their legs; snakes have lost theirs, though boas and pythons, the most primitive of snakes, still have the vestiges of hind legs protruding from their bodies.

Surprising as it might seem, losing one's legs can be an advantage. Without legs, snakes can slip into very small openings, such as the nests and burrows of prey. Also, they can take refuge in hiding places inaccessible to enemies – other and larger snakes, birds of prey and hunters such as the mongoose.

To give them swift movement, snakes have developed long and extremely supple backbones. Each of the several hundred vertebrae that make up a snake's spine is joined to a pair of mobile ribs by a complex battery of muscle tendons. Some of these tendons connect adjacent ribs; others join ribs that are several vertebrae apart; and chains of tendons span as many as thirty vertebrae. Combined

Tell-tale tracks in the sandy desert mark the trail of a sidewinder snake, which moves rapidly sideways in a bewildering way. It touches the ground at only two points.

with muscles, the tendons enable a snake's ribs to swivel, and exert a rippling, backward pressure on the surface over which the snake travels. Wherever and whenever this push meets resistance from uneven ground or an obstacle such as a tree branch or rock, the snake is shot forward a little way.

Squirming, the familiar serpentine side-to-side flexing, gives most snakes their maximum purchase on the ground. Some snakes of the American and African deserts use an exaggerated form of squirming, called sidewinding, to move quickly across sand. And many snakes, especially boas and vipers, can move efficiently, if slowly, in a straight line. They do so by hitching their wide belly scales forward, then tilting them back to force the trailing edges against the ground.

Tall tales are told of the great speeds at which some snakes can travel, but the truth is that most can't go much faster than about 7 km/h (4.3 mph). The world's fastest is the African black mamba, which has been clocked at 11.2 km/h (7 mph).

Why do snakes have forked tongues?

Snakes may appear to us to be equipped with an array of supersenses. They are cunningly camouflaged, move swiftly and almost silently, and deliver their deadly poisons with alarming speed.

But in fact their senses are restricted. Their eyes detect movement at close quarters, allowing a strike on target, but they can't define distant objects. And their ears, lacking external openings, serve mainly to control balance and to sense ground vibrations.

As compensation, most snakes use their tongues to lead them to prey. In the roof of its mouth the snake has what is known

as its Jacobson's organ. This consists of two sacs with many nerve endings that are extremely sensitive to smell. When a snake repeatedly flicks out its tongue through a notch in the upper lip, it is not just tasting but smelling what lies ahead. Its tongue has in fact very few taste buds.

The forked tongue picks up scent particles from the air, the ground and other surfaces. The twin prongs of the fork carry these traces to their complementary twin sacs of the Jacobson's organ where, in a kind of test centre, they are sampled and identified. Aided also by its nostrils, this combined action of smelling and tasting enables a snake to follow prey and to track down a mate.

Some snakes, such as rattlesnakes, pit vipers, boas and pythons, can home in on prey by tracking the creature's body heat. In pit vipers and rattlesnakes, pit organs

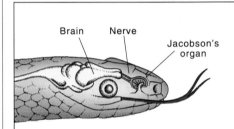

*A **snake's tongue** has few taste buds and is used more for smelling than tasting. The Jacobson's organ detects odours picked up on the tongue. The grass snake (below) is venomous only to small animals, such as mice*

below the eyes and on each side of the head detect minor changes in temperature – as little as 0.2°C (0.4°F). Flicking out its tongue and moving its head from side to side to keep it on target, a snake of this kind can move in as relentlessly as a heat-seeking missile, striking warm-blooded prey accurately even in the dark.

Snakes commonly hunt rats, mice, frogs, lizards and birds. All snakes can swim, and some catch fish. A few specialise in eating birds' eggs. An African egg-eating snake of finger thickness can engulf eggs four times the size of its head.

Why don't snakes choke on their food?

Judged by the large size of its prey, a snake frequently takes on more than it can chew. In fact, snakes can't chew at all. Their teeth are small, point backwards, and are used only to draw food into the mouth. Even so, the size of a snake's kill commonly exceeds that of its mouth.

The reticulated python of southeast Asia – the world's largest snake, reaching nearly 10 m (33 ft) in length – is on record for eating an 80-kg (176-lb) bear; another swallowed a fourteen-year-old boy; many other snakes have been photographed with their mouths jammed open by gargantuan meals. Whatever it kills, a snake must swallow whole and usually headfirst so that limbs, fur or feathers don't get trapped on the way down.

A snake can consume such feasts because its jaws have developed two unusual features. One involves a freeing mechanism that unlocks the jaws so that they can open wide. As well, the lower jaw

*A **gargantuan feast** has a rock python's jaws at full stretch. Prey of this size, a Thomson's gazelle, is usually swallowed headfirst. The snake may not feed again for weeks*

is multi-hinged, giving even greater expansion. These factors combine to allow the mouth to cover prey greater in diameter than the snake's body.

It's a laborious process, which in other animals would block off the air supply. A snake continues to breathe because its windpipe has a mobile, reinforced opening, which is thrust out safely from one side of its mouth.

Why do crocodiles let their food rot?

Crocodiles, alligators and their relatives like fresh food. Fed in captivity, they ignore tainted meat. So why is it generally believed that crocodiles prefer their meat

strong, and in their natural habitat store it until it is going off?

The misconception arises from the practice of some crocodiles, powerful enough to kill such prey as the buffalo and hippopotamus, of leaving their victims underwater until the hides soften. Then they feed, sometimes communally, on relatively fresh meat. Often, the feast is too big for even a group of crocodiles, and the meat goes rotten, leading to a belief that this is how they like it.

Few creatures are so feared, yet not all twenty or so species of the crocodilian family are meat-eaters. Several smaller types have slender jaws, and feed mainly on fish. But the biggest and most dangerous, the estuarine crocodile found from India through southeast Asia to northern

FASCINATING RHYTHM

Piping their haunting melodies, Indian snake charmers play a harmless trick on spectators. A cobra rises from its basket and sways in time with the music, apparently hypnotised. In fact, as far as the snake is concerned, the music is irrelevant – the cobra can't hear a thing. What prompts it to perform is the snake charmer's clever manipulation of the cobra's natural tendencies. When suddenly thrust into the open air from the darkness of the basket, the snake rises up and spreads its hood, its normal reaction to a threat. It sees the swaying pipe and mistakes it for another snake. That error, together with the charmer's movements in time with the music, holds the snake's attention. As the charmer moves the pipe, so the cobra bobs its head. That is the only way for the snake to follow the pipe's movements, because it cannot swivel its eyes.

King cobras, the biggest of poisonous snakes, sway as their young master plays. It's a clever but harmless trick

Australia, is a bold hunter reaching 9 m (30 ft) in length and weighing as much as 3 tonnes. It fiercely defends its territory, seizing intruders in its awesome jaws and using its great strength to drag them beneath the water to drown.

Though powerful crocodiles do kill humans, the Indian gharial does not deserve its gruesome reputation for such slaughter. Gharials grow to a great size, but live mainly on fish. Jewels discovered in their stomachs were found to have come from corpses floated ceremonially on rafts downriver – not from victims seized from the bank.

Why are reptiles called cold-blooded?

A number of reptiles are most comfortable when their body temperature is about the same as ours – close to 37°C (98.6°F). But, unlike us, all reptiles lack a mechanism for keeping a constant level of inner warmth. Their body temperature is ruled by their surroundings.

The notion of cold-bloodedness arose when Europeans first handled reptiles in winter. In that season, the creatures are sluggish and easily caught. Pick up a reptile in winter and its skin feels cold; so is its blood. Catch one in summer and, if it has been lying in the Sun, it will feel hot and be in danger because of it. Air temperatures of 40°C (104°F) or more produce so much heat in thinner-skinned reptiles, such as snakes and some lizards, that their tissue proteins are destroyed and they die.

Reptiles gain heat when they need it by basking in the Sun, and they avoid overheating by seeking shade. Many snakes hunt by night during the hottest months. Crocodiles cool off by going into water. In colder weather, many reptiles become less active; in extreme cold, they hibernate, slowing their breathing and heart rate to a minimum.

Restricted as to when and where they can thrive, reptiles nevertheless enjoy an advantage over mammals and birds. Humans, for example, require much more food because we turn about 80 per cent of it into heat to maintain our body temperature. A reptile can stay alive on one-tenth of the nourishment needed by a mammal of the same weight.

Why do lizards lose their tails?

People who have picked up a lizard by its tail are sometimes surprised when the reptile escapes, leaving a violently wriggling tail in their hands.

Many lizards have tails with a built-in weakness, designed to snap off with the slightest pull. It's an unusual method of defence, allowing rapid escape from a predator or tormentor.

When alarmed, some small skinks and geckoes can cast off their tails by flicking them. Automatic nerve impulses make the detached tail wriggle for a few seconds, distracting an enemy's attention while the bulk of its intended meal makes a quick getaway. Zoologists call this mechanism autotomy, a term that literally means 'self-cutting'.

Little blood is lost at the point of breakage, and the wound heals quickly. Tail tissue regenerates readily, although new growth is coarser than old. Sometimes regrowth comes with such a surge that more than one new tail is formed. Geckoes with up to seven tails are on record.

*A **strange ritual** starts the marine iguana's day. At dawn it exposes its flanks to the rising Sun to absorb heat. As the Sun grows warmer, the iguana turns to face it, reducing the heat on its body. The reptile has no sweat glands and could soon simmer inside its scaly skin*

Why did dinosaurs die out?

The word dinosaur, from Greek words meaning 'terrible lizard', first came into use in the 1840s to describe a few gigantic extinct animals known from their fossilised bones. Only gradually did scientists come to learn how many different kinds of reptiles once dominated the land, skies and oceans. They came in a wide variety.

Among reptiles of the dinosaur age were crocodiles – their modern forms are virtually unchanged after 200 million years – turtles and tortoises, the tuatara and ancestors of modern lizards and snakes. The survival of these types makes the sudden extinction of so many species, some sixty-three million years ago, all the more puzzling.

Many theories have been advanced. One is that a large meteorite collided with our planet. Another is that huge volcanic upheavals brought massive changes. Whatever happened at that time, most scientists agree that the global climate turned suddenly cold, cutting or destroying food supplies. The cold undoubtedly forced reptiles with a narrow range of temperature tolerance into hibernation, perhaps so prolonged that they died.

Some species may have withstood the immediate effects of the catastrophe, only to be wiped out in bizarre fashion later. Studies of crocodiles, alligators and turtles, all of which bury their eggs and rely on natural heating to hatch them, show that incubation temperature determines the sex of their young. A difference of just 1°C (2°F) changes the ratio of females to males. Among American alligators, for example, the lower the temperature, the greater the proportion of females born. If dinosaurs had a similar characteristic, they may have survived for a while, only to find that their populations were all of the same sex.

Why do turtles and tortoises live so long?

Turtles and tortoises are truly ancient creatures, having survived as a group (the order Chelonia) since long before dinosaurs walked the planet. Turtles live mostly in water; true tortoises go to water only to drink or cool down.

Both types live to a great age. One turtle, landed on the island of Mauritius

Scientists puzzle over how tortoises reached the Galápagos Islands. One theory is that they floated there on driftwood. In their isolation they became distinctively different

by the French explorer Marion de Fresne in 1766 and believed to have come from the Seychelles Islands of the Indian Ocean, lived until 1918 – 152 years later. Its age on capture was estimated to be twenty-eight, making its life span about 180 years.

Other tortoises are said to have lived for more than 200 years, claims based on dates carved into their carapaces. Archbishop Laud kept a common tortoise in the garden of London's Lambeth Palace from 1633. Records are conflicting, but its age at death was at least 120.

A prime reason these reptiles live so long is that their vital organs don't degenerate with age, as do those of birds and mammals. Another is that their energy demands are low, enabling them to apply most of their food intake to body building. Cells regenerate and the reptiles continue to grow, if very slowly, for as long as they live.

The greatest risks to turtles and tortoises come from predation in infancy by birds, fish and small mammals – in some species only one in a hundred survives – and from infections, destruction or pollution of their habitat and starvation through competition.

Once the shells of infants have hardened completely, which may take several months, turtles and tortoises are superbly armoured against most enemies. The shells of a number of species incorporate clever defensive devices. Some have hinged lobes that shut down tightly when the occupant is securely inside; land tortoises block the openings with the armoured soles of their feet.

Whether the reptiles are vegetarian or carnivorous, their choices of food are wide. Many can tolerate fasting or thirst for extensive periods, and those living in cold climates hibernate in winter. Though adult males sometimes squabble over mates, they do not fight to the death for

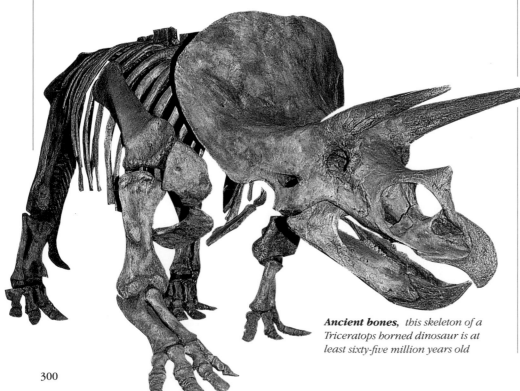

Ancient bones, *this skeleton of a Triceratops horned dinosaur is at least sixty-five million years old*

CHAMPIONS OF THE LONGEVITY LEAGUE

Each branch of the animal kingdom has its clear champions in long living. Here are estimates of their potential life spans, based in most cases on reliable records and in others on known growth rates. Keep in mind that animals in the wild almost never reach these potential ages. They are usually killed off long before by predators, disease, adverse weather conditions, starvation due to competition, or the destruction of their habitat by humans.

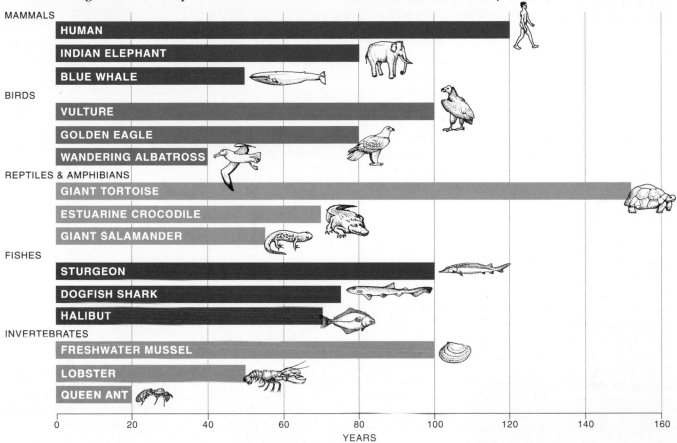

MAMMALS
HUMAN
INDIAN ELEPHANT
BLUE WHALE

BIRDS
VULTURE
GOLDEN EAGLE
WANDERING ALBATROSS

REPTILES & AMPHIBIANS
GIANT TORTOISE
ESTUARINE CROCODILE
GIANT SALAMANDER

FISHES
STURGEON
DOGFISH SHARK
HALIBUT

INVERTEBRATES
FRESHWATER MUSSEL
LOBSTER
QUEEN ANT

0   20   40   60   80   100   120   140   160
YEARS

territories, as do some crocodiles and many mammals. Over the centuries, humans have been the greatest enemy of turtles and tortoises. Records show that, between 1831 and 1868, some 10 000 tortoises were taken from the Galápagos Islands in the eastern Pacific by American whalers alone. But with greater awareness of the urgent need to safeguard all wild creatures, some turtles and tortoises living today should be enjoying life at the close of the next century.

Giant tortoises live in a wild state only on coral cays and atolls of the Aldabra group in the Indian Ocean and on the Galápagos Islands. Strict vegetarians, they grow to prodigious size, weighing up to 250 kg (550 lb), with shells 1.5 m (5 ft) long, having hatched from eggs no bigger than a hen's. Their ancestors are thought to have reached the islands on driftwood from homelands in South America and India, where human hunting has now wiped them out. The tortoises of the Galápagos comprise different subspecies on different islands, and are distinguished by their shell shapes. This was one of the observations that led Charles Darwin to his theory of evolution.

Why does the axolotl keep its gills?

Some amphibians seem to have reversed the trend of evolution, and rejected life on the land. Best known, because of its weird appearance and popularity with aquarium owners, is the Mexican axolotl.

Whereas most amphibians lose their gills as tadpoles, the axolotl normally retains them. Fed experimentally with thyroxine, a growth hormone, it loses its gills and develops lungs. But this rarely happens naturally. The key is water. While it has water, the axolotl keeps its gills. If the water dries up, it loses them, and becomes a land-dwelling tiger salamander.

Gills or no gills – *it's a matter that makes the Mexican axolotl a rarity of its kind*

Why are frogs vanishing?

During the 1980s, naturalists noted a decline in frog populations around the world. Many of the world's 3700 or more species had disappeared; others had abnormalities, such as deformed limbs and loss of digits, which showed they were under threat.

The life cycle of frogs makes them extremely vulnerable to water pollution, from agricultural and industrial chemicals, pesticides, sewage, acid rain. Forest clearances and water-management schemes, such as hydroelectric dams and irrigation, have a profound effect on their environment. Because they absorb air through the skin they are vulnerable also to poisons in the atmosphere. To compound the problem, frogs have limited mobility and can't move easily elsewhere when a habitat is affected.

When scientists met in Britain in 1989 for the world's first congress of herpetology, surprising and disturbing evidence was given that frogs are vanishing in some of the world's seemingly pristine areas, including parks in Costa Rica, Australia, Switzerland and the United States. No specific causes had yet been found for such a widespread and simultaneous reduction in numbers, but many naturalists advanced the view that the frog acts as a barometer of the general health of our planet, and that the frog's decline is an early warning of dangers to come.

Why do tadpoles lose their tails?

Millions of years ago, long before the time of birds and mammals, the first fishlike creatures crawled from a steaming swamp to breathe air on land. Aeons later, their descendants developed ways to breathe more easily, enabling them to move farther from their watery birthplaces. Today, three orders of animals lead this double life – confined to water as eggs and infants and living as adults mainly on land. Called amphibians (meaning 'leaders of a double life'), they include frogs and toads in one group, newts and salamanders in another, and rarely seen, wormlike creatures in the third.

To complete the change from fishlike larvae into land-dwellers that breathe air, amphibians require water of suitable

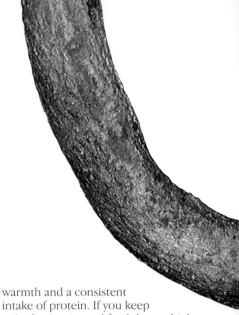

No tadpoles hatch from the spawn of Costa Rica's coral-spotted rain frog, which lays its eggs (inset) on land in the rainforest. A typical tadpole develops within each egg, but emerges as a froglet. These frogs, like so many others, are under threat

warmth and a consistent intake of protein. If you keep tadpoles in a jar and feed them a high-protein diet, they will advance into frogs more swiftly. In ponds, tadpoles eat insect larvae and other tiny aquatic organisms. Also, they obtain extra protein by absorbing their tails. But they may not lose their tails if their habitat has too little protein to ensure their full development. When kept experimentally on a low-protein diet, tadpoles grow bigger but do not mature as adults. Scientists believe that this explains why giant tadpoles of the European edible frog are occasionally found. Sometimes these are far bigger than the frogs themselves.

Newts and salamanders keep their tails, which may explain why their development is more frequently retarded. A number of species – usually those living in cold, deep water – reach sexual maturity without taking on other adult characteristics. They may develop lungs and retain their feathery gills.

Lake-dwelling salamanders in Mexico and the southern United States turn into air breathers only if they have to, when their watery homes dry out because of drought. If water is plentiful, they grow and eventually breed – as larvae that resemble tadpoles.

Why do frogs blink when they swallow?

With lightning speed, too fast for the eye to follow, a frog shoots out its tongue and captures a nearby insect. The action seems routine enough, but it has taken the slow-motion camera to show us precisely what happens.

The frog's tongue, like that of the toad, is fastened to the creature's lower jaw at the front of the mouth. When the mouth is closed the tongue points down the throat. As soon as it spots its prey the frog opens its mouth and the tongue, coated with a kind of glue, springs out like a power-charged hinge. Scientists have noticed that with the opening of the

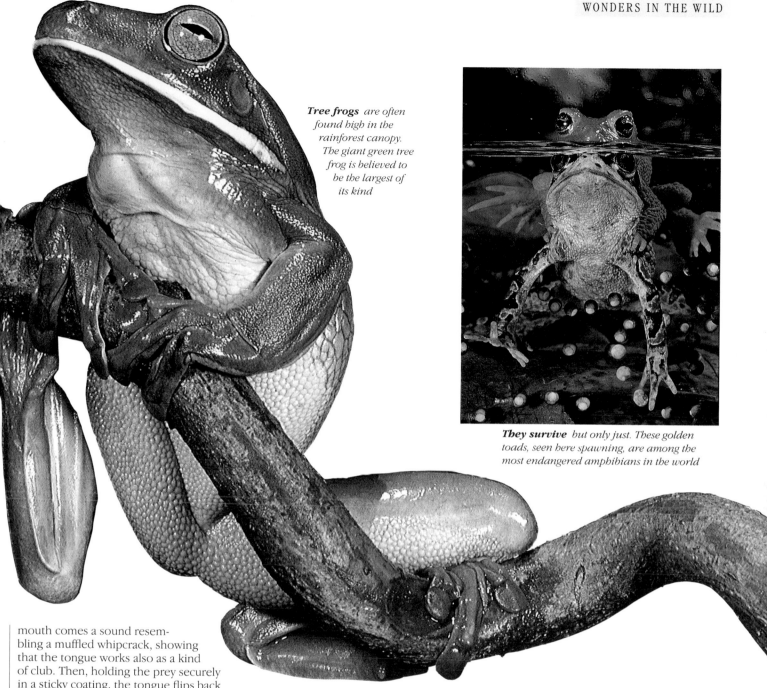

Tree frogs are often found high in the rainforest canopy. The giant green tree frog is believed to be the largest of its kind

They survive but only just. These golden toads, seen here spawning, are among the most endangered amphibians in the world

mouth comes a sound resembling a muffled whipcrack, showing that the tongue works also as a kind of club. Then, holding the prey securely in a sticky coating, the tongue flips back into the mouth.

A frog can't chew its prey, so food goes straight down its gullet. To help and speed up the process, the frog blinks. This pushes its eyes inwards, creating two bulges in the roof of the mouth. These, aided by the backward shove of the tongue, assist the frog in swallowing.

The frog's tongue is not only a formidable weapon. It acts also as a kind of windscreen wiper, flipping across the frog's eyeballs to remove any dust.

Why can't frogs drink?

Water governs frogs' lives. As tadpoles they are born in it and as adults they rarely stray far from it. But for all their dependence on water, frogs can't drink it

as we do through the mouth. They lack the equipment to do so.

Even though they were the first animals with backbones to walk on land, their lungs have never provided them with all the oxygen they need. They take in more through a highly permeable skin.

The disadvantage of such a skin is that, just as air flows in, so body fluids may evaporate and flow out. That's why the frog needs to stay close to water – in a pond, puddle, marsh or on moist earth beneath a stone. By keeping the skin moist, it can absorb water instead of drinking it, and prevent its inside from drying out.

Frogs and toads need water also for reproduction: their eggs must stay moist. And they usually need more than is found

in a puddle, which may easily dry out before the eggs have hatched. Tadpoles, too, must have adequate quantities of water for their development.

In hot climates, where water may soon dry up, frogs and toads have adopted clever strategies to beat a dry spell, if it comes. Their eggs hatch fast – within a few days, compared with as long as four months for those of other frogs – and the tadpoles also grow quickly. A small pool of rainwater collected by a plant may be all that the frogs need to start a family. Some tree frogs seal clutches of eggs inside nests of foam, which gradually harden, or within purses of leaves. These they suspend over water. When rain comes, the eggs hatch, causing the nests to disintegrate; the tadpoles fall into the water.

Lone rangers and swarming hordes

Why don't all spiders have webs?

Despite the evidence of the cobwebs that accumulate in our cellars and gardens, relatively few of the world's spiders regularly weave webs. Most of them regard it as too laborious and risky a means of trapping their food. Webs give weaving spiders a monopoly of aerial prey, and they position them cunningly to take full advantage. But webs are easily broken, and building them exposes spiders to attacks by birds.

Many spiders rely on their mobility to hunt down food on the ground or to steer clear of danger. The common house spider, for example, is a fast runner, travelling proportionally six times as fast as an Olympic sprinter.

Other spiders lurk in burrows, trees and buildings until their prey comes to them. These spiders are invariably more venomous than web-weavers, because they need to overpower their quarry more quickly, instead of leaving it to a lingering death, glued to the larder.

Scientists say that the world's 40 000 or so species of spiders came originally from marine creatures that invaded the land some 400 million years ago. Their evolution hasn't resulted in earlier kinds dying out. Trapdoor and funnel-web spiders, for example, have lived almost unchanged in form for millions of years. In a process known as adaptive radiation, more and more spiders of different kinds have developed, successfully filling every available ecological niche and sporting a wonderful mix of lifestyles.

All spiders share a predatory habit and a unique method of mating. The male spins a strand of web onto which he drops his sperm. He sucks the web and sperm into organs known as palps, and then hunts for a female. Swiftly, to avoid retaliation and possible injury, he discharges the sperm into her genitals, and makes his getaway.

Spiders spin silk by squirting it from modified excretory glands. Originally the silk was used to protect eggs and to line nesting burrows. Now it serves many purposes. As well as webs, it makes triplines to alert trapdoor spiders to approaching visitors; it wraps up prey; it provides safety lines for jumping spiders, so that if they fall they are suspended by a thread, much as mountaineers are saved by safety ropes. On slender strands of gossamer, hatchling spiders, which may

*A **spider lurks** at the centre of a web that is distorted by pearls of dew. The silk's elasticity and strength are remarkable. It will stretch by a third before breaking – twice as far as nylon*

Wiles galore have been devised by spiders to trap their prey. The hunting spider, seen feeding on a katydid (far left), relies on sharp eyesight to spot a meal, and pounces with speed. The trapdoor spider lies in wait under the lid of its silk-lined burrow. The trapdoor is cunningly designed and is sometimes rimmed with teeth to give it an exact fit in the ground

number up to 1000 from one cocoon, can disperse by riding the wind.

Members of the worldwide Theridiidae family of spiders, which includes the American black widow, lay gum-footed lines on which to catch their food. First, they spin a tangle of web as an anchor, attaching it to the ground, a tree or a rock. Then they stretch a sticky thread to their hideout. An unsuspecting insect becomes caught on the line, and the spider hauls it in.

Net-throwing spiders weave a napkin of elastic silk, which they hold with their front four feet as they hang upside down. As their prey approaches, they lunge, capturing it in the net. The victim's struggles serve only to imprison it more tightly. But

for originality and simplicity, nothing beats the ploys of tropical bolas spiders. The bolas spider dangles a large, sticky globule on the end of a single silk thread. The adhesive attracts moths. The spider senses a moth's vibrating wings, and swings the lure, like a bolas, faster and faster. When it traps a moth on the sticky bait, the spider hauls it up, like an angler landing a fish.

Spider silk is extremely light and strong. A strand stretching from London to New York, a distance of 5536 km (3440 miles) would weigh less than a pullet's egg, yet have a breaking strain proportionally greater than that of steel. The silk of the golden orb spider, found worldwide, is the strongest natural fibre known.

Why don't spiders get stuck in their webs?

A spider building a web is an artist at work. And when it races from hiding to pick up its prey, it is like a high-wire performer on skates. It can do this, where flies and other insects get trapped, because it has special, hard bristles on the underside of its feet.

These slot over the thread, and act as runners, allowing the spider to move freely over the silk without getting stuck. Elsewhere, to resist its own snare, a spider's body has an oily, non-stick coating. If all fails, a spider entangled in its web eats its way out. most spiders that construct webs reabsorb unwanted silk as a matter of course.

Not all of a typical web is sticky. A weaving spider controls carefully how much adhesive coats its silk. Often, it loads the first strand with a heavy blob of gum. This swings like a pendulum in the wind and catches eventually on a distant branch or clump of foliage. Next, the spider weaves the spokes and spirals of a complete web with dry silk. Finally, it follows the outline of this web, eating some strands and replacing them with spirals of sticky silk. In bright sunlight, the shiny threads identify the sticky part of a web.

A DOSE OF PUZZLING POISON

All spiders, except members of the family Uloboridae found in warm regions worldwide, are venomous. The chemical composition of their poisons is as varied as the spiders themselves. Some components are intended to kill or paralyse prey – usually insects; others liquefy a victim's body contents so that spiders can suck them out.

In humans, bites from spiders may cause pain or sickness, but few are fatal. The venom of one kind of funnel-web spider, found in Sydney, Australia, puzzles entomologists. It contains atratoxin, which can kill people, especially children. But pets, livestock and wild animals are immune to it.

Pets survive bites from a funnel-web but humans may die

Why are cicadas so noisy?

The sound made by the cicadas in one tree can measure 100 decibels at a distance of 18 m (60 ft). That of a pneumatic drill at an equal range clocks up about 90 decibels. No wonder that cicadas in full crescendo cause ear-splitting pain to some people. The volume from cicadas in chorus can blot out almost any other noise in the animal world.

You can imitate the sound, but not necessarily its pitch, by pressing down on the flexible lid of a metal container, and then releasing it. You will get two sharp clicks – one as you press and another as you release.

Male cicadas, which usually make the noise, do something similar, and at a furious rate of up to 600 times a second. Their abdomens have drumlike chambers covered by stiff membranes. Powerful pulsating muscles snap these membranes in and out. Hollows in the abdominal region amplify the sound, and other organs add resonance.

The purpose of this din is, like the songs of birds, to attract females to mate and to warn off other males of the same species. What our ears miss in this confusion of sound is an intricate variation in rhythm that distinguishes one species from another.

We shouldn't begrudge cicadas their right to be heard. In their larval stages they spend an extraordinary time underground – at least four years in mild climates. In parts of America, where the soil freezes in winter, some species wait seventeen years before coming into the open. After all that, they have no more than a month to find mates and produce eggs before they die.

Why do scorpions dance?

Looking like a bizarre imitation of partners in a ballroom, the scorpions approach, interlock their huge pincers, and shuffle around in a dance.

For a minute or more, they move ponderously over the ground, their venomous tails raised. Though only their claws touch, the couple are mating. As they rock back and forth in this dance of love, they brush aside stones and other debris. As the dance approaches its end, the male squirts sperm onto a cleared

patch of ground from an opening in his underside. Still holding his mate by the claws, he manoeuvres her over the spot. The sperm then enters her body, impregnating her eggs. The locking of claws apparently neutralises their natural instinct to lash out with their stinging tails.

The first young, born one at a time, arrive after a few months. The last may not come for almost a year. All are born alive, or in soft sacs from which they quickly hatch. In about two weeks, they are fully independent. Until then, they group together, riding around on their mother's back.

Some 1200 scorpion species are found throughout the world, and all have poisonous stings. Those inhabiting hot, dry regions, such as Egypt, can be deadly to humans.

Why do fireflies shine in the dark?

Fireflies aren't flies, but beetles. And there is nothing fiery about them. Their flashing, rhythmical signals are cool light, the most efficient light known. Most electric bulbs convert only about 5 per cent of energy into light; the rest produces unwanted heat. Fireflies do the reverse: only 5 per cent goes into heat. Scientists who have tried to copy this way of producing light say that a candle shining with the same brightness would be about 80 000 times as hot as a firefly's signal.

When fireflies get amorous, they stay cool. Their flashing lights are mating calls. Like those from a lighthouse, these signals are very different from one another. Some flash steadily, others intermittently,

Lights flash in unison as these Asian fireflies send their mating signal

depending on sex and species. Male fireflies flash their message, sometimes on the wing, then watch. Large, bulging eyes help them to pick up a signal from the beacon of a stationary female.

One study showed that 2.1 seconds elapsed between the male of one species flashing his signal and the female of the same species showing a welcoming response. The time difference was the all-important key in bringing them together; the male will ignore a reply that comes at any other interval of time.

Members of two families of beetles are known as fireflies. One is seen in and among trees in moist areas in Europe, North America and Australia; the other is found in South America and the Pacific islands. In both sexes of the first group, members of the Lampyridae family, insects have transparent panels towards the rear of their abdomens. Inside are cells of organic crystals that are broken down at short intervals by a special enzyme. This chemical conversion discharges energy in the form of light. The colour, as well as the frequency of flashing, varies between species, and so do the dancing patterns that males make during their flight.

Some Lampyridae beetles look more like grubs, and emit a softer, steadier light. These are usually known as glow-worms. However, the cave glow-worms that attract tourists in Australia and New Zealand are quite different from those found in other parts of the world. They are the larvae of fungus gnats, and their way of snaring food is unique – even more remarkable than that of spiders. Light from the larvae lures flying insects to head towards them, where they blunder into curtains of sticky silk.

No soft-shoe shuffle can match the ponderous love dance of scorpions. First the couple rock and roll. Then the male entices his partner to a spot impregnated with his sperm

Why aren't insects bigger?

Of all the different classes of animals in the world, insects are the most successful and numerous. They outnumber humans by at least a million to one. By evolving into so many forms – so abundant that we can't count all the species, let alone guess at the numbers in each – they have adapted to the widest possible range of living conditions. Insects are just about everywhere. Entomologists say that 1 hectare (2½ acres) of pastureland contains about 890 million insects.

Under attack, insects are resistant. Despite our best efforts, we have failed to exterminate a single pest species. The shells of insects protect them even from doses of radiation lethal to humans. It is often claimed that after the worst imaginable disaster only insects would survive to inherit the world.

For all their assets, insects lack the power to grow bigger. This is because they breathe through tiny openings in their shells. These pores connect with fine tubes that run to all parts of their bodies. Oxygen is absorbed directly into muscle tissues, not into the blood stream.

This system works well in a small body, where the tubes are short. As the tubes grow longer, the intake of oxygen and the discharge of carbon dioxide becomes less efficient. A few insects use abdominal muscles to pump air through their bodies, but even this method doesn't allow them to grow bigger. Only a radical, evolutionary change in which insects found a new way to breathe would permit that.

Atomic radiation *turns ants into giants but only in the movie,* Them! *Insects can't grow bigger, but can survive large doses of radiation*

An army of workers *attends the queen (centre of photograph and carrying the beekeeper's yellow spot on her thorax). As the queen lays eggs, she secretes pheromones. These stop the workers, all females, from developing ovaries, and also transmit codes of social behaviour*

Why do honeybees dance?

In the highly structured society of a bee-hive, an elaborate system of communications keeps everything running with extraordinary efficiency. The residents, numbering anything from about 1000 to 100 000, include two categories: house bees and field bees. An army of house bees keeps the hive clean and well ventilated, and builds new combs to store honey. Field bees, older bees that have graduated from household duties, search for nectar.

When foraging bees find new sources of nectar, they report their discoveries to others in the hive. Karl von Frisch, an Austrian pioneer in the study of bees and beekeeping, noticed that returning bees perform two kinds of dances. In one, which he first described in 1923 as 'the round', a scout bee swings its body vigorously for anything from one second to several minutes, turning first to the right, then to the left. The round dance is performed when the source of food is quite close, and its length and liveliness show other bees how rich the food is. If the nectar is more distant – more than about 100 m (330 ft) – the scout bee does a tail-

wagging dance. First it runs straight for a short distance, the angle of the run indicating the direction of the source. Then it wags its abdomen and tail before turning a full circle. The slower the rate of the dance, the farther away the nectar.

Many factors influence the bees' level of excitement and the vigour of the dances. Most important is the sweetness of the nectar. Researchers have noticed that in colonies where the level of honey is low the discovery of a rich source of nectar leads to greater excitement and more dancing than such a find by bees in a well-stocked hive.

Even though bees may be forced by big rocks or other obstacles to fly a circuitous route home, they can work out precisely

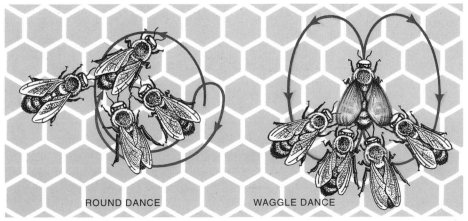

ROUND DANCE WAGGLE DANCE

Dancing with delight, *scout bees inform the hive of a rich new food source by running in a tight circle. A round dance declares that the food is less than 100 m (330 ft) distant. A waggle dance, in which the bees turn in a figure-of-eight and wag their tails, shows that the feast is farther away. If the dance is in a slow tempo, the food is more distant. The waggle sometimes indicates a great new place to live, which may set the bees swarming*

the direct line between a new feeding source and the hive. They take their bearings from the position of the Sun and continuous landmarks, such as a shoreline, forest or highway.

When the Sun is hidden, the extreme sensitivity of a bee's eye to ultraviolet light enables it to keep on track. Studies of bee swarms searching for a new nest site show that sometimes they dance by night, and even then correctly indicate the Sun's position. Bees that were moved experimentally from the southern to the northern hemisphere were at first disoriented, but in little more than a month they had learned to compensate for the Sun's 'reverse' movement.

Von Frisch observed, 'What these animals can tell each other about feeding places they have discovered … is beyond anything we should have expected of insects. And their brains are no bigger than a grain of millet. Nothing could more clearly illustrate the marvellous structure of the nerve cells. It would be presumptuous to say that we can understand it.'

Why do honeybees swarm from their hives?

The sight of many thousands of bees flying in a dense cloud rarely fails to provoke alarm. A century ago, distraught villagers rang bells and beat tin pans in the belief that this would induce the bees to settle. In time they did, but not because of the clamour: scientific tests using loudspeakers show that swarming bees take no notice of noise.

Beekeepers know that swarming – the migration of some or all of an average hive's 50 000 bees – is an instinctive reaction, part of a honeybee colony's life cycle. They know, too, that good management can prevent colonies breaking up; if migrating bees aren't captured, bee stocks are seriously depleted and honey yields reduced.

Many factors cause bees to swarm. The chief is believed to be overcrowding of the hive, particularly if this occurs when nectar is scarce and the colony is not producing much honey. If a hive's population is well balanced and making plenty of honey, it rarely splits up.

Swarming is also part of the honeybees' method of reproduction. At the height of the honey-gathering season, when bees work furiously, a honeybee lives for not much longer than a month. In an active hive, some 2000 of a colony's bees may die every day.

Only the queen bee lays eggs, and only she can replenish the hive's rapidly changing population. The queen, who is in fact more like a slave-labourer, spends

Hives of straw existed 400 years ago and for centuries before that. Decorations on ancient Egyptian tombs show that people have kept bees for some 2500 years. Honey was valued as one of few readily available sweeteners and provided a potent beverage, mead

her life laying eggs. At the age of about two weeks she makes the first of her three or four nuptial sorties, often flying a kilometre (more than half a mile) from the hive. She carries a powerful scent that has the colony's males pursuing her, even though the shock of mating kills them. The initial impregnations by as many as five million sperm ensure that she never needs to mate again. Then, for possibly five years, the queen does little but lay eggs. Records show that some queens lay 3000 eggs a day – two eggs a minute, day and night, nonstop.

In a stable hive, where the population doesn't increase too rapidly, where the flow of honey is good and where the queen remains young and active, the bees do nothing to produce another queen. If, however, the queen is ageing and cannot lay eggs in sufficient number, the bees work to raise another. They do this by feeding a small number of larvae with what is known as royal jelly, a creamy and complex secretion, high in protein and rich in B vitamins.

If two or more queens develop at the same time, they fight for supremacy, one usually killing her rivals. Two queens rarely inhabit the same hive. The older one usually departs, often taking with her as much as half the hive's population.

While beekeepers agree that such factors as overcrowding, poor ventilation and an ageing queen are likely to cause bees to swarm, they are still puzzled about why some colonies break up and others, seemingly enjoying similar conditions, do not.

Why can't we make honey?

Worldwide, about 50 million colonies of bees, tended by some 6.5 million beekeepers, produce an estimated 900 000 tonnes of honey a year. They turn it out in a wide and wonderful variety of flavours and aromas, according to the type of flowering trees and plants on which the bees feed. In some countries, such as Australia and the United States, commercial beekeepers move their hives great distances to exploit new and high-yielding nectar and pollen sources as particular trees come into flower.

If bees can produce honey so efficiently and in such variety, it may seem pointless to try to make honey in a factory. Yet many food scientists have tried to find a cheap substitute. The most successful process uses corn syrup, but few would deny that it lacks the subtle flavour of honey, which is a complex mixture of many ingredients.

Honey contains several different sugars; a dozen elements such as potassium, calcium, sulphur and iron; and a range of organic acids, proteins and free amino acids. The precise composition depends greatly on the kind of nectar and pollen that the bees have fed on. The kind of nectar affects a honey's proportions of fructose and glucose.

The bees' way of making honey, too, is complex and difficult to copy. Honeybees collect nectar and store it in their honey sacs for the return flight to the hive. Already the process of converting nectar to honey has begun. In the hive, the bees regurgitate the fluid from their sacs. Fellow workers swallow it, adding proteins and evaporating more of its water. The fluid is put into cells of the honeycomb, and more water is evaporated by the constant fanning of the bees' wings.

The bees keep the hive at a constant temperature of 34 to 35°C (93 to 95°F). If the hive gets too hot, they increase their fanning. Already, as part of the hive's air-conditioning system, they have deposited reserves of water, which their fast-beating wings evaporate. If the hive needs further cooling, the colony may disperse, with some bees clustering outside. If the hive becomes too cold, the bees cluster more tightly inside, using their body warmth to raise the temperature.

When they have evaporated water from the fluid in the cells to 20 per cent or less, they instinctively judge the honey to be ripe, and not liable to ferment. They seal off the cells by covering them with wax.

Not surprisingly, all our attempts to imitate this meticulous process have failed. Producing honey without bees is like trying to make champagne without grapes.

Why do ants work as a team?

In our everyday talk, we commonly refer to social insects with admiration and a touch of envy. If only we could always be 'as busy as bees' or tackle jobs 'like an army of ants', most of our work problems would vanish, we believe, and civil strife would end.

Certainly, that might seem to be so. Drop a grain of sugar on the ground, and an ant scurries in. If the treasure is too heavy to move, along comes a team of assistants. For a brief moment, they appear to chat, head to head, as if discussing the best way to tackle the job. In fact, they are exchanging particles of food, if they have some, and/or traces of saliva. Also, ants give off an odour containing chemicals called pheromones, by which they identify themselves and signal to one another. These pheromones constantly reinforce their drive to work as a team. Without them, insects such as ants would have no way of communicating or joining forces. Research on pheromones is in its infancy. Scientists believe that these chemicals control such activities as sexual attraction, species identification and hibernation. Pheromones can signal alarm, and stir insects to show aggression.

All kinds of ants and many kinds of bees, wasps and termites form communities in which individuals are divided physically into distinct classes. Each class performs a special task for the common good. Cooperation is essential. Only as a group are they biologically complete. Some members can breed, others obtain food. No individual can do both. The understood maxim is: unite or perish!

A long-living, egg-laying queen controls each community. Along with her food

supply comes a mass of pheromone signals that report the population balance. If more workers are needed, she adjusts her routine. Queens mate only once a year, storing the sperm and doling it out gradually. Most eggs hatch into females. But unless they are fed special foods from the queen's secretions – royal jelly in the case of honeybees – their sexual development is arrested. By her use of pheromones, the queen sterilises them so that they form a neutered working class of food gatherers, builders and nursemaids and, if necessary, a fighting force. In all honeybees and some ants, what might have been egg-laying organs develop as venomous stings.

A few females are reared as princesses to succeed their queens. And a few unfertilised eggs are laid. These produce just enough males to ensure that the new queens will have mates. The winged ants seen in summer are short-living males that have followed a new queen in her mating flight from the nest.

ANCIENT HOME – WITH ALL MOD CONS

Although we have been building houses for many centuries, we have not always constructed them in a way that achieves maximum warmth in winter and coolness in summer.

Termites, probably the most prolific insects of the world's warmer areas, learned that lesson aeons ago. But their building style left us puzzled. Why do some of them build mounds shaped like axe heads? And why does the mound's sharper end point due north?

The explanations have nothing to do with the Earth's magnetic field, as was once believed. Compass termites, found on grasslands in some tropical regions, build in this way to make the most of their environment. Their summer is cloudy and moist. In winter, nights are cool, but unremitting sunshine produces fierce midday heat. The termites build so that the broadest faces of their mounds catch the gentler rays of early morning sunshine which temper the night-time chill; the smallest surface – the axe head – faces the greatest heat.

Termites are not 'white ants'. In fact they are not even related to ants. And not all termites construct mounds. But whether they live above ground or obscurely in the soil, they have a social order much like those of bees and ants, except that it includes a long-reigning king as well as a queen.

Houses for humans built on a similar scale to this African termites' mound would stand at least 1.5 km (about 1 mile) high

Why do mosquitoes bite?

No matter where you go, you will almost certainly find mosquitoes. Not all bite humans. If anything can be said without qualification about mosquitoes, it is that most prefer to bite something else.

In Africa, some mosquitoes feed on plant nectar. Others, in Canada, breed in melted snow and attack in such numbers that, unhindered, they could exhaust a human's blood supply in about four hours. Another kind sets its proboscis, its needle-sharp feeding tube, into the mouths of ants to steal their food.

Male mosquitoes don't bite. Their only purpose in life is to mate. Usually, a female mates only once in her life and, just before or soon afterwards, she goes on the hunt for blood, which she needs to

Day and night *leafcutter ants toil to take food to the nest. With their powerful jaws they cut and carry the leaves. These they deliver to gardener ants whose job is to store them away*

feed her eggs with protein and vitamins. She stores the male's sperm in her body, then fertilises her eggs as she lays them. But first she finds a suitable place for them to hatch, usually a pool of water or a hollow where water will gather. In some species, the eggs will lie dormant for years until the water supply and temperature are just right.

Apart from repellents, will anything prevent mosquito bites? Over the years, devices of all kinds, from coloured lights to high frequency buzzers, have been tried without significant success.

If you keep a pet, it is more likely to get bitten than you are. One entomologist noted that the incidence of malaria was lower in countries where people slept with a pig in the room. The pig decoyed the nightly invaders.

Spraying furiously with pesticides will reduce mosquito numbers for a time, but is not a practical long-term solution. Some mosquitoes lay about 400 eggs at a time, and may lay several batches. If conditions are right, a new generation of females will be on the wing and hunting for blood in two to three weeks. Trying to defeat such a fast-growing airforce is like aiming to empty an ocean by sucking through a straw.

Why do mosquitoes bite some people and not others?

Everybody gets bitten by mosquitoes at some time or another. Whether one person is bitten more frequently than others may be just a matter of luck. If a female mosquito flies into a room looking for blood, which she needs to nourish her eggs, she may take enough in one bite

and fly away. Studies indicate that a mosquito may feed for as long as two and a half minutes, if it is undisturbed. The likelihood of that happening on a watchful human is remote, so invariably the mosquito moves on. If several people are in a group, two or three may be bitten, and the cry will go up: 'Why me?'

As with bites from other insects, some people are allergic to those from mosquitoes, and react more strongly than others. People living in regions that are heavily infested tend to build up an immunity. That is why, though they are bitten, they are less disturbed, and may indeed believe that they haven't been bitten at all. Rubbing or scratching a bite aggravates the effects, which usually wear off quite swiftly if ignored.

Entomologists know that a variety of chemicals and climatic conditions attract mosquitoes. We are all aware that on warm, humid evenings they seem to abound. As well, they favour dark places, but this could simply be because dark places are often shielded from breezes, which mosquitoes dislike. One way to avoid bites is to sit near a fan.

Paradoxically, some mosquitoes are attracted by far-distant light. Researchers have tracked them heading in droves towards the bright lights of a city. But at close quarters something else draws them towards a victim. We know that carbon dioxide, exhaled in our breath, is a powerful magnet. And our individual body odours, a mixture of sweat and chemicals such as amino acids, also play a part.

Mosquitoes carry with them the bacteria and viruses of several diseases. Every year some 1.2 million people die from

malaria which, as the eighth most prevalent human disease, affects 270 million people worldwide. Mosquito-borne encephalitis afflicts many thousands more. Millions of dollars have been poured into the search for better repellents and exterminants, as well as for effective vaccines.

Efforts, so far unsuccessful, have been made to isolate what precisely draws a mosquito towards its target. Many scientists fear that as long as we, and other animals, continue to exhale warm breath, laden with moisture and carbon dioxide, the war against the mosquito and its bite will not be won.

Scientists know that malarial mosquitoes seek out people suffering from malaria. This disease reduces the number of red cells in the blood, making it thinner and easier to suck out. That fact may provide further clues in the search for something that will throw mosquitoes off our scent.

Wartime poster *and peacetime cartoon show the danger and nightly annoyance caused by mosquitoes. Dengue and malaria are just two diseases transmitted by mosquito bites in tropical regions*

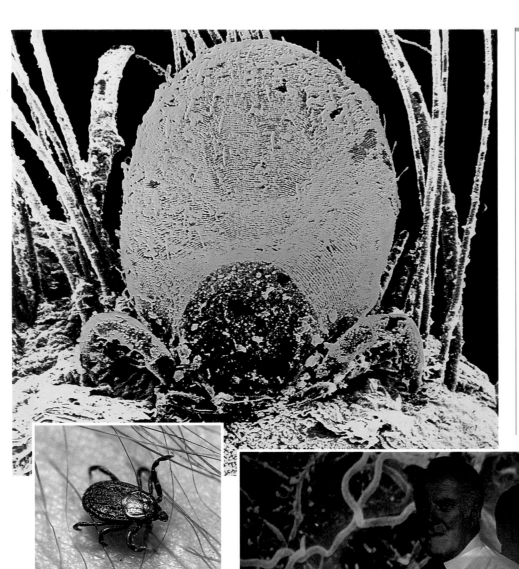

Lying in wait for some unsuspecting victim, a sheep tick (top) lurks in damp underbrush. A tick settles on the leg of a human host (above) and prepares to feed. Some ticks carry the bacterium that causes Lyme disease, a discovery made in 1981 by entomologist Willy Burgdorfer

Why do ticks endanger our health?

In 1975, doctors identified a strange disease among children at Old Lyme, Connecticut, USA. Its symptoms were skin rashes, joint pains, chronic fatigue and signs of flu.

After painstaking medical detective work, the cause was found to be the bacterium *Borrelia burgdorferi*, which is transmitted by ticks. Thousands of cases of Lyme disease, as it is now called, occur in the northeastern United States. It is found also in Britain, continental Europe, China and Australia.

One explanation for its upsurge in the United States is the protection of deer from hunters. As deer populations have increased, so has the danger to humans of bites from ticks. The deer invariably carry blood-sucking ticks, which do them no great harm. Unfortunately, a tick's life cycle requires the insect to move to another host. Under natural conditions, deer ticks transfer to white-footed mice, but in settled areas they can just as easily infest livestock and pets. In grass alongside a walking trail or among shrubs in a garden, they lie in wait for a secondary host, which by accident might be human.

Tick bites usually cause a red spot on the skin. This may soon expand to a reddened blotch. With some victims, the first signs may be feverish symptoms, headache, muscle pains and swelling in the larger joints. If it isn't treated, the disease may last for years.

Anybody who suspects a tick bite should seek immediate treatment from a doctor. A blood test will quickly detect Lyme disease, and the treatment, usually with antibiotic drugs, soon brings a cure.

As well as Lyme disease, ticks cause a number of other diseases and conditions by spreading viruses and bacteria. Some ticks also have toxins which, as part of their saliva, they excrete into their victims. Unless the tick is removed, the toxins can lead to paralysis and, in extreme cases, death.

Why do mosquitoes whine?

It's a familiar experience. No sooner are we settled comfortably in bed, lights out and ready to sleep, than somewhere close by and getting closer comes the high-pitched buzz of a mosquito.

The noise of fast-beating wings is the mating call of the female mosquito. The name mosquito is Spanish for 'little fly', and is given to some 3000 members of the family Culicidae. Few places in the world have no mosquitoes, and many have several kinds living in close proximity. Among different species occupying the same locality the mating calls of the females need to be different, so they vary slightly in pitch. They are signals that must be obeyed.

Sound waves of exactly the right frequency cause fine hairs on a male mosquito's two antennae to vibrate in unison. That motion agitates sensory cells at the bases of the antennae. These, in turn, trigger nerve impulses that put the male into automatic flight. Like a missile homing in on a target, the male mosquito heads directly towards the source of the sound. He has no choice but to answer the female's command, and has only one purpose in life – to mate.

Why do flies walk over food?

As we are repeatedly reminded by television advertisements for flysprays, houseflies will tread all over our food, spreading dangerous germs. It's true that illnesses passed on by flies range from minor stomach upsets to dysentery and typhoid fever. But causing disease isn't their aim. When flies walk over food, they are tasting it. Countless sensory hairs on their legs and feet tell them what's suitable to eat – and transmit disease from one feeding ground to another.

Only after doing the walk test is a fly sufficiently stimulated to lower its trunk-like proboscis, which draws up fine particles of food. To liquefy hard foods, such as sugar, the fly regurgitates digestive juices, pumps them down its proboscis, and then sucks up the solution.

High-speed photography *has solved the riddle of how most centipedes travel. Groups of legs move in waves. When those on one side are bunched, those opposite stretch out*

Why doesn't a centipede have a hundred feet?

When the ancient Romans found worm-like creatures with a multitude of feet lurking under logs and in leaf litter, they named them *centipeda*, meaning 'hundred-footed'. The name lacks precision, but is certainly memorable.

A centipede doesn't have 100 feet – and can never have, without a remarkable change in its structure. A centipede's body is divided into segments, each carrying one pair of legs. Every centipede among some 3000 known species distributed worldwide has an odd number of body segments: none has the required 50 that would give it exactly 100 legs. Some centipedes have only 30 legs; others have more than 350.

The creatures are in a zoological class of their own, called Chilopoda. Some are shorter than a fingernail. Others – for example, *Scolopendra giganta*, found in South and Central America – are by comparison true giants, growing longer than a man's hand. All centipedes prey on other small creatures, such as insects and earthworms, and have venomous fangs. Some larger species are capable of delivering bites that are very painful to humans.

Millipedes – 'thousand-footers' – are even more loosely named. Of about 8000 known species, none has more than 200 legs, and some get along on only 28. Superficially resembling centipedes, but not closely related to them, they make up a class called Diplopoda. Their bites aren't poisonous, but in some species the skin gives off foul-smelling, acidic secretions that kill insects.

Countless sensory hairs *on a fly's leg act as food tasters, telling their owner what's fit to eat. This horse fly sucks blood through a needlelike proboscis and is distinguished by its large and highly developed eyes. These have hundreds of individual facets, giving the flies remarkable vision*

Vivid patterns, as in this swallowtail, help butterflies to find mates and sometimes serve to scare off predators moving in for a kill

Why do moths eat clothes?

Moths form such a large and varied group of insects that, in one way or another, they have learned to live in almost every environment. Inevitably, many of them conflict with our own interests. Among these are moths that have become scavengers, which find an easy living by invading our homes to feed on woollens, furs and other fibres of animal origin.

Scavenger moths come principally from two huge families, known as Tineidae and Pyralidae. The majority feed on scraps of dead plants and animals, usually after bacteria and fungi have already caused them to decay. Among the Tineidae family are several different clothes moths, so named because they lay their eggs in the cosy depths of a sweater or suit, which their larvae eat into holes. Wool, cashmere, mohair and felts top their menu, but no fabric is immune. Freshly cleaned clothes usually escape attack, but even synthetics will be eaten if they are tainted with sweat and grease. As the caterpillars tunnel into a garment, they line their holes with silken web.

Other moths that hover near the larder are often mistaken for clothes moths. They are more likely to be scavengers of another kind, Indian meal moths, which are pests where flour, cereals and grains are stored. Similar moths or their caterpillars attack rice crops, sugar cane and even hives of bees. In 1908, the European corn borer arrived in the United States from southern Europe, where its effects were little noticed. In America's corn belt, however, it became a notorious and feared destroyer.

The activities of moths are not entirely harmful. Many of them are essential in pollinating plants. One, the silkworm moth, we have harnessed to give us silk. And when, early this century, the prickly pear cactus spread rapidly across vast expanses of eastern Australia, rendering grazing land useless, scientists in 1925

imported its natural enemy, the cactoblastis moth, from Argentina. The moth's caterpillars drilled holes into the fleshy stems of the cactus plants, and disease organisms did the rest. The operation was so successful that it was commemorated by the opening of the Cactoblastis Memorial Hall at Boonarga, in Queensland – the world's only monument to a moth.

Why are butterflies more colourful than moths?

Essentially, moths and butterflies are the same creatures. Together, they are known as Lepidoptera, one of the largest orders in the vast array of insects. Many moths are brightly coloured, but compared to butterflies they are in general plain and dowdy. Because butterflies are usually

*A **million or more*** overlapping scales cover the wing of a large butterfly or moth and are grouped to create complex effects. Part of this sunset moth's wing is shown magnified

active only by day, they have developed powerful eyesight. In bright sunlight, when they tend to be more active, they have the ability to identify prospective mates solely by colour and pattern.

To a butterfly, these colours and patterns are even more vivid and complex than they are to us. A butterfly's wing is made up of a million or more tiny, overlapping scales, some of which contain no

pigment. Instead, their transparent structures break up light into its component colours, including the ultraviolet and infrared that we cannot see. The huge, multifaceted eyes of butterflies take in the whole brilliant spectrum.

Many butterflies are distinctively colourful for their own protection. The monarch, for example, which is renowned for its annual migration from parts of Canada and the United States to Mexico, carries juices that are poisonous to some predators. Its colours advertise the fact so successfully that they are copied by other, edible butterflies.

Some moths that fly by day also sport brilliant colours, rivalling those of the most spectacular butterflies. The sunset moth of Madagascar has hind wings glowing with an iridescent sheen. As the wings move, their colour changes from gold to copper to purple.

These day-flying moths use colour in the same way and for the same reasons as butterflies, and also have keen eyesight. Nocturnal lepidopterans, which include some dull-coloured butterflies, rely on odours, sounds and ultraviolet light for identification and protection. They have developed highly sensitive membranes to guide them after dark.

Why are moths drawn to a flame?

Fluttering around burning candles or blundering into glowing light bulbs, moths seem bent on self-destruction. In fact, they are driven by their mating instinct. It isn't the illumination that we see that attracts them, but the ultraviolet light of radiant heat, which to us is invisible.

Ultraviolet vision helps moths get together in the dark. Their body temperatures soar when they are in flight, and they home in on one another like heat-seeking missiles. Warmth from the flame of a candle must seem to them like an overwhelmingly powerful summons from a supermoth.

Within range of a female moth of the right species, the male's sense of smell takes over. His antennae detect the sex-attractant odour given off by a suitable mate. Some male moths have extraordinarily elaborate antennae resembling feathery plumes. These carry an array of small sense organs that can pick up a scent from more than 10 km (6 miles) and enable the male to fly unerringly towards a mate.

That may seem to be an immense distance for a moth to fly, but among this order – with butterflies, they number more than 150 000 species – are some giant specimens. The Atlas moth, found

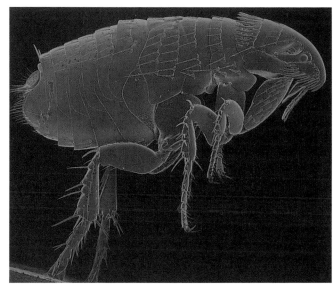

Perfect takeoff for a flea in its mission to board a new host. Fleas have powerful hind legs to propel them. Once a flea has touched down among a host's hair or fur, comblike spines on its body help it to stay there. Fleas draw blood and most leave a host soon after feeding

in parts of east and southeast Asia, has a wingspan of about 30 cm (1 ft); the Hercules moth has a wingspread that is almost as great, with a total wing area of more than 260 sq cm (40 sq in).

Why did grey moths turn sooty black?

Before the era of smoking chimneys and air pollution, the peppered moth *Biston betularia*, found extensively in Europe, was normally light grey, with some scribbly black markings. Another variety of the same moth, a natural mutation, is almost black, but it was once far outnumbered by grey members of the species.

As city buildings and trees were gradually blackened by soot, the grey moths became more conspicuous – and easy prey for birds – while the darker moths became better camouflaged and harder to find. As fewer grey moths survived to breed, their numbers fell; the sooty moths grew more prevalent. By 1900, the peppered moths in European cities and industrial areas were almost entirely black; in the country, away from soot and smog, the speckled grey moths predominated, as they do today.

In recent years, as some cities have cleaned smoke from their air, the grey peppered moth is making a comeback; the black moths, more conspicuous again, are dwindling in number.

Why don't fleas fly?

If you have ever had the misfortune to be troubled by fleas – which, in some parts of the world, is not uncommon among people with high standards of hygiene – you may wonder how they came to single

you out for attention. Fleas don't fly. They have never flown, and they don't need to. They are specialised parasites that thrive on close and continuous association with host animals. As they never need to look elsewhere for food or a breeding ground, long-distance travel is not part of their lifestyle.

A flea wants only to share the resting place of its host and to climb aboard whenever it needs a meal of blood. Females lay their eggs amid the warmth of a host's fur or hair. The eggs and the young when hatched fall into the resting place, where the new generation finds a home and a visiting larder.

Fleas are champion high jumpers, achieving heights of at least 100 times their body length. If we could do that, we'd clear about 190 m (620 ft), roughly halfway up New York's Empire State Building. Try catching a flea and you will soon find how swift and elusive they can be. This jumping-jack talent enables a flea to escape from danger and to leap upon any new host passing by.

Fleas seldom jump from furry animals on to people. They are specific to their hosts: cats, dogs, rats and other animals have their own special fleas. So do people, but in modern societies these are rare. If we keep pets and are bitten by fleas, the trouble comes usually from young fleas taking a trial leap into life. They have hatched possibly in areas of carpet or upholstery, remote from the vacuum cleaner's reach.

Eggs may lie dormant for a number of months until something, usually the right temperature and humidity, triggers them to hatch. In homes that have been unoccupied, the sudden tread of feet over carpet or floorboards tells the dormant eggs that a new host – and food supply – has arrived.

Plants – nature's cunning tricksters

Why do some plants eat animals?

When John Wyndham wrote his novel about the triffids, man-eating plants that tried to take over the Earth, readers took comfort that it was science fiction, far removed from real life. Yet more than 500 plant species have between them devised such ingenius ways to trap their prey that fiction truly pales before fact. The idea that plants can trap and eat animals sounds preposterous. The usual order is for animals, when not eating other animals, to eat plants. But here's an empire that strikes back.

The best known carnivorous plants are sundews, pitcher plants, bladderworts and the Venus flytrap. Plants of this kind often grow in acid, boggy soils that lack essential foods, particularly nitrogen. Laboratory studies show that carnivorous plants can survive without killing prey. Like other plants, they use light, carbon dioxide and water to make food. But without animal nutrients, they lose vigour. Competitors would soon wipe them out.

These plants have turned leaves into complex traps, which catch prey and then absorb their nutrients. Some, such as the sun pitchers, rely on bacteria to break down their victims. Others, sundews and bladderworts, excrete enzymes and acids.

Some traps are of a passive kind, in which victims contribute to their own

Beware the trap! Many plants survive by eating insects or small animals. They lure and capture their prey with the aid of some devilish devices. The Malaysian pitcher plant (below) tricks an ant into a well from which it cannot escape. The sundew (right) holds a damselfly with glue, and grabs it in its tentacles. The Venus flytrap snaps shut on a hapless frog

disaster. Pitcher plants, for example, use a pitfall device. Insects head for nectar near the trap's entrance, but greed lures them towards the richest source, just inside the pitcher's mouth. They lose their footing on the slippery slope, and fall right into the trap. Some pitchers are big enough to kill small mammals, scorpions and reptiles. One species in Borneo, *Nepenthes rajah*, has pitchers up to 35 cm long and 18 cm wide (14 by 7 in), large enough to ensnare a small rat.

Sundews catch their victims with a sticky secretion, a kind of glue, then grab their prey in tentacles. The Venus flytrap and the bladderworts have developed highly sophisticated active traps. When an insect touches the sensitive trigger hairs of the Venus flytrap, the leaf folds along its midrib, closing with such speed behind the victim that it cannot escape.

The ultimate, hi-tech device belongs to the mainly water-dwelling bladderworts, a mousetrap system baited with mucus and sugar. The trap includes a kind of bladder – hence the plants' name – which is located underwater and sealed to maintain a partial vacuum. Guarding the bladder's entrance is a trapdoor. When an aquatic animal arrives to sip the sugary solution, it brushes against trigger hairs, and the trapdoor flies open. The vacuum sucks in water, the prey is swept along helplessly, and the trapdoor closes. All of this happens in ten to fifteen thousandths of a second, so fast that human

eyes may not be able to take in the action.

Carnivorous flowering plants are not the only animal killers. Some fungi also are into the act. The genus *Dactylella* strangles eelworms. The fungi send out threads known as hyphae, which form loops. When a worm puts its head or tail into the loop, the noose tightens. The fungus sends down other hyphae to eat the corpse.

If all this disturbs you about taking a countryside walk, stay calm. As yet, no plant has succeeded in capturing anything larger than a small rat.

Why do grass seeds catch in our socks?

The only time a plant is free to travel is when it is a seed or fruit. As soon as the seed germinates, the plant is stuck for life.

Seeds need to travel away from their parents to avoid overcrowding and competition for light and water. Also, new ground gives plants a fresh chance. It doesn't always work out, of course, because some seeds land on stony ground when they should be in loam. But it's clearly an advantage for the seeds of plants on poor land to be able to move on and maybe reach richer soil.

Plants use water, wind or animals to disperse their seeds. Coconuts, the fruit and seeds of coconut palms, float so that the water can carry them away. Often they travel across oceans before taking root on a distant shore. Sometimes, as when they lodge on a volcanic reef just peeping above the ocean's surface, they help to create new islands. By taking root, then dropping their leaves and seeds, they gradually enrich the soil, enabling more coconut palms – and an island – to grow. Many trees, such as alders and sedges, which grow along river banks also use water for seed dispersal.

Some plants have developed particularly light seeds that carry well on the

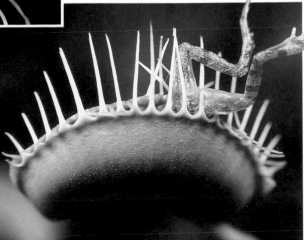

*A **puff of wind** and parachutes from a dandelion are airborne. The chutes, made up of fine hairs, disperse the seeds widely*

wind. Orchid seeds, which look like fine dust, may be blown 160 km (100 miles) from the parent plant. Other plants, such as dandelions and clematis, use parachutelike plumes that drift on the breeze. Ash and sycamore trees have much heavier seeds with wings that spin like propellers, designed to fly and travel when caught by the wind.

We have all had the experience of trying to get grass seeds out of our socks. They are not there by accident. The seeds carry tiny hooks, built to catch in the furry coats of passing animals. Other plants produce succulent fruits, so that animals and birds will eat them. The seeds pass unharmed through the animal's body, and are deposited with the excreta, which helps give them a good start in life. Birds eat mistletoe berries, then wipe their beaks on a tree to get rid of the sticky, unpalatable seeds. The seeds germinate, and the parasitic mistletoe, which lives on trees, has probably found a new host.

Many plants won't trust anything but themselves to disperse their seeds. They use explosive techniques. As the seeds of gorse and iris mature, the pods become dry. Then they burst, throwing the seeds possibly several metres away. To gain further distance, some plants have round seeds, which will roll down hill.

Ripe fruit of impatiens and the squirting cucumber are so swollen with water that the slightest touch by an animal makes the fruit explode, shooting out the seeds. A puffball of average size – 20 to 30 cm (8 to 12 in) in circumference – holds a million million spores, the equivalent of seeds in higher plants. Touched by an animal, the puffball explodes, shooting its tiny spores into the air. One of the biggest fungi ever found was an American puffball *Calvatia gigantea*, which had a circumference of 196 cm (6 ft 5 in). Just how many millions of spores this giant contained is beyond calculation.

Why does a seed grow, even if it lands upside down?

When we plough the fields and scatter the seed, we are concerned perhaps about the state of the soil and the vagaries of the weather, but rarely give much thought to the seed itself. Whether it is delivered by hand or from a modern seed drill, we are sure it will germinate, no matter how it lands. That's lucky for us. Imagine the farmer's toil, if seeds had a right and wrong side up.

Seeds are designed, of course, to grow irrespective of how they fall. Otherwise, in nature, a high percentage would be wasted. When a seed germinates, gravity affects both the roots and the shoot. A plant hormone known as auxin triggers the growth. The pull of gravity concentrates auxin in cells on the lower sides of the roots and shoots. High concentrations make shoot cells grow faster, but inhibit the growth of root cells.

On germination, the roots emerge first. Whether the seed is on its side or upside down, the hormone ensures that they head in the right direction. The tip of the young root is capped with expendable cells. If they are damaged as they push through the soil, the plant sheds them without inhibiting its growth.

When the shoot breaks through the seed's casing, no matter whether it appears above or below, the hormone guides it upwards. After roots have sprouted in such plants as marigolds, mung beans and cucumbers, the shoot carries the residue of the seed above ground, where it turns green and functions as the first leaves.

Plants protect the delicate shoot as it pushes upwards. Grasses cover their tips with a sheath. The tips emerge looking like tiny arrowheads. Then the sheath ruptures, allowing the shoot to develop. In other plants, such as onions, the first sign of growth is a loop breaking through the soil. As it grows, it drags the tip upwards. Tough cells on the upper side of the loop protect the shoot from abrasion.

With a few exceptions, seeds don't germinate immediately – and for good reason. In temperate climates, most plants release their seeds not long before cold weather sets in. Delicate seedlings would be killed by frost.

To ensure that their seeds aren't fooled into sprouting prematurely, plants adopt many delaying tactics. Seeds from roses, magnolias, apples, pears and spruces won't germinate until they have felt the cold. Those of the pea family have coats impermeable to water. Only after the coat is worn by a winter's abrasion in the soil and the action of frosts, bacteria and fungi are the seeds ready to germinate. That is why, before sowing, some farmers soak pea seeds in a mild acid, or scratch them in a scarifying machine.

In a number of species, the same plant drops some seeds with harder coats; if one crop fails in, say, a drought, a reserve batch of armour-coated seeds is in reserve. Tomato and sugar-beet seeds contain water-soluble inhibitors; when the inhibitor is washed away, germination occurs. Others, such as short-lived desert plants, contain salt. Only prolonged heavy rain will wash the salt from the seed, conditions in which the new plant will thrive to maturity. Some eucalypts germinate only after fire, which removes nearby competitors and puts useful nutrients into the soil.

*A **root emerges** and develops from a wheat seed. No matter how the grain falls on the soil, the root will always grow downwards*

Why are lichens two plants in one?

Lichens, commonly seen as grey-green or orange growths on roof tiles, are among the world's most extraordinary plants. Some 16 000 different species make up this group, and all consist of two plants – a fungus and an alga living as partners. These two grow so closely entwined that they look like one. A microscope shows that in the thallus, or body, of lichen a network of fungal strands holds millions of algae cells.

Lichens are excellent examples of symbiosis, the state in which two species live together for mutual benefit. The fungus dominates this partnership, sending out threads known as hyphae to form the main part of the plant. The hyphae entrap single-celled algae, which have a skill denied the fungus – an ability to use light to make carbohydrates, mainly sugars. The fungus takes food from the algae as a form of rent, offering shelter and mineral salts in return.

Fungi that form lichens are completely dependent on the algae, and cannot survive alone. Not so the algae: others of their kind live independently.

Lichens occur in three forms: crustose, seen closely compressed on rocks, trees and tiles; foliose, which have a leaflike appearance and prefer moist conditions, such as in a rainforest; and fruticose, whose stringy branches often hang from trees in coastal and tropical regions.

Few places are without lichens, which are among the world's hardiest plants. They grow in deserts, where temperatures reach 80°C (176°F), and in icy regions of -10°C (14°F) cold. In the Arctic they are the reindeer's staple food. Nothing puts on weight faster than desert lichens after rain, increasing their bulk by 50 per cent in ten minutes. Crustose lichens are pioneers in preparing the

way for other plants. The fungus excretes acids, which break down rocky surfaces, enabling the plant's hyphae to penetrate. The rock gradually disintegrates into soil particles, and other plants move in.

Lichens have many uses. For centuries they have provided dyes for clothes. Many scholars believe that the manna, or bread from Heaven, which saved the Israelites from starvation after their flight from Egypt, was a kind of lichen. It grows as pale grey lumps on barren land from Algeria, through Israel to the Volga River.

Because they grow at a constant but slow rate, lichens are used to date ancient woodlands, roofs from old houses and rocks exposed to retreating glaciers. Most are reliable indicators also of air quality. They can't stand pollution so, wherever you see them, the air is safe to breathe. But just to prove the family's versatility, one lichen enjoys polluted air. In recent years, *Lecanora conizaeoides* has increased its distribution in Britain because of a rise in air pollution.

The world's longest seaweed *is giant kelp. Some kinds reach 65 m (215 ft) in length*

Few places *are without lichens, which combine (inset) the round globules of algal cells and the threadlike hyphae of a fungus*

Why are seaweeds many different colours?

Next time you walk beside the sea, look closely at the seaweed. A striking feature of some rocky shorelines is how seaweeds grow in distinct colour bands, marking different water levels. Green seaweeds dominate the upper shore, from the high-tide mark down. Below the low-tide region brown weeds thrive. Farther out, you may see rocks encrusted with colourful red seaweeds, known as coralline algae because they resemble coral.

These different colours come from pigments within the seaweed cells. All seaweeds have the green pigment chlorophyll, which captures light and helps plants make food through a process known as photosynthesis. Brown and red seaweeds also have chlorophyll but, according to their depth, they mask it with other pigments. These absorb particular wavelengths of light and reflect others that we see as reds or browns.

Sea water absorbs different wavelengths of light at different depths. Red wavelengths are absorbed very quickly, and none penetrates below about 5 m (16 ft). Green plants need red light to photosynthesise, so seaweeds containing chlorophyll alone tend to grow only in very shallow waters. To use the light at greater depths, plants such as brown and red seaweeds need extra light-gathering pigments. Blue-green light has the deepest penetration, reaching to 200 m (650 ft) in clear water. Below that is darkness.

Why do cacti have spines?

If desert cacti didn't grow in such dry conditions, they would have leaves, not spines. Cactus spines are leaves that have changed during the plant's evolution to enable it to survive. Leaves take up most of a plant's surface area, and they lose a lot of water through their pores, particularly in hot climates.

This loss doesn't matter where water is abundant – in a rainforest, for example. But in the American deserts where many cacti grow it may not rain for a year or more. That's why most cacti cannot afford the luxury of leaves. Among all the world's enormous variety of plants, they are the great survivors. One cactus left with light but no water on a laboratory bench was still alive six years later.

Surprisingly, perhaps, some cacti of tropical regions have small leaves, but they drop them if conditions become too dry. Other species haven't entirely lost their inborn instinct to grow leaves. If you take a stem cutting – a new side shoot – of a prickly pear, place it in sand in a light-proof box and water it frequently, it will grow leaves, not spines.

Because most cacti have no leaves, their stems perform all the functions of food manufacture, and they store water

and food. To reduce evaporation, the stem is covered by a thick outer skin, the epidermis. Many cacti have stems with ridges or furrows. This enlarges the stem's area, enabling it to catch more light. Increased area usually means an equivalent loss of water, but by forming stem ridges in this way a cactus achieves a balance: it catches the maximum light, with minimum exposure to heat. The furrows act like pleats in an accordion. With ample water, the stem swells; in a severe drought, it shrinks.

Cacti have another cunning tactic to conserve water. Like other plants, they turn carbon dioxide into food. Plants take in carbon dioxide through pores called stomata. When the stomata open to admit carbon dioxide, precious water vapour escapes. Cacti open their stomata only at night, when temperatures are much lower. Because they can't use the carbon dioxide until daylight, they bank it overnight in special cells.

If cacti don't need leaves, why bother to grow spines? The spines shield the stems from drying breezes or low temperatures by trapping an insulating layer of air. As well, spines protect the plants from thirsty desert animals, which recognise certain cacti as life-saving sources of water. In Arizona, giant saguaro cacti grow 18 m (60 ft) tall. To collect water, their roots radiate up to 100 m (330 ft) outwards. The stems of these cacti are like huge sponges and store up to 3000 litres (660 UKgal; 790 USgal) of water. But don't try to tap this tempting desert reservoir. The saguaro's water has a sickening taste.

*A **desert landmark**, the organ-pipe cactus of Arizona is prized by many for its fruit*

MANY PLANTS MAKE LIGHT WORK

Unlike animals, almost all plants use light to make food. Special cells trap the light, which is used to produce simple sugars and oxygen from carbon dioxide and water. The process is known as photosynthesis, the formation of a compound with the aid of light.

All plants using photosynthesis contain an important pigment called chlorophyll, which colours leaves green.

*A **plant's food** comes partly from its leaves, which use light, carbon dioxide and water before releasing oxygen*

Sunlight

Sugars

Water

Carbon dioxide

Oxygen

Chlorophyll is similar in chemical structure to haemoglobin in our red blood cells, except that chlorophyll contains magnesium, and haemoglobin has iron. In some ways, both perform similar functions. For example, each in its own system deals with carbon dioxide and oxygen.

Leaves absorb some 83 per cent of the light striking them, but use only 4 per cent in photosynthesis. The rest is dispelled through the leaves as heat. Plants growing in shade are often a darker green: their leaves have a greater concentration of chlorophyll to trap more of the little light they receive.

Photosynthesis is important not only for plants. Without it, animal life as we know it could never have evolved; nor could it continue. In producing food, plants absorb carbon dioxide from the atmosphere, an important factor in controlling the greenhouse effect, and they give out oxygen.

Land plants make only some 10 per cent of the Earth's oxygen. Most comes from a myriad array of algae in the sea. That is why, as well as conserving the land, we need to keep the oceans clean. If marine plants die, so do we.

Sex problems solved by the birds and bees

When it comes to sex, plants have a problem. To fertilise their seeds, the male cell of one plant must contact the female cell of another. The difficulty is that the plants may live far apart, and cannot move. During the mating season, they use a variety of agents – courier services of one kind or another – to bring their male and female cells together.

Mosses, algae and other plants of a lower order transport their male cells by water. Some 20 per cent of plants, including many trees, all cereals and grasses, are pollinated by the wind. The plants produce vast quantities of dust-like pollen, hoping that one grain will land on the female part, or stigma, of a flower of the same species. One gram (⅕ oz) of pollen from the common cat's-tail grass has 210 million grains. No wonder that many of us suffer from hay fever when pollen is in the wind.

Wind-pollinated plants produce small, dull flowers, because they don't need to attract any other agent. To disperse their pollen, the long male anthers dangle in the wind. To trap the pollen, the female stigma are large and protruding.

Plants relying on animal couriers use many lures. Brightly coloured flowers, heavy perfumes and sweet nectar are all part of the bait. Some flowers, such as foxgloves and rhododendrons, may have stripes and spots to guide an insect on to the runway and show it where to park. Insects are more sensitive to ultra-violet light, and can see flower-petal patterns invisible to our eyes.

Successful pollination occurs only if pollen moves between plants of the same species. The couriers must visit one rose after another, rather than roam haphazardly. To ensure this, flowers have a number of tricks. One is colour. Birds tend to prefer green, red and orange flowers. Bees like white, cream, yellow, blue and purple. Beetles, flies, bats and nocturnal moths go for dull-coloured, pale flowers.

Flower shape is another factor. Trumpets, tubes and brushes attract birds, butterflies, moths and bees; dish-shaped flowers draw flies and beetles. Kapok-tree flowers open between 5 pm and eight next morning, when bat pollinators are busy. Those of a moth-pollinated cactus, *Selenicereus grandiflorus*, are in business from 8 pm until 2 am.

These ploys, aimed to keep couriers faithful, work very well. A study of 207 honeybees shows that 121 visited only one plant species, 67 carried pollen from two, 18 from three; the remaining busy bee sucked flightily on four.

Some plants go to extraordinary lengths to attract a particular visitor. Bee and wasp orchids produce flowers resembling either female bees or wasps. Also, they carry pheromone scents that mimic those of female insects. When misguided male bees or wasps try to copulate with the flower, they get covered with pollen. Understandably frustrated, they move on – usually to another flower mimic, exchanging one load of pollen for another.

The Central American yucca has formed a complex relationship with its pollinating moth. After laying eggs in the yucca's ovary, the moth protects them with sticky pollen, collected from another yucca. The moth's eggs hatch into caterpillars, which eat some seeds, but the rest propagate the plant. If the moths died, the yucca would become extinct; if the yucca disappeared, the moths would vanish also.

Not all scented flowers smell sweet to humans. Some stink deliberately to attract carrion feeders, especially flies. When flies land on the lords-and-ladies flower, it traps them with stiff hairs until pollination is completed. When the hairs wither, the flies are free to go, taking pollen with them.

The stapelia of southern Africa stinks of carrion, and its wrinkled brown flowers are covered with hairs to represent a dead animal's decaying skin. To complete the deception, the stapelia generates heat, simulating the warmth of a decaying body.

Self-pollination – the fertilising of a plant's seeds by its own pollen – brings

Many ploys attract insects and birds to flowers in a two-way deal that fertilises the seeds. Bees seek nectar from a dandelion and a spider orchid (left). The honeyeater has to probe – and gets coated with pollen

some mixing of the genes, but is only one step better than asexual reproduction, in which the offspring are clones of the parent. In cross-pollination, a plant pollinates other plants of the same species, and genes are more widely spread; the offspring can cope better with varied conditions.

Plants have an array of tricks to ensure cross-pollination. Some, such as papaya, willows and hollies, are either male or female. Others, including melons, cucumbers and begonias, have developed what is known as self-sterility. Plants bear separate male and female flowers, but the flowers mature at different times. When pollen lands on the stigma of a flower on the same plant, it cannot fertilise the female cells.

If plants have so many ingenious ways to fertilise their seed, why do they also reproduce without sex? Sexual reproduction, which involves the growing of flowers, seeds and fruit, makes great demands. A plant needs extra food. Also, the seeds' fate is uncertain. A plant may produce thousands of seeds that are never fertilised and millions of grains of unproductive pollen.

For this reason, most plants choose asexual, or vegetative, forms of reproduction, in which the offspring are genetically identical to the parent plant. Gardeners often grow new plants this way by taking cuttings; or they divide

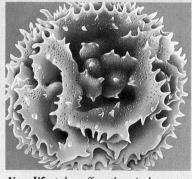

New life *takes off on the wind as a puffball releases a cloud of minute spores. An enlarged pollen grain shows its sculpted outer wall, with hooks that assist its dispersal*

clumps of such plants as daisies and peonies into separate plants. Those are two of many asexual ways of reproduction. Single-celled algae multiply by dividing one cell into two. Plants such as crocuses and gladioli make corms – short, underground stems capable of growing a new plant. Onions, tulips, daffodils and hyacinths produce bulbs, underground leaves joined to a disclike stem. Potatoes, turnips and dahlias multiply from tubers. Each eye of a potato is a small bud, capable of sprouting a new plant.

As gardeners know, some plants – strawberries, for example – spread rapidly by sending out stolons, runners above ground; mints and many grasses produce similar runners, called rhizomes, below ground. In favourable conditions, blackberries and lantana are perhaps the swiftest occupiers of vacant land. A hanging branch touches the ground, the tip swells and takes root, and the plant grows in all directions.

Another asexual method of reproduction that sometimes has dire economic fallout is fragmentation, when winds or water tear a plant apart. After the South American water hyacinth was introduced to Africa, it blocked the Aswan and Kariba dams. In the 1870s, Canadian pondweed – which possibly came originally from aquariums – blocked

canals in Britain, and was a major factor in a switch of goods to the railways.

Asexual reproduction is surer and less costly to a plant, but has considerable disadvantages and long-term dangers. Most often, the progeny are not dispersed. In time, they may have nowhere to spread. Also, the method fails to bring variety within a species. That is useful for us in providing seedless fruit and crops of genetically identical potatoes. If humans bred by cloning, millions of us would look alike. Every disease might become an epidemic.

An example of the dangers came when Britain's immemorial elms were devastated by Dutch elm disease in the 1970s. Elms, poplars, cherries and other trees in temperate climates multiply by sending out suckers. Fortunately, many elm trees sent up late suckers, which escaped the plague, and in time will bring elms back to the landscape.

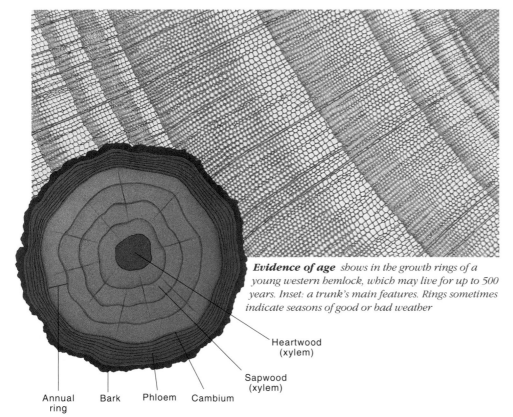

Evidence of age *shows in the growth rings of a young western hemlock, which may live for up to 500 years. Inset: a trunk's main features. Rings sometimes indicate seasons of good or bad weather*

Heartwood
(xylem)

Sapwood
(xylem)

Annual
ring

Bark   Phloem   Cambium

Why do growth rings show a tree's age?

If you look at a fallen tree or a tree stump, you will probably see that its cross section shows a series of concentric rings. A tree forms a new ring once a year, during each growing season. So, if you count the rings, you can tell a tree's age.

Underneath the bark and surrounding the trunk lies a thin layer of glistening white tissue known as cambium. During each growing season the cambium's cells divide to increase the tree's girth. New cells grow on the inner and outer sides of the cambial layer.

The inner cells form a network of tubes known as the xylem, which makes up most of the wood supporting the stem. To add strength, a tough and complex compound called lignin – about 25 per cent of a tree's wood – impregnates and waterproofs the xylem cell walls.

The xylem is a vital part of the tree's food-transport system, carrying water and minerals from the roots through the trunk and into the branches. Sequoias, the giant redwoods of northwestern America, grow 100 m (330 ft) tall. For water to feed the topmost branches and leaves, it must travel from the ground, overcoming the downward pull of gravity. Scientists calculate that this requires a force equal to that in lifting a weight of 1.6 tonnes. Trees are nourished not only

by their roots but also by their leaves, which make sugar, proteins and minerals. On the cambium's outside, they have another vital supply line in tissue known as phloem, which carries this food to every part of the tree.

A tree produces new xylem and phloem all its life but not at a constant rate. In temperate climates, growth spurts in the spring, resulting in large, wide xylem cells. In autumn, growth slows. A tree's rings tell us more than its age. They show what the weather was like centuries ago. Given rain and warmth, the rings grow wider; narrow rings indicate a poor season.

The world's oldest trees are bristlecone pines. Core samples from one specimen in east Nevada, USA, show that it started growing in 2926 BC. By examining growth rings of these and other old trees, climatologists can detect changes in weather patterns. Because of their long life, giant sequoias give a climate history for up to 4000 years. The growth rings on ancient fossil trees show that 100 000 years ago Canada had an eleven-year cycle of heavier rainfall – just as it has today.

Rings are a reasonably reliable guide, but they do not always show a tree's precise age. At any time, disease or insect attack may interrupt the growth of xylem cells. In tropical climates, trees grow uniformly all year round, without any discernible rings. But in temperate regions, rings are often a remarkably revealing autobiography of a tree.

Why do some trees lose their leaves for winter?

In many parts of the world, the changing colours of trees in the autumn, or fall, is one of nature's spectacular sights. Gone is the green of spring and summer, to be replaced by a glorious succession of yellows, reds and golds before the leaves drop and carpet the ground. Some trees, such as maples, are renowned for their truly brilliant display.

By the time winter comes, deciduous trees – a wide variety that includes oaks, elms, willows and birches – are completely bare. Evergreens, such as holly, spruces, pines and gums, cast their leaves gradually all the year round.

In temperate climates, tree roots lose their power to absorb water during cold winter months. Sometimes, of course, the soil may be frozen, limiting the water supply. Because the roots can't draw much water, the tree has to reduce evaporation from its leaves. Getting rid of them is one way to survive. At the same time, the falling leaves carry away the toxins

and wastes accumulated by the tree during the growing season.

Leaf fall is not brought about solely by colder weather. Even an Indian summer, a burst of unseasonable warmth after summer has gone, won't stop trees dropping their leaves. Also, European trees transplanted to places that never experience really cold weather, still lose their leaves. The loss is triggered by fewer hours of daylight as winter approaches. Trees growing near streetlights often keep their leaves for a time after others in unlit parts of the street lose theirs.

Before a leaf falls, tissue in what is known as the abscission zone, the point of separation at the base of the leaf-stalk, begins to disintegrate. Green pigment – chlorophyll – breaks down, exposing other pigments within the leaf. That is why leaves change colour. Once the green has gone, the other colours show through. The tree then withdraws any food in the leaves, and deposits in them its toxic and other waste products. Finally, a layer of corklike, fatty cells forms in the

In winter's grip a forest of oak trees stands leafless. Leaf fall anticipates a cut in water supplies should the ground freeze

abscission zone of each leaf to protect the scar left when the leaf falls.

Leaves on deciduous trees have thin cuticles, the outer skin, and cannot control water lost through evaporation. Leaves on evergreens are built to limit water loss. The needles of pine trees, for example, expose little surface area. Holly leaves have a thick and shiny outer skin. To withstand the fierce Sun and occasional prolonged droughts, those of eucalypts are covered in wax.

By trapping light, leaves supply a tree with food. Evergreens gain because their leaves produce food all year round.

Why does ringbarking kill a tree?

Sweethearts carving messages of undying love on tree trunks should take care. If the cut encircles the tree – ringbarks it – the tree will die. Farmers and foresters sometimes use ringbarking to kill trees that they intend later to cut down.

It is almost impossible to remove bark from a tree without taking away essential tissue. This material, known as phloem, carries food made by the leaves to the rest of the tree. By removing a complete ring of bark, the food-supply system is cut. The roots and all the tree below the cut will starve to death. When the roots die, the tree loses water and mineral ions collected by the root system. Leaves, particularly, depend on water, because they evaporate so much through their

Preparing for battle, a red-deer stag rubs velvet from its antlers. Many trees die after losing their bark in this way

pores. When they go thirsty, they drop, further depriving the tree of food.

Hungry wild animals, such as rabbits, may ringbark small trees by nibbling repeatedly at their bases. Deer kill larger trees by rubbing their new antlers against the trunks to remove the velvet. And domestic cats, which sharpen their claws on tree trunks, sometimes scratch the bark from young trees. That is why it's wise to protect vulnerable trees with an encircling guard of wire mesh.

A tree can survive partial ringbarking. Cutting halfway round the trunk won't kill it, because the remaining tissue will take sufficient food to the roots. Also, a ringbark high in the trunk, above the lower branches, may not be fatal, but the tree's health and growth would be impaired. However, cuts of this kind are rare. Human and animal ringbarkers usually keep their feet on the ground.

Why are trees called hardwoods and softwoods?

Hardwood and softwood, terms often used to describe timber, have little to do with the hardness or softness of the wood. Some hardwoods, such as balsa, are extremely soft: you can easily mark them with your fingernails. By contrast, many softwoods, such as some kinds of cypress, juniper and pine, are quite hard.

Softwoods are usually faster growing, and come from cone-bearing trees such as firs, spruces and pines, which today are often plantation grown. Their chief use is for house frames, furniture and paper pulp. High-grade furniture, veneers, musical instruments and tool handles are usually made of hardwoods.

The two types of wood are clearly distinguished by the make-up of their cells. Hardwoods have a greater proportion of long, pipelike cells known as vessels. Also, hardwoods are more varied. The heaviest, South African ironwood, weighs 1490 kg per cubic metre (93 lb per cu ft). It is so dense, with a specific gravity of 1.49, that it sinks in water, which has a specific gravity of 1.0. By contrast, balsa normally has a specific gravity of about 0.12, but it is a wood that varies considerably according to its growing conditions. For this reason, a cubic metre of balsa may weigh anything between about 40 and 390 kg (a cu ft of balsa weighs from 2½ to 24 lb).

If you have wood fires, beware of softwoods. They make good kindling, because they burn rapidly, but large pieces often throw out hot sparks. Most hardwoods, on the other hand, are ideal, burning slowly with a cosy glow and not too much flame.

Hazelnut

Raspberry

Tomato

Apple

Plum

Pea

Why do plants bear fruit?

When most of us think of fruit, we have a picture of apples, pears, oranges – the contents of a fruit shop. But the fruit store of the wild has much wider variety, and includes many items, such as cucumbers, cereal grains and the 'keys' of elm, ash and maple trees, that perhaps only botanists would recognise as fruit.

Plants produce fruit for three reasons: to feed, protect and eventually disperse their seeds. In many ways, a fruit can be likened to a female womb. Plants protect their embryos – seeds – in much the same way as a mother shields her baby. The whole structure is known as a fruit.

The fruit's body guards its store of developing seeds, and nourishes them. A coconut's thick husk protects the seed against predators and during its fall. Its hollow centre ensures that it will float on water. Unripe fruits are sour to deter animals and birds from eating them before the seeds have developed. After that, a fruit's sweet ripeness encourages its removal to some distant place, dispersing the seeds.

Fruit production saps a plant's food resources, and many die soon after fruiting.

To a botanist all these, including the pea-pod, are fruits. They guard the plant's seed and are designed to help its dispersal

WHEN JUST A SCRATCH WAS A DEADLY BLOW

The poison in a *death-cap mushroom could kill three men*

Many plants pack a powerful dose of poison, a fact known since earliest times. The ancient Greeks used infusions of aconite, an extract from the roots of monkshood (wolfsbane), to dispose of the aged and infirm. Spears dipped in aconite were a deadly weapon in many ancient battles, causing severe and often fatal poisoning from just a scratch.

Until recent times, natives of Java used to smear hunting arrows with the deadly sap of the upas tree. Amazonian tribesmen coat their arrowheads in curare, which they get by boiling the bark of the pareira vine *Chondrodendron tomentosum*.

Some east African tribesmen dip arrows in a toxin held in the wood and roots of *Acokanthera* plants. The poison also provides a crafty way to kill enemies. The spiny fruit of *Tribulus terrestris*, a form of caltrops, are soaked in the toxin and scattered along a likely path. A barefoot victim may scarcely notice the fatal prick, and the tribe probably decides that death was from natural causes.

Georgi Markov, a Bulgarian broadcaster in the BBC's external service, died mysteriously in London in September 1978, after being prodded – accidentally, it seemed at first – with another pedestrian's umbrella. Investigators decided he'd been murdered. The umbrella's spike, they deduced, carried a shot of ricin, a deadly derivative of the castor-oil plant.

Most people know that some mushrooms are highly toxic. Without swift medical attention, eating the death cap *Amanita phalloides* is fatal in 50 per cent of cases. But for its grim effects, a microscopic fungus called ergot is in a class of its own. The fungus sometimes infects rye. Bread made from the rye is poisonous.

In AD 994, some 40 000 people died in France from ergot poisoning. At the time, it was believed a deadly plague had swept the land. Those who sought sanctuary in monasteries and convents survived because the monks and nuns made bread from wheat flour. A peculiar form of madness overcame visitors to the German town of Aachen in 1374. They had arrived there to celebrate the mid-summer feast of St John, and for no apparent reason started to dance. Foaming at the mouth, they danced until they dropped. In the next fifty years, dancing mania spread. Many historians today believe that rye bread infected with the ergot fungus was to blame. Some say that it caused the famous trials at Salem, Massachusetts, in 1692, after which fourteen women, mostly teenagers, and five men, all of whom had hallucinations, were hanged as witches.

Plant poisons come from many sources. The toxin in a cup of apple seeds could kill a man. Surprisingly, some creatures don't suffer the poisons' effects. A tiny slug can eat a whole death-cap mushroom that could kill at least three men. Cabbages, cauliflowers and broccoli are highly toxic to most insects, but give a feast to aphids and caterpillars of the cabbage-white butterfly.

Some animals have adapted to plant toxins. Grazing animals and most insects avoid the bitter poison of milkweed, but caterpillars of the monarch butterfly feed on it, storing the toxin in special tissues. Bird predators ignore the monarch, because they have learned that its stored poisons will make them vomit.

A witch on trial at Salem in 1692. Some historians say that a fungus caused the outbreak of hallucinations

MATTERS OF MOMENT & IDLE CURIOSITY

'The time has come,' the Walrus said, 'to talk of many things: of shoes and ships and sealing wax – of cabbages and kings.' A miscellany of problems, some of serious concern, others of light-hearted but lasting interest

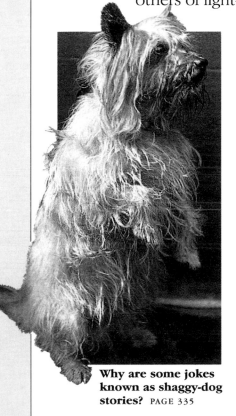

Why were frankincense and myrrh gifts fit for a king? PAGE 340

Why are some jokes known as shaggy-dog stories? PAGE 335

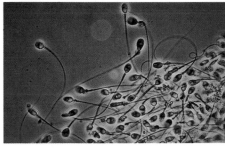

Why do males produce millions of sperm to fertilise one egg? PAGE 337

Present signs of future danger

Why should we worry about acid rain?

There is nothing new about the problem of acid rain. In the late nineteenth century, Robert Smith, a chemist in Manchester, northern England, used the term when describing how air pollution was eroding the city's buildings. Just before World War I, experiments in Leeds, another British industrial city, showed that the size and quality of lettuces grown there was seriously affected by the amount of sulphur dioxide in the air.

Sulphur dioxide gets into the atmosphere naturally from rotting vegetation and volcanic eruptions, but in Europe's highly polluted air about 85 per cent comes from the burning of fossil fuels, particularly in coal-fired power stations. Sulphur dioxide pollutes not only the air we breathe but the rain that falls.

Scientists measure acid levels on what they call a pH scale, in which 1 is very acid and 14 is very alkaline. Normal rain is slightly acidic. It collects carbon dioxide and other acidic particles from the air to form a solution with a pH of about 5.5. In recent years, rain in some parts of Central Europe has had a pH of 4.1. During severe fogs and smogs, which are loaded with sulphur dioxide, the air itself may become more acid than lemon juice, which has a pH of 2.

The consequences of acid rain are serious. It damages buildings, attacks

Smoke billows from a power station and factories in Leipzig, eastern Germany. The fumes cause acid rain, which kills trees. The cost in Europe is estimated at 118 million cu m (4200 million cu ft) of wood a year for the next century, plus erosion of buildings and sculptures, such as the Italian gargoyle

stone and iron, and destroys vegetation. As acid rain seeps through the soil, it dissolves heavy metals, and carries poisons into waterways. Rivers and lakes become acidic, fish die or stop breeding, and other organisms vanish. In Scandinavia, lakes and rivers that once held abundant stocks of trout and salmon are now fishless. So are many lakes in northeastern United States and Canada.

In a Canadian experiment, scientists slowly added acid to a lake with a pH of 6.5 – almost neutral, neither acidic nor alkaline. At a pH of 6, the shrimps and minnows died. Without their natural food, trout starved. As the lake became more acid, crayfish and their eggs were attacked by parasites. Soon the once-bountiful lake was almost lifeless.

The chain reaction doesn't stop when a lake or river dies. Birds and waterside animals suffer next. When they vanish, so too may other birds and animals.

Acid rain attacks trees, particularly conifers. Because it robs the soil of some nutrients, vegetation is starved. Forest surveys show that some 15 per cent of Europe's forests, covering an area about the size of Germany, are affected. This again has wider consequences for birds

and animals, which lose their habitat. Also, it brings soil erosion. This in turn causes an increasing runoff of acid rain and soil into lakes and rivers.

Sulphur dioxide is not the only villain. Car exhausts put nitrogen oxides into the air, which mix with rain to form nitric acid. Also, in bright sunshine these exhaust gases turn into ozone, causing the brown, photochemical smog that blankets some cities. Ozone speeds the creation of acid rain. One sample of Los Angeles smog had a pH of 1.7, corrosive not only to buildings and vegetation but also to human lungs.

To clean up the worldwide problem of acid rain will take decades of work, huge sums of money and worldwide determination. The only encouraging signs are that many governments have already recognised its gravity, and informed groups are pressing them into action.

Why can't we design buildings to survive earthquakes?

Buildings designed to withstand the shock of an earthquake already exist in some major cities, where it is not solely a question of whether an earthquake will occur but more a matter of when.

When an earthquake strikes a city, the toll of dead and injured depends how its buildings are constructed and what they stand on. Tall office blocks that collapse may bring down others nearby. Recent research shows that those erected on landfill areas are particularly vulnerable.

A typical earthquake brings an initial shock, moving at enormous speed, up to 32 000 km/h (20 000 mph). This is followed by a series of waves that can twist, rattle and shake a building to pieces. Architects, guided by seismic engineers, have designed some modern tower blocks to sway with the force, much as a tree bends in the wind.

Others, such as New York's World Trade Center, are said to be so resistant that a person standing on the roof might see many buildings collapse but otherwise would not know an earthquake was taking place. Some buildings in Tokyo and elsewhere use huge counterweights to stop them jostling their neighbours. In others, computers detect any motion caused by earthquake or wind, and activate massive blocks to counteract swaying and twisting.

These devices, plus shock-absorbent rubber piles sunk deep into the foundations and anchored in bedrock, can prevent an earthquake's vibrations bringing down a city's building. If earthquakes can't be predicted, goes the theory, we must learn to live with them.

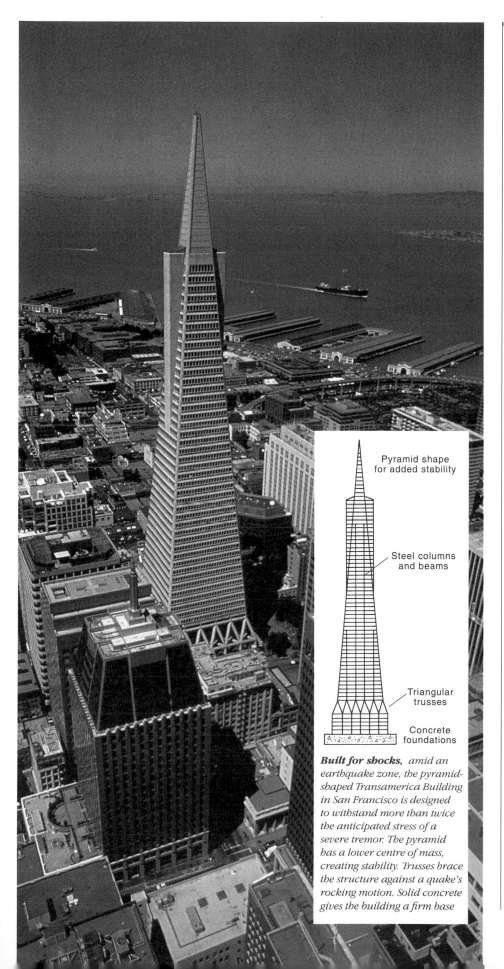

Pyramid shape
for added stability

Steel columns
and beams

Triangular
trusses

Concrete
foundations

Built for shocks, *amid an
earthquake zone, the pyramid-
shaped Transamerica Building
in San Francisco is designed
to withstand more than twice
the anticipated stress of a
severe tremor. The pyramid
has a lower centre of mass,
creating stability. Trusses brace
the structure against a quake's
rocking motion. Solid concrete
gives the building a firm base*

Why does the greenhouse effect threaten our climate?

The greenhouse effect has acted like a friendly thermostat on the Earth's temperature ever since our planet began to cool and first got its atmosphere.

On the Moon, which has no air, the surface temperature rises by day to 110°C (230°F); at night, it drops to -150°C (-238°F). The Moon and the Earth are roughly the same distance from the Sun, about 150 million km (93 million miles) away. Without the blanket of air that shields our planet, the Earth's temperature would be about the same as the Moon's, and life could not exist.

Some of the Sun's enormous energy pierces the layers of the atmosphere to reach the ground. As Earth's surface heats up, it radiates infrared (heat) energy back into space. Some of this heat is absorbed by what are known as greenhouse gases, chiefly water vapour and carbon dioxide, which together make up a tiny percentage of the atmosphere. The trapped heat warms the atmosphere, which in turn heats the land and oceans. This natural greenhouse effect ensures that our planet is kept at a habitable temperature. If there were no greenhouse gases, the Earth's average surface temperature would drop from its present level of about 15°C (59°F) to a chilly -18°C (-0.4°F).

If the levels of water vapour and carbon dioxide remain constant, the Earth's average temperature doesn't change. Everything stays in balance. But in the past century, the burning of fossil fuels, particularly coal and oil, has increased the carbon dioxide in the atmosphere. The extra carbon dioxide absorbs more of the heat that would otherwise vanish into space.

Scientists first discussed the greenhouse effect more than a century ago, and speculated then how a build-up of carbon dioxide would affect global temperatures. Accurate temperature records exist only from the 1850s. They show that between 1880 and 1940 the world warmed up by about 0.25°C (0.45°F). In the next thirty years, it cooled down by almost as much. Since then, global temperatures have risen rapidly by about 0.3°C (0.54°F), along with a steady increase in the atmosphere's carbon dioxide. The year 1990 was the warmest since the 1850s.

A joint Australian–United States study suggests that the temperature in the past twenty-five years may have risen more rapidly than at any time since AD 900. The scientists looked at tree rings in ancient Huon pines growing in northwest Tasmania, Australia. The size of a tree's annual growth rings are a guide to the climate in times past. Since 1965, the tree-ring index, a barometer of growth and climate, has risen by 50 per cent.

Higher global temperatures will lead to a rise in the sea level as the polar ice caps melt and the warmed oceans expand. During the last century, the sea level has risen by between 10 and 15 cm (4 and 6 in). But researchers are not yet sure that global warming has caused this rise.

Scientists are reluctant to say that this warming or any changes in the world's weather are due to the greenhouse effect. We know from air trapped in polar ice that the amount of carbon dioxide before the Industrial Revolution was about 270 parts per million and that this level persisted for the past 10 000 years.

Computer models show that a doubling of that level of carbon dioxide would raise global temperatures by an average 2°C (4°F). A doubling in carbon-dioxide levels may occur before the end of the next century. In addition to producing more carbon dioxide, we are releasing more methane, another greenhouse gas. The combined effect is that by as early as 2030

the temperature of our planet may be on average 2.5°C (4.5°F) warmer.

Higher temperatures would not apply everywhere. The tropics might stay much as they are, but polar regions could become much warmer. That in itself would change prevailing wind and rainfall patterns. Inland areas may dry out, with severe results for agriculture and forestry. Other regions may get more rain. Nobody knows just what changes the greenhouse effect will bring, except that it could change the world and our lives. No long-term plans can afford to ignore it.

Why is there a hole in the ozone layer?

If they were exposed to the Earth's upper atmosphere during a flight into space, astronauts would notice a remarkable change in temperature. As their space vehicle climbed from ground level to a height of about 12 km (7½ miles), they would feel the temperature drop steadily to -60°C (-76°F). After that, for some

Loss of ozone over the Antarctic is clearly seen in these false-colour images of the upper atmosphere sent by the Nimbus-7 satellite. Colours show the concentration of ozone, from white (highest), red, yellow, green and blue to purple (lowest). The ozone hole, serious ozone loss, appears in blue in 1979–82. A few years later, in 1989–92, the depletion (purple) is far more widespread. Ozone loss is linked to chemicals such as chlorofluorocarbons, used in refrigerators, plastic foam and some aerosol sprays. Ozone protects us from the cancer-causing effects of sunshine

40 km (25 miles) in what is known as the stratosphere, the temperature doesn't fall with increasing altitude, but gets markedly warmer, so that at 40 km the temperature is -23°C (-9°F).

This blanket of warmer air is known as the ozone layer. It is warmer because it absorbs heat from ultraviolet rays in sunlight. Ozone is formed when sunlight acts on oxygen. The oxygen molecule, chemical symbol O_2, consists of two atoms of oxygen. Ultraviolet radiation in sunlight splits these molecules into two separate atoms. Some of these free atoms join up with oxygen molecules to form another kind of oxygen, one with three atoms, whose chemical symbol is O_3. This is sometimes called trioxygen, but is more commonly known as ozone.

Because solar radiation is strongest over the equator and the tropics, most of the ozone is made there. The process is happening constantly. As ozone is produced, stratospheric winds drive it from the tropics towards polar regions.

In the mid-1950s, scientists began monitoring the atmosphere at Halley Bay in Antarctica. Since 1982, their studies have intensified, and each spring they have detected a loss of ozone. Data from satellites, balloons and aircraft confirm their findings. In some regions of the stratosphere, at an altitude of about 18 km (11 miles), the ozone all but vanishes during the Antarctic spring. Scientists describe this as a hole in the ozone layer.

When the darkness of winter arrives in Antarctica, strong winds sweep the continent, virtually sealing it off from the rest of the world. Temperatures in the stratosphere drop to -90°C (-130°F), and icy clouds build up. Chlorine, released from man-made chemicals, is locked up in different chemical compounds on ice particles within these clouds. The chlorine comes mainly from chlorofluorocarbons (CFCs), which are used in refrigerators, air-cooling systems, plastic foam, some cleansers and aerosol sprays. When spring arrives in the Antarctic, sunlight causes the ice clouds to yield their store of chlorine. In a series of reactions, the

ALL ABOARD FOR MISSION IMPOSSIBLE

Three great quests have lured the world's scientists through the centuries. Medieval alchemists sought to find 'the philosopher's stone', a substance that could change base metals such as lead into gold. Others aimed to discover the secret of eternal life. A long-lasting dream was to invent a machine that, when set in motion, would run without power for ever.

We know now that perpetual motion would defy the basic laws of our Universe. Everything that moves depends on energy. The energy may come from a variety of sources. Wind drives windmills, water turns turbines, and the Sun's heat can produce electricity.

It may seem that a waterwheel in running water uses no energy, but scientists can prove that the stream loses some energy in heat or friction. The number of waterwheels that a stream can drive is limited. The laws of thermodynamics say that, whenever one kind of energy is changed into another, energy is lost.

The closest we have come to our dreams of perpetual motion is in launching probes into space, where their speed cannot be slowed by friction. But eventually these vehicles, along with Earth and other planets in the solar system, will lose their initial motion. At some time in the far-distant future, the Sun will burn out and the entire solar system will vanish.

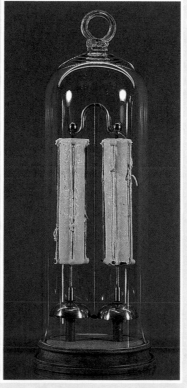

A ringing success is this bell, which has sounded at Oxford since 1840. It may seem like perpetual motion, but its pillars are long-lasting batteries

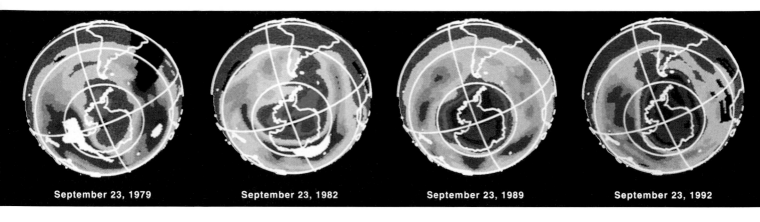

September 23, 1979   September 23, 1982   September 23, 1989   September 23, 1992

chlorine atoms attack the ozone, turning it into ordinary oxygen. In the end, the chlorine itself is free to repeat the cycle many thousands of times.

The loss of ozone is most serious above the Antarctic, but is spreading elsewhere. Environmental scientists analysed more than twelve years' data from the Nimbus-7 satellite, and found that in some places at certain times of the year, the northern hemisphere loses about 6 per cent of its ozone shield.

The loss is gradually replaced, but for part of the summer we risk greater exposure to dangerous ultraviolet rays. By absorbing ultraviolet light, ozone protects us from these rays, which cause skin cancer and reduce crop yields. Medical scientists estimate that in the next fifty years skin-cancer deaths will rise in the United States alone from the current level of 9300 to some 200 000 a year.

Why can't we use hydrogen as a fuel?

The world's supplies of fossil fuels are slowly running out. As they do so, they create a range of problems. Dwindling resources bring political tensions. Increased consumption by expanding industries obviously affects our atmosphere and may even change our climate.

Many scientists have already pointed to hydrogen, a clean and easily obtained gas, as a promising long-term answer. When hydrogen burns it combines with oxygen in the air to make water. Its only pollution problem is minor: hydrogen burned in an engine may result in the release of nitric oxide. This, caused by nitrogen in the air combining with unburned oxygen in the cylinders, occurs in all internal combustion engines, irrespective of the fuel.

If ways can be found to use hydrogen in an internal combustion engine, many forms of transport will benefit. Already major manufacturers have made great strides in solving

the basic technology. Mazda, Daimler-Benz and BMW have prototypes. The problems are many. To store sufficient hydrogen in a small tank, such as that in a car, the gas must be liquefied. Liquid hydrogen has a temperature of -253°C (-423°F). Without effective insulation, liquid hydrogen rapidly vaporises. BMW developed a 93-litre (21-UKgal; 25-USgal) 'double-wall vacuum, superinsulated tank' to overcome this difficulty. Even so, some 2 per cent of the hydrogen leaked from a parked car.

Liquid hydrogen makes metals brittle. Unlike petrol, hydrogen has no lubricating properties. And the low-temperature fuel presents major handicaps to the development of an efficient fuel pump and injection system. But, for all that, automotive scientists are confident that they will succeed.

The most forbidding challenge may lie elsewhere. Filling stations would need radically new equipment to store and deliver hydrogen fuel – highly insulated tanks, possibly with refrigeration systems, and a unique type of pump. Hoses now used for petrol would be useless: liquid hydrogen would make them as brittle as dried twigs. Self-service might be banned as too dangerous.

Making hydrogen is relatively easy. Any country could do it and possibly become

independent of the world's energy suppliers. Usually, hydrogen is produced by passing steam over coke heated to about 1000°C (1800°F). One snag is that this uses energy. Another is that a by-product is carbon monoxide, a poisonous gas. If this is converted to non-poisonous carbon dioxide, we are back to our starting point. In trying to replace today's petrol engines, which puff out carbon dioxide, we've found another way to contribute to the greenhouse effect.

Now for the good news. Solar scientists point to a way of making hydrogen without pollution at any stage of the process. As school science teachers often demonstrate, an electric current passed through water will produce hydrogen bubbles at one electrode and oxygen at the other. Solar cells, generating electricity from sunshine, could be used to make hydrogen from water, without producing carbon dioxide and with no adverse effects on global warming.

To today's scientists that sounds like a dream more wonderful than turning base metals into gold.

Tomorrow's cars may run on hydrogen, a readily available, non-polluting fuel. This high-performance Mazda HR-X prototype can travel up to 200 km (125 miles) before refuelling, making it a useful city car

Why are so many animals and plants at risk?

In our thirst for knowledge about the Earth and the Universe, we know surprisingly little about the animals and plants that share our planet. Many species have never been identified; relatively few of those classified and named have been studied in any detail.

One reliable authority, the World Conservation Union (IUCN), says that 2750 vertebrates and 2250 invertebrates are at risk. So possibly are some 25 000 plants. IUCN acknowledges that its records have significant gaps, particularly about creatures of tropical rainforests, whose habitat decreases daily.

Since the first spark of life on Earth, some 500 million different species have existed. About 490 million are extinct. Most of those vanished in the natural process of evolution – the survival of the fittest. They failed to adapt successfully to meet competition from rivals or the demands of a changing environment.

In the past 200 years, and with increasing pace since 1950, animals and plants have succumbed in far greater numbers, helpless against competition from the most rapacious of all Earth's animals. As the human population has risen to its current 5400 million, we have destroyed the homes of our fellow creatures in a multitude of ways.

Towns have expanded, eating up woods and grasslands. Bulldozers have obliterated great tracts of countryside to build new roads. Mines, mills and factories have poisoned rivers. We have cut down forests for timber, drained marshlands and dammed great valleys. In the United States, urban areas in 1960 covered 8.5 million hectares (21 million acres); by 2000, they are expected to occupy 18 million hectares (45 million acres).

To feed our growing numbers, we have ploughed the land, depriving wild animals of food. We have let domestic animals overgraze pastures. By degrading the land, we have damaged or destroyed the habitat of plants and animals; in turn, we have allowed rivers to silt up, often rendering them lifeless. We have killed animals for food, and shot them for sport. We have overfished the seas, and still do so. Our motor vehicles kill millions of animals every year.

Wherever our ancestors went, they took plants and animals, often with devastating effects. Introduced species, such as dogs, cats, foxes and rabbits, have run wild in many parts of the world, sometimes wiping out native creatures. We have put brown and rainbow trout, European carp and perch into rivers and lakes to satisfy the passions of anglers. Competition from exotic fish has destroyed local species.

As the world's wildlife vanishes, demand rises among collectors and tourists for rare specimens. Poachers raid sanctuaries for skins, ivory and horns. Others smuggle live animals, birds and rare plants across the world's frontiers. The US Fish and Wildlife Service estimates that every year smugglers take some 350 000 African and Amazon parrots into the United States.

World population is expected to reach 8500 million by 2025, increasing the demand for housing, food and jobs. Fortunately, in recent years, more people have become aware of the urgent need to save the world's plants and animals – for our own good.

Some 40 per cent of drugs essential for our health come from plants, microbes and animals. Madagascar's tiny rosy periwinkle, for example, provides two drugs that have virtually eliminated deaths from the childhood cancers of Hodgkin's disease and lymphocytic leukaemia. The Pacific yew yields taxol, a valuable weapon against ovarian cancers. Yet scientists have examined only some 3 per cent of the world's flowering plants for possible drugs. And every day, somewhere in the world, one or two plant species become extinct, plants that could be essential in our fight against epidemic diseases.

It may be that only by working with nature can humanity survive.

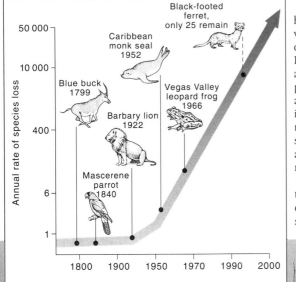

Habitat destruction, *particularly of forests, is a major reason why animals are vanishing. The graph shows their rate of extinction since 1800, together with some notable losses and the years in which the last of their kind were seen. America's black-footed ferret is in great danger because farmers poison its food, the prairie dog. As the world's human population expands, demand for housing, farm land, timber and minerals increases the annual death rate of animals and plants*

The puzzling things we say

The demon drink *has brewed its own collection of sayings, many of which predate this scene from fourteenth-century England*

Why do we say 'as drunk as a newt'?

Americans claim that the saying 'drunk as a newt', which spread particularly among US servicemen during World War II, is the result of a mishearing. The expression should be, 'drunk as an Ute', and refers to the infamous drunkenness of Ute Indians on their reservations, which led to a ban on alcohol there.

Britons give the saying greater antiquity. In medieval times, it was common for mice and rats to fall into vats of beer and cider. Some brewers believed that this enhanced the flavour and, with barbarous disregard, deliberately put small creatures into their brew. Newts, which are amphibians and better swimmers than mice, lasted longer, but got helplessly drunk.

Why do we say that the show's not over till the fat lady sings?

A saying that started with American basketball has spread to other events worldwide, possibly through the medium of television. Today it is as likely to be used by spectators at a British football match as by those watching Canadian ice hockey. In meaning, it equals other expressions about the uncertainty of predicting the outcome of close contests, such as: 'Wait till the final whistle!' However, it is not confined to sport, and frequently crops up in political speeches.

Sports journalist Dan Cook, from San Antonio, Texas, is credited with saying in 1975, 'The opera ain't over till the fat lady sings.' He was voicing what may have been a popular view that all operas ended with an aria from an overweight diva. Cook's local basketball team had just taken the lead in a championship series, and he was warning fans that it wasn't 'all over bar the shouting'. The series was won by the Washington Bullets, which resulted in politicians picking up the quip.

Some people believe that the saying originated with baseball, and it does have a link with that game. During their 1988 season, the Baltimore Orioles could do nothing right. To counter the taunts of rival fans, an Orioles supporter is said to have put up a poster showing a diva of Wagnerian proportions, complete with Viking helmet and spear. A caption announced, 'She ain't sung yet!'

Why do we talk about Dutch courage?

The English language is strewn with derogatory references to foreigners and foreign lands. Many of these expressions take an unfair shot at the Dutch, implying meanness and particularly a tendency towards alcoholism.

Dutch courage is that shown under the influence of drink; a Dutch bargain is a transaction settled while both parties are drinking; in a Dutch treat, each participant pays; a Dutch uncle is not benign and avuncular but stern and critical.

Most English expressions critical of foreigners probably originated during wars against them, a brand of propaganda to denigrate the enemy.

In the late seventeenth century, England fought a series of wars against Holland. These gave rise to many such phrases, some of which have long since vanished from the language. For example, Dutch consolation meant no consolation at all. Citizens who wanted to imply that something was 'old hat' would dismiss a news-bearer with the remark, 'I hear that the Dutch have taken Holland.'

Why do we say 'as sick as a parrot'?

Some sources record that 'sick as a parrot' is a corruption of 'as sick as a pierrot'. The French pantomime character, traditionally dressed in floppy white clothes and having a whitened face, always looked miserably sick.

Others say that the popularity of parrots as pets led to the spread of psittacosis, a viral disease common in parrots and easily passed to humans, in whom it causes high fever and respiratory problems similar to those of pneumonia. In the late 1920s, the disease became particularly prevalent, and the saying, it is claimed, was born.

A third explanation is that, because of disease in parrots, the United States enforced strict quarantine laws. Smugglers of parrots from South America tried to dodge the laws by doping the birds and concealing them in suitcases, as many bird smugglers try to do today. Often the birds were discovered, and invariably looked pathetically sick. Their plight gave rise to the saying.

Pathetic but appealing, *Pierrot drew sympathy in French pantomimes through his wan expression of lovesick helplessness*

High-living tycoon *Gordon Bennett spent some $30 million during a life that ended in 1918. Scandal forced him to leave America*

Why do we sometimes exclaim with dismay, 'Oh, Gordon Bennett!'?

The expression, like so many others, has spread round the English-speaking world from the United States. James Gordon Bennett was a renowned American publisher who, in 1869, commissioned Henry Morton Stanley to find the British missionary and explorer, David Livingstone.

The flamboyant Bennett became the talk of New York through bouts of ill-mannered behaviour and wild escapades in which, it seems, he spared no one. At a party arranged by his fiancée, he is said to have drunk too much and behaved disgracefully. His fiancée's brother threw Bennett into the street, and laid on some blows with a horsewhip.

When news of Bennett's latest escapade reached society gossips, they shook their heads in dismay, exclaiming, 'Oh, Gordon Bennett!' They never knew what he might do next. In 1877, scandal drove Bennett to France, where his interest in polo, yachting and flying made him one of Europe's best-known sportsmen.

Why do we say that somebody has a chip on the shoulder?

When we accuse others of having a chip on the shoulder, we mean that they are spoiling for a fight, or are carrying a grudge. The saying originated in American bars in the 1830s. A man who felt like a fight picked up a woodchip from the sawdust floor, put it on his shoulder and defied anybody to knock it off. Such a challenge was rarely refused. It was invariably a fight to the finish, lasting long after the woodchip fell to the floor.

Parts of England and Ireland had a similar custom. Would-be brawlers 'trailed a coat', dangling it behind in the hope that somebody would step on it and give cause for a fight.

Why do we say that a person has crossed the Rubicon?

To cross the Rubicon means to take a decisive step, from which there is no retreat. The Rubicon is a small Italian stream flowing from the Etruscan Apennines to the Adriatic Sea, which it enters at Gatteo a Mare, some 15 km (9 miles) north of Rimini. In Roman times, it formed the boundary between what was known as Cisalpine Gaul, that part of Gaul south of the Italian Alps, and the Roman Republic. When Julius Caesar crossed the Rubicon with his army in 49 BC, he was in effect declaring war against the Senate and his great rival, Pompey.

At one time, the exact location of the Rubicon was a cause of dispute, and claims were made for three rivers, the Pisciatello, the Uso and the Fiumicino di Savignano. A papal bull of 1756 decided that the Uso was indisputably the Rubicon, but scholars later did not agree. By comparing distances given in the accounts of Suetonius, Plutarch and Lucan, they proved that the Fiumicino was the river that Caesar crossed. In 1932, the Fiumicino was renamed the Rubicon.

Why was there a craze for writing, 'Kilroy was here'?

The craze sprang up during World War II for scrawling 'Kilroy was here' in the most remarkable places. It was introduced to Europe and other war theatres by American servicemen. According to some sources, James Kilroy was an inspector at a yard building liberty ships. Kilroy's job was to inspect and approve the welds as one plate or section was joined to another. This had to be done as soon as the weld was completed, because new work might cover the join, making inspection impossible. Kilroy chalked his name across each weld.

Most of his chalk marks were soon obliterated by footsteps or weather. Others, in inaccessible spots within the hull, remained. Sometimes, crewmen would open a locker or remove a fitting, and reveal Kilroy's name. Soon they began to conjecture about this mystical figure, whose name popped up in unexpected places. Fresh discoveries of his mark were greeted with cries of 'Kilroy was here!'

Before long, servicemen were competing to write 'Kilroy' or 'Kilroy was here' wherever they thought it might cause surprise and amusement: inside locked drawers, at great heights on walls, in offices of strict security – to show that Kilroy could be just about everywhere.

Postwar shortages in Britain and elsewhere gave birth to a parallel mania but one of protest. Chad, a chalked figure of a human head peering over a wall, appeared in countless places, with the caption, 'Wot, no — ?'

The fateful decision *of Caesar to cross the Rubicon was a breach of Roman law. He was allowed to command an army only within his province. Once over the river boundary, he could not return*

In case you've ever wondered...

Like a giant balloon, *the rising Moon hangs over the towers of New York's World Trade Center. The TV antenna's tip is 521 m (1710 ft) above street level*

Why does the Moon on the horizon look bigger than when it is high in the sky?

To stand on the seashore or an open plain and watch the huge globe of the Moon appear majestically over the horizon is a commonplace but wonderful experience. Strangely, the Moon's orb looks enormous, and it appears to rise quite fast, like a huge gas balloon ascending into the heavens. A short time later, when the Moon is higher in the sky, it seems to be much smaller, and it may be difficult to detect that it is still rising.

The Moon's size and speed are constant. It moves, in relation to us, at 97 200 km/h (60 400 mph) and in an orbit that keeps it about 384 400 km (238 900 miles) from the Earth. (The Moon's orbit isn't exactly a circle.) Any perceived change in its size or speed is a trick of the eye, an optical illusion. It is not caused, as some people believe, by a form of atmospheric distortion that magnifies the Moon or speeds it up. In fact, atmospheric effects cause the Moon's measured diameter at the horizon to be slightly smaller than when it is measured higher in the sky.

The illusion is caused by the way our brain interprets information. A rising Moon is placed on the horizon, and perceived as being more distant than one immediately overhead. Nearly two centuries ago, English mathematician and astronomer Robert Smith concluded that at the horizon the sky appears to be three times as far away as it does at its zenith – overhead. This is because land-based objects, such as trees and buildings, lead us into a wrongful comparison.

The same trick makes the Moon look bigger. When it is high in the sky, we have nothing to compare it with. Similarly, we think that it is rising faster, because we can see the gap between it and the horizon constantly widening. Later, the gap is too vast for us to detect any movement of the Moon at all.

Another curious example of our brain leading us into mistaken conclusions may come when viewing the Moon through binoculars. Many people claim that the image looks smaller than it does with the naked eye, the reverse of what is seen when looking at other objects through binoculars. The explanation for this is probably that when we use binoculars other objects are excluded, thus removing any basis for comparison.

If you want to see the Moon shrink suddenly in size, try this: hold up a pea at arm's length, and compare it with the Moon. You may be surprised to find that the Moon looks about half the size of an average pea.

Why does soil smell sweet after rain?

We've all noticed and enjoyed the delightful sweet smell of the earth after rain, particularly in summer when a brief, heavy shower may be followed by warm sunshine. One result of such showers is that the rain quickly settles any dust in the air.

Another, say scientists, is that the rain releases from the soil some sweet-smelling chemicals known as geosmins. These are produced by microbes such as the filamentous actinomycetes. Some of these microbes, for example the Streptomyce, give us material from which we produce streptomycin and other antibiotics.

Heat from the Sun induces vapour to rise from the ground, making the sweet smell more apparent.

Why did beaux and belles wear wigs?

Wigs were worn in ancient times. Egyptians shaved their heads and donned wigs, neatly woven, to protect themselves from the Sun. But not until the reign of Elizabeth I of England did wigs again become everyday apparel, enhancing the hairy heads of some and disguising the vanishing locks of others.

Queen Elizabeth I, whose red hair began to turn white, pushed the fashion along by never appearing without her auburn wig. Across the Channel in France, Louis XIII set a new style in 1624 by sporting a peruke or periwig, a full-flowing wig that covered the head and sometimes the shoulders. French aristocrats followed their king with such élan that suddenly the wig was big. A new industry was born.

By 1665, the wigmakers of France were organised into a guild. Some professions adopted distinctive wigs as part of their official dress, and wigs were produced on a scale never seen before. For the well-dressed squire and lady of the seventeenth and eighteenth centuries, a stylish wig was as essential an item of fashion as are jeans for partygoers today. It was also an unmistakable badge of class, to be swept away in

High-and-mighty fashions, such as the wearing of elaborate wigs, became a popular target for satirists in the late eighteenth century. Female wigs were sometimes ornate constructions requiring hours of work. Many, built over wire cages and padded with animal hair, were over a metre (about 3 ft) high and decorated with feathers, jewels and ribbons. A British engraving of 1776, marking the Battle of Bunker Hill, lampoons the fashion. The battle was the first major engagement of the American War of Independence. The British won but with heavy losses. American troops retreated only after their ammunition ran out

the aftermath of the French and American revolutions. Portrait paintings and pictures of formal occasions during the seventeenth and eighteenth centuries often show society ladies and gentlemen bewigged in silver grey. Whereas today's culture idolises youth, and millions are spent in trying to recapture it, in times past grey was great, the true mark of wisdom. 'Everyone wants to look old,' said a lady-in-waiting of King Louis XIV's powder-wigged court at Versailles. 'For to look old is to appear wise.'

Why do we refer to a ship as 'she'?

Scholars argue about how sex reared its head in language ... why, in English, ships are feminine; why some people declare optimistically that 'she'll be right'; why some creatures irrespective of their sex are assigned one, as when whalers declare, 'Thar she blows!'

It's not a case of sex but of gender. And as students know, sometimes to their despair, in most European languages nouns may be one of two or three genders, and often logic doesn't seem to apply. In German, for example, a woman is feminine but a young girl is neuter.

Many theories attempt to explain why this is so. In the earliest European languages, objects were classified according to their function. Those that played an active part in society, or in changing things within it, were considered to be masculine; those that brought other things into being were said to be feminine; passive or childish objects were neuter. By this reasoning, weapons and tools were masculine; the earth and the sea, which yielded food, were feminine.

The rule of three genders survived in languages such as Latin, German and Russian. As Romance languages evolved from Latin, neuter nouns, both singular and plural, lost their distinctive forms, leaving them with only two genders.

Another explanation points to cultures, such as those of some South American tribes, where men spoke one language and the women another. An object was masculine or feminine, depending on whether a man or woman referred to it. When the languages combined, two genders survived.

In English, the gender of nouns and pronouns is usually straightforward: in general, living creatures are masculine or feminine, and inanimate things are neuter. For centuries, sailors have referred to a ship as 'she'. One theory is that, next to their own mothers, nothing was more revered than the ships that guarded them from often-perilous seas.

Why are some jokes known as shaggy-dog stories?

Shaggy-dog stories are like verbal practical jokes, often enjoyed more by the teller than the audience. The longer the story, the funnier it may seem – to the teller, that is – because at the end may come a pointless or irrelevant punchline. Some say that the first shaggy-dog story originated in America, and went (in abbreviated form) something like this:

A man took his dog into a bar. The dog told the barman to get a big glass, put in some ice, a measure of rye, a drop of gin, some brandy, and top it off with cider. 'How strange,' said a bystander. 'Yes,' said the dog's owner. 'He can't be feeling too good. I've never known him order anything but beer.'

A more likely candidate for the original shaggy-dog story is one of epic length about a man who lost his dog. He inserted an advertisement in his local paper: 'Lost. Very shaggy dog. Finder rewarded.' In the following weeks, queues of people with shaggy dogs formed outside his house. Meticulously, the man went up and down the lines but without success. Several weeks later, when all hope seemed lost, a boy leading a very shaggy dog arrived at the man's house. 'I believe you've lost a shaggy dog,' said the boy. The man looked at the dog with disgust. 'I did lose a shaggy dog,' he said, 'but it wasn't as shaggy as that.'

During World War II, the shaggy-dog vogue spread and the nature of the jokes changed, so that today a definition of a shaggy-dog story might include the long and pointless, stories about talking animals and a catalogue of anecdotes about absurd custom-made goods for which the customers never turned up.

Why don't Americans have English accents?

When the Pilgrim Fathers landed in the New World in 1620, they took with them the English language and their English accent, that of their native Devonshire. Today's Americans, however, don't have the distinctive burr that characterises the speech of natives of southwest England.

It could be argued that, because America was colonised also by immigrants from many parts of Britain, the Devonshire

Shaggy-dog jokes brought laughter in Britain more than a century ago, but their humour was quite different

accent vanished, swamped by Irish or Scottish brogue or by cockney dialect. But Americans who speak what is known as General American English, standard speech without a distinctive regional accent such as that of the South, have a sound unmistakably their own.

Since English was first spoken in the New World, the language has of course changed. Surprisingly perhaps, the biggest change has come in Britain and particularly in southeastern England. One key example is the loss in England of the rolling 'r' sound that many recognise as a delightful feature of Scottish speech. If the English had always spoken as they do today, many words, such as bird, start, lord, would be spelled differently. Americans generally have kept a slight 'r' in their speech.

Another English diversion is the change in pronunciation of the 'a' in words such as dance, father, bath. In southern England, the 'a' has a broader and longer sound; north-country speech and General American English share the older, original sound, made in the front of the mouth.

Speech authorities say that southeastern English has changed so much in the past 200 years that well-spoken citizens of the eighteenth century would be shocked if they could hear speeches by British VIPs today. They would find that General American English had a more acceptable ring, closer to the English accent of centuries past.

Why don't birds die when they perch on high-voltage power lines?

On a drive through the countryside or in cities where power lines run on poles above ground, you may have been surprised to see birds sitting unperturbed on the wires, even during rain. If you have wondered why they aren't electrocuted, it is because they aren't touching anything directly connected to the ground.

An electric current will flow only if a circuit is completed. A bird on a high-voltage line is safe because special insulators, usually of glass or ceramic, prevent the current flowing to earth via the power poles. If the bird touches an overhanging tree, the current might flow through the bird to the ground, completing the circuit and electrocuting the bird.

During rain this is even more likely, because water conducts electricity. That is why power-company staff lop trees near power lines. Also, it explains why, if you

High-wire artists such as these galahs often perch in flocks. On wires mounted one above another, the birds' antics and their weight have sometimes caused short circuits

are forced to shelter under a tree during a thunderstorm – never a wise thing to do – you should pick one with a smooth bark. If lightning strikes the tree, it will find a direct path down the wet trunk to the ground, instead of jumping from the tree to you.

Why does fruit in a packet of muesli rise to the top?

If you mix up beads of different sizes in a jar and give the mixture a gentle shake, you will see an interesting effect. Provided you keep the container upright, the smallest beads, though obviously lighter in weight, will sink gradually to the bottom and the larger and heavier beads will rise to the top.

A little thought explains why this must obviously be so. Only the smaller beads can sink, because only they can fit into some of the spaces. If a group of small beads moved simultaneously from one area, a larger bead would drop down to fill the space. But in a well-balanced

BRAVO FOR ITALIAN DESIGN!

In the past thirty years, Italy has become the indisputable source of stylish and innovative design in everything from cars and clothes to cutlery and furniture. The design collection of New York's Museum of Modern Art includes more products from Italy than from any other country. Some economists attribute Italy's high postwar growth rate to the artistic skills of its industrial designers, which have created a demand for its products.

Before World War II, the Germans were renowned for industrial design. In modern times they were the first, through their Bauhaus movement in the 1920s, to marry function and style in everyday objects. In the 1950s, Scandinavian designers took the lead, particularly with a rather stark, geometric look in teak furniture and abundant use of glass and laminates.

Since then, Italians have dominated, making a wide range of objects that are not just reliably functional but sometimes worth keeping just to look at when their working parts are worn out. The reason for this success lies partly in Italy's cultural history. The nation's designers, often trained in formal art, grow up in a treasurehouse of great architecture and painting. The respect for classical beauty is fostered by industry's leaders, who at the same time more readily accept innovation in colour and form.

The skill of Italian designers is sought by manufacturers worldwide, many of whom join the queue to have new inventions given an exclusive and often more workable form. Fortunately for all of us, good design isn't a prerogative of the wealthy. Today, in what is sometimes called the high-touch generation, one in which the feel of objects is regarded as an important facet of their design, our daily lives are enriched by things that are both beautiful to look at and to use.

Stylish and practical, these products are typical examples of Italian design that has won worldwide praise. Clockwise from the top: a whistling kettle made by Alessi, a tractor-seat stool designed by Achille Castiglioni and Lamborghini's eye-catching Countach car

mixture that is unlikely. In its travels to the supermarket, a packet of muesli gets many hours of gentle shaking. This creates smaller and smaller spaces between the items in the mixture. These spaces act like a screen, through which only the fine particles can pass.

Gradually, all the smaller items sink to the bottom, forcing the nuts and fruit, which are usually the largest constituents, to the top. Even though they are bulkier, gravity can't pull them down. By the time it reaches the supermarket shelves, muesli that is well blended by its makers may look as though all the fruit and nuts were added as an afterthought.

Why do males produce millions of sperm to fertilise one egg?

Scientists researching the sexual behaviour of primates have made some remarkable discoveries about their sperm counts. The 200 or so species of primates include tiny lemurs, huge gorillas, baboons and humans, and they have a variety of mating habits.

Gorillas, for example, live in small groups, in which one dominant male controls several females. Macaques, the most widespread and versatile of monkeys, live in large groups in which competition for females is fierce.

The size of a primate's testicles is a reliable guide to sperm production. Remarkably, the gorilla has small testicles and produces about sixty-five million sperm with each ejaculation. Some macaques, by comparison, have extremely large testicles and ejaculate several thousand million sperm.

Scientists say that this difference is a measure of the competition that males face in trying to reproduce. The gorilla, with his harem of females, has no immediate rivals. Male macaque monkeys have many. But even in what seem to be stable relationships, research shows that females are fickle. In all species, insects included, females are rarely faithful. To ensure that their eggs are fertilised, they try to mate with as many males as they can, frequently outside their own group.

This in turn affects male behaviour. Studies show that sperm counts may suddenly change if a male feels threatened. Rats with steady partners ejaculated an average 29.7 million sperm; given the uncertainty of different partners, their sperm counts almost doubled.

Fidelity may possibly affect sperm production in humans. Researchers have found that, if couples spend more time together, the male's sperm count, which

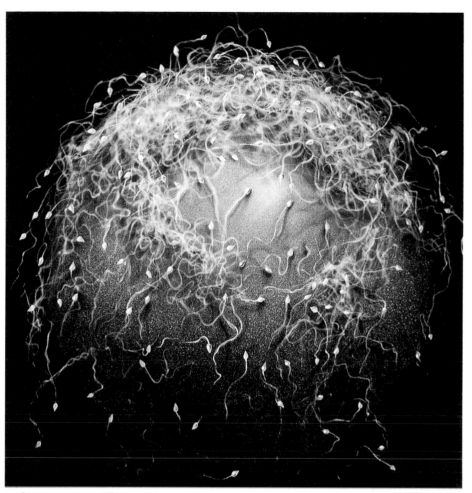

Only one among millions *of these sperm may successfully penetrate the egg to fuse with the female nucleus. The illustration is based on a micrograph of a human ovum and spermatozoa*

is normally between 200 and 500 million, declines. Separated from his partner, the male's sperm count increases, even though the interval between each ejaculation remains constant.

Why are some nuts so hard to crack?

If you have battled over a bowl of nuts, struggling to crack the shells without turning the kernels to pulp, you are not alone. Tough nuts present a minor but universal challenge. Some, such as macadamias and brazils, are regularly the last survivors in a mixed bowl.

Scientists have discovered that nutshells are almost indestructible. Every year, Americans discard some 50 000 tonnes of pecan shells alone, which creates a considerable disposal problem. Some nutshells go into garden mulches. Another use, because they are so hard, is as an abrasive in sandblasting. In some plywoods, finely ground nutshells bulk out the glues to make them go

farther. Chemical analysis of nutshells shows that they are mainly made up of cellulose, hemicellulose and lignins, substances known as polymers that give hardwoods their toughness. These substances exist in nutshells in similar proportions to those in some hardwoods. So, when we try to crack a nut, we are in fact trying to break open a hardwood case, which often has an in-built springiness to improve its defences.

Bone-hard shells *make macadamia nuts extremely difficult to crack. Now Hawaii is growing macadamias with softer shells*

The centuries-old quest for perfect timing

Time, according to a witty piece of graffiti, is nature's way of keeping everything from happening all at once. Of the many definitions of time that have been given throughout history that may be as clear as any.

Most of us probably see time as a kind of river, flowing steadily year after year. That is how many scientists regarded it until Albert Einstein produced his theory of relativity, which presented time as another dimension, and changed how we look at our planet and the Universe.

When astronomers study light from a distant galaxy, they are seeing something as it was thousands of millions of years ago. If they go back to the origins of the Universe, they are travelling mentally to the moment when time began.

Our measurement of time comes from the movements of our planet and the heavens. By studying these, our distant ancestors divided time into days, months and years. All are natural measures. A day marks one complete revolution of the Earth, the period between one sunrise and the next. A month is roughly how long the Moon takes to orbit the Earth. A year embraces all the seasons – spring, summer, autumn and winter – before the seasonal cycle starts again.

The week is an invention dating back thousands of years, possibly to times when markets were first held. Ancient people needed a shorter measure than a month. Some, in Africa, held a

Portable sundials were popular in the sixteenth century. Hinged tablets opened to tighten a string which acted as the gnomon

market every four days, and fixed a four-day week. Others, such as the Assyrians, had a week of six days. Ancient Egyptians had a ten-day week and the early Romans one of eight days.

The Babylonians of about 4000 BC set their week by the Moon's four phases, each of which takes about seven days. They regarded seven as a magical number. They counted seven supreme bodies in the sky – the Sun, Moon, Mercury, Mars, Jupiter, Venus and Saturn – each of which, they said, ruled events on one day of the week. The Jews also had a seven-day week. They, too, believed that seven, which is mentioned many times in the Old Testament, had great significance. God created the world in six days and rested on the seventh.

In the fourth century AD, the Romans adopted the seven-day week throughout their empire. When the Roman Empire fell, the Saxons spread across northern Europe. They kept some Roman names for the days, but called others after their own gods. Thus, we have three

Designed to last, a perpetual form of the Julian calendar from Germany in 1520 has rings giving months and days, saints' days and zodiac signs. The V-shaped segment lists fixed religious days. Sandglasses were made to measure periods as long as four hours

Roman names – Saturday (after Saturn), Sunday and Monday. The other four are Saxon: Tuesday (after Woden's son, Tiu), Wednesday (after Woden), Thursday (Thor's day) and Friday (after the goddess, Frigga).

The lunar year, measured by the passing of twelve moons, each of twenty-nine and a half days, has only 354 days. As a rough guide it worked reasonably well, but soon got out of step with the seasons. In 46 BC, Julius Caesar decreed that the Roman world would adopt a calendar proposed by an astronomer, Sosigenes of Alexandria. This, the Julian calendar, had three years of 365 days, with an extra day every four years.

The early Romans had begun their year in Martius (March). That is why the seventh, eighth, ninth and tenth months were named September, October, November and December. Sosigenes suggested that alternate months should have either thirty-one or thirty days. Februarius was given twenty-nine days and thirty in a leap year. This meant that September and November had thirty-one days instead of their current thirty.

When Augustus Caesar came to power, he wanted a month named after himself. In 8 BC, he changed Sextilis, originally the sixth month, to Augustus (our August). Because Sextilis had thirty days and Julius thirty-one, Augustus gave his own month an extra day, so that it would not be shorter than that named after his uncle, Julius Caesar. To do this, he cut back Februarius to twenty-eight days, with twenty-nine in a leap year.

To preserve as closely as he could the pattern of alternate months of thirty or thirty-one days, he gave September and November thirty days and added a day to October and November, setting the lengths of each month as they are now.

Augustus Caesar's revisions left the length of the year unchanged, and in the Julian calendar it had a basic fault. It was 11 minutes, 10.3 seconds too long. By the sixteenth century the calendar was about ten days out.

In 1582, Pope Gregory XIII introduced the Gregorian calendar to correct the flaw. First, he set back the Catholic world by declaring October 5 to be October 15, which angered many people because they thought their lives had been shortened. Then, the pope declared that centenary years would be leap years only if they could be divided by 400. Thus, even though 1896, divisible by four, was a leap year, 1900 was not. This minor correction means that the Gregorian calendar will not be even one day out until the year 4906.

Pope Gregory wanted all Christian countries to introduce his calendar at once, but Protestant Britain and its then American colonies waited until 1752, when the Julian calendar was eleven days out. The day after September 2, 1752, was declared to be September 14. That is why the anniversary of George Washington who, according to the Julian calendar, was born on February 11, 1732, is now celebrated on February 22.

Along with the need to devise a calendar to denote the years, early societies

*A **king's clock,** built for Henry VIII at Hampton Court Palace in 1540, shows the time, the motion of the Sun and Moon, and degrees of the zodiac. The central solar plate revolves once in twenty-four hours*

found they required a way to measure parts of the day. The ancient Egyptians divided their day into twenty-four parts, possibly for religious reasons. From dawn, they kept track of the Sun god Re, using primitive sundials made by the shadows of sticks stuck in the ground. The appearance of certain stars or constellations on the eastern horizon marked the twelve parts of the night. This gave them hours that varied in length in summer and winter.

The first clocks, made by the Chinese nearly 6000 years ago, were water clocks. The ancient Egyptians used them, too, as did the Greeks, who named them clepsydras. Similar to sand-filled hourglasses, they measured time by the emptying or filling of vessels as water dripped in or out. These were later improved to include a drum dial, but the Greeks retained the Egyptian idea of having hours of varying length.

Moslem scientists of the early Middle Ages gave the hour a fixed span. The first mechanical clocks, possibly built in China as early as AD 800, gained or lost at least a quarter of an hour a day.

In the sixteenth century, the great Italian scientist Galileo Galilei is said to have watched a freshly lit lamp swinging in the cathedral at Pisa. He timed it by counting the beats of his pulse, and noticed that each complete swing took about the same time, irrespective of the distance travelled. Galileo's discovery of the pendulum made clocks more accurate, and brought a new age of precise timekeeping.

In today's world, we need much finer measurements of time than those given by the second hand of a stopwatch. Spacecraft are guided by radio signals timed to thousand-millionths of a second (nanoseconds). Atomic physicists reckon in picoseconds (a million-millionth of a second) and even femtoseconds (thousandths of a picosecond). These ultra-precise timekeepers will tell you that there are more femtoseconds in one second than there were seconds in the past thirty-one million years.

Next-century's timekeeping will demand precision that cannot be met by clocks today. At the US National Institute of Standards, a scientist works on a prototype atomic clock which, when completed, is expected to be 100 000 times more accurate than the best available now

Why were frankincense and myrrh gifts fit for a king?

In the Bible story of the Nativity, the three wise men brought gifts of gold, frankincense and myrrh to the infant Jesus. Gold is still treasured. Frankincense and myrrh, resins of trees native to Arabia, were once as valuable as gold, but would hardly make acceptable gifts today.

The myrrh tree, which is small, scrubby and spiny, exudes resin from its whitish bark. Frankincense is produced by tapping into the trunk of a tree that grows on limestone rocks in southern Arabia and the Horn of Africa; resin oozes out, much as latex does from a rubber tree.

The importance of frankincense and myrrh came from their use in worship. When burned, both give off aromatic smoke; today, some Christian churches still use myrrh in incense burners. Ancient Egyptians used myrrh to prepare mummies, filling the body cavities with the resin and spices. Myrrh contains an antiseptic oil, and arrests decay.

Frankincense also has a long history. In about 1495 BC, Hatshepsut, Egypt's queen, ordered the first recorded expedition to collect plants. Her courtiers returned with some thirty frankincense trees which were planted around her temple at Deir el Bahri. Smoke rising from an altar fire burning frankincense was thought to take prayers to the gods. At cremations, the smoke was believed to secure immortality; also, its fragrance masked unpleasant odours.

In ancient times, frankincense soared in price. Caravans travelling the Incense Road to the Egyptian coast brought the resin from Arabia. The route ran through desolate regions, and the caravans were frequently raided. When the Queen of Sheba visited King Solomon in 950 BC, she took him a gift of myrrh. She is said to have asked him to intervene personally to make the Incense Road safe. Her territory of Sheba, now known as Yemen, was a major source of frankincense. Historians say that the queen was undoubtedly trying to safeguard the income she obtained from a product so valuable that only nobles and royalty could afford it.

Why does the Leaning Tower of Pisa lean?

The tower of Pisa, 58.4 m (192 ft) high, started to lean soon after building began, in 1174. Five years later, when stonemasons reached halfway, money ran out and work stopped. It was a good job it did. Studies show that, had building continued, the tower would have collapsed.

In its early stages, the tower leaned to the north. Masons varied the marble blocks in a bid to correct the fault, which got worse as they went higher. On the first storey's north side, the blocks are 1 cm (0.4 in) thinner than those on the south; on the fourth storey, they are 10 cm (4 in) thinner.

Building restarted in 1272, by which time the tower had almost straightened. But now it began to lean to the south. At

Decline and fall? *Pisa's famous tower has tilted for more than 800 years without toppling over. But recently its rate of tilt has speeded up, renewing fears of impending disaster*

the seventh storey, work stopped for about eighty years. Again, the delay was fortuitous. In a final bid to straighten the tower, the bell chamber was built out of line. Four steps lead to it on the north side and six on the south.

Today, the tower still leans to the south, where it is 2.5 m (8 ft) lower than on the north. For a structure weighing 14 453 tonnes, its foundations are inadequate, just 3 m (10 ft) deep. Also, the soil to the north has more sand. To the south it is richer in silt. This compresses more easily, allowing the tower to sink on that side.

Over the years, almost every move to correct the tilt has worsened it. In 1934, Benito Mussolini, the Italian dictator, tried to save the tower. Engineers poured tonnes of cement into 361 holes drilled in the foundations. That year the tower lurched more than in the previous fifteen.

In 1989, a similar but upright tower at Pavia collapsed. The Italian government closed Pisa's tower, and set up an international commission to stabilise the building.

Some twenty years earlier, engineers discovered that the tower moves hour by

Treasure flows *from a frankincense tree, tapped for its gum in Oman. The gum soon hardens (inset). In Christ's time about 3000 tonnes of frankincense were exported every year from Arabia to consecrate temples, treat ailments and mask unpleasant odours*

hour, reacting to the warmth of the Sun. Recently, electro-levels – highly sensitive detectors – were installed in the foundations. These showed that as the tower warms up it rocks its foundations, increasing its tilt. Since the end of World War II, the rate of tilt has doubled. The tower leans nearly 2 mm (0.01 in) more each year, moving closer to the point where it will topple over.

Some structural engineers fear that internal stresses may make the building explode. In 1992, as a safeguard, they girdled it with eight metal cables. A year later they loaded the foundations with 600 tonnes of lead.

Suggestions arrive daily from all over the world. One is to dismantle the tower and rebuild it straight. Citizens fiercely oppose the idea. After the tower closed, tourism fell by 25 per cent. It seems that everybody wants a leaning tower, provided it is safe.

Why was the V-sign used in World War II?

For centuries and in many countries the two-fingered V-sign had only one meaning, an insult. A British survey shows that it is still the most frequent gesture of abuse, even among children.

If the two fingers are raised but held steady, the sign may have several interpretations. The most common is that it means 'victory'. Another is that it signifies the number two.

How the gesture became a sexual insult is in dispute. In Roman times it was done with one finger or with the thumb, which could be seen as phallic symbols. In some countries today that interpretation still applies, which is why hitchhikers thumbing a lift may get a hostile reception.

The obscene gesture undoubtedly existed long before the V-for-Victory sign, which Winston Churchill, Britain's prime minister during World War II, made internationally famous. Churchill gave the sign to bolster the confidence of troops going into battle, to inspire munitions workers to increase their production, to boost the morale of bomb victims. His V-sign was slightly but significantly different, because invariably he turned the palm of his hand towards his viewers.

Some close associates say that the use of the sign, with its more customary meaning, amused Churchill. He was, in effect, giving a victory symbol to Britons and their allies and an insulting gesture to the enemy. Some researchers say that this switch has a parallel in the use of KO, for knock-out, as the opposite of OK.

Churchill made the V-sign famous, but he did not invent it. After the German occupation of Belgium in 1940, underground fighters began a campaign of chalking R A F (for Royal Air Force) on walls as a sign of resistance. The letters had obvious flaws: many people didn't know what the abbreviation meant and it took too long to scrawl in a prominent place that was probably under the watching eyes of the Gestapo.

Early in 1941, a Belgian lawyer, Victor de Lavelaye, came up with one of the most brilliant propaganda ideas of all time. Inspired perhaps by his own first name, he broadcast from London to occupied Belgium and proposed a V-for-Victory campaign. The letter V stood for victory in English, French (*victoire*) and Flemish (*vrijheid*).

Other propagandists gave the idea new dimensions. In the Morse code, the sound for V is dot-dot-dot-dash, which could be rapped out by radio and by the knuckles knocking on wood. The opening bars of Beethoven's Fifth Symphony have that precise rhythm, and became a familiar prelude to Britain's wartime broadcasts to occupied Europe.

The total campaign was so successful that the Nazis tried to hijack it, using V to symbolise *Viktoria*, an outdated Teutonic word for victory. They even displayed a huge V-sign on the Eiffel Tower. But they were already too late. With the V-for-Victory campaign well established on the radio, Churchill extended it visually by turning an ancient gesture of obscenity into a symbol inspiring hope. Today, the rapped-out V-sign has vanished, but Churchill's victory symbol lives on – in one way or another.

Gesture of triumph *from Margaret Thatcher when, as Britain's prime minister, she heralds an election victory. Churchill popularised the V-sign, calling it a 'symbol of unconquerable will'*

*A **triumph too late**, the Me 262 was the first operational jet aircraft. Inset: its designer, Willy Messerschmitt*

Why did it take so long to invent jet aircraft?

In 1929, British inventor Frank Whittle foresaw that conventional aircraft would have difficulty flying above 20 000 ft (6000 m). He reasoned that the air there is too thin for propellers to drive efficiently and for piston engines to breathe. Almost ten years before World War II broke out, he patented his idea for a jet engine, but could find no one in private industry willing to pursue it.

In 1934, Hans von Ohain, a twenty-three-year-old German physics postgraduate, had a similar idea. Two years later, aircraft manufacturer Ernst Heinkel offered him a job, pledging him to secrecy, because he feared that bureaucrats in Adolf Hitler's Air Ministry might insist on taking over the work.

In 1935, Whittle found two businessmen interested in developing his idea. Britain's Air Ministry allowed Whittle, an officer in the Royal Air Force, to work on the project, but for only six hours a week and only if he gave the government 25 per cent of his commercial interest. On April 12, 1937, he tested the world's first jet engine, but couldn't get it to run consistently for more than a short time.

Had Whittle received support, Britain would have entered World War II with overwhelming air superiority. His money almost ran out as he tried to cure his engine's faults. In June 1939, the Air Ministry finally gave him a contract to build a lightweight jet engine.

By July that year, von Ohain also had produced a successful jet engine, and

Heinkel invited Hitler to its unveiling. The Führer wasn't enthusiastic. To persuade him, Heinkel put the engine into the first jet aircraft, the He 178, which on August 27, 1939, had its test flight. Luftwaffe officials refused Heinkel's persistent invitations to see it take to the skies.

On May 15, 1941, Britain finally tested a small jet aircraft, the E28/39, and Winston Churchill later watched the test flight of a second version, to which Whittle wasn't even given an invitation.

Hitler believed that the war wouldn't last more than a year after the fall of France, and the German High Command banned long-term military research. Two Air Ministry engineers disobeyed the order. They heard about Heinkel's jet aircraft, and offered contracts to his rival, Willy Messerschmitt, for a jet fighter, the Me 262. Remarkably, the General Staff insisted that work should stop immediately.

Messerschmitt ignored the directive, and by late 1943 had a jet fighter ready for mass production. Fortunately for the Allies, Hitler wanted the fighter adapted as a bomber. That decision wasted ten months, and had enormous impact on the war. Without air superiority, the D-Day landings in June 1944 would certainly have been more costly and might even have failed.

On March 18, 1945, Germany put the high-speed Me 262 into battle with devastating results against B-17 Flying Fortresses and Liberators. In that encounter, American gunners couldn't swivel their turrets fast enough to keep pace with their attackers, and eighteen bombers were shot down.

Why is it blue for boy babies and pink for girls?

Researchers say that in Anglo-Saxon Britain, in the fifth and sixth centuries, boy babies were more prized than girls. The belief spread that ever-present evil spirits would visit the cradle and harm or carry off a boy child. Blue, a power colour because it came from the sky, would scare away these malevolent forces.

At that time, girl babies didn't warrant a protective colour. Later, in Germany, a widespread legend held that girl babies sprang from a pink rose, and it became customary to dress baby girls in pink. That custom merged with the British one of dressing boys in blue, and the fashion of blue for boys and pink for girls spread to other parts of the Western world.

Psychiatrists and designers have long recognised that colour can convey a specific meaning. A common example in Western countries is the use of red as a warning. Traffic signals at red are an urgent command to stop; in the days of the Cold War, a red alert indicated a possible nuclear attack.

In our culture, red for danger comes possibly from the colour of blood or of fire. To the Chinese, red conveys happiness. Similarly, other colours often mean different things in different places. For example, black is our colour of mourning. In China, it is white.

Newborn babies in a Chicago hospital are neatly distinguished. The girls snuggle under pink blankets, the boys beneath blue

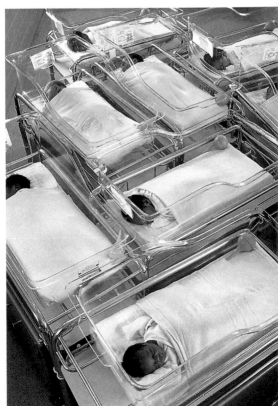

Why is it said that Loch Ness holds a monster?

When the *Inverness Courier*, a respected Scottish local newspaper, reported on May 2, 1933, an unusual sighting in nearby Loch Ness, it set off a controversy that has surfaced on and off for more than half a century.

The report came from a Fort Augustus resident, Alex Campbell, who revived stories that the loch held 'a fearsome-looking monster'. For at least 200 years, soldiers, fishermen and country trades-men had told of strange creatures inhabit-ing the loch. Some historians claimed, without much evidence, that the loch was named after Nessa, a Celtic water nymph. Others said that in AD 565 St Columba, the Irish poet who converted the Picts to Christianity, had attended the burial on the banks of the River Ness of a man who was killed by the monster. At the saint's command, the terrified creature fled.

Loch Ness, the largest body of fresh water in Britain, is about 39 km (24 miles) long and 1.6 km (1 mile) wide. Its shores fall sharply into murky, peat-stained depths, reaching in places to more than 300 m (nearly 1000 ft). Often, the loch is hit by sudden squalls, or it may be cloaked in mist. Much of it can be seen easily only from a boat. At times, it is a wild and forbidding place; always it holds a sense of mystery.

For some strange reason, the reports of 1933 caught attention when earlier ones did not. By the early summer, Inverness was crowded with journalists from news-papers in many parts of the world, includ-ing New York and Tokyo. In April 1934, R. K. Wilson, a London surgeon on holi-day, photographed what seemed to be the head and neck of a strange creature pro-truding from the water. Some biologists thought it might be a plesiosaur, a marine reptile that had been extinct for some seventy million years.

Soon, flimsy rumour became hard fact. The monster was reported to have left the loch, captured a sheep, and leaped a road before returning to its haunt. When an elderly woman disappeared, the monster was blamed. A visiting big-game hunter reported he had found the monster's spoor on a beach. Researchers identified the tracks as a hoax, made by a collector's hippopotamus foot.

Every day brought a fresh report or a new explanation. One story was that a pet crocodile brought back from Africa had escaped. Another explained that a Ger-man zeppelin, shot down over the loch in World War I, had surfaced temporarily.

For several years until World War II, newspapers reported new sightings of the

Rumour and hoax helped to establish the legend that Loch Ness holds a monster. It was all good for the tourist trade and brought a demand for postcards, curios and memorabilia

·A SOUVENIR OF LOCH NESS·

THE LOCH NESS MONSTER
NESSUM·MONSTROSUM

Loch Ness Monster. These came particu-larly in high summer, a time sometimes known as 'the Silly Season', when holi-days made hard news rarer and editors were even more keen to chase the bizarre and sensational.

During World War II, Nessie, as the monster was called, went unnoticed. But in 1960, Tim Dinsdale, an English aero-nautical engineer, filmed a black-humped shape moving briskly across the loch. The Royal Air Force's Joint Air Reconnaissance Intelligence Centre studied the film, and declared that the strange apparition was 'probably an inanimate object'. Remark-ably, the findings did little to quell interest

in Nessie, and demands came to solve the mystery once and for all.

In 1972, an American team from the Academy of Applied Science searched the loch with underwater cameras and sonar devices. One image, enhanced by com-puter, seemed to show the flipper of possibly a very large animal. A second survey in 1975 led the academy to con-clude that the loch held a very large aquatic creature. One year later, the *New York Times* contributed $25 000 to help fund a new expedition. This, like others, found nothing conclusive. As many scien-tists have said, only Nessie's capture will finally set the puzzle to rest.

NOBEL'S LEGACY OF DYNAMITE

In six fields of human endeavour, no greater honour exists than to win a Nobel prize. These prizes, a cash award of about $900 000 and a medallion, are given each year for the most significant work in physics, chemistry, medicine, literature and econom-ics, and to the person who has made the greatest contribution to the cause of peace.

Swedish chemist Alfred Nobel invented dynamite, and killed his younger brother in the process. Ironi-cally, after creating the means of such destruction in the world, he left on his death in 1896 a will stipu-lating that income from much of his fortune should provide annual prizes to those who had given humanity the greatest benefit.

The Nobel medal has a profile of the inventor

Interpreting Nobel's will brought four years of argument before the Nobel Foundation was set up. One measure of the prizes' value is that they have provoked annual bitterness and envy. Some scientists have been accused of speeding up or slowing down publication of their work to make it eligible in a particular year and avoid possible competition.

Always the prizes have caused public controversy and sometimes interna-tional incident. When Boris Pasternak was given the Nobel prize for literature in 1958, the Soviets ordered him to refuse it. In 1970, they argued that the award to Aleksandr Solzhenitsyn was politically motivated. He defied them by accepting the prize, and four years later was exiled.

Whatever Nobel's intentions, nobody can justly claim that his prizes have promoted greater understanding and peace.

INDEX

347

PICTURE CREDITS

Abbreviations: l = left; c = centre; r = right; t = top; b = bottom; bg = background; APL = Australian Picture Library; BAL = Bridgeman Art Library; BC = Bruce Coleman; Coo-ee H = Coo-ee Historical Picture Library; HD = Hulton Deutsch; MEPL = Mary Evans Picture Library; NHPA = Natural History Photographic Agency; OSF = Oxford Scientific Films; PEP = Planet Earth Pictures; PhRes = Photo Researchers Inc.; PLA = The Photo Library Australia; SPL = Science Photo Library; SpPix = Sporting Pix; TBA = The Bettmann Archive; TGC = The Granger Collection; TIB = The Image Bank; TSA = Tom Stack & Associates; TSW = Tony Stone Worldwide; V&A = reproduced by permission of the Board of Trustees of the Victoria and Albert Museum.
Reader's Digest has made every effort to trace the copyright owners of the illustrations in this book. Any person or organisation we have failed to reach is invited to contact the publishers.
All diagrams are by Jon Gittoes, except where stated.

7 t, David Malin/ROE/AAT Board 1985; bl, MEPL; br, NASA/SPL/PLA. **8** TGC. **9** t, Photri; b, SPL/PLA; r, Margaret Harwood/American Institute of Physics/Emilio Segré Visual Archives. **10** tr, NASA/SPL/PLA; tl, *Artist Oliver Rennert*. **11** t, Jack Finch/SPL/PLA; b, Mt Wilson Palomar Observatories/CIT. **12** t and bl, TGC; br, Culver. **13** Photri. **14** Fred Spenak/SPL/PLA. **15** TGC. **16** Reg Morrison/Auscape. **17** NASA/SPL/PLA. **18** t, Lionel F. Brown/TIB; b, NASA. **19** MEPL. **20-1** bg, TGC. **20** l, TGC; r, E.T. Archive; b, Culver. **21** t, Coo-ee H; bl, Manfred L. Kreiner/QUICK/Camera Press/Austral; br, NASA/SPL/PLA. **22** TGC. **23** Culver. **24** t, NASA/SPL/PLA; b, TGC; bl, Venus's orbit, after an illustration in W.J. Kaufmann, *The Universe* (W.H. Freeman & Co. 1985). **25** NASA/SPL/PLA. **26** t, MEPL; b, Planetary Society. **27** l, TGC; r, Photo Research Int./PLA. **28-9** NASA/SPL/PLA. **30** SPL/PLA. **31** t, TGC; b, Dario Perla/Horizon. **32-3** t, stellar evolution, after an illustration in *The Children's Space Atlas* (Quarto Publishing 1991). **33** Ronald Grant Archive. **34** b, expansion of the Universe, after an illustration in *The Children's Space Atlas* (Quarto Publishing 1991). **35** t, FPG/Austral; bl, Jay Maisel/TIB; br, Comstock. **36** Erich Schrempp/PhRes. **37** Nicolas Foster/TIB. **38** Alex Bartel/SPL/PLA. **39** t, Robert Harding Pic. Lib.; b, TGC. **40** John Sandford/SPL/PLA. **41** NASA. **42** l, MEPL; r, John Cleare. **43** Michael Holford. **44** l, APL; r, UPI/Bettmann. **45** UPI/Bettmann. **46** Christie's London/BAL. **47** t, Bettmann; b, M. Krafft/Auscape. **48** t, Simon Fraser/SPL/PLA; b, Durieux/Sipa/Austral. **49** M. Krafft/Auscape. **50** t, Anthony Howard/Comstock; b, P.V. Tearle/PEP. **51** t, TGC; b, TBA. **52** t, Ron Ryan/Coo-ee; b, *Courier Mail*. **53** l, Francis Alain/Explorer/Auscape; r, John & Gillian Lythgoe/PEP; b, Studio 9. **54-5** bg, SPL/PLA. **54** b, NASA. **55** l, Kalt/Zefa/APL; r, David R. Austen; b, Reuters/Bettmann; br, Walker/Shooting Star/Austral. **56** l, Howard Platt/PEP; r, Steve Dunwell/TIB; b, Nuridsany & Perennou/SPL/PLA. **57** t, UPI/Bettmann; b, Coo-ee H. **58** t, FPG/Austral; b, MEPL. **59** t, Michel Klinec/BC; bl and br, John Lythgoe/PEP. **60** Pictor/Austral. **61** t and b, Hans Reinhard/BC. **63** t, Philip Fischer; b, TGC. **64** Wolfgang Steche/VISUM. **65** tl, Oliver Strewe/APL; tr, *Artist David Carroll*; b, Joseph Lee/*Evening News*/Centre for the Study of Cartoons and Caricature/University of Kent at Canterbury. **66** t, NASA/Science Source/PhRes; b, Walter Bibikow/TIB. **67** t, Yan/Rapho/PhRes. **68** t, Picturepoint; bl, *Artist David Carroll*. **69** t, Nick Rains; b, Richard Woldendorp/Photo Index. **70** *Artist David Carroll*. **70-1** Jay Maisel/TIB. **71** t, Manfred Kage/SPL/PLA; b, Tommaso Guicciardini/SPL/PLA. **72** l, *Artist David Carroll*; r, David Parker/SPL/PhRes. **73** t, Prof. P. Motta/SPL/PLA; bl, Richard Hutchins/PhRes; br, Dennis Stock/MAGNUM. **74** Mark Grimberg/TIB. **75** t, Bob Martin/Allsport/APL; b, Dr Jeremy Burgess/SPL/PLA. **76** t, Popper/SpPix; b, Courtesy Phillip Bush. **77** l, TGC; r, MEPL. **78** t, K. Parker/Zefa/APL; b, Coo-ee H. **79** t, MEPL; b, Gerard Champlong/TIB. **80** t, Sheila Terry/SPL/PLA; b, APL. **81** MEPL. **82** Rory McClenaghan/SPL/PLA. **83** International Ph. Lib. **84** TSW/PLA. **85** b, Robert Farber/TIB; r, colour blindness tests reproduced by permission from *Ishihara's Tests for Colour Blindness* (Kanehara & Co., Tokyo). Colour blindness can be detected accurately only by using the original plates. **86** c, corneal transplant, after an illustration by Theres Biedermann in *Graphis Diagram 1* (Graphis Press Corp. 1988); br, Fotopic/APL. **87** TGC. **88** t, Prof. P. Motta/SPL/PLA; b, SPL/PLA. **89** TBA. **90** SPL/PLA; *Artist Oliver Rennert* (how blood clots), after an illustration in *American Medical Association, Home Medical Encyclopedia* (Dorling Kindersley and AMA 1989). **91** l, SPL/PLA; r, TBA; b, TGC. **93** t, SPL/PLA; bl, International Ph. Lib.; br, Dan Smith/TSW/PLA. **94** l, TGC; r, TBA; b, HD/PLA. **95** SPL/PLA. **96** t, Picturepoint; b, George Bernhard/SPL/PhRes. **97** TGC. **98** HD/PLA. **99** l, TBA; r, Howard Sochurek/The Stockmarket. **100** SPL/PLA; brain cross section, after an illustration in *AMA Medical Library, The Brain and Nervous System* (Dorling Kindersley and AMA 1989). **101** Manfred Kage/SPL/PLA. **102** Scott Kamazine/PhRes. **103** Bill Robbins/TSW/PLA. **104** SPL/PLA. **105** t, TGC; b, Bill Holden/APL. **106** t, Barts Medical Library; bl, *Artist David Carroll*; br, Dale O'Dell/The Stockmarket. **107** SPL/PLA. **108** t, SPL/PLA; b, Dr Michael Klein. **109** Pictor/Austral. **110** l, John Fairfax Group; r, TBA; b, SPL/PLA. **111** l, Harry Langdon/Shooting Star/Austral; r, David Woods/The Stockmarket. **112** Nick Rains. **113** Roger Ressmeyer/Starlight. **114-5** bg, David J. Carol/TIB. **114** t, Phototake/Stockphotos; b, Cecil Fox/Science Source/ PhRes; br, SPL/PLA. **115** t, Art Stein/PhRes; b, HD/PLA. **116** l and r, Dr Rob Stepney/SPL/PLA; b, SPL/PLA. **117** t and b, Lennart Nilsson/Boehringer Ingelheim Int. GmbH. **118** t, Coo-ee H; b, Robin Ekta/Orop/Austral. **119** t, Prado Madrid/Index/BAL; b, *Artist Oliver Rennert* (sleep patterns), after an illustration in *The Guinness Encyclopedia* (Guinness Publishing 1990). **120** Otto Greule/Allsport/APL. **121** l, TGC; rt, TBA; rc, Vinnie Zuffante/Starfile/APL; rb, Archive/PhRes. **122** APL. **123** t, J.M. La Roque/Auscape; bl, Anne Sager/PhRes; br, Jean-Paul Ferrero/Explorer/PhRes. **124** t, A.B. Dowsett/SPL/PLA; b, Coo-ee H; **125** t, Ronny Jaques/PhRes; b, Nick Rains. **126** Nestlé S.A. **127** t, C.P. Fischer/Zefa/APL; b, Hanya Chlala/APL. **128** t, Michael Melford/TIB; b, Olympia/APL. **130-1** bg, TSW/PLA; t, Laynia Yann/Explorer/Auscape. **131** r and c, TGC; b, MEPL. **132** t, MEPL; b, Tessa Traeger. **133** TGC. **134** Adam Woolfitt/Comstock. **135** t, Nick Rains; c, Olympia/APL; b, J.N. Reichel/PhRes. **136** l, FPG/Austral; r, Champagne Bollinger. **137** l, MEPL; r, Philip Quirk/Wildlight; b, Coo-ee H. **138** t, T.D. Winter/Robert Harding; b, Scoopix. **139** l, MEPL; r, David Beatty/Comstock. **140** t and b, TGC. **141** l, Sygma/Austral; r, Angela Fisher/Robert Estall Photographs; b, Stephen Dalton/PhRes. **142** Carol Beckwith/Robert Estall Photographs. **143** t, Jane Burton/BC; b, TGC. **144** tr, reproduced from L. Kybalova, O. Herbenova and M. Lamarova, *The Pictorial Encyclopedia of Fashion* (Aventinum, Prague 1966); bl, Popper/SpPix; br, Sipa/Austral. **145** t and b, MEPL. **146** t, Nick Rains; b, Pictor/Austral; r, British Textile Council. **147** l, Rex/Austral; r, C. Barthelmy/Sipa/Austral. **148** t, HD/PLA; b, Henry Ausloos/NHPA. **149** t, Laurie Campbell/NHPA; b, Cath Wadforth/University of Hull/SPL/PLA. **150** l, London News Service/Austral; r, Gérard Lacz/NHPA. **151** t, Pierre Sun/Sipa/Austral; r, Erika Stone/APL; c, Chris Bell/Rex/Austral; b, FPG/Austral. **152** l, Coo-ee H; r, J.M. Labat/Auscape; c, Private Collection/BAL. **153** C.A. Henley/Auscape. **154** l, Jane Burton/BC; r, Nick Rains; b, Beatrix Potter/Frederick Warne & Co. **155** l, Science Museum London/Michael Holford; r, Sygma/Austral. **156** V&A/Design Council London. **157** t, Dr Jeremy Burgess/SPL/PLA; b, Bob Martin/Allsport/APL. **158-9** l and r, Ron Ryan/Coo-ee. **160-1** bg, MEPL. **160** t, MEPL; bl, SPL/PLA; br, Dr Jeremy Burgess/SPL/PLA. **161** l, TBA; tr, MEPL; br, TGC. **162** TBA. **162-3** APL. **164** t, Dr Jeremy Burgess/SPL/PLA; c and b, TCG. **165** Dr Jeremy Burgess/SPL/PLA. **166** Arthur Meyerson/TIB. **167** t, Pictor/Austral; b, Lux by Electrolux. **168** t, Ormond Gigli/Camera Press/Austral; b, *Illustrated London News*/MEPL. **169** t, Mitchell Library/APL; b, Rex/Austral. **170** t, Woodprint by K. Utamaro/TBA; b, Rex/Austral. **172** t, Michael Holford/V&A; b, Hanns-Frieder Michler/SPL/PLA. **173** r, Pictor/Austral. **174** t, Coll. Robert Wyatt/BAL; br, Dr Tony Brain/SPL/PLA; bl, alphabet, after a table in *The Guinness Encyclopedia* (Guinness Publishing 1990). **175** t, TGC; bl, UPI/Bettmann; br, New York Public Library, with permission of New York *Daily News*. **176** t, Francisco Hidalgo/TIB; b, Nick Rains. **177** TBA. **178** l, Nick Nicholson/TIB; r, Picturepoint. **179** *Artist David Carroll*. **180** tr, *Artist David Carroll*; bl, MEPL; bc, Dr Jeremy Burgess/SPL/PLA; br, TBA. **181** t, TBA; b, UPI/Bettmann. **182** UPI/Bettmann. **183** t, FPG/Austral; bl, *Artist David Carroll*; b, Paul Slaughter/TIB. **184** l, UPI/Bettmann; r, Reuters/Bettmann; b, Dick Hanley/PhRes. **185** t, HD/PLA; c, MEPL; b, Sygma/Austral. **186** b and **186-7** TSW/PLA. **188** t, Coo-ee H; b, Don Skirrow. **189** l, Images; tr, Alpha/Austral; br, Popper/SpPix. **190** Musée de la Chartreuse, Douai/Giraudon/BAL. **191** t, MEPL; bl, Pictor/Austral; br, Mark Lang/Wildlight. **192** t, MEPL; c, APL; b, TGC. **193** t, V&A/BAL; b, MEPL. **194** Private Collection/BAL. **195** l and r, MEPL. **196** t, MEPL; b, Images. **197** t, MEPL; b, UPI/Bettmann. **198** t, TBA; b, Brian Shuel/Collections. **199** Sonia Halliday. **200** t, MEPL; b, Leigh Clapp/PLA. **201** tl, C.M. Dixon; tr, Sipa/Austral; c, Michael Dixon; b, MEPL. **202** TBA. **203** t, Sandy Roessler/Stockshots; b, Syndicated Features/Austral. **204-5** Graham Monro. **205** Popper/SpPix. **206** t, G. & M. David de Lossy/TIB; b, Graham Monro. **207** t, Murray White/Sipa/Austral; b, Pictor/Austral. **208** Kim Taylor/BC. **209** t, Larry Dale Gordon Studio/TIB; b, UPI/Bettmann. **210** Images. **211** t, MEPL; b, TBA. **212** Images. **212-3** Ancient Art & Architecture. **214-5** bg, Nick Rains. **214** t, Ancient Art & Architecture; b, TGC. **215** l, Coo-ee H; r, TGC; c, TBA; b, MEPL. **216** Dr Scott Nielsen/BC. **217** t, Popper/SpPix; b, MEPL. **218** TGC. **219** t, Michael Freeman/BC; b, C.M. Dixon. **220** t, TGC; b, Anthony Blake Photo Library. **221** Herbert Kranawetter/BC. **222** t, Collections; b, Giraudon. **223** l, Bob Martin/Allsport/APL; r, Shooting Star/Austral; b, R. Landau/WL/APL. **224** London *Daily Express*/Archive/APL. **225** t, Picturepoint; b, Scala. **226** t, Robert Harding. **226-7** b, Adam Woolfitt/*National Geographic*/Nippon Televison. **227** l and r, Vatican Museums/Nippon Televison. **228** l, V&A/BAL; r, Erich Hartmann/MAGNUM. **229** t, Mansell Coll.; l, Coram Foundation/BAL; r, Private Collection/BAL. **230** t, Picturepoint; b, Aquarius PhLib. **231** t, TBA; b, Camera Press/Austral. **232** Springer/Bettmann Film Archive. **233** l, Culver; r, Kobal Coll. **234** l, TGC; r, Pictor/Austral. **235** TGC. **236** t, Kobal Coll.; c, Shooting Star/Austral; b, Nick Nicholson/TIB. **237** t, Fotos Int./Austral; b, UPI/Bettmann. **238** l and r, Sygma/Austral. **239** t, Kobal Coll.; b, UPI/Bettmann. **240** t, Austral; b, Picturepoint. **241** t, Rex/Austral; c and b, TGC. **242** t, Paul Bryden Coll./Nick Rains; b, Giraudon. **243** t, Sipa/Austral; c, Glenn A. Baker Coll.; b, Fotofest/Retna/APL. **244** l, UPI/Bettmann; c, Coo-ee H; b, G. Vandystadt/Allsport/APL. **245** t, MEPL; b, TGC. **246** t, HD/PLA; b, TSW/PLA. **247** t, Allsport/APL; b, UPI/Bettman. **248** t, *Illustrated London News*; b, Allsport/APL. **249** t, Picturepoint; b, TGC. **250** t, TGC. **251** t, Lo Linkert; b, Tony Feder. **252-3** t, Picturepoint. **252** b, UPI/Bettmann. **253** c, HD/PLA; b, David Rogers/Bob Thomas/SpPix. **254-5** bg, Kishimoto/Live Action. **254** l, Popper/SpPix.; r, Coo-ee H; b, HD/PLA. **255** l, APL; r, Dave Cannon/TSW/PLA; b, International. **256** Marylebone Cricket Club/BAL. **257** l, Nick Rains; r, Simon Bruty/Allsport/APL. **258** t, Professional Sport, London; b, MEPL. **259** t, Michel Hans/Vandystadt/APL; b, City of Edinburgh Museum & Art Gallery/BAL. **260** t, Clive Brunskill/Bob Thomas/SpPix; b, Chris Cole/Allsport/APL. **261** t, Günter Ziesler/BC; bl, Michael & Patricia Fogden; br, Rod Planck/TSA. **262** Günter Ziesler/BC. **263** t, Hans Reinhard/BC; b, E.A. Jones/NHPA. **264** l, *Artist Oliver Rennert*; t, John Shaw/Auscape. **265** t, Raghu Rai/MAGNUM; b, G.D. Plage/BC. **266** t, Günter Ziesler/BC; b, Jane Burton/BC. **267** t, Y. Arthus-Bertrand/Ardea London; cats' eyes, after an illustration in *Grzimek's Encyclopedia of Mammals* (Kindler Verlag); b, Sue Earle/PEP. **268** tl, cat's claws, after illustrations in *Grzimek's Encyclopedia of Mammals* (Kindler Verlag) and *Great Cats* (Weldon Owen 1991); b, TGC. **269** M. Tuttle/Bat Conservation Society. **270** t, Jones/APL; b, MEPL. **271** t, V&A/BAL; b, J. & G. Lythgoe/PEP. **272** t, David E. Rowley/PEP; b, Jeff Foott/Auscape. **273** P. Morris/Ardea London. **274-5** bg, William Curtsinger/Zefa/All Stock/APL. **274** l, J.L.B. Smith Institute; c, UPI/Bettmann; r, Dr Hans W. Fricke. **275** t, c and b, Dr Hans W. Fricke. **276** TGC. **277** D. Parer & E. Parer-Cook/Auscape. **278** t, Jean-Paul Ferrero/Auscape; b, APL. **279** t, Ron & Valerie Taylor/Ardea London; b, Dr Frieder Sauer/BC. **280** t, MEPL; b, APL. **281** bg, Larry Tackett/TSA; tl, Bill Wood/NHPA; tr, Kelvin Aitken/A.N.T. Photo Library; c, Ed Robinson/TSA; bl, Brian Parker/TSA; br, Ron & Valerie Taylor/A.N.T. Photo Library. **282** George I. Bernhard/NHPA. **283** Frances Furlong/BC. **284** l, Dr Jeremy Burgess/SPL/PLA; r, J.B. & S. Bottomley/Ardea London; b, Jane Burton/BC. **285** l, Andy Purcell/BC; r, John Markham/BC. **286** George McCarthy/BC. **287** l, G.C. Kelly/TSA; cl, Peter Jackson/BC; cr, Mike Brown/OSF; r, Günter Ziesler/BC; c, Jeff Foott/BC. **288-9** bg, John Downer/PEP. **288** l, David Hosking/FLPA; r, Michael & Patricia Fogden/BC. **289** l, Yves Lanceau/Auscape; cl, Hans Reinhard/BC; cr, Marie Read/BC; r, Ralph & Daphne Keller/A.N.T. Photo Library. **290** tl, A.S. Weaving/Ardea London; tr, *Artist Oliver Rennert*; b, Jean-Paul Ferrero/Auscape. **291** t, TGC; b, G. Lewis/APL. **292** t, Graham Robertson/Auscape; b, Cyril Webster/A.N.T. Photo Library. **293** t, Coo-ee H; b, John Carnemolla/APL. **294** t, Private Collection/BAL. **294-5** Bob & Clara Calhoun/BC. **295** t, Nigel Blake/BC; birdsong sonagrams redrawn from W.H. Thorpe's *Bird Song* (Cambridge University Press 1958). **296** Michael & Patricia Fogden. **297** cr, *Artist Oliver Rennert*; b, Mark Mattock/PEP. **298** t, Günter Ziesler/BC; b, Hugh Jones/PEP. **299** D. Parer & E. Parer-Cook/Auscape. **300** t, Frans Lanting/Zefa/All Stock/APL; b, Dr Alex Ritchie. **301** t, *Artist Oliver Rennert*; b, Jane Burton/BC. **302** t, Michael & Patricia Fogden; b, Michael Fogden. **303** l, Jean-Paul Ferrero/Auscape; r, Michael & Patricia Fogden. **304** J. Lotter/TSA. **305** l, Michael & Patricia Fogden; r, Dr J.A.L. Cooke/OSF; b, Densey Clyne/A.N.T. Photo Library. **306** tl, Ivan Polunin/A.N.T. Photo Library; tr, Ivan Polunin/NHPA; b, G.I. Bernard/OSF. **307** Kobal Coll. **308** t, Jacques Six/Auscape; b, *Artist Oliver Rennert*. **309** TGC. **310** t, Michael & Patricia Fogden; b, John Downer/PEP. **311** l, LSF/OSF; r, Culver; b, N.S.W. Health Department/Coo-ee H. **312** t, SPL/PLA; c, Sinclair Stammers/OSF; b, Stuart Franklin/MAGNUM. **313** t, Leonard Lee Rue/BC; b, Otto Rogge/A.N.T. Photo Library. **314** t, S. Wilson/A.N.T. Photo Library; c, Stephen Dalton/NHPA; b, Don & Esther Phillips/TSA. **315** SPL/PLA. **316** l, Dr Paul A. Zahl/PhRes; c, Adrian Davies/BC; r, Sean Morris/OSF. **317** t, Stephen Dalton/NHPA; b, Adam Hart-Davis/SPL/PLA. **318** t, Jeff Foott Prod./BC; bl, Ardea London; br, Carol Gilkson/Macquarie University. **319** Michael Freeman/BC. **320-1** bg, Larry Mulvehill/PhRes. **320** l, John Shaw/BC; c, Eric Lindgren/Ardea London; r, Bert Wells/OSF. **321** l, Michael Fogden/OSF; r, John Bavosi/SPL/PLA. **322** E.J. Cable/TSA. **322-3** Jean-Paul Ferrero/Auscape. **323** Hans Reinhard/BC. **324** tl, Ian Beames/Ardea London; br, TGC. **325** l, Coo-ee H; r, Lynn Abercrombie; b, John Walsh/PhRes. **326** t, Dirk Reinhartz/VISUM; b, Rolf Nobel/VISUM. **327** Luis Castaneda/TIB. **328** Catherine Lee/Physics Photography Unit/University of Oxford. **329** t, NASA/SPL/PLA; b, Rex/Austral. **330** Walt Anderson/TSA. **331** t, British Library, London/BAL; b, MEPL. **332** t, TBA; b, HD/PLA. **333** Robert J. Herko/TIB. **334** TGC. **335** MEPL. **336** Ron Ryan/Coo-ee; bl, Murray Alcosser/TIB; c, Alessi s.p.a.; br, Zanotta s.p.a. **337** t, Francis Leroy/Biocosmos/SPL/PhRes.; b, Stuart Owen Fox. **338-9** bg, TBA. **338** t, TGC; c, TBA; b, BAL. **339** t, Coo-ee H; b, SPL/PLA. **340** b and c, Lynn Abercrombie; r, Gianni Giansanti/Sygma/Austral. **341** AP/AAP. **342** l, Süddeutscher Bilderdienst; r, Ullstein Bilderdienst; b, Kay Chermush/TIB. **343** t, Valentines Postcards/Coo-ee H; b, Mitchell Lib./State Lib. of NSW/permission of Nobel Foundation.